Dictionary of Battles and Sieges

Dictionary of Battles and Sieges

A Guide to 8,500 Battles from Antiquity
through the Twenty-first Century

Volume 3
P–Z

Tony Jaques

Foreword by Dennis Showalter

GREENWOOD PRESS
Westport, Connecticut • London

Library of Congress Cataloging-in-Publication Data

Jaques, Tony.
  Dictionary of battles and sieges : a guide to 8,500 battles from antiquity through the twenty-first century /
Tony Jaques ; foreword by Dennis Showalter.
      p. cm.
  Includes bibliographical references and index.
  ISBN 0–313–33536–2 (set : alk. paper)—ISBN 0–313–33537–0 (vol. 1 : alk. paper)—ISBN 0–313–33538–9
(vol. 2 : alk. paper)—ISBN 0–313–33539–7 (vol. 3 : alk. paper)   1. Battles—History—Encyclopedias.   2. Sieges—
History—Encyclopedias.   3. Military history—Encyclopedias.   I. Title.
  D25.J33 2007
  355.403—dc22   2006015366

British Library Cataloguing in Publication Data is available.

Library of Congress Catalog Card Number: 2006015366
ISBN: 0–313–33536–2 (set)   ISBN-13: 978–0–313–33536–5 (set)
       0–313–33537–0 (vol. 1)   978–0–313–33537–2 (vol. 1)
       0–313–33538–9 (vol. 2)   978–0–313–33538–9 (vol. 2)
       0–313–33539–7 (vol. 3)   978–0–313–33539–6 (vol. 3)

First published in 2007

Greenwood Press, 88 Post Road West, Westport, CT 06881
An imprint of Greenwood Publishing Group, Inc.
www.greenwood.com

Printed in the United States of America

The paper used in this book complies with the
Permanent Paper Standard issued by the National
Information Standards Organization (Z39.48–1984).

10 9 8 7 6 5 4 3 2 1

This dictionary is dedicated to the memory of my father, Pat Jaques, 1903–1980.

Contents

P

Paardeberg ❙ 1900 ❙ 2nd Anglo-Boer War

Pursued east from **Kimberley**, Piet Cronjé was unwisely attacked near Paardeberg by advance British units under General Sir Horatio Kitchener. The rash frontal assault was driven off with over 1,200 men lost although the main force under General Lord Frederick Roberts then besieged the Boer laager. Cronjé and over 4,000 men were finally starved into surrender (18–27 February 1900).

Padaghe ❙ 1780 ❙ 1st British-Maratha War
See **Doogaur**

Padua ❙ 1509 ❙ War of the League of Cambrai

Four months after France, Germany and the Papacy defeated Venice at **Agnadello**, Venetian troops recaptured Padua and held it against a massive army under Emperor Maximilian. Although the siege failed, the Imperial army's savagery against an Italian city persuaded Pope Julius II to abandon the League and ally himself with Venice to drive the powers out of Italy (September–3 October 1509).

Paducah ❙ 1864 ❙ American Civil War (Western Theatre)

Confederate General Nathan B. Forrest led a large-scale raid north across Tennessee into Kentucky where he attacked the town of Paducah, on the Ohio. While the raiders caused widespread damage, the Union garrison of Colonel Stephen D. Hicks successfully defended nearby Fort Anderson and Forrest withdrew.

The next month he attacked **Fort Pillow** on the Mississippi (25 March 1864).

Paekchon ❙ 663 ❙ Sino-Korean Wars

Attempting to restore the southwest Korean Kingdom of Paekche after conquest at **Sabi** by China and neighbouring Silla, rebel Pung Chang sought aid from Japan, which sent 170 ships under Abe Hirafu. In a decisive naval action against Tang commander Liu Rengui at the mouth of the Paekchon (Japanese Hakusukinoe—modern Kum), Japan lost 40 ships and was forced to abandon Paekche.

Pagahm-mew ❙ 1826 ❙ 1st British-Burmese War

Advancing against King Bagyipaw of Burma in the ancient capital at Ava, British General Sir Archibald Campbell captured **Wattee-Goung** and **Melloone**, then attacked Chief Na-wing Phuring and 16,000 men at nearby Pagahm-mew (modern Pagan). Campbell stormed the town and two weeks later the King signed a peace treaty ceding Arakan and Tenasserim to Britain (9 February 1826).

Pagan ❙ 1826 ❙ 1st British-Burmese War
See **Pagahm-mew**

Pagasae ❙ 352 BC ❙ 3rd Sacred War

After a failed intervention to help **Thessaly** against Phocis, Philip II of Macedon returned to seize Pagasae, the port of Pherae, then met Onomarchus of Phocia on nearby Crocus Field. Brutal action cost the Phocians over 6,000 men killed, including Onomarchus, and Philip reputedly had 3,000 captives thrown into the sea. He was later blocked by Athenians at Thermopylae and returned home.

Pago Largo ▮ 1839 ▮ Argentine Civil Wars

When Governor Genaro Berón de Astrada of Corrientes led a campaign against Argentine Dictator Juan Manuel de Rosas, he was defeated and killed in battle at Pago Largo, south of Corrientes, by General Pascual Echague of Entre Rios. Other leaders were executed after the battle, temporarily suppressing the rising. Astrada was avenged two years later at **Caaguazú** (31 March 1839).

Pakozd ▮ 1848 ▮ Hungarian Revolutionary War

At the start of the rising against the Habsburgs, Hungarian General Johann Moga was met southwest of Budapest near Stuhlweissenberg, between Pakozd and Velencze, by Imperial General Joseph Jellacic, appointed Ban of Croatia to combat Hungarian nationalism. An indecisive action led to an armistice, but the Hungarians soon resumed fighting and advanced on **Vienna** (29 September 1848).

Palacé ▮ 1811 ▮ Colombian War of Independence

In the first substantial action of Colombia's independence struggle, Colonel Antonio Baraya, aided by Atanasio Jirardot, met the Royalist forces of Governor Miguel Tacón at the Rio Palacé, in the Cauca Valley. Following a decisive Patriot cavalry charge led by Miguel Cabal, Tacón withdrew towards Pasto with heavy losses in casualties and prisoners. Baraya occupied Popayán (28 March 1811).

Palacé ▮ 1813 ▮ Colombian War of Independence

When Spanish Royalists under Juan de Samano invaded southern Colombia and occupied Popayán, Republican General Antonio Nariño marched south from Bogotá with 1,200 infantry and 200 cavalry. His vanguard under Colonel José María Cabal routed the Royalists on the Palacé Heights. Nearby Popayán fell two weeks later following further victory at **Calibio** (30 December 1813).

Palanan ▮ 1901 ▮ Philippine-American War

American General Frederick Funston landed at Casiguran Bay in eastern Luzon, then aided by Macabebe soldiers under Hilario Tal Palcido and Gregorio Cadhit, marched 100 miles north to surprise Revolutionary President Emilio Aguinaldo in his headquarters at Palanan. Funston entered the town by ruse and captured Aguinaldo, though the guerrilla war continued (23 March 1901).

Palau Islands ▮ 1944 ▮ World War II (Pacific)

With the **Mariana Islands** secured, the Allied decision to attack the Philippines rather than Formosa sent Admiral Theodore Wilkinson and General Roy Geiger southwest against the Palau Islands, held by General Sadao Inoue. Some of the highest losses of the war saw about 1,500 Americans and perhaps 12,000 Japanese killed before Geiger took **Peliliu** and **Angaur** (September–November 1944).

Palawan Passage ▮ 1944 ▮ World War II (Pacific)

As Japanese Admiral Takeo Kurita sailed from Brunei to disrupt American landings at **Leyte Gulf**, his fleet was ambushed in Palawan Passage, off the western Philippines, by the American submarines *Dace* and *Darter*. Kurita had two cruisers sunk (including his flagship) and one badly damaged. He then transferred his flag and continued east into the **Sibuyan Sea** (23 October 1944).

Palembang ▮ 1942 ▮ World War II (Pacific)

Regrouping after losses in the **Madoera Strait**, a Dutch-British-American squadron under Admiral Karel Doorman tried to intercept a Japanese force heading for Palembar in southeast Sumatra. The Allies were driven off by air attack and a Japanese parachute assault opened the landing on Palembang. Another Allied interception failed days later in **Lombok Strait** (13–14 February 1942).

Palencia I 1870 I Central American National Wars

In a prelude to Guatemala's Liberal Revolution, the seasoned rebel Serapio Cruz led a force against President Vicente Cerna. Just west of Guatemala City at Palencia, Cruz was defeated and killed by government troops under General Antonio Solares. The following year renewed fighting began at **Tacaña** and ended with rebel victory at **San Lucas Sacatepéquez** (23 January 1870).

Palermo I 830–831 I Byzantine-Muslim Wars

Arab invaders of Byzantine Sicily were driven off from a failed siege of **Syracuse** (827–828) and held only Mazara and Mineo when they were reinforced from Spain and North Africa and advanced against Palermo. The key northern city was taken by storm after a long siege and became the capital of Muslim Sicily, renamed by the Arabs as Balarm (August 830–12 September 831).

Palermo I 1071–1072 I Norman Conquest of Southern Italy

Crossing into Sicily to aid his younger brother Roger d'Hauteville (who had secured a great victory at **Misilmeri** in 1068), Robert Guiscard Duke of Apulia besieged the nearby key city of Palermo. A five-month land and naval blockade ended when some of Robert's men scaled the walls at night and the Muslims surrendered next day. Guiscard became Count Roger I of Sicily (1071–5 January 1072).

Palermo I 1647 I Allesi's Insurrection

The hungry people of Palermo were inspired by a popular insurrection in **Naples** to rise against Pedro Fajardo Marquis de los Vélez, the Spanish Viceroy of Sicily. Rebel leader Guiseppe d'Alessi proclaimed himself Captain-General but, like Mansaniello in Naples, he was eventually killed by his own supporters and the

rising was suppressed amid bloody violence (15–22 August 1647).

Palermo I 1676 I 3rd Dutch War

Two months after the Dutch-Spanish naval loss at **Augusta**, in which Dutch Admiral Michiel de Ruyter was fatally wounded, French forces supporting Sicily against Spain attacked the Allies at anchor off Palermo. French Marshal Louis Victor de Vivonne and Marquis Abraham Duquesne defeated and killed Dutch Admiral Jan de Haan, securing command of the Mediterranean (12 June 1676).

Palermo I 1860 I 2nd Italian War of Independence

Giuseppe Garibaldi and "The Thousand" landed in western Sicily for victory at **Calatafimi**, then marched on Palermo, held by 18,000 Neapolitans under General Ferdinando Lanza. Garibaldi broke into the city although the Neapolitans resisted strongly before finally surrendering with heavy losses. Garibaldi then marched east for his decisive victory at **Milazzo** (27 May–6 June).

Palermo I 1943 I World War II (Southern Europe)

American General George Patton landed in southwest Sicily around **Gela** and advanced north through Agrigento (16 July), then swept into the northwest where General Geoffrey Keyes seized Palermo from General Giusseppe Molinaro. While the advance secured many Italian prisoners, it was of doubtful strategic value and the Americans turned east towards **Messina** (22 July 1943).

Palestrina I 1849 I 1st Italian War of Independence

Advancing to support the French siege of the self-declared Republic of Rome, Ferdinand II of the Two Sicilies sent General Carlo Zucchi and 7,000 men against Giuseppe Garibaldi at Palestrina, 25 miles southeast of **Rome**. A fierce action saw the numerically superior Neapolitans driven off and the Bourbon advance was repulsed again ten days later at nearby **Velletri** (9 May 1849).

Palestro I 1859 I 2nd Italian War of Independence

When King Victor Emmanuel II of Sardinia-Piedmont mobilised in support of independence, he faced an Austrian invasion under General Philipp Stadion von Thannhausen. Ten days after being repulsed at **Montebello**, the Austrians attacked Piedmontese General Enrico Cialdini crossing the Sesia near Palestro. The Austrians were heavily repulsed and driven out of Palestro (30 May 1859).

Pali I 1857 I Indian Mutiny

The British-supported Rajah of Jodhpur faced rebellion by his vassal Kusal Singh, Thakur of Awah, and sent his forces under Anad Singh to hold Pali, southeast of Jodhpur. Unwisely leaving his well-defended position, Anad Singh was routed and killed in a surprise dawn assault and the army of Jodhpur suffered severe losses. The Thakur lost the following January at **Awah** (8 September 1857).

Palikao I 1860 I 2nd Opium War
See **Baliqiao**

Palkhed I 1728 I Later Mughal-Maratha Wars

As the Marathas expanded their power into northern India, Mulhar Rao Holkar in the service of Baji Rao I trapped the army of Nizam-ul-Mulk of Hyderabad in dry hills at Palkhed, 20 miles west of Aurangabab. With his supplies cut off, the Nizam was forced to make terms. Holkar quickly rose to senior command in the Peshwar's army (28 February 1728).

Pallet I 1793 I French Revolutionary Wars (Vendée War)

Royalist rebel leader Charles Bonchamp defeated Republican General Jean-Baptiste Kléber at **Torfou** (19 September) then pursued him north as far as Pallet, just 20 miles from Nantes, where he inflicted a sharp defeat on the retreating army, killing many of their wounded. However, Kléber was saved by reinforcements from Nantes itself and Bonchamp eventually withdrew (24 September 1793).

Palmar, Mexico I 1812 I Mexican Wars of Independence

In support of the soldier-priest José María Morelos after **Cuautla**, insurgent leaders Pablo Galeana and Nicolás Bravo took 600 men against Colonel Juan Labaqui at Palmar, southeast of Puebla. Heavy fighting saw Labaqui and 47 others killed and the Royalists surrendered, yielding the rebels 200 prisoners and a large quantity of arms, including three guns (19 August 1812).

Palmar, Mexico I 1813 I Mexican Wars of Independence

Continuing the fight for independence under soldier-priest José María Morelos, Mariano Matamaros attacked a large Royalist convoy led by Colonel Manuel Martínez near Palmar, southeast of Puebla. The Royalists were routed, losing over 200 dead and almost 400 prisoners. Morelos was soon defeated at **Valladolid** and Matamaros lost in January 1814 at **Puruarán** (14 October 1813).

Palmar, Uruguay I 1838 I Uruguayan Civil War

Despite defeat at **Carpinteria** (September 1836), former Uruguayan President Fructuoso Rivera renewed his rising against Manuel Oribe and met the President's brother Ignacio Oribe at Palmar del Arroyo Grande, in western Uruguay near Cordobesa. The government army suffered decisive defeat after which Manuel Oribe fled to Buenos Aires and Rivera regained the Presidency (15 June 1838).

Palmira I 1831 I Colombian Civil Wars

General Rafael Urdaneta seized power after victory at **Santuario**, then faced rebellion in the Cauca Valley led by Liberal Generals José María Obando and José Hilario López. Government forces under General Pedro Muguerza and Colonel Manuel José Collazos were badly defeated near Palmira, northeast of Cali, and by early

May Urdaneta was forced to resign (10 February 1831).

Palmito Ranch I 1865 I American Civil War (Trans-Mississippi)

The reputed last battle of the war saw Union Colonel Theodore H. Barrett lead about 300 men from Brazos Santiago inland along the Rio Grande to attack the Confederate camp at Palmito Ranch, just outside Brownsville, Texas. Barrett was eventually driven off by Colonel John S. Ford, losing over 100 men in heavy fighting, and the war soon came to an end (12–13 May 1865).

Palmyra I 272 I Roman-Palmyrean War

With her army routed by Emperor Aurelian at **Immae** and **Emessa**, Queen Zenobia of Palmyra withdrew under siege to her capital in the Syrian desert. Expected Persian aid did not come and, after Aurelian stormed Palmyra, he spared the city and started for Rome with Zenobia as a captive. However, when the Palmyreans massacred Aurelian's garrison, he turned back and razed the city to the ground.

Palmyra I 1941 I World War II (Middle East)

Despite the fall of **Damascus**, Vichy forces continued fighting in central Syria along the strategic pipeline from Iraq. General George Clarke's Habforce, including the Arab Legion, converged on Palmyra (modern Tadmur), which was captured after hard fighting. It was one of the last major actions in Syria and Vichy commander Henri Dentz soon sued for peace (23 June–3 July 1941).

Palo I 1815 I Colombian War of Independence

While Spanish General Pablo Morillo besieged **Cartagena**, other Royalists led by Aparico Vidaurrázaga occupied Popayán then faced a large Patriot army under General José María Cabal. Marching out to the nearby Palo River, Vidaurrázaga was decisively defeated, losing 350 casualties and 500 prisoners. Po-

payán was lost until Spanish victory in June 1816 at **El Tambo** (5 July 1815).

Palo Alto I 1846 I American-Mexican War

American General Zachary Taylor advancing from the mouth of the Rio Grande to relieve besieged **Fort Texas** was met to the northeast at Palo Alto by a much larger Mexican force under General Mariano Arista. After suffering heavy losses to artillery fire, the Mexicans fled with 400 casualties and were defeated again next day at **Resaca de la Palma** (8 May 1846).

Palo Duro I 1874 I Red River Indian War

With Indians in northern Texas on the warpath over destruction of buffalo, Colonel Ranald Mackenzie attacked the stronghold in Palo Duro Canyon, southeast of Amarillo, held by Kiowa under Lone Wolf and some Comanche. While few lives were lost, massive supplies and over 1,000 captured horses were destroyed, effectively ending the Indian capacity to fight the war (28 September 1874).

Palo Hincado I 1809 I Napoleonic Wars (5th Coalition)

See **Santo Domingo**

Palonegro I 1900 I Colombian War of the Thousand Days

In the most decisive action of Liberal revolt against President Manuel Antonio Sanclemente, government forces recovered from defeat at **Peralonso** (December 1899) and General Gabriel Vargas Santos beat Liberal General Próspero Pinzon at Palonegro, just west of Bucaramanga. Sanclemente was soon replaced by José Manuel Marroquín, though war dragged on for two years (11–16 May 1900).

Palosina I 1919 I Waziristan Campaign

In the wake of the Third Afghan War, Wana and Mahsud tribesmen in Waziristan, southwest of Peshawar, rebelled and an Indian army column under General Andrew Sheen marched to the Palosina Plain. Sikh infantry suffered costly losses failing to drive the rebels from nearby hills, but the rebels also lost heavily to machine-gun and artillery fire and withdrew to **Ahnai Tangi** (19–22 December 1919).

Paltzig ▌ 1759 ▌ Seven Years War (Europe)

See **Kay**

Pa Mok ▌ 1585 ▌ Burmese-Siamese Wars

The Burmese client state of Chiang Mai sent a force reputed to be over 100,000 men, with war elephants and cavalry, against King Naresuan of Siam, who marched north from Ayutthaya to meet them at Pa Mok. Using barge-mounted heavy cannon, Naresuan secured a bloody and decisive victory, forcing Chiang Mai to withdraw. In 1593 he finally overthrew Burmese overlordship at **Nong Sarai**.

Pampa Grande ▌ 1933 ▌ Chaco War

Attacking Bolivian forces in the Chaco Boreal, Paraguay's 7th Division under Colonel José A. Ortiz assaulted and seized Pampa Grande, taking more than 600 Bolivian prisoners. The same day Colonel Eugenio Garay's 8th Division took 250 more prisoners further east at Pozo Favorito. The main offensive soon commenced to the southwest against **Alihuatá** (15 September 1933).

Pamplona ▌ 1813 ▌ Napoleonic Wars (Peninsular Campaign)

As Allied forces advanced into the western Pyrenees after **Vitoria**, British General Sir Rowland Hill and later Spanish General Henry O'Donnell blockaded Pamplona, held by Governor Louis-Pierre Cassan. After a threat to execute the French officers, the fortress was starved into surrender and Arthur Wellesley Lord Wellington was able to press his invasion of France (25 June–31 October 1813).

Pamunkey ▌ 1625 ▌ Powhatan Indian Wars

English settlers in Virginia under Governor Sir Francis Wyatt responded to the massacre at **Jamestown** (March 1622) with a bloody war against the Algonquin confederation, led by Opechancanough. Under the pretense of making peace, the settlers fell on the Indian village at nearby Pamunkey, reportedly killing 1,000. With both sides exhausted a peace treaty was signed in 1632.

Panama ▌ 1671 ▌ Morgan's Raids on Panama

Two years after taking **Porto Bello**, on the Panama Isthmus, Welsh-born Henry Morgan took about 2,000 buccaneers through the jungle to attack the city of Panama, held by Don Juan Perez de Guzman. The Spanish were driven off in very heavy fighting and the city was sacked and burned. Morgan was later knighted by Charles II and returned as Deputy Governor of Jamaica (16 January 1671).

Panama ▌ 1989 ▌ American Invasion of Panama

After President Manuel Noriega of Panama declared war on the United States, a large American invasion force was sent to seize the President and restore democracy. By the time fighting ended, 26 Americans had been killed, plus about 300 Panamanian military and over 200 civilians. Noriega was taken to the United States, where he was imprisoned for drug trafficking (20–31 December 1989).

Panay Incident ▌ 1937 ▌ Sino-Japanese War

American and British civilians sailing up the Yangzi in a small convoy to escape the Japanese advance on **Nanjing** were bombed and strafed by Japanese aircraft. The American gunboat *Panay* was sunk (with three killed and many wounded) along with two oil barges sunk. Anxious to avoid war, America demanded and received an apology and compensation (12 December 1937).

Pancalia ▌ 978 ▌ Byzantine Military Rebellions

When Byzantine General Bardas Sclerus was proclaimed Emperor by his troops and seized much of Asia Minor, Emperor Basil II sent for the great warrior Bardas Phocas, who marched east to meet the usurper on the Plain of Pancalia, near Amorium. Phocas was defeated and fell back on the Halys. They fought again the following year at **Aquae Saravenac** and Bardas Sclerus was defeated (19 June 978).

Panchgaum ▮ 1775 ▮ Maratha Wars of Succession

During civil war against Raghunath Rao (who had murdered his nephew to make himself Peshwa), Sabaji Sindhia—on behalf of the legitimate government in Poona—fought his own brother Mudhoji at Panchgaum, ten miles south of Nagpur. The usurper secured a major victory when Mudhoji defeated and killed Sabaji, but Raghunath was soon beaten and deposed at **Adas** (26 January 1775).

Pancorbo ▮ 1808 ▮ Napoleonic Wars (Peninsular Campaign)

Spanish General Joachim Blake was defeated at **Zornoza** (29 October) then had to abandon **Bilbao** when the French attacked at **Durango**. The same day further south at Pancorbo near Miranda, he was attacked by French Marshals Francois Lefebvre and Claude Victor. Blake lost about 600 casualties before disengaging to withdraw through **Valmaseda** towards **Espinosa** (31 October 1808).

Pandapatan ▮ 1902 ▮ American-Moro Wars

See **Bayan**

Pandhana ▮ 1720 ▮ Mughal-Hyderabad War

See **Ratanpur**

Pandjeh ▮ 1885 ▮ Russo-Afghan War

See **Penjdeh**

Pandosia ▮ 331 BC ▮ Macedonian Conquests

Alexander of Epirus attempted to emulate his nephew Alexander the Great by invading southern Italy to support Greek residents of Tarentum against the Lucanians and Samnites. Despite some early success, Alexander was decisively defeated by a force of Lucanians and Bruttians at Pandosia, on the Acheron in Bruttium near the border with Lucania. He was then assassinated.

Pandu Nadi ▮ 1857 ▮ Indian Mutiny

Advancing northeast from Allahabad to recapture Cawnpore, General Sir Henry Havelock secured victory at **Aong**, but the rebels attempted to hold the bridge on the flooded Pandu Nadi. After a sharp action the same day in very hot conditions, Havelock's exhausted men seized the bridge when explosive charges failed. The next day they advanced eight miles to **Cawnpore** (15 July 1857).

Paneas ▮ 198 BC ▮ 5th Syrian War

Antiochus III of Syria failed to conquer Palestine in 217 BC at **Raphia** and returned 19 years later with a huge army to defeat an Egyptian force under the Greek Commander Scopas in the Jordan Valley at Paneas (later Baniyas). Flushed with victory, Antiochus then captured Gaza and Jerusalem and Ptolemy V Epiphanes of Egypt renounced any claim to Palestine and Lower Syria.

Pangani ▮ 1889 ▮ German Colonial Wars in Africa

Defeated in German East Africa near **Bagamoyo**, Arab rebel leader Abushiri ibn Salim was driven out of Sadani (7 June) then was bombarded and defeated at his main stronghold in Pangani (in modern Tanzania) by Commissioner Hermann von Wissmann. After nearby Tanga also fell, Abushiri fled into the interior where he was later captured and hanged, effectively ending the rising (July 1889).

Pange ▮ 1870 ▮ Franco-Prussian War

See **Colombey**

Pangpang ▮ 1904 ▮ American-Moro Wars

Major Hugh Scott recovered from a wound suffered as the rebel Panglima Hassan escaped from capture at **Lake Seit**, then led a fresh offensive against the Muslim Moro leader on Jolo, in the southern Philippines. The rebel fortress at Pangpang was destroyed by artillery fire with about 80 Moros killed. Hassan escaped again but was cornered and shot down at nearby **Bud Bagsak** (5 March 1904).

Pangul ▌ 1418–1420 ▌ Vijayanagar-Bahmani Wars

On his last campaign, Bahmanid Sultan Firuz Shah attacked Pangul, north of the Krishna, held by Vira Vijaya of Vijayanagar. Firuz suffered heavy losses securing a costly victory then besieged the town. After two years, with the Bahmani army decimated by disease, Vira Vijaya attacked and the Sultan was routed and withdrew. The costly failure shattered Firuz and within two years he was dead.

Panhala ▌ 1660 ▌ Bijapur-Maratha Wars

Maratha commander Shivaji killed the Bijapur General Afzal Khan at **Pratabgarh** then captured Panhala near Kolhapur, where he was besieged by the Bijapur army under Fazl Khan, son of the murdered General. Shivaji fled after the fall of nearby Pavingarh (13 July) and Panhala finally had to surrender when Sultan Ali Adil Shah sent further reinforcements (2 March–22 September 1660).

Panhala ▌ 1673 ▌ Bijapur-Maratha Wars

When Ali Adil Shah of Bijapur died (1672) Maratha General Shivaji sent Annaji Pant in a fresh assault against the Sultan's four-year-old son Sikander and Regent Khawas Khan. Approaching Panhala, near Kolhapur, a Maratha advance unit of just 60 under Kondaji Farzand mounted the walls in a courageous night-time escalade. They killed the commander and secured the fortress (6 March 1673).

Panhala ▌ 1701 ▌ Mughal-Maratha Wars

On a renewed offensive south of Bombay, Emperor Aurangzeb and Zulfiqar Khan besieged the Maratha leader Trimbak at the powerful fortress of Panhala, near Kolhapur. A relief force under Dhanaji Jadhav was heavily repulsed (23 January) and mines were prepared to destroy the walls. Instead the Mughals negotiated a massive payment to achieve a negotiated surrender (January–28 May 1701).

Paniani ▌ 1782 ▌ 2nd British-Mysore War

After victory at **Trikalur**, Colonel Thomas Humberston again advanced inland from the Malabar Coast of southern India, then had to withdraw in the face of 20,000 Marathas under Tipu Sultan (son of Haidar Ali of Mysore). Falling back on the British position on the Paniani, he repulsed a huge Maratha attack and Tipu withdrew on the death of his father (27 November 1782).

Paniar ▌ 1843 ▌ British-Gwalior War
See **Panniar**

Panion ▌ 198 BC ▌ 5th Syrian War
See **Paneas**

Panipat ▌ 1526 ▌ Mughal Conquest of Northern India

Babur, Ruler of Kabul, marched from Afghanistan into northern India, where he conquered the Punjab then advanced against Ibrahim Lodi, Afghan Sultan of Delhi. Ibrahim attacked the enemy defensive position to the north at Panipat with a vastly superior army, but was decisively defeated and killed. Babur then occupied Delhi and Agra to establish the 300-year Mughal Empire (21 April 1526).

Panipat ▌ 1556 ▌ Mughal Conquest of Northern India

After victory at **Sirhind** (June 1555), the 14-year-old Mughal Emperor Akbar and Regent Bairam Khan marched towards **Delhi** against Afghan-Hindu forces under the Hindu usurper Hemu, who had recaptured the capital. Despite being heavily outnumbered, Akbar crushed Hemu 50 miles north at Panipat. Delhi was retaken and Akbar restored the 300-year Mughal Empire (5 November 1556).

Panipat ▌ 1761 ▌ Indian Campaigns of Ahmad Shah

Afghan General Ahmad Shah Durrani beat a Maratha force at **Barari Ghat** then a year later marched against the main Maratha army under the Peshwa's cousin Sadashiv Bhao. North of Delhi, at Panipat, Bhao and the Peshwa's teenage son

Viswas Rao were killed, along with up to 200,000 troops and camp followers, and Maratha military power in the north was destroyed (14 January 1761).

Panium I 198 BC I 5th Syrian War
See **Paneas**

Panjkora I 1895 I Chitral Campaign
As General Sir Robert Low marched northeast from Nowshera to relieve a British force besieged by rebels in the Kashmir Kingdom of **Chitral**, Colonel Fred Battye over-ambitiously pursued Umra Khan's Chitralis across the Panjkora, north of Chakdara. When the river bridge was washed away Battye was killed in the withdrawal. However, Low soon resumed his advance (13 April 1895).

Panjshir Valley I 1982 I Afghan Civil War
On a large-scale offensive north of Kabul, 12,000 Afghan and Soviet troops in the Panjshir Valley attacked Mujahaden rebels under Ahmad Shah Massud fighting the Kabul government. Two separate operations failed after intense fighting cost up to 3,000 government and Soviet killed and wounded, plus the loss of 60 armoured vehicles and 35 aircraft and helicopters (May–September 1982).

Panjshir Valley I 1984 I Afghan Civil War
About 15,000 Afghan and Soviet troops led by Russian General Saradov renewed their offensive in the Panjshir Valley north of Kabul, attacking Mujahaden rebels under Ahmad Shah Massud. Supported by heavy bombing and helicopter assault, the Kabul government troops forced Massud to withdraw and they captured high-profile rebel commander Abdul Wahed (April–May 1984).

Panjwin I 1983 I Iraq-Iran War
Iranian forces campaigning in Iraqi Kurdistan took **Haj Omran** (29 July) then launched a fresh offensive east of Suleimaniya. Despite Iraqi air attack and chemical weapons, Iran and its Kurdish allies secured much of the Panjwin Valley, but were halted outside Panjwin itself. By early 1985,

anti-Baghdad forces reportedly controlled over one-third of Kurdistan (20 October–30 November 1983).

Panniar I 1843 I British-Gwalior War
During a disputed succession of the Maharaja of Gwalior in central India, Governor General Lord Ellenborough sent a large force under General Sir Hugh Gough. On the same day that Gough routed the Marathas at **Maharajpur**, his left wing led by General John Grey defeated a separate Maratha force at Panniar, southwest of Gwalior, bringing the war to an end (29 December 1843).

Panormus, Greece I 429 BC I Great Peloponnesian War
See **Naupactus**

Panormus, Sicily I 251 BC I 1st Punic War
When Rome captured Panormus (modern Palermo), Carthaginian General Hasdrubal launched a massive assault to recover his former base in Sicily. However, he was heavily defeated by Lucius Caecilius Metellus, with all his war-elephants killed or captured. The victory encouraged the Roman Senate to provide fresh ships to attack remaining Carthaginian strongholds in western Sicily.

Panowce I 1633 I Polish-Tatar Wars
See **Kamieniec**

Pantano de Vargas I 1819 I Colombian War of Independence
Patriot leader Simón Bolívar advanced through **Gámeza** towards Bogotá, crossing the Sogamoso to attack Spanish Colonel José María Barreiro at Pantano de Vargas, northeast of Tunja. Both sides lost heavily in a fierce yet indecisive action, though the day was saved by Bolívar's llaneros under Juan José Rondon. Barreiro was later forced to fall back towards **Boyacá** (25 July 1819).

Pantin I 1814 I Napoleonic Wars (French Campaign)
See **Paris**

Paoki I 1948 I 3rd Chinese Revolutionary Civil War
See **Baoji**

Paoli I 1777 I War of the American Revolution
Pursuing General George Washington after victory at **Cooch's Bridge** and the **Brandywine**, British commander Sir William Howe sent General Charles Grey against an American rearguard under General Anthony Wayne. Grey surprised and routed Wayne in a night attack at Paoli, near the Schuylkill, and a few days later Howe marched into Philadelphia (21 September 1777).

Paoting I 1928 I 2nd Chinese Revolutionary Civil War
See **Baoding**

Papremis I 459 BC I Greco-Persian Wars
In support of revolt against Persia in Egypt by Inaros of Libya, Athens sent a large fleet to the Nile Delta, where Persian commander Achaemenes (brother of Xerxes) was defeated and killed at Papremis. The Athenians then advanced south and seized most of Memphis. The citadel held out for four years until a Persian relief force arrived overland from Syria for victory at **Prosopitis**.

Papua I 1942–1943 I World War II (Pacific)
With an invasion of Port Moresby thwarted in the **Coral Sea** (May 1942), Japanese landed on the north coast of Papua and marched overland towards the capital. With a landing repulsed in the east at **Milne Bay**, the invaders were finally halted outside Port Moresby. Driven back across the **Kokoda Trail**, they were destroyed at **Gona**, **Buna** and **Sanananda** (23 July 1942–21 January 1943).

Parabiago I 1339 I Condottieri Wars
During the brutal condottieri campaigns in northern Italy, large bodies of mercenaries ravaged the countryside for booty, with one such band formed by Lodrisio Visconti to attack Milan. The so-called "company of adventurers" was repulsed with heavy losses at Parabiago, northwest of Milan. The threat of the roaming bands continued for many years (21 February 1339).

Paraetacene I 317 BC I Wars of the Diadochi
Amid war between the successors of Alexander the Great, Antigonus invaded Persia and met Eumenes near Isfahan at Paraetacene. After a massive battle, with more than 40,000 men on either side, the action was broken off inconclusively and the two armies withdrew with both Generals claiming tactical victory. The following winter Antigonus won the decisive action at **Gabiene**.

Paraguarí I 1811 I Argentine War of Independence
See **Cerro Porteño**

Parana I 1865 I War of the Triple Alliance
See **Riachuelo**

Parana I 1866 I War of the Triple Alliance
See **Estero Bellaco**

Paredón I 1914 I Mexican Revolution
With Federal forces falling back in central Mexico after disaster at **Torréon** (3 April), rebel General Francisco (Pancho) Villa detoured to attack a strong government position at Paredón, north of Saltillo. After a total rout in which more than half the government troops became casualties or deserted, the Federal garrison abandoned Saltillo and Villa advanced on **Zacatecas** (17 May 1914).

Parí I 1816 I Argentine War of Independence
A year after Spain secured western Bolivia at **Sipe-Sipe**, Royalist General Francisco Javier Aguilera in the east attacked Argentine Colonel Ignacio Warnes at Parí, near Santa Cruz (seized by Warnes after battle at **Florida**). A decisive Argentine defeat saw Warnes captured and beheaded and Aguilera executed over 900 Patriots, including many women and children (21 November 1816).

Paris I 885–886 I Viking Raids on France

In one of the largest-scale Viking actions in Europe, Siegfrid and Sinric besieged Paris, heroically defended for almost a year by Odo (Eudes) Marquess of Neustria and Bishop Gozelin. After Frankish victory at **Montfaucon**, King Charles III—the Fat—bought the Norse army off and allowed it to plunder Burgundy. He was soon deposed and Odo became King (November 885–October 886).

Paris I 1429 I Hundred Years War

Following French victory at **Patay** (19 June), Jeanne d'Arc captured Troyes, Chalons and Rheims from the English, then rashly attempted an attack on Paris on the religious festival of Our Lady's Nativity, despite lack of support from the newly crowned King Charles VII. She was wounded by an arrow in the thigh and her impetuous attack was driven off (8 September 1429).

Paris I 1436 I Hundred Years War

Philip Duke of Burgundy abandoned support for the English when they were repulsed from central France and joined King Charles VII, ending the long-running Burgundian-Armagnac Civil War. The reconciled French allies then marched on Paris and Arthur Count of Richemont captured the city after the English garrison of the Bastille were starved into surrender (13 April 1436).

Paris I 1590 I 9th French War of Religion

Henry of Navarre, who had claimed the French throne as Henry IV, defeated the Holy League at **Ivry** (14 March) then besieged the Catholics in Paris where they were led by Charles Duke of Mayenne. The city was nearly starved into submission when Alessandro Farnese Duke of Parma arrived with a Spanish relief force and the siege ended (May–August 1590).

**Paris I 1814 I Napoleonic Wars
(French Campaign)**

As the Allies closed in on Paris, Marshals Auguste Marmont and Édouard Mortier attempted to defend the capital against the massive combined army of Prince Karl Philipp Schwar-

zenberg and General Gebhard von Blucher. After action at Pantin, Romainville and Montmartre, Marmont surrendered Paris. Two weeks later Bonaparte abdicated and went into exile (30 March 1814).

Paris I 1870–1871 I Franco-Prussian War

With much of the French army besieged at **Metz** or captured at **Sedan**, Marshal Helmuth von Moltke and Prince Friedrich Wilhelm laid siege to Paris itself, defended by troops and militia under General Louis Jules Trochu. After failed French sorties, including **Villiers** and **Le Bourget**, a massive siege bombardment forced the starving city to surrender (20 September 1870–28 January 1871).

Paris I 1871 I Paris Commune

In the wake of humiliating defeat by Germany, Republicans tried to establish an independent government in Paris and faced a massive assault by Royalist troops. The damaging conflict that followed saw about 750 troops killed. Over 20,000 Communards died in the fighting or were executed and thousands more were deported as Royalist Government was restored (18 March–21 May 1871).

**Paris I 1944 I World War II
(Western Europe)**

As Allied armies broke out from **Normandy** and advanced across France, Resistance units in Paris rose against the remaining German garrison. After heavy street fighting, Free French forces under General Philippe Leclerc arrived to liberate Paris and General Dietrich von Cholitz surrendered the city. General Charles de Gaulle arrived next day to claim victory (19–24 August 1944).

**Parkany I 1683 I Later Turkish-
Habsburg Wars**

John III Sobieski of Poland destroyed the Turkish siege of **Vienna** and pursued his enemy to Parkany, near **Esztergom**, where he was initially repulsed. Two days later Charles V arrived with his cavalry and the Turks suffered a terrible defeat, with over 20,000 reported killed. Esztergom itself soon fell and Grand Vizier Kara

Mustafa Pasha was later executed for failure (7–9 October 1683).

Parker's Cross Roads | 1862 | American Civil War (Western Theatre)

Returning from raiding western Tennessee, Confederate General Nathan Bedford Forrest was intercepted by Union forces under General Jeremiah C. Sullivan north of **Lexington** at Parker's Cross Roads. Forrest repulsed a brigade under Colonel Cyrus L. Dunham, but was surprised by Colonel John W. Fuller and lost about 500 men before withdrawing across the Tennessee River (31 December 1862).

Parma | 1247–1248 | Imperial-Papal Wars

When the north Italian city of Parma revolted against Emperor Frederick II, its struggle became a trial of strength between the pro-Imperial Ghibellines and the pro-Papal Guelfs of cities such as Milan. The reinforced garrison of Parma sortied after a bloody six-month siege and destroyed the Emperor's camp, forcing him into a humiliating withdrawal (July 1247–February 1248).

Parma | 1734 | War of the Polish Succession

In support of the former King Stanislas Leszcynski of Poland, his son-in-law Louis XV sent French troops into Austrian-held Lombardy, where Marshal François de Coigny narrowly defeated and killed Austrian Field Marshal Claudius von Mercy in a brutal battle at Parma. Coigny went on to capture Milan, though it was returned to Austria after the war (29 June 1734).

Parrot's Beak | 1985 | Afghan Civil War

Having repulsed a guerrilla offensive at **Khost**, up to 20,000 Russian and Afghan government troops converged on the area near the Pakistan border southeast of Kabul known as the Parrot's Beak, held by Mujahaden commander Jalaluddin Haqqani. Massive guerrilla supply dumps were captured, though the rebel base at **Zhawar** did not fall until the following year (August–September 1985).

Parsa | 1815 | British-Gurkha War

As General Bennet Marley advanced slowly north into central Nepal, huge Gurkha forces surprised and overwhelmed his advanced post southwest of Kathmandu at Parsa, killing 120 (including Captain Henry Sibley) and wounding another 130. A second attack the same day also destroyed the smaller post at nearby Samanpur. Marley was dismissed and fled in disgrace (1 January 1815).

Parwan Durrah | 1221 | Conquests of Genghis Khan

Leading a counter-offensive against the Mongol Genghis Khan, Prince Jalal-ud-din of Khwarezm (who succeeded on his father's death after defeat at **Hamadan** in 1220) marched north from Ghazni in southern Afghanistan. Jalal-ud-din defeated Mongols under the Khan's Tatar adopted son Sigi Khutukhu near Kabul at Parwan Durrah, but was soon destroyed by Genghis Khan at the **Indus**.

Parwan Durrah | 1840 | 1st British-Afghan War

Former Amir Dost Muhammad was defeated in northern Afghanistan at **Bamian** and soon after was driven off by part of General Sir Robert Sale's brigade in a close-fought battle at Parwan Durrah, near Charikar north of Kabul (despite the shameful withdrawal of the 2nd Bengal Cavalry). Dost Muhammad soon surrendered and was exiled in India until he was restored in 1843 (2 November 1840).

Pasajes | 1836 | 1st Carlist War
See **San Sebastian**

Pasang Santol | 1897 | Philippines War of Independence
See **Dasmariñas**

Pasaquina | 1871 | Central American National Wars

When Honduras and El Salvador accused each other of supporting domestic rebellion, war broke out and Honduran troops marched into El Salvador. Near the border at Pasaquina, Honduran exile

Florencio Xatruch defeated the invaders and led Salvadoran forces into Honduras. He had little further success and fled when rebels ousted the Salvadoran government at **Santa Ana** (16 March 1871).

Pasaquina **I** 1876 **I** Central American National Wars

Two years after securing a friendly government in Honduras with victory at **Comayagua**, President Justo Ruffino Barrios of Guatemala invaded El Salvador to win at **Apaneca**, while a smaller column under General Gregorio Solares attacked in the east. Near Pasaquina, north of La Union, Solares won a second victory and Barrios installed his friend Rafael Zaldivar as President (19 April 1876).

Paso de Cuevas **I** 1865 **I** War of the Triple Alliance

Recovering from losses at **Riachuelo**, near Corrientes (11 June), Brazilian Admiral Francisco Manuel Barroso tried to advance down the Parana through the pass at Cuevas, just south of Bellavista, defended by Paraguayan Colonel José Maria Bruquez with 3,000 men and 34 guns. Barroso suffered severe damage, with 24 dead and 42 wounded, and retired on Rincon de Soto (12 August 1865).

Paso de Patria **I** 1866 **I** War of the Triple Alliance
See **Tuyutí**

Paso Real **I** 1896 **I** 2nd Cuban War of Independence

Insurgent leader Antonio Maceo marched east from Mantua in western Cuba where he was attacked by Spanish General Agustin Luque on the railway northeast of Pinar del Río at Paso Real. The Cubans sustained the heavier losses in severe fighting along very extended lines, but managed to drive off the Spanish, with Luque severely wounded. Maceo soon struck back at **Candelaria** (January 1896).

Pasques **I** 1870 **I** Franco-Prussian War
See **Dijon (2nd)**

Passaro **I** 1718 **I** War of the Quadruple Alliance
See **Cape Passaro**

Passchendaele (1st) **I** 1917 **I** World War I (Western Front)

Despite shocking losses during Third **Ypres**, most recently around **Poelcappelle**, British commander Sir Douglas Haig was determined to reach his original objective, the village of Passchendaele, northeast of Ypres. Fighting in terrible mud, Generals Sir Herbert Plumer and Hubert Gough were driven off with heavy losses. They attacked again two weeks later (12 October 1917).

Passchendaele (2nd) **I** 1917 **I** World War I (Western Front)

In the final effort of his offensive northeast of **Ypres**, British commander Sir Douglas Haig again sent Generals Sir Herbert Plumer and Hubert Gough against Passchendaele, which was finally taken by the newly arrived Canadian Corps. The Third Battle of Ypres ended and Passchendaele came to symbolise the pointless loss of life in the mud of Flanders (26 October–6 November 1917).

Passo do Rosario **I** 1827 **I** Argentine-Brazilian War
See **Ituzaingó**

Pastrengo **I** 1799 **I** French Revolutionary Wars (2nd Coalition)
See **Verona**

Patan **I** 1790 **I** Mughal-Maratha War of Ismail Beg

When renegade Mughal General Ismail Beg and his Rajput allies were besieged near Ajmer at Patan Tanwar (Turavati) by Mahadji Sindhia and General Benoit de Boigne, Ismail attacked the Marathas but his cavalry failed to break de Boigne's squares. De Boigne then routed Ismail, capturing massive plunder in guns, elephants and horses, and the renegade fled to the Punjab (20 June 1790).

Patay ▌ 1429 ▌ Hundred Years War

Six weeks after defeating the English at the siege of **Orleans**, French forces led by Jean Duke of Alencon and Jeanne d'Arc surprised the retreating English under John Talbot Earl of Shrewsbury and Sir John Fastolfe at Patay, northwest of Orleans. An unexpected attack led by Etienne de Vignolles, La Hire, routed the English and Shrewsbury was captured and held for four years (19 June 1429).

Paterangi ▌ 1864 ▌ 2nd New Zealand War
See **Mangapiko**

Patiala ▌ 1857 ▌ Indian Mutiny

Colonel Thomas Seaton campaigning east of Aligarh won near **Kasganj** then marched to Patiala, northeast of Etah, against a large rebel force under Ahmed Yir Khan and Mohson Ali. An artillery duel and a bayonet charge forced the rebels to flee, leaving perhaps 600 dead. Seaton then returned for Aligarh for his convoy before advancing southeast on **Mainpuri** (17 December 1857).

Patila, Plain of ▌ 1393 ▌ Conquests of Tamerlane
See **Shiraz**

Patna ▌ 1759 ▌ Seven Years War (India)

Encouraged by Nawab Shuja-ud-Daula of Oudh, the Shahzada Ali Gauhar (son of Emperor Alamgir II) invaded Bengal against English-supported Nawab Mir Jafar and besieged Patna, defended by Raja Ramnarain. With a British force approaching under Robert Clive, a final assault by the Shahzada and Muhammad Kuli of Allahabad was heavily repulsed and they withdrew (4–5 April 1759).

Patna (1st) ▌ 1763 ▌ Bengal War

Mir Kasim, the warlike new Nawab of Bengal, threatened William Ellis, the local East India Company agent, who led a small column of troops which surprised and captured Patna. However, a counter-attack by Bengali troops under Armenian mercenary Maskarian drove them out with most

taken captive. The prisoners, including Ellis, were later murdered (25 June 1763).

Patna (2nd) ▌ 1763 ▌ Bengal War

Following his defeat at **Udaynala** (5 September) Mir Kasim, deposed Nawab of Bengal, murdered prisoners earlier captured at Patna, then faced a substantial British-Sepoy force under Major Thomas Adams, who advanced to besiege Patna. Adams captured the town after heavy fighting which caused severe Bengali losses. Mir Kasim fought on until late 1764 at **Buxar** (6 November 1763).

Patna ▌ 1764 ▌ Bengal War

Advancing to attack Nawab Shuja-ud-Daula of Oudh, British Colonel John Carnac withdrew to prepared positions outside Patna when Shuja counter-attacked. A daylong action saw Shuja repulsed with heavy losses. However, Carnac did not pursue and the Nawab remained a month before the rains forced him to withdraw. The decisive action was fought in October at **Buxar** (3 May 1764).

Patras ▌ 429 BC ▌ Great Peloponnesian War

When Sparta sent Admiral Cnemus against Acarnania, at the mouth of the Corinthian Gulf, the Athenian Phormio allowed the large main fleet to pass then attacked a reinforcement of 47 Peloponnesian ships crossing the Gulf of Patras. Commanding just 20 vessels, Phormio secured a great victory and returned with 12 prizes to **Naupactus**, where he soon attacked the main fleet.

Patriot Hill ▌ 1861 ▌ American Civil War (Trans-Mississippi)
See **Shoal Creek**

Patton Nagar ▌ 1965 ▌ 2nd Indo-Pakistan War
See **Khem Karan**

Paulus Hook ▌ 1779 ▌ War of the American Revolution

Encouraged by success at **Stony Point** (16 July), American General George Washington sent Major Henry Lee against the Hudson River fort at Paulus Hook, New Jersey City, held by Major William Sutherland. A pre-dawn raid by Lee inflicted 50 casualties and he withdrew with 150 prisoners. Lee received a gold medal from Congress and Sutherland was court-martialled (19 August 1779).

Pavia ∎ 271 ∎ Roman-Alemannic Wars

Emperor Aurelian quickly recovered from defeat at **Placentia** to rout an invading army of Alemanni tribesmen on the east coast of Italy at **Fano**. The invaders started to return north with Aurelian in pursuit and, at the city of Pavia (Ticinum) south of Milan, he crushed the remaining Alemanni forces, effectively ending the threat to Rome. The Emperor then turned his attention to **Palmyra**.

Pavia ∎ 351 ∎ Later Roman Military Civil Wars

The Western usurper Flavius Magnus Magnentius fled his disastrous defeat at **Mursa** (28 September) and reached northern Italy before turning on his pursuers near Pavia. While he dealt a sharp defeat to the Imperial army, Emperor Constantius refused to make peace with the man who had murdered his brother. Magnentius was chased back into Gaul where he was beaten in 353 at **Mons Seleucus**.

Pavia ∎ 476 ∎ Fall of the Western Roman Empire

Leading a mutiny by barbarian mercenaries in the Roman army of General Orestes, the German Odoacer defeated and executed Orestes at Pavia, south of Milan. Odoacer then marched on Ravenna, where he defeated and slew Orestes' son Paulus and overthrew his other son, the Emperor Romulus Augustulus (4 September 476), marking the effective fall of the Western Roman Empire.

Pavia ∎ 569–572 ∎ Lombard Invasion of Italy

The Lombard invasion of Gothic Italy quickly secured major cities, including Verona, Milan, Ravenna and Rome, but Pavia strongly resisted Lombard King Alboin. When the city fell after a three-year siege, a purported sign from God prevented the intended massacre. Pavia became the capital of the region, which became known as Lombardy.

Pavia ∎ 1524–1525 ∎ 1st Habsburg-Valois War

Francis I of France was driven out of Lombardy at **Bicocca** (1522) and **Sesia** (April 1524), then led another invasion to invest Pavia, held by Antonio de Levya. Following a long siege, Imperial forces under Fernando d'Avalos Marquis of Pescara routed the French and their Swiss mercenaries. Francis gave up all claims in Italy but revoked his promise when released (28 October 1524–24 February 1525).

Pavón ∎ 1861 ∎ Argentine Civil Wars

A final attempt to break away from the Argentine confederation of President Justo José de Urquiza saw General Bartolomé Mitre lead the army of Buenos Aires against Federalist Santiago Derqui just to the northwest at Pavón. Reversing his defeat two years earlier at **Cepeda**, Mitre secured a decisive victory and became the first constitutional President of a united Argentina (17 September 1861).

Paxos ∎ 229 BC ∎ Illyrian War

When Illyria laid siege to Corcyra (modern Corfu), a fleet from Achaea and Aetolia sailed to its aid. But the Illyrians won a decisive victory near Paxos after which they seized Corcyra and sailed north to besiege Dyrrhachium. Concerned by piracy in the Adriatic, Rome then intervened to end the siege and landed troops on the mainland. Queen Teuta of Illyria (roughly Albania) soon sued for peace.

Payne's Farm ∎ 1863 ∎ American Civil War (Eastern Theatre)

See **Mine Run**

Paysandú ∎ 1864–1865 ∎ War of the Triple Alliance

In Brazil's undeclared war against the Blancos of Uruguay, Brigadier João Propício Mena

Barreto attacked Paysandú on the Uruguay, already besieged by Uruguayan Colorados under Venancio Flores. Garrison commander Colonel Leondro Gómez surrendered after a 35-day siege and was executed. The fall of Montevideo saw Flores become President (December 1864–2 January 1865).

Peach Orchard | 1862 | American Civil War (Eastern Theatre)
  See **Savage's Station**

Peachtree Creek | 1864 | American Civil War (Western Theatre)
  Three days after succeeding to command the Confederate army defending Atlanta, Georgia, General John B. Hood sent General William J. Hardee against the Union bridgehead a few miles to the north across the Peachtree Creek. However, Union General George H. Thomas fought a brilliant, stubborn defence and "Hood's First Sortie" was driven back on **Atlanta** (20 July 1864).

Peacock vs *Epervier* **| 1814 | War of 1812**
  See **Florida, USA**

Pea Ridge | 1862 | American Civil War (Trans-Mississippi)
  As he attempted to intercept Confederate forces withdrawing from southwest Missouri, Union General Samuel R. Curtis took a position at Pea Ridge, just inside Arkansas, where he was attacked by Confederates under General Earl Van Dorn. Van Dorn lost over 4,000 men in a bloody action and withdrew to Memphis, yielding southern Missouri and northern Arkansas (6–8 March 1862).

Pearl Harbour | 1941 | World War II (Pacific)
  With Japan determined to pre-empt American naval power, Admiral Chuichi Nagumo launched a massive air strike at Pearl Harbour, on Oahu in Hawaii. Within minutes, 350 carrier-borne aircraft sank or damaged eight battleships and three cruisers. Over 2,400 Americans died and unprepared Admiral Husband Kimmel and General Walter Short were dismissed (7 December 1941).

Pecan Bayou | 1839 | Cherokee Indian Wars
  See **San Saba**

Pecatonica | 1832 | Black Hawk Indian War
  On campaign east of the Mississippi, the Sauk Chief Black Hawk defeated some militia at **Rock River**, Illinois (14 May), then marched north into Wisconsin, where he was attacked on the Pecatonica near Woodford by experienced Michigan mounted volunteers under Colonel Henry Dodge. Black Hawk suffered a sharp defeat and lost again a month later at **Wisconsin Heights** (16 June 1832).

Pech David | 1799 | French Revolutionary Wars (2nd Coalition)
  See **Toulouse**

Peckuwe | 1780 | War of the American Revolution
  See **Piqua**

Pedestal | 1942 | World War II (War at Sea)
  See **Convoy Pedestal**

Peebles' Farm | 1864 | American Civil War (Eastern Theatre)
  See **Poplar Springs Church**

Peekskill Raid | 1777 | War of the American Revolution
  Colonel John Bird assumed the offensive in New York State, taking 500 men by boat against the American depot on the east bank of the Hudson at Peekskill. Garrison commander General Alexander McDougall was forced to retire and the British burned substantial stores before withdrawing. British commander General William Howe sent another raid in April against **Danbury** (23 March 1777).

Pegu I 1539 I Burmese Dynastic Wars

King Tabinshwehti of Toungoo was deter-mined to unite the kingdoms of Burma and took his army against Pegu. He eventually took the city by storm after a lengthy siege and failed assaults, then captured other key cities, includ-ing Prome (1542). Tabinshwehti made himself King of Burma, with his capital at Pegu. He was assassinated in 1550 after failure in Arakan and against Siam at **Ayutthaya**.

Pegu I 1551 I Burmese Dynastic Wars

When King Tabinshwehti of Burma was as-sassinated by Mon rebels in the southern capital of Pegu, his brother-in-law and successor Bayinnaung led a large force, with Portuguese mercenaries, to crush the rebels. A decisive ac-tion near Pegu saw rebel leader Smim Htaw defeated and executed and other Mon leaders soon submitted at **Prome**. Bayinnaung then turned to defeat Shan rebels at **Ava**.

Pegu I 1599 I Burmese Dynastic Wars

Weakened by civil war and war against Siam, King Nanda Bayin of Burma was attacked by his brothers, aided by Arakanese troops and Portu-guese adventurer Felipe de Brito. In a brutal assault, Nanda Bayin was captured and executed and Pegu was burned to the ground. (King Naresuan of Siam took part but was driven off by his erstwhile allies.) De Brito was granted the nearby port of **Syriam**.

Pegu I 1757 I Burmese Civil Wars

The Chieftain Alaungpaya resolved to unify Burma and launched a campaign against the Mon King Binnya Dala, who had secured vic-tory in 1752 at **Ava**. After capturing Ava, Prome and Rangoon, Alaungpaya led a final assault against Pegu, where the King was captured. Alaungpaya founded a 120-year dynasty and Binnya Dala was executed in 1774 by Alaung-paya's son Hsinbyushin (May 1757).

Pegu I 1852 I 2nd British-Burmese War

Britain resumed war with Burma and General Henry Thomas Godwin captured **Rangoon** and **Bassein**, then advanced north to capture Pegu, but lacked the forces to hold it. Five months later, with 4,000 men and naval support from Commodore George Robert Lambert, Godwin recaptured the city. The war ended and Britain annexed Pegu Province (4 June & 20 November 1852).

Pegu I 1942 I World War II (Burma-India)

Two weeks after British disaster at the **Sit-tang**, east of Rangoon, Brigadier Noel Hugh-Jones tried to hold the city of Pegu against General Hiroshi Takeuchi. Despite courageous defence, especially by Gurkha units, the small force was overwhelmed and had to withdraw. Rangoon was abandoned the same day and the main British army retreated north towards **Prome** (6–7 March 1942).

Pei-ts'ang I 1900 I Boxer Rebellion
See **Beicang**

Peiwar Kotal I 1878 I 2nd British-Afghan War

Concerned at Russian influence over Amir Sher Ali Khan, Britain sent General Sir Freder-ick Roberts into Afghanistan through the Kar-ram Valley. At the Peiwar Kotal Pass, southeast of Kabul, Roberts routed an Afghan force under Karim Khan, capturing their guns. Sher Ali fled when Roberts marched into **Kabul** (September 1879) and his son Yakub Khan sued for peace (2 December 1878).

Peking I 1214–1215 I Conquests of Genghis Khan
See **Beijing**

Peking I 1644 I Manchu Conquest of China
See **Beijing**

Peking I 1900 I Boxer Rebellion
See **Beijing**

Peking I 1917 I Manchu Restoration
See **Beijing**

Peking ▌ 1928 ▌ 2nd Chinese Revolutionary Civil War
  See **Beijing**

Peking ▌ 1937 ▌ Sino-Japanese War
  See **Beijing**

Peking ▌ 1949 ▌ 3rd Chinese Revolutionary Civil War
  See **Beijing**

Pelacanon ▌ 1328 ▌ Byzantine-Ottoman Wars
  Two years after losing **Brusa** to Ottoman expansion in northern Turkey, Byzantine Emperor Andronicus III led an expedition south from the Bosphorus along the eastern end of the Sea of Marmara to aid Nicaea. Near Chalcedon at Pelacanon (modern Maltepe) he was routed by Sultan Orkhan Gazi and fled back to Constantinople. Nicaea soon surrendered and Orkhan besieged **Nicomedia**.

Pelagonia ▌ 1259 ▌ 3rd Latin-Byzantine Imperial War
  Byzantine Emperor Michael VIII of Nicaea at war with the Latin rulers in Constantinople, won western Macedonia when his brother John Paleologus routed the Despot Michael of Epirus and the Frankish and German knights of Manfred of Sicily and William of Villehardouin (who was captured). Victory at Pelagonia, near modern Bitola, led directly to Greek recapture of **Constantinople** in 1261.

Pelham Manor ▌ 1776 ▌ War of the American Revolution
  See **Throg's Neck**

Peliklahaka ▌ 1842 ▌ 2nd Seminole Indian War
  During a final offensive against the Seminole in Florida, Colonel William Worth pursued the elusive warrior Halleck Tustenuggee to the well-defended village of Peliklahaka, southwest of Lake Apopka. Although casualties were light, Tustenuggee was decisively defeated. He was captured ten days later, ending the war that virtually exterminated the Seminole (19 April 1842).

Peliliu ▌ 1944 ▌ World War II (Pacific)
  To secure airbases to attack the Philippines, General William Rupertus landed on Peliliu in the **Palau Islands** and faced unexpectedly stiff resistance, particularly at **Bloody Nose Ridge**. The brutal campaign cost over 1,300 Americans and about 10,000 Japanese killed. Only 300 Japanese survived to be captured, including General Sadae Inoue (15 September–25 November 1944).

Pelischat ▌ 1877 ▌ Russo-Turkish Wars
  In an attempt to break out from the Russian siege of **Plevna**, on the Vid south of the Danube, Turkish commander Osman Nuri Pasha led a large sortie with perhaps 25,000 men southeast towards nearby Pelischat. However, he was driven back by General Pavel Zotov with an estimated 3,000 casualties and the siege continued with a massive Russian assault a month later (30 August 1877).

Pella ▌ 635 ▌ Muslim Conquest of Syria
  See **Fihl**

Pellene ▌ 241 BC ▌ Wars of the Achaean League
  Aratus of Sicyon secured the Achaean League with victory at **Corinth** then two years later took a force to defend the neighbouring city-state of Pellene, south of the Gulf of Corinth, against a raiding party from the rival Aetolian league. Surprised in the sack of Pellene, the raiders were badly defeated, with a reported 700 put to the sword, and Aratus seized the city for the Achaean League.

Pellinge ▌ 1918 ▌ Finnish War of Independence
  See **Porvoo**

Pellschat ▌ 1877 ▌ Russo-Turkish Wars
  See **Pelischat**

Pell's Point I 1776 I War of the American Revolution

British General William Howe, attempting to outflank General George Washington's defence of New York City, landed at **Throg's Neck**, then moved by land and sea three miles north to Pell's Point, defended by Colonel John Glover. While the Americans fell back after a costly skirmish, Washington had already left **Harlem Heights** to meet Howe at **White Plains** (18 October 1776).

Pelusium I 525 BC I Persian Invasion of Egypt

Marching west to continue the empire building of his father Cyrus II, King Cambyses II of Persia invaded Egypt. Outside the city of Pelusium, east of modern Port Said, Cambyses destroyed the army of Pharoah Psamthek III, who fled to Memphis, which surrendered after a brief siege. Lower Egypt passed under Persian control, though Cambyses failed in attempts to conquer the Upper Nile.

Pelusium I 640 I Muslim Conquest of Egypt

Muslim General Amr ibn al-As was buoyed by the Arab conquest of Syria and took a very small force into Egypt and besieged the key city of Pelusium, guarding the eastern approach to the Nile Delta. Pelusium fell after 30 days and Amr advanced up the eastern branch of the Nile to a decisive victory at **Heliopolis**, near modern Cairo (January 640).

Pemaquid I 1696 I King William's War
See **Fort William Henry, Maine**

Pembroke I 1648 I British Civil Wars

When Parliamentary forces in southern Wales declared for the King and were defeated at **St Fagan's**, General Oliver Cromwell determined to crush the rebels. He quickly took Tenby and Chepstow then attacked massive Pembroke Castle, held by General Rowland Laugharne and Colonel John Poyer. After a brutal siege, Pembroke was starved into surrender (May–11 July 1648).

Pen I 1016 I Danish Conquest of England
See **Penselwood**

Peñacerrada I 1833 I 1st Carlist War

Early in the war against Carlists in Navarre, forces loyal to Spanish Regent Maria Cristina under Generals Pedro Sarsfield and Manuel Lorenzo took Logroño at **Los Arcos**, then crossed the Ebro and routed 1,500 Carlists blocking their way at Peñacerrada. Within a week the Liberals had entered Vitoria and Bilbao unopposed. They were later checked at **Guernica** and **Asarta** (19 November 1833).

Peñacerrada I 1838 I 1st Carlist War

Liberal Commander-in-Chief Baldomero Espartero continued his offensive in northern Spain, where he advanced through Burgos and attacked Carlist commander Juan Antonio Guergué south of Vitoria at Peñacerrada. The bloody action was decided by a cavalry charge by Colonel Juan Zabala and the Carlists were crushed. A year later Don Carlos V left the country forever (22 June 1838).

Penang I 1945 I World War II (Pacific)

Sent to evacuate the Andamans, the Japanese cruiser *Haguro* (Admiral Shintaro Hashimoto) was damaged by British carrier-borne aircraft north of Sumatra and turned back for Singapore. Hunted down by a British destroyer squadron led by Captain Manley Power, *Haguro* was sunk after midnight off Penang, with 900 killed. It was the last major surface action of the war (15–16 May 1945).

Peñas de San Fausto I 1834 I 1st Carlist War

On campaign against the Carlists northwest of Estella in Navarre, a Spanish Liberal division under Baron Luis Angel de Carondolet was surprised by General Tomás Zumalacárregui at Peñas de San Fausto on the Urederra River. The Liberals were routed and fled, losing 250 men, including some drowned in the river. Carondolet was soon defeated again at Viana (19 August 1834).

Pendleton I 1878 I Bannock Indian War

Pursued after defeat at **Birch Creek**, Bannock and Paiute under Chief Egan were cornered near Pendleton, northern Oregon, and heavily defeated by the 21st infantry under Captain Evan Miles. Umatilla Indians murdered Egan next day. When Paiute medicine man Oytes surrendered (12 August) the war was effectively over and both tribes returned to their reservations (12 July 1878).

Penebscot I 1779 I War of the American Revolution

Massachusetts militia General Solomon Lovell and American Commodore Dudley Saltonstall attacked the British timber port at Penebscot Bay, Maine, where they failed in a siege of the fort held by General Francis MacLean. British Commodore Sir George Collier then arrived and destroyed the rebel squadron. The complete fiasco cost almost 500 American lives (25 July–14 August 1779).

Pengcheng I 205 BC I Chu-Han War

Collapse of the Qin (Ch'in) Dynasty at **Xianyang** (207 BC) triggered a bloody war for succession and warlord Lui Bang of Han seized Pengcheng, capital of Chu. His rival Xiang Yu returned and Liu Bang suffered a terrible defeat, with a claimed 100,000 men killed and his wife and father captured. A subsequent truce after defeat at **Chenggao** (204 BC) finally saw the hostages returned.

Penghu I 1683 I Chinese Conquest of Taiwan

When Ming General Zheng Chenggong (known as Koxinga) seized Taiwan at **Fort Zeelandia** (1662), his son and grandson held the island against repeated Manchu attack until Emperor Kangxi sent Admiral Shilong (Shih Lang) with 300 warships and 20,000 men. The Ming were decisively defeated on nearby Penghu and the Manchu secured Taiwan until it was ceded to Japan in 1895 (8 July 1683).

Peñíscola I 1812 I Napoleonic Wars (Peninsular Campaign)

Soon after capturing the strategic city of **Valencia**, French Marshal Louis Suchet sent General Philippe Severoli north against the stubborn coastal fortress of Peñíscola. While the inaccessible site was securely defended against siege, Spanish garrison commander General Garcia Navarro prematurely surrendered after just two weeks, apparently to secure his own safety (20 January–2 February 1812).

Penjdeh I 1885 I Russo-Afghan War

Russian General Alexander Vissarionovich Komarov occupied Merv in Afghanistan then led just 1,200 men towards Herat. They were blocked by 40,000 Afghans under Ghausuddin Khan at Penjdeh and a one-sided disaster saw the Afghans dispersed with very heavy losses. When Britain then began to prepare for war, Amir Abdur Rahman made peace, ceding land to Russia (30 March 1885).

Pennagadam I 775 I Indian Dynastic Wars

Amid continuing war between the Kingdoms of southern India, Varaguna of Pandya (also known as Nedunjadayan), son of the great Rajasimha, attacked the army of Pallava at Pennegadam, on the Kaveri near modern Thanjavur (Tanjore). The Pallava forces under Nandivarman I were decisively defeated, giving Varaguna one of his greatest victories (disputed date c 775).

Peno Creek I 1866 I Red Cloud's War
See **Fetterman Massacre**

Penrith I 1745 I Jacobite Rebellion (The Forty-Five)
See **Clifton Moor**

Pensacola I 1781 I War of the American Revolution

A year after he secured **Mobile** in British West Florida, Don Bernardo de Galvez, Spanish Governor of Lousiana, took 7,000 men and a strong naval squadron against Pensacola, where General John Campbell tried to defend Fort

George. However, heavy bombardment forced Campbell to surrender and after the war Spain retained both East and West Florida (10 March–9 May 1781).

Pensacola I 1814 I War of 1812

A British expedition into the Gulf of Mexico under Admiral Sir Alexander Cochrane landed at Pensacola in Spanish West Florida, but his advance towards Mobile was repulsed at **Fort Bowyer**. A major counter-attack by American General Andrew Jackson then forced Spanish Governor Gonzalez Manriquez of Pensacola to surrender and the British abandoned their bridgehead (7 November 1814).

Pensacola I 1818 I 1st Seminole Indian War

American General Andrew Jackson marched into Spanish West Florida with 800 regulars, supported by Georgia militia and William Mac-Intosh's Creeks and captured St Marks (1 April), burned the village of Seminole Chief Boleck on the Suwanee (12 April), then laid siege to Pensacola. The city fell after three days to end the war. Spain later ceded Florida to the United States (24 May 1818).

Penselwood I 658 I Anglo-Saxon Territorial Wars

As he attempted to expand the power of Wessex, King Cenwalh (Coenwalch) defeated the Welsh on the Avon at **Bradford** and six years later achieved another substantial victory at Penselwood, near Wincanton in Somerset. The defeated Welsh were driven back across the River Parrett which then became established as the West Saxon boundary.

Penselwood I 1016 I Danish Conquest of England

Knut, son of the great Sweyn Forkbeard of Denmark, attempting to complete his conquest of England, faced a spirited resistance by Edmund Ironside, son of King Aethelred of Wessex. A hard-fought battle at Penselwood, near Wincanton in Somerset, saw Edmund's Barons achieve a sharp victory and shortly afterwards he

became King. Edmund was soon defeated by Knut at **Ashingdon**.

Pentland Hills I 1666 I Scottish Covenanter Rebellion

Rising against Episcopalianism, Covenanters led by Colonel James Wallace were repulsed marching on Edinburgh against the Secretary of State for Scotland, John Maitland Duke of Lauderdale. Pursued to the Pentland Hills, they were defeated at Rullion Green by General Thomas Dalzell, who brutally crushed the rising with execution and transportation (28 November 1666).

Peparethus I 361 BC I Wars of the Greek City-States

Encouraged by the death of Epaminondas of Thebes at **Mantinea** (362 BC), Alexander of Pherae recovered from defeat at **Cynoscephalae** and renewed the offensive by besieging Peparethus, off the coast of Thessaly. A relief force under Athenian Admiral Leosthenes was beaten and Alexander plundered Piraeus before withdrawing. A few years later he was murdered at his wife's instigation.

Peralejo I 1895 I 2nd Cuban War of Independence

In the first major check to Spanish forces in eastern Cuba, insurgent leader Antonio Maceo, supported by Jesús Rabi and Quintín Banderas, attacked a column under General Arsenio Martínez Campos at Peralejo, east of Manzanillo. General Fidel Alonso de Santocildes arrived in support, but he was defeated and killed. Martínez Campos led the survivors to Bayamo (13 July 1895).

Peralonso I 1899 I Colombian War of the Thousand Days

Amid Liberal revolt against President Manuel Antonio Sanclemente and Vice President José Manuel Marroquín, rebel forces led by General Benjamín Herrera met government troops under General Vicente Villamizar at Peralonso in Norte de Santander. The Liberals won their first substantial victory in the Three-Year War, though five months later they lost at **Palonegro** (15–16 December 1899).

Perambakam ▌ 1780 ▌ 2nd British-Mysore War

Haidar Ali of Mysore, resuming war against Britain, threatened Madras and faced separate forces under Colonel William Baillie and General Sir Hector Munro. Without support Baillie was routed and captured at Perambakam, near Conjeveram. Munro withdrew and lost command before the decisive battle at **Porto Novo** (July 1781), while Haidar Ali approached **Arcot** (10 September 1780).

Pered ▌ 1849 ▌ Hungarian Revolutionary War

With Austrian forces driven out of Hungary by defeat at **Hatvan**, **Isaszeg** and **Waitzen**, Russia intervened to help and Russian General Ivan Paskievich joined Austrian Field Marshal Alfred Windischgratz to attack General Artur Gorgey at Pered, northwest of Neuhausel. The Hungarians were driven back with heavy losses through **Acs** to defeat in August at **Temesvár** (21 June 1849).

Peregonovka ▌ 1919 ▌ Russian Civil War

As White commander Anton Denikin advanced north towards Moscow, his General Iakov Slashchev suffered a surprise pre-dawn attack at Peregonovka by Ukrainian anarchists under Nestor Makhno. The guerrillas were eventually driven off, but the costly attack threatened Denikin's over-extended supply lines and encouraged October's Red counter-offensive at **Orel** (26 September 1919).

Pereiaslav ▌ 1630 ▌ Cossack-Polish Wars

On a fresh offensive in the Ukraine after previous action at **Borovitsa**, Polish commander Stanislas Koniecpolski was checked southeast of Kiev near Korsun (4 April) by Cossack leader Taras Fedorovych, then a few weeks later was badly defeated in heavy fighting at nearby Pereiaslav. The Poles were forced to sue for peace, though Fedorovych was soon replaced as Hetman (25 May 1630).

Perekop ▌ 1736 ▌ Austro-Russian-Turkish War

Russian Marshal Count Burkhard Christoph von Münnich took a large force against the Crimean Tatars and attacked the defensive lines at Perekop, guarding the isthmus to the Crimea. The key fortress of Or-Kapi soon fell by assault, but after the sack of nearby Perekop an army mutiny forced Münnich back to the Ukraine. **Azov**, further to the east, fell a few weeks later (15–19 May 1736).

Perekop ▌ 1771 ▌ Catherine the Great's 1st Turkish War

After successes against Turkish Moldavia, the Russian spring campaign of 1771 saw Prince Vasili Dolgoruki besiege a reputed 50,000 Tatars at Perekop, guarding northern Crimea. After the city fell, Dolgoruki conquered the entire Crimea in just three weeks—earning himself the honorific Krimski—and Khan Selim III of Crimea was replaced by a Russian puppet (14–15 June 1771).

Perekop ▌ 1920 ▌ Russian Civil War

Having made peace with Poland after battle on the **Vistula**, the Red Army turned south on White commander Pyotr Wrangel, who had attempted a last offensive through **Melitopol**. Brutal action at the Perekop Isthmus saw Red General Mikhail Frunze storm into the Crimea. Wrangel had to evacuate his army by sea to Constantinople, ending the war on Russian soil (7–12 November 1920).

Perekop ▌ 1941 ▌ World War II (Eastern Front)

General Erich von Manstein helped destroy the Soviet pocket further east at **Chernigovka**, then launched a massive assault on the Crimean Peninsula. In very heavy fighting at the five-mile wide Perekop Isthmus, Manstein's Eleventh Army broke through the Russian defences and quickly over-ran the whole of the Crimea except for **Sevastopol** and **Kerch** (19–28 October 1941).

Perekop I 1944 I World War II (Eastern Front)

Weeks after supporting Russia's offensive in the Ukraine at **Krivoy Rog**, General Fedor Tolbukhin led a huge assault across the Perekop Isthmus into the Crimean Peninsula. Aided by a flank attack at the Sivas, Tolbukhin broke through in three days against General Erwin Jaenecke's Seventeenth Army and raced south for **Sevastopol**. Other Russians entered the Crimea at **Kerch** (8–11 April 1944).

Perembacum I 1780 I 2nd British-Mysore War
See **Perambakam**

Perez Dasmariñas I 1897 I Philippines War of Independence
See **Dasmariñas**

Pergamum I 230 BC I Pergamum-Seleucid Wars

When Attalus of Pergamum refused to pay tribute to Gallic tribes ravaging Asia Minor, he faced an invasion by the Galatians, supported by their Seleucid ally, Antiochus Hierax. Close to Pergamum (Bergama in western Turkey) Attalus won a brilliant victory. He then took the title King and turned against his rival Hierax the following year at **Lake Koloe** and the **Harpasus**.

Perinthus I 339 BC I 4th Sacred War

An heroic defence against King Philip II of Macedon saw the small fortified port of Perinthus, on the Sea of Marmara, resist a lengthy siege by land and sea. With Byzantine and Persian support, the Perinthians fought off the attack until Athenian ships attacked Philip at sea. In a rare reversal, the Macedonian King was forced to withdraw and also lifted his siege of nearby Byzantium.

Perinthus I 191 I Civil Wars of Emperor Severus

While the Emperor Septimius Severus marched east from Rome against Pescennius Niger, his rival's proconsul Asselius Aemilius occupied Byzantium and met advanced units of the Emperor's army further west at Perinthus. Aemilius inflicted a costly defeat, though the advancing Severans forced the victor back to **Byzantium**. Three years later he was defeated across the Sea of Marmara at **Cyzicus**.

Perm I 1918 I Russian Civil War

Admiral Aleksandr Kolchak seized control of White forces in the east at Omsk and launched a large-scale mid-winter offensive west across the Urals, where General Rudolf Gajda attacked Perm, defended by Generals Rheinhold Berzin and Mikhail Lashevich. The Reds suffered terrible losses in the fall of the city, though further south they captured and held **Ufa** (24 December 1918).

Perm I 1919 I Russian Civil War

With Red forces defeated in the Urals at Perm and Ufa, commander Mikhail Tukhachevski launched a bold counter-offensive and General Sergei Mezheninov advanced east across the Viatka to occupy Sarapul (20 May). Following the fall of **Ufa**, further to the south (9 June), Mezheninov marched northeast to seize Perm. The White Army then began its long retreat towards **Omsk** (1 July 1919).

Pernambuca I 1630 I Dutch-Portuguese Colonial Wars
See **Recife**

Péronne I 1870–1871 I Franco-Prussian War
See **Bapaume**

Perryville I 1862 I American Civil War (Western Theatre)

General Braxton Bragg led the Confederate invasion of Kentucky which secured **Munfordville** and **Richmond**. However, southeast of Louisville at Perryville he met a stubborn Union force under General Don Carlos Buell. While a brief yet very bloody action caused Buell greater losses, Bragg suffered a costly strategic defeat and his offensive was driven back south to Tennessee (8 October 1862).

Perth I 1312–1313 I Rise of Robert the Bruce

A determined attack against the second most heavily fortified place in Scotland after Berwick saw Robert the Bruce besiege the strategic town of Perth, defended by the veteran knight Sir William Oliphant. Bruce's force feigned a withdrawal after seven weeks, then returned in the night and scaled the walls after wading through the deep moat (November 1312–8 January 1313).

Perth I 1339 I Anglo-Scottish War of Succession

In the Scottish Royalist war against the English-backed claimant Edward Baliol, Robert the Steward (later Robert II) was appointed Regent for David II and besieged Perth. Aided by French ships and the ecclesiastic William Bullock, Robert forced the surrender of Perth. The subsequent capture of Stirling prepared the way for the return from exile of the lawful King (August 1339).

Perth I 1644 I British Civil Wars
See **Tippermuir**

Perusia I 41–40 BC I Wars of the Second Triumvirate

Amid renewed civil war, Mark Antony's wife Fulvia united with his brother Lucius Antonius against Octavian, who joined with Marcus Agrippa to besiege Lucius at Perusia (modern Perugia), 90 miles north of Rome. A relief attempt by Ventidius Bassus was driven off and Lucius capitulated after a costly failed sortie. Perusia was then plundered and burned (December 41–March 40 BC).

Peshawar I 1001 I Muslim Conquest of Northern India

On campaign from Afghanistan into India, Mahmud of Ghazni attacked the powerful Raja Jaipal of Punjab, previously defeated at **Lamghan** (989). Outside Peshawar, the Raja and a coalition of Hindu Princes were heavily defeated and Jaipal commited suicide in captivity. Jaipal's son Anandpal was similarly defeated near Peshawar at **Waihand** in 1006 and 1008 (27 November 1001).

Peshawar I 1006 I Muslim Conquest of Northern India
See **Waihand**

Peshawar I 1008 I Muslim Conquest of Northern India
See **Waihand**

Peshawar I 1834 I Afghan-Sikh Wars

The great Sikh leader Ranjit Singh twice gained then lost Peshawar before he sent General Hari Singh, who surrounded the city and forced Sultan Muhammad Khan to evacuate after brief fighting. A large Afghan force under his brother Dost Mohammad Khan appeared in support, but they shamefully withdrew and Sultan Mohammad Khan was reinstated as Governor of the Sikh city (6 May 1834).

Peta I 1822 I Greek War of Independence

As Reshid Pasha advanced into western Greece, a largely foreign Greek army marched north to Peta, near Arta, where Alexandros Mavrocordatos left command to General Karl Normann, aided by Pietro Tarella and André Dania. The Greek force was overwhelmed and crushed (with 400 killed including Tarella and Dania executed) and the Turks marched south on **Missolonghi** (16 July 1822).

Peterborough I 1071 I Norman Conquest of Britain
See **Ely**

Petersburg (1st) I 1864 I American Civil War (Eastern Theatre)

While the main armies fought at **Cold Harbour**, east of Petersburg, Virginia, General Benjamin F. Butler of the Union Army of the James sent General Quincy A. Gillmore against the city from the south. His mismanaged assault was driven off by a much smaller Confederate force led by General Pierre G. T. Beauregard.

The main Union army tried again a week later (9 June 1864).

Petersburg (2nd) I 1864 I American Civil War (Eastern Theatre)

Union commander Ulysses S. Grant advanced west days after victory at **Cold Harbour**, leading more than 60,000 men against the key city of Petersburg, Virginia, defended by heavily outnumbered Confederate General Pierre G. T. Beauregard. Despite heavy fighting and about 10,000 casualties, Grant failed to take the city by assault and began a bloody 12-month siege (15–18 June 1864).

Petersburg I 1865 I American Civil War (Eastern Theatre)

The day after decisive Union victory, southwest of Petersburg at **Five Forks**, General Ulysses S. Grant made his final assault on the besieged Confederate city. Following bloody fighting (including Confederate General Ambrose P. Hill killed) and defeat further west at **Sutherland Station**, General Robert E. Lee evacuated the city and his forces withdrew towards **Amelia Springs** (2 April 1865).

Petersham I 1787 I Shays' Rebellion

Sent to suppress a Massachusetts rebellion against high taxes, General Benjamin Lincoln dispersed the rebels at **Springfield** (27 January), then led a night-time march through a snowstorm to surprise leader Daniel Shays at Petersham, north of Worcester. Shays was routed, with 150 captured, ending the rebellion. He fled and was sentenced to death but was later pardoned (3 February 1787).

Peterwardein I 1526 I Turkish-Hungarian Wars

Sultan Suleiman I advancing along the Danube north of Belgrade sent Grand Vizier Ibrahim Pasha ahead to besiege Peterwardein (modern Petrovaradin). While the town fell after just three days, the citadel held out bravely until mining destroyed part of the defences and it fell by storm. The garrison were massacred or sold into slavery and the Turks marched on to **Mohacs** (12–27 July 1526).

Peterwardein I 1716 I Austro-Turkish War

With the end of the War of the Spanish Succession, Austria joined Venice against Turkey and sent a large army to the Danube under Field Marshal Prince Eugène of Savoy. Grand Vizier Damad Ali Pasha was fatally wounded in a disastrous defeat at Peterwardein (Petrovaradin) and lost 6,000 men killed and over 100 guns. Eugène pressed his advantage and besieged **Temesvár** (5 August 1716).

Petorca I 1851 I 1st Chilean Liberal Revolt

Liberal officers José Miguel Carrera Fontecilla and Justo Arteaga Cuevas opposing President Manuel Montt Torres were intercepted and crushed northeast of Valparaiso at Petorca by Conservative government forces under Juan Viduarra Leal. Carrera Fontecilla fled to exile (returning for **Cerro Grande** in 1859) and a rising in the south was defeated in December at **Loncomilla** (14 October 1851).

Petra I 548–549 I Byzantine-Persian Wars

Chosroes I of Persia invaded Lazica on the east coast of the Black Sea and in 541 seized the Roman fortress city of Petra. Emperor Justinian later sent 7,000 men under Dagisthaeus, who joined King Gobazes of Lazica to besiege Petra. The Allies defeated two Persian field armies, but could not retake the city. Dagisthaeus withdrew when Mermeroes arrived with a claimed 30,000 Persians.

Petra I 551 I Byzantine-Persian Wars

When Dagisthaeus failed to recapture Petra, on the Black Sea coast of modern Georgia (548–549), Emperor Justinian replaced him with the veteran Bessas, who began a second siege. After bitter fighting, the city fell by storm with many defenders burned to death when they tried to hold out in the citadel. The city walls were destroyed to prevent Petra again becoming a Persian base.

Petrograd ‖ 1917 ‖ Russian Civil War

When Bolsheviks seized power at Petrograd (St Petersburg), Prime Minister Aleksandr Kerenski marched on the capital with a Cossack force under General Pyotr Krasnov. After bloody fighting in the surburb of Pulkovo, Kerenski fled into exile, effectively ending the Provisional government, and the Bolsheviks soon began peace talks with Germany (7–12 November 1917).

Petrograd ‖ 1919 ‖ Estonian War of Independence

With Soviet forces expelled from Estonia after **Cesis**, Estonian troops reluctantly joined White Russian commander Nikolai Yudenich in an advance on Petrograd (St Petersburg). Heavy fighting saw them driven out by a desperate defence of the city under the personal command of Leon Trostky. A month later the Estonians faced a Russian counter-offensive on the **Narva** (10–21 October 1919).

Petropavlosk ‖ 1854 ‖ Crimean War

As a diversion against Russia in the Pacific, an Anglo-French force bombarded Petropalvosk on the Kamchatka Peninsular. Led by Admiral Auguste Febvrier-Despointes (after British Admiral David Price unaccountably shot himself), the Allies landed 700 men to capture the Russian guns. However, they were heavily repulsed with about 300 casualties and the expedition withdrew (4 September 1854).

Petropavlosk ‖ 1919 ‖ Russian Civil War
See **Tobol**

Petrovaradin ‖ 1526 ‖ Turkish-Hungarian Wars
See **Peterwardein**

Petrovaradin ‖ 1716 ‖ Austro-Turkish War
See **Peterwardein**

Petsamo ‖ 1939 ‖ Russo-Finnish War

When the **Winter War** began, Russians invaded northern Finland and seized the strategic ice-free port of Petsamo and its nickel mines. When Hitler attacked Russia, German forces from Norway captured Petsamo (21 June 1941), while the Lapland War saw Russian Marshal Kirill Meretskov regain the area in September 1944, then "invade" Norway and take **Kirkenes** (2–3 December 1939).

Pevensey ‖ 1088 ‖ Norman Dynastic Wars

Immediately following the death of William the Conqueror, his half-brother Odo raised rebellion for his nephew Robert of Normandy against the new King William II Rufus. Odo captured Pevensey Castle in Sussex to await Robert, though an attempted landing from Normandy was driven off. After a six-week siege by William, Odo was starved out and withdrew to **Rochester**.

Pharsalus ‖ 48 BC ‖ Wars of the First Triumvirate

Julius Caesar retired to Thessaly after defeat at **Dyrrhachium** and fought his decisive battle against Pompey at Pharsalus, near the Enipeus. Reinforced by Mark Antony and Domitius Calvinus, Caesar secured a brilliant victory over Pompey and Titus Labienus. The defeated Generals fled north towards Larissa then later to **Alexandria**, where Pompey was murdered (9 August 48 BC).

Pharsalus ‖ 1897 ‖ 1st Greco-Turkish War

Two weeks after the Greek army lost in northern Thessaly at **Mati**, Crown Prince Constantine abandoned the important city of Larissa and fell back on Pharsalus, where he attempted to turn against Edhem Pasha's Ottoman army. Facing a fierce attack and a simultaneous assault on their right wing at **Velestino**, the demoralised Greeks were defeated and withdrew south to **Domokos** (5 May 1897).

Phasis ‖ 692 ‖ Early Byzantine-Muslim Wars
See **Sebastopolis**

Pherushahr ‖ 1845 ‖ 1st British-Sikh War
See **Ferozeshah**

Philiphaugh I 1645 I British
Civil Wars

While victory at **Kilsyth** gave the Royalists effective command of Scotland, defeat of Charles I at **Naseby** released Parliamentary lowlanders under General David Leslie to attack James Graham Marquis of Montrose. Outnumbered four to one at Philiphaugh, near Selkirk, the Royalists were destroyed, with many prisoners murdered and Montrose fled (13 September 1645).

Philippi, Macedonia (1st) I 42 BC I Wars
of the Second Triumvirate

Mark Antony and Octavian joined after battle at **Mutina** (43 BC) and marched to Philippi (near modern Kavalla) in eastern Macedonia against Marcus Brutus and Gaius Cassius Longinus. A fierce action Brutus saw repulse Octavian, but on the other wing Antony defeated Cassius (who killed himself), then joined Octavian to secure victory. Brutus lost at the same site three weeks later (3 October 42 BC).

Philippi, Macedonia (2nd) I 42 BC I Wars
of the Second Triumvirate

Three weeks after the death of Gaius Cassius Longinus at the first Philippi, in eastern Macedonia, Octavian and Mark Antony fought a further battle against the surviving enemy commander Marcus Brutus. The second action at Philippi saw Brutus decisively defeated. He subsequently committed suicide and the Republic effectively perished with him (23 October 42 BC).

Philippi, West Virginia I 1861 I American
Civil War (Eastern Theatre)

Union General Thomas A. Morris commenced operations in West Virginia by surprising about 1,500 Confederates under Colonel George A. Porterfield at Philippi. Defeated by Colonels Ebenezer Dumont and Benjamin F. Kelley, Porterfield withdrew south to Huttonsville. This skirmish—with only a handful of casualties—challenges **Big Bethel** as the war's first land battle (3 June 1861).

Philippines I 1941–1942 I World War II
(Pacific)

Within hours of **Pearl Harbour**, Japanese General Masaharu Homma sent large forces against the Philippines and General Douglas MacArthur's aircraft were destroyed on the ground. Manila quickly fell (2 January) and American and Filipino forces withdrew to **Corregidor** and **Bataan**. When the Allies finally surrendered, the Philippines were lost (8 December 1941–18 May 1942).

Philippines I 1944–1945 I World War II
(Pacific)

When American forces launched a massive offensive against the Philippines, an all-out Japanese effort was defeated on **Leyte** and in the **Leyte Gulf**. The Americans then moved north against **Luzon** and south towards **Mindanao**. The campaign cost 13,000 Americans killed, over 300,000 Japanese and perhaps 100,000 Filipinos, mainly civilians (22 October 1944–August 1945).

Philippine Sea I 1944 I World War II
(Pacific)

While American forces invaded the **Mariana Islands**, Admiral Jizaburo Ozawa led massive forces against Admiral Ray Spruance's support fleet in the Philippine Sea. The largest carrier action of the war saw three Japanese aircraft carriers sunk and 330 planes lost in "The Great Marianas Turkey Shoot." Ozawa's defeat was decisive and he withdrew north towards **Okinawa** (19–20 June 1944).

Philippopolis I 250 I 1st Gothic War

Driven off from a siege at **Nicopolis** in Moesia, the Goth Kniva joined the rest of his army besieging Philippopolis (modern Plovdiv, Bulgaria), where he was pursued by Emperor Decius. At nearby Beroea, Decius suffered a severe loss and Philippopolis was taken with terrible slaughter. Kniva then ravaged Thrace. The following year he was driven back to the Danube and battle at **Abrittus**.

Philippopolis I 1208 I Bulgarian Imperial Wars

Three years after his brother Baldwin was defeated and captured by the Bulgars at **Adrianople**, the new Latin Emperor Henry at Constantinople faced a fresh advance by the new Bulgar Tsar Boril. At Philippopolis (Plovdiv), Boril was routed by Crusader Knights and withdrew behind the Balkan Mountains. He soon made peace with Henry and in 1218 he was overthrown at **Trnovo**.

Philippopolis I 1878 I Russo-Turkish Wars

See **Plovdiv**

Philippsburg I 1688 I War of the Grand Alliance

Louis XIV of France sent his son, the Dauphin Louis, to invade Germany and most of the Palatinate quickly surrendered. However Philippsburg, south of Heidelberg, held out under the Count Ernst von Starhemberg. Utilising the siegecraft of Marshal Sebastien Vauban, the Dauphin forced the surrender of Philippsburg after a month of terrible assault (27 September–29 October 1688).

Philippsburg I 1734 I War of the Polish Succession

In support of the former King Stanislas Leszcynski of Poland, his son-in-law Louis XV sent French troops into Austrian-held Lorraine, where Marshal James Duke of Berwick besieged Philippsburg, south of Heidelburg. When Berwick was decapitated by a cannonball, Count Maurice of Saxe drove off Prince Eugène of Savoy and the city fell by storm (13 May–20 June 1734).

Phillora I 1965 I 2nd Indo-Pakistan War

Indian forces under Colonel Ardeshir Burzorji Tarapore attempting to secure a foothold for a fresh attack on **Chawinda**, southeast of **Sialkot**, boldly advanced to the north at Phillora. The Indian tanks secured a hard-fought victory to threaten Chawinda, but Indian command fatally delayed four days before resuming the offensive further west at **Buttar Dograndi** (11 September 1965).

Philomelion I 1116 I Byzantine-Turkish Wars

In his attempt to recover territory in Anatolia (lost by his father Kilij Arslan at the time of the First Crusade), Sultan Malik Shah of Rum was defeated by Byzantine Emperor Alexius I at **Cotyaeum**, then renewed his campaign three years later. Near Philomelion (modern Aksehir in central Turkey) he was again defeated by Alexius and was forced to recognise to the borders of Byzantium.

Phnom Penh I 1599 I Cambodian-Spanish War

Spanish commander Blaz Ruiz, supported by Portuguese adventurer Diego Veloso, intervened in Cambodia's succession and installed Crown Prince Barom Reachea II as puppet (1597). However, the Cambodians soon rose in revolt and a brutal massacre in Phnom Penh saw almost every Spaniard killed. Spain's ambition on Asia's mainland was halted and Cambodia became a Siamese vassal.

Phnom Penh I 1975 I Cambodian Civil War

With North Vietnam using Cambodia to attack South Vietnam, pro-western General Lon Nol overthrew Prince Norodom Sihanouk (18 March 1970). However, North Vietnamese and Cambodian Communists (Khmer Rouge) gradually seized the country then shelled and seized Phnom Penh. When the capital fell, Lon Nol fled and the Khmer Rouge began their genocidal rule (16 April 1975).

Phnom Penh I 1979 I Vietnamese-Cambodian War

After years of border clashes, Vietnam launched a major invasion of Cambodia under General Van Tien Dung, who had taken **Saigon** in 1975. Up to 100,000 Vietnamese and 18,000 Cambodian rebels routed the Khmer Rouge army and seized Phnom Penh to replace the Pol Pot Government with a puppet regime. Civil war continued until the Vietnamese left in 1989 (7 January 1979).

Phraaspa ∎ 36 BC ∎ Roman-Parthian Wars

Two years after a Parthian invasion of Roman Syria was repulsed at **Gindarus**, Mark Antony led a large army into Parthia and besieged the capital, Phraaspa. With his baggage and siege-train under Oppius Stationus destroyed by Phraates IV of Parthia and King Artavasdes of Media, Antony lifted the siege and withdrew in severe winter weather. The expedition cost him half his army (June–October 36 BC).

Phu Doan ∎ 1952 ∎ French Indo-China War

See **Nghia Lo**

Phung-tao ∎ 1894 ∎ Sino-Japanese War

An act which helped precipitate war between Japan and China over Korea saw Admiral Kozo Tsuboi attack a Chinese convoy off the west coast of Korea, taking reinforcements to Asan. Near Phung Island in Asan Bay, two Chinese vessels were sunk, including the chartered British troopship *Kowshing* lost with over 1,000 lives. Asan soon fell to land assault at **Songhwan** (25 July 1894).

Phuoc Binh ∎ 1974–1975 ∎ Vietnam War

Violating the Paris Peace Treaty to begin North Vietnam's campaign to conquer the south, General Tran Van Tra led about 8,000 men into Phuoc Long Province, north of Saigon, where they attacked with artillery and rockets, and stormed the capital Phuoc Binh. Two months later the main offensive began in the central highlands at **Ban Me Thuot** (13 December 1974–6 January 1975).

Phuoc Ha ∎ 1965 ∎ Vietnam War

South Vietnamese General Hoang Xuan Lam tried to clear the Phuoc Ha Valley, southwest of Danang, and suffered heavy losses before US Marines arrived under General Melvin Henderson (later General Jonas Platt). Operation Harvest Moon saw costly action, including Marines ambushed at Ky Phu, before the Communists

withdrew with over 400 killed. The Allies lost 130 (8–18 December 1965).

Piacenza ∎ 200 BC ∎ Gallic Wars in Italy

See **Placentia**

Piacenza ∎ 271 ∎ Roman-Alemannic Wars

See **Placentia**

Piacenza ∎ 456 ∎ Later Roman Wars of Succession

See **Placentia**

Piacenza ∎ 1746 ∎ War of the Austrian Succession

Austria recovered from defeat at **Bassignano** and sent reinforcements to northern Italy, where Prince Joseph Wenzel von Lichtenstein took command of the Austro-Sardinian army. Near Piacenza at San Lazaro he beat French Marshal Jean-Baptiste Desmarets Marquis de Maillebois and Infante Philip of Spain. A further French loss at **Rottofredo** in August virtually drove them out of Italy (16 June 1746).

Piacenza ∎ 1796 ∎ French Revolutionary Wars (1st Coalition)

Napoleon Bonaparte captured Piedmont in Northern Italy then sent General Pierre Augereau to cross the Po at Piacenza, where Austrians under General Jean-Pierre de Beaulieu attacked his bridgehead in a night action near the village of Fombio. Although French General Amédée Emmanuel La Harpe was killed, the Austrians were driven back towards the Adda and lost two days later at **Lodi** (7–8 May 1796).

Piatka ∎ 1593 ∎ Cossack-Polish Wars

In revolt against Polish Governor Konstantin Ostrozhsky in the Ukraine, Cossack leader Kristof Kosinsky seized Ostopol and was attacked by Ukrainian nobles and mercenaries under the Governor's son Janush. Rashly marching out against Ostrozhsky, he was routed at nearby Piatka and was subsequently killed. Another Cossack rising in 1596 was crushed at **Lubny** (February 1593).

**Piave ∎ 1809 ∎ Napoleonic Wars
(5th Coalition)**

Prince Eugène de Beauharnais regrouped after defeat in northern Italy at **Sacile** (16 April), gathering his French and Italian army at the Piave north of Venice to advance across the river against Archduke John of Austria near Conegliano. The Austrians were heavily defeated in a daylong action and Eugène drove the Archduke out of Italy and to eventual defeat in June at **Raab** (8 May 1809).

**Piave (1st) ∎ 1918 ∎ World War I
(Italian Front)**

With the Italians routed at **Caporetto** (November 1917), Austrian forces began a renewed offensive along the Piave. General Conrad von Hotzendorf in the north was checked around **Monte Grappa**, but further south General Svetozar Boroevic forced a crossing. New Italian commander Armando Diaz counter-attacked and Boroevic was forced back with heavy losses (10–22 June 1918).

**Piave (2nd) ∎ 1918 ∎ World War I
(Italian Front)**

See **Vittorio Veneto**

**Pichi-Carhué ∎ 1872 ∎ Argentine
Civil Wars**

See **San Carlos, Argentina**

**Pichincha ∎ 1822 ∎ Ecuadorian War
of Independence**

Campaigning in southwestern Colombia after **Bomboná**, Patriot leader Simón Bolívar sent General Antonio José de Sucre against Quito in northern Ecuador. Advancing through **Ríobambo**, de Sucre routed Spanish commander Melchior Aymerich just southwest of Quito at Pichincha. Quito surrendered next day and Bolívar became President of independent Ecuador (24 May 1822).

**Pickett's Mill ∎ 1864 ∎ American Civil
War (Western Theatre)**

As Union commander William T. Sherman pursued Confederate General Joseph E. John-ston through Georgia towards **Atlanta**, he attempted to turn him at Allatoona and was repulsed to the southwest at **New Hope Church**. Next day at nearby Pickett's Mill, General Oliver O. Howard was also repulsed and the Confederates attempted a counter-attack southwest at **Dallas** (27 May 1864).

Picuiba ∎ 1934 ∎ Chaco War

See **Yrendagüe**

**Piedmont ∎ 1864 ∎ American Civil War
(Eastern Theatre)**

Resuming the offensive in the Shenandoah Valley after repulse at **New Market**, Union commander David Hunter advanced south from Winchester and at Piedmont, southwest of Port Republic, Virginia, met Confederate General William E. Jones, who was defeated and killed in severe fighting. Hunter then occupied Staunton and continued south towards **Lynchburg** (5–6 June 1864).

**Piedra-Gorda ∎ 1863 ∎ Mexican-
French War**

Amid fighting in Guanajuato, Liberal General José López Uraga met an Imperial force led by General Leonardo Márquez at Piedra-Gorda, east of San Luis de la Paz. One of the first actions between Mexicans without French involvement saw Márquez wounded and lose many casualties. However, Uraga withdrew and defected to the French after the fall of Guadalajara (17 December 1863).

**Piedras ∎ 1812 ∎ Argentine War of
Independence**

See **Río Piedras**

Piercebridge ∎ 1643 ∎ British Civil Wars

William Cavendish Earl of Newcastle marched south from Newcastle with a large Royalist army and found his way across the Tees blocked at Piercebridge by Captain John Hotham, son of Sir John Hotham, Governor of Hull. The young Parliamentary commander, with just three troops of horse and four companies of foot, was swept aside and Earl Newcastle captured York (1 December 1643).

Pierre's Hole I 1832 I Blackfoot Indian War

While operating west of the Teton Range, in eastern Idaho, beaver hunters from the Rocky Mountain Fur Company under Milton G. Sublette were met at Pierre's Hole by Blackfoot Indians. When a chief attempting a parley was shot down, the battle which followed saw seven trappers and seven friendly Indians killed. Within a few more years the rich fur trade was exhausted (17 June 1832).

Pieter's Hill I 1900 I 2nd Anglo-Boer War
See **Tugela Heights**

Pigüé I 1858 I Argentine Civil Wars

When Indians of the pampas under Juan Calfucurá continued raiding eastern Argentina after victory at **Sierra Chica** (1855), the government sent a large force under Colonel Wenceslao Paunero, supported by Colonels Nicolás Granada and Emilio Conesa. Calfucurá was badly beaten near Pigüé, north of Bahia Blanca, yet fought on until 1872 at **San Carlos** (16 February 1858).

Pilawce I 1648 I Cossack-Polish Wars

Cossack rebel Bogdan Chmielnicki won at **Zolte Wody** and **Korsun** in May, then marched west across the Polish Ukraine and at Pilawce, southwest of Kiev, met a new force under Aleksander Koniecpolski, Mikolaj Ostrorog and Ladislav-Dominic Zaslawski. The brash Poles and their German mercenaries were routed. In 1649, Chmielnicki took Kiev and won at **Zborov** (23 September 1648).

Pilkem Ridge I 1917 I World War I (Western Front)

The British offensive at **Ypres** began with bombardment by over four million shells before General Hubert Gough attacked north and east against General Friedrich von Arnim. Despite terrible mud and 30,000 casualties, strategic Pilkem Ridge was taken before heavy rain ended the advance. Gough wanted to halt but was soon ordered to attack again at **Langemark** (31 July– 2 August 1917).

Pillau I 1945 I World War II (Eastern Front)

With the fall of **Königsberg** (9 April), survivors fled west to join German forces attempting to hold the Samland Peninsula, where thousands of civilians and wounded were evacuated. After a massive assault by Marshal Aleksandr Vasilevksy and Admiral Vladimir Tributs' Baltic fleet, General Dietrich von Saucken surrendered the key city of Pillau, effectively ceding East Prussia (13–15 April 1945).

Pilleth I 1402 I Glendower's Rebellion

In a largely guerrilla-style rebellion, Welsh nationalist Owen Glendower (Owain Glynn Dwr) lost at **Welshpool** (1400), then achieved a rare victory in open battle when he surprised an English force of Hereford levies under Sir Edmund Mortimer at Pilleth near Ludlow, Shropshire. Mortimer was captured but later married Glendower's daughter and embraced the Welsh cause (22 June 1402).

Pilot Knob I 1864 I American Civil War (Trans-Mississippi)
See **Fort Davidson**

Pilsen I 1618 I Thirty Years War (Bohemian War)

Supporting the Protestants of Bohemia against the appointment of the Catholic Ferdinand of Styria as King, the Elector Palatinate Frederick V and Duke Charles Emmanuel of Savoy sent a mercenary army of 20,000 under Count Ernst von Mansfeld against Pilsen, southwest of Prague. The Catholic city fell after fierce fighting but Mansfeld was defeated in 1619 at **Sablat** (21 November 1618).

Pinaglabanan I 1896 I Philippines War of Independence
See **San Juan del Monte**

Pine Bluff | 1863 | American Civil War (Trans-Mississippi)

Confederate General John S. Marmaduke withdrew down the Arkansas River from Little Rock after defeat at nearby **Bayou Fourche** (10 September) and attempted to recapture Pine Bluff, to the southeast, from a small Union garrison under Colonel Powell Clayton. Marmaduke was unable to take the town despite heavy shelling and was driven off with about 150 casualties (25 October 1863).

Pine Creek | 1858 | Yakima Indian Wars

As Kamiakin of the Yakima continued to resist removal, he was joined by other tribes in southeastern Washington and met Major Edward Steptoe leading a small Federal force north towards Spokane. At Pine Creek, near modern Rosalia, Steptoe was routed by 1,000 Coer d'Alanes, Spokanes and Palouses. However, they were later defeated at **Four Lakes** and on **Spokane Plain** (18 May 1858).

Pine Mountain | 1864 | American Civil War (Western Theatre)

See **Marietta**

Pingcheng | 200 BC | Wars of the Former Han

Emperor Gao Zu consolidated his new Han Dynasty after **Gaixia**, then led a claimed 300,000 troops against the Xiongnu leader Maodun, who had united tribes on China's northwestern frontier. Pursuing the Xiongnu as far as Pingcheng, in northern Shanxi, Gao Zu was ambushed by a massive force and only just escaped capture. He agreed to make peace and sent Maodun a Chinese princess as a bride.

Pingjiang | 1926 | 1st Chinese Revolutionary Civil War

Nationalist General Chiang Kai-shek opened his offensive against the warlords of northern China by advancing northeast from **Changsha** and ordered Li Zongren against Pingjiang, defended by Li Zhuozang for Wu Beifu. When Wu himself counter-attacked, Chiang arrived to secure a bloody victory and then drove north against **Tingsiqiao** (18–19 August 1926).

Pingjin | 1948–1949 | 3rd Chinese Revolutionary Civil War

See **Beijing-Tianjin**

Pingkiang | 1926 | 1st Chinese Revolutionary Civil War

See **Pingjiang**

Pingsingguan | 1937 | Sino-Japanese War

With **Beijing** taken, Japanese General Seishiro Itagaki's advance southwest into Shanxi was attacked on the flank in the Wutai Mountains at Pingsingguan by a Communist force under Lin Biao and Nie Rongzhen. The Japanese were badly defeated with perhaps 5,000 casualties, but the Red Army failed to follow up and the invaders continued towards **Taiyuan** (25 September 1937).

Pingyang | 234 BC | China's Era of the Warring States

Zhao Zheng, King of Qin (Ch'in), attempting to unify China, renewed war against his Zhao rivals who had been beaten in 260 BC at **Changping**. In a subsequent decisive battle at Pingyang, Zheng routed his enemy, with a claimed 100,000 beheaded. By 221 BC, Zheng had overcome all rival states and proclaimed himself Emperor of China as Qin Shi Huang. His Qin Dynasty fell in 207 BC at **Xianyang**.

Pingyang | 576–577 | Wei Dynastic Wars

In the prolonged struggle for northern China, Emperor Wu of Northern Zhou (Western Wei) took a large army into Northern Qi (Eastern Wei), where he besieged and seized the border town of Pingyang on the Fen River. Qi Emperor Gao Wei arrived to besiege the captured town, but in battle nearby, he was defeated and driven off by Wu, who then proceeded upriver towards **Taiyuan**.

Pinkie | 1547 | Anglo-Scottish Royal Wars

In a failed attempt to marry his nephew Edward VI to the infant Mary Queen of Scots,

Edward Seymour Duke of Somerset invaded Scotland and on Falside Hill at Pinkie Cleugh, near Musselburgh, destroyed a much larger Scots army under the Regent James Hamilton Earl of Arran. The English captured nearby Edinburgh but were driven out three years later (10 September 1547).

Pinnacle Mountain I 1860 I Pyramid Lake Indian War

When Paiute in western Nevada avenged the rape of two Indian girls, then defeated a pursuing force of miners at the **Truckee**, 800 California militia—the Carson Valley expedition—set out under former Texas Ranger Colonel Jack Hays. Near Pinnacle Mountain, south of Pyramid Lake, the Indians were scattered with 25 killed, effectively ending the brief war (14 May–15 July 1860).

Piombino I 1646 I Thirty Years War (Franco-Habsburg War)

See **Porto Longone**

Piperdean I 1436 I Anglo-Scottish Border Wars

In response to Henry Percy Earl of Northumberland preparing for war against Scotland in violation of an existing truce, William Douglas Earl of Angus and Adam Hepburn were sent to Piperdean, near Cockburnspath, where they heavily defeated an English force under Sir Robert Ogle. In a further response to England's invasion, James I then laid siege to **Roxburgh** (10 September 1436).

Piqua I 1780 I War of the American Revolution

Colonel George Rogers Clark and 1,000 Kentucky militia retaliating for a Loyalist attack at **Ruddle's Station**, destroyed Indian Chillicothe in Ohio. Clark then attacked 300 Shawnee and Delaware under Chief Black Hoof at nearby Piqua and, after costly losses on both sides, burned the town and crops. Following **Blue Licks** in 1782, Clark returned and destroyed what remained (8 August 1780).

Piraeus I 87–86 BC I 1st Mithridatic War

King Mithridates VI of Pontus sent his General Archclaus to invade Greece and Rome sent a counter-invasion. General Lucius Sulla blockaded Archelaus in Piraeus and Aristion in nearby Athens. Following a long siege and heavy fighting, Athens fell (1 March 86 BC). While a further assault soon drove Archelaus to abandon Piraeus, he soon continued the war at **Chaeronea**.

Piraja I 1822 I Brazilian War of Independence

Under attack at **Salvador**, in northern Brazil's Bahia Province, Portuguese commander Colonel Ignacio Luis Madeira de Melo led a counteroffensive against the blockading Brazilians about 15 miles north of the city at Piraja. Madeira was badly defeated by French-born insurgent leader Brigadier Pedro Labatut and withdrew under siege to Salvador (8 November 1822).

Piribebuy I 1869 I War of the Triple Alliance

One of the bloodiest actions of the war provoked by Paraguayan Dictator Francisco Solano López saw Brazilians under Gaston d'Orleans Comte d'Eu storm Piribebuy, southeast of Ausunción, held by Colonel Pedro Pablo Caballero. Caballero was taken and executed, along with many soldiers and civilians, and the survivors withdrew through **Acosta-Ñu** to **Cerro Corá** (12 August 1869).

Pirisabora I 363 I Later Roman-Persian Wars

In response to attacks on Roman Mesopotamia by Shapur II of Persia, Emperor Julian led a large army from Syria down the Euphrates, where he attacked Pirisabora (Anbar) guarding the vital canal linking to the Tigris. The Sassanian garrison fought fiercely, but Roman siege machines smashed the walls and the city was razed to the ground. Julian continued east to **Maiozamalcha** (27–29 April 363).

Pirmasens I 1793 I French Revolutionary Wars (1st Coalition)

Advancing across the Rhine, Austrian General Dagobert Wurmser besieged Landau before French under General Charles Landrémont counter-attacked along the Lauter between Pirmasens and Wissembourg, heavily repulsing the Austrians. Wurmser attacked again a month later and new French commander General Jean Carlenc was driven back and fled (14 September & 13 October 1793).

Pirna I 1756 I Seven Years War (Europe)

Frederick II of Prussia invaded Saxony in force to open his war and occupied undefended Dresden (9 September) as the Saxon army under Marshal Friedrich von Rutowski withdrew southeast to siege at Pirna. When an Austrian relief army was defeated at **Lobositz**, the starving Saxons surrendered and about 18,000 were pressed into Prussian service (September–14 October 1756).

Pirna I 1813 I Napoleonic Wars (War of Liberation)

As a prelude to Napoleon Bonaparte's decisive victory at **Dresden**, French General Dominique Vandamme crossed the Elbe and attacked the Allied flank held by Prince Eugene of Württemberg ten miles southeast at Pirna. The Allies were forced to divert reinforcements in support, which helped secure Bonaparte's success on the main battlefield on the first day (26 August 1813).

Pirot I 1885 I Serbo-Bulgarian War

In a dispute over eastern Rumelia, King Milan IV of Serbia marched into newly independent Bulgaria, where he was repulsed at **Slivnitza** by Prince Alexander (Battenberg) of Bulgaria, who drove him out and invaded Serbia. While the Bulgarians stormed Pirot on the Nisava, Austria intervened to save Serbia and an armistice next day brought the brief war to an end (26–27 November 1885).

Pirvan I 1221 I Conquests of Genghis Khan
See **Parwan Durrah**

Pisa I 1406 I Florentine-Pisan Wars

After Gerhardo Appiani of Pombio murdered Piero Gambacorti to seize Pisa (1392), he sold it to the Dukes of Milan (1400), who traded it to Florence (1405). The humiliated people of the city rose in revolt, but they were starved into surrender after a terrible six-month siege. The once-powerful Maritime Republic lost its independence apart from a brief period under Charles VIII (April–9 October 1406).

Pisco I 1819 I Peruvian War of Independence

Chilean commander Lord Thomas Cochrane regrouped after a repulse at **Callao** (29 September), sending Captain Martin Guise south against Royalist Pisco. A landing party under Major William Miller and Colonel Jagrae Charles met heavy fire—with Charles killed and Miller wounded—but the Chileans captured the garrison, along with large supplies of arms, ammunition and rum (7 November 1819).

Pistoria I 62 BC I Catiline Revolt

An attempted coup in Rome by Lucius Sergius Catiline failed when the conspiracy was exposed by the orator Cicero. Trying to flee across the Apennines, Catiline's army was trapped in the Arno Valley at Pistoria (modern Pistoia) by General Gaius Antonius and the veteran Marcus Petreius. The rebels were routed in a brutal battle and Catiline died in a suicidal last charge.

Pitgaveney I 1040 I Scottish War of Succession
See **Elgin**

Pitiantuta I 1932 I Chaco War
See **Carlos Antonio López**

Pittsburgh I 1763 I Pontiac's War
See **Fort Pitt**

Pittsburgh Landing I 1862 I American Civil War (Western Theatre)
See **Shiloh**

Piva I 1861 I Turko-Montenegran Wars
Following the assassination of Danilo II of Montenegro, his nephew and successor Prince Nicholas Petrovich supported Slavs in Herzogovina to rebel against the Turks. At Piva, in the southwest, Turkish forces under Omar Pasha routed the Herzogovina rebels. The following year Omar invaded Montenegro itself for victory at **Rijeka** (21 November 1861).

Piva Forks I 1943 I World War II (Pacific)
While American forces established a beachhead on **Bougainville**, severe fighting developed in heavy jungle inland from **Empress Augusta Bay** between the Piva River and the Numa Numa Trail. The Japanese were eventually repulsed with 1,200 killed and successful defence of the American perimeter at "Cibik Ridge" helped turn the tide in Bougainville (18–26 November 1943).

Pi-yang I 563 BC I Wars of China's Spring and Autumn Era
See **Biyang**

Pla I 1811 I Napoleonic Wars (Peninsular Campaign)
As French Marshal Jacques Macdonald marched through Valls towards Lérida, his vanguard under Italian General Francisco Orastelle Eugenio determined to march north against the Spanish. Five miles from Valls at Pla, they found themselves facing a force three times as large under General Pedro Sarsfield and were routed, with Eugenio killed and about 600 men lost (11 January 1811).

Placentia I 200 BC I Gallic Wars in Italy
In the aftermath of the Punic Wars, Carthaginian General Hamilcar roused the Boii, Insubres and Cenomani of Cisapline Gaul (Po Valley in northern Italy) to attack Placentia (modern Piacenza). The Roman city was taken by storm and then sacked, with terrible losses and damage.

However, the Gauls were routed when they laid siege to nearby **Cremona**.

Placentia I 271 I Roman-Alemannic Wars
Three years after defeat in Italy at **Lake Benacus**, Alemanni tribesmen joined with Juthungi allies to again cross the Alps onto the northern plains. New Emperor Aurelian rushed back from fighting Vandals on the Danube and met the invaders near Placentia (modern Piacenza). Rome's army suffered a severe defeat and the Alemanni marched south towards Rome, turning to meet Aurelian at **Fano**.

Placentia I 456 I Later Roman Wars of Succession
During the decline of **Rome** following its sack in 455, the Roman general, the Sueve Ricimer, drove the Vandals out of Sicily, defeated a raiding party on **Corsica**, then attacked the Emperor Avitus who had returned from Gaul. At Placentia (modern Piacenza), Avitus was defeated and overthrown. Six months later, Ricimer established his ally Majorian as the new Emperor (16 October 456).

Placilla I 1891 I Chilean Civil War
In civil war against Chilean President José Manuel Balmaceda, Congressist Colonel Estanislao del Canto Arteaga won at **Concón** near Valparaiso then a week later met 14,000 Loyalist troops under Colonel Orozimbo Barbosa Puga further north at Placilla. Barbosa Puga was routed with over 3,500 casualties and was later murdered. Valparaiso fell and Balmaceda committed suicide (28 August 1891).

Plain of Reeds I 1966 I Vietnam War
American and Australian troops on their first ground offensive in the Mekong Delta, advanced into the marshy Plain of Reeds against a large, well-entrenched Viet Cong formation. Exercising strategic air mobility east of the Oriental River, the Allied forces of Operation Marauder effectively destroyed one Viet Cong battalion and the headquarters of another (1–8 January 1966).

Plains of Abraham | 1759 | Seven Years War (North America)
See **Quebec**

Plains Store | 1863 | American Civil War (Lower Seaboard)
As Union commander Nathaniel P. Banks moved into position around Confederate Port Hudson, Louisiana, a division under General Christopher C. Augur was met by Colonels Frank P. Powers and William R. Miles to the north, near Springfield Road at Plains Store. The Confederates were defeated in heavy fighting and fell back under siege at **Port Hudson** (21 May 1863).

Plamam Mapu | 1965 | Indonesian-Malaysian Confrontation
Indonesia refused to recognise Malaysia and began a border war, which saw a decisive action when Indonesian troops entered Borneo to attack the village of Plamam Mapu. In very heavy fighting against British paratroops under Captain John Fleming, the Indonesians were driven off with costly losses. It is claimed they never again tried to cross the border in such force (25 April 1965).

Plaridel | 1899 | Philippine-American War
See **Quinqua**

Plassey | 1757 | Seven Years War (India)
British commander Robert Clive resumed war in Bengal and marched north from Calcutta to aid Mir Jafar against the French-supported Nawab Siraj-ud-Daula. At Plassey, in the most decisive battle in Bengal, Clive's hugely out-numbered army routed the Nawab, who was soon assassinated. Mir Jafar became Nawab and the British commander was created Baron Clive of Plassey (23 June 1757).

Plataea | 479 BC | Greco-Persian Wars
A year after defeat at **Salamis** and the return of King Xerxes to Persia, a Persian army left in Greece under Mardonius reoccupied Athens until confronted by Greeks under the Spartan Pausanias south of Thebes near Plataea. A terrible rout saw Mardonius and about 50,000 killed. A naval defeat at the same time in Asia Minor at **Mycale** ended the Persian campaign in Greece (August 479 BC).

Plataea | 429–427 BC | Great Peloponnesian War
Spartan King Archidamus II was determined to punish Plataea for bloodily suppressing a Theban coup and led a large Spartan-Theban force against the city south of Thebes, held by just 400 Plataeans and 80 Athenian allies. After a long siege, in which about half the garrison escaped to Athens, the starving survivors surrendered and over 200 were executed (May 429–August 427 BC).

Platrand | 1900 | 2nd Anglo-Boer War
See **Wagon Hill**

Platte Bridge | 1865 | Cheyenne-Arapaho Indian War
Lieutenant Caspar Collins, attempting to protect a wagon supply train, rashly rode out from Platte Bridge stockade (modern Casper, Wyoming) and immediately came under a massive attack, with Collins and half his men killed. Meantime, in a four-hour battle east of Red Buttes against Roman Nose, Sergeant Amos Custard and the incoming 20-man wagon escort were annihilated (26 July 1865).

Plattsburg | 1814 | War of 1812
A large-scale British offensive south from the St Lawrence saw General Sir George Prevost and 10,000 men attack Plattsburg, on the western shore of Lake Champlain. American General Alexander Macomb then withdrew across the Saranac. After days of delay and a naval defeat on **Lake Champlain**, Prevost broke off his attack and withdrew to Canada in disgrace (6–11 September 1814).

Platzberg | 1794 | French Revolutionary Wars (1st Coalition)
After the French were repulsed west of the Rhine at **Kaiserslautern**, General Laurent

Gouvion Saint-Cyr attacked to the southeast against well-fortified positions on Platzberg. The Prussians were heavily defeated and driven off, with 3,000 killed including their commander General Theodore Von Pfau. A second French attack began further west next day at **Trippstadt** (13 July 1794).

Playa Girón I 1961 I Bay of Pigs Incident
See **Bay of Pigs**

Pleasant Hill I 1864 I American Civil War (Trans-Mississippi)
Union commander Nathaniel P. Banks advanced 150 miles up the Red River through Louisiana before being checked at **Mansfield**. He then fell back southeast to Pleasant Hill, where he was attacked next day by Confederate General Richard Taylor. Although Banks inflicted greater casualties in a hard-fought victory, he abandoned his objective and began the retreat through **Monett's Ferry** (9 April 1864).

Plechenitzi I 1812 I Napoleonic Wars (Russian Campaign)
See **Bolshoi-Stakhov**

Pleiku I 1965 I Vietnam War
Emboldened by their attack on the airbase at **Bien Hoa** and at **Binh Gia**, Viet Cong forces attacked the major US airbase near Pleiku, in the central highlands, where eight Americans were killed, 126 wounded and ten aircraft were destroyed. Next day the US launched its first reprisal air attacks on North Vietnam and a month later the first American ground combat troops arrived (7 February 1965).

Plei Me I 1965 I Vietnam War
At the start of a major offensive in Pleiku, Viet Cong and North Vietnamese regulars under Gen Chu Huy Man attacked the Montagnard camp at Plei Me near the Cambodian border. Very heavy fighting saw South Vietnamese troops and US airborne forces relieve the siege, inflicting costly losses. This was followed by the American counter-offensive at nearby **Ia Drang** (19–27 October 1965).

Plevna (1st) I 1877 I Russo-Turkish Wars
Russian Grand Duke Nicholas captured the Danube fortresses of **Svistov** and **Nicopolis** then marched south against Plevna, held by Osman Nuri Pasha. General Nikolai Krudener launched a powerful assault, followed by a second attack ten days later. However, both assaults were driven back with heavy losses and the Russians settled down to a long and bloody siege (20 & 30 July 1877).

Plevna (2nd) I 1877 I Russo-Turkish Wars
With the Danube fortresses of **Svistov** and **Nicopolis** secured, Grand Duke Nicholas marched south against Plevna, defended by 30,000 Turks under Osman Pasha. Following costly Russian assaults in July General Mikhail Skobelev led a fresh attack, which captured two redoubts. However, he was driven out with a claimed 20,000 casualties and the siege continued (10–12 September 1877).

Plevna (3rd) I 1877 I Russo-Turkish Wars
Russian forces captured the Danube fortresses of **Svistov** and **Nicopolis** then marched south against Osman Pasha and 30,000 Turks at Plevna. Following costly Russian assaults in July and September, Osman led a final sortie, which broke the Russian siege lines. But after terrible losses to both sides Osman was driven back and surrendered to King Carol of Romania (9–10 December 1877).

Pliska I 811 I Byzantine-Bulgarian Wars
See **Verbitza**

Ploermel I 1351 I Hundred Years War
See **Thirty**

Ploesti I 1943 I World War II (Western Europe)
Determined to destroy the petroleum plants at Ploesti, Romania, 177 Liberator bombers under General Uzal Ent set off North Africa. Facing heavy attack, especially at low altitude over Ploesti, 54 of the American aircraft failed to return, with over 300 aircrew killed and almost 200 men captured in Romania or interned in

Turkey. Damage to the refineries was quickly repaired (1 August 1943).

Plotchnik I 1387 I Ottoman Conquest of the Balkans

With the Ottoman army absent in Asia, Lazar I of Serbia rebelled against Sultan Murad I and attacked a depleted Turkish force at Plotchnik (Plocnic), on the Toplitsa, southwest of Nish in central Serbia. Aided by Turtko of Bosnia, Lazar secured a decisive victory. However, two years later he was defeated and killed by Murad at **Kossovo**.

Plovdiv I 1878 I Russo-Turkish Wars

General Ossip Gourko advanced through Bulgaria after Russian victory near the Shipka Pass at **Senova** then days later stormed the fortified city of Plovdiv, held by the great Turkish commander Suleiman Pasha. Plovdiv fell at the cost of 5,000 Turkish casualties and 2,000 prisoners. Suleiman soon abandoned Adrianople and Turkey sued for peace (17 January 1878).

Plowce I 1331 I Wars of the Teutonic Knights

Despite Papal intervention, the Teutonic Order refused to relinquish Pomerania and **Gdansk**. After seizing Estonia, they raided south into the territory of their former ally Ladislav of Poland. Ladislav badly defeated the knights at Plowce, west of Wroclawek, though they retained their conquests. The Order later turned east against Lithuania and in 1410, was routed at **Tannenberg** (27 September 1331).

Plum Creek, Nebraska I 1867 I Cheyenne-Arapaho Indian War

When Cheyenne derailed a Union Pacific train west of Plum Creek (near modern Lexington, Nebraska) General Christopher Augur sent Captain James Murie and 50 Pawnee scouts who attacked Indians looting the wreck. In a fierce delaying action to protect their fleeing women and children, the Cheyenne had seven killed and lost a further 17 in the pursuit until nightfall (17 August 1867).

Plum Creek, Texas I 1840 I Comanche Indian Wars

Pursuing Comanche under Buffalo Hump after the raid on Victoria and Linnville in southern Texas, militia under Generals Felix Huston and Edward Burleson and Texas Ranger Ben McCulloch attacked the invaders at Plum Creek, near modern Lockhart, northeast of San Antonio. Buffalo Hump lost all his loot and about 80 killed. He was beaten again in October on the **Colorado** (12 August 1840).

Plymouth, England I 1588 I Anglo-Spanish Wars

See **Spanish Armada**

Plymouth, England I 1652 I 1st Dutch War

Admiral Michiel de Ruyter attempted to escort a Dutch convoy through the English Channel and was confronted off Plymouth by a large English fleet under Sir George Ayscue. While both fleets suffered severe damage, neither managed to gain the advantage and action broke off at nightfall. Both sides claimed victory, though the Dutch convoy was able to continue on its journey (26 August 1652).

Plymouth, North Carolina I 1864 I American Civil War (Eastern Theatre)

In a combined assault on Union forces in North Carolina, Confederate General Robert F. Hoke, supported by the ram vessel *Albermarle*, attacked the city of Plymouth and drove off nearby Union ships. Colonel Henry W. Wessells surrendered over 2,000 men after Hoke captured key positions. An assault on **Albermarle Sound** two weeks later was far less successful (17–20 April 1864).

Po I 1431 I Venetian-Milanese Wars

See **Cremona**

Po I 1945 I World War II (Southern Europe)

See **Po Valley**

Po-chü I 506 BC I Wars of China's Spring and Autumn Era

See **Boju**

Podgoritza I 1712 I Ottoman Invasions of Montenegro

When Ottoman Sultan Ahmed III led a large invasion of Montenegro, his army was met on the plain of Podgoritza, east of the old capital of Cetinje, by Prince Danilo Petrovich. In the greatest battle between Montenegro and Turkey—on a field later known as Tzarevlatz—the Sultan was utterly defeated. Two years later, Grand Vizier Damad Ai invaded again and captured Cetinje (29 July 1712).

Podhajce I 1667 I Russo-Polish Wars

With Poland weakened after war with Moscow, Russian-aligned Tatar and Cossack forces reunited and up to 30,000 men under Piotr Doroshenko and Devlet Girei ravaged parts of Ukraine then besieged Polish Hetman John Sobieski at Podhacje (modern Pidhaytsi). After heavy fighting the greatly superior Tatar-Cossack force was defeated and withdrew from Polish Western Ukraine (October 1667).

Podol I 1866 I Seven Weeks War

Prince Friedrich Karl invaded Austrian Bohemia with the Prussian 1st Army and sent General Heinrich von Horn against **Liebenau**, just west of Turnau, then continued down the Iser to capture the bridges at Podol. A fierce night-time infantry action forced the Austrians to retreat and Count Edouard von Clam-Gallas fell back southwest towards **Münchengratz** (26–27 June 1866).

Podubnie I 1812 I Napoleonic Wars (Russian Campaign)

See **Gorodeczno**

Podul Inalt I 1475 I Moldavian-Turkish War

See **Rakhova**

Poelcappelle I 1917 I World War I (Western Front)

Following success east of **Ypres** at **Broodseinde**, General Sir Herbert Plumer, supported by General Hubert Gough, attacked in the northeast around Poelcappelle, where much of the fighting fell on the Australians. Despite very heavy losses for no substantial gain, British Commander-in-Chief Sir Douglas Haig then launched his exhausted forces against **Passchendaele** (9 October 1917).

Poggibonzi I 1479 I Florentine-Neapolitan War

When a dispute developed between Pope Sixtus IV and Lorenzo de Medici of Florence, a large army from Naples, supported by Siena, advanced into Tuscany. After months of inconclusive combat the Florentines were routed north of Siena at Poggibonzi by the Allies under Alfonzo, Duke of Calabaria. A courageous embassy by Lorenzo to King Ferdinand of Naples then ended the war.

Point Pelee I 1763 I Pontiac's War

With **Detroit** under siege by the Ottawa Chief Pontiac, Lieutenant Abraham Cuyler was despatched from Fort Niagara with 96 men and ten boats of supplies. At Point Pelee, near the mouth of the Detroit River, the column was ambushed. About 60 men were killed or captured, with many later tortured to death. Cuyler and the survivors escaped by boat back to Niagara (28 May 1763).

Point Pleasant I 1774 I Dunmore's War

After mutual atrocities between Indian and settlers, Virginian Governor John Murray Earl of Dunmore sent Colonel Andrew Lewis against Shawnees in Kentucky. Near the mouth of the Kanawha on the Ohio at Point Pleasant, Shawnee Chief Cornstalk was decisively defeated and made peace. In the subsequent Revolutionary War, Lewis defeated Dunmore at **Gwynn Island** (10 October 1774).

Poison Spring ▌ 1864 ▌ American Civil War (Trans-Mississippi)

Union General Frederick Steele marched across Arkansas through **Elkin's Ferry** and **Prairie d'Ane** to capture Camden, then sent a foraging party west under Colonel James M. Williams. About 15 miles away at Poison Spring, Williams was surprised and routed by Generals John S. Marmaduke and Samuel B. Maxey, returning to Camden after losing all his wagons (18 April 1864).

Poitiers ▌ 732 ▌ Muslim Invasion of France
See **Tours**

Poitiers ▌ 1356 ▌ Hundred Years War

In the disputed Breton succession, Edward III of England supported Charles of Navarre against John II of France and sent Edward Prince of Wales raiding into central France. The Black Prince met John's force at Maupertuis, near Poitiers, and inflicted a terrible defeat. John was taken prisoner to England and the ensuing truce gave Edward new French territory (19 September 1356).

Poitiers ▌ 1569 ▌ 3rd French War of Religion

Four months after the Protestant rout at **Jarnac**, Huguenot leader Admiral Gaspard de Coligny received German reinforcements and joined 15-year-old Henry of Bearnais (later Henry IV) besieging Poitiers. Catholic commander Marshal Gaspard de Tavennes eventually drove off the prolonged siege and quickly followed up with a decisive victory at **Moncontour** (July–September 1569).

Pola ▌ 1379 ▌ War of Chioggia
See **Pula**

Poland ▌ 1939 ▌ World War II (Western Europe)

A lightning campaign to start the war saw German Panzer forces sweep into Poland while battleships shelled the naval bases at **Westerplatte** and **Hel**. Despite heavy fighting and a bold Polish counter-attack at the **Bzura**, War-saw surrendered and resistance ended at **Kock**. The campaign cost up to 200,000 Poles killed and wounded and perhaps 40,000 Germans (1 September–5 October 1939).

Pollentia ▌ 402 ▌ Goth Invasion of the Roman Empire

Soon after an inconclusive action at **Asta**, the Roman-Vandal General Flavius Stilicho attacked the Goth leader Alaric on the Tanarus River near Pollentia (modern Pollenza), southwest of Ancona. While both sides suffered very heavy losses, after initial success Alaric was forced to withdraw north into the Alps. The following year he advanced against Stilicho near **Verona** (6 April 402).

Pollilore ▌ 1780 ▌ 2nd British-Mysore War
See **Perambakam**

Pollilore ▌ 1781 ▌ 2nd British-Mysore War

Haidar Ali of Mysore was decisively defeated at **Porto Novo**, in southeast India (4 July), and pulled back towards **Perambakam**, where he had gained a clear victory a year before. He attempted to make a stand at the nearby village of Pollilore, where he suffered another loss at the hands of General Sir Eyre Coote. Haidar Ali lost again a month later at **Sholinghur** (27 August 1781).

Polo ▌ 1899 ▌ Philippine-American War

American commander Arthur MacArthur marched north from Manila through **Caloocan** (10 February) advancing on Philippine General Antonio Luna's headquarters at the railway town of Polo. American Colonel Harry C. Egbert was killed leading a charge in heavy fighting at nearby Malinta, but Polo fell later the same day. Luna led a scorched-earth retreat towards **Malolos** (26 March 1899).

Polonka ▌ 1660 ▌ Russo-Polish Wars

Prince Yuri Dolgorukov defeated the Poles near **Vilna** (1658) then supported a fresh Russian invasion of Lithuania led by Ivan Khovanski. At Polonka, south of Novogrudok in Belorus, the Allies lost over 5,000 men to Polish

Hetman Stefan Czarniecki. The following year Khovansky was beaten again at **Kushliki** and the Poles gradually recovered most of Lithuania (27 June 1660).

Polonyye I 1660 I Russo-Polish Wars
  See **Polonka**

Polotsk I 1563 I Livonian War
  When Sigismund II Augustus of Poland and Lithuania declared war on Russia to defend Livonia, Tsar Ivan IV himself took a strong army to the Lithuanian border and besieged Polotsk. Two weeks of brutal siege in severe winter conditions forced the city to surrender, but Ivan agreed to an armistice and returned to Moscow. Fighting later resumed at **Chashniki** and **Nevel** (15 February 1563).

Polotsk I 1579 I Livonian War
  Formally declaring war on Russia over Livonia, King Stephen Bathory of Poland determined to cut Moscow's communications with the disputed territory and marched into Russia with a large army to besiege Polotsk. The city fell to Bathory after heavy fighting and the following year he campaigned deeper into enemy territory to the northeast against **Velikie Luki** (11–30 August 1579).

Polotsk (1st) I 1812 I Napoleonic Wars (Russian Campaign)
  As Napoleon Bonaparte advanced into Russia, he sent Marshal Laurent Gouvion Saint-Cyr to reinforce Marshal Nicolas Oudinot near Polotsk against Prince Ludwig Wittgenstein. With Oudinot and Bavarian commander Prince Karl von Wrede both wounded, St-Cyr took over and drove the Russians out, securing the French left flank and gaining his Marshal's baton (17–18 August 1812).

Polotsk (2nd) I 1812 I Napoleonic Wars (Russian Campaign)
  At the start of his retreat from Moscow, Napoleon Bonaparte ordered Marshal Laurent Gouvion Saint-Cyr to secure Polotsk and prevent Prince Ludwig Wittgenstein and Admiral Paul Tchitchakov joining to block his route. After St-Cyr was badly wounded, his French and Bavarian force was heavily defeated and was forced to abandon Polotsk (18 October 1812).

Poltava I 1658 I Russo-Polish Wars
  Cossack leader Ivan Vyhovsky opposed the Russian-aligned Cossack faction in the Ukraine and attacked Poltava, held by Colonel Martyn Pushkar and Zaporozhian Cossacks under Yakov Barabash. After initial failure (25 January) a second assault stormed and burned Poltava, with Pushkar killed. Barabash was later caught and executed and Vyhovsky soon turned against **Kiev** (1 June 1658).

Poltava I 1709 I 2nd "Great" Northern War
  Advancing into Russia after victory at **Holowczyn** (July 1708), Charles XII of Sweden besieged Poltava and faced a Russian relief army under Tsar Peter I. With Charles wounded, his army under Count Carl Gustav Rehnskjold was trapped and destroyed between the Dneiper and Vorska. Only about 2,000 out of 20,000 Swedes escaped, with Charles fleeing to Turkish Moldavia (1 May–1 July 1709).

Polygon Wood I 1917 I World War I (Western Front)
  In renewed fighting east of Ypres in the Third Battle of **Ypres**, General Sir Herbert Plumer followed success along the **Menin Road** with a large-scale assault north on Polygon Wood. German forces of General Friedrich von Arnim's Sixth Army were driven out in heavy fighting and Plumer immediately launched a third attack further north at **Broodseinde** (26 September–3 October 1917).

Pombal I 1811 I Napoleonic Wars (Peninsular Campaign)
  French Marshal Michel Ney, on retreat from the failed invasion of Portugal, fought some remarkable rearguard actions against the cautious pursuit led by Arthur Wellesley Lord Wellington. At the town of Pombal, east of the Tua, Ney attempted to defend the nearby castle,

but was driven out by Colonel Friedrich Arentschildt and withdrew towards the Soure at **Redhina** (10 March 1811).

Pompeii I 89 BC I Roman Social War

When the Marsi and Samnite tribes of central Italy revolted against Roman rule over citizenship, victory at **Asculum** virtually secured the north. Meanwhile Lucius Cornelius Sulla in the south besieged the rebel stronghold at Pompeii, where a Samnite relief army under Cluentius was decisively defeated. After the fall of Pompeii the revolt in the south was soon crushed.

Poncha Pass I 1855 I Ute Indian Wars

On campaign against the Utes in central Colorado, Colonel Thomas T. Fauntleroy led 250 men north from Fort Union and found the camp of Chief Blasco and 150 warriors at Poncha Pass, southwest of Salida. Attacking at night, Fauntleroy's force killed 40 men and scattered the rest, then destroyed the camp and all the Indian possessions, effectively ending Ute resistance (28 April 1855).

Ponda I 1675 I Bijapur-Maratha Wars

During an offensive on India's west coast, Maratha King Shivaji besieged the Bijapuri fortress of Ponda, near Goa. After Mughal Bahlol Khan of Bijapur failed to send aid, the fortress fell by storm and garrison commander Muhammad Khan was one of the few who escaped the ensuing massacre. The victory largely secured the Western Carnatic for Shivaji (8 April–6 May 1675).

Pondicherry I 1748 I 1st Carnatic War

British Admiral Edward Boscawen relieved besieged **Fort St David** on India's southeast coast, then determined to take almost 6,000 European and Indian troops against French Governor General Joseph Dupleix in his nearby capital at Pondicherry. However, after monsoon rains flooded the British trenches Boscawen withdrew with loss of 1,000 men (6 September–17 October 1748).

Pondicherry I 1759 I Seven Years War (India)

Having relieved the French siege of **Madras** (17 February), British Admiral Sir George Pocock patrolled the southeast coast of India and met French Admiral Comte Ann-Antoine d'Aché off Pondicherry. As in their previous encounters off **Cuddalore** and **Negapatam**, the result was indecisive, though d'Aché suffered heavy damage and casualties and withdrew to Mauritius (10 September 1759).

Pondicherry I 1760–1761 I Seven Years War (India)

The last major clash between France and Britain in India saw Colonel Eyre Coote follow **Wandewash** (January 1760) with a large-scale siege of the main French base at Pondicherry, supported at sea by Admiral Charles Steevens. Despite storm damage to the fleet, Coote maintained the siege and forced surrender, virtually ending France's presence in India (8 December 1760–15 January 1761).

Pondicherry I 1778 I War of the American Revolution

On the resumption of war in Europe, British General Hector Munro was sent against French Pondicherry in southeast India, defended by Governor Guillaume de Bellecombe. While Pondicherry was under siege, French Admiral Tronjolly was repulsed by Admiral Edward Vernon (10 August) and the city finally surrendered. Munro was knighted for his success (16 October 1778).

Pont-à-Chin I 1794 I French Revolutionary Wars (1st Coalition)

The Austrian-British-Hanoverian allies retreating from defeat at **Tourcoing** in Belgium turned against General Charles Pichegru at Tournai, east of Lille. An otherwise indecisive battle saw the British right wing under General Henry Fox repulse the French from the village of Pont-à-Chin, before both sides disengaged after heavy losses. The Allied withdrawal continued (22 May 1794).

Ponta Delgada ▌ 1582 ▌ Spanish-Portuguese War
See **Terceira**

Ponta della Priula ▌ 1809 ▌ Napoleonic Wars (5th Coalition)
See **Piave**

Pont à Noyelles ▌ 1870 ▌ Franco-Prussian War
See **Hallue**

Pontarlier ▌ 1871 ▌ Franco-Prussian War
After a French attempt to relieve **Belfort** was repulsed at **Héricourt**, General Charles-Denis Bourbaki was replaced by General Justin Clinchant, who was driven south by General Edwin von Manteuffel. Defeated near Pontarlier and nearby La Cluse, Clinchant led his 90,000 men across the border to internment in Switzerland just as the war came to an end (29 January–1 February 1871).

Pont-Charrault ▌ 1793 ▌ French Revolutionary Wars (Vendée War)
See **Pont de Gravereau**

Pont-de-Ce ▌ 1620 ▌ French Civil War
See **Ponts-de-Ce**

Pont de Gravereau ▌ 1793 ▌ French Revolutionary Wars (Vendée War)
General Louis Marcé, advancing towards the Lay near the start of the Royalist counter-revolution in western France, routed Republicans at the Pont de Gravereau, then occupied nearby Chantonnay, while the defeated army fled south towards **Fontenay**. Regarded as the first Royalist victory over Republican regulars, it is mistakenly also known as Pont-Charrault (19 March 1793).

Pontesbury ▌ 661 ▌ Anglo-Saxon Territorial Wars
Wulfhere of Mercia, son of the great King Penda, became increasingly concerned by the expanding power of Wessex and took a large force against King Cenwalh (Coenwalch) of Wessex. The army of the West Saxons was heavily defeated at Pontesbury, southwest of Shrewsbury in central Shropshire and Wulfhere went on to seize the Isle of Wight.

Pontoise ▌ 1441 ▌ Hundred Years War
Five years after French forces recaptured **Paris** from the English, Thomas Lord Clifford seized Pontoise on the northwestern outskirts (June 1441). Despite reinforcements under Richard Duke of York and John Talbot Earl of Shrewsbury, the English were eventually driven out by Jean Bureau Master of Artillery. The battle was the last major action before a five-year truce in 1444 (14 September 1441).

Ponts-de-Ce ▌ 1620 ▌ French Civil War
In a struggle for power in France, Queen Mother Marie de Medici became the focus for nobles opposing the young Louis XIII and his unpopular Minister Alfred de Luynes. Louis II de Bourbon Prince of Condé defeated the Queen's adherents under Jean-Louis Duke d'Epernon south of Angers at Ponts-de-Ce and a Royal reconciliation was negotiated (7 August 1620).

Pontvallain ▌ 1370 ▌ Hundred Years War
During a period of intermittent fighting in France, the rearguard of an English force led by Sir Robert Knolles was surprised in camp near Pontvallain, south of Le Mans, by the great warrior Bertrand du Guesclin. The English were heavily defeated and the main English army was driven back to Brittany (4 December 1370).

Poona ▌ 1663 ▌ Mughal-Maratha Wars
A brilliant exploit in western India saw Maratha warlord Shivaji and his lieutenant Chimnaji Bapuji lead about 400 men on a night-time raid on the camp of Mughal Viceroy Shaista Khan just outside Poona. Surprised in his harem, Shaista Khan was slightly wounded, while his son Abdul Fath and about 40 men were killed. The Viceroy withdrew in shame to Aurangabad (5 April 1663).

Poona ▌ 1781 ▌ 1st British-Maratha War
See **Bhorghat**

Poona I 1802 I Maratha Territorial Wars

In bloody war between rival Maratha Princes, Maharaja Jaswant Rao Holkar of Indore came back from defeat at **Indore** (October 1801) and, outside Poona, he defeated Daulat Rao Sindhia of Gwalior and overthrew his ally Peshwa Baji Rao II. British demands to restore the deposed Peshwa led to the 2nd British-Maratha War, when Sindhia changed sides to support Holkar (25 October 1802).

Poonch I 1947–1948 I 1st Indo-Pakistan War

Soon after the fall of **Uri**, Pakistan-backed tribal rebellion broke out in southwest Kashmir and over 45,000 refugees crammed into Poonch, where Indian regulars arrived with orders to hold the city at all cost. Aided by a bold airlift, and despite facing trumped-up charges, Brigadier Pritam Singh held out against a yearlong siege and Poonch was finally relieved (November 1947–23 November 1948).

Poplar Grove I 1900 I 2nd Anglo-Boer War

General Lord Frederick Roberts advancing east from **Kimberley** through **Paardeberg** met a Boer defensive line on the Modder at Poplar Grove. A badly managed action saw a failed British flanking attack and a bold rearguard action by Christiaan de Wet. The Boers, including President Paul Kruger himself, then withdrew through **Driefontein** to Bloemfontein (7 March 1900).

Poplar Springs Church I 1864 I American Civil War (Eastern Theatre)

While Union forces attacked northeast of **Petersburg**, Virginia, at **New Market Heights**, Generals Gouvernor K. Warren and John G. Parker advanced southwest near Poplar Springs Church. In heavy fighting at Peebles' Farm, a Confederate counter-attack by Generals Ambrose P. Hill and Wade Hampton failed and the Union line was extended to the west (30 September–2 October 1864).

Porici I 1420 I Hussite Wars

When Sigismund of Hungary invaded to seize Bohemia and threatened Prague, the city sent for help from the Hussite Jan Zizka at Tabor. A Royalist force under Pipo Spano (Count Filippe de Scolari) and Wenceslas of Duba intercepted the approaching Hussites near Porici, on the Sásava, south of Prague. However, they were heavily defeated and Zizka entered the capital next day (19 May 1420).

Pork Chop Hill I 1953 I Korean War

Chinese forces attacking southwest of Chorwon seized **Old Baldy** but failed to take nearby Pork Chop Hill (23–26 March). A second attempt also failed (16–18 April) before the Chinese launched a third, overwhelming assault. After heavy losses for no strategic purpose, General Maxwell Taylor abandoned the hard-fought position. Two weeks later the armistice was signed (6–11 July 1953).

Pornic I 1793 I French Revolutionary Wars (Vendée War)

General André Jean Saint-André opened the Royalist rebellion in western France by taking Pornic, near the mouth of the Loire. But after his men got drunk on looted liquor, it was retaken by National Guardsmen with over 200 killed. Saint-André retired in disgrace and Pornic was easily captured again five days later by Royalist General Francois-Athanese Charette (22 March 1793).

Port Arthur I 1894 I Sino-Japanese War

While Japanese forces crossed the **Yalu** from Korea into China, Marshal Iwao Oyama landed 40,000 men on the Liaodong Peninsula, where he captured Jinzhou (5 November), then marched on Port Arthur (modern Lüshun). After a massive bombardment by land and sea, General Maresuke Nogi took the vital port by storm and soon marched north into Manchuria towards **Kaiping** (21 November 1894).

Port Arthur I 1904 I Russo-Japanese War

Just before midnight on the first day of the war, Japanese Admiral Heihachiro Togo engaged a Russian squadron outside Port Arthur (modern Lüshun) badly damaging three capital ships. In the "First Pearl Harbour," he then heavily shelled the city and harbour. A simultaneous attack was made on **Chemulpo** and Japan declared war the following day (8–9 February 1904).

Port Arthur I 1904–1905 I Russo-Japanese War

Following victory at **Nanshan** (May 1904), Japanese General Maresuke Nogi advanced down the Liaodong Peninsula to besiege Port Arthur (modern Lüshun). Months of suicidal assaults on outlying positions cost about 60,000 Japanese casualties before Russian General Anatole Stoessel finally surrendered, yielding 30,000 prisoners and massive supplies (June 1904–2 January 1905).

Port-au-Prince I 1803 I Napoleonic Wars (Santo Domingo Rising)

With French forces in **Santo Domingo** suffering a British naval blockade and terrible losses to fever, rebel leaders Jean Jacques Dessalines and Alexander Pétion launched an offensive on the western plain and besieged Port-au-Prince. The capital fell after three weeks of heavy fighting. Remaining French forces withdrew on Cap Francais and tried to defend nearby **Vertieres** (17 October 1803).

Portela I 982 I War of Leonese Succession

When King Ramiro III of Leon lost Zamora and was routed by Muslims at **Rueda** (981), a group of rebellious nobles supported his cousin Bermudo as pretender and the rivals met at Portela de Arenas, near Monterroso southwest of Lugo. Although the battle produced no decisive outcome, the unpopular Ramiro died soon afterwards and his cousin succeeded as Bermudo II (15 May 982).

Porte St Antoine I 1652 I War of the 2nd Fronde

See **St Antoine**

Port Gibson I 1863 I American Civil War (Western Theatre)

General John S. Bowen defended the southern approaches to Confederate Vicksburg on the Mississippi, repulsing a naval assault at **Grand Gulf**. Days later he marched to meet General Ulysses S. Grant who had crossed further south. Bowen was defeated in heavy fighting at Port Gibson, near Pierre Bayou, Mississippi. He abandoned Grand Gulf, opening the route to **Vicksburg** (1 May 1863).

Port Harcourt I 1968 I Biafran War

After the fall of **Onitsha**, Federal Colonel Benjamin Adckunle advanced west from **Calabar** against the Nigerian city of Port Harcourt with its airport, oil refineries and the last sea access for rebel Biafra. Attacking behind a decisive artillery bombardment, Adekunle overwhelmed Colonel Joe "Hannibal" Achuzie in two days, then moved north towards Aba and **Owerri** (16–18 May 1968).

Port Hudson I 1863 I American Civil War (Lower Seaboard)

Union General Nathaniel P. Banks followed victory at **Plains Store** by besieging the nearby Confederate stronghold at Port Hudson, Louisiana, on the Mississippi north of Baton Rouge, held by General Franklin Gardner. The garrison surrendered after six weeks' siege and the fall of **Vicksburg**. Union forces soon attacked again further south at **Cox's Plantation** (21 May–9 July 1863).

Portland, Dorset I 1653 I 1st Dutch War

Admiral Robert Blake built up the English fleet after defeat at **Dungeness** (December 1652) and attacked Dutch Admiral Maarten Tromp escorting a large merchant convoy off Portland, Dorset. In running action as far as Beachy Head Tromp lost nine warships and 24 merchantmen. While Blake also lost several ships, the Channel was effectively closed to Dutch trade (28 February–2 March 1653).

Portland, Maine ∎ 1813 ∎ War of 1812

In a morale-boosting American victory, the sloop *Enterprise* (Captain William Burrows) attacked the British brig *Boxer* (Captain Samuel Blyth) off Portland, Maine. Both captains were killed in an hourlong exchange of broadsides, though the mortally wounded Burrows lived long enough to accept the British surrender. He and Blyth were later buried side by side (5 September 1813).

Port Mahon ∎ 1756 ∎ Seven Years War (Europe)

Without a declaration of war, France sent Admiral Marquis Augustine de la Galissonière and Louis Duke de Richelieu against the English-held Mediterranean island of Minorca, where they captured Ciudadela then besieged the capital, Port Mahon. General William Blakeney surrendered the port after 70 days and the repulse of a British fleet off **Minorca** (18 April–28 June 1756).

Porto Bello ∎ 1668 ∎ Morgan's Raids on Panama

With England at war against Spain, Welsh-born buccaneer Henry Morgan attacked Porto Principe in Cuba, then took 12 ships and about 500 men against well-fortified Porto Bello on the Panama Isthmus. The city fell after heavy fighting and was then looted and burned. Morgan later attacked Spanish possessions in Venezuela and in 1671 destroyed the city of **Panama** (28 August 1668).

Porto Bello ∎ 1739 ∎ War of the Austrian Succession

A preliminary campaign known as the War of Jenkin's Ear saw English Admiral Edward Vernon attack Porto Bello, in Spanish Panama, and capture the key fortress of San Felipe after heavy gunfire. The city surrendered next day, then Vernon seized all the ships in the harbour and destroyed the fortifications. In 1741 he was heavily repulsed at **Cartagena** in Colombia (20–21 November 1739).

Porto Calvo ∎ 1635 ∎ Dutch-Portuguese Colonial Wars

While campaigning against Portuguese Brazil, Dutch under the mulatto Domingo Fernandez Calabar captured Porto Calvo (March 1635), where they were besieged by a Portuguese force from the fall of Fort Nazaré. Calabar capitulated and was executed as a traitor, but the Portuguese soon withdrew. The town was regained in 1636 from Dutch commander Sigismund von Schoppe (July 1635).

Porto Calvo ∎ 1637 ∎ Dutch-Portuguese Colonial Wars

Dutch Governor John Maurice of Nassau had scarcely arrived in Brazil when he sailed south from Recife to recapture Portuguese Porto Calvo. With a reported 3,000 soldiers, 1,000 sailors and 1,000 Indian allies he took the town after two weeks' siege from the Italian adventurer Joao Vicente Sao Felix Conde de Bagnuoli. A year later Maurice was heavily repulsed at **Salvador** (18 February 1637).

Porto Conte ∎ 1353–1354 ∎ Aragon's Conquest of Sardinia
See **Alghero**

Porto Farina ∎ 1665 ∎ Corsair Wars

With the end of the First Dutch War, English Admiral Robert Blake was sent to the Mediterranean against Barbary pirates. Leading a large squadron, he attacked the corsair fleet at Porto Farina, near Bizerta in the Gulf of Tunis. Shielded by the smoke of their own cannonade the English set fire to all nine pirate ships and withdrew, losing just 25 killed and 40 wounded (4 April 1665).

Portolongo ∎ 1354 ∎ Venetian-Genoese Wars
See **Sapienza**

Porto Longone ∎ 1646 ∎ Thirty Years War (Franco-Habsburg War)

When Allied forces were driven back at **Orbetello** in June, a fresh advance into Italy was led by French Marshals Charles de la Porte Duke de la Meilleraie and Cesar de Choiseul du Plessis-Praslin who seized Piombino, opposite Elbe. They then besieged and captured Porto Longone (modern Porto Azzurro) on Elbe itself and Pope Innocent X soon agreed to a treaty with France (September 1646).

Porto Novo I 1781 I 2nd British-Mysore War

General Sir Eyre Coote resolved to lure Haidar Ali of Mysore into open battle in southeast India and led 8,000 men against a massively superior Mysorean army at Porto Novo, just north of the British base at Cuddalore. With his cavalry commander Mir Sahib killed amid very heavy casualties, the Maharaja was forced to retreat. He lost again two months later at **Pollilore** (1 July 1781).

Porto Praya I 1781 I War of the American Revolution

As British and French fleets sailed to secure the Dutch Cape of Good Hope, French Admiral Pierre André Suffren surprised Commodore George Johnstone at anchor in Porto Praya in the Cape Verde Islands. Ignoring Portuguese neutrality, Suffren attacked and badly damaged the British ships. He sailed on to reinforce the Cape Colony then to India and battle at **Sadras** in 1782 (16 April 1781).

Port Republic I 1862 I American Civil War (Eastern Theatre)

Manoeuvering in the Shenandoah Valley against Union Commander John C. Frémont, Confederate forces won at **Cross Keys** then next day General Thomas "Stonewall' Jackson attacked and heavily defeated the isolated brigades of Union Generals Erastus Tyler and Samuel S. Carroll across the river at Port Republic. Frémont had to retreat and was relieved of command (9 June 1862).

Port Royal, Nova Scotia I 1614 I Anglo-French Wars in North America

British colonists in Virginia were reluctant to accept French presence in Acadia (modern Nova Scotia) and sent Sir Samuel Argall against Port Royal (later Annapolis Royal), held by Charles de Biencourt Baron de Saint-Just. Argall (famous for abducting Pocahontas) captured and burned the port then took his prisoners to England, eventually returning as Deputy Governor of Virginia.

Port Royal, Nova Scotia I 1690 I King William's War

In the largest action during King William's War—the American phase of the War of the Grand Alliance—colonial militia under Sir William Phips surprised the French at Port Royal in Acadia (modern Nova Scotia). The port fell after a short siege though Phips failed against **Quebec**. Port Royal was retaken the following year and was retained by France at the war's end (11 May 1690).

Port Royal, Nova Scotia I 1704 I Queen Anne's War

Early in Queen Anne's War—the American phase of the War of the Spanish Succession—militia Colonel Benjamin Church of Massachusetts led an expedition against the French base at Port Royal in Acadia (modern Nova Scotia). However, the French avoided decisive action and he eventually withdrew. Another attempt was repulsed in 1707, though the port later fell to a larger force (July 1704).

Port Royal, Nova Scotia I 1710 I Queen Anne's War

Colonel Francis Nicholson attacked France in North America, taking 1,500 colonial militia against Port Royal in Acadia (modern Nova Scotia) held by Daniel de Subercase. Supported by ships under Captain George Martin, the expedition captured the fortress after a short siege. Acadia became British and the port was renamed Annapolis Royal for Queen Anne (24 September–5 October 1710).

Port Royal, South Carolina I 1779 I War of the American Revolution

See **Beaufort**

Port Said ❙ 1956 ❙ Suez Crisis

When Egypt nationalized the Suez Canal, Anglo-French forces under General Sir Charles Keightley and Admiral Pierre Barjot landed at Port Said and nearby Port Fuad against General Salah ed-Din Moguy. Sharp fighting cost about 30 allies and up to 1,000 Egyptians killed before American pressure forced a ceasefire and the invasion ended in disastrous failure (5–6 November 1956).

Port Say ❙ 1907 ❙ French Colonial Wars in North Africa
See **Wadi Kiss**

Port Stanley ❙ 1982 ❙ Falklands War
See **Stanley**

Portugalete ❙ 1812 ❙ Napoleonic Wars (Peninsular Campaign)

British Admiral Sir Home Popham led an offensive on the northern coast of Spain to relieve pressure on the Allied campaign around **Salamanca**, attacking **Lequeitio**, **Guetaria** and **Castro Urdiales**, before he and Spanish Colonel Francsico Longa bombarded Portugalete in Bilbao Bay. However, they were driven off and Popham returned to attack **Guetaria** (11 July 1812).

Port Walthall Junction ❙ 1864 ❙ American Civil War (Eastern Theatre)

Supporting the Union offensive in the **Wilderness**, General Benjamin F. Butler advanced against railways northeast of Petersburg, Virginia, where General William T. H. Brookes attacked Port Walthall Junction, defended by Confederate General Johnson Hagood. After heavy fighting and some track destroyed, the superior Union force withdrew with almost 300 men lost (6–7 May 1864).

Porvoo ❙ 1918 ❙ Finnish War of Independence

Red commander Ali Aaltonen seized **Helsinki**, then despatched a force east against White troops near Porvoo. After costly fighting, the Whites fell back to the nearby island of Pellinge.

Attacking across the ice, the Reds were driven off, but the Whites were out of ammunition and withdrew, eventually to Estonia. Red forces soon attacked west of Helsinki at **Sigurds** (6–12 February 1918).

Posadas ❙ 1832 ❙ Mexican Civil Wars

General Antonio de Santa Anna led the rebellion against President Anastasio Bustamente and captured **Puebla**, then held it against an advancing government force under Bustamente himself. Following heavy fighting in the northwestern suburb of Posadas, Bustamente was decisively defeated. He soon resigned and Santa Anna became President in early 1833 (5 December 1832).

Poserna ❙ 1813 ❙ Napoleonic Wars (War of Liberation)
See **Rippach**

Poson ❙ 863 ❙ Byzantine-Muslim Wars

At the start of a counter-offensive against Islam in Asia Minor, Byzantine Emperor Michael III sent his uncle Petronas (brother of the former Regent Theodora) and a large force against Omar of Melitene (modern Malatya), who had sacked Amisus (Samsun). Omar was driven back then defeated and killed in battle at Poson, stalling Muslim expansion. Petronas returned to Constantinople in triumph.

Potidaea ❙ 432–429 BC ❙ Great Peloponnesian War

When the former Corinthian colony of Potidaea, on the Pallene Isthmus, revolted against Athens, it was quickly supported by the Corinthian Aristeus and 2,000 Peloponnesian volunteers. An Athenian expedition initially under Archestratus won a battle outside the city, then settled into a long siege, precipitating renewed war. When the garrison finally surrendered they were allowed to go free.

Potidaea ❙ 356 BC ❙ 1st Greek Social War

While Athens was enmeshed in the Social War, Philip II of Macedon seized Amphipolis and Pydna, then besieged Athenian-controlled

Potidaea, on the Pallene Isthmus. Supported by Olynthian troops, Philip forced the town to capitulate and sold the citizens into slavery. He gave Potidaea to his allies to keep them detached from Athens, but in 348 BC he turned on them and attacked **Olynthus**.

Potrerillos I 1817 I Chilean War of Independence

As Patriots led by Juan Gregorio Las Heras marched on Uspallata, northwest of Mendoza, an advance column under Colonel Enrique Martínez was surprised by the government forces of Miguel Marqueli to the south at Potrerillos, near Cacheuta. The Royalists were defeated and withdrew to the west, while Las Heras crossed the Andes into Chile in May and captured **Gavilán** (25 January 1817).

Potrero de Chacón I 1831 I Argentine Civil Wars

See **Rodeo de Chacón**

Potrero del Sauce I 1866 I War of the Triple Alliance

See **Boquerón, Nhembucu**

Potrero Obella I 1867 I War of the Triple Alliance

Brazilian Marshal Luíz Aldes, Marquis of Caxias, was determined to isolate besieged **Humaitá** in southwest Paraguay. He won at **Tatayiba** then sent General Joao Manoel Mena Barreta and 4,000 men against nearby Potrero Obella. A three-hour action saw Paraguayan Captain Gonsalez forced to withdraw with 136 casualties. The Allies won again five days later at **Tuyutí** (29 October 1867).

Potsdam I 1806 I Napoleonic Wars (4th Coalition)

The Prussian army was retreating north past Berlin after the twin defeats at **Jena** and **Auerstadt** when Napoleon Bonaparte's pursuing forces crashed into their rear west of the city at Potsdam. Marshals Joachim Murat and Jean Lannes heavily repulsed Prussian units under Prince Friedrich-Ludwig of Hohenloe, who soon lost again at **Zehdenick** and **Prenzlau** (24 October 1806).

Poupry I 1870 I Franco-Prussian War

See **Loigny**

Poutoko I 1863 I 2nd New Zealand War

Maoris in southern Taranaki recovered from defeat on the **Katikara** in June and threatened the redoubt at Poutoko, five miles south of New Plymouth, held by British Regulars under Major Henry Butler. A relief force under Colonel Henry J. Warre was heavily outnumbered by hostile Maoris. After heavy fighting (with two Victoria Crosses won) the redoubt was saved (2 October 1863).

Po Valley I 1945 I World War II (Southern Europe)

Stalled in northern Italy around **Bologna**, new Allied commanders Sir Richard McCreery and the American General Lucian Truscott launched a spring offensive against the **Gothic Line**, now commanded by General Heinrich von Vietinghoff. The Allies drove into the Po Valley, taking Ferrara Mantua and Venice, and German forces in Italy soon formally surrendered (5 April–2 May 1945).

Powder I 1865 I Cheyenne-Arapaho Indian War

On campaign north of the Black Hills, 2,000 men led by the inexperienced Colonels Nelson Cole and Samuel Walker became disoriented in extremely hot conditions, losing hundreds of horses to thirst. Attacked on the Powder River in Montana by Cheyenne under Roman Nose, they held off the Indians and were eventually rescued by Major Frank North's Pawnee scouts (September 1865).

Powder I 1876 I Sioux Indian Wars

General George Crook marching through the Big Horn Mountains against the Sioux, sent Colonel Joseph Reynolds against Old Bear's Northern Cheyenne and Ogala Sioux under He Dog in camp near the junction of the Powder and Little Powder in southeast Montana. Most of the

Indians escaped the dawn attack and a few months later joined Crazy Horse at **Little Big Horn** (17 March 1876).

Powick Bridge I 1642 I British Civil Wars

Marching south towards London, King Charles I met units of the Parliamentary army of Robert Devereux Earl of Essex south of Worcester at Powick Bridge. One of the first actions of the war saw Colonel Nathaniel Fiennes' Ironsides cavalry ambushed and dispersed by Prince Rupert's dragoons. Essex withdrew and met the King again a month later at **Edgehill** (23 September 1642).

Poyang Lake I 1363 I Rise of the Ming Dynasty

Han leader Chen Yuliang took a large armada down the Yangzi to besiege **Nanchang** then turned to meet Zhu Yuanzhang's Ming fleet on Poyang Lake. A four-day battle cost the Han terrible losses before the Ming withdrew. A month later, Chen tried to break out to the Yangzi, but was defeated and killed. In 1364 his capital Wuchang fell to the Ming (30 August–2 September & 3 October 1363).

Poza I 1813 I Napoleonic Wars (Peninsular Campaign)

When French forces under General Giuseppe Palombini made an aggressive sweep south of the Ebro, Spanish General Francisco Longa attempted to cut them off and sent forces to attack the invaders at Poza de le Sal, northeast of Burgos. A poorly managed action allowed Palombini to drive off the Spanish assault and return across the Ebro to Vitoria (10–11 February 1813).

Poza de las Carmelos I 1832 I Mexican Civil Wars

General Esteban Moctezuma supported a rising against President Anastasio Bustamente by attacking a government force under General Pedro Luciano Otero at Poza de las Carmelos, near San Luis Potosi. Otero was defeated and killed and Moctezuma seized San Luis Potosi. However, he was subsequently defeated by Bustamente in September at **Gallinero** (3 June 1832).

Pozières I 1916 I World War I (Western Front)

During the Battle of the **Somme**, newly arrived Australian Divisions under Sir William Birdwood attacked towards Pozières Ridge on the Albert-Bapaume Road. Supported by English units, the Australians eventually took the Ridge and Pozières Village after very heavy fighting. However, they lost about 6,000 men, 4,000 of them killed and 400 taken prisoner (23 July–3 September 1916).

Poznan I 1945 I World War II (Eastern Front)

As Soviet Marshal Georgi Zhukov swept across Poland in the massive **Vistula-Oder** offensive, he bypassed a large German force in the fortress city of Poznan, which was then surrounded by part of his army under General Vasilii Chuikov. Intense street fighting saw costly losses in a long siege before Poznan finally fell with perhaps 25,000 prisoners (26 January–23 February 1945).

Pozo Almonte I 1891 I Chilean Civil War

In civil war between Chile's Congress and President José Manuel Balmaceda, Congressist Colonel Estanislao del Canto Arteaga seized Iquique after victory at **San Francisco**. After a check at **Huara** he defeated and killed Loyalist Colonel Eulogio Robles Pinochet to the east at Pozo Almonte, securing northern Chile for the rebels, who then sailed south against **Concón** (7 March 1891).

Pozo Favorito I 1933 I Chaco War
See **Pampa Grande**

Pozzolo I 1800 I French Revolutionary Wars (2nd Coalition)
See **Mincio**

Praga I 1794 I War of the 2nd Polish Partition

Russian Field Marshal Alexander Suvorov secured victory at **Maciejowice** (10 October) then attacked Generals Tomasz Wawrzecki and Jakob Jasinski at Warsaw. The suburb of Praga was stormed, with up to 30,000 Poles butchered, including Jasinski. After Wawrzecki was surrounded and captured, the rest of Warsaw fell and a new Great Power treaty wiped Poland off the map (4–8 November 1794).

Praga I 1831 I Polish Rebellion

When Poland deposed Duke Constantine, brother of Tsar Nicholas I, a massive Russian retaliatory invasion was halted just east of Warsaw at **Grochow**. A few days later, in the northeastern Warsaw suburb of Praga, Poles under General Jan Skrznyecki dealt another bloody check to Field Marshal Hans von Diebitsch and the invaders were forced to withdraw (25 February 1831).

Prague I 1420 I Hussite Wars
See **Vitkov Hill**

Prague I 1620 I Thirty Years War (Bohemian War)
See **White Mountain**

Prague I 1648 I Thirty Years War (Franco-Habsburg War)

Count Hans Christoph Königsmarck led a fresh Swedish invasion of Bohemia, advancing to besiege Prague, which was stubbornly defended by a largely citizen militia. A relief attempt by Imperial General Ottavio Piccomolini was driven off and Königsmarck was preparing to take the city by assault when the Treaty of Westphalia ended the war (June–24 October 1648).

Prague I 1744 I War of the Austrian Succession

Re-entering the war, Frederick II of Prussia launched a large-scale invasion of Bohemia and besieged Prague, held for Prince Charles of Lorraine. Despite suffering heavier casualties, Frederick seized the city, along with a large number of prisoners, then advanced to threaten Vienna. However, he was denied aid by his French and Bavarian allies and had to withdraw (2–16 September 1744).

Prague I 1757 I Seven Years War (Europe)

Frederick II of Prussia advanced into Bohemia and met Prince Charles of Lorraine at the Moldau outside Prague. Bloody action caused heavy losses on both sides (including the deaths of Prussian Marshal Kurt von Schwerin and Austrian Marshal Maximilian von Browne) before the Austrians were finally driven off. Frederick besieged Prague but withdrew after defeat in June at **Kolin** (6 May 1757).

Prague I 1945 I World War II (Eastern Front)

With **Vienna** secured, Marshal Rodion Malinovsky drove deep into Czechoslovakia, while Marshal Ivan Konev advanced from the north towards Prague. The people rose in revolt and the city fell after a four-day Soviet attack. However, Marshal Ferdinand Schörner's Army Group Centre held out nearby and did not surrender until 11 May, said to be the last act of the war in Europe (6–9 May 1945).

Praia Bay I 1828 I Miguelite Wars

After Don Miguel de Braganza usurped the throne of Portugal as Miguel I, supporters of his niece, the legitimate Queen Maria da Gloria, established a constitutional government on Terceira in the Azores. An attempt by Miguel to seize the island was defeated at sea off Praia Bay and the Azores became the base for eventual restoration of lawful government (12 August 1828).

Prairie d'Ane I 1864 I American Civil War (Trans-Mississippi)

Union General Frederick Steele led an expedition southwest from Little Rock, Arkansas, and fought across the Little Missouri at **Elkin's Ferry** before facing a Confederate blocking force under General Sterling Price further south at Prairie d'Ane. Despite an initial repulse, Steele and General John M. Thayer drove off the Confederates and marched east to capture **Camden** (9–13 April 1864).

Prairie Dog Creek I 1860 I Comanche Indian Wars

When Colonel John Sedgewick led an expedition to punish Comanche and Kiowa attacks on the Santa Fé trail, one of his columns under Captain Samuel Sturgis from Fort Cobb met the Indians near Prairie Dog Creek in northern Kansas. With Cheyenne and Arapaho aid, Sturgis inflicted a decisive defeat after an eight-day chase before the expedition returned to camp (9 August 1860).

Prairie du Chien I 1814 I War of 1812

Governor William Clark of Missouri seized the British outpost at Prairie du Chien—on the Wisconsin and Missisippi Rivers—and built Fort Shelby, which was later attacked by Michigan militia and Indians under Major William McKay. The small American garrison surrendered after two days and the gunboat *Governor Clark* escaped downstream towards **Rock Island Rapids** (18–19 July 1814).

Prairie Grove I 1862 I American Civil War (Trans-Mississippi)

Campaigning in northwest Arkansas, Confederate commander Thomas C. Hindman found himself southwest of Fayetteville between General James G. Blunt advancing from Arkansas through **Cane Hill** and General Francis J. Herron marching south from Missouri. Both sides lost about 1,200 men in bloody action at Prairie Grove and Hindman retreated south to Van Buren (7 December 1862).

Pratabgarh I 1659 I Bijapur-Maratha Wars

With the Muslim state of Bijapur determined to deal finally with the growing power of Maratha commander Shivaji, General Afzal Khan led the army of Bijapur west from Wai towards well-prepared Maratha positions near Pratabgarh, northwest of Satara. Shivaji lured Afzal Khan to his death, then ambushed and utterly destroyed the leaderless Bijapuri army (10 November 1659).

Prenzlau I 1806 I Napoleonic Wars (4th Coalition)

As the Prussian army retreated north across Germany after the twin defeats at **Jena** and **Auerstadt**, Prince Friedrich-Ludwig of Hohenloe's retreating force lost at **Potsdam** and **Zehdenick**. Two days later French Marshal Joachim Murat caught up with Hohenloe at Prenzlau. The exhausted Prussians were routed and the Prince surrendered with over 10,000 men (28 October 1806).

President vs *Endymion* I 1815 I War of 1812

See **Connecticut**

Pressburg I 907 I Magyar Invasion of Germany

On a renewed invasion of Bavaria, Magyar horsemen from Hungary were challenged near Pressburg (modern Bratislava) by a force under the Margave Luitpold, who was defeated and killed and the raids continued. Fourteen-year-old Ludwig III, the nominal King of Germany, was ill-advisedly present on the battlefield and only just escaped being taken prisoner (4 July 907).

Pressburg I 1866 I Seven Weeks War

See **Blumenau**

Preston I 1648 I British Civil Wars

Scottish Royalist James Duke of Hamilton, aided by English under Sir Marmaduke Langdale, invaded England in support of Charles I and was massively defeated in a two-day action at Preston, Lancashire, by the Parliamentary army of Sir Thomas Fairfax. Hamilton was captured and executed and the fall of **Colchester** at the end of August virtually ended the King's second war (17–18 August 1648).

Preston I 1715 I Jacobite Rebellion (The Fifteen)

In support of James Stuart—the Old Pretender—English forces under James Radcliffe of Derwentwater and Thomas Forster captured Preston, Lancashire, supported by Scots under William Mackintosh of Borlum. After repulsing

Hanoverian General Sir Charles Wills, the rebels were forced to surrender and Derwentwater and Lord Kenmure were executed (12–14 November 1715).

Prestonpans I 1745 I Jacobite Rebellion (The Forty-Five)

Leading renewed rebellion in the Highlands Charles Stuart—Bonnie Prince Charlie—raised an army and found his way south blocked at Prestonpans east of Edinburgh by General Sir John Cope. A decisive ten-minute action was sufficient for the Prince and Lord George Murray to rout the hastily raised militia, who fled with heavy losses. The Highlanders then invaded England (21 September 1745).

Preussich-Eylau I 1807 I Napoleonic Wars (4th Coalition)

See **Eylau**

Preveza I 1538 I Later Venetian-Turkish War

A year after repulsing an Ottoman siege of **Corfu**, Venice sent Admiral Andrea Doria against the Turkish naval base on the Albanian mainland at Preveza. A mismanaged campaign against Admiral Khair-ed-Din Barbarossa saw Doria attempting to avoid a decisive battle. In action off Preveza the Venetian was driven off and in 1539 he turned his attention to **Castelnuovo** (26–28 September 1538).

Primolano I 1796 I French Revolutionary Wars (1st Coalition)

Napoleon Bonaparte faced a renewed Austrian attempt to relieve the French siege of **Mantua** and, after defeating an Austrian force at **Calliano**, he turned against General Dagobert Wurmser in the Brenta Valley. At Primolano, northeast of Vicenza, General Pierre Augereau captured Wurmer's Croat rearguard, followed by the decisive battle next day at **Bassano** (7 September 1796).

Primosole Bridge I 1943 I World War II (Southern Europe)

See **Catania**

Prince of Wales and Repulse I 1941 I World War II (Pacific)

Belatedly trying to protect **Malaya**, the British battleship *Prince of Wales* and battle cruiser *Repulse* arrived in **Singapore** under Admiral Tom Phillips. Sent to meet a reported Japanese landing, but without air support, the ships were sunk by land-based aircraft off the east coast with 840 killed, including Phillips. They were the first capital ships sunk at sea by air attack alone (10 December 1941).

Princes I 1856 I Zulu Wars of Succession

See **Ndondakusuka**

Princeton I 1777 I War of the American Revolution

Confronted by British General William Howe at **Trenton**, New Jersey, General George Washington slipped away at night and to the east met Colonel Charles Mawhood with reinforcements outside Princeton. American General Hugh Mercer was initially repulsed and killed, but Washington arrived to defeat the British, then withdrew to winter quarters in Morristown (3 January 1777).

Prinitza I 1263 I 3rd Latin-Byzantine Imperial War

After Byzantine restoration in **Constantinople** in 1261, Emperor Michael VIII sent a large army under his brother Constantine to invade Greece against William of Villehardouin, Prince of Achaea. In a semi-mythic action at Prinitza, near Olympia, a force claimed to be just 312 Frankish knights under Jean de Catavas scattered the Byzantine army. A year later Constantine was routed at **Makry Plagi**.

Proctor's Creek I 1864 I American Civil War (Eastern Theatre)

See **Drewry's Bluff**

Prokhorovka I 1943 I World War II (Eastern Front)

The decisive action of the massive offensive towards **Kursk** saw Panzer General Herman Hoth attack east of Oboyan around Prokhorovka with 700 tanks (including 100 of the new Tigers) to outflank Kursk from the southeast. Facing 850 Russian tanks under General Pavel Rotmistrov, the Germans lost 350 tanks and 10,000 men and fell back onto the defensive (12–13 July 1943).

Prome ▌ 1552 ▌ Burmese Dynastic Wars

King Bayinnaung of Burma was determined to crush Mon opposition in the south and, with the aid of Portuguese mercenaries, seized the southern capital **Pegu**. The following year he marched north to attack Prome, where other Mon leaders had taken refuge. This key city on the Irriwaddy was eventually starved into surrender. Bayinnaung then crowned his success by turning against the Shan at **Ava**.

Prome ▌ 1825 ▌ 1st British-Burmese War

While resuming his offensive on the Irriwaddy, British General Sir Archibald Campbell came under attack at Prome by a large Burmese army under the veteran Maha Nemyo. A very hard-fought battle saw Maha Nemyo defeated and killed and the Burmese General Kee Wyunji was repulsed at nearby Napadi, opening the way for the British advance through **Melloone** (1–5 December 1825).

Prome ▌ 1852 ▌ 2nd British-Burmese War

British General Henry Thomas Godwin returned to the offensive in Burma, advancing north along the Irriwaddy from **Rangoon** to the river city of Prome, supported by naval forces under Commodore George Robert Lambert. After a heavy bombardment of shell and cannister from the river, British forces landed and stormed the city, then continued on to **Pegu** (9 October 1852).

Prome ▌ 1942 ▌ World War II (Burma-India)

As the British retreated north from Rangoon, General David "Punch" Cowan was ordered to hold Prome, on the west bank of the Irriwaddy, while Chinese to the east tried to hold **Toungoo**. Severe fighting south and southeast of Prome at Schwedaung and Paungde saw heavy British losses in men and tanks and they were forced to withdraw upriver to **Yenangyaung** (20 March–1 April 1942).

Prosopitis ▌ 456–454 BC ▌ Greco-Persian Wars

In support of revolt in Egypt by Inaros of Libya, Athens defeated Persia at **Papremis** (459 BC) then advanced up the Nile and besieged the Citadel at Memphis. Four years later the Persian Megabyzus relieved Memphis and surrounded the Athenians on Prosopitis, an island in the Nile. After 18 months they surrendered—at the cost of perhaps 200 ships and 50,000 men—and Inaros was put to death.

Provence ▌ 109 BC ▌ Rome's Gallic Wars

After defeating Rome in central Europe at **Noreia**, the Cimbri and Teutone tribes migrated west across the Rhine and eventually arrived in Roman-occupied Provence, where the Senate sent an army under Marcus Junius Silanus. In battle at an unidentified site on the lower Rhone, the Consul was badly beaten. Two years later another Consular army was defeated further west across Gaul at **Aginnum**.

Providien ▌ 1782 ▌ War of the American Revolution

In the second of five indecisive naval actions off the east coast of India, British Admiral Edward Hughes was carrying reinforcements to Trincomalee in Ceylon and met French Admiral Pierre André Suffren in a violent rain squall off Providien. While Hughes suffered heavy damage, Suffren declined to resume battle next day. They met three months later off **Negapatam** (12 April 1782).

Pruth ▌ 1711 ▌ Russian Invasion of Moldavia

See **Stanilesti**

Pruth ▌ 1770 ▌ Catherine the Great's 1st Turkish War

Russian General Pyotr Rumyantsev defeated Turks and Tatars at **Kagul**, on the Pruth north of its junction with the Danube (21 July), then gathered further forces and attacked Grand Vizier

Khalil Pasha in powerful entrenchments along the east bank of the River. A series of attacks by Rumyantsev expelled the Turks with heavy losses and he advanced on **Bucharest** (September 1770).

Przasnysz **I** 1915 **I** World War I (Eastern Front)

Despite a check at the **Masurian Lakes**, Germans north of Warsaw seized the key fortress at Przasnysz, then faced counter-attack by Russian Northern commander Mikhail Alexeyev. His troops suffered terrible losses to enemy machine-gun fire before the Germans were driven out, losing over 5,000 prisoners. Przasnysz was retaken (14 July) in the advance on **Warsaw** (25–28 February 1915).

Przemysl (1st) **I** 1914 **I** World War I (Eastern Front)

Austria was driven from Poland at **Rawa Russka** and **Gorodok**, leaving only General Hermann Kusmanek at the fortress at Przemysl, west of Lemberg. Aided by a German advance on **Warsaw**, Austrian General Svetozar Boroevic counter-attacked against General Radko Dmitriev and relieved Przemysl. However, he was checked at the **San** and the siege resumed (24 September–9 October 1914).

Przemysl (2nd) **I** 1914–1915 **I** World War I (Eastern Front)

With Austria again driven out of Galicia, General Andrei Selivanov resumed the Russian siege of Przemysl, held by General Hermann Kusmanek. Following the failure of a winter relief offensive by Austrian General Eduard Böhm-Ermolli, Kusmanek destroyed his fortifications and ammunition and surrendered about 100,000 men and 1,000 guns (6 November 1914–22 March 1915).

Psara **I** 1824 **I** Greek War of Independence

Soon after Muslim forces desolated **Kasos** (19 June), Turkish Admiral Khosrew Pasha led a large fleet and 8,000 troops from the Dardanelles into the Aegean against Psara, just northwest of

Chios. A brutal assault left Psara utterly ravaged. About 4,000 residents escaped by sea, though 8,000 others were killed or enslaved before Khosrew withdrew to Mytilene with 100 captured ships (3–4 July 1824).

Psie Pole **I** 1109 **I** Polish-German Wars

When Emperor Henry V invaded Poland in support of former King Zbiginiew and laid siege to Glogow, Boleslaw III returned south from defeating the Pomeranians at **Naklo** to drive off the siege. He then attacked and routed the Emperor at Psie Pole, just outside Wroclaw (Breslau). The Imperial army fled, abandoning their dead to the dogs, and the battleground was named Dog's Field.

Pskov **I** 1502 **I** 1st Muscovite-Lithuanian War

See **Lake Smolino**

Pskov **I** 1581–1582 **I** Livonian War

At war with Moscow over Livonia, Stephen Bathory of Poland captured **Polotsk** and **Velikie Luki**, then attacked the powerful fortress of Pskov, defended by Prince Ivan Shuiski. After repeated assaults, Bathory left the siege to Jan Zamoysky and the city held out until the fall of **Narva** made Tsar Ivan IV sue for peace. Russia kept Pskov but abandoned Livonia (26 August 1581–4 February 1582).

Pskov **I** 1615 **I** Russo-Swedish Wars

With **Gdov** retaken, Gustavus Adolphus of Sweden renewed his offensive in Russia and attacked Pskov, defended by Dimitri Trubetskoi and Vasili Buturlin. Despite massive assaults (with Swedish Marshal Evert Horn killed) the city held out. Threatened by Poland's alliance with Sweden, Russia sued for peace, gaining Novgorod but losing her Baltic access (June–October 1615).

Pteria **I** 547 BC **I** Persian-Lydian War

In order to support his allies in Babylon and forestall a Persian invasion of Asia Minor, King Croesus of Lydia crossed the Halys River and captured Pteria in Cappadocia (modern central

Turkey). However, a huge Persian army under Cyrus II the Great routed the Lydians and drove them on a retreat westwards, falling back through further defeat at **Thymbria** on their capital at **Sardis**.

Ptolemais I 150 BC I Seleucid Dynastic War

Alexander Balas, pretended son of Antiochus IV, claimed the Seleucid throne and gained aid from Ptolemy VI of Egypt to enter Syria. He was initially repulsed by Demetrius I, who later advanced from Antioch and was defeated and killed near Ptolemais. Alexander took the throne, marrying Ptolemy's daughter Cleopatra Thea. After five years he was overthrown by Ptolemy at **Oenoparas**.

Pucará I 1882 I War of the Pacific

A year after defeat at **Chorrillos** and **Miraflores**, Peruvian General Andrés Avelino Cáceres regrouped in Huancayo, then advanced southeast on Pucara, where Colonel Francisco Seceda secured a strong position. A surprise attack by Chilean José Francisco Gana Castro was driven off after costly fighting and Cáceres secured the town. Chileans soon lost again at nearby **Tongos** (5 February 1882).

Puck I 1462 I Thirteen Years War

In a war to regain Baltic land lost to the Teutonic Knights, Casimir IV of Poland was initially defeated at **Chojnice** but gradually regained the initiative and took Marienburg (1457). The decisive action was near Puck, south of Tczew, where a largely mercenary Polish army secured bloody victory. The Order eventually yielded considerable territory yet retained East Prussia (17 September 1462).

Puebla I 1832 I Mexican Civil Wars

General Antonio de Santa Anna defended **Veracruz** then advanced on Puebla, held for President Anastasio Bustamente by Generals Antonio Azcárate and José Antonio Facio. Azcárate was defeated and killed when Facio withdrew precipitately and Santa Anna captured Puebla and a large number of prisoners and arms. In December Bustamente lost at nearby **Posadas** (29 September 1832).

Puebla I 1847 I American-Mexican War

With Mexico City lost after **Chapultepec** (12 September), Mexican General Antonio de Santa Anna sent General Joaquin Rea to retake Puebla to the southeast, held by Colonel Thomas Childs. After a bloody siege, later reinforced by Santa Anna himself, Puebla was finally relieved by General Joseph Lane from Veracruz, ending the last major action of the war (14 September–12 October 1847).

Puebla I 1862 I Mexican-French War

French General Charles Latrille Comte de Lorencez advanced into central Mexico and days after driving General Ignacio Zaragoza out of **Acultzingo**, met him again near Fort Guadalupe outside Puebla. In a brilliant victory—still celebrated as Cinco de Mayo—Zaragoza heavily repulsed the French. However, Lorencez soon won again at **Orizaba** and France sent massive reinforcements (5 May 1862).

Puebla I 1863 I Mexican-French War

Arriving in Mexico with large-scale reinforcements, new French commander General Elie Fréderic Forey advanced through **Orizaba** against Puebla, held by General Jesus González Ortega. After the very costly loss of nearby San Xavier fortress (29 March) and the repulse of a relief army at **San Lorenzo**, Puebla surrendered and the French soon entered Mexico City (16 March–18 May 1863).

Puebla I 1867 I Mexican-French War

With the French puppet-Emperor Maximilian besieged at **Querétaro**, Liberal Mexican General Porfirio Diaz laid siege to Puebla, held by about 2,500 Conservatives under General Manuel Noriega. Following a bloody assault (2 April) Noriega surrendered. While his men were freed, Noriega and all 74 officers were executed. Diaz then advanced west on **Mexico City** (9 March–4 April 1867).

Pueblo de Taos I 1847 I American-Mexican War

Colonel Sterling Price advanced up the Rio Grande against insurgents in New Mexico who had murdered Governor Charles Bent. He won at **La Cañada** and **Embudo** before cornering the rebels at Pueblo de Taos. The rising was crushed after two days of artillery bombardment with 150 Mexicans killed. Price was promoted to General and became Governor of Chihuahua (3–4 February 1847).

Puente de la Bateria I 1865 I War of the Triple Alliance
See **Corrientes (2nd)**

Puente de la Reina I 1873 I 2nd Carlist War
See **Mañeru**

Puente de Márquez I 1829 I Argentine Civil Wars

When General Juan Galo Lavalle seized power in late 1828 with victory at **Navarro**, he faced Federalist forces under Estanislao López of Santa Fe and General Juan Manuel Rosas, losing part of his army at **Vizcacheras**. Outside Buenos Aires at Puente de Márquez, Lavalle was decisively beaten. Despite Unitarist victory at **La Tablada** in June, he made peace and went into exile (26 April 1829).

Puente Larga I 1812 I Napoleonic Wars (Peninsular Campaign)

As he withdrew from the failed siege of **Burgos**, Arthur Wellesley Lord Wellington ordered evacuation of Madrid and General Sir Rowland Hill ordered Colonel John Skerrett east to delay French Marshals Nicolas Soult and Jean-Baptiste Jourdan. Skerrett checked the French at Puente Larga on the Jarama before being driven back and Madrid was abandoned next day (30 October 1812).

Puerto Cabello I 1812 I Venezuelan War of Independence

A year after Francisco Miranda declared Venezuelan independence, a disastrous earthquake created devastation and Spanish commander Juan Domingo Monteverde counter-attacked. When Miranda capitulated, Simón Bolívar was forced to surrender the powerful fortress at Puerto Cabello. Spanish authority was re-established until defeat a year later at **Taguanes** (6 July 1812).

Puerto Cabello I 1962 I Venezuelan Porteñazo Uprising

After a failed uprising at Carúpano (4 May) democratically elected President Rómulo Betancourt of Venezuela faced a larger scale revolt by leftist officers at the naval base of Puerto Cabello, led by Captain Pedro Medina Silva. Before the rising was crushed, severe fighting cost the rebels 300 killed and 700 wounded. Loyalist forces lost 136 killed and 300 wounded (2–5 June 1962).

Puerto del Gallinero I 1832 I Mexican Civil Wars
See **Gallinero**

Puerto Rico I 1898 I Spanish-American War
See **Guánica**

Puesto del Márquez I 1815 I Argentine War of Independence

Colonel Francisco Fernandéz de la Cruz and the Patriot Army of the North on a fresh offensive in northern Argentina, surprised and defeated Royalist troops under Joaquín de la Pezuela at Puesto del Márquez, east of Lago de Pozuelos in Jujuy. Victory opened the way for commander José Rondeau's advance north into modern Bolivia and his defeat in October at **Venta y Media** (17 April 1815).

Pukekohe East I 1863 I 2nd New Zealand War

On campaign against settlements south of Auckland after action at **Camerontown**, about 200 Ngati Maniapoto attacked the church stockade at Pukekohe East, held by just 17 troops and nine volunteers. After a courageous daylong defence without loss, the Maoris were driven off by troops from Drury with about 60 killed. Another action followed in October at nearby **Mauku** (14 September 1863).

Pukenui I 1845 I 1st New Zealand War
See **Te Ahuahu, Bay of Islands**

Puketakauere I 1860 I 2nd New Zealand War
Despite defeat at **Waitara**, north of New Plymouth (17 March) Ngatiawa Chief Wiremu Kingi built a powerful fortified pa at nearby Puketakauere, where he was rashly attacked by Major Thomas Nelson and Captain Frederick Seymour-Beauchamp of *Pelorus*. Slaughtered in ambush, the British retreated with 30 killed and 34 wounded. They were soon avenged at **Mahoetai** (27 June 1860).

Puketutu I 1845 I 1st New Zealand War
Colonel William Hulme resolved to avenge the attack on **Kororareka** in New Zealand's far north, leading 400 troops to Hone Heke's pa (fortified village) at Puketutu, near Lake Omapere. While the Maoris lost about 50 men in a fierce attack, mainly in an unwise sortie led by Kawiti, the Europeans suffered 52 casualties and withdrew to Kerikeri. They soon counter-attacked at **Ohaewai** (8 May 1845).

Pula I 1379 I War of Chioggia
In the resumed war between Genoa and Venice, Genoese Admiral Luciano Doria approached the city of **Chioggia**, near Venice, and Venetian Admiral Vittore Pisani reluctantly led his outnumbered fleet from Pula, across the Adriatic. Doria was killed before victory near Pula was complete, though Pisani was routed with heavy losses and Venice was ousted from Pula (7 May 1379).

Pulau Aur I 1804 I Napoleonic Wars (3rd Coalition)
French Admiral Charles Durand de Linois took his squadron to Malacca to attack British merchantmen and intercepted a 30-strong unescorted China convoy off Pulau Aur. But Commodore Nathaniel Dance had three vessels disguised as warships and opened fire. After a half-hearted attack, Linois withdrew with Dance in pursuit. Dance received a knighthood and a fortune (14 February 1804).

Pul-i-Sanghin I 1511 I Mughal-Uzbek Wars
Following Persian defeat of the Uzbeks at **Merv**, the Mughal Babur of Kabul crossed from India and, joined by Persians, marched on Gissar in Uzbekistan. After a fierce yet indecisive battle at Pul-i-Sanghin, Timur Sultan, son of Shaybani, withdrew and Babur went on to capture Bokhara and Samarkand itself. Within a year, he was beaten by the Uzbeks at **Kul-i-Malik** and **Ghujduwan**.

Pulkkila I 1808 I Napoleonic Wars (Russo-Swedish War)
After halting the Russian invasion of Finland in the west at the **Siikajoki** (18 April) some Swedish forces pursued the invaders down the coast towards **Revolax** while Swedish General Johan August Sandels marched southeast towards Kuopio. South of Oulu at Pulkkila he surrounded and defeated Russian General Sergei Timofevich Obuhoff, who was forced to surrender (2 May 1808).

Pullalur I 610 I Indian Dynastic Wars
Pulakesin II of Chalukya secured his northern border, then moved south against his great rival Mahendravarman of Pallava. In battle at Pullalur, just southwest of his capital Kanchi, Mahendra and General Paranjothi were decisively defeated and Pulakesin besieged Kanchi itself. Mahendra's son Narashimavarman was avenged in 642, when he killed Pulakesin at **Vatapi** (disputed date c 610).

Pultawa I 1658 I Russo-Polish Wars
See **Poltava**

Pultawa I 1709 I 2nd "Great" Northern War
See **Poltava**

Pultusk I 1703 I 2nd "Great" Northern War

Charles XII of Sweden defeated a Saxon-Polish army in southern Poland at **Kliszow** (19 July 1702), then wintered over before marching north to seek out Augustus II, Elector of Saxony and King of Poland. At Pultusk, north of Warsaw, a large Saxon army under Field Marshal Adam von Steinau fled, suffering about 600 casualties and 1,000 prisoners. Charles then besieged **Thorn** (21 April 1703).

Pultusk I 1806 I Napoleonic Wars (4th Coalition)

Having destroyed the Prussians at **Jena** and **Auerstadt** in October, Napoleon Bonaparte invaded Poland and captured Warsaw. Marching north to Pultusk Marshal Jean Lannes attacked a Russian Corps under General Levin Bennigsen, who drove off the outnumbered French in a desperate, indecisive action. He withdrew during the night to avoid a battle of attrition (26 December 1806).

Pungu-a-Ndongo I 1671 I Portuguese Colonial Wars in West Africa

Six years after crushing the Kingdom of Kongo at **Ambuila**, Portuguese forces attacked the rebellious Kingdom of Ndongo along the River Kwanza. Marching inland southeast from Luanda, the Portuguese attacked the fortified capital at Pungu-a-Ndongo (modern Pungo Andongo), where Ngola Ari II of Ndongo was defeated and killed. The once-powerful Kingdom was annexed to Portuguese Angola.

Punitz I 1704 I 2nd "Great" Northern War

While Charles XII of Sweden was occupied in southern Poland, the deposed king—Augustus II—gathered a Russian-Saxon-Polish force and recaptured Warsaw. Two months later he faced Charles at Punitz (modern Poniec), southeast of Leszno. Augustus was forced to retreat and Charles restored his candidate—Stanislaus Leszczynski—to the Polish throne (October 1704).

Punniar I 1843 I British-Gwalior War

See **Panniar**

Punta Brava I 1896 I 2nd Cuban War of Independence

Boldly advancing towards Havana, the insurgent leader Antonio Maceo was met to the southwest by a Spanish column under Major Francisco Cirujeda marching out of Punta Brava. In a terrible blow for the cause, Maceo was defeated and killed, along with Francisco Gómez, son of rebel commander Máximo Gómez, who continued the war until American intervention (7 December 1896).

Punta Stilo I 1940 I World War II (War at Sea)

See **Calabria**

Purandar I 1665 I Mughal-Maratha Wars

Emperor Aurangzeb responded to a Maratha raid on **Surat** in early 1664, sending Jai Singh and Dilir Khan, who besieged the rebel Shivaji in the hill fortress of Purandar, south of Poona. After General Murar Baji Prabhu was killed in a brave but costly sortie (2 June), Shivaji surrendered and signed a treaty yielding up 23 fortresses. Most of them were later recaptured (31 March–12 June 1665).

Puray I 1897 I Philippines War of Independence

After defeat south of Manila at **Naic**, Revolutionary leaders Emilio Aguinaldo and Licerio Geronimo fled northeast to Puray, in the mountains near Montalban, where they brilliantly defeated a Spanish attack under Colonel Dujiols. Governor Fernando Primo de Rivera negotiated a peace and Aguinaldo went into exile in Hong Kong until America won in May 1898 at **Manila Bay** (14 June 1897).

Puruarán I 1814 I Mexican Wars of Independence

Soon after the terrible insurgent loss at **Valladolid**, rebel leader Mariano Matamaros, who won so decisively at **Palmar** (October 1813) was besieged at Puruarán, south of Tacambaro,

Michoacán, by a large Royalist force led by Brigadier Ciriaco de Llano and Agustin de Iturbide. Matamaros was defeated and captured, and his execution a month later effectively ended the rising (5 January 1814).

Pusan (1st) | 1592 | Japanese Invasion of Korea

At the start of Toyotomi Hideyoshi's invasion of Korea, an advance Japanese force landed at Pusan, where Konishi Yukinaga attacked the naval fortress in the harbour, while So Yoshitomo attacked the town garrison, led by Chong Bal. Pusan was taken by storm with terrible Korean losses, including Chong Bal killed, and the Japanese advanced inland against **Tongnae** (23 May 1592).

Pusan (2nd) | 1592 | Japanese Invasion of Korea

Korean naval hero Yi Sun-shin won at **Hansan** and **Angolpo**, then boldly determined to attack more than 500 Japanese ships at Pusan Harbour under Wakizaka Yasuharu, Kuki Yoshitaka, Kato Yoshiaki and Todo Takatora. With support from Yi Ok-ki and Won Kyun, Yi's massively outnumbered force sank about 100 Japanese ships before withdrawing, reportedly without loss (6 October 1592).

Pusan Perimeter (1st) | 1950 | Korean War

As North Korean forces invaded, Americans and South Koreans withdrew southeast to the Pusan Perimeter, where General Walton Walker's "stand or die" order saw the heaviest American losses of the war. After desperate defensive actions—including **Taejon**, **Yongchon** and the **Naktong Bulge**—the Allies held the line, then regrouped to break out for **Seoul** (5 August–16 September 1950).

Pusan Perimeter (2nd) | 1950 | Korean War

Despite heavy casualties defending the Pusan Perimeter in southeast Korea, Americans and South Koreans under General Walton Walker launched a large counter-offensive to coincide with the landing in the north at **Inchon**. Very heavy fighting saw the North Koreans driven back, with massive losses in killed and captured, and the Allies broke out north towards **Seoul** (16–22 September 1950).

Putaendo | 1817 | Chilean War of Independence

As General José de San Martin crossed the Andes into Chile, his vanguard under Major Mariano Pascual Necochea met a strong Spanish force led by Colonel Miguel Atero on the Rio Aconcagua near Putaendo, northeast of Valparaiso. A bold action saw Necochea rout the Royalists, securing nearby San Felipe and helping ensure victory further south at **Chacabuco** (7 February 1817).

Put-in Bay | 1813 | War of 1812
See **Lake Erie**

Pydna | 168 BC | 3rd Macedonian War

Determined to avenge defeat at **Callicinus** (171 BC), Roman General Lucius Aemilius Paullus led a fresh invasion of Greece, where he was attacked on the Gulf of Salonika at Pydna by ambitious young King Perseus of Macedon. The Macedonian army was utterly destroyed, reputedly losing 20,000 killed and 8,000 captured. Perseus was dethroned, ending the Macedonian Empire (23 June 168 BC).

Pydna | 149 BC | 4th Macedonian War

Attempting to revive the throne of Macedon, Andriscus, claiming to be Philip son of Perseus, defeated and killed the Roman Praetor Juventius Thalna. The pretender then faced a large force under Quintus Caecilus Metellus and was crushed near Pydna, on the Gulf of Salonika. Andriscus was later executed, while Metellus was styled Macedonicus and Macedonia became a Roman Province.

Pyle's Defeat | 1781 | War of the American Revolution
See **Haw River**

Pyliavsti I 1648 I Cossack-Polish Wars
See **Pilawce**

**Pylos-Sphacteria I 425 BC I Great
Peloponnesian War**

A year after victory at **Olpae**, the Athenian Demosthenes was sent to fortify the headland of Pylos, in Navarino Bay, as a base to raid Spartan territory. When Spartans occupied nearby Sphacteria, the Athenian Cleon arrived with reinforcements and a fierce action saw the island captured. Athens held this outpost until wider pressure in the Aegean led to its evacuation in 409 BC (May–August 425 BC).

**Pyokjekwan I 1593 I Japanese Invasion
of Korea**

Ming Chinese General Li Rusong crossed the Yalu into Korea and drove the Japanese out of **Pyongyang**, then advanced towards Seoul, gathering heavy Korean reinforcements. In a massive action north of the city at Pyokjekwan, Kobayakawa Takakage and Kato Kiyomasa halted the Chinese-Korean army. However, a Japanese counter-offensive was soon defeated at **Haengju** (25 February 1593).

**Pyokjeyek I 1593 I Japanese Invasion
of Korea**

See **Pyokjekwan**

Pyongyang I 668 I Sino-Korean Wars

The eastern Kingdom of Silla conquered Paekche in southwest Korea at **Sabi** (660), then sent General Kim Yinmun against the northern Kingdom of Koguryo, aided by a large Tang Chinese army under 74-year-old General Li Ji. The invaders stormed and captured Pyongyang, ending the 700-year-old Kingdom of Koguryo. It was placed under Tang Governors, causing hostility between China and Silla.

**Pyongyang (1st) I 1592 I Japanese
Invasion of Korea**

Japanese General Kato Kiyomasa marched north along the Korean Peninsula through Seoul after victory at **Chongju** (7 June) and fought his way across the **Imjin** to advance on Pyongyang,

where he was halted outside the city at the Tadong. When a Korean assault across the river was repulsed by Kuroda Nagamasa, the Japanese counter-attacked and Pyongyang soon fell by storm (20 July 1592).

**Pyongyang (2nd) I 1592 I Japanese
Invasion of Korea**

With the fall of **Pyongyang** (20 July), Korean King Songju appealed for help to Ming China, which sent just 5,000 men under General Zu Zhengxun. The inadequate Chinese force was ambushed and routed in a brutal night action by Japanese commander Konishi Yukinaga. Low supplies and naval defeat in the south at **Hansan** and **Angolpo** then forced Konishi to accept a truce (3 October 1592).

**Pyongyang I 1593 I Japanese Invasion
of Korea**

Reinforced after a truce, Chinese General Li Rusong led 40,000 veteran Ming troops on a mid-winter offensive against the Japanese at Pyongyang. Facing a massive assault on the city, the courageous Japanese commander Konishi Yukinaga was forced to withdraw across the frozen Tadong. He then retreated towards Seoul, where the Chinese were finally halted at **Pyokjekwan** (10 February 1593).

**Pyongyang I 1627 I Manchu Conquest
of Korea**

When the great Manchu leader Nurhachi died after his repulse in Ming China at **Ningyuan** (February 1626), his son and successor Abahai (Hong Taiji) sent his brother Amin east against Korea and a lightning invasion seized Pyongyang to secure northern Korea. A second Manchu invasion ten years later completed the conquest of Korea, which became a long-time vassal of Manchu China.

Pyongyang I 1894 I Sino-Japanese War

With war declared against China after victory in Korea at **Songhwan** (29 July), Japanese commander Michitsura Nozu advanced north on Pyongyang (then Heijo), held by 12,000 Chinese under Generals Wei Rugui and Ma Yugun.

Heavy fighting across the Tadong cost 650 Japanese casualties before the Chinese fell back to the **Yalu** with about 2,000 killed and 600 captured (15 September 1894).

Pyongyang ∎ 1950 ∎ Korean War

With the fall of **Seoul**, Allied forces entered North Korea and, overcoming resistance at Kumchon and Sariwon, raced for Pyongyang. Americans entered the capital almost simultaneously with South Koreans, who took the city centre by storm next day. A Chinese offensive later saw Pyongyang evacuated (3 December) and much of it was destroyed by fire (19–20 October 1950).

Pyramids ∎ 1798 ∎ French Revolutionary Wars (Middle East)

Three weeks after invading Egypt and seizing **Alexandria**, Napoleon Bonaparte advanced to near the Pyramids, where he faced a massive Mamluk army under General Murad Bey. Using defensive squares against the swarming Mamluk cavalry, Bonaparte achieved a decisive victory and many fleeing Mamluk infantry drowned in the Nile. Nearby Cairo fell the next day (21 July 1798).

Pyrenees ∎ 1813 ∎ Napoleonic Wars (Peninsular Campaign)

See **Roncesvalles**

Q

Qadesh ▌ 1275 BC ▌ Egyptian-Hittite Wars
See **Kadesh**

Qadirganj ▌ 1751 ▌ Pathan War
Wazir Safdar Jang of Delhi lost to invading Pathans in northern India at **Farrukhabad** and **Kasganj** before Jayappa Sindhia and Mulhar Rao Holkar took 20,000 Maratha troops to his aid. At Qadirganj, south of Budaun, they routed the Bangash army of Shadil Khan. Ahmad Khan Bangesh then had to lift his siege of Allahabad and the Pathans soon lost again at Farrukhabad (20 March 1751).

Qadisiyya ▌ 636 ▌ Muslim Conquest of Iraq
With Syria conquered at **Damascus**, Caliph Omar renewed his invasion of the Sassanian Persian Empire, stalled after victory at **Buwayb** (April 635). On the Euphrates canal at Qadisiyya, near Hira, Sa'ad ibn Abi Waqqas decisively beat a large Persian force under Chancellor Rustam, who was killed. **Madain** quickly fell and the Persians tried to make a stand at **Jalula** (disputed date 636 or 637).

Qala-i-Jangi ▌ 2001 ▌ Afghanistan War
When mainly foreign Taliban prisoners from **Kunduz** were taken to Qala-i-Jangi fortress, near Mazar-i-Sharif, they overpowered their Northern Alliance guards and stormed the armoury. Tanks, air-strikes and Allied special forces were used to retake the prison, where perhaps 400 Taliban fought to the death. About 40 Northern Alliance troops and an American observer also died (24–27 November 2001).

Qara Chaman ▌ 1762 ▌ Persian Wars of Succession
Determined to finally secure control in Azerbaijan, Persian Regent Karim Khan Zand marched towards Tabriz and was met to the southeast at Qara Chaman (modern Siah Chaman) by Fath Ali Afshar, whose cavalry initially repulsed the Zand army. Karim Khan's General Shayk Ali Khan then rallied for a great victory and the Regent moved to besiege Fath Ali at **Urmiya** (June 1762).

Qarah Bagh ▌ 1842 ▌ 1st British-Afghan War
See **Ghoaine**

Qarqar ▌ 854 BC ▌ Early Assyrian Wars
King Shalmaneser III of Assyria invaded southern Syria, where he faced his largest enemy army—an alliance under King Benhadad of Damascus, King Ahab of Israel and Irkhuleni, King of Hamath. At Qarqar, in the Orontes Valley, Shalmaneser defeated this confederacy, though was unable to extend his power. Twelve years later King Ahab's son Joram accepted Assyria as overlord.

Qarqar ▌ 720 BC ▌ Assyrian Wars
Shortly after the accession of King Sargon of Assyria, a coalition of vassal provinces in Palestine rose against him, led by Iaubi'di, King of Hamath. Marching south into the Orontes Valley,

Sargon inflicted a massive defeat on the rebels at Qarqar, site of a similar battle 130 years earlier. As a result the vassal Princedom of Hamath became a fully dependent Assyrian province.

Qatia ∎ 1916 ∎ World War I (Middle East)
See **Katia**

Qianshuiyuan ∎ 618 ∎ Rise of the Tang Dynasty
Soon after proclaiming the Tang Dynasty at Chang'an, Gaozu sent his son Li Shimin and General Liu Wenjing against the rival Xue family at Qianshuiyuan, where the Tang army was routed in a confused fiasco by Xue Jue. Li Shimin later advanced again and lured Xue Ren-'gao to a decisive defeat. Qianshuiyuan fell next day, securing Tang control of northwest China (6 August & 29 November 618).

Qingdao ∎ 1914 ∎ World War I (Far East)
Attacking Germany in China, Admiral Hika-nojo Kamimura took about 23,000 men against Qingdao (Tsingtao) on the Shandong Peninsula. Aided by a small British force, the Japanese bombarded and besieged the port, held by about 4,500 Germans under Governor Alfred Meyer-Waldeck. The city fell after heavy fighting and Japanese forces held Qingdao until 1922 (27 August–7 November 1914).

Qingpu ∎ 1860 ∎ Taiping Rebellion
Campaigning west of Shanghai to block the Taiping army of Li Xiucheng, foreign troops under American Colonel Fredrick T. Ward captured **Songjiang** but were driven off further north at Qingpu (Tsingpu) by General Zhou Wenjia. In a second attack, supported by Imperial General Li Hengsong, Ward was defeated by Li Xiucheng himself and fell back on **Shanghai** (2 & 8 August 1860).

Qinis ∎ 1885 ∎ British-Sudan Wars
See **Ginniss**

Qiqihar ∎ 1900 ∎ Russo-Chinese War
Russian General Deian Subotich crossed the Amur into Manchuria, where he seized **Aigun**

(5 August) then marched south through Mergen (Nenjiang) towards Qiqihar (Tsitsihar) on the Chinese Eastern railway. Chinese commander Shou Shan refused a truce and Qiqihar fell by storm after heavy fighting. With other Russians advancing east from **Xing-an**, General Shou killed himself (28 August 1900).

Qomsheh ∎ 1753 ∎ Persian Wars of Succession
In the struggle for control of Persia, Azad Khan Afghan of Azerbaijan captured Isfahan then sent his ally Fath Ali Afshar south to Qomsheh, where he was repulsed by the Regent Karim Khan Zand. However, after Azad arrived with reinforcements (and Karim's brother Es-kander Khan was killed attempting to assassinate him), Karim fought a courageous rearguard action and withdrew.

Quaker Hill ∎ 1778 ∎ War of the American Revolution
See **Rhode Island**

Quaker Road ∎ 1865 ∎ American Civil War (Eastern Theatre)
See **Lewis's Farm**

Quang Ngai ∎ 1965 ∎ Vietnam War
See **Ba Gia**

Quang Ngai ∎ 1966 ∎ Vietnam War
See **Chau Nhai**

Quang Tri (1st) ∎ 1972 ∎ Vietnam War
At the start of the **Eastertide Offensive**, North Vietnamese regulars attacked across the demilitarised zone and advanced towards Hue, attacking the key city of Quang Tri, held by South Vietnamese troops and marines. With heavy artillery support, the invaders besieged and took Quang Tri by storm. Further south their offensive struck against **Kontum** (26 April–1 May 1972).

Quang Tri (2nd) ∎ 1972 ∎ Vietnam War
After halting the North Vietnamese **Easter-tide Offensive** in the central highlands at

Kontum and at An Loc, South Vietnamese forces began a bloody counter-offensive in the north, aided by American bomber strikes and naval guns. Prolonged fighting saw Quang Tri City retaken to effectively end the offensive and four months later a ceasefire ended the war (28 June–15 September 1972).

Quanzhou I 1852 I Taiping Rebellion

As Taiping forces withdrew northeast from Guilin past Quanzhou (Ch'uan-chou), a sniper on the city wall fatally wounded the great leader Feng Yunshan and the rebels turned on the city, held by magistrate Cao Xiepei. After breaching the walls with explosives, the vengeful Taiping massacred the residents before continuing north across Suo'yi Ford (24 May–3 June 1852).

Quatre Bras I 1815 I Napoleonic Wars (The Hundred Days)

In a prelude to Waterloo, south of Brussels, Napoleon Bonaparte took his centre and right wing against General Gebhard von Blucher's Prussians at Ligny while Marshal Michel Ney led the left against the British-Dutch Allies at Quatre Bras. After initial success, Ney was driven back by Arthur Wellesley Duke of Wellington, though both sides had approximately equal losses (16 June 1815).

Quebec I 1629 I Anglo-French Wars in North America

Scottish adventurer David Kirke campaigned against France on the St Lawrence, where he captured Tadoussac, southeast of Quebec, then sent his brothers Thomas and Louis against the starving settlement at Quebec. Governor Samuel de Champlain evacuated Quebec after a brief show of force. When war in Europe ended, King Charles I of England returned the city to France (19 July 1629).

Quebec I 1690 I King William's War

Having taken Port Royal, New England commander Sir William Phips led 35 ships against French Quebec where Governor Louis de Buade Comte de Frontenac declined to surrender. A landing under Major John Walley was repulsed, though French leader Jacques le Moyne de Saint-Hélène was fatally wounded. Phips was driven off with 90 casualties and several ships lost (16–20 October 1690).

Quebec I 1711 I Queen Anne's War

Admiral Sir Hovenden Walker took a large fleet and almost 6,000 troops into the St Lawrence in his campaign against French Quebec. After a storm sank eight of his transports, Walker turned back and ordered Colonial militia under Colonel Francis Nicholson to withdraw from their advance on Montreal. Walker was later court-martialled and dismissed (18 August–16 September 1711).

Quebec I 1759 I Seven Years War (North America)

In the decisive action of the conquest of Canada, British General James Wolfe scaled the Heights of Abraham above the St Lawrence River and defeated a French force under Marquis Louis de Montcalm on the Plains above. Although both commanders were mortally wounded in the fighting, the victory opened the way to nearby Quebec, which surrendered five days later (13 September 1759).

Quebec I 1760 I Seven Years War (North America)

French General Francois de Lévis resolved to recover Quebec, lost six months earlier, and advanced from Montreal with over 8,000 men. He defeated British commander General James Murray outside Quebec at Saint-Foy and the heavily outnumbered British withdrew into the city under siege. They were eventually relieved by a naval squadron and Lévis retreated to Montreal (27 April 1760).

Quebec I 1775–1776 I War of the American Revolution

Six weeks after capturing Montreal, American forces invading Canada under General Richard Montgomery and Colonel Benedict Arnold attacked Quebec, held by General Guy Carleton. With Montgomery killed and Arnold wounded, Captain Daniel Morgan was defeated and captured in a costly assault next day and the Americans were driven off (31 December 1775–1 January 1776).

Quebracho Herrado | 1840 | Argentine Civil Wars

Defeated at **Sauce Grande** in Entre Rios, Unitarist General Juan Galo Lavalle was pursued west by General Manuel Oribe, the new commander for Dictator Manuel de Rosas. At Quebracho Herrado, between Santa Fe and Córdoba, Lavalle suffered a crushing defeat, followed by a massacre, which virtually destroyed his army. He met final defeat a year later at **Famaillá** (28 November 1840).

Queenston | 1812 | War of 1812

American General Stephen van Rensselaer led a rash offensive across the Niagara River between Lake Erie and Lake Ontario, attacking from Lewiston against General Isaac Brock at Queenston. Although Brock was killed during initial American success, a counter-attack by General Roger Sheaffe forced the Americans to surrender. Rensselaer resigned his command (13 October 1812).

Queetz | 1807 | Napoleonic Wars (4th Coalition)

During a fresh spring offensive in eastern Prussia following the winter carnage at **Eylau** (8 February), Russian Generals Levin Bennigsen and Anton Lestocq campaigned east of the Passarge River, repulsing Marshal Jean Baptiste Bernadotte with heavy losses at Mehlsack and Lomitten. Bernadotte then halted the Russians at Queetz and Russia lost again a week later at **Friedland** (5 June 1807).

Querétaro | 1867 | Mexican-French War

Re-conquering Mexico after Napoleon III withdrew his forces, Mexican General Mariano Escobeda advanced south through **San Jacinto** to besiege Querétaro, held by Emperor Maximilian and 20,000 men under Miguel Miramón and Tomás Mejía. After the city fell by storm, the Emperor, Miramón and Mejía were executed. **Mexico City** surrendered a day later (6 March–14 May 1867).

Queseras del Medio | 1819 | Venezuelan War of Independence

Patriot leader Simón Bolívar recovered after **La Puerta** and met General Pablo Morillo on the Apure in southwest Venezuela, where a small force under General José Antonio Páez lured the Spanish cavalry into pursuit. At Queseras del Medio, northeast of San Fernando, the Royalist horse were defeated with 400 casualties. But within days Bolívar was routed at **Rincón de los Toros** (2 April 1819).

Questa de los Angeles | 1880 | War of the Pacific

See **Los Angeles, Peru**

Quetzaltenango | 1524 | Spanish Conquest of Guatemala

Conquistador Pedro de Alvarado set out from Mexico City (**Tenochtitlan**) and marched into Guatemala, where he recruited Cakchiquel Mayas against their traditional rivals, the Quiché. On the plain near Totonicapan, at a site later named Quetzaltenango, King Tecún Umán of Quiché was defeated and killed, reputedly by Alvarado himself. The Spaniards then marched on **Ututlán** (28 February 1524).

Quiberon | 1795 | French Revolutionary Wars (1st Coalition)

In support of a local insurrection in Brittany, over 3,000 French émigrés were landed from British warships on the Quiberon Peninsula. Republican General Louis Lazare Hoche repulsed the invasion, capturing massive armaments and a large number of Royalists who failed to reach the departing British ships. About 700 of the prisoners were executed (27 June–20 July 1795).

Quiberon Bay | 56 BC | Rome's Later Gallic Wars

See **Morbihan Gulf**

Quiberon Bay I 1759 I Seven Years War (Europe)

With the French Toulon squadron dispersed at **Lagos Bay** (19 August), Admiral Sir Edward Hawke blockaded the Brest fleet in order to frustrate the planned invasion of Britain. French commander Hubert Comte de Conflans eluded the blockade, but Hawke destroyed the French fleet off Quiberon, with seven ships lost and over 2,000 men killed. This ended the planned invasion (20 November 1759).

Quilmes I 1826 I Argentine-Brazilian War

While Brazilian Admiral Rodrigo Pinto Guedes attempted to blockade Buenos Aires, Argentine commander William Brown made repeated attacks, culminating in a violent action just to the east off Quilmes. Brown was heavily outgunned and had to abandon his damaged flagship. However, the Brazilians failed to destroy the Argentine fleet and in early 1827 were routed at **Juncal** (29 July 1826).

Quilmes I 1827 I Argentine-Brazilian War

Despite defeat at **Quilmes** and **Juncal**, Brazil sent another squadron comprising ten vessels into the Rio de la Plata. Off Quilmes, just east of Buenos Aires, Admiral William Brown, now commanding 24 ships, routed the Brazilians, who fled after one vessel blew up with all hands. Brown lost just 17 killed and wounded, but a month later he was defeated **Monte Santiago** (24 February 1827).

Quilmo I 1819 I Chilean War of Independence

On campaign northeast of Concepción, Royalist irregulars led by Vicente Elizondo (second in command to Vicente Benavides) met Patriot forces under Pedro Nolasco Victoriano, Governor of Chillan, just southeast of Chillan at the nearby Rio Quilmo. Elizondo was defeated in a sharp and bloody encounter and Victoriano returned safely to Chillan (19 September 1819).

Quilo I 1814 I Chilean War of Independence

See **Alto de Quilo**

Quimperlé I 1342 I Hundred Years War

English commander Sir Walter Manny intervened in Brittany in support of Jean de Montfort, relieving **Hennebont** then marching west against Louis of Spain, who had landed to aid rival claimant Charles of Blois. Manny captured the poorly guarded enemy fleet, then routed the much larger Spanish army near Quimperlé, northwest of Lorient. Louis escaped with just a small retinue (June 1342).

Quinby Bridge I 1781 I War of the American Revolution

Threatened northeast of Charleston, South Carolina, British Colonel John Coates withdrew behind the partially demolished Quinby Bridge on the Cooper. Boldly facing a poorly managed attack by Generals Thomas Sumter and Francis Marion and Colonel Henry Lee, Coates inflicted costly American casualties. When reinforcements approached, Sumter withdrew (17 July 1781).

Quinqua I 1899 I Philippine-American War

As the Americans prepared to advance from **Malolos**, a column under Major James F. Bell was met near Quinqua (modern Plaridel) by a Philippine force under Pablo Tecson and Gregoria del Pilar. The Americans suffered costly losses (including Colonel John Stotesenburg killed) before the insurgents finally withdrew. Commander Arthur MacArthur then advanced to **Bagbag** (23 April 1899).

Quintanilla de Valle I 1811 I Napoleonic Wars (Peninsular Campaign)

See **Benavides**

Qurna I 1914 I World War I (Mesopotamia)

Anglo-Indian troops under General Sir Arthur Barrett captured **Basra**, near the mouth of the

Euphrates, then advanced upstream to Qurna, where Turkish forces attempted to defend the strategic confluence with the Tigris. Attacking by land and from both rivers, the British were initially repulsed, but reinforcements arrived and the Turkish garrison of over 1,000 surrendered (4–9 December 1914).

Qurna I 1915 I World War I (Mesopotamia)
See **Amara**

Quy Nhon I 1773 I Vietnamese Civil War
Leading a rebellion against the dominant Nguyen in the south of Vietnam, the brothers Nguyen Hue, Nguyen Nhac and Nguyen Lu from Tay Son met the Nguyen army at Quy Nhon. A decisive victory for the Tay Son forces secured much of the country. Nguyen Hue declared himself Emperor Quang Trung in 1788 and defeated a Chinese army the following year at **Thang Long**.

R

Raab I 1044 I German-Magyar War

After King Peter of Hungary was overthrown by Magyar nobles, the usurper "King" Samuel Aba continually raided into Bavaria until German Emperor Henry III took a small army to the River Raab in Hungary, where he defeated and scattered the Magyar host. Peter was restored as a German vassal and executed Aba, though he lost the throne again within two years.

Raab I 1664 I Later Turkish-Habsburg Wars
See **St Gotthard**

Raab I 1809 I Napoleonic Wars (5th Coalition)

Concentrating his forces on the Danube after defeat at **Aspern-Essling** (22 May), Napoleon Bonaparte recalled Prince Eugène de Beauharnais from Italy, who pursued Archduke John of Austria across the Alps to Raab, near Graz. John was beaten and driven off towards Pressburg. When besieged Raab fell ten days later, Eugène joined Bonaparte for the decisive battle at **Wagram** (14 June 1809).

Raate Road I 1940 I Russo-Finnish War

As invading Russians converged on **Suomussalmi** in central Finland, General Hjalmar Siilasvuo destroyed the invaders' northern division then turned against the southern force blocked from advancing along the Raate Road. Hard fighting along a 20-mile stretch saw Russia's 44th Division destroyed with terrible los-

ses. General Anton Vinogradov fled and was executed (1–8 January 1940).

Rabat-i-Pariyan I 1598 I Persian Reconquest of Khorasan

Shah Abbas of Persia took advantage of Uzbek confusion following the death of their great leader Abdullah II, leading a major expedition to recover his northern territories in the Khorasan. At Rabat-i-Pariyan, Shah Abbas decisively defeated Uzbeks under Din Muhammad Khan to recover Herat. He also seized Nishapur and Meshed but was checked at Balkh and made peace (9 August 1598).

Rabaul I 1943–1944 I World War II (Pacific)
See **New Britain**

Rachaya I 1925 I Druze Rebellion
See **Rashaya**

Raclawice I 1794 I War of the 2nd Polish Partition

In a renewed Polish rising against Russia, Tadeusz Kosciuszko returned to take command of the Polish army at Cracow, then marched against a Russian force under General Alexander Tormazov. The Russians were defeated northeast of Cracow at Raclawice by 4,000 Polish regulars and 2,000 peasants armed with scythes. However, Cracow was recaptured a few months later (4 April 1794).

**Radcot Bridge I 1387 I English
Barons' Revolt**

Richard II of England faced rebellion by
Barons under his uncle Thomas Woodstock
Duke of Gloucester and the King sent Robert de
Vere Earl of Oxford to meet the rebels at Radcot
Bridge, near Oxford. Supported by Richard
Fitzalan Earl of Arundel, Thomas Mowbray Earl
of Nottingham and Henry Bolingbroke (later
Henry IV), Gloucester routed de Vere, who fled
into exile (20 December 1387).

**Radenivela I 1630 I Later Portuguese
Colonial Wars in Asia**

Facing expansion by the Kingdom of Kandy, in
central Ceylon (modern Sri Lanka), under King
Senarat and his son Rajasinha, Portuguese Captain-
General Constantino de Sa de Noronha led an invasion towards the capital, Kandy. To the southeast
at Radenivela, he was attacked by Rajasinha.
When his Sinhalese militia deserted, de Sa was
defeated and killed and his force was destroyed.

**Radnor I 1282 I English Conquest
of Wales**

See **Aber Edw**

**Radom I 1914 I World War I
(Eastern Front)**

The Austro-German army of Count Franz
Conrad von Hotzendorf and Victor Dankl was
repulsed from the Vistula at **Ivangorod** and fell
back on Radom, where they were attacked by
General Nikolai Ivanov's Russians. The Germans withdrew north after very heavy losses and
later counter-attacked at **Lodz**, while the Austrians retreated southwest towards **Cracow** (24–
28 October 1914).

Rafa I 1916 I World War I (Middle East)

Just weeks after victory at **Magdhaba** in
eastern Sinai, British forces under General Philip
Chetwode attacked fortified Turkish positions at
Rafa. After artillery bombardment, the Turkish
trenches and nearby Magruntein Hill were taken
by storm with many prisoners captured. Victory
cleared the last Turks from Sinai and opened the
route to Palestine and **Gaza** (9 January 1917).

Rafa I 1956 I Arab-Israeli Sinai War

As Israel launched its war against Egypt in
Sinai, General Haim Laskar marched north against
a strong Arab concentration behind minefields
around Rafa, which was taken by storm. Further
west, Israeli forces drove the Egyptians out of El
Arish, capturing hundreds of vehicles (including
Russian-made tanks). They then turned north
against **Gaza** (31 October–1 November 1956).

Rafa I 1967 I Arab-Israeli Six Day War

Opening the Sinai campaign, General Israel
Tal, with Colonel Shmuel Gonen's armour, advanced on Rafa, held by Egyptian General Abd
el Azizi Soliman with 100 tanks supporting
well-fortified lines. Rafa fell by storm and the
Israelis fought their way west through the fiercely contested El Jiradi defile to take El Arish,
then broke out into the Sinai towards **Jebel
Libni** (5–6 June 1967).

Rahatgarh I 1858 I Indian Mutiny

General Sir Hugh Rose and about 3,000 men
advancing northeast from Mhow to relieve the
small British garrison at **Sagar**, were blocked by
the army of the Rajah of Banpur 30 miles to the
west at the strong hilltop fort at Rahatgarh. Using
artillery to smash the walls of the fort, Rose forced
the rebels to flee. Most escaped east to a new
defensive position at **Barodia** (24–28 January
1858).

**Rahmaniyya I 1786 I Mamluk-
Ottoman Wars**

Amid inter-factional anarchy in Mamluk
Egypt, Turkish Admiral Djeza'irli Ghazi Hasan
Pasha led a large expeditionary force and on the
Rosetta branch of the Nile at al-Rahmaniyya, he
routed Murad Bey and recovered Egypt for the
Ottomans. However, Hasan Pasha soon had to
withdraw and Murad Bey later recovered power.
He held Cairo until defeat by Bonaparte at the
Pyramids in 1798 (July 1786).

Rahon I 1710 I Mughal-Sikh Wars

When Sikh leader Banda Singh Bahadur marched towards Jullundur, in the Punjab, he was attacked by local Mughal ruler Shams Khan 35 miles

southeast near the fort of Rahon. Banda withdrew after a fierce battle, but when Shams Khan left the fort next day to return to Sultanpur, his rearguard was routed. The Sikhs took the fort then advanced to capture Jullundur (11 October 1710).

Raichur I 1520 I Wars of the Deccan Sultanates

Amid rivalry between states following the break-up of the Bahmani Sultanate, Ismail Adil Shah of Muslim Bijapur seized the fortress of Raichur, southwest of Hyderabad, then faced a siege by Krishnadeva Raya of Hindu Vijayanagar. The Bijapuri army was routed and Raichur fell to Krishnadeva Raya in battle nearby. Bijapur and her allies were avenged in 1565 at **Talikota** (19 May 1520).

Raigarh I 1689 I Mughal-Maratha Wars

Emperor Aurangzeb executed Maratha King Sambhaji then dispatched General Zulfiqar Khan against the new teenage King Rajaram at Raigarh (Rayagad), southwest of Poona. Rajaram escaped and fled to **Gingee** (5 April). When Raigarh fortress eventually fell by treachery, Sambhaji's widow Yesu Bai and son Shahu were captured and held for 17 years (25 March–19 October 1689).

Raigarh I 1703–1704 I Mughal-Maratha Wars

On campaign against the Marathas southwest of Poona, Emperor Aurangzeb sent Hamid-ud-din Khan and Tarbiyat Khan against the huge hill fortress of Raigarh, held by Santaji Silimkar. A fierce attack eventually captured most of the fort, though the citadel held out for ten days before the Marathas surrendered. The Mughals then turned against **Torna** (30 November 1703–16 February 1704).

Rain I 1632 I Thirty Years War (Swedish War)

Gustavus Adolphus of Sweden secured victory at **Breitenfeld** (September 1631) then occupied the Rhineland, marching into Bavaria against Duke Maximilian and Imperial commander Johan Tserclaes Count Tilly. On the Lech near Donauwörth at Rain, Gustavus inflicted another decisive loss, with Tilly fatally wounded. The Protestants seized nearby Augsburg and later Munich (15 April 1632).

Raisin River I 1813 I War of 1812
See **Frenchtown**

Rajahmundry I 1758 I Seven Years War (India)

To take pressure off the British in **Madras**, Governor Robert Clive of Bengal sent Colonel Francis Forde south from Calcutta to support Raja Ananda Raj against the French under Herbert de Brienne Comte de Conflans. Forde and the Raja's infantry routed and scattered the French on the Godaveri near Rajahmundry, then continued south against the city of **Masulipatam** (7 December 1758).

Rajgarh I 1858 I Indian Mutiny

Marching in pursuit of Tantia Topi, General John Michel advanced through intense heat and heavy rain and met the rebel at the walled town of Rajgarh, 60 miles northwest of Bhopal. Supported by cavalry under Major William Gordon, Michel attacked and routed the rebels, capturing 26 guns. Tantia Topi then retreated east to Sironj (15 September 1858).

Rajmahal, Bengal I 1576 I Mughal Conquest of Northern India

Daud Khan, the young Afghan ruler of Bengal, was beaten by the Mughal army at **Tukaroi** in March 1575, but soon rebelled against his new masters and faced a second expedition under Mughal Emperor Akbar. Near Rajmahal, on the Ganges southeast of Bhagalpur, Daud was defeated and executed, giving Akbar the province of Bengal and effective control of northern India (July 1576).

Rajmahal, Rajasthan I 1747 I Mughal Wars of Succession

Following the death of Sawai Jaysingh of Rajput Jaipur, his elder son, Ishwarisingh, faced armed resistance from the younger son, Madhorsingh. A two-day battle at Rajmahal, on the Banas southeast of Ajmer, saw Ishwarisingh

decisively defeat his brother and Rana Ja-
gatsingh of Udaipur. Maratha Peshwa Mulhar
Rao Holkar eventually brokered a settlement (1–
2 March 1747).

Rakhova I 1475 I Moldavian-Turkish War

Despite disaster at **Scutari** in 1474, Ottoman
commander Hadim Suleiman Pasha was given a
fresh army to invade Wallachia against a Christian
coalition led by Stephen the Great of Moldavia,
who was aided by Hungary and Poland. Suleiman
suffered a further defeat at Rakhova (modern
Oryakhovo) near Vaslui in northeast Romania,
but the Turks were soon avenged at **Valea Alba**
(10 January 1475).

**Rakshasbhuvan I 1763 I Later Mughal-
Maratha Wars**

Nizam Ali of Hyderabad took advantage of
civil war in Maharashtra to launch an invasion.
But on the Godaveri at Rakshasbhuvan, Maratha
Peshwa Madhav Rao and his uncle Ragunath Rao
destroyed the Nizam's army, killing a claimed
10,000, including commander Vithal Sundar.
Nizam Ali sued for peace and yielded all the land
he had recovered in late 1762 after **Alegaon** (10
August 1763).

**Rakshasi-Tangadi I 1565 I Wars of the
Deccan Sultanates**

See **Talikota**

**Rakvere I 1268 I Early Wars of the
Teutonic Knights**

Twenty-five years after Novgorod's great
victory at **Lake Peipus**, Mikhail Fedorovich of
Novgorod, supported by Pskov, Pereiaslav and
Suszdal, attacked Danes and Teutonic Knights
of the Livonian Order near Rakvere, east of
Tallinn in Estonia. The Danes and Germans
were badly beaten and a failed attack on Pskov
in May 1269 further weakened the Livonian
Order (18 February 1268).

**Ramadi I 1917 I World War I
(Mesopotamia)**

With **Baghdad** secured, Anglo-Indian commander Sir Frederick Maude attacked west

along the Euphrates to Ramadi, where he was
driven back in extreme heat (11 July). A second
expedition in cooler conditions, with General Sir
Harry Brooking, forced Turkish commander
Ahmad Bey to surrender 3,500 men and all his
guns. Maude soon contracted cholera and died
(28–29 September 1917).

Ramgarh I 1814 I British-Gurkha War

See **Mangu**

**Ramillies I 1706 I War of the Spanish
Succession**

Allied commander John Churchill Duke of
Marlborough was returning to the Spanish Netherlands after his great victory at **Blenheim** when
he met a Franco-Belgian army under Maximilian
Emanuel of Bavaria and Francois de Neufville
Marshal Villeroi. Another decisive French defeat
north of Namur near Ramillies made Villeroi
abandon Flanders and he later lost his command
(23 May 1706).

Ramleh I 1101 I Crusader-Muslim Wars

Two years after being repulsed at **Ascalon**,
Fatimid Egyptian Vizier al-Afdal sent another
substantial army into Palestine under Saad ed-
Daulah. The hugely outnumbered Crusaders
were driven back in a bitterly fought action at
Ramleh, southeast of Jaffa, before a heroic intervention by King Baldwin I of Jerusalem saved
the day and the Fatimids withdrew with heavy
losses (6 September 1101).

Ramleh I 1102 I Crusader-Muslim Wars

Fatimid Egyptian Vizier al-Afdal lost at
Ramleh, between Joppa and Jerusalem, but a
year later sent his son Sharaf al-Maali with another large army. At Ramleh, Baldwin I of Jerusalem and a small force of knights without infantry were routed and took refuge in the local
fortress. Most were killed or captured next day
though the King escaped and soon repulsed the
invaders at **Joppa** (17–18 May 1102).

Ramleh I 1105 I Crusader-Muslim Wars

Despite defeat at **Ramleh** in 1101 and **Joppa**
in 1102, Egyptian Vizier al-Afdal sent a third

large army into Palestine under his son Sena al-Mulk Husein. Aided by Turks from Damascus, the Fatimid Egyptians once again advanced as far as Ramleh, southeast of Joppa (modern Jaffa) where King Baldwin I of Jerusalem defeated and drove back this last full-scale Egyptian invasion (27 August 1105).

Ramnagar I 1848 I 2nd British-Sikh War

With Sikh forces defeated and besieged at **Multan**, northwest of Lahore, General Sir Hugh Gough attempted to cross the Chenab at Ramnagar and came under heavy artillery fire from Sikhs under Sher Singh. Gough was repulsed with heavy losses and withdrew to await reinforcements from the fall of Multan, but impatiently tried again two weeks later at **Sadulapur** (22 November 1848).

Ramón de las Yaguas I 1895 I 2nd Cuban War of Independence
See **Sao del Indio**

Ramosch I 1799 I French Revolutionary Wars (2nd Coalition)

During a fresh Austrian offensive in eastern Switzerland, Count Heinrich von Bellegarde repulsed General Jean-Joseph Dessoles at **St Maria**, then turned against General Claude Lecourbe on the River Inn. Lecourbe managed to drive off the Austrians with heavy losses at Ramosch but had to withdraw along the Inn to Suss, then west through the mountains to Bellinzona (30 April 1799).

Rampura I 1818 I 3rd British-Maratha War

Defeated by General Sir Thomas Hislop at **Mehidpur** in December, Marathas of Mulhar Rao Holkar marched north across the Chambal to Rampura, where they were threatened by cavalry and infantry under Major-General Sir Thomas Brown advancing from Sind. Brown inflicted heavy losses in a dawn attack and captured 10 guns. Holkar's commanders escaped into Mewar (10 January 1818).

Rancagua I 1814 I Chilean War of Independence

Juan José Carrera overthrew Spanish government in Chile then fell out with fellow rebel Bernardo O'Higgins. When Loyalist General Mariano Osorio attacked at Rancagua, south of Santiago, the "Disaster of Rancagua" saw O'Higgins defeated when Carrera and his brother José Miguel failed to provide support. Santiago City fell and Spanish authority was re-established (1 October 1814).

Rancho Dominguez I 1846 I American-Mexican War

In a rash attempt to capture Los Angeles, about 300 Americans advancing from San Pedro under naval Captain William Mervine were blocked at Rancho Dominguez (in modern North Long Beach) by Californian troops led by José Antonio Carillo. Driven off by a single four-pounder, Mervine was forced to withdraw but Los Angeles fell after battle in January at **San Gabriel** (8–9 October 1846).

Rangiaowhia I 1864 I 2nd New Zealand War

With the Maoris defeated at **Rangiriri** and **Paterangi**, General Sir Duncan Cameron continued south into New Zealand's Waikato, seizing the strategic pa (fortified village) at Rangiaowhia. When Maori forces began to dig in at nearby Hairini, Cameron led a bloody counter-attack and drove them off with the bayonet. Another action at **Orakau** in April ended the Waikato War (21–22 February 1864).

Rangiriri I 1863 I 2nd New Zealand War

A major British force under General Duncan Cameron advanced south from Auckland down the Waikato to secure Meremere, then attacked a powerful Maori position at nearby Rangiriri. A rash frontal assault saw two Victoria Crosses won, but Cameron lost 39 killed and over 100 wounded. However, the Maoris surrendered next day and he continued south to **Paterangi** (20 November 1863).

Rangoon ▌ 1824 ▌ 1st British-Burmese War

When Burma conquered Arakan and threatened British India, Britain declared war and General Sir Archibald Campbell secured Rangoon (May 1824) where he was later besieged by Maha Bundoola and a reported 60,000 men. Bundoola was heavily defeated in a fierce battle (1–7 December) then was repulsed at nearby Kokein and pursued towards **Danubyu** (30 November–16 December 1824).

Rangoon ▌ 1852 ▌ 2nd British-Burmese War

Britain resumed war against Burma for commercial gain and General Henry Thomas Godwin and Admiral Charles John Austen captured the strategic fortress of **Martaban**, controlling the Salween, then moved west against Rangoon. The key city fell at the cost of under 150 British casualties and Godwin then took his force northwest against **Bassein** (14 April 1852).

Ranod ▌ 1858 ▌ Indian Mutiny

The rebel Firuz Shah crossed the Ganges into Gwalior intending to sack Ranod, 40 miles southwest of Jhansi, where he was intercepted by General Sir Robert Napier. Arriving at Ranod to find that Napier had reached the town the same day, Firuz Shah was defeated and repulsed. A month later he joined up with Tantia Topi but was defeated again at **Dausa** (17 December 1858).

Raor ▌ 712 ▌ Muslim Conquest of Sind

In response to attacks on Arab shipping, Caliph Al-Hajjaj in Baghdad sent his nephew Muhammad ibn Qasim with a large force against Sind, where he besieged Debal (near modern Karachi, Pakistan). Hindu King Dahir of Sind then rashly tried to make a stand at Raor, where he was defeated and killed. The capital Alor quickly fell and Sind became the first Muslim foothold in India (June 712).

Raphia ▌ 720 BC ▌ Assyrian Wars

Although Prince Hanun of Gaza supported a rebellion by Palestinian provinces against King Sargon of Assyria, he was not present when his allies were routed at **Qarqar**. Later that year Sargon continued his march through Palestine and at Raphia, south of Gaza, Hanun was also defeated and captured, ending the rebellion and securing the Assyrian Empire's southern boundary with Egypt.

Raphia ▌ 217 BC ▌ 4th Syrian War

Tempted by apparent military decline in Egypt, the Seleucid Antiochus III took an army into Palestine. After initial success, Ptolemaic General Sosibius destroyed the invaders in a massive battle at Raphia, south of Gaza. Antiochus had to acknowledge Ptolemaic authority over Palestine, but he returned 19 years later and the Battle of **Paneas** finally ended 100 years of Ptolemaic rule in Palestine.

Rapidan River ▌ 1864 ▌ American Civil War (Eastern Theatre)

See **Morton's Ford**

Rapido ▌ 1944 ▌ World War II (Southern Europe)

Following a British advance across the **Garigliano** in support of the Allied landing south of Rome at **Anzio**, American General Frederick Walker attempted to cross the Rapido to the east near Sant'Angelo. Facing heavy German reinforcements, the Americans were repulsed with 1,600 casualties and the Allied offensive stalled in the shadow of **Monte Cassino** (20–22 January 1944).

Rappahannock ▌ 1862 ▌ American Civil War (Eastern Theatre)

Union General John Pope was advancing through northern Virginia towards Gordonsville when part of his army was repulsed by General Thomas "Stonewall" Jackson at **Cedar Mountain** and fell back on the Rappahannock. Pope attempted to secure the river with a series of actions, but when Jackson turned the Union flank at **Kettle Run**, Pope withdrew towards **Bull Run** (22–25 August 1862).

Rappahannock Station ∎ 1863 ∎ American Civil War (Eastern Theatre)

Repulsed at **Bristoe Station**, Virginia, from a failed advance on Manassas, Confederate commander Robert E. Lee was pursued southwest to the Rappahannock by Union General George G. Meade, who attacked at Rappahannock Station and nearby Kelly's Ford. Lee's troops were defeated with about 1,600 captured and he retired south of the Rapidan to **Mine Run** (7 November 1863).

Rapperswil ∎ 1656 ∎ 1st Villmergen War

During resumed religious warfare in Switzerland, the Protestant forces of Zurich under General Rudolf Werdmüller attempted to seize the castle at Rapperswil in the Catholic Canton of Schwyz. The men from Zurich were driven off, while the army of Berne was repulsed even more heavily at **Villmergen**. A troubled peace was then established (January 1656).

Rapti ∎ 1859 ∎ Indian Mutiny

After rebel leader Nana Sahib fled into Nepal after defeat at **Banki** in December, General Alfred Horsford was invited across the border against the fugitives and advanced up the Rapti. Meeting over 1,000 rebels on the river at Sitka Ghat, he drove them off and captured 15 guns. Colonel Thomas Kelly pursued the survivors into the hills where Nana Sahib later died in obscurity (9 February 1859).

Ras al-Khaimah ∎ 1809 ∎ Anglo-Arab Wars

In the prolonged struggle against Arab pirates in the Persian Gulf, British Colonel Lionel Smith took a small force against the Bani Bu Ali stronghold of Ras al-Khaimah, on the southern side of the Strait of Hormuz. Smith stormed the fortress and largely dismantled its defences. However, it was partially rebuilt and a second British expedition was required ten years later (13 November 1809).

Ras al-Khaimah ∎ 1819 ∎ Anglo-Arab Wars

General Sir William Grant Keir renewed Britain's attack on piracy in the Persian Gulf and landed with 3,000 men at the Strait of Hormuz near Ras al-Khaimah, held by the Qawasim Chief Hasan Ibn Rahmah. The pirate fortress surrendered after heavy bombardment and the death of the chief's brother Ibrahim in a costly sortie. The Qawasim then agreed to end piracy (3–9 December 1819).

Rasboeni ∎ 1476 ∎ Moldavian-Turkish War

See **Valea Alba**

Rashaya ∎ 1925 ∎ Druze Rebellion

Soon after Druze forces captured **Suwayda** in southeast Syria, fighting spread to Lebanon, where 3,000 rebels under Zayd Beg attacked Rashaya fortress, held by Captain Granger. Rebels who broke in were repulsed in bloody fighting. With ammunition spent, the Legionnaires were preparing a final suicidal charge (as at **Camerone** in 1863) when relief arrived just in time (20–24 November 1925).

Rastatt ∎ 1796 ∎ French Revolutionary Wars (1st Coalition)

After crossing the Rhine at Strasbourg, French General Jean Victor Moreau advanced against Archduke Charles Louis of Austria, who immediately began to withdraw north and east. Moreau defeated Austrian General Maximilian Latour on the River Murg, southwest of Karlsruhe at Rastatt, and Charles was forced to continue his withdrawal over the river towards Swabia (4 July 1796).

Raszyn ∎ 1809 ∎ Napoleonic Wars (5th Coalition)

Facing an advance on Warsaw by Archduke Ferdinand of Austria, Polish-French forces under Prince Josef Poniatowski marched southwest to the small town of Raszyn (a modern suburb of Warsaw) where they were defeated and driven back with heavy losses. Three days later (22 April) the capital surrendered to the Austrians (19 April 1809).

Ratanpur | 1706 | Mughal-Maratha Wars

Mughal Prince Bidar Bakht countered a Maratha offensive into Gujarat under Dhanaji Jadhav by advancing towards Ratanpur, on the Narmada. On the east bank near Rajpipla he was routed by the Marathas, with his Generals Safdar Khan Babi and Nazar Alim Khan captured. Although they were later ransomed, Mughal power in the Deccan had suffered a grave blow (15 March 1706).

Ratanpur | 1720 | Mughal-Hyderabad War

On campaign in central India against the ambitious Nizam-ul-Mulk and General Iwaz Khan, Dilawar Ali Khan led a large Imperial army towards Ratanpur, north of Burhanpur. However, further north at Husainpur, Mughal Generals Sher Khan and Babar Khan were killed, as was Dilawar himself when he took command. The Nizam soon defeated another Imperial army at **Balapur** (19 June 1720).

Rathenow | 1675 | Scania War

When Sweden joined France against Brandenburg and the Netherlands, Swedish Count Karl Gustav Wrangel invaded Brandenburg. After a forced march across Germany, Field Marshal Georg von Derfflinger attacked the invaders at the fortress of Rathenow, west of Berlin. The Swedes were driven out in heavy fighting and withdrew north to a decisive defeat at **Fehrbellin** (25 June 1675).

Rathgarh | 1858 | Indian Mutiny
See **Rahatgarh**

Rathmines | 1649 | British Civil Wars

When Irish Royalists commanded by James Butler Earl of Ormonde advanced on Dublin, the city's Parliamentary garrison under Colonel Michael Jones launched a powerful counter-attack at nearby Rathmines. The Royalists were heavily repulsed, losing over 4,000 casualties and all their guns. Oliver Cromwell soon arrived to brutally crush remaining resistance (2 August 1649).

Ratisbon | 1634 | Thirty Years War (Swedish War)
See **Regensberg**

Ratisbon | 1809 | Napoleonic Wars (5th Coalition)
See **Regensberg**

Ratnagiri | 1783 | 1st British-Maratha War

Unaware that peace had been signed with the British, Maratha naval commander Anand Rao Dhulap took his fleet and attacked a squadron under the sloop *Ranger* off the coast south of Bombay. A hard-fought action near Ratnagiri cost about 100 Maratha and 30 British lives and Dhulap captured five British ships. However, they were quickly returned and peace was secured (8 April 1783).

Rat's Gap | 1853 | Taiping Rebellion
See **Wuxue**

Rattlesnake Springs | 1880 | Apache Indian Wars

Crossing the Rio Grande into Texas, the Apache Chief Victorio was repulsed at **Tinaja de las Palmas**, then tried to march north through the Sierra Diablo. At Rattlesnake Springs, on Salt Flat, he was driven off by Buffalo Soldiers under Colonel Benjamin Grierson and Captain Louis Carpenter. Victorio then withdrew into Mexico, where he was killed in October at **Tres Castillos** (6 August 1880).

Raucoux | 1747 | War of the Austrian Succession
See **Rocoux**

Rautu | 1918 | Finnish War of Independence

Local White commander Captain Yrjo Elfvengren launched a bold offensive in eastern Karelia, leading an outnumbered force against Rautu (modern Sosnovo, Russia). While heavy fighting cost the Whites 220 killed and over 400 wounded, the Russians lost 400 killed and 700 captured and the railway from Petrograd (St Petersburg). Karelia was secured just weeks later at **Vyborg** (1–5 April 1918).

Ravenna I 307 I Roman Wars of Succession

When Maxentius usurped the Western throne, his rival Severus II attempted to besiege Rome, but was driven off when part of his army changed sides. Severus fled to Ravenna, where he was then besieged by Maximianus Herculius, former Emperor and father of Maxentius. Facing defeat, Severus and his force surrendered and soon after he was mysteriously put to death.

Ravenna I 425 I Later Roman Wars of Succession

When Honorius died, the throne at Ravenna was usurped by his minister John, opposed by Eastern Emperor Theodosius II, who sent an army under Aspar. Besieged at Ravenna, John was deposed and killed before Hun mercenaries could arrive or his ally Aetius could return from Africa. Six-year-old Valentinian III, son of Constantius, was enthroned and his mother Placidia effectively ruled in the west.

Ravenna I 432 I Later Roman Wars of Succession

When Placidia, mother of the boy-Emperor Valentinian III, dismissed her over-ambitious General Flavius Aetius, she recalled Bonifacius, who abandoned his besieged city of **Hippo Regius** in North Africa. Bonifacius defeated Aetius in battle outside Ravenna, though he was mortally wounded. When Aetius returned a year later with Hun troops he became virtual ruler in the west.

Ravenna I 475 I Fall of the Western Roman Empire

Roman General Orestes was ordered to raise a large army against the tribal rulers of Gaul but instead led his force against Emperor Julius Nepos in his capital at Ravenna, where Nepos was defeated and deposed. Nepos fled to Dal-

matia and Orestes enthroned his own son Romulus Augustulus, who was in turn overthrown in September 476 after the Roman defeat at **Pavia** (28 August 475).

Ravenna I 490–493 I Goth Invasion of Italy

After invading Italy and defeating the German ruler Odoacer on the **Sontius** and at **Verona**, Theodoric the Ostrogoth besieged Odoacer at his capital in Ravenna. The siege continued for more than three years until a naval blockade forced Odoacer to make peace. Theodoric invited Odoacer to a banquet, where he was murdered and Theodoric became undisputed ruler of Italy (27 February 493).

Ravenna I 539–540 I Gothic War in Italy

Driven back from failed sieges at **Rome** and Rimini, the Ostrogoths of King Witiges were in turn besieged in their capital at Ravenna. For six months they held out against General Belisarius, who eventually pretended to accept an offer to become the Ostrogoth King. Belisarius then captured the city and sent Witiges to Constantinople as a prisoner (December 539–May 540).

Ravenna I 1512 I War of the Holy League

With successive victories in northern Italy, 22-year-old French commander Gaston de Foix Duke of Nemours marched towards Ravenna to face the Papal-Spanish forces of the Holy League. One of Italy's bloodiest battles saw de Foix killed, but Raymond of Cardona was routed by French artillery. The Holy League defeat brought the Swiss and Germans into the war against France (11 April 1512).

Ravenspur I 1471 I Wars of the Roses

Edward IV returned to England after briefly escaping his ambitious younger brother George Duke of Clarence and Kingmaker Richard Neville Earl of Warwick, landing with about 2,000 men on the Humber at Ravenspur. After little more than token resistance, a defending force under Martin de la See withdrew and Edward marched south to meet Warwick a month later at **Barnet** (16 March 1471).

Ravi ▮ 1306 ▮ Mongol Invasions of India

Sent to avenge defeat at **Amroha** (December 1305), a fresh Mongol invasion of northern India under Kabak was met at the River Ravi by Sultan Ala-ud-din's army under Malik Naib Kufur and Ghazi Malik. The Mongols were routed, with Kabak and thousands of prisoners executed and their women and children enslaved. It was the last great Mongol invasion until Tamerlane 90 years later.

Ravine-à-Coulevres ▮ 1802 ▮ Napoleonic Wars (Santo Domingo Rising)

See **Gonaives**

Rawal ▮ 1857 ▮ Indian Mutiny

When mutineers attacked the small British garrison at Mehidpur, northwest of Ujain, 400 Hyderabad cavalry under Major Sutherland Orr set off in pursuit. Orr relieved Mehidpur and 12 miles north met the rebels in a very strong defensive position at the village of Rawal. After losing about 100 dead, the rebels abandoned their captured guns and stores and fled to **Mandasur** (12 November 1857).

Rawa Russka ▮ 1914 ▮ World War I (Eastern Front)

As Russian forces crossed the **Gnila Lipa** towards Lemberg (Lvov) in southeast Poland, General Aleksei Brusilov circled north and smashed into Austrian General Moritz von Auffenberg around Rawa Russka. While action was indecisive, following defeat further south at **Gorodok** and the fall of Lemberg, Austria abandoned Galicia except for **Przemysl** (3–11 September 1914).

Rawdhat al Muhanna ▮ 1906 ▮ Saudi-Rashidi Wars

While Turkish garrisons tried to separate rival Rashidi and Saudi forces, Abd al-Aziz ibn Rashidi was ambushed at the oasis of Rawdhat al Muhanna, north of Buraydah, by Abd al-Aziz (Ibn Saud) of Riyadh. The Rashidi ruler was routed and his head was cut off as a trophy. Ottoman forces withdrew from central Arabia and were eventually ejected in the east in 1913 at **Hofuf** (13 April 1906).

Rawiya ▮ 1903 ▮ British Conquest of Northern Nigeria

As General George Kemball marched northwest from **Kano** to **Sokoto**, a 45-strong patrol under Captain Wallace Wright defeated about 200 Nigerians near Rawiya, then next day formed square and repulsed 2,000 infantry and 1,000 cavalry returning to threaten Kano. The Emir's army lost 300 casualties, including the Wazir killed, and Wright won a Victoria Cross (25–26 February 1903).

Rawka ▮ 1794 ▮ War of the 2nd Polish Partition

See **Szczekociny**

Raymond ▮ 1863 ▮ American Civil War (Western Theatre)

In support of the besieged Confederate stronghold of **Vicksburg**, on the Mississippi, General John Gregg advanced from the east to intercept approaching Union forces under General James B. McPherson. Severe fighting at Raymond, Mississippi, saw Gregg delay the much-larger Union force before falling back northeast to **Jackson**, which was lost two days later (12 May 1863).

Rayy ▮ 1059 ▮ Seljuk Wars of Expansion

The Great Seljuk Sultan Toghril Beg was repulsed in Byzantine Armenia at **Manzikert** (1054) and withdrew to Rayy, southeast of modern Tehran, where he later faced revolt by Muhammad and Ahmad, sons of his kinsman Er-tash, and their uncle Ibrahim Inal. With the aid of his nephew Alp Arslan, Toghril won a decisive victory and the three rebels were executed (22 July 1059).

Reading ▮ 871 ▮ Viking Wars in Britain

Having secured East Anglia following victory in late 870 at **Hoxne**, Viking leaders Halfdan and Bagsecq invaded Wessex and were repulsed at **Englefield** by Aethelwulf, Ealdorman of Berkshire. Joined by King Aethelred's main Saxon army, Aethelwulf attacked the Danish camp at Reading, but was driven off and killed. Aethelred soon faced the decisive battle at nearby **Ashdown** (January 871).

Reading ∎ 1643 ∎ British Civil Wars

At the end of failed negotiations, Parliamentary commander Robert Devereux Earl of Essex resumed the offensive and, supported by General John Hampden, besieged Reading. King Charles I personally led a relief force from Oxford and the Royalists were repulsed just to the north at Caversham Bridge. Charles withdrew to Wallingford, leaving Reading to surrender next day (15–25 April 1643).

Reams Station (1st) ∎ 1864 ∎ American Civil War (Eastern Theatre)

Returning from a cavalry raid south of besieged **Petersburg**, Virginia, Union Generals James Wilson and Augustus V. Kautz were defeated at **Sappony Church** then met Confederate forces under Generals Fitzhugh Lee and William Mahone at Reams Station on the Weldon Railroad. Under heavy attack, Wilson abandoned his wagons and guns and withdrew north to the Union lines (29 June 1864).

Reams Station (2nd) ∎ 1864 ∎ American Civil War (Eastern Theatre)

Union General Gouvernor K. Warren attacked the Weldon Railroad south of besieged **Petersburg**, Virginia, by securing **Globe Tavern**, then sent General Winfield Hancock and cavalry under General David M. Gregg five miles south against Reams Station. They were routed by Confederate General Henry Heth and withdrew with 2,700 men lost, mainly captured (25 August 1864).

Rebecco ∎ 1524 ∎ 1st Habsburg-Valois War

Driven from Lombardy after **Bicocca** in 1522, Francis I of France sent a fresh army under Admiral William de Bonnivet, who advanced to Milan, where he unwisely ordered Chevalier

Pierre Terrail de Bayard to hold nearby Rebecco. The French were overwhelmed by Spanish commander Fernando Francesco d'Avalos Marquis of Pescara and retreated to further defeat at the **Sesia**.

Recife ∎ 1630 ∎ Dutch-Portuguese Colonial Wars

After losing **Salvador** in Portuguese Brazil, the Dutch sent Admiral Hendrik Lonck and Colonel Diedrik van Waerdenburgh further north against Olinda, capital of Pernambuca, and its port of Recife. After fierce fighting, the Dutch troops routed Governor Matthias de Albuquerque to storm Olinda, then captured the forts of Recife, securing Pernambuca (15–16 February 1630).

Recife ∎ 1632 ∎ Dutch-Portuguese Colonial Wars

When Dutch forces seized Pernambuco in Portuguese Brazil, a large relief force despatched from Lisbon under Admiral Antonio de Oquendo was met off Recife by Dutch Admirals Adriaen Pater and Martin Thijssen. A hard-fought action saw Pater killed, but Oquendo withdrew north. A fresh relief fleet, which arrived in 1640, was defeated **Itamaraca** (12 September 1632).

Recife ∎ 1640 ∎ Dutch-Portuguese Colonial Wars

See **Itamaraca**

Recife ∎ 1650–1654 ∎ Dutch-Portuguese Colonial Wars

Through costly defeats at nearby **Guararapes**, the Dutch settlement at Recife, Pernambuco, remained under long-term siege and the 3,000-strong garrison and over 8,000 civilians eventually faced starvation. When a large Portuguese fleet arrived (20 December 1653) the Dutch soon surrendered Recife and all remaining possessions in Brazil (February 1650–26 January 1654).

Redan (1st) ∎ 1855 ∎ Crimean War

In a poorly co-ordinated assault on the defences of the besieged Black Sea fortress of

Sevastopol, British forces under General Fitzroy Somerset Lord Raglan attacked the key position known as The Redan, while French troops attacked the **Malakov**. A costly failure—commonly blamed on the French—saw the British repulsed. Raglan died soon afterwards (17–18 June 1855).

Redan (2nd) ▮ 1855 ▮ Crimean War

Three months after costly Anglo-French failure at the **Malakov** and The Redan, which guarded besieged **Sevastopol**, General Sir William Codrington seized The Redan, then lost it to a Russian counter-attack. However, French gunfire from the captured Malakov expelled the Russians and General Mikhail Gorchakov evacuated Sevastopol next day, effectively ending the war (8 September 1855).

Redaniyya ▮ 1517 ▮ Ottoman-Mamluk War

See **Ridanieh**

Red Buttes ▮ 1865 ▮ Cheyenne-Arapaho Indian War

See **Platte Bridge**

Red Canyon ▮ 1879 ▮ Ute Indian Wars

Major Thomas Thornburgh and 200 men marching to support the **White River** Agency in northwest Colorado were besieged near the Milk River in Red Canyon by 300 Utes under Jack (Nicaagat) and Colorow. The Americans had lost 60 casualties (including Thornburgh killed) before they were relieved. Chief Ouray then intervened to restore peace (29 September–3 October 1879).

Red Cliffs ▮ 208 ▮ Wars of the Three Kingdoms

With northern China secured, the great warlord Cao Cao (Ts'ao Ts'ao) turned south, where he defeated Liu Bei at **Changban** and soon after was blocked at Red Cliffs, on the Yangzi near Jiangling, by Liu Bei and Sun Quan of Wu. In a decisive battle on the river, Cao Cao's fleet was destroyed and he withdrew. He later consoli-

dated his power in the northwest at **Huayin**, then turned south into Hanzhong.

Reddersburg ▮ 1900 ▮ 2nd Anglo-Boer War

Days after victory at **Sannah's Post**, Boer commander Christiaan de Wet led his raiders against the 600-strong garrison at Reddersburg, south of Bloemfontein. Following a 24-hour attack, the entire garrison under Captain William McWhinnie of the Irish Rifles surrendered for lack of water, with 45 killed and wounded and 546 captured. De Wet then marched east against **Wepener** (3 April 1900).

Redencão ▮ 1866 ▮ War of the Triple Alliance

See **Ilha de Redencão**

Redhina ▮ 1811 ▮ Napoleonic Wars (Peninsular Campaign)

Marshal Michel Ney retreated from the failed French invasion of Portugal and fought a series of remarkable rearguard actions against the cautious Allied pursuit. At the bridge of Redhina on the River Soure, Ney held off the Anglo-Portuguese Allies under Arthur Wellesley Lord Wellington, then continued his withdrawal through **Cazal Novo** and **Foz d'Aronce** (12 March 1811).

Red Idol Gorge ▮ 1904 ▮ British Invasion of Tibet

Britain suspected Russian intervention in Tibet and sent 1,000 men under General James Macdonald, who advanced through **Guru** to a narrow defile on the Nyang Chu, known as Red Idol Gorge for its pigmented Buddhas. Gurkhas climbed the steep sides and fired down into the defenders, who lost 200 killed and 70 captured. The invaders then marched on to **Gyantse** (9 April 1904).

Red Mound ▮ 1862 ▮ American Civil War (Western Theatre)

See **Parker's Cross Roads**

Red River Delta I 1950 I French Indo-China War

After routing the French in northern Vietnam at **Cao-Bang**, Viet Minh commander Vo Nguyen Giap launched a sustained offensive into the Red River Delta around Hanoi. Prolonged fighting saw Giap lose to the northwest at **Vinh Yen**, to the northeast at **Mao Khé** and in the south on the **Day River** before he withdrew. In September 1951 he attacked again at **Nghia Lo** (January–June 1950).

Refugio I 1836 I Texan Wars of Independence

Sent to delay General José Urrea's Mexicans advancing from **San Patricio**, Texan forces under Amon King and William Ward attempted to hold the Nuestra Senora del Rosario mission at Refugio. In confused actions nearby, King was defeated and then executed with 15 others. Ward was also defeated, though he escaped capture until later and died in the **Goliad Massacre** (12–15 March 1836).

Regensberg I 1634 I Thirty Years War (Swedish War)

Bernard of Saxe-Weimar led his Protestant forces into Bavaria, where he captured the Danube city of Regensberg (14 November 1633). Threatened by Ferdinand of Hungary approaching from Bohemia, Bernard counter-attacked at **Landshut**. In his absence however, Regensberg capitulated to the Imperial army and the garrison were permitted to march out with the honours of war (26 July 1634).

Regensberg I 1809 I Napoleonic Wars (5th Coalition)

The Austrian army of Archduke Charles which invaded Bavaria was defeated over three days at **Abensberg**, **Landshut** and **Eckmühl**, before retiring on the fourth day to Regensberg on the Danube. A well-judged defensive action enabled Charles to hold the city against the exhausted French until most of the Austrian army had successfully escaped towards **Vienna** (23 April 1809).

Rei I 1194 I Wars of the Great Seljuk Sultanate
See **Shahr Rey**

Reichenbach, Germany I 1813 I Napoleonic Wars (War of Liberation)

In the aftermath of victory on the Spree at **Bautzen**, Napoleon Bonaparte encountered Prince Ludwig Wittgenstein's Russians again next day west of Gorlitz at Reichenbach, near Markersdorf in Saxony. In the course of a brief action, Bonaparte's favorite aide, General Geraud Duroc, was killed by a cannonball, reputedly while standing close to the Emperor (22 May 1813).

Reichenbach, Poland I 1762 I Seven Years War (Europe)

With Russia out of the war, Frederick II of Prussia defeated Austrian Marshal Leopold von Daun at **Burkersdorf** in Silesia in July, then besieged the key fortress of Schweidnitz. Von Daun's last attempt to relieve the siege was heavily repulsed at Reichenbach (modern Dzierzoniow), southwest of Breslau, and Schweidnitz capitulated (9 October) securing Silesia for Frederick (16 August 1762).

Reichswald I 1945 I World War II (Western Europe)

Months after Allied failure at **Arnhem**, a fresh attack was made to outflank the **Siegfried Line** in Holland. Anglo-Canadian forces under General Henry Crerar advanced east from Nijmegen but were stalled by heavy losses and bad weather in the Reichswald Forest. With American aid, Crerar finally cleared the forest and General Alfred Schlemm fell back across the Rhine (8 February–9 March 1945).

Reimerswaal I 1574 I Netherlands War of Independence
See **Walcheren**

Reims I 356 I Alemannic Invasion of Roman Gaul
See **Rheims**

Reims I 1359–1360 I Hundred Years War
See **Rheims**

**Reims I 1814 I Napoleonic Wars
(French Campaign)**
See **Rheims**

Rellano (1st) I 1912 I Mexican Revolution
Mexican rebel Pascual Orozco turned against former ally President Francisco Madero and Federal General José González-Salas took 6,000 men north to Rellano, where his train was blown up by 800 Orozquistas under Emilio Campa. During a decisive rout with up to 300 killed, the Federal troops mutinied, fleeing southeast to Torreon, and the wounded Salas killed himself in shame (23 March 1912).

Rellano (2nd) I 1912 I Mexican Revolution
With Federal forces routed at Rellano in Chihuahua, hard-drinking veteran General Victoriano Huerta took a fresh government force against the rebel Pascual Orozco. Huerta repulsed a rebel force at Conejos (12 May), then northwest at Rellano, his artillery delivered a second, decisive victory. Over 200 insurgents were killed and Orozco's movement was effectively ended (22 May 1912).

**Remagen I 1945 I World War II
(Western Europe)**
In fighting for the **Rhineland**, all bridges over the Rhine were destroyed except at Remagen, south of Cologne, where the Ludendorff Bridge was seized by an American armoured patrol just as German forces failed to fully demolish it. Five divisions crossed the vital bridge before it collapsed ten days later, opening the way for the American advance on the **Ruhr Pocket** (7 March 1945).

Remolina I 1873 I Kickapoo Indian Wars
See **Nacimiento**

**Renchen I 1796 I French Revolutionary
Wars (1st Coalition)**
As French forces under General Jean Victor Moreau advanced across the Rhine at Stras-

bourg, General Louis Desaix marched against Austrian General Count Anton Sztaray and 10,000 men at Renchen, north of Offenberg. The Austrians suffered a costly defeat, losing 1,200 men and ten guns, before withdrawing north to join Archduke Charles Louis' main force at **Rastatt** (26 June 1796).

**Rennell Island I 1943 I World War II
(Pacific)**
As the **Guadalcanal** campaign ended, an American task force with reinforcements under Admiral Robert Giffen was intercepted to the southeast near Rennell Island by land-based torpedo bombers. A hard-fought night attack saw the American cruiser *Chicago* badly damaged for seven Japanese aircraft lost. *Chicago* was attacked again and sunk next day (29–30 January 1943).

Rennes I 1356–1357 I Hundred Years War
In the disputed Breton succession, English forces won a great victory at **Poitiers**, then Henry of Lancaster laid siege to Rennes. A relief army sent by the Dauphin Charles VII was driven off but young Betrand de Guesclin broke in with reinforcements. The siege then continued despite an official truce until Lancaster accepted a large cash tribute and withdrew (3 October 1356–5 July 1357).

**Resaca I 1864 I American Civil War
(Western Theatre)**
Near the start of his march through Georgia from **Chattanooga**, Union commander William T. Sherman drove General Joseph E. Johnston's Confederate army off **Rocky Face Ridge** (11 May) then advanced south through Dalton on Resaca. While both sides lost almost 3,000 casualties in a sharp action, Johnston was unable to check the Union advance and fell back to **Adairsville** (13–15 May 1864).

**Resaca de la Palma I 1846 I American-
Mexican War**
American General Zachary Taylor advanced from the mouth of the Rio Grande to relieve besieged **Fort Texas**, then won at **Palo Alto** before meeting the main army of Mexican

General Mariano Arista next day at Resaca de la Palma. Arista's force was decisively defeated and fled. When the United States officially declared war a few days later, Taylor crossed into Mexico (9 May 1846).

Resaena ∎ 243 ∎ Roman-Persian Wars

When Shapur I of Sassanid Persia continued the invasion of Roman Syria commenced by his father Ardashir, teenage Emperor Gordian III sent his father-in-law Timesitheus, who routed the Persians west of Nisibis at Resaena (modern Ras al-Ayn, Syria), effectively recovering Syria and Mesopotamia. Timesitheus then died and Gordian was defeated at **Misiche** (244) and murdered.

Reshire ∎ 1856 ∎ Anglo-Persian War

Britain responded to Persia's capture of **Herat** in Afghanistan (25 October) by sending forces to the Persian Gulf under Colonel Foster Stalker, who landed near Reshire (modern Rishahr), held by about 1,500 tribesmen. Stalker inflicted a heavy bombardment then took the fortress by a costly frontal assault, driving the Persians a few miles north towards **Bushire** (7–9 December 1856).

Rethel ∎ 1650 ∎ War of the 2nd Fronde

See **Champ Blanc**

Retief Massacre ∎ 1838 ∎ Boer-Zulu War

Boer leader Piet Retief resolved to negotiate with the Zulus and marched northeast from Durban in Natal with 70 men to parley with Zulu King Dingane. After several days' discussion in the Zulu capital at Gingindlovu, Retief and his entire party were suddenly seized and executed. All-out war started a few days later with an attack on the Trekker camp at **Bloukranz** (6 February 1838).

Réunion ∎ 1810 ∎ Napoleonic Wars (5th Coalition)

After a previous raid at **St Paul** on the Indian Ocean island of Réunion (French Bourbon), British Commodore Josias Rowley returned with almost 4,000 troops under Colonel Henry

Keating. They landed at key points and a rapid advance forced French Colonel Jean Ste. Susanne to surrender the island. A later British attack further east on Mauritius was defeated **Grand Port** (8–9 July 1810).

Reutlingen ∎ 1377 ∎ War of the Swabian League

South German cities of the Swabian League opposed Charles IV trying to secure succession for his son Wenceslas and repulsed him at **Ulm** (1376), then marched against his Governor, Count Eberhard of Württemberg. The Count's son Ulrich was badly beaten at Reutlingen, south of Stuttgart, and Charles had to acknowledge the liberty of the cities until his victory ten years later at **Doffingen** (May 1377).

Reval ∎ 1219 ∎ Danish Wars of Expansion

While campaigning against the pagan Ests of the eastern Baltic, Waldemar II of Denmark—the Conqueror—was losing a battle at Reval (modern Tallinn) when the purportedly miraculous appearance of a Danish flag turned likely defeat to victory. Waldemar conquered Estonia and Denmark became the dominant power in northern Europe until defeat in 1227 at **Bornhoved**.

Reval ∎ 1343 ∎ Wars of the Teutonic Knights

The St George's Night Rebellion saw northern Estonians rise against their Danish and German rulers and try to besiege Reval. Master Burckhardt von Dreileben of the Livonian Order seized and hanged the insurgent leaders at truce talks then routed their army outside Reval before Swiss aid could arrive. After the rising was suppressed on Oesel, Denmark sold northern Estonia to the knights.

Reval ∎ 1570–1571 ∎ Livonian War

Tsar Ivan IV appointed Danish Prince Magnus, Duke of Holstein, as vassal King of Livonia, then sent 25,000 Russians to help Magnus and his Germans capture Reval (Tallinn in modern Estonia) from the Swedes, who had entered the war to support Poland. Despite massive assault, the city remained supplied by sea and Magnus finally had to withdraw (21 August 1570–16 March 1571).

Reval ▮ 1577 ▮ Livonian War
On a fresh campaign in Livonia, Tsar Ivan IV led 50,000 Russians in a renewed attempt to seize Reval (Tallinn in modern Estonia), defended by its courageous citizens and a Swedish garrison. After repeated costly assaults, with commander Ivan Vasilevich Sheremetev killed, the Tsar finally withdrew and turned south to vent his anger on the city of **Wenden** (23 January–13 March 1577).

Reval ▮ 1790 ▮ 2nd Russo-Swedish War
Gustav III of Sweden renewed his offensive against Russia and sent a flotilla under his brother Duke Charles of Sodermanland against the Russian fleet at Reval (modern Tallinn) in Estonia. Russian Admiral Paul Vasili Tchitchakov repulsed the attack, with one Swedish ship captured and another run aground, and Duke Charles withdrew to support Gustav at **Fredriksham** (11 May 1790).

Revolax ▮ 1808 ▮ Napoleonic Wars (Russo-Swedish War)
Halted by a Swedish counter-offensive at the **Siikajoki** (18 April), Russia's invasion of western Finland was driven further south to Revolax, where General Mikhail Bulatoff attempted to make a stand. In a major Swedish victory, General Johann Cronstedt utterly routed the Russians, who were forced to withdraw further down Finland's west coast towards **Nykarleby** (27 April 1808).

Rewi's Last Stand ▮ 1864 ▮ 2nd New Zealand War
See **Orakau**

Reynosa ▮ 1808 ▮ Napoleonic Wars (Peninsular Campaign)
Withdrawing before Napoleon Bonaparte's invasion of northern Spain, General Joachim Blake fell back from his defeat at **Espinosa** and, two days later, found his retreat in Castile cut off

at Reynosa by Marshal Nicolas Soult, marching north from his victory at **Gamonal**. Blake's survivors were beaten again and General Pedro La Romana was appointed in his place (13 November 1808).

Rezonville ▮ 1870 ▮ Franco-Prussian War
See **Mars-la-Tour**

R'Fakha ▮ 1908 ▮ French Colonial Wars in North Africa
Five weeks after failure east of Casablanca at **Wadi M'Koun**, General Albert d'Amade was patrolling along the wadi and unwisely sent Colonel Luigné's cavalry across the river, where they were heavily ambushed on R'Fakha Ridge, losing 12 killed and 25 wounded. The main force drove the Moroccans off and the following month d'Amade attacked a camp at **Bou Nouala** (29 February 1908).

Rhandeia ▮ 62 ▮ Later Roman-Parthian Wars
See **Arsanias**

Rheims ▮ 356 ▮ Alemannic Invasion of Roman Gaul
Flavius Claudius Julianus, cousin of the Emperor Constantius, attempted to recover western territory from the Franks and Alemanni, crossing into Gaul while the Emperor was advancing up the Rhine. Marching out of camp at Rheims, the small Roman army was attacked by Alemanni tribesmen, who inflicted heavy casualties on the rearguard before Julianus was able to recover. He soon won at **Sens**.

Rheims ▮ 1359–1360 ▮ Hundred Years War
On his last campaign into France, Edward III of England marched from Calais to besiege Rheims, defended by Gaucher de Châtillon Comte de Porcien. Supported by Henry of Lancaster and Edward Prince of Wales, the King captured nearby towns, although Rheims held out. Edward eventually withdrew but imposed a hard peace on France (4 December 1359–15 March 1360).

Rheims I 1814 I Napoleonic Wars (French Campaign)

Napoleon Bonaparte withdrew northeast through Soissons following defeat at **Laon**, then marched to recapture Rheims, which had fallen after the battle to an independent Russian-Prussian force under General George St Priest. Bonaparte inflicted heavy casualties retaking Rheims, but it is regarded as his last real victory. He abandoned the city days later after French defeat at **Fismes** (13 March 1814).

Rheims I 1918 I World War I (Western Front)

See **Marne**

Rheinberg I 1945 I World War II (Western Europe)

See **Wesel**

Rheinfelden I 1638 I Thirty Years War (Franco-Habsburg War)

Crossing the Rhine into Alsace, advance units under Bernard of Saxe-Weimar were heavily repulsed east of Basel at Rheinfelden by Imperial General Johann von Werth and Count Friedrich von Savelli, with Duke Henry of Rohan killed. A second advance saw Bernard himself win a decisive victory—capturing Werth and Savelli—and he marched on towards **Breisach** (28 February & 2 March 1638).

Rhineland I 1945 I World War II (Western Europe)

After breaching the **Siegfried Line** and repulsing German counter-attacks in the **Ardennes** and **Alsace**, the Allied offensive resumed in the Rhineland to clear the **Colmar Pocket** and advance through the **Reichswald**. The Germans were driven back behind the Rhine with 50,000 killed and 250,000 captured and the Allies crossed at **Remagen** and **Wesel** (8 February–21 March 1945).

Rhode Island I 1778 I War of the American Revolution

American General John Sullivan landed on Rhode Island to besiege **Newport** then secured Butts Hill, at the northern end of the island, where he was later counter-attacked by General Sir Robert Pigot. Sullivan repulsed the assault at nearby Quaker Hill, but with major British reinforcements arriving he abandoned his campaign and returned to Providence (29 August 1778).

Rhodes I 305–304 BC I Wars of the Diadochi

In war among the successors of Alexander the Great, Demetrius Poliorcetes, son of Antigonus, seized Cyprus from Ptolemy of Egypt with victory at **Salamis** (306 BC) then tried to capture Rhodes, which was supported by Ptolemy. Demetrius landed with a massive force and advanced siege equipment, but after two years and costly losses, he could make no impression against heroic defence and withdrew.

Rhodes I 88 BC I 1st Mithridatic War

King Mithridates VI of Pontus renewed his expansion in Asia Minor, where he reportedly massacred 80,000 Roman and Italian residents, then led a force against Rhodes. Despite initial repulse at sea by the Rhodian navy, Mithridates landed but failed to take the city by storm and withdrew. His forces later lost in Greece at **Piraeus**, **Chaeronea** and **Orchomenus**, and he soon sued for peace.

Rhodes I 654 I Early Byzantine-Muslim Wars

See **Mount Phoenix**

Rhodes I 1310 I Later Crusader-Muslim Wars

Following Crusader withdrawal from the Holy Land, the Knights Hospitallier of St John of Jerusalem under Grandmaster Fulke de Villaret assaulted the Byzantine island of Rhodes, off Asia Minor, disputed between Byzantines and Turks. The knights gradually secured the island and held it as a Christian outpost until they were defeated and expelled by the Turks in 1522 (15 August 1310).

Rhodes I 1480 I Turkish Imperial Wars

Ottoman Sultan Mehmed II made peace with Venice then ordered Masih Pasha against the

Aegean island of Rhodes, held by the Knights of St John under Grand Master Pierre d'Aubusson. Using massive siege guns, the Turks forced their way into the town, but an unwise order against looting led the troops to withdraw and the Grand Vizier had to give up the siege (23 May–20 August 1480).

Rhodes I 1522 I Turkish Imperial Wars

After 200 years on the Aegean island of Rhodes, with a heavy siege repulsed in 1480, the Knights of St John faced a massive expedition by Ottoman Sultan Suleiman I. Five months of siege saw terrible losses on both sides before Grand Master Philip de l'Isle Adam was starved into surrender. The knights were permitted to evacuate and eventually moved to **Malta** (28 July–21 December 1522).

Rhodes I 1912 I Italo-Turkish War

See **Dardanelles**

Rhyndacus I 1211 I 1st Latin-Byzantine Imperial War

Byzantine Emperor Theodore Lascaris in Nicaea defeated the Seljuk Turks of Rum and their Latin allies in southwest Anatolia at **Antioch**, then later that year met Latin Emperor Henry in the north at the Rhyndacus (modern Kemalpasa) near Bursa, where Henry won a great victory. When the rivals finally made peace and divided Asia Minor, the Latins secured northwest Anatolia (15 October 1211).

Riachuelo I 1865 I War of the Triple Alliance

In a bold assault across the Parana River, President Francisco Solano Lopéz of Paraguay sent his fleet under Captain Pedro Ignacio Meza against Brazilian Admiral Francisco Manuel Barroso at Riachuelo, near **Corrientes**, Argentina. While the Brazilians suffered heavy losses, Meza was mortally wounded and defeated. The Paraguayan invaders soon lost again at **Yatay** (11 June 1865).

Riade I 933 I Magyar Invasion of Germany

German Emperor Henry I broke a truce with the Magyar horsemen of Hungary and launched a large-scale counter-offensive, attacking the invaders on the Unstrut at Riade (modern Rothenburg). For the first time, the seemingly invincible Hungarians were routed, suffering massive casualties. They did not re-enter Germany until 20 years later, when they were routed at **Lechfeld** (15 March 933).

Rice's Station I 1865 I American Civil War (Eastern Theatre)

While Confederates retreating from **Petersburg**, Virginia, surrendered at **Sayler's Creek**, others under General James Longstreet reached Rice's Station, a few miles south, where they were blocked by Union forces led by General John Gibbon. Scattered fighting forced Longstreet to withdraw northwest towards **High Bridge** on the Appomattox River (6 April 1865).

Richmond, Kentucky I 1862 I American Civil War (Western Theatre)

At the start of the Confederate offensive into Kentucky, General Edmund Kirby Smith marched north from Tennessee and met a Union force under General William Nelson, southeast of Louisville at Richmond. Nelson was routed in a bloody action, losing over 4,000 men captured. Meanwhile the main Confederate army advanced further west through **Munfordville** (29–30 August 1862).

Richmond, Virginia I 1781 I War of the American Revolution

Determined to destroy American supplies in Virginia, British troops led by the Loyalist General Benedict Arnold secured the battery at Hood's Point near Jamestown (3 January) and marched towards Richmond on the James River, which was under the nominal command of Governor Thomas Jefferson. Arnold burned warehouses and buildings then withdrew to Portsmouth (5–7 January 1781).

Rich Mountain ▮ 1861 ▮ American Civil War (Eastern Theatre)

In the first full-scale action in West Virginia after the skirmish at **Philippi**, Union Generals George B. McClellan and William S. Rosecrans attacked and heavily defeated Colonel John Pegram's Confederates at Rich Mountain, just northwest of Beverly. Pegram and over 500 men surrendered and General Robert S. Garnett was pursued and killed two days later at Corrick's Ford (11 July 1861).

Ridanieh ▮ 1517 ▮ Ottoman-Mamluk War

Ottoman Sultan Selim I advanced into Egypt after victory at **Yaunis Khan** (October 1516) and was blocked outside Cairo by Mamluk Sultan Touman Beg. The Mamluks were defeated in a desperately hard-fought battle at Ridanieh, though Selim's Vizier, Hadim Sinan, was killed. Selim then ravaged nearby Cairo and later executed Touman, ending Egypt's Mamluk Dynasty (22 January 1517).

Ridgefield ▮ 1777 ▮ War of the American Revolution

See **Danbury Raid**

Ridisiya ▮ 1799 ▮ French Revolutionary Wars (Middle East)

See **Er Ridisiya**

Rietfontein ▮ 1899 ▮ 2nd Anglo-Boer War

As General James Yule withdrew from **Talana Hill**, General Sir George White came out from Ladysmith to cover the British retreat and attacked a Boer interception force about eight miles north at Rietfontein. White lost about 100 men in an indecisive action and withdrew to **Ladysmith**. However, Yule's force was saved and days later White led an offensive at **Nicholson's Nek** (24 October 1899).

Rieti ▮ 1821 ▮ Italian Revolt against Austria

After an army revolt to depose Ferdinand IV of Naples, General Guglielmo Pepe's 10,000 Neapolitans faced a massive Austrian army of about 80,000 under Count Johann Maria Frimont. At Rieti, northwest of Rome, Pepe was crushed and banished. A further Austrian victory at **Novara** in April saw the King restored as Ferdinand I of the Two Sicilies (7 March 1821).

Riga ▮ 1617 ▮ 2nd Polish-Swedish War

On a fresh offensive in Livonia, a small Swedish force under Nils Stiernskold secured Dunamunde then captured the strategic Duna Redoubt outside Riga. However, the hesitant Stiernskold failed to press his attack against Riga and the Redoubt was retaken by the city's militia army. Stiernskold later changed sides to join Polish commander Krystof Radziwill (23 July–September 1617).

Riga ▮ 1621 ▮ 2nd Polish-Swedish War

Renewing war against Poland in Livonia, Gustavus Adolphus of Sweden invaded with 14,000 men and besieged Riga (in modern Latvia). A weak relief attempt by Polish General Krystof Radziwill was driven off (30 August) and after the garrison had repulsed three heavy Swedish assaults, the great fortress capitulated. It remained Swedish for nearly 90 years (1 August–15 September 1621).

Riga ▮ 1656 ▮ Russo-Swedish Wars

While Sweden was attacking Poland at **Warsaw**, Tsar Alexius entered Swedish-occupied Livonia, where he and Prince Yakov Kudenetovich seized several cities before being blocked at Riga (in modern Latvia). When Swedish reinforcements arrived, Magnus de la Gardie led a bloody sortie which caused very heavy Russian losses, forcing the Tsar to withdraw (July–August 1656).

Riga ▮ 1700 ▮ 2nd "Great" Northern War

See **Jungfernhof**

Riga ▮ 1701 ▮ 2nd "Great" Northern War

Charles XII of Sweden followed his great victory over Russia at **Narva** (November 1700) by marching into Livonia to relieve Riga, under siege by a Russian-Polish-Saxon force under

Augustus II, Elector of Saxony and King of Poland. The besieging force was defeated after sharp fighting and Riga did not fall to Russia until 1710, when starvation forced the city into submission (17 June 1701).

Riga ∎ 1709–1710 ∎ 2nd "Great" Northern War

With the Swedish army destroyed at **Poltava** (July 1709), Tsar Peter I sent General Boris Sheremetev into Livonia to besiege Riga. After eight months, with massive losses to disease on both sides and the city pounded by a reported 8,000 Russian shells, the garrison of almost 5,000 surrendered and Sweden was finally expelled from Estonia and Livonia (December 1709–10 July 1710).

Riga ∎ 1916 ∎ World War I (Eastern Front)

As part of the Russian offensive around **Lake Naroch**, at the northern end of the Eastern Front, General Aleksei Kuropatkin attempted a subsidiary advance against Riga (in modern Latvia). The Russians lost over 10,000 men in the first few days for very little gain and, by the end of April, Colonel Georg Bruchmüller's counterattack had retaken all lost ground (21 March–30 April 1916).

Riga ∎ 1917 ∎ World War I (Eastern Front)

In the final Russo-German battle of the war, General Oskar von Hutier followed up the destruction of the **Kerensky Offensive** with a large-scale attack in the north around Riga. A few days of fighting saw General Valdislav Klembovsky driven out and the front smashed open. Russia's government quickly collapsed and the new Communist leaders sued for peace (1–3 September 1917).

Riga (1st) ∎ 1919 ∎ Latvian War of Independence

Shortly after revolution in Russia, Karlis Ulmanis formed an independent Latvian government but was forced out of Riga by Red Army units (3 January 1919). German General Rudiger

von der Goltz then took command and his German and Latvian troops defeated and repulsed the Russians. However, after defeat further north at **Cesis** in June, Goltz had to withdraw from Riga (22 May 1919).

Riga (2nd) ∎ 1919 ∎ Latvian War of Independence

Despite Germany abandoning Riga after defeat at **Cesis**, German volunteers under Colonel Pavel Bermondt-Avalov renewed the attack on the city. Aided by Estonian troops and Anglo-French naval forces, Latvian General Janis Balodis eventually repulsed the Bermondtists. A subsequent treaty with the Soviet Russia secured recognition of Latvian independence (8 October–10 November 1919).

Riga ∎ 1944 ∎ World War II (Eastern Front)

With German Army Group Centre destroyed at **Minsk** and **Vilna**, Soviet Generals Ivan Bagramyan and Andrei Yeremenko converged on Army Group North in Latvia, where General Ferdinand Schörner counter-attacked strongly. However, he was forced back and the Russians seized Riga, while the Germans evacuated to the Courland Peninsula (14 September–13 October 1944).

Rijeka ∎ 1862 ∎ Turko-Montenegran Wars

Omar Pasha led a fresh Turkish invasion of Montenegro and was briefly held off at the Monastery of Ostrog by the Regent Mirko Petrovich and just a handful of men. Withdrawing towards Cetinje, Mirko attempted to make a stand to the east at Rijeka Crnojevica and was heavily defeated. The Powers once again intervened and the subsequent peace saw the Regent banished (23 August 1862).

Rimini ∎ 1944 ∎ World War II (Southern Europe)

In the largest battle of the Italian campaign, the British Eighth Army under General Sir Oliver Leese attacked the Adriatic end of the **Gothic Line** towards the key city of Rimini, defended by General Heinrich von Vietinghoff.

Severe fighting saw Leese eventually break through the line to seize Rimini, while further west the Americans stalled at **Bologna** (25 August–20 September 1944).

Rimnic Sarat I 1916 I World War I (Balkan Front)

Driven out of **Bucharest**, Romanian commander Alexandru Averescu, with Russian support, attempted to hold Rimnic Sarat to the northeast. A massive assault by Erich von Falkenhayn smashed through the front and the Allies withdrew into Moldavia. The line stabilised along the Sareth until a Russo-Romanian counter-offensive in August 1917 towards **Maracesti** (22–27 December 1916).

Rimnik I 1789 I Catherine the Great's 2nd Turkish War

Following Turkish defeat at **Focsani** in July, Vizier Yusuf Pasha gathered a massive force against Russian General Alexander Suvorov and Austrian Prince Friedrich Josias of Saxe-Coburg. On the Rimnik near Martinesti (modern Maicanesti, Romania), the Turkish army was virtually destroyed. The Turks retreated to the Danube and Suvorov was created Count Rimnikski (11 September 1789).

Rincón de los Toros I 1819 I Venezuelan War of Independence

Patriot leader Simón Bolívar recovered after **La Puerta** to secure tactical victory at **Queseras del Medio**, but was attacked in camp at Rincón de los Toros, northwest of Calabozo near San José, where an assassination attempt was foiled. Although Spanish commander Colonel Rafael Lopez was killed in the attack, Bolívar's infantry was virtually destroyed and he fled to Calabozo (16 April 1819).

Rincón de Vences I 1847 I Argentine Civil Wars

When the northeastern province of Corrientes formed an alliance with Paraguay, Argentine Dictator Manuel de Rosas sent Justo José de Urquiza against his former ally Joaquín Madariaga. Southeast of Corrientes at Rincón de Vences, Urquiza secured a decisive victory. His troops looted then destroyed the town of General Paz and Madariaga fled to Brazil (27 November 1847).

Rineen I 1920 I Anglo-Irish War

In a well-known typical guerrilla action against Britain in Ireland, Republicans avenging the murder of Martin Devitt ambushed a Royal Irish Constabulary (Black and Tan) lorry at Dromin Hill, Rineen, in County Clare to capture rifles and ammunition. After initial success, the heavily outnumbered IRA met and defeated reinforcements and got away with their booty (22 September 1920).

Ringgold Gap I 1863 I American Civil War (Western Theatre)

Union commander Joseph Hooker broke out of besieged **Chattanooga**, Tennessee, with victory at **Missionary Ridge** and set off southeast after the Confederates. At Ringgold Gap, on Taylor's Ridge, he ran into a brilliant rearguard action by General Patrick Cleburne, aided by Generals Lucius E. Polk and Mark P. Lowery. Their courage helped the Confederate army to get away (27 November 1863).

Ríobambo I 1822 I Ecuadorian War of Independence

As fighting continued in southwestern Colombia after **Bomboná** (7 April), Patriot leader Simón Bolívar ordered General Antonio José de Sucre to Quito in northern Ecuador. North from Guayaquil, de Sucre advanced across the Cordillera of El Azuay and led a brilliant assault on the city of Ríobambo. He then continued north towards Quito and the key action on 24 May at **Pichincha** (21 April 1822).

Rio Barbate I 711 I Muslim Conquest of Spain
See **Guadalete**

Rio Caliente I 1854 I Apache Indian Wars

Days after ambushing government troops at **Cieneguilla** in northern New Mexico, 150 Jicarilla Apache under Chacon ambushed another pursuing force under Captain James Quinn at Rio Caliente, a tributary of the Chamba. However, troops under Colonel Philip Cooke counter-attacked and Chacon fled, having lost five killed, six wounded and all his equipment and ponies (8 April 1854).

Rio Cuarto I 1831 I Argentine Civil Wars

Despite defeat at **La Tablada** (1829) and **Oncativo** (1830), Federalist leader Juan Facundo Quiroga again invaded Córdoba, where he decisively defeated the local Unitarists Juan Pascual Pringles and Juan Gualbert Echevarria at Rio Cuarto. Pringles was captured and shot ten days later at Rio Quinto by a band under Ruiz Huidobro. Quiroga then marched to **Rodeo de Chacón** (9 March 1831).

Rio de Janeiro I 1710 I War of the Spanish Succession

Attacking Portuguese territory in Brazil, French Captain Jean-Francois du Clerc landed near Rio de Janeiro, held by Governor Francisco de Castro de Moràes. Heavily outnumbered by a large Portuguese and local force, du Clerc was defeated and captured along with about 700 of his men. He was subsequently murdered and most of his troops died in captivity (6 August–18 September 1710).

Rio de Janeiro I 1711 I War of the Spanish Succession

Admiral René Duguay-Trouin was determined to avenge a French disaster at Rio de Janeiro, arriving the following year with eight ships and 2,800 men. After a brilliant attack, Portuguese Admiral Gaspar da Costa Ataide scuttled his fleet and Governor Francisco de Castro de Moràes surrendered the city. The French then sacked Rio and withdrew with a vast treasure (12–20 September 1711).

Riofrio I 1841 I Colombian War of Supreme Commanders

Amid continued fighting in southern Colombia, government troops under General Joaquín Posada Gutiérrez, supported by Manuel María Franco, met rebel forces led by Colonel Pedro Antonio Sánchez in Huila at Riofrio, east of Popayán. Sánchez suffered a heavy defeat and he was killed two months later in the bloody rebel rout at **La Chanca** (4–5 May 1841).

Rionegro I 1851 I Colombian Civil Wars

Facing Conservative rebellion, government forces loyal to President José Hilario López won in the south at **Buesaco**, then General Tomás Herrera secured the Cauca Valley and advanced north into Antioquia against rebel General Eusebio Borrero. Just southwest of Medellín at Rionegro, Borrero suffered a crushing defeat and the rising was effectively over (10 September 1851).

Río Piedras I 1812 I Argentine War of Independence

Patriot General Manuel Belgrano was ordered to withdraw from Upper Peru towards Córdoba, but his rearguard surprised advance units of General Pío Tristán's pursuing Spanish army at Río Piedras, southeast of Salta near Metan. Colonel Eustoquio Díaz Vélez routed the Royalists in a brilliant cavalry action, encouraging Belgrano to make a stand at **Tucumán** (3 September 1812).

Rio Salado I 1340 I Later Christian Reconquest of Spain

A large-scale Muslim offensive in southern Spain saw the Nasrid Emir Yusuf I of Granada reinforced by fresh troops from Morocco to besiege Tarifa, on the Strait of Gibraltar. Supported by Alfonso IV of Portugal, Alfonso XI of Castile led a large Christian army to the relief of the city. To the west at the Rio Salado they gained a brilliant victory, repulsing the Muslim advance (30 October 1340).

Río Seco, Argentina I 1821 I Argentine Civil Wars

During confused fighting in northwest Argentina, Francisco Ramirez of Entre Rios marched into Córdoba against Juan Bautista Bustos and was attacked on the Río Seco near San Francisco by soldiers of the Bustos ally Estanislao López of Santa Fe. Escaping after defeat, Ramirez returned for his lover Delfina and was captured and shot, ending years of inter-provincial war (10 July 1821).

Rio Seco, Spain I 1808 I Napoleonic Wars (Peninsular Campaign)
See **Medina del Rio Seco**

Rippach I 1813 I Napoleonic Wars (War of Liberation)
In a prelude to Napoleon Bonaparte's great battle at **Lützen**, units of the advancing French army were blocked by the Allies between the villages of Rippach and Poserna, east of Weissenfels. Marshal Jean-Baptiste Bessières was killed outright by a cannonball in the course of a sharp action, though the French continued east for the battle next day at **Lützen** (1 May 1813).

Ripple Field I 1643 I British Civil Wars
Advancing across the Severn into Gloucestershire, Royalist commander Prince Maurice encountered Parliamentarians Sir William Waller and Sir Edward Massey returning from capturing Tewkesbury. Waller had been repulsed the previous day at Little Dean and, just north of Tewkesbury at Ripple Field, Maurice inflicted a sharp defeat on the Puritans (13 April 1643).

Rivas I 1855 I National (Filibuster) War
Amid ongoing war between the Liberal and Legitimist parties in Nicaragua, the Liberals sought aid from the American Filibuster William Walker, who attempted to invade from Costa Rica with 55 Americans and about 100 Indian allies. His heavily outnumbered force was badly beaten near Rivas and in September Legitimist troops attacked him in camp at **La Virgen** (29 June 1855).

Rivas I 1856 I National (Filibuster) War
American adventurer William Walker was driven out of Costa Rica after defeat at **Santa Rosa** (20 March) and President Juan Rafael Mora and General Jose Maria Cañas pursued the Filibusters back to Rivas in Nicaragua. Walker

was beaten in an action, which created the boy-martyr Juan Santamaria. The Central American Republics soon formed an alliance and drove him out of **Masaya** (11 April 1856).

Rivas I 1857 I National (Filibuster) War
Pursuing American Filibuster William Walker through western Nicaragua, Central American alliance commander José Maria Cañas defended **San Jorge** then attacked Walker at nearby Rivas. After costly Allied losses in a failed assault (11 April), Walker destroyed his stores and surrendered to the US Navy. In 1860 he returned from America to seize **Trujillo** in Honduras (23 March–1 May 1857).

River of Blood I 633 I Muslim Conquest of Iraq
See **Ullais**

River Plate I 1939 I World War II (War at Sea)
After sinking nine merchant ships, the German pocket battleship *Graf Spee* was pursued and attacked off the River Plate by Commodore Henry Harwood's cruiser squadron. The outgunned British ships suffered heavy damage before driving *Graf Spee* into neutral Uruguay. Three days later, Captain Hans Langsdorf scuttled his ship off Montevideo and committed suicide (13 December 1939).

Rivers' Bridge I 1865 I American Civil War (Western Theatre)
As Union commander William T. Sherman began his march across the Carolinas, his right wing under General Francis P. Blair was blocked at Rivers' Bridge, on the Salkehatchie just east of **Savannah**, South Carolina. Facing a dangerous flank attack, Confederate General Lafayette McLaws retreated north towards Branchville and Sherman continued on through Columbia (3 February 1865).

Riviera I 1944 I World War II (Western Europe)
Six weeks after the Allied invasion of **Normandy**, American General Lucian Truscott

invaded southern France along the Riviera between Cannes and St Tropez, where almost
100,000 men were landed for fewer than 100
killed. Truscott then raced up the Rhone Valley
through **Montélimar** and **Montrevel**, while
French forces swung west towards **Marseilles**
and **Toulon** (15 August 1944).

Rivoli I 1797 I French Revolutionary Wars (1st Coalition)

A fourth attempt to relieve the French siege of
Mantua saw a fresh Austrian army under Baron
Josef Alvinzi advance down the Adige Valley. A
complex battle east of Lake Garda at Rivoli saw
Napoleon Bonaparte and General André Masséna smash the Austrians, inflicting heavy losses
in casualties and prisoners. Mantua surrendered
two weeks later (14 January 1797).

Rivolta I 1509 I War of the League of Cambrai

See **Agnadello**

Riyadh I 1887 I Saudi-Rashidi Wars

During the destructive struggle between the
sons of Faisal ibn Saud of Riyadh, the sons of
Saud ibn Faisal seized Riyadh and imprisoned
their Uncle Emir Abd Allah, who appealed for
aid to Muhammad ibn Rashid of Hail. Riyadh
fell after a siege and the rebels withdrew. Abd
Allah was taken prisoner to Hail and Al Rashid
was appointed governor, effectively conquering
the Wahhabi state.

Riyadh I 1891 I Saudi-Rashidi Wars

See **Mulaydah**

Riyadh I 1902 I Saudi-Rashidi Wars

Ten years after Abd al-Rahman was driven out
of Riyadh by Rashidi victory at **Mulaydah**, his
young son Abd al-Aziz (Ibn Saud) and 40
companions returned to the city. In one of Saudi
Arabia's most celebrated military exploits, they
seized the fortress of Musmak, killing Governor
Ajlam. In November, Abd al-Aziz defeated a
Rashid counter-attack south of Riyadh at **Dilam**
(16 January 1902).

Roanoke Island I 1862 I American Civil War (Eastern Theatre)

Union General Ambrose E. Burnside opened
his coastal expedition against North Carolina by
landing over 7,000 men on Confederate Roa-
noke Island, defended by General Henry Wise
and Senator Colonel Henry M. Shaw. During a
bold action of manoeuvre, Burnside forced the
surrender of more than 2,500 men and over 30
guns, then sailed south to attack **New Bern** (7–8
February 1862).

Roanoke River I 1864 I American Civil War (Eastern Theatre)

See **Albermarle Sound**

Roan's Tan Yard I 1862 I American Civil War (Trans-Mississippi)

Determined to secure northeastern Missouri,
Union Major William M. G. Torrence marched
against the Confederate camp at Roan's Tan Yard,
on Silver Creek northwest of Fayette, where
Colonel John A. Poindexter was reinforced by
survivors from **Mount Zion Church**. Poindexter
was routed, losing over 100 men and valuable
supplies, then fled under the cover of fog (8 January 1862).

Roble I 1813 I Chilean War of Independence

When Chileans under Bernardo O'Higgins
and José Miguel Carrera attacked the Royalist
stronghold at Chillan, Spanish commander
Francisco Sanchez sent Juan Antonio Olate to
take the Patriots in the rear. Badly surprised at
Roble on the Itata, Carrera was rescued from
defeat by O'Higgins and his brother Juan José
Carrera, who rallied the troops for victory (17
October 1813).

Roche-Derrien I 1347 I Hundred Years War

In the continuing struggle for the Dukedom
of Brittany, Charles of Blois besieged Roche-
Derrien, on the Jaudy, captured a year earlier by
Sir Thomas Dagworth before he defeated Blois
at **St Pol de Léon**. English Governor Richard

Totsham held out until Dagworth arrived with a relief force and routed the French. Blois was captured wounded and taken to the Tower of London (20 June 1347).

Rochensalm I 1790 I 2nd Russo-Swedish War

See **Svenskund**

Rochester I 1088 I Norman Dynastic Wars

Following the death of William the Conqueror, his half-brother Odo raised rebellion for his nephew Robert of Normandy against new King William II Rufus. Having surrendered **Pevensey**, Odo undertook to yield his main fortress at Rochester, then refused to do so. Rufus took the castle by storm to end the rebellion. Odo returned to Normandy and died in 1097 on Crusade (May 1088).

Rochester I 1215 I 1st English Barons' War

Soon after forcing King John of England to sign the Magna Carta, his Barons rebelled and William d'Aubigny of Belvoir seized Rochester Castle on the Medway in Kent, where he was forced to surrender after seven weeks' siege by John's army. The King's forces defeated his opponents again at **Dover**, but John died before the Royalist victory in 1217 at **Lincoln** (11 October–30 November 1215).

Rochester I 1264 I 2nd English Barons' War

Henry III and his son Prince Edward faced rebellion by Simon de Montfort Earl of Leicester and defeated the Earl's son Simon the Younger at **Northampton**. They then marched to Rochester, where de Montfort and Gilbert Earl of Gloucester had taken the town and besieged the castle. The rebels were defeated but later renewed the siege, leading to the decisive battle at **Lewes** in May (April 1264).

Rockcastle Hills I 1861 I American Civil War (Western Theatre)

See **Camp Wild Cat**

Rock Island Rapids I 1814 I War of 1812

Soon after British forces recovered Fort Shelby at **Prairie du Chien**, 400 Sauk, Fox and Kickapoo Indians pursued the American gunboat *Governor Clark* down the Mississippi. At Rock Island Rapids they attacked a relief force approaching too late under Captain John Campbell, who suffered 35 casualties and heavy damage to his boats and was forced to return to St Louis (July 1814).

Rock River I 1832 I Black Hawk Indian War

With Sauk Chief Black Hawk raiding east of the Mississippi, Generals Henry Atkinson and Samuel Whiteside sent advance units under Major Isaiah Stillman, who opened fire on a truce party on the Rock River, south of Rockford, Illinois. Attacking Black Hawk and just 40 warriors, the 275 militiamen lost 12 killed and fled. Black Hawk was later repulsed at the **Pecatonica** (14 May 1832).

Rocky Face Ridge I 1864 I American Civil War (Western Theatre)

At the start of his offensive through Georgia towards **Atlanta**, Union commander William T. Sherman marched southeast from **Chattanooga** against General Joseph E. Johnston's Confederate army along the well-defended Rocky Face Ridge. While Sherman suffered heavy losses in repeated attacks, Johnston eventually abandoned nearby Dalton and withdrew south to **Resaca** (8–11 May 1864).

Rocky Mount I 1780 I War of the American Revolution

Rebel Colonel Thomas Sumter was encouraged by success at **Williamson's Plantation** (12 July) and advanced on the British outpost at Rocky Mount, South Carolina, northwest of their main base at **Camden**. Attempting to storm a well-defended position held by Tory militia under Colonel George Turnbull, Sumter was repulsed and instead turned east against **Hanging Rock** (1 August 1780).

Rocoux I 1747 I War of the Austrian Succession

With Prussia out of the war, Prince Charles of Lorraine took his Austrian army against France in the Netherlands, where he and his Dutch allies came under attack by Marshal Maurice de Saxe at Rocoux, just north of Liège. The Austrian Prince was defeated with over 5,000 casualties. Despite the return of his English allies, he lost again the following year at **Lauffeld** (11 October 1746).

Rocroi I 1643 I Thirty Years War (Franco-Habsburg War)

General Francisco de Mello invaded France from the Spanish Netherlands and besieged Rocroi, west of the Meuse near Mézières. Attacked by a French relief force under 22-year-old Louis II Duke d'Enghien, the Spanish infantry suffered one of its most decisive defeats, with a reported 8,000 killed and 7,000 captured. Louis then marched southeast against **Thionville** (19 May 1643).

Roda I 1812 I Napoleonic Wars (Peninsular Campaign)

As French General Honoré Rielle campaigned to secure Catalonia, he sent General Jean Raymond Bourke against Baron Jaime Eroles, who had taken a strong defensive position at Roda, near the Noguera Ribagorzana, north of Lérida. Despite much greater numbers, Bourke was heavily repulsed in an unwise frontal assault and Eroles continued to divert Rielle's offensive (5 March 1812).

Rodeo de Chacón I 1831 I Argentine Civil Wars

Federalist leader Juan Facundo Quiroga recovered from defeat at **La Tablada** and **Oncativo** to win in Córdoba at **Rio Cuarto** (9 March), then marched west into Mendoza against Unitarist Governor José Videla Castilla. Near Las Catitas at Rodeo de Chacón, Videla Castilla suffered a decisive defeat and fled to Bolivia, while Quiroga won again in November at **La Ciudadela** (28 March 1831).

Rodeo del Medio I 1841 I Argentine Civil Wars

Shortly after Unitarist defeat at **Famaillá**, another force opposed to Dictator Manuel de Rosas under General Gregorio Araoz Lamadrid attempted to march into Mendoza and was caught at Rodeo del Medio, southeast of Mendoza, by converging Rosas armies under Generals Angel Pacheco, José Felix Aldao, and Juan Antonio Benavídez. Lamadrid was routed and fled to Chile (24 September 1841).

Rogensalm I 1789 I 2nd Russo-Swedish War

See **Svenskund**

Rohilla I 1621 I Early Mughal-Sikh Wars

An early campaign against the growing influence of the Sikhs saw 4,000 Mughal troops sent to northern Punjab to support local Governor Abdul Khan against Guru Hargobind. Although Sikh General Jattu died in heavy fighting northeast of Amritsar at Rohilla, Abdul Khan was defeated and killed, along with his sons Nabi Bakhsh and Karim Bakhsh, greatly enhancing the Sikh cause.

Rohtas I 1795 I Punjab Campaigns of Shah Zaman

Shah Zaman of Kabul advanced into the Punjab and seized Hassan Abdal, then attacked the fortress of Rohtas, near the Jhelum, held by the young Sikh leader Ranjit Singh. After failing to gain Maratha support, the Sikhs fled to the hills and Shah Zaman seized Rohtas. However, he was later forced to return home to deal with threatened insurrection (November–December 1795).

Roi-Namur I 1944 I World War II (Pacific)

Opening the offensive in the **Marshall Islands**, General Harry Schmidt attacked Roi and Namur, on the northern edge of the massive **Kwajalein** Atoll. The twin islets, joined by a causeway, were taken after heavy fighting, which cost over 750 Marine casualties. The Japanese lost about 3,500, many of them in the massive preliminary bombardment (1–3 February 1944).

Rokuhara I 1160 I Heiji War

Minamoto Yoshitomo helped suppress a coup at **Shirakawa** (1156) then joined Fujiwara Nobuyori to seize Japan's Imperial Palace at Kyoto, capturing Emperor Nijo and murdering Counsellor Fujiwara Michinori. Just southeast of Kyoto at Rokuhara, Taira Kiyomori crushed the rising and killed both rebels, reasserting Taira power until the disaster in 1185 at **Dannoura** (4 February 1160).

Rolica I 1808 I Napoleonic Wars (Peninsular Campaign)

When a British force under General Sir Arthur Wellesley landed at Mondego Bay in central Portugal, French General Androche Junot sent General Henri Delaborde to delay the invasion while he concentrated his forces north of Lisbon. The heavily outnumbered French were beaten in a courageous action at Rolica before withdrawing south in good order to join Junot at **Vimeiro** (17 August 1808).

Romagnano I 1524 I 1st Habsburg-Valois War

See **Sesia**

Romainville I 1814 I Napoleonic Wars (French Campaign)

See **Paris**

Romani I 1916 I World War I (Middle East)

A large German-Turk army under Colonel Friedrich von Kressenstein, advancing west towards the Suez Canal, retook **Katia** and threatened Romani. After a confused assault, Australian and New Zealand forces under General Harry Chauvel counter-attacked and the Turks were driven off with about 8,000 casualties. They then fell back through **Magdhaba** and **Rafa** to Palestine (4–5 August 1916).

Romanov I 1812 I Napoleonic Wars (Russian Campaign)

At the beginning of Napoleon Bonaparte's advance into Russia, Polish cavalry leading General Marie Latour-Mauberge's Corps were ambushed southwest of Minsk at Romanov (modern Dzerzhinsk) by Cossack General Matvei Platov, who had been driven off further west

at **Mir**. The Poles lost over 200 men before the main force arrived and the Russians withdrew (15 July 1812).

Rome I 505 BC I Early Roman-Etruscan Wars

This semi-legendary battle saw Lars Porsena, King of Clusium, besiege Rome in support of the deposed last Roman King, Tarquinius. At the nearby hill of Janiculum, the outnumbered Romans were driven back across the Tiber, their escape made possible by the mythic defence of the bridge by Horatius Cocles. Some historians now believe Lars Porsena went on to capture the city (trad date 505 BC).

Rome I 408–410 I Goth Invasion of the Roman Empire

Following the murder of the great Roman-Vandal General Stilicho, Alaric the Visigoth led a new invasion of Italy and besieged Rome. With nearby **Ostia** captured (409) and the breakdown of negotiations with Emperor Honorius, Alaric seized Rome and put it to the sack. However, he died soon afterwards and his brother-in-law Ataulf took the Goths against Roman Gaul (408–24 August 410).

Rome I 455 I Roman-Vandal Wars

With the Western Empire unstable following the murder of Valentinian, his widow Eudoxia sought aid from the Vandal King Gaiseric against the murderer and usurper Petronius Maximus. Arriving from **Carthage**, Gaiseric attacked Rome itself. Petronius Maximus was killed and the Vandals sacked and plundered the city before returning with Eudoxia to North Africa (2–16 June 455).

Rome I 472 I Fall of the Western Roman Empire

The Suevic king-maker Ricimer established Anthemius as Emperor, then fell out with his nominee and attacked Rome, supported by Burgundian allies and the German Odoacer. Rome fell after five months of siege and defeat of a relief army from Gaul under Bilimer. Anthemius was killed, but Ricimer also died soon afterwards.

After years of chaos Odoacer won at **Pavia** in 476 to secure Italy.

Rome ∎ 537–538 ∎ Gothic War in Italy

A yearlong defence of Rome saw General Belisarius hold out against a massive army under the Goth King Witiges. The Goths suffered costly losses in attacks and counter-attacks during the siege and, when heavy Roman reinforcements arrived from the east, Witiges withdrew under siege to his capital at **Ravenna** (1 March 537–12 March 538).

Rome ∎ 545–546 ∎ Gothic War in Italy

During the fresh Goth offensive in Italy, which began under their new King Totila, Rome changed hands several times. However, the key campaign began in May 545 when Totila imposed a renewed siege of the city. After driving off a relief force under the famous General Belisarius, Totila launched his final assault and took the city by storm (May 545–17 December 546).

Rome ∎ 849 ∎ Byzantine-Muslim Wars

See **Ostia**

Rome ∎ 1167 ∎ Wars of the Lombard League

In support of Emperor Frederick Barbarossa, Archbishops Rainald of Cologne and Christian of Mainz invaded central Italy and defeated a Papal army outside Rome (29 March). The Emperor himself joined the siege in July and, after another defeat, the city finally submitted. However, the German army was struck by a terrible pestilence and withdrew in disarray (March–August 1167).

Rome ∎ 1527 ∎ 2nd Habsburg-Valois War

Francis I of France repudiated a treaty made following battle at **Pavia** (1525) and once again invaded Italy against the Imperial army of Charles, Duke of Bourbon. To punish Pope Clement VII for supporting France, Duke Charles led Spanish and German troops in a terrible sack of Rome. Although the Duke died in the assault, the Pope recognised Charles V of Spain as Emperor (6 May 1527).

Rome ∎ 1849 ∎ 1st Italian War of Independence

When a Republic was declared in Rome, France sent 8,000 troops under General Nicolas Oudinot to besiege the city, which was held by 20,000 men, including 5,000 followers of Giuseppe Garibaldi. After an initial repulse, and a second reinforced attack driven off a month later, Oudinot eventually forced the city to capitulate. Garibaldi fled to America (30 April–2 July 1849).

Rome ∎ 1944 ∎ World War II (Southern Europe)

See **Liri Valley**

Rometta ∎ 1038 ∎ Later Byzantine-Muslim Wars

The great Byzantine commander George Maniakes led a determined attack on Muslim Sicily with a force including Normans from Italy and Varangians under King Harald Hardrada of Norway. A long campaign saw Maniakes capture Messina then secure a bloody victory at nearby Rometta. He was recalled to Constantinople in 1040 to meet the Bulgarians and the Muslims recovered Sicily.

Roncesvalles ∎ 778 ∎ Wars of Charlemagne

After a campaign against Muslim northern Spain, Charlemagne, King of the Franks, was returning through the Pyrenees to put down a Saxon revolt when the rearguard of his army was attacked by Christian Basques. While the ambush at Roncesvalles was no major battle, the death of the King's nephew Roland was glorified in the epic poem "The Song of Roland" (15 August 778).

Roncesvalles ∎ 1813 ∎ Napoleonic Wars (Peninsular Campaign)

During the weeklong "Battles of the Pyrenees," French General Honoré Reille met British General Sir Lowry Cole west of Roncesvalles on the Linduz Plateau, while General Bertrand

Clausel met General Sir John Byng to the east near Altobiscar. As at **Maya** the same day, the outnumbered Allies fell back, though only after delaying the French advance on **Pamplona** (25 July 1813).

Roodewal, Cape Province I 1802 I 3rd Cape Frontier War

Amid renewed fighting in eastern Cape Province, Boer commander Tjaart van der Walt led the Swellendam commando against the fortified village at Roodewal (Rooiwal) on the Sundays River, held by a large Xhosa force under Klaas Stuurman. After ten days of fruitless attack, with his son killed, van der Walt agreed to an armistice, but fighting soon resumed along the **Sundays** (13 February 1802).

Roodewal, Orange Free State I 1900 I 2nd Anglo-Boer War

On campaign southwest of Johannesburg, Christiaan de Wet captured a convoy at Heilbron, attacked Vredefort Station, then attacked the supply dump and railway station at Roodewal, forcing the garrison to surrender. After inflicting over 150 casualties and capturing almost 500 prisoners, de Wet seized what he could carry, then burned a massive quantity of supplies and mail (7 June 1900).

Roodewal, Transvaal I 1902 I 2nd Anglo-Boer War

The last major action of the war saw Boers under Jan Kemp and Commandant Ferdinand J. Potgieter attack 3,000 men armed with field guns under Colonel Robert Kekewich at Roodewal, in the western Transvaal south of **Tweebosch**. Recklessly charging over open ground, the Boers suffered terrible losses, including Potgieter killed. Peace talks resumed and the war soon ended (11 April 1902).

Rooilaagte I 1899 I 2nd Anglo-Boer War
See **Graspan**

Rooiwal I 1900 I 2nd Anglo-Boer War
See **Roodewal, Orange Free State**

Roosebeke I 1382 I Hundred Years War

In a Flemish popular uprising, Philip van Artevelde captured **Bruges** (3 May) before joining workers from Ghent at Roosebeke, east of Brussels. The untrained artisan army was crushed by Louis II, the French Count of Flanders, with massive losses, including van Arteveldt—whose father led a similar rising 80 years before. Bruges was retaken and Ghent fell a few weeks later (27 November 1382).

Rorke's Drift I 1879 I Anglo-Zulu War

On the same day as the British rout at **Isandhlwana**, about 4,000 Zulus besieged just 139 soldiers and 50 Natal native auxiliaries under Lieutenants John Chard and Gonville Bromhead further west at Rorke's Drift. In one of the British army's most celebrated defences—with 11 Victoria Crosses won—the Zulus were held off and withdrew at dawn with about 400 dead (22–23 January 1879).

Rosaires I 1898 I British-Sudan Wars
See **Dakhila**

Rosas I 1645 I Thirty Years War (Franco-Habsburg War)

Henri Comte d'Harcourt replaced Philippe de la Motte-Houdancourt as French commander in Spain after failure at **Lérida** (1644) and besieged the coastal fortress town of Rosas, northeast of Barcelona, supported by Cesar de Choiseul du Plessis-Praslin. Rosas was forced to capitulate after stubborn resistance, but Harcourt failed a year later at **Lérida** and was recalled (2 April–28 May 1645).

Rosas I 1794–1795 I French Revolutionary Wars (1st Coalition)

With Spanish invasion of France repulsed, French forces invaded Catalonia to capture **Figueras** (18 November) and General Claude Victor moved against the seemingly weaker city of Rosas, a few miles east. However, the 4,000-strong Spanish garrison fought on for two months. By the time the port fell, most of the garrison had escaped by sea (December 1794–3 February 1795).

**Rosas I 1808 I Napoleonic Wars
(Peninsular Campaign)**

Advancing into Spain to relieve the siege of
Barcelona, French General Laurent Gouvion
Saint-Cyr was blocked at the coastal port of
Rosas, defended by Governor Pedro O'Daly.
The town stubbornly resisted for a month, sup-
ported by British naval Captain Lord Thomas
Cochrane, before it finally fell. St-Cyr then
moved on towards Barcelona (7 November–4
December 1808).

**Rosbach I 1382 I Hundred
Years War**
See **Roosebeke**

**Rosbecque I 1382 I Hundred
Years War**
See **Roosebeke**

**Rosburgh I 1460 I Anglo-Scottish
Border Wars**
See **Roxburgh**

Rosebud I 1876 I Sioux Indian Wars

At war with the Sioux in southeast Montana,
General George Crook and about 1,000 men
were attacked on the Rosebud River, outside
modern Kirkby. Although Crook claimed victory, he had lost 28 dead and 56 wounded in very
heavy fighting and was forced to withdraw.
Encouraged by his success, Crazy Horse launched his famous attack a week later at **Little Big
Horn** (17 June 1876).

**Rosetta I 1807 I Napoleonic Wars
(4th Coalition)**

To undermine the Ottoman Empire, now
supporting France, Britain unwisely sent General Alexander Mckenzie Fraser to seize Egypt.
After capturing **Alexandria** (21 March), Fraser
took a force against Rosetta (modern Rashid),
where he was routed by Mehemet Ali Pasha. A
treaty was arranged—with British prisoners returned—and the disastrous expedition withdrew
three days later (20 April 1807).

**Roshangaon I 1616 I Mughal-
Ahmadnagar Wars**

While campaigning in central India, Mughal
Emperor Jahangir sent his son Prince Parwiz and
General Shah-Nawaz Khan against a large army
raised by Malik Ambar, Minister of Ahmadnagar. Ambar suffered a crushing defeat on the
Dudhna, west of Jalna at Roshangaon, though he
kept fighting the Mughals for many years and
was eventually avenged in 1624 at **Bhatavadi** (4
February 1616).

**Rosillo I 1813 I Gutiérrez-Magee
Expedition**

The army of Spanish Texas withdrawing from
La Bahía tried to block Republican Bernardo
Gutiérrez and American Filibusters under Samuel Kemper (following the death of Augustus
Magee). Near the Rosillo, southeast of San Antonio, Royalist commander Simón de Herrera
and Governor Manuel Maria de Salcedo were
decisively defeated, then executed after surrendering (29 March 1813).

Roslin I 1303 I William Wallace Revolt

At the expiry of a truce with Scotland, Edward
I sent a large army under Sir John de Segrave
advancing towards Edinburgh. Just to the south
at Roslin, the English were attacked and destroyed by Sir Simon Fraser and John Comyn
the Younger, nephew of King John Baliol. King
Edward himself then captured Edinburgh and in
mid-1304 defeated the rebellious Scots at **Stirling** (24 February 1303).

**Rossbach I 1757 I Seven Years War
(Europe)**

Fredrick II of Prussia marched west to counter
the Allied invasion of Saxony and secured a decisive victory at Rossbach, southwest of Leipzig.
Supported by cavalry General Friedrich von
Seydlitz, Frederick routed Austrian Prince Joseph
of Saxe-Hildburghausen and the French of Duke
Charles of Soubise, then hastened east to meet
another Austrian army at **Leuthen** (5 November
1757).

Rostov I 1918 I Russian Civil War

When the Ukraine seceded from Russia, Red General Vladimir Antonov-Ovseyenko stormed into the Don Basin (10 January) and Don Cossack Ataman Aleksei Kaledin killed himself in despair. The key city of Rostov fell after heavy fighting, followed by nearby Novocherkassk. White General Anton Denikin withdrew to the Kuban and in July attacked **Ekaterinodar** (22–24 February 1918).

Rostov I 1920 I Russian Civil War

The decisive battle for the **Don Basin** saw Anton Denikin's White Army try to defend the last key cities against Red General Aleksandr Yegorov. Over two days of terrible fighting, Novocherkassk fell with huge losses in men and equipment and Rostov fell with further losses, including over 10,000 prisoners. The Reds then invaded the Kuban through **Torgovaya** (7–9 January 1920).

Rostov I 1941 I World War II (Eastern Front)

Following the fall of **Kiev**, Marshal Gerd von Rundstedt drove southeast on Rostov, taken after heavy fighting by General Ewald von Kleist (21 November) before Russian Marshal Symeon Timoshenko launched a massive counter-attack. Refusing Hitler's order to stand firm, Rundstedt withdrew (and resigned days later) giving Russia her first major victory (9–29 November 1941).

Rostov I 1942 I World War II (Eastern Front)

German Army Group A under Marshal Wilhelm List opened an offensive south from **Kharkov** and crossed the Don towards Rostov. Attacked from the vulnerable northeast, Rostov fell amid widespread panic, opening the way into the **Caucasus**. Six months later Rostov was used for withdrawal following Germany's failed Caucasus campaign and surrender at **Stalingrad** (15–23 July 1942).

Rotebro I 1497 I Wars of the Kalmar Union

King John I of Denmark resolved to secure his birthright in Sweden and made peace with Grand Prince Ivan III of Moscow, then led German mercenaries and rebel Swedish nobles against Chancellor Sten Sture, who had ruled since **Brunkeberg** (1471). Sture was defeated north of Stockholm at Rotebro and John secured Sweden's throne, but lost it at **Hemmingstedt** in 1500 (28 September 1497).

Rotorua I 1870 I 2nd New Zealand War
   See **Waikorowhiti**

Rotterdam I 1940 I World War II (Western Europe)

As Germany invaded the Lowlands, airborne forces led a lightning assault on the Netherlands and the Dutch Queen and government fled to Britain. German bombers then launched an unprecedented terror raid on Rotterdam. The air attack cost very heavy civilian casualties in killed or wounded and General Henri Winkelman surrendered next day to avoid further casualties (10–14 May 1940).

Rottofredo I 1746 I War of the Austrian Succession

After victory near **Piacenza** (16 June), Austrian commander Prince Joseph Wenzel von Lichtenstein pursued the French and attacked their rearguard at nearby Rottofredo. While both sides suffered costly casualties, French Marshal Jean-Baptiste Desmarets Marquis de Maillebois was beaten. The garrison of Piacenza surrendered and France effectively abandoned Italy (12 August 1746).

Rottweil I 1643 I Thirty Years War (Franco-Habsburg War)

Reinforced by infantry and cavalry under General Josias von Rantzau, French Marshal Jean-Baptiste Guébriant led the army of Weimar east across the Rhine into Württemberg and besieged Rottweil, 40 miles northeast of Freiburg. The city was forced to capitulate, but

Guébriant died of a wounds. France lost Rott-weil after defeat at **Tuttlingen** just a few days later (19 November 1643).

Roubaix I 1794 I French Revolutionary Wars (1st Coalition)
See **Tourcoing**

Rouen I 1418–1419 I Hundred Years War
Seizing much of Normandy after victory at **Agincourt** (1415), Henry V of England captured **Caen** then advanced up the Seine against Rouen. The city, which had a powerful garrison but little food, surrendered after a seven-month siege and widespread starvation. Shortly afterwards, Henry married the daughter of the King of France and was recognised as his heir (29 July 1418–19 January 1419).

Rouen I 1449 I Hundred Years War
Charles VII of France ended a five-year truce and invaded English Normandy, where he attacked Rouen. Despite support by John Talbot Earl of Shrewsbury, the incompetent Edmund Beaufort Duke of Somerset was defeated and surrendered the city, handing Shrewsbury over as a hostage. Further English defeat at **Formigny** six months later led directly to the loss of Normandy (29 October 1449).

Rouen I 1562 I 1st French War of Religion
Following the massacre of Protestants at **Vassy** (1 March), Huguenots led by Louis I de Bourbon Prince of Condé seized cities, including Rouen, which was then besieged by Catholic commander Francis de Guise. Despite aid from England, Rouen fell, leading to battle at **Dreux** in December. Condé's brother, Anthony of Navarre, died fighting on the Catholic side (26 October 1562).

Rouen I 1591–1592 I 9th French War of Religion
After a failed siege of Catholic **Paris**, Protestant forces under Henry of Navarre invested Rouen, held for the Holy League by Governor Pierre de Villars. While Henry left to meet the

Spanish relief force at **Aumâle**, Villars led a brilliant sortie against Marshal Charles Biron (24 February). The reimposed siege was relieved after two months by the Duke of Parma (November 1591–21 April 1592).

Roulers I 1794 I French Revolutionary Wars (1st Coalition)
Austrian Count Charles von Clerfayt advanced to relieve the French siege of the Netherlands city of Ypres and sent his left wing through the village of Roulers, where the French were defeated and lost many guns and prisoners. Further south at **Hooglede**, Clerfayt's right wing was defeated and repulsed by General Charles Pichegru. Ypres capitulated the following day (16 June 1794).

Roumeli I 1948 I Greek Civil War
On the offensive in south central Greece, 20,000 government troops under General Thrasyvoulos Tsakalotos began a sweep through the Roumeli Mountains. Heavy fighting at Artotina and in the Mornos Valley near Lidoriki cost 640 insurgents killed and 1,300 captured, as well as 145 government casualties. Tsakalotos then moved north against **Grammos** (15 April–7 May 1948).

Round Island I 1904 I Russo-Japanese War
See **Yellow Sea**

Round Mountain I 1861 I American Civil War (Trans-Mississippi)
Confederate Colonel Douglas H. Cooper followed failed peace talks by attacking Chief Opothleyahola and a large band of pro-Union Creeks and Seminoles in camp at Round Mountain, near the Red Fork of the Arkanas in Oklahoma. The so-called first Indian battle of the Civil War was indecisive and Opothleyahola withdrew northeast towards **Bird Creek** (19 November 1861).

Roundway Down I 1643 I British Civil Wars
Retiring on Devizes after the costly battle at **Lansdown** (5 July), the wounded Royalist Sir

Ralph Hopton was besieged by Sir William Waller from nearby Roundway Down. Caught between Hopton's Cornish garrison and a large cavalry relief force led by Henry Wilmot, the Parliamentarians surrendered, losing 600 killed, 800 prisoners and all their guns and ammunition (13 July 1643).

Rouvray I 1429 I Hundred Years War

During the English siege of **Orleans**, a wagon convoy of supplies commanded by Sir John Fastolfe (including barrels of fish for Lent) was attacked at Rouvray, east of Avallon, by a French-Scottish force under Etienne de Vignolles "La Hire" and Count Charles of Clermont. The attackers were driven off with heavy losses in an action known as the "Battle of the Herrings" (12 February 1429).

Roveredo I 1796 I French Revolutionary Wars (1st Coalition)

Within weeks of being repulsed at **Lonato** and **Castiglione**, Austrian General Dagobert Wurmser made a fresh attempt to relieve the French siege of **Mantua**, but once again ill-advisedly split his force. Marching east of Lake Garda, Napoleon Bonaparte drove General Paul Davidovich out of Roveredo before his decisive victory over Davidovich next day at **Calliano** (4 September 1796).

Rovine I 1395 I Ottoman Conquest of the Balkans

Facing rebellion in Romania, Ottoman Sultan Bayazid sent Yildirim Khan across the Arges and west of Arad at Rovine Prince Mircea of Wallachia was defeated (though the reluctant Ottoman ally Marko Kraljevic of Serbia was killed). Bayazid then executed John Sisman of Trnovo to put Vlad on the Wallachian throne. In 1396 the Sultan defeated a Christian Crusade at **Nicopolis** (17 May 1395).

Rowde Ford I 1643 I British Civil Wars

As wounded Royalist General Sir Ralph Hopton withdrew following **Lansdown**, Prince Maurice ordered Major Walter Slingsby with Mohun's Cornish Regiment of Foot to hold a ford on the Rowde, commanding the road from Chippenham. The rearguard held the line at heavy cost as Hopton fell back on Devizes. Days later the Parliamentarians were routed at **Roundway Down** (9 July 1643).

Rowlett's Station I 1861 I American Civil War (Western Theatre)

Determined to destroy the newly repaired bridge on the Green River near Woodsonville, in eastern Kentucky, Confederate General Thomas C. Hindman attacked Indiana German volunteers under Colonel August Willich, north of the river at Rowlett's Station. While both sides withdrew after inconclusive fighting, the important railway line was secured for the Union (17 December 1861).

Rowley Burn I 634 I Anglo-Saxon Territorial Wars

See **Heavenfield**

Rowton Heath I 1645 I British Civil Wars

King Charles I was marching from Oxford to relieve the Parliamentary siege of Chester, when he was taken in the rear at nearby Rowton Heath by the Yorkshire Horse of Parliamentary General Sydenham Poyntz. The advancing Royalist force was driven off with 600 killed and 800 prisoners lost and the King then withdrew to Oxford for the winter (24 September 1645).

Roxburgh I 1314 I Rise of Robert the Bruce

As Scotland secured her border areas following victory at **Loudon Hill** in 1307, Robert the Bruce sent Sir James "Black" Douglas against the large and powerful border town of Roxburgh. Lacking men to capture the castle by storm, Douglas took advantage of drunken Shrove Tuesday celebrations and scaled the walls at night to surprise and overwhelm the garrison (6 March 1314).

Roxburgh I 1436 I Anglo-Scottish Border Wars

In response to an English invasion, driven back at **Piperdean** (10 September), James I of

Scotland took his army to besiege Roxburgh. After 15 days he was ignominiously driven off by Henry Percy Earl of Northumberland and was soon murdered by his own Barons. Coincidentally, the King's son died 24 years later in another siege of the same border fortress (October 1436).

Roxburgh I 1460 I Anglo-Scottish Border Wars

James II of Scotland crushed the Douglas Rebellion at **Arkinholm** (May 1455) then moved against the last English outposts and besieged the border town of Roxburgh. During an otherwise insignificant action, a misloaded cannon accidentally exploded and the King standing nearby was killed instantly. Roxburgh fell a few days later and was completely destroyed (August 1460).

Royushan I 1904 I Russo-Japanese War
See **Hill 203**

Ruapekapeka I 1845–1846 I 1st New Zealand War

Following costly repulse at **Ohaewai**, near Waimate, Colonel Henry Despard took 1,100 men against Hone Heke and Kawiti further east at Ruapekapeka. After heavy bombardment, the fortified pa was taken with about 42 European casualties and unknown Maori losses. Heke and Kawiti sued for peace and were later pardoned, ending war in the far north (27 December 1845–11 January 1846).

Rubio-Ñu I 1869 I War of the Triple Alliance
See **Acosta-Ñu**

Ruddle's Station I 1780 I War of the American Revolution

Colonel William Byrd led a Loyalist offensive into Kentucky, taking about 1,000 men—mainly Wyandot Indians—against Ruddle's Station in Harrison County, then against Martin's Station in Bourbon County, killing about 200 men, women and children. Unable to control his Indians, Byrd withdrew. The Wyandot attacked

again two years later at **Little Mountain** (20 & 28 June 1780).

Rudnik Ridges I 1914 I World War I (Balkan Front)
See **Kolubara**

Rudsar I 1757 I Persian Wars of Succession
See **Lahijan**

Rueda I 981 I Later Christian-Muslim Wars in Spain

Renewing the Muslim offensive in central Spain, Vizier Ibn Abi-Amir invaded Leon and sacked Zamora before marching east to Rueda, where Ramiro III of Leon was decisively defeated and later deposed. Leon became a Muslim tributary and the Vizier took the name Al-Mansor—the Victorious—by which title he became known as one of Islam's greatest warriors in Spain.

Rufiji Delta I 1915 I World War I (African Colonial Theatre)

Having sunk the British cruiser *Pegasus* at Zanzibar (29 September 1914), the German cruiser *Königsberg* (Captain Max Loof) was driven deep into the swampy Rufiji Delta, south of Dar Es Salaam. After a prolonged blockade and fruitless pursuit, British Admiral Herbert King-Hall sent the monitors *Severn* and *Mersey*, which shelled *Königsberg* and sank her in the mud (11 July 1915).

Rügen I 1168 I Danish Wars of Expansion
See **Arkona**

Rugley's Mill I 1780 I War of the American Revolution

As rebel General Daniel Morgan began an offensive in South Carolina, he sent Colonel William Washington against Tory Colonel Henry Rugley at his home near modern Clermont. After failing to take the Tory defensive position by force, Washington used a fake gun to deceive the garrison into surrender and over 100 Tory militia were captured (4 December 1780).

Ruhr I 1794 I French Revolutionary Wars (1st Coalition)
See **Aldenhoven**

Ruhr I 1945 I World War II (Western Europe)
American Generals William Simpson and Courtney Hodges advanced from the Rhine, closing from **Wesel** and **Remagen** to surround Germany's Army Group B on the Ruhr, where the encirclement closed at Lippstadt (1 April). After heavy fighting, Marshal Walther Model shot himself and 320,000 men were captured, contributing directly to the fall of **Berlin** (28 March–21 April 1945).

Ruiya I 1858 I Indian Mutiny
Marching north from Lucknow against the fort at Ruiya, ten miles east of the Ganges, General Robert Walpole ignored intelligence that rebel commander Nirpat Singh was considering surrender and ordered a disastrous frontal assault. This blunder cost 57 British dead, including Brigadier Adrian Hope, before the rebels evacuated next day and were pursued to **Sirsa** (15 April 1858).

Rullion Green I 1666 I Scottish Covenanter Rebellion
See **Pentland Hills**

Rumaithah I 1920 I Iraqi Revolt
When Arab insurgents besieged Rumaithah, on the Shatt al Hillah south of Baghdad, a relief force under Colonel Donald McVean was driven off with heavy losses (7 July). A larger column under General Frank Coningham later fought their way in to save Captain Harry Bragg's starving garrison. The town was evacuated next day and the revolt rapidly spread south to **Samawah** (1–20 July 1920).

Rumani I 1916 I World War I (Middle East)
See **Romani**

Ruovesi I 1918 I Finnish War of Independence
Russian Colonel Mikhail Svetchnikov led a renewed offensive on the **Vilppula** front, advancing west from Ruovesi towards Kankanpää against Whites under Colonel Ernst Linder. Later reinforced by troops from **Aland**, Linder led a brilliant weeklong defense and by month's end the poorly co-ordinated Red offensive had ground to a halt (21–28 February 1918).

Ruschuk (1st) I 1811 I Russo-Turkish Wars
Defeated at **Loftche** in February, Grand Vizier Ahmed Pasha led fresh forces to the Danube and was overcome in battle at Ruschuk (modern Ruse) by General Mikhail Kutuzov. However, the Russian commander was forced to abandon the city. After destroying its defences he withdrew across the river to nearby Slobodzeya, where he routed the Turks in October to retake **Ruschuk** (4 July 1811).

Ruschuk (2nd) I 1811 I Russo-Turkish Wars
In a fresh offensive on the Danube, Ottoman Grand Vizier Ahmed Pasha was defeated at Ruschuk (modern Ruse) by General Mikhail Kutuzov, who withdrew across the river. Three months later Kutuzov destroyed the Turkish army in a powerful counter-offensive at nearby Slobodzeya and retook Ruschuk. More than 12,000 Turks surrendered and Turkey sued for peace (15 October 1811).

Rushen I 1314 I Rise of Robert the Bruce
Seven years after victory at **Loudon Hill**, Robert the Bruce crossed to the Isle of Man against Duncan McDougal of Galloway, who had captured the Scottish leader's brothers Thomas and Alexander at **Lochryan** (February 1307) and delivered them for execution to Edward II of England. At Rushen Castle McDougal was routed and Bruce imposed his rule on the island (June 1314).

Rush Springs ❙ 1858 ❙ Comanche Indian Wars

Following Texas Ranger success in Indian Territory at **Antelope Hills** (12 May), Major Earl van Dorn crossed the Red River and attacked Buffalo Hump at Rush Springs, southwest of modern Oklahoma City. A dawn attack saw van Dorn severely wounded, but 56 Comanche men, women and children were killed, with massive supplies and the Indian pony herd captured (1 October 1858).

Ruspina ❙ 46 BC ❙ Wars of the First Triumvirate

Julius Caesar defeated Pompey at **Pharsalus** (48 BC), then landed in Tunisia against Pompey's sons and their ally King Juba of Numidia. After months preparing, Caesar marched towards Utica and was surprised at Ruspina (modern Monastir) by Titus Labienus and Marcus Petreius. Caesar was saved by a brilliant battle of manoeuvre and marched to victory in February at **Thapsus** (3 January 46 BC).

Russian ❙ 1850 ❙ Pit River Indian War

Sent to northern California to punish the Pit River Indians for killing Captain William Warner and two white settlers, Captain Nathaniel Lyon dealt out terrible retribution at **Clear Lake** and a few days later marched west to the Russian River against another band of about 100. Trapped in a swampy area, few of the Indians escaped alive, but Captain Warner's murderers were never found (19 May 1850).

Rustaq ❙ 1955 ❙ Imam Revolt

Sultan Said ibn Taymur of Muscat faced rebellion by Imam Ghalib ibn Ali of Oman and took the rebel capital Nizwa. He then sent his Bartinah force under Colonel Colin Maxwell against Ghalib's brother Talib at Rustaq, on the northern slopes of the **Jebel Akhdar**. After Maxwell besieged and stormed the fortress, Ghalib abdicated and Talib fled into exile (12–15 December 1955).

Rustumiyah ❙ 1920 ❙ Iraqi Revolt

Indian troops and a company of the Manchester Regiment attempting to relieve Kifl, south of Baghdad, set out from Hillah under Colonel Richard Hardcastle. Attacked by Arab insurgents at the Rustumiyah Canal, the "Manchester Column" lost 20 killed, 60 wounded and 160 captured and fled back to Hillah. Captain George Henderson won a posthumous Victoria Cross (24 July 1920).

Rutherford's Farm ❙ 1864 ❙ American Civil War (Eastern Theatre)

See **Stephenson's Depot**

Ruthven ❙ 1306 ❙ Rise of Robert the Bruce

See **Methven**

Rutland ❙ 1798 ❙ French Revolutionary Wars (Irish Rising)

In support of Irish rebellion, rebel James Napper Tandy and 270 French troops in the corvette *Anacreon* broke through the British naval blockade and landed on Rutland Island, off Donegal, with guns and artillery. The town was captured without bloodshed, but hearing of the French defeat at **Ballinamuck**, they sailed away—ending the last French landing on British soil (16 September 1798).

Rutland Stockade ❙ 1847 ❙ 1st New Zealand War

Withdrawing from **Boulcott's Farm**, near Wellington, Topine Te Mamaku returned north to threaten Wanganui, protected by the Rutland Stockade, built by Captain Joseph Laye. To avenge the execution of four Maoris for killing a settler family, Te Mamaku and 30 men attacked Rutland and other stockades. He was bravely repulsed but attacked again in July at **St John's Wood** (19 May 1847).

Ryabaya Mogila ❙ 1770 ❙ Catherine the Great's 1st Turkish War

A new Russian offensive in the Balkans saw General Pyotr Rumyantsev cross the Pruth with 37,000 men, and at Ryabaya Mogila he attacked the Turks under Abaza Pasha and Crimean Khan Kaplan Girai. With Rumyantsev advancing in a dispersed square formation, General Grigori Potemkin's reserves took the Turks in the rear and they fled downstream towards **Larga** (17 June 1770).

Ryazan | 1237 | Mongol Conquest of Russia

On campaign against the Princedoms of Russia, the Mongol Batu and his General Subetai captured Bulgar City, capital of the Volga Bulgars, then besieged Ryazan, on the Oka southeast of Moscow. The city (now called Staraya Ryazan) fell after a desperate defense and Prince Yuri Igorevich and his wife were executed. The Mongols then marched north against **Kolomna** (15–21 December 1237).

Rymenant | 1578 | Netherlands War of Independence

Spanish Viceroy Don John of Austria followed his decisive victory at **Gembloux** (31 January) by attacking a Dutch army under French veteran Francois de la Noue at Rymenant (modern Rymenam), just northeast of Brussels. The Dutch were initially driven back, but a large English contingent under Sir John Norris held their ground and the Spanish were repulsed with over 1,000 killed (1 August 1578).

Rzhev | 1942 | World War II (Eastern Front)

While the world focussed on **Stalingrad**, four Soviet armies under Marshal Georgy Zhukov launched a mid-winter offensive against the Rzhev Salient, north of Moscow. Successive battles of annihilation cost the Russians perhaps 100,000 killed and about 1,600 tanks before they fell back exhausted. General Walter Model withdrew from Rzhev in March 1943 (November–December 1942).

S

Saalfield I 1806 I Napoleonic Wars (4th Coalition)

With Napoleon Bonaparte's army converging on Prussia, an isolated force of Prussians and Saxons under Prince Ludwig Ferdinand attempted to block the advance of Marshal Jean Lannes at Saalfield, where the outnumbered Allies were overwhelmed. After the Prince was killed in a cavalry charge, Lannes advanced north to the French victory four days later at **Jena** (10 October 1806).

Saarbrucken I 1870 I Franco-Prussian War

As Napoleon III's army advanced towards Germany, forward units under Charles Auguste Frossard encountered about 1,000 Prussians at Saarbrucken, led by Colonel Eduard von Pestel, who withdrew across the Saar after heavy bombardment. France claimed a great victory and baptism of fire for the young Prince Imperial, though the city was lost four days later after **Spicheren** (2 August 1870).

Saaz I 1421 I Hussite Wars

See **Zatec**

Sabac I 1476 I Turkish-Hungarian Wars

With Turkish forces occupied in Croatia, King Mathias of Hungary took a large force into Serbia against Shabatz (modern Sabac), west of Belgrade, garrisoned by just 1,200 men. After a heavy bombardment and the repulse of a Turkish relief force, the city surrendered yielding massive supplies of ammunition. Mathias then ad-

vanced further down the Danube (16 January–15 February 1476).

Sabac I 1521 I Turkish-Hungarian Wars

Determined to invade Hungary against Louis II, Sultan Suleiman I and Grand Vizier Mehmed Piri Pasha had first to seize the Balkan fortresses and besieged Shabatz (modern Sabac), on the Drava west of Belgrade. A brief yet hard-fought siege saw Shabatz fall by assault before Hungary could mobilise, enabling the Ottoman army to concentrate against **Belgrade** (8 July 1521).

Sabac I 1914 I World War I (Balkan Front)

When Austrian Generals Liborius von Frank and Oskar Potiorek invaded Serbia they were defeated in the **Cer** Mountains west of Belgrade by the Serbians Stepa Stepanovic and Zivojin Misic, and fell back across the Drina to defend Sabac (previously Shabatz). Further heavy fighting saw Sabac retaken and the Austrians were driven out, but they later invaded again across the **Drina** (21–24 August 1914).

Sabalah I 1929 I Ikhwan Rebellion

The Ikhwan brotherhood of central Arabia was reluctant to accept Wahhabi authority and turned on former ally Abd al-Aziz (ibn Saud) of Nejd, whose army met rebel leaders Faisal al-Dawish and Ibn Humayd at as-Sabalah, near al-Artawiya. The hugely outnumbered rebels were destroyed by Saudi machine-guns and cavalry. They were crushed again in August at **Umm Urdhumah** (March 1929).

Sabi I 660 I Sino-Korean Wars

Supported by Tang China, the Korean Kingdom of Silla sent Kim Yusin against western neighbour Paekche. Aided by a massive Chinese army under Su Ding Fang, the capital Sabi (modern Puyo) was taken by storm and the Kingdom of Paekche came to an end. A counteroffensive failed at **Paekchon** and a Tang army with Sillan support seized Koguryo in the north with victory at **Pyongyang**.

Sabila I 1929 I Ikhwan Rebellion
See **Sabalah**

Sabine Cross Roads I 1864 I American Civil War (Trans-Mississippi)
See **Mansfield**

Sabine Pass I 1862 I American Civil War (Trans-Mississippi)

Campaigning against the coast of Texas, Captain Frederick Crocker in the Union steamer *Kensington*, supported by two schooners, attacked Sabine Pass, outside Port Arthur, defended by a Confederate garrison under Major Josephus Irvine. Crocker captured it without loss after brief bombardment and two weeks later Union forces to the west captured **Galveston** (24 September 1862).

Sabine Pass I 1863 I American Civil War (Trans-Mississippi)

An attempted landing on the Texas coast saw Captain Frederick Crocker and four Union gunboats escort seven troop transports past Sabine Pass outside Port Arthur, where Crocker had previously won an easy victory. Accurate gunfire from Lieutenant Richard W. Dowling at Fort Griffin forced the expedition to retire, with one gunboat and 200 crew captured (8 September 1863).

Sabis I 57 BC I Rome's Later Gallic Wars
See **Sambre**

Sablat I 1619 I Thirty Years War (Bohemian War)

Count Ernst von Mansfeld saved Protestant Bohemia by capturing **Pilsen** (November 1618), then took his mercenaries southeast towards Budweis to continue rebellion against Catholic Ferdinand of Styria. Intercepted near Sablat, Mansfeld was routed by the Imperial army of Charles-Bonaventure de Longueval Comte de Bucqoi, who won again 18 months later at **White Mountain** (10 June 1619).

Sabraon I 1846 I 1st British-Sikh War
See **Sobraon**

Sabugal I 1811 I Napoleonic Wars (Peninsular Campaign)

While retreating from the failed French invasion of Portugal, Marshal Michel Ney fought a series of successful rearguard actions against pursuit by Arthur Wellesley Lord Wellington. But on the Coa River at Sabugal, an isolated French Corps under General Jean Reynier came under attack and lost over 1,000 men before withdrawing across the border towards **Ciudad Rodrigo** (3 April 1811).

Sabzavar I 1755 I Persian-Afghan Wars

On a fresh advance into northeast Persia after capturing **Meshed** (November 1754), Afghan ruler Ahmad Shah Durrani marched west through Sabzavar against Muhammad Hasan Khan of Qajar. However, at nearby Mazinan, Ahmad's advance units led by Shahpas and Khan were heavily defeated by part of Muhammad's army under Hosayn Khan Develu. The Afghans then withdrew from Persia.

Sachon I 1592 I Japanese Invasion of Korea

Following the initial invasion of Korea and capture of **Pusan** (23 May), the main Japanese fleet arrived and sailed to Sachon, west of Pusan, where they were lured out to battle by Korean Admiral Yi Sun-shin, supported by Won Kyun. Despite being heavily outnumbered, Yi secured a brilliant victory. He attacked the Japanese again three days later to the southeast off **Tangpo** (8 July 1592).

Sachon I 1598 I Japanese Invasion of Korea

General Dong Yiyuan recovered from a failed Chinese assault on **Ulsan** in February to attack the Japanese fort at Sachon in southern Korea, south of Chinju. Lured into a trap by Shimazu Yoshihiro, the Chinese division was destroyed, with tens of thousands of severed ears sent to Kyoto as proof of victory. Shimazu soon sailed west to support the besieged garrison at **Sunchon** (30–31 October 1598).

Sacile I 1809 I Napoleonic Wars (5th Coalition)

To prevent Austrian troops in Italy joining the campaign on the Danube, French and Italian forces under Prince Eugène de Beauharnais attacked Archduke John of Austria north of Venice on the Livenza at Sacile. Eugène was forced to withdraw in defeat after a confused engagement, but the Austrians had also suffered heavy losses and weeks later were beaten at the **Piave** (16 April 1809).

Sackets Harbour I 1813 I War of 1812

Responding to the American assault on the British naval base on Lake Ontario at **York**, Commodore Sir James Yeo attacked the American base at Sackets Harbour, supported by 750 troops under Colonel Edward Baynes. General Jacob Brown and about 1,000 New York militia fiercely defended the habour and the British were driven off with almost 300 casualties (29 May 1813).

Sacramento I 1847 I American-Mexican War

American Colonel Alexander Doniphan marching south from Santa Fe repulsed a Mexican force at **Brazito**, then met a much larger force on the Sacramento River near Chihuahua. A one-sided action forced General José Heredia and Governor Angel Trias to withdraw with heavy losses. Doniphan completed his 3,000-mile trek just too late to join the fight at **Buenavista** (28 February 1847).

Sacriportus I 82 BC I Sullan Civil War

After returning from Greece to take control of Rome, veteran General Lucius Cornelius Sulla won at **Mount Tifata** then marched against Gaius Marius the younger. At Sacriportus, in the Trerus Valley southeast of Rome, Marius was heavily defeated and his supporters suffered further losses when pursued towards nearby Praeneste. His allies were also defeated in the north at **Faventia**.

Sacsahuana I 1548 I Spanish Civil War in Peru

See **Xaquixaguana**

Sadowa I 1866 I Seven Weeks War

See **Königgratz**

Sadras I 1758 I Seven Years War (India)

See **Cuddalore**

Sadras I 1782 I War of the American Revolution

In the first of five indecisive naval actions off the east coast of India, French Admiral Pierre André Suffren attempted to recover prizes captured by British Admiral Edward Hughes. Fighting in flukey winds off Sadras, near Madras, Suffren was driven off and withdrew that night to Pondicherry. The two Admirals met again two months later off **Providien** (17 February 1782).

Sadulapur I 1848 I 2nd British-Sikh War

With Sikh forces defeated and besieged at **Multan**, northwest of Lahore, General Sir Hugh Gough was repulsed attempting to cross the Chenab at **Ramnagar**. Two weeks later he sent General Sir Joseph Thackwell across the river to turn the flank of Sher Singh's army. After a largely artillery action at Sadulapur, the Sikhs fell back to even stronger positions at **Chilianwallah** (3 December 1848).

Sadusam I 1848 I 2nd British-Sikh War

At the start of renewed war against the Sikhs of Punjab, Lieutenant Herbert Edwardes and a mixed Pathan and Baluchi force joined with Nawab Futteh Mohammed Khan of Bhawalpur to defeat the rebels at **Kineyre**. They then attacked Sikh Governor Dewan Mulraj outside the walls of Multan at Sudusam, where the Sikhs were badly beaten and withdrew under siege into **Multan** (1 July 1848).

Sa-erh-hu Mountain I 1619 I Manchu Conquest of China
    See **Sarhu**

Safad I 1948 I Israeli War of Independence
    Palmach commander Ygal Allon seized **Tiberias** in northern Galilee (18 April), then moved north to besiege the important town of Safad (modern Zefat), fiercely defended by Iraqi irregulars and local Palestinian militia. The Jews were initially repulsed with costly losses but resumed the attack to seize key outposts. The Arab population of Safad and surrounding villages fled (30 April–11 May 1948).

Saga I 1874 I Saga Rebellion
    Rising against Japan's newly restored Imperial Government, about 3,000 Saga Samurai under Eto Shimpei attacked offices in Saga, Kyushu, and were bloodily suppressed by Home Minister Okubo Toshimichi. Fleeing to Kagoshima, Eto and co-rebel Shima Yoshitaka failed to enlist Saigo Takamori and were eventually executed. A few years later, Saigo himself rebelled at **Kagoshima** (January 1874).

Sagar I 1680 I Mughal-Berad Wars
    Withdrawing from failure at **Bijapur**, Mughal Viceroy Dilir Khan besieged the fortress of Sagar, held by Pam Nayak, Chief of the Berad tribesmen, whose territory lay between the Krishna and Bhima Rivers. After heavy losses in a humiliating defeat, Dilir Khan abandoned the siege and returned home in disgrace. In 1705 Emperor Aurangzeb himself attacked the Berad at their capital, **Wagingera**.

Sagar I 1858 I Indian Mutiny
    When rebels besieged Sagar, northeast of Bhopal, General Sir Hugh Rose set out from Mhow to relieve the tiny British garrison and about 170 European women and children. Having defeated rebel forces at **Rahatgarh** and **Barodia**, Rose reached the town on 26 January. Sagar was relieved when artillery fire breached the walls and Rose then advanced against **Jhansi** (3 February 1858).

Sagiuyne I 713 I Muslim Conquest of Spain
    See **Scgoyuela**

Sagrajas I 1086 I Early Christian Reconquest of Spain
    See **Zallaka**

Sagunto I 1811 I Napoleonic Wars (Peninsular Campaign)
    French Marshal Louis Suchet captured **Tarragona** before advancing south to capture Murviedro, east of Valencia, then besieged the nearby fortress of San Fernando de Sagunto, defended by Colonel Luis Andriano. The siege ended when Suchet's outnumbered force destroyed a Spanish relief army under General Joachim Blake and Sagunto surrendered (23 September–25 October 1811).

Saguntum I 219 BC I 2nd Punic War
    In renewed war against Rome (which had defeated his father Hamilcar), the Carthaginian Hannibal Barca attacked the Roman-protected city of Saguntum, north of modern Valencia. The assault provoked Rome to declare war. After Saguntum fell by storm following an eight-month siege, Hannibal began his famous advance through Gaul and across the Alps to Italy.

Saguntum I 212 BC I 2nd Punic War
    After beating Hasdrubal at **Ibera**, Roman forces under Publius Scipio the Elder and his brother Gnaeus recovered much of Spain south of the Ebro before they finally besieged and captured Saguntum, which had been lost to Hannibal seven years earlier and partly destroyed. However, the Scipio brothers were soon defeated and killed in a Carthaginian counter-offensive at the **Baetis** and **Ilurci**.

Saguntum I 75 BC I Sertorian War
    See **Murviedro**

Sahagun I 1808 I Napoleonic Wars (Peninsular Campaign)
    Embarking on an ill-advised invasion from Spain into Portugal, across the Duoro at Zamora

and Toro, newly appointed British commander Sir John Moore surprised French mounted units at Sahagun, east of the Esla in Leon. General Henry Paget's cavalry destroyed the French squadrons, though the British were soon in retreat towards **Corunna** (21 December 1808).

Sahay I 1742 I War of the Austrian Succession

French Marshal Francois de Broglie took advantage of Prussian victory at **Chotusitz** (17 May) to attack Austrian General George Christian Lobkowitz advancing towards Frauenberg. Defeated at Sahay, near Budweis, Lobkowitz fell back north towards Prague. A few weeks later Empress Maria Theresa made peace with Prussia in order to turn against France and Bavaria (27 May 1742).

Sahil I 1914 I World War I (Mesopotamia)

When Turkey attacked Russia at **Sevastopol**, an Anglo-Indian force under General Sir Arthur Barrett landed in Turkish Mesopotamia to seize Basra. Beating off initial resistance, the British advanced to Sahil, where an entrenched superior Turkish force was badly defeated. Basra fell a few days later and the British continued up the Euphrates towards **Qurna** (17 November 1914).

Saigon I 1859 I French Conquest of Indo-China

In supposed response to execution of Spanish Bishop José María Díaz, Franco-Spanish troops under Admiral Charles Rigault de Genouilly captured **Danang**, then sailed south against Saigon. The citadel of Saigon fell after heavy fighting and was later held against siege by veteran Marshal Nguyen Tri Phuong until victory at **Chi Hoa** in 1861 secured southern Vietnam for France (17 February 1859).

Saigon I 1968 I Vietnam War

As part of the **Tet Offensive**, thousands of Viet Cong and North Vietnamese launched a surprise attack on Saigon, where General Fred Weyand led a bloody Allied defence. The offensive was eventually defeated with terrible losses, though TV images of enemy troops inside the US Embassy shocked the American public and undermined the political will to continue the war (31 January–7 March 1968).

Saigon I 1975 I Vietnam War

Climaxing the 55-day offensive to conquer South Vietnam, up to 100,000 North Vietnamese troops converged on Saigon through **Xuan Loc** and Bien Hoa. With rockets falling on the airport and downtown Saigon, the capital was doomed. As the last Americans were airlifted from their embassy, President Doung van Minh surrendered to end the long war (23–30 April 1975).

Sailor's Creek I 1865 I American Civil War (Eastern Theatre)

See **Sayler's Creek**

St Albans I 1455 I Wars of the Roses

Richard Duke of York and Richard Neville Earl of Warwick were marching on London, when they were met 20 miles to the northeast at St Albans by Henry VI and Edmund Beaufort Duke of Somerset. The Lancastrians were heavily defeated, with Somerset killed, after which York seized the King and had himself appointed Constable of England (22 May 1455).

St Albans I 1461 I Wars of the Roses

Two weeks after Yorkist victory at **Mortimer's Cross**, Richard Neville Earl of Warwick marched north from London to intercept the Lancastrian army and took a strong position at St Albans, where he was defeated by Henry Beaufort Duke of Somerset and Sir Andrew Trollope. Henry VI was then released from captivity but turned away north and lost next month at **Towton** (16 February 1461).

St Amand I 1793 I French Revolutionary Wars (1st Coalition)

See **Condé-sur-l'Escaut**

St Antoine I 1652 I War of the 2nd Fronde

Rebelling against the power of Cardinal Jules Mazarin during the minority of Louis XIV,

Louis II de Bourbon Prince of Condé withdrew to Paris after defeat at **Etampes** (4 May). However, Marshal Henri de Turenne brought up fresh Royalist troops and defeated the rebels outside Paris at the Gate of St Antoine. The battle virtually ended the war and Condé fled to the Spanish army (2 July 1652).

St Aubin du Cormier I 1488 I Mad War

In response to revolt by Duke Louis of Orleans and Duke Francis of Brittany, Charles VIII of France sent a large army led by Louis de la Trémouille, who defeated the rebels at St Aubin du Cormier, northeast of Rennes. With Duke Louis and the Prince of Orange captured, the revolt was virtually over. When Francis died, Charles obtained Brittany by marrying his daughter Anne.

St Augustine I 1586 I Drake's Caribbean Raid

At the end of a large-scale raid against Spain in the Caribbean, where he had attacked **Santo Domingo** and **Cartagena**, English Admiral Sir Francis Drake took his fleet, now said to be almost 50 ships, against St Augustine in Spanish Florida, held by General Pedro Menéndez Marqués. Drake sacked and burned the town after a brief action, before returning home with his booty (6 June 1586).

St Augustine I 1702 I Queen Anne's War

Governor James Moore of South Carolina opened Queen Anne's War—the American phase of the War of the Spanish Succession—when he took 600 English troops and 600 Indians against St Augustine in Spanish Florida. After a month's siege, with little damage done to either side, two Spanish frigates appeared. Moore burned his ships and returned overland to Charleston (August 1702).

St Augustine I 1740 I War of the Austrian Succession

Leading an attack on Spanish Florida, James Oglethorpe, founder of Georgia, besieged St Augustine, on the Matanzas River southeast of Jacksonville, supported by Commodore Vincent Pearce. However, Oglethorpe eventually had to withdraw. Despite repulsing a Spanish counter-offensive two years later at **Bloody Swamp**, he failed again at St Augustine in 1743 (10 May–5 July 1740).

St Augustine I 1778 I War of the American Revolution

In an attempt to engage Britain in the south, General Robert Howe took a militia force against East Florida, held by General Augustine Prevost, where he attacked St Augustine, southeast of Jacksonville. Faced by sickness in his troops and insubordination in his ally, Governor William Houston of Georgia, the expedition became a disaster and Howe returned to **Savannah** (May 1778).

St Bartholomew's Eve I 1572 I 4th French War of Religion

The so-called Fourth War of Religion centered largely on the notorious Massacre of St Bartholomew's Eve, when thousands of Huguenots were murdered in Paris, including the great commander Gaspard de Coligny. Following the massacre, Huguenot forces regrouped and gained considerable power in western France, holding off a siege of **La Rochelle** (23–24 August 1572).

St Cast I 1758 I Seven Years War (Europe)

Returning to Brittany after attacking **Cherbourg**, Commodore Sir Richard Howe and General Thomas Bligh landed near St Malo, where the port was too well defended. Attempting to re-embark further west at St Cast Bay, the British were heavily attacked by Emmanuel Duke d'Aiguillon, losing General Alexander Dury killed among 800 casualties, mainly captured (7–12 September 1758).

St Charles, Arkansas I 1862 I American Civil War (Trans-Mississippi)

Union gunboats under commander Augustus H. Kilty, with Colonel Graham N. Fitch, advanced up the White River in Arkansas to attack the Confederate batteries at St Charles, commanded by Captain Joseph Fry. A severe action saw St Charles taken, although the Union gunboat *Mound City* was hit and her boiler exploded, with 125 killed and many wounded, including Kilty (17 June 1862).

St Charles, Quebec I 1837 I French-Canadian Rebellion

When French Canadians in Quebec declared independence, they repulsed British and Canadian Loyalists east of Montreal at **St Denis**. Two days later, further south at St Charles, rebel militia under Thomas Storrow Brown were badly beaten by Loyalist Colonel George Augustus Wetherall. Further defeat in a few weeks at **St Eustache** effectively ended the rising (25 November 1837).

St Clair's Defeat I 1791 I Little Turtle's War

General Arthur St Clair, attempting to avenge **Harmar's Defeat** (October 1790), entered Ohio with 600 regulars and 1,500 militia. On the Wabash at the site of Fort Recovery, his camp was attacked by Little Turtle of the Miami and the Shawnee Blue Jacket. Over 900 troops and camp followers were killed in the worst white defeat in North America, though St Clair was exonerated (4 November 1791).

St Croix I 1807 I Napoleonic Wars (4th Coalition)

See **St Thomas**

St Denis, France I 1567 I 2nd French War of Religion

At risk of fresh attacks by Catholic Royalists, Huguenot leader Louis I de Bourbon Prince of Condé regathered his forces and met Anne Duke of Montmorency northeast of Paris at St Denis. Despite an heroic Huguenot defence and the death of 74-year-old Montmorency, the battle was a narrow Catholic victory. A new peace was quickly secured (10 November 1567).

St Denis, France I 1678 I 3rd Dutch War

Four days after a treaty ended war between France and Holland, William of Orange, apparently unaware, attacked Duke Francois Henri of Luxembourg besieging Mons in modern Belgium. The Dutch suffered heavy losses in a violent clash near the Abbey of St Denis before the armies disengaged. News of the peace treaty was confirmed next day (14 August 1678).

St Denis, Quebec I 1837 I French-Canadian Rebellion

When French Canadians in Quebec declared independence, British and Canadian Loyalists led by Colonel Charles Gore marched against rebel leader Wolfred Nelson at St Denis, northeast of Montreal. Gore was repulsed in a badly handled action and retreated when reinforcements approached under George Étienne Cartier. Other Patriots were defeated at **St Charles** (23 November 1837).

St Denis, Réunion I 1810 I Napoleonic Wars (5th Coalition)

See **Réunion**

St Dizier (1st) I 1814 I Napoleonic Wars (French Campaign)

While manoeuvring east of Paris to prevent a junction of the Prussian and Austrian armies, Napoleon Bonaparte sent Marshal Claude Victor against General Gebhard von Blucher at St Dizier, southeast of Chalons. Blucher had left for **Brienne** and a sharp action forced a Russian rearguard under General Sergei Lanskoi to withdraw. The Emperor then entered the town (27 January 1814).

St Dizier (2nd) I 1814 I Napoleonic Wars (French Campaign)

Just days after withdrawing at **Arcis-sur-Aube**, Napoleon Bonaparte continued to manoeuvre in the rear of the Allied advance on Paris. At St Dizier, southeast of Chalons-sur-Marne, he checked Baron Ferdinand von Winzingerode, probing south from Vitry. The Prussians lost 1,500 men and nine guns, but Bonaparte was unable to fight his way through to his capital (26 March 1814).

St Dogmael I 1088 I Welsh Dynastic War

See **Llandudoch**

St Domingo I 1806 I Napoleonic Wars (4th Coalition)
See **Santo Domingo**

St Étienne I 1814 I Napoleonic Wars (Peninsular Campaign)
British General Sir John Hope and the German Legion under General Heinrich Hinuber led the Allies closing in on **Bayonne** in southwestern France, where they attacked the eastern suburb of St Étienne. The area finally fell to the combined assault, though at the cost of over 300 mainly German casualties. French losses were around 100 (25 February 1814).

St Eustache I 1837 I French-Canadian Rebellion
Three weeks after rebels in Quebec were defeated at **St Charles**, Governor Sir John Colborne and Loyalist Colonels George Augustus Wetherall and John Maitland attacked the final holdouts under Jean-Olivier Chénier at St Eustache, 18 miles northwest of Montreal. Chénier and about 70 others were killed in a violent attack. The town was then destroyed and the rising was crushed (14 December 1837).

St Eustatius I 1781 I War of the American Revolution
When Britain declared war on Holland, Admiral George Rodney was sent to attack the rich Dutch West Indies trading island of St Eustatius. Rodney secured a massive amount of treasure, although much was recaptured off the **Scilly Isles** in May. St Eustatius was retaken by Admiral Francois-Claude de Bouillé (25 November) but was eventually returned to Holland (3 February 1781).

St Fagan's I 1648 I British Civil Wars
With war virtually over, Parliamentary forces in south Wales mutinied over pay and declared for the King. Up to 8,000 under General Rowland Laugharne advanced on Cardiff and attacked about 3,000 Parliamentarians under Colonel Thomas Horton at St Fagan's. Perhaps the largest battle on Welsh soil saw the Royalist rebels routed and they fell back on **Pembroke** (8 May 1648).

St Foy I 1760 I Seven Years War (North America)
See **Quebec**

St Francis I 1760 I Seven Years War (North America)
Determined to punish Indians who supported the French and had taken hundreds of English scalps, General Jeffrey Amherst sent New Hampshire militia under Major Robert Rogers against the Abenaki at St Francis in northern Maine. A dawn attack saw "Rogers Rangers" kill about 200 warriors and destroy the village. They suffered heavy losses during the return to Charlestown (April 1760).

St Fulgent I 1793 I French Revolutionary Wars (Vendée War)
Royalist rebel leader Francois-Athanase Charette defeated Republican General Jean-Baptiste Kléber at **Torfou**, then marched southeast to St Fulgent against some of Kléber's defeated force plus fresh troops from the south under General Jean Mieskowski. Charette won the resulting confused night-time action, though most of the Republicans slipped away in the dark (23 September 1793).

St Gall I 1403 I Habsburg-Swiss Wars
See **Speicher**

St George's Battle I 1774 I Rohilla War
See **Miranpur Katra**

St George's Channel I 1813 I War of 1812
After a highly successful campaign against merchant shipping campaign off England, the 18-gun American brig *Argus* (Captain William H. Allen) was attacked to the west in St George's Channel by the 20-gun British sloop *Pelican* (Captain John F. Maples). Allen was mortally wounded in a heavy broadside and, with her rigging shot away and boarded, *Argus* was forced to strike (14 August 1813).

St Giovanni I 1799 I French Revolutionary Wars (2nd Coalition)
See **Trebbia**

St Gotthard I 1664 I Later Turkish-Habsburg Wars

Facing an advance into Hungary by an Ottoman army under Grand Vizier Ahmed Fazil Koprulu, Imperial Field Marshal Raimondo Montecuccoli established himself on the right bank of the Raab at St Gotthard, on the route to Graz and Vienna. A fierce battle prevented the Ottomans from crossing the river and a week later they signed a treaty of peace with the empire (1 August 1664).

St Jakob on the Birs I 1444 I Old Zurich War

During a truce in the Hundred Years War, Charles VII of France sent the Dauphin Louis to intervene in Switzerland on behalf of Emperor Frederick III and relieve the Confederate siege of Zurich. While the French and their mercenaries destroyed the outnumbered Swiss at Saint Jakob on the Birs, south of Basel, heavy losses persuaded Louis to make peace and withdraw (24 August 1444).

St Jakob on the Sihl I 1443 I Old Zurich War

When Zurich entered into a special alliance with the Habsburg House of Austria, the Swiss Forest Cantons and Glarus marched against Zurich itself and inflicted a sharp defeat to the south at St Jakob on the Sihl, killing Zurich Burgomaster Rudolf Stussi. However, when Confederate forces besieged Zurich a year later, France intervened at the battle of **St Jakob on the Birs** (22 July 1443).

St James I 1426 I Hundred Years War
   See **Avranches**

St James Day I 1666 I 2nd Dutch War
   See **North Foreland**

St Jean I 1775 I War of the American Revolution
   See **St Johns**

St Jean d'Angely I 1621 I 1st Huguenot Rebellion

In response to French Huguenots holding an unauthorised assembly in La Rochelle, Louis XIII and his Minister Alfred de Luynes sent an army, which besieged the nearby fortress of St Jean d'Angely, defended by Benjamin of Soubise. Duke Francois de Lesdiguieres forced a capitulation after almost a month and the Royalist army turned its attention to **Montauban** (30 May–25 June 1621).

St Jean de Losne I 1636 I Thirty Years War (Franco-Habsburg War)

Imperial forces under Count Matthias Gallas led a fresh invasion of France, crossing the Rhine while General Johann von Werth invaded the north and captured **Corbie**. West of Dole, Gallas was delayed by the fortress of St Jean de Losne. Inspired by their courageous resistance, Louis XIII personally took command of his army and the Allies finally had to withdraw (August–November 1636).

St Jean de Luz I 1813 I Napoleonic Wars (Peninsular Campaign)

Creating a large-scale diversion the day before his main attack on the **Nivelle**, Arthur Wellesley Lord Wellington sent General Sir John Hope against St Jean de Luz, on the French right near the Franco-Spanish border. Hope's feint, involving about 20,000 men, was a brilliant opening to the main advance the following day further inland along the Nivelle (9 November 1813).

St Johns (1st) I 1775 I War of the American Revolution

As part of the attack on **Fort Ticonderoga**, Americans Colonel Benedict Arnold and Major Ethan Allen marched north against St Johns, southeast of Montreal, commanding the route from Lake Champlain to the St Lawrence. The Americans captured the strategic fort and a small sloop before they were forced to withdraw by a large British relief column approaching from Chambly (17 May 1775).

St Johns (2nd) I 1775 I War of the American Revolution

Determined to block America's advance towards Montreal, Major Charles Preston held the strategic fort at St Johns to the southeast against repeated attacks by Generals Richard Montgomery and Philip Schuyler. The fort had to surrender after the fall of nearby **Chambly** and defeat of a relief column at **Longueuil** (30 October). **Montreal** fell ten days later (5 September–2 November 1775).

St John's Bluff I 1862 I American Civil War (Lower Seaboard)

Union General John M. Brannan determined to secure shipping on Florida's St John's River, taking a force supported by ships under Captain Charles Steedman against the Confederate battery at St John's Bluff, guarding the river near Jacksonville. Attacked by land and on the river, Confederate artillery commander Colonel Charles F. Hopkins was forced to abandon the position (1–3 October 1862).

St John's Wood I 1847 I 1st New Zealand War

Two months after a failed attack on the **Rutland Stockade**, protecting Wanganui, Topine Te Mamaku launched a fresh attack on the settlement, now garrisoned by 1,200 men under Colonel William A. McCleverty, supported by Maori allies. Heavy fighting near the stockades at St John's Wood saw Te Mamaku eventually driven off. He later sued for peace and was pardoned (19 July 1847).

St Julien I 1915 I World War I (Western Front)

Opening the Second Battle of **Ypres**, Duke Albrecht attacked around **Gravenstafel** to the northeast, then further north, where he seized the village of St Julien from the Canadians. After a failed counter-attack, British commander Sir Horace Smith-Dorrien was dismissed for withdrawing to shorten the line. Sir Herbert Plumer faced the Germans days later at **Frezenberg** (24 April–4 May 1915).

St Kitts I 1667 I 2nd Dutch War
See **Nevis**

St Kitts I 1782 I War of the American Revolution

French Admiral Francois Comte de Grasse landed a large force on the West Indian island of St Kitts and drove British General Thomas Fraser into a defensive position at Brimstone Hill. Admiral Sir Samuel Hood (1724–1816) arrived and repulsed de Grasse with victory at sea off Basseterre (25–26 January). But he was unable to assist the garrison ashore and Fraser had to surrender (11 January–12 February 1782).

St Kitts I 1805 I Napoleonic Wars (3rd Coalition)

A few days after unsuccessfully attacking the British West Indian island of **Dominica**, French General Joseph Lagrange sailed north and landed on St Kitts, where the outnumbered garrison took to the hills. Having plundered the city of Basse-Terre, Lagrange withdrew, taking five merchants ships he captured in the harbour (27 February 1805).

St Laurent I 1794 I French Revolutionary Wars (1st Coaltion)
See **San Lorenzo**

St Lazaro I 1746 I War of the Austrian Succession
See **Piacenza**

St Lo I 1944 I World War II (Western Europe)

After the great Allied landing in **Normandy**, American General Charles Corlett drove inland against the strategic transport center of St Lo on the River Vire. Brutal defence under Panzer General Fritz Bayerlein saw severe house-to-house fighting before St Lo was finally taken at the cost of 11,000 American casualties. The Americans then attacked west towards **Avranches** (7–18 July 1944).

St Louis I 1780 I War of the American Revolution

On campaign against Spanish presence in Missouri Territory, British under Emanuel Hesse, with a large force of Indian allies led by

Chiefs Wabasha and Matchekewis, attacked San Luis de Ylinoises (modern St Louis). Governor Don Fernando de Leyba's outnumbered Spanish regulars and militia boldly drove off the attack and the Spaniards later hit back at **Fort St Joseph** (26 May 1780).

St Lucia | 1778 | War of the American Revolution

French Admiral Charles-Hector Comte d'Estaing arrived in the West Indies just too late to prevent Admiral Sir Samuel Barrington and General James Grant invading St Lucia, so instead landed troops to relieve the capital, Castries. Driven off with heavy losses by General Sir William Meadows, d'Estaing re-embarked, leaving the local French garrison to surrender (12–28 December 1778).

St Lucia | 1780 | War of the American Revolution

A month after returning to St Lucia from failure off **Martinique**, British Admiral George Rodney faced the approaching fleet of Admiral Luc-Urbain Comte de Guichen. After days of manoeuvring off St Lucia, they met in a brief action, then again four days later. Three British ships were disabled, but de Guichen's supplies were running low and he withdrew (15 & 19 May 1780).

St Lucia | 1794 | French Revolutionary Wars (1st Coalition)

Progressing south after capturing **Martinique** (23 March), a British expedition under Admiral Sir John Jervis and General Sir Charles Grey landed on St Lucia. The fortress of Morne Fortunee quickly fell and General Nicolas Ricard surrendered. However, the small British garrison evacuated in June 1795 in the face of a bloody Negro revolt. The island had to be re-taken in 1796 (1 April 1794).

St Lucia | 1796 | French Revolutionary Wars (1st Coalition)

When France recaptured St Lucia in 1795, Admiral Sir Hugh Christian took a large force to the West Indies under Generals Sir Ralph Abercromby and John Moore. General Goyrand surrendered St Lucia after three weeks' fighting and Moore became Governor. However, St Lucia was returned to France under treaty in 1802 and had to be taken a third time in 1803 (27 April–24 May 1796).

St Lucia | 1803 | Napoleonic Wars (3rd Coalition)

After the French West Indian island of St Lucia had been taken in 1794 and again in 1796, then returned to France in 1802, British Commodore Samuel Hood (1762–1814), Commander in Chief of Leeward Islands Station, and General William Grinfield took a third expedition. When they stormed Morne Fortunee, the island fell for the last time and was ceded to Britain in 1814 (21 June 1803).

St Malo | 1944 | World War II (Western Europe)

American forces broke out from **Normandy** and captured **Avranches**, while General Troy Middleton was sent west into Brittany to seize the key German-held ports. First objective was St Malo, protected by a series of strong fortresses. Nearby Dinard was taken and vicious house-to-house fighting saw St Malo itself fall. The Americans then continued west against **Brest** (3–16 August 1944).

St Maria | 1799 | French Revolutionary Wars (2nd Coalition)

French General Jean-Joseph Dessoles faced a fresh Austrian offensive in eastern Switzerland, where he was attacked by Count Heinrich von Bellegarde at St Maria, east of St Moritz. Driven back by massively superior forces, Dessoles led a remarkable withdrawal west through Zernetz, then south through the mountains to Tirano on the Upper Adda in Italy (22 April 1799).

St Mary's | 1645–1646 | Ingle's Rebellion

With England racked by religious war, skirmishing occurred in the colonies between Puritan Virginia and Catholic Maryland, where the Puritan trader Richard Ingle captured and plundered the Maryland capital, St Mary's.

Catholic leader Philip Calvert later retook the settlement and its Assembly later passed its famous Tolerance Act guaranteeing religious freedom (February 1645–August 1646).

St Mary's Church I 1864 I American Civil War (Eastern Theatre)

As Union General Philip Sheridan returned from raiding the Confederate rear at **Trevilian Station** (12 June), he crossed the Chickahominy at Jones Bridge southeast of Richmond and was intercepted by General Wade Hampton's cavalry at St Mary's Church near Charles City, Virginia. Sheridan managed to drive off the attack and he rejoined the Union army on the James (24 June 1864).

St Mary's Clyst I 1549 I Western Rebellion

When pro-Catholic forces in Cornwall and Devon besieged **Exeter**, Lord John Russell awaited reinforcement by German and Italian mercenaries, then marched to relieve the siege. About 6,000 rebels attacked Russell just east of the city at St Mary's Clyst but were badly defeated with about 1,000 killed. The rebels had to lift the siege and were routed by Russell at **Sampford Courtenay** (4 August 1549).

St Michael-Leoben I 1809 I Napoleonic Wars (5th Coalition)

Two weeks after driving Archduke John of Austria out of northern Italy with victory at the **Piave**, Prince Eugène de Beauharnais marched north and crashed into Austrian Field Marshal Franz von Jellichich northwest of Graz at St Michael and Leoben. Routed by General Paul Grenier, the beaten Austrian force withdrew to join Archduke John and soon shared his defeat at **Raab** (25 May 1809).

St Mihiel I 1918 I World War I (Western Front)

In the wake of Allied success at the **Marne** and **Amiens**, American commander John Pershing, with French support, attacked the St Mihiel salient, southwest of Verdun. The surprised Germans lost 15,000 prisoners and over

250 guns, but most of their army escaped the American pincer movement. The Allied offensive was soon renewed north of Verdun on the **Meuse** (12–16 September 1918).

St Nazaire I 1942 I World War II (Western Europe)

Attacking the German battleship dock at St Nazaire on the Loire, commander Robert Ryder rammed the destroyer *Campbelltown*, packed with explosives, into the dock gates while commandos demolished port facilities. Next day, *Campbelltown* blew up, wrecking the dock and killing many Germans. The raid cost the British 169 killed and 200 captured out of 611 (28 March 1942).

St Omer I 1677 I 3rd Dutch War
See **Cassel**

St Paul I 1809 I Napoleonic Wars (5th Coalition)

British Commodore Josias Rowley took six ships west from Rodrigues to the Indian Ocean island of Réunion and landed with about 600 troops and seamen under Captain Nesbit Willoughby near the main harbour at St Paul. Attacking from the landward side, they seized the batteries and joined the squadron taking a French frigate and two prizes before they withdrew (21 September 1809).

St Paul vs *Terror* I 1898 I Spanish-American War
See **San Juan, Puerto Rico (2nd)**

St Petersburg I 1917 I Russian Civil War
See **Petrograd**

St Petersburg I 1919 I Estonian War of Independence
See **Petrograd**

St Pierre and Miquelon I 1793 I French Revolutionary Wars (1st Coalition)

A minor skirmish against France's overseas territories saw British forces from Halifax, Canada, under General James Ogilvie attack the small fishing islands of St Pierre and Miquelon, south of Newfoundland. The garrisons capitulated without bloodshed and were removed, along with the French civilian inhabitants, to the Canadian mainland (14 May 1793).

St Pierre d'Irube I 1813 I Napoleonic Wars (Peninsular Campaign)

Three days after being defeated on the **Nive**, near the Franco-Spanish border, French Marshal Nicolas Soult skillfully moved his troops through Bayonne to attack in the east, between the Nive and Adour. General Sir Rowland Hill personally led a courageous counter-attack and hard fighting around the village of St Pierre forced Soult back to **Bayonne** (13 December 1813).

St Pol de Léon I 1346 I Hundred Years War

Amid the struggle for the Dukedom of Brittany, Sir Thomas Dagworth captured Roche-Derrien after three days' siege, then faced a heavy assault by Charles of Blois at St Pol de Léon, northwest of Morlaix. Standing firm, the outnumbered English longbowman caused heavy French losses and Blois withdrew. He attempted a further attack a year later at **Roche-Derrien** (9 June 1346).

St Privat la Montagne I 1870 I Franco-Prussian War

See **Gravelotte**

St Quentin I 1557 I 5th Habsburg-Valois War

Emperor Phillip II resumed the war in northern France by sending Emmanuel Philibert Duke of Savoy to recover territory seized by Henry II. While the Spanish army and its English allies besieged St Quentin, bravely defended by Admiral Gaspard de Coligny, a French relief force under Duke Anne of Montmorency was utterly routed. The city fell two weeks later (10 August 1557).

St Quentin I 1871 I Franco-Prussian War

The final outside attempt to relieve besieged **Paris** saw General Louis Léon Faidherbe take 50,000 men against a force of about 30,000 Germans under General August von Goeben near St Quentin, east of **Péronne**. Seven hours of fighting saw Faidherbe driven off with the loss of 3,000 casualties and 10,000 prisoners. Paris capitulated a week later (19 January 1871).

St Quentin I 1914 I World War I (Western Front)

See **Guise**

St Quentin Canal I 1918 I World War I (Western Front)

Assaulting the **Hindenburg Line**, British General Sir Henry Rawlinson and French under General Marie Debeney stormed over the St Quentin Canal, north of St Quentin. Despite heavy losses, the Allies seized the key tunnelled canal section near Bellicourt and the strategic Riqueval Bridge near Bellinglise. They then advanced on **Cambrai** and **Le Cateau** (29 September–2 October 1918).

St Thomas I 1746 I 1st Carnatic War

See **St Thomé**

St Thomas I 1807 I Napoleonic Wars (4th Coalition)

In order to prevent France seizing the Danish-held West Indian islands of St Thomas and St Croix, which had been temporarily occupied by Britain in 1801, a fresh force was sent under Admiral Sir Alexander Cochrane and General Henry Bowyer. Both islands were taken after brief resistance by the Danish garrison. They were returned to Denmark after the war (22–25 December 1807).

St Thomé I 1746 I 1st Carnatic War

After British surrender of **Madras** (21 September), French commander Duval D'Espréménil faced 10,000 Indians under Maphuz Khan, whose father Anwar-ud-Din, Nawab of Arcot, had been promised the city for remaining neutral. A sortie with 900 men saw French Colonel Paradis rout the Indian force at nearby St Thomé and Madras was secured for France (3 November 1746).

St Vincent ∎ 1606 ∎ Netherlands War of Independence
See **Cape St Vincent**

St Vincent ∎ 1779 ∎ War of the American Revolution
Admiral Charles-Hector Comte d'Estaing, French commander in the West Indies, having failed to prevent British forces capturing **St Lucia** (December 1778), took a force south from Martinique. Eluding British Admiral John Byron, he seized the island of St Vincent and a few weeks later also captured **Grenada**. Both territories were regained by Britain at the end of the war (16 June 1779).

St Vincent ∎ 1796 ∎ French Revolutionary Wars (1st Coalition)
With the West Indian island of **Grenada** secured in June, General Sir Ralph Abercromby sailed to St Vincent to put down a French-supported rebellion against British rule by negroes and Carib Indians. Unlike the quick success in Grenada, it took four months and 4,000 troops before Negro leader Martin Padre finally surrendered (June–4 October 1796).

St Vincent ∎ 1797 ∎ French Revolutionary Wars (1st Coalition)
See **Cape St Vincent**

St Vincent ∎ 1780 ∎ War of the American Revolution
See **Cape St Vincent**

St Vincent ∎ 1833 ∎ Miguelite Wars
See **Cape St Vincent**

St Vith ∎ 1944 ∎ World War II (Western Europe)
At the start of the German advance into the **Ardennes**, General Hasso von Manteuffel sent Panzer forces across the **Schnee Eifel** Ridge against the Belgian crossroads town of St Vith. American armoured units under General Bruce Clarke fought a classic delaying defence before they were forced to withdraw. The German offensive then swung south against **Bastogne** (17–23 December 1944).

Saintes ∎ 1242 ∎ Anglo-French Wars
Henry III of England was trying to regain Angevin land lost by his father King John when he was defeated by Louis IX at **Taillebourg**, near the Charente River southeast of Rochefort. Henry was then abandoned by his French ally, the Count de la Marche and next day lost again at nearby Saintes. The two kings made peace and Louis forbade his nobles to hold fiefs from both crowns (22 July 1242).

Saintes ∎ 1351 ∎ Hundred Years War
When French Marshals Guy de Nesle and Arnaud d'Endreghem advanced into Poitou and besieged St Jean d'Angely and Saintes, an English force under Sir John Beauchamp marched north from Bordeaux. They met and fought dismounted near Saintes, where the French were badly defeated. Nesle and d'Endreghem were both captured but were eventually ransomed (7 April 1351).

Saints ∎ 1782 ∎ War of the American Revolution
Admiral Francois Comte de Grasse, sailing from Martinique against Jamaica, fought indecisively off **Dominica** and days later met British Admiral George Rodney in a large engagement near the Saints, small islands between Guadaloupe and Dominica. A brilliant victory saw Rodney break the French line and capture six ships, effectively ending the naval war in the west (12 April 1782).

Saipan ∎ 1944 ∎ World War II (Pacific)
With the **Marshall Islands** secured (20 February), General Holland Smith and Admiral Kelly Turner sailed into the **Mariana Islands**, first attacking the northern island of Saipan. After shocking losses on both sides, many Japanese committed suicide, including Admiral Chuichi Nagumo and General Yoshitsugu Saito. Defeat triggered the fall of Premier Tojo, just 1,200 miles away in Tokyo (15 June–9 July 1944).

Sajo ∎ 1241 ∎ Mongol Invasion of Europe
Sweeping into Eastern Europe, the Mongol Batu (grandson of Genghis Khan) and his brilliant commander Subetai conquered much of Russia and Poland, advancing west from **Kiev** (1240) to

force the **Carpathian Passes** into Hungary. Northeast of Budapest near Mohi, King Bela IV was routed on the Sajo River. On the death of the Khan Ogedai in December the Mongols withdrew from Europe (11 April 1241).

Sakarya I 1921 I 2nd Greco-Turkish War

King Constantine of Greece advanced into Anatolia through a bloody action at **Eskisehir** (17 July), attacking Turkish positions along the Sakarya, 40 miles west of Ankara, where Mustafa Kemal had taken personal command. After three weeks of heavy fighting, the Greeks finally had to withdraw. Kemal counter-attacked a year later through **Afyon** (23 August–13 September 1921).

Saladillo I 1869 I 1st Cuban War of Independence
See **Bayamo**

Salado I 1340 I Later Christian Reconquest of Spain
See **Rio Salado**

Salado I 1813 I Gutiérrez-Magee Expedition
See **Rosillo**

Salado I 1842 I Texan Wars of Independence

Having occupied **San Antonio**, Mexican General Adrian Woll was lured out to attack 200 appoaching Texans under Colonel Mathew Caldwell in camp seven miles to the northeast at the Salado. When 800 charging Mexicans were driven off with about 120 casualties, Woll withdrew to San Antonio, though a small American force was destroyed in **Dawson's Massacre** (18 September 1842).

Salaita I 1916 I World War I (African Colonial Theatre)

General Wilfred Malleson attempted an offensive in German East Africa, sending 6,000 men against Major Georg Kraut in a strong position at Salaita, east of Kilimanjaro near Taveta. Terrible losses in a frontal assault against ma-chine-guns saw the mixed British force flee towards Serengeti. General Jan Smuts soon took command and attacked around **Morogoro** (12 February 1916).

Salala I 1817 I Chilean War of Independence

During his advance into Chile, General José de San Martin sent the northern wing of his Army of the Andes under Juan Manuel Cabot against the port of Coquimbo. On the nearby Salala Plains, Cabot defeated the Spanish-Chilean garrison to secure the fort and the coast. Two days later San Martin's main force fought the decisive battle further south at **Chacabuco** (11 February 1817).

Salamanca, Mexico I 1858 I Mexican War of the Reform

Opposing the new Liberal constitution, Conservative commander Luis Osollo, supported by Generals Miguel Miramón and Tomás Mejía, attacked Liberal commanders Anastasio Parrodi and Leandro Valle at Salamanca, east of Guadalajara. The Conservatives secured a decisive victory, with Guadalajara taken two weeks later, and Liberal leader Benito Juarez left for Panama (10 March 1858).

Salamanca, Spain I 1812 I Napoleonic Wars (Peninsular Campaign)

Arthur Wellesley Lord Wellington advancing north from the capture of Salamanca was surprised by a counter-offensive by French Marshal Auguste Marmont. Withdrawing to the plain south of Salamanca, Wellington achieved one of his most outstanding victories, with heavy French casualties including Marmont wounded. Wellington then advanced to seize Madrid (22 July 1812).

Salamanca Forts, Spain I 1812 I Napoleonic Wars (Peninsular Campaign)

As part of his offensive in central Spain, Arthur Wellesley Lord Wellington advanced against the three heavily fortified convents controlling the River Tormes at Salamanca. Two weeks of desperate fighting saw Wellington's Anglo-Portuguese troops seize all three—San Vincente, San Cayetano and La Merced—before capturing the unfortified city of **Salamanca** (14–27 June 1812).

Salamaua I 1943 I World War II (Pacific)

With **Papua** secured at **Sanananda** (22 January), Australian General Edmund Herring, with American support, advanced northwest into New Guinea against General Hotazo Adachi. In severe fighting for key airfields, the Allies took Salamaua (11 September) and Lae four days later. They then led a co-ordinated land and sea attack north against the **Huon Peninsula** (May–15 September 1943).

Salamcheh I 1988 I Iraq-Iran War

Five weeks after a stunning victory to regain **Al Faw**, Iraq launched another offensive east and southeast of Basra towards the town of Salamcheh. Facing a massive barrage of artillery and nerve gas, the Iranian defenders fought bravely before being forced into retreat, abandoning huge quantities of arms and equipment, effectively bringing the war in the south to an end in a single day (25 May 1988).

Salamina I 1841 I Colombian War of Supreme Commanders

Marching into Antioquia to support rebel leader Colonel Salvador Córdoba, Colonel José María Vesga was met 23 miles north of Manizales, at Salamina, by government forces under General Braulio Henao. Vesga was heavily defeated and captured. After the rebels were routed two months later at **La Chanca** (11 July), Vesga was executed (9 August) in the Plaza at Medellín (5 May 1841).

Salamis, Cyprus I 497 BC I Greco-Persian Wars

Darius I of Persia secured victory at **Ephesus** (498 BC), then sent a force to recapture Cyprus, where Onesilus, brother of the King of Salamis, was besieging Phoenician Amathus. The Ionian fleet arrived to beat the Persians at sea, but on the plains outside Salamis, Onesilus was defeated and killed. Salamis surrendered and the Persians

reconquered Cyprus before returning to Ionia to besiege **Miletus**.

Salamis, Cyprus I 450 BC I Greco-Persian Wars

During a truce in the Peloponnesian War after victory at **Oenophyta** (457 BC), Athens sent a large fleet under Cimon against Persian-held Cyprus and the southern city of Citium (near modern Larnaca). Although Cimon died during the siege, his forces won a major victory over a Phoenician and Cilician fleet further east off Salamis. However, Athens then withdrew and made peace with Persia.

Salamis, Cyprus I 306 BC I Wars of the Diadochi

In war among the successors of Alexander the Great, Demetrius Poliorcetes, son of Antigonus, attacked Cyprus, held for Ptolemy of Egypt by his brother Menelaus, who was defeated outside Salamis and fell back under siege. Ptolemy sailed with a relief force and was defeated off Salamis, losing over 100 ships. Salamis surrendered, but Demetrius soon failed against **Rhodes**.

Salamis, Greece I 480 BC I Greco-Persian Wars

When King Xerxes of Persia occupied Athens after victory at **Thermopylae**, his advancing ships were met to the west at Salamis by the much smaller Athenian-Spartan fleet led by Themistocles and Eurybiades. One of history's decisive naval actions saw the Persian fleet mauled and Xerxes withdrew, leaving Mardonius to occupy central Greece until defeat at **Plataea** (23 September 480 BC).

Salangarh I 1781 I 2nd British-Mysore War

See **Sholinghur**

Sala Phou Khoun I 1975 I Laotian Civil War

Coinciding with the renewed North Vietnamese advance towards **Saigon**, North Vietnamese and Communist Pathet Lao forces launched a new offensive in northern Laos. General Vang Pao's

Meo tried to hold a strategic position at Sala Phou Khoun, but without air support they were defeated and withdrew into exile. Vientiane fell without a fight and the Pathet Lao seized Laos (March–April 1975).

Saldanha Bay ∎ 1796 ∎ French Revolutionary Wars (1st Coalition)

When the Batavian fleet under Admiral Engelbertus Lucas arrived at Saldanha Bay in South Africa to recapture **Cape Colony** from the British, a small force under General James Craig marched overland to oppose the landing. Meanwhile, Admiral Sir George Keith Elphinstone arrived with a British squadron and after a sharp action the Dutch were forced to surrender (7–17August 1796).

Salem Church ∎ 1863 ∎ American Civil War (Eastern Theatre)

Having taken **Fredericksburg** on the Rappahannock, Union General John Sedgewick marched west to support General Joseph Hooker at **Chancellorsville**, Virginia. Attacked front and rear at Salem Church next day by units of Robert E. Lee's Confederate army, Sedgewick was forced to retire. With his reinforcements beaten, Hooker was decisively defeated and retreated east (3–4 May 1863).

Salerno ∎ 1943 ∎ World War II (Southern Europe)

With **Sicily** secured in mid-August, Anglo-American forces under General Mark Clark began a massive amphibious landing at Salerno, 50 miles south of Naples. General Heinrich von Vietinghoff led a powerful counter-attack, which seriously threatened the beachhead before reinforcements and naval and air bombardment broke the defence and the Allies advanced to **Naples** (9–18 September 1943).

Salgótarján ∎ 1919 ∎ Hungarian-Czech War

Czech troops were poised on the northern border of Bolshevik Hungary when Hungarian General Aurél Stromfeld led an offensive into Slovakia and secured a brilliant victory at Sal-

gótarján, then captured Miskolc further east. Two days later a Czech counter-offensive at Miskolc was driven off with costly Hungarian losses and the Hungarians were soon checked at **Nove Zamky** (20–23 May 1919).

Salher ∎ 1671–1672 ∎ Mughal-Maratha Wars

Maratha General Shivaji defeated the Mughals at **Dindori**, then captured the mountain fortress of Salher, southeast of **Surat**, near Mulher (January 1671). Salher was subsequently besieged by Dilir Khan, who then left to attack Poona and Shivaji sent Moropant Pingle and Pratap Rao Gujar. A great victory saw Mughal General Ikhlas Khan routed and captured (September 1671–February 1672).

Salices ∎ 377 ∎ 5th Gothic War

See **Ad Salices**

Salihiyya ∎ 1773 ∎ Mamluk Wars

Driven out of **Cairo** by his former lieutenant Abu'l-Dhahab, the Great Mamluk Ali Bey fled to his ally Shayk Zahir al-Umar of Acre and, after helping him capture Jaffa, raised a fresh army and attempted to recover power in Egypt. In the eastern Nile Delta at al-Salihiyya, Ali Bey was defeated and fatally wounded, dying a week later in Cairo. In 1775 Abu'l-Dhahab recaptured **Jaffa** (1 May 1773).

Salinas, Peru ∎ 1538 ∎ Spanish Civil War in Peru

After Diego del Almagro seized control of Peru at **Abancay** (July 1537), he faced an attack at Cuzco by Hernando Pizarro, who secured a decisive victory at nearby Salinas. Almagro's General, Rodrigo Orgoñez, was beheaded and Almagro himself was executed ten weeks later. The victor's brother Francisco Pizarro was restored to power, but he was assassinated four years later (26 April 1538).

Salinas, Spain ∎ 1812 ∎ Napoleonic Wars (Peninsular Campaign)

In a battle-scale guerrilla action in the mountains of southern Navarre, insurgent leader

Francisco Espoz y Mina attacked a massive French convoy heading for Mondragon (modern Arrasate). Battle at the Pass of Salinas, 15 miles northeast of Vitoria, cost the French over 500 killed, while the guerrillas seized invaluable booty as well as releasing more than 400 Spanish prisoners (9 April 1812).

Salineville I 1863 I American Civil War (Western Theatre)

Confederate General John H. Morgan ended his destructive raid into Kentucky and Ohio by escaping the disastrous defeat at **Buffington Island** (19 July) only to be pursued north along the Ohio through Salineville by Union forces under General James M. Shackelford. Defeated and surrounded at nearby New Lisbon, Ohio, Morgan and his last 360 men were forced to surrender (26 July 1863).

Salisbury I 552 I Anglo-Saxon Conquest of Britain

See **Searobyrg**

Salkehatchie I 1715 I Yamasee Indian War

When the Yamasee of South Carolina united with other Indian tribes in well co-ordinated attacks on settlers on the Ashley River (15 April 1715), Governor Charles Craven led a 1,200-strong militia force against the Indian allies on the Salkehatchie, west of Charleston. The Yamasee were routed in a decisive campaign and the survivors fled across the Savannah into Spanish Florida.

Salkehatchie River I 1865 I American Civil War (Western Theatre)

See **Rivers' Bridge**

Salmas I 1605 I Turko-Persian Wars

See **Sufiyan**

Salmon Falls I 1690 I King William's War

Six weeks after the Canadian raid on **Schenectady**, New York, Governor Louis de Buade Comte de Frontenac sent a Canadian and Indian force under Joseph-Francois Hertel against Salmon Falls, near Rollinsford, New Hampshire. Having brutally destroyed the town, Hertel heavily defeated pursuing militia from nearby Portsmouth before withdrawing. He soon joined the attack on **Fort Loyal** (18 March 1690).

Salonika I 1430 I Venetian-Turkish Wars

When the Byzantines sold Salonika (modern Thessalonika) to Venice, Ottoman Sultan Murad II declared war on his former ally and attacked Venetian possessions in the Adriatic and southern Greece. Building up his fleet, Murad besieged the Greek city and overwhelmed the Venetian garrison. Venice was forced to accept peace and continued trade under Ottoman authority (March 1430).

Salonika I 1915–1918 I World War I (Balkan Front)

Anglo-French forces attempting to aid Serbia against German and Bulgarian attack made scant headway when they landed at Salonika in Greece. Although offensives were attempted at the **Vardar**, **Florina**, **Monastir**, **Lake Prespa** and **Doiran**, the Salonika campaign tied up huge numbers of Allied troops for little gain until the final advance on the **Vardar** (6 October 1915–29 September 1918).

Salonta I 1636 I Transylvanian-Turkish Wars

Hussein Nasuh, commander of Buda and son of Grand Vizier Nasuh Pasha, rebelled against centralised Ottoman control and invaded Transylvania, held by Prince George Rákóczi I under Turkish suzereignty. A brilliant night attack on the Turkish camp at Salonta, near the Hungarian border, saw Rákóczi's troops inflict a terrible defeat, which greatly enhanced his reputation (October 1636).

Salsette I 1774 I 1st British-Maratha War

See **Thana**

Salsu I 612 I Sino-Korean Wars

Leading a claimed million men against the North Korean Kingdom of Koguryo, Sui Emperor Yang Di sent General Yu Chong Sheng advancing towards Pyongyang. Ambushed at the Salsu (modern Chongchon) by Korean General Ulchi Mundok, the Chinese suffered a terrible rout and withdrew with perhaps 300,000 men lost. Another invasion was blocked 33 years later at **Ansi-song** (August 612).

Salt **I** 1918 **I** World War I (Middle East)
See **Es Salt**

Salta **I** 1813 **I** Argentine War of Independence

Five months after defeat at **Tucumán**, in northwestern Argentina, Spanish General Pío Tristán withdrew further north to Salta, where he was attacked in a well-entrenched position by Patriot General Manuel Belgrano. A decisive victory for Belgrano secured 3,500 prisoners, 10 cannon and 2,000 rifles. By November he had lost all his strategic gains at **Vilcapugio** and **Ayohuma** (20 February 1813).

Saltah **I** 1847 **I** Russian Conquest of the Caucasus

Count Mikhail Vorontsov campaigned against Imam Shamil of Dagestan, capturing the rebel village of **Girgil**, then besieging Saltah, aided by Corsican-born General Charles Burnod. An initial assault was repulsed with 400 Russian casualties, with a further 1,000 casualties a week later when Saltah fell by storm. Vorontsov destroyed the village and withdrew (8 August–26 September 1847).

Saltanovka **I** 1812 **I** Napoleonic Wars (Russian Campaign)
See **Mogilev**

Salt Creek **I** 1871 **I** Kiowa Indian War

When Kiowa attacked ten freight wagons on the Salt Creek Prairie, northwest of Fort Worth, Texas, seven out of 12 teamsters were killed and a force was sent from nearby Fort Richardson. After a dangerous confrontation, General William Sherman arrested the Chiefs Satanta, Satank and Big Tree. Satank was killed trying to escape, while the other two were convicted, then pardoned (17 May 1871).

Saltillo **I** 1840 **I** Mexican Federalist War

Regrouping in the United States after defeat at **Santa Rita de Morelos** (25 March), Federalist General Antonio Canales Rosillon sent an American-Mexican vanguard under Samuel Jordan, who took Ciudad Victoria, then met Centralist General Rafael Vasquez near Saltillo. Massively outnumbered, Jordan fought clear and withdrew to Texas, but Canales Rosillon soon capitulated (25 October 1840).

Salt River **I** 1872 **I** Apache Indian Wars
See **Skeleton Cave**

Saltville (1st) **I** 1864 **I** American Civil War (Western Theatre)

Union General Stephen G. Burbridge led a raid from Kentucky into southwestern Virginia, advancing on the strategic saltworks near Saltville, defended by Generals Alfred E. Jackson and John S. Williams. After heavy fighting and the loss of about 350 men, the badly outnumbered Union force was repulsed. A number of black prisoners left behind were reportedly murdered (2 October 1864).

Saltville (2nd) **I** 1864 **I** American Civil War (Western Theatre)

Leading a second Union raid into southwest Virginia against the saltworks at Saltville, General George Stoneman feinted towards the leadworks at nearby **Marion**, then marched west on Saltville itself. The Confederate defenders under General John C. Breckinridge were driven off and Stoneman captured and destroyed the works before returning to Knoxville (20–21 December 1864).

Salvador **I** 1624–1625 **I** Dutch-Portuguese Colonial Wars

Dutch Admiral Jacob Willekens, with Colonel Jan van Dorth, campaigned against Salvador in Portuguese Brazil, landing a large force at Bahia Bay and Governor Diogo de Mendonca Furtado surrendered after very heavy fighting (9 May 1624). Salvador was besieged next year by a great Spanish armada under Fadrique de Toledo

Osorio and had to capitulate (30 March 1624–28 April 1625).

Salvador I 1627 I Dutch-Portuguese Colonial Wars

Returning to Salvador in Portuguese Brazil, which had been captured, then lost, by Dutch forces, Admiral Piet Heyn attacked Spanish and Portuguese shipping in the port at Bahia. Although massively outnumbered, the Dutch destroyed or captured 22 vessels and Heyn went home with his prizes. He returned to capture the silver fleet in September 1628 off **Matanzas** (3 March 1627).

Salvador I 1638 I Dutch-Portuguese Colonial Wars

Determined to expand Dutch conquests in Portuguese Brazil, new Governor John Maurice of Nassau recaptured **Porto Calvo**, then a year later took a force of almost 5,000 men further south against the key city of Salvador. A bold assault nearly secured victory (17–18 May), but Maurice was eventually forced to withdraw. By 1654 Holland had lost all its Brazilian possessions (8 April 26 May 1638).

Salvador I 1822–1823 I Brazilian War of Independence

Early in the war, Portuguese commander in Bahia, Colonel Ignacio Luis Madeira de Melo was besieged at Salvador by Brazilian Colonel Pedro Labatut (later Colonel Joaquim de Lima e Silva). After defeat at **Piraja** and naval action off Salvador, Madeira eventually evacuated by sea for Lisbon, leaving Portugal's only remaining forces in **Montevideo** (February 1822–2 July 1823).

Salvador I 1823 I Brazilian War of Independence

Brazilian naval commander Lord Thomas Cochrane sailed from Rio de Janiero against besieged Salvador, where he met Portuguese Admiral João Félix Pereira de Campos in a badly handled battle off the port. Cochrane had to break off the action and withdrew south to Morro de San Paulo, yet claimed victory because

the Portuguese fleet remained under blockade in Salvador (4 May 1823).

Salween I 1944–1945 I World War II (China)

To break the land blockade of China, General Wei Lihuang crossed the Salween in Yunnan against Japan's General Yuzo Matsuyama. Fighting in high mountains, the Chinese took **Tengchong**, **Longling**, **Songshan** and then **Wanting** on the border to reopen the Burma Road. The much-delayed campaign cost 19,000 Chinese and 15,000 Japanese killed (11 May 1944–20 January 1945).

Samakov I 1371 I Ottoman Conquest of the Balkans

See **Samokov**

Samala I 1901 I Wars of the Mad Mullah

On the first expedition against Muhammad Abdullah Hassan of Somaliland, General Eric Swayne led a mainly Somali force southeast from Burao, where his camp at Samala, north of Damot, was attacked by about 5,000 Dervishes under the Mullah himself. The Dervishes were driven off with heavy losses by Captain Malcolm McNeill and soon met Swayne further south at **Ferdiddin** (2–3 June 1901).

Samalu I 780 I Byzantine-Muslim Wars

Abbasid Caliph al-Mahdi retaliated for the sack of **Hadath** (779) by sending a large army into Byzantine Cilicia under his teenage son Harun, with command assigned to Hasan ibn Kahtaba and the Prince's tutor Khalid ibn Barmaki. The fortress of Samalu, near Massissa east of Adana, was forced to surrender after a 38-day bombardment. A second expedition in 782 won at **Nicomedia**.

Samana I 1709 I Mughal-Sikh Wars

At the head of a massive peasant army, the Sikh leader Banda Singh Bahadur rebelled against Emperor Bahadur Shah and attacked the wealthy Mughal city of Samana, southwest of Patiala in the Upper Punjab. The city fell by storm after three days' fighting in what is claimed to have been the first notable offensive for Sikh arms, followed by a terrible sack and massacre (26 November 1709).

Samanpur | 1815 | British-Gurkha War
See **Parsa**

Samar | 1900 | Philippine-American War
See **Balangiga**

Samar | 1944 | World War II (Pacific)
Despite losses in the **Sibuyan Sea** in the northern Philippines, Admiral Takeo Kurita sailed east through the San Bernadino Strait and the following day surprised Admiral Clifton Sprague off Samar. The massively out-gunned Americans lost two escort carriers and three destroyers, but Kurita lost three cruisers and withdrew, effectively deciding the battle of **Leyte Gulf** (25 October 1944).

Samara | 1918 | Russian Civil War
Counter-attacking against the Czech Legion of former prisoners of war, Red forces retook **Kazan** (10 September) and advanced down the Volga through Simbirsk (12 September). Then at Samara, the Czech units and their White allies were utterly routed. Czech Colonel Svec killed himself when his troops mutinied and the Red offensive continued east towards **Ufa** (8 October 1918).

Samaria | 724–722 BC | Assyrian Wars
When King Hoshea of Israel revolted against his Assyrian overlord, King Shalmaneser V of Assyria took a large army to attack the ancient Israeli capital Samaria, northwest of Jerusalem. While Shalmaneser died during the siege, his successor Sargon II stormed and destroyed Samaria, ending the Kingdom of Israel. Its citizens were deported to Media and Israel became an Assyrian Province.

Samarkand | 1025 | Eastern Muslim Dynastic Wars
Campaigning north of the Oxus, Mahmud of Ghazni attacked Ilek Khan Ali Tegin of Bokhara, who was suppported by Arslan Israil, son of the great leader Seljuk. Aided by Tegin's rival, Yusuf Kadir Khan of Kashghar, Mahmud secured a decisive victory near Samarkand. Arslan and his followers were permitted to settle in Khorasan, though he was later imprisoned and died in captivity.

Samarkand | 1032 | Eastern Muslim Dynastic Wars
See **Dabusiyya**

Samarkand | 1141 | Wars of the Great Seljuk Sultanate
Seljuk Sultan Sanjar of Khorasan supressed a rebellion by the Turkoman tribes of Transoxonia, then faced a new alliance between the Qara-Khitai Tatars and neighbouring Turkish Qarluqs. Decisively defeated near Samarkand, Sanjar was forced to abandon Transoxonia and the continuing Turkoman invasion eventually led to the collapse of his kingdom.

Samarkand | 1220 | Conquests of Genghis Khan
On a massive offensive against the Khwarezmian Empire, the Mongol Genghis Khan captured and destroyed **Bokhara**, then besieged Samarkand, held by Governor Turghay Khan after Sultan Muhammad II fled. When Samarkand fell, it too was destroyed and its inhabitants were massacred. Muhammad was then pursued through his empire to defeat near **Hamadan** (19 March 1220).

Samarkand | 1497–1498 | Mughal-Uzbek Wars
The 15-year-old Mughal Babur led a bold advance to Samarkand, where his small force captured the capital of his ancestor Tamerlane. He then faced a massive army nearby, under the Uzbek leader Muhammad Shaybani Khan and was driven back into the city under siege. Babur was starved into surrender after five months but was allowed to withdraw (November 1497–March 1498).

Samarkand | 1501 | Mughal-Uzbek Wars
See **Sar-i-Pul**

**Samarra I 1917 I World War I
(Mesopotamia)**
  See **Istabulat**

Samawah I 1920 I Iraqi Revolt
  While British troops south of Baghdad ad-
vanced down the Euphrates towards **Kufah**,
General Frank Coningham advanced upriver
from Nasiriyah towards besieged Samawah,
held by Major Arthur Hay. After heavy fighting
at Khidir (6 October) and Hasbah (13 October),
Samawah was relieved. The war soon ended and
Britain established Prince Faisal as King of Iraq
(July–14 October 1920).

**Sambre I 57 BC I Rome's Later
Gallic Wars**
  As he advanced into northern Gaul across
the **Aisne**, Julius Caesar was confronted by
the Belgic Nervii people camped near the Sambre. After some advanced Roman units were
ambushed with heavy losses, Caesar counter-
attacked and routed his enemy, inflicting massive casualties. Thousands more, including
women and children, were sold into slavery and
the Nervii were virtually destroyed.

**Sambre I 1914 I World War I
(Western Front)**
  See **Charleroi**

**Sambre I 1918 I World War I
(Western Front)**
  With his army driven back across the **Selle**,
German commander Erich von Ludendorff re-
signed. The Allies launched their final offensive
along the Sambre between Valenciennes and the
Oise, supported by the Americans in the south on the
Meuse. Brutal fighting saw Le Quesnoy, Tournai,
Mauberge and Mons fall and Germany sued for
peace to end the war (1–11 November 1918).

**Samgamner I 1679 I Mughal-
Maratha Wars**
  Maratha King Shivaji was returning from the
sack of Jalna, northeast of Bombay, when he
was attacked at Samgamner by Mughal General
Ranmast Khan. The King's rearguard held the

Mughals for three days of hard fighting before
Maratha commander Sidhoji Nimbalkar was
eventually killed, along with about 2,000 of his
men. It was Shivaji's last battle and he died six
months later (November 1679).

**Samhud I 1799 I French Revolutionary
Wars (Middle East)**
  Having routed Mamluk General Murad Bey at
the Battle of the **Pyramids** in July 1798, Napoleon
Bonaparte sent Generals Louis Desaix and Louis-
Nicolas Davout in pursuit along the Nile. With
Murad defeated at **Sediman** (7 October), they
advanced to Samhud, near Garga, where another
major Mamluk force was beaten. Murad withdrew
and lost again at **Aswan** (22 January 1799).

**Samland I 1945 I World War II
(Eastern Front)**
  See **Pillau**

**Samokov I 1371 I Ottoman Conquest
of the Balkans**
  Fresh from victory at the **Maritza**, Ottoman
Sultan Murad I marched against a coalition of
Bulgarian and Serbian Princes under his brother-
in-law Prince John Sisman of Trnovo. Supported
by General Lala Shahin Pasha, Murad routed
and dispersed the Christians at Samokov,
southeast of Sofia, marking the beginning of the
end of independent Bulgaria.

**Samos I 1824 I Greek War of
Independence**
  Turkish Admiral Khosrew Pasha was determined to seize Samos and landed troops before
his fleet was met between Ikaria and Samos by
Greek Admiral Georgios Sachtouris with Kon-
staninos Kanaris. With three ships, 100 cannon
and 1,000 men lost in heavy fighting, Khosrew
was forced to abandon his expedition. He fought
again next month further south off **Bodrum**
(11–17 August 1824).

**Sampford Courtenay I 1549 I
Western Rebellion**
  Pro-Catholic insurgents in Cornwall and
Devon who besieged **Exeter** were driven off at

St Mary's Clyst (4 August), then regrouped to the northwest under Sir Humphry Arundell at Sampford Courtenay. In the final brutal action of the rebellion, they were crushed by Lord John Russell with many prisoners killed. Arundell and other leaders were executed and Russell was ennobled (17 August 1549).

Samugargh I 1658 I War of the Mughal Princes

Bitter war between the sons of ailing Mughal Emperor Shahjahan saw the younger brothers Aurangzeb and Murad Baksh defeat an Imperial army at Dharmat, then march on Agra against the eldest brother, Dara Shikoh. Dara was defeated eight miles east at Samugargh and fled. Aurangzeb then imprisoned his own father and brother Murad and seized the throne (29 May 1658).

Samur I 1583 I Turko-Persian Wars
See Vilasa

San I 1914 I World War I (Eastern Front)

Aided by a German advance on Warsaw, Austrian General Svetozar Boroevic launched a fresh offensive into southern Poland and managed to relieve besieged Przemysl, west of Lemberg (Lvov). Russian forces under General Radko Dmitriev fought a courageous defence along the San and, with the Germans checked around Warsaw, Boroevic began to fall back (13–14 October 1914).

Sanaa I 1967–1968 I Yemeni Civil Wars

Encouraged by the withdrawal of Egyptian forces supporting the Republican government of North Yemen, Saudi-backed Royalists under Prince Muhammad Hussein attacked the highland city of Sanaa. After an epic 70-day defence, aided by Republicans from South Yemen, the siege was broken and the Royalist war to restore the Imamate was effectively lost (1 December 1967–8 February 1968).

Sanananda I 1942–1943 I World War II (Pacific)

Australian General George Vasey and American Robert Eichelberger took Buna and Gona on the north coast of Papua, but stalled outside the main Japanese beachhead at Sanananda. With both sides reinforced, there was heavy fighting before Sanananda fell and the surviving Japanese were evacuated northwest towards Salamaua (20 November 1942–22 January 1943).

San Andrés I 1913 I Mexican Revolution

Francisco (Pancho) Villa resumed the war in northern Mexico, attacking a Federal force of almost 1,000 men under General Feliz Terrazas advancing towards Chihuahua at San Andrés. Major Benito Artalejo took the town by storm after a daylong action, capturing massive arms and booty. The Federals lost 300 casualties in the action and Villa executed over 300 prisoners (26 August 1913).

San Antonio, El Salvador I 1828 I Central American National Wars

On campaign against President Manuel José Arce of the Central American Federation, General Francisco Morazán of Honduras again invaded El Salvador and defeated Colonel Antonio de Aycinena at San Antonio, on the Rio Lempa near Gualcho. The Federal army capitulated and Morazán entered San Salvador in triumph, then advanced on Guatemala City (9 October 1828).

San Antonio, Texas I 1835 I Texan Wars of Independence

Advancing through Goliad to occupy San Antonio, Mexican General Martin Perfecto de Cos and 1,200 troops were besieged at the Presidio (known as Bexar) by Texan volunteers. In the final assault by Ben Milam and Frank W. Johnson (5 December), Milam was killed. However, Cos soon surrendered and the Texans captured plentiful guns and ammunition (October–9 December 1835).

San Antonio, Texas (1st) I 1842 I Texan Wars of Independence

Eight years after losing Texas at San Jacinto, Mexico sent a raiding force of 500 Regular cavalry under General Ráfael Vásquez, who seized San Antonio. Contrary to Texan fears, Vásquez proved not to be the vanguard of a full-scale invasion and he returned across the Rio Grande after indecisive skirmishing. A much larger force tried again six months later (5 March 1842).

San Antonio, Texas (2nd) ∎ 1842 ∎ Texan Wars of Independence

French-born Mexican General Adrián Woll led a second large-scale raid into Texas, marching 1,200 troops north to once again secure San Antonio. However, after a week's occupation, Woll was defeated by Texan forces at the nearby **Salado** River and withdrew towards Mexico with his prisoners. The Texans retaliated in December with a raid against **Laredo** (11–20 September 1842).

San Bernadino Strait ∎ 1944 ∎ World War II (Pacific)

See **Samar**

San Carlos, Argentina ∎ 1872 ∎ Argentine Civil Wars

Despite aiding the government at **Cepeda** in 1859, Indian leader Juan Calfucurá continued to attack towns on the Pampas in Buenos Aires Province and was met at San Carlos de Bolivar by a large force under General Ignacio Rivas and Indian ally Cipriano Catriel. Calfucurá suffered a decisive defeat with about 200 men killed, effectively ending the Indian raids. He died a year later (8 March 1872).

San Carlos, Falklands ∎ 1982 ∎ Falklands War

When a British amphibious force landed 4,000 men on East Falkland at San Carlos, Argentine planes sank two British ships and badly damaged two others, while the destroyer *Coventry* was sunk to the northwest. Over 30 Argentine aircraft were lost before a second British landing secured the bridgehead. The troops then marched east towards **Stanley** and south towards **Goose Green** (21 26 May 1982).

Sand Creek ∎ 1864 ∎ Cheyenne-Arapaho Indian War

Colonel John Chivington took a force of cavalry 40 miles northeast of Fort Lyon in eastern Color-

ado against 500 Cheyenne and some Arapaho led by Black Kettle in camp under a flag of peace at Sand Creek. In a brutal attack at dawn, Chivington's men destroyed the camp, killing about 300, more than half of them women and children, and provoking a bitter war (29 November 1864).

Sandepu ∎ 1905 ∎ Russo-Japanese War

During an attempted offensive south of **Mukden** (modern Shenyang), Russian General Aleksei Kuropatkin advanced at the western end of the entrenched positions between **Shaho** and the Hun River. Launched in heavy snow near the villages of Sandepu and Heigoutai, the mismanaged Russian initiative stalled with severe losses and achieved nothing (25–29 January 1905).

Sandershausen ∎ 1758 ∎ Seven Years War (Europe)

As Duke Charles of Soubise counter-attacked through Hesse, his French vanguard under Duke Victor-Francois of Broglie was met at Sandershausen, on the Fulda northeast of Kassel, by Hessians and Hanoverians under Prince Johann Casimir of Isenburg. Broglie overwhelmed the outnumbered Allies and in October Soubise won a decisive victory at nearby **Lutterberg** (23 July 1758).

Sandfontein ∎ 1914 ∎ World War I (African Colonial Theatre)

As South African forces invaded German Southwest Africa, General Henry Lukin in the south took Raman Drift on the Orange, while Colonel Ronald Grant advanced upriver to Sandfontein. Attacked by German Colonel Joachim von Heydebreck, the South Africans suffered heavy losses and surrendered. A need to deal with a Boer rising then stalled the Allied campaign (26 September 1914).

Sand Mountain ∎ 1863 ∎ American Civil War (Western Theatre)

See **Day's Gap**

Sandomierz ∎ 1656 ∎ 1st Northern War

Charles X of Sweden renewed his offensive into Poland through **Golab**, advancing on Lvov.

However, he failed trying to storm Zamosc and fell back to the Vistula near Sandomierz, blockaded in the west by Stefan Czarniecki and Jerzy Lubomirski and in the east by Pavel Sapeiha's Lithuanians. A relief force was beaten at **Warka**, but Charles broke out and recaptured **Warsaw** in July (March–April 1656).

San Domingo I 1802–1803 I Napoleonic Wars (Santo Domingo Rising)
　See **Santo Domingo**

Sand River I 1900 I 2nd Anglo-Boer War
　See **Zand**

Sandwich I 851 I Viking Raids on Britain
　Threatened by continued Viking raids on the south English coast, Athelstan, under-King of Kent and brother of Aethelwulf of Wessex, led the Saxon fleet to sea supported by Ealdorman Ealchere. In what is sometimes called England's first naval victory, Athelstan defeated the Danes off Sandwich, reputedly taking ten prizes. The Danes withdrew to the Thames and imminent defeat at **Aclea**.

Sandwich I 1217 I 1st English Barons' War
　See **South Foreland**

Sandwich I 1460 I Wars of the Roses
　Despite their disaster at **Ludford Bridge** (October 1459), a Yorkist force returned from Calais and landed near Sandwich, Kent, defended by Sir Osbert Mountfort. A fierce action saw John Dinham seize the town, supported by Sir John Wenlock and William Neville Earl of Fauconberg. Richard Neville Earl of Warwick then landed and in July defeated Henry VI at **Northampton** (20 June 1460).

Sandy Creek I 1814 I War of 1812
　American barges moving guns and cables from Oswego to new ships at Sacket's Harbour were met at Sandy Creek on the east shore of Lake Ontario by 200 English marines and sailors under Captain Stephen Popham. Ambushed by 250 riflemen and Oneida Indians led by Captain

Daniel Appling, Popham had to surrender and America soon regained naval superiority on Lake Ontario (30 May 1814).

San Esteban de Gormaz I 918 I Christian-Muslim Wars in Spain
　Ordono II of Leon led a major offensive against the Muslims, advancing across the Douro to campaign as far south as Merida before being challenged by a massive army raised by the Andalusian Umayyad Caliph Abd-ar-Rahman III. Near San Esteban de Gormaz, southwest of Soria, Ordono achieved a brilliant victory, though he was beaten by Abd-ar-Rahman in 920 at **Val-de-Junquera**.

San Felasco Hammock I 1836 I 2nd Seminole Indian War
　While campaigning in northern Alachua County, northwest of modern Gainesville, Florida, 100 local militia on reconnaissance under Colonel John Warren were attacked by Seminoles at San Felasco Hammock, south of Newnansville. A hard-fought action saw Warren's troops almost surrounded before they were saved by effective use of their cannon (18 September 1836).

San Felice I 1810 I Napoleonic Wars (Peninsular Campaign)
　See **Barba de Puerco**

San Felipe I 1863 I Central American National Wars
　President Gerardo Barrios of El Salvador repulsed Guatemalan invaders at **Coatepeque** (24 February), then turned south to support Liberal rebellion in Nicaragua. However, Barrios was defeated by President Tomás Martínez at San Felipe, a suburb of Leon, and had to return to El Salvador. He soon faced a fresh Guatemalan invasion and siege of his own capital **San Salvador** (29 April 1863).

San Felix I 1817 I Venezuelan War of Independence
　With Revolutionary forces besieging **Angostura** in eastern Venezuela, Spanish commander Pablo Morillo sent 1,500 reinforcements under

General Miguel de La Torre, who met General Manuel Piar 60 miles to the northeast at San Felix. De La Torre was routed and narrowly escaped capture, losing 500 killed and 500 prisoners. Angostura fell to Piar in July (11 April 1817).

San Fermo I 1859 I 2nd Italian War of Independence

At war with Austria in northern Italy east of Lake Maggiore, Giuseppe Garibaldi and 3,000 men captured **Varese**, then advanced on Como next day, meeting over 6,000 infantry under Marshal Karl von Urban at San Fermo. Despite brave resistance, the Austrians were driven out at bayonet-point. Garibaldi won again at **Tre Ponti** (15 June), though he achieved little strategic benefit (27 May 1859).

San Fiorenzo I 1794 I French Revolutionary Wars (1st Coalition)

With the British navy forced out of **Toulon** in December 1793, Admiral Sir Samuel Hood (1724–1816) invaded Corsica and landed near San Fiorenzo (St Florent). A storming party under Captain William Beresford seized the town, while survivors of the garrison fled to **Bastia**. Two French frigates in the harbour were sunk, though one was later recommissioned (7 February 1794).

San Francisco I 1879 I War of the Pacific

When Chile won command of the sea at **Angamos** (8 October), a 6,000-strong Chilean army under Emilio Sotomayer Baeza landed at Pisagua and captured Dolores, then faced General Juan Buendía's Peruvians marching north from Iquique. Buendía was utterly routed on the nearby Plain of Dolores at Cerros de San Francisco. The Chileans then captured Iquique (19 November 1879).

San Francisco I 1891 I Chilean Civil War

Amid civil war against Chilean President José Manuel Balmaceda, 1,000 Congressist troops led by Colonel Estanislao del Canto Arteaga defeated Loyalist Colonel Eulogio Robles Pinochet and 350 troops northeast of Iquique at Cerros de San Francisco, on the plain of Dolores. Iqique fell next day. After a check at **Huara**, Canto Arteaga won again weeks later at **Pozo Almonte** (15 February 1891).

San Gabriel, California I 1847 I American-Mexican War

Commodore Robert Stockton and General Stephen Kearney continued the offensive against Spanish California and were met northeast of Los Angeles at the San Gabriel by Spanish-Californian forces under Captain José Maria Flores. Falling back with few casualties, Flores was beaten again next day on the plain of La Mesa and American forces re-entered Los Angeles (8–9 January 1847).

San Gabriels, Texas I 1839 I Texan Wars of Independence

Unaware of the defeat of the Mexican insurrectionist Vicente Córdova at **Mill Creek**, Manuel Flores set out from Matamaros with food and munitions, escorted by about 30 Indians and Mexicans. Intercepted near the San Gabriels, west of modern Georgetown, Texas, by Texas Ranger James O. Rice, Flores was defeated and killed and the so-called Córdova Rebellion was finally over (17 May 1839).

Sanganer I 1858 I Indian Mutiny

Bogged down by heavy rain and unable to cross the swollen Chambal following defeat at **Jawra Alipur** (20 June), the rebel Tantia Topi made a stand near Sanganer, just south of Jaipur city, against the pursuing Rajputana Field force under General Henry Gee Roberts. The rebels fled after terrible losses to artillery fire and a week later tried to hold the Banas at **Kankrauli** (7 August 1858).

Sangerhausen I 1758 I Seven Years War (Europe)

See **Sandershausen**

Sanggiyan Hada I 1619 I Manchu Conquest of China

See **Siyanggiayan**

San Giovanni ▌ 1799 ▌ French Revolutionary Wars (2nd Coalition)
See **Trebbia**

San Giuliano ▌ 1799 ▌ French Revolutionary Wars (2nd Coalition)
See **Alessandria**

Sangju ▌ 1592 ▌ Japanese Invasion of Korea
As Toyotomi Hideyoshi's massive invasion force advanced up the Korean Peninsula from **Pusan**, Konishi Yukinaga, supported by So Soshitomo, reached Sangju, northwest of Taegu, where General Yi Il attempted to halt the invaders. The largely untrained Korean peasant force was routed and fled with thousands beheaded. Konishi continued north through **Chongju** (3 June 1592).

San Gregorio ▌ 1817–1818 ▌ Mexican Wars of Independence
See **Los Remedios**

Sangro ▌ 1943 ▌ World War II (Southern Europe)
German General Traugott Herr lost **Termoli** (7 October) but held the Sangro, the eastern end of the **Gustav Line** across Italy. A British bridgehead across the river was heavily counter-attacked and almost lost before tanks were brought up. General Sir Bernard Montgomery then drove on across the Moro and took **Ortona** before heavy losses made him call off his offensive (20–28 November 1943).

Sanguesa ▌ 924 ▌ Christian-Muslim Wars in Spain
In reprisal for Christian capture of the castle of Viguera, Abd-ar-Rahman III led an expedition from Cordova into northeastern Spain against Sancho I of Navarre. The opposing forces met at Sanguesa, southeast of Pamplona, and Sancho was routed. The Muslim ruler then went on to sack the abandoned city of Pamplona (22 July 924).

San Ignacio ▌ 1867 ▌ Argentine Civil Wars
Rebels led by General Juan Sáa and Juan de Dios Videla rose in western Argentina against President Bartolomé Mitre and faced a large force under General Wenceslao Paunero. At San Ignacio, on the Rio Quinto east of San Luis, the Loyalist vanguard under Colonel José Miguel Arredondo inflicted a decisive defeat. The rebels fled to Chile and Arredondo was promoted General (1 April 1867).

San Isidro ▌ 1896 ▌ Philippines War of Independence
At the start of the war, 2,000 ill-armed rebels in Nueva Ecija under Mariano Llanera and Pantaleon Belmonte seized the town of San Isidro and besieged Governor Leonardo Walls and the Spanish garrison in their barracks. However, Major Lopez Arteaga arrived with reinforcements next day and the Patriots were driven out after a brutal all-night counter-attack (3–4 September 1896).

San Isidro ▌ 1899 ▌ Philippine-American War
After American forces captured the Revolutionary capital at **Malolos**, 30 miles northwest of **Manila** (31 March), General Henry W. Lawton advanced to the northeast on the newly designated insurgent capital at San Isidro, Nuevo Ecija. The town fell following heavy fighting, but President Emilio Aguinaldo's government eluded capture and retreated upriver to Cabanatuan (17 May 1899).

San Isidro del General ▌ 1948 ▌ Costa Rican Civil War
In the wake of a disputed election, rebels under José María Figueres Ferrer seized San Isidro, commanding the Pan America highway, from the government forces of President Teodoro Picado. Very heavy fighting drove off a counter-attack by Carlos Luis Fallas and General Toribia Tijerno (killed in the withdrawal) and Figueres advanced north towards **Cartago** (12–14 March 1948).

San Jacinto, Mexico I 1867 I Mexican-French War

Imperial-Mexican Conservative forces under General Miguel Miramón, attempting to block the Liberal re-conquest of Mexico, seized Zacatecas then faced a counter-offensive by General Mariano Escobedo at nearby San Jacinto. Miramón was routed and over 100 prisoners—including his brother Joaquin—were executed. Escobedo continued south against **Querétaro** (12 February 1867).

San Jacinto, Nicaragua I 1856 I National (Filibuster) War

East of Lake Managua, 300 of William Walker's Filibusters led by American Byron Cole attacked 160 troops under Colonel José Dolores Estrada at San Jacinto. In a celebrated action, the outnumbered Nicaraguans were roused by heroic Sergeant Andrés Castro and drove Cole off. Their courage inspired another defensive victory a month later at **Masaya** (14 September 1856).

San Jacinto, Texas I 1836 I Texan Wars of Independence

General Sam Houston's battered Texans fell back after the disasters at the **Alamo** and **Coleto Creek** in March and took a defensive position on the San Jacinto River, southeast of modern Houston, against Mexican General Antonio de Santa Anna. The outnumbered Texans won a brilliant victory, with almost every Mexican killed or captured, effectively securing independence for Texas (20 April 1836).

San Jorge I 1857 I National (Filibuster) War

Soon after the Central American allies drove the American William Walker out of **Granada** in western Nicaragua, their new commander José Maria Cañas advanced south on Rivas and seized nearby San Jorge. Repeated costly attacks by Charles Henningsen and later by Walker himself failed to dislodge the allies, who then resumed the offensive against **Rivas** itself (29 January–16 March 1857).

San José I 1835 I Central American National Wars

Twelve years after Costa Rica's capital was moved to San José following victory at **Ochomogo**, the cities of Cartago, Alajuela and Heredia formed a secessionist League and besieged President Braulio Carrillo in San José. However, League troops were repeatedly defeated and peace assured the dominance of San José. Carrillo was eventually overthrown in 1842 (October 1835).

San José la Arada I 1851 I Central American National Wars

See **La Arada**

San Juan, Puerto Rico (1st) I 1898 I Spanish-American War

American naval commander William T. Sampson, on the hunt for the Spanish fleet under Admiral Pascual Cervera, arrived at San Juan, Puerto Rico, where he found no ships, but launched a controversial bombardment of the city. After inflicting heavy damage, Sampson withdrew to blockade Puerto Rico. A Spanish attempt to break the blockade the following month failed (12 May 1898).

San Juan, Puerto Rico (2nd) I 1898 I Spanish-American War

One of the best-known ship-to-ship actions of the war saw the Spanish destroyer *Terror* and the old cruiser *Isabel II* leave San Juan, Puerto Rico, to attack the blockading American auxiliary cruiser *St Paul* (Captain Charles D. Sigsbee). *Isabel II* turned back and *Terror* was badly damaged by very fierce gunfire and run ashore. A month later American forces landed at **Guánica** (22 June 1898).

San Juan Bridge I 1899 I Philippine-American War

See **Manila**

San Juan del Monte I 1896 I Philippines War of Independence

In their first major action, 800 ill-trained Katipuneros under Andrés Bonifacio and Emilio

Jacinto attacked the Spanish depot at San Juan del Monte, then advanced on nearby Manila. Met by Spanish reinforcements under General Bernard Echaluse, the insurgents were routed with 153 killed and over 200 captured. Next day Governor Ramon Blanco declared a state of war (30 August 1896).

San Juan de los Llanos I 1817 I Mexican Wars of Independence

Spanish adventurer Francisco Javier Mina landed on the east coast of Mexico at **Soto La Marina** to raise rebellion and met a much larger Royalist army under Colonel Felipe Castañon at the hacienda of San Juan de los Llanos, near San Felipe, Guanajuato. A one-sided defeat saw Castañon mortally wounded and over 300 men lost. Mina then took his force to **Sombrero** (29 May 1817).

San Juan de Ulúa I 1838 I Pastry War

When Mexico refused compensation for French nationals looted during an army mutiny—including a pastrycook—French Admiral Charles Baudin besieged San Juan de Ulúa, off Veracruz, held by General Antonio Gaona. After failed negotiations, a brief bombardment forced the "Gibraltar of America" to surrender and Mexico agreed to pay compensation (26 October–27 November 1838).

San Juan Epatlán I 1876 I Diaz Revolt in Mexico

A week after rebels against President Sebastián Lerdo de Tejada were defeated at **Icamole**, Generals Ignacio Alatorre and Diódoro Corella attacked rebel Generals Fidencio Hernandez and Antonio Couttolenne at San Juan Epatlán in Puebla. After a protracted action—with Corella fatally wounded—the insurgents had to withdraw. Alatorre was routed later that year at **Tecoac** (28 May 1876).

San Juan Hill I 1898 I Spanish-American War

Generals Samuel Sumner and Jacob F. Kent advanced through **Las Guásimas** against **Santiago de Cuba**. Supported by Colonels Leonard Wood and Theodore Roosevelt, they attacked Spanish outer defences held by General Arsenio Linares. San Juan Hill and Kettle Hill were taken at a cost of over 1,500 American casualties and Santiago surrendered two weeks later (1 July 1898).

San Lazaro I 1746 I War of the Austrian Succession

See **Piacenza**

San Lorenzo, Argentina I 1813 I Argentine War of Independence

When a Spanish squadron of 11 ships from Montevideo attempted to ascend the Parana River in support of Royalist forces in the Upper Provinces, a landing party under Juan Antonio Zabala was surprised at San Lorenzo, 15 miles northwest of Rosario, by Colonel José San Martin's Mounted Grenadiers. San Martin was badly wounded but the Patriots won a decisive victory (3 February 1813).

San Lorenzo, Mexico I 1863 I Mexican-French War

With the strategic Mexican city of **Puebla** under siege by French General Elie Fréderic Forey, General Ignacio Comonfort led a relief army east from Mexico City. At San Lorenzo, the Mexicans were surprised in an early morning ambush by a French force detached by Forey under General Achille Bazaine. Comonfort was routed and fled and Puebla surrendered ten days later (8 May 1863).

San Lorenzo, Mexico I 1867 I Mexican-French War

While Liberals under General Porfirio Diaz besieged **Puebla**, an Imperial-Mexican relief force led by General Leonardo Márquez marched east from Mexico City. When Puebla fell (4 April), Diaz pursued Márquez and attacked the government troops at San Lorenzo. Márquez was decisively defeated and abandoned his guns as he withdrew under siege to **Mexico City** (10 April 1867).

San Lorenzo, Spain (1st) I 1794 I French Revolutionary Wars (1st Coalition)

General Pierre Augereau responded to the Spanish invasion of southeastern France by crossing the Spanish border to divert Spanish forces away from the French siege of the fortress at **Bellegarde**. At San Lorenzo de la Muga, Augereau repulsed Spanish General Amarillas Comte de la Union with heavy losses before being forced to withdraw. However, the siege of Bellegarde continued (13 August 1794).

San Lorenzo, Spain (2nd) I 1794 I French Revolutionary Wars (1st Coaltion)
See **Figueras**

San Lucas Sacatepéquez I 1871 I Central American National Wars
Liberal revolution against President Vicente Cerna of Guatemala began with the heroic stand at **Tacaña** (2 April). Miguel Garcia Granados and Justo Rufino Barrios then won several actions before defeating the main government army near Antigua at San Lucas Sacatepéquez. Cerna fled into exile while Garcia Granados entered Guatemala City next day to secure the Presidency (29 June 1871).

San Luis de Ylinoises I 1780 I War of the American Revolution
See **St Louis**

San Luis Potosi I 1832 I Mexican Civil Wars
See **Gallinero**

San Luis Potosi I 1863 I Mexican-French War
When Tomás Mejía led a large Imperial force against San Luis Potosi, Liberal General Miguel Negrete abandoned the city without a fight, then gathered reinforcements and launched a bloody counter-offensive. Mejía repulsed the Liberals after heavy fighting, capturing all of Negrete's guns and 800 prisoners, most of whom joined the Imperial cause (December 1863).

San Marcial I 1813 I Napoleonic Wars (Peninsular Campaign)
In a co-ordinated effort to relieve the Allied siege of San Sebastian on the Spanish north coast,

French Marshal Nicolas Soult led a powerful force across the **Bidassoa** near San Marcial, where they were heavily repulsed by Spanish General Manuel Freire. Another relief attempt was driven off near **Vera**, and **San Sebastian** town fell by storm the same day (31 August 1813).

San Marcos, Honduras I 1876 I Central American National Wars
José María Medina briefly regained power in Honduras with victory at **La Esperanza** in January, then faced a rapid counter-offensive by President Ponciano Levía, whose General Luis Bográn Baraona attacked at San Marcos River. Medina's army under his namesake Juan Antonio Medina was badly beaten. The usurper lost again at El Naranja (21 February) and fled (13 February 1876).

San Marcos, Venezuela I 1813 I Venezuelan War of Independence
Buoyed by his victory over Spanish Royalists at **Araure**, in western Venezuela, three days later Patriot leader Simón Bolívar sent 1,000 men against the brutal llaneros irregulars under José Tomás Boves at San Marcos on the Guárico. Bolívar's outnumbered Republican force was utterly destroyed and Boves advanced to a further victory in two months at **La Puerta** (8 December 1813).

San Marcos de Colón I 1907 I Nicaraguan-Honduran War
When President José Santos Zelaya of Nicaragua invaded Honduras, President Manuel Bonilla sent Salamón Ordóñez to defend San Marcos de Colón, near the border northeast of Choluteca. The Hondurans were routed and the invaders seized the city, proclaiming Miguel Bustillo as provisional President. Another disaster followed in March, further south at **Namasigue** (25 February 1907).

San Mateo, Philippines I 1896 I Philippines War of Independence
Recovering from heavy losses at **San Juan del Monte**, Katipunero rebels under Andrés

Bonifacio and Emilio Jacinto withdrew to the Montalban hills and soon attacked San Mateo. The rebels seized the town for their first significant victory, but the Spanish quickly counterattacked. After heavy fighting along the Langka River, Bonifacio's forces retreated to Balara (September 1896).

San Mateo, Philippines I 1899 I Philippine-American War

Threatened by Philippine insurgent activity near Manila, American commander Elwell S. Otis sent a small column under General Henry W. Lawton against General Licerio Geronimo, 15 miles to the northeast on the Mariquina at San Mateo, Morong. The courageous Lawton was killed during a fierce action fought in heavy rain and his defeated force returned to Manila (19 December 1899).

San Mateo, Venezuela I 1814 I Venezuelan War of Independence

Patriot Simón Bolívar followed defeat at **La Puerta** in north Venezuela (3 February) by taking a defensive position at San Mateo, east of Lake de Valencia, against Spanish irregulars led by José Tomás Boves. Another Spanish force was beaten at nearby **La Victoria** and Boves was repulsed in two brutal attacks on San Mateo before Bolívar withdrew west to **Valencia** (28 February & 25 March 1814).

San Miguel de Tucumán I 1812 I Argentine War of Independence
See **Tucumán**

San Miguelito I 1860 I Mexican War of the Reform
See **Calpulalpam**

San Millan I 1813 I Napoleonic Wars (Peninsular Campaign)

As part of the manoeuvring before the great Allied victory at **Vitoria**, a French division under General Antoine-Louis Maucune was unexpectedly intercepted south of the Ebro at San Millan de la Cogolla by British units un-

der Generals John Vandeleur and James Kempt. The French were badly mauled and took no part in the main battle three days later (18 June 1813).

San Munoz I 1812 I Napoleonic Wars (Peninsular Campaign)
See **Huebra**

Sannah's Post I 1900 I 2nd Anglo-Boer War

Christiaan de Wet abandoned Bloemfontein after **Driefontein** and led an offensive against the Sannah's Post pumping station on the Modder, 20 miles east of Bloemfontein. Despite reinforcements being available within sound of the guns, no help was sent to General Robert Broadwood, who lost 117 wagons, seven guns and 480 prisoners. De Wet continued south to **Reddersburg** (31 March 1900).

Sannaiyat I 1916 I World War I (Mesopotamia)

After another attempt to relieve **Kut-al-Amara** was repulsed at **Dujaila** (8 March), new Anglo-Indian commander General George Gorringe led 30,000 men in a final effort to save the besieged city on the Tigris. Four major assaults were launched against the Turks at nearby Sannaiyat—with five Victoria Crosses won—but the British were driven off and Kut fell a week later (5–22 April 1916).

Sannaspos I 1900 I 2nd Anglo-Boer War
See **Sannah's Post**

San Nicolás I 1811 I Argentine War of Independence

Near the start of Argentina's war against Spain, a small Patriot squadron under Juan Bautista Azopardo was sent up the Parana to aid General Manuel Belgrano's campaign in Paraguay. At San Nicolás, 37 miles southeast of Rosario, the squadron was intercepted and destroyed by Spanish ships from Montevideo and Spain retained control of the rivers (2 March 1811).

San Pascual I 1846 I American-Mexican War

American General Stephen Kearney, marching overland into Spanish California, was blocked northeast of San Diego at San Pascual by a Spanish-Californian force under Captain Andrés Pico. Reinforced from the north by Lieutenant Andrew Gray, Kearney fought a hard but inconclusive action. However, he took San Diego six days later then marched north to **San Gabriel** (6 December 1846).

San Patricio I 1836 I Texan Wars of Independence

While Mexican commander General Antonio de Santa Anna invaded Texas to retake **San Antonio**, a smaller force under General José Urrea advanced along the Gulf Coast. At San Patricio, Urrea destroyed a Texan force under Frank Johnson. He then defeated other Texan forces at **Refugio** and **Agua Dulce Creek** as he advanced inland towards **Coleto Creek** (27 February 1836).

San Payo I 1809 I Napoleonic Wars (Peninsular Campaign)
    See **Oitaven**

San Pedro, Cuba I 1896 I 2nd Cuban War of Independence
    See **Punta Brava**

San Pedro, Venezuela I 1892 I Venezuelan Civil Wars

When President Raimondo Andueza Palacio tried to extend his power, Joaquín Crespo led the "Legalist Revolution," which overthrew Palacio and his successor, Guillermo Tell Vellegas. After numerous engagements over six months, General Domingo Monagas was finally defeated at San Pedro, near Los Tegues. Crespo entered Caracas next day and became President (5 October 1892).

San Pedro Perulapán I 1839 I Central American National Wars

Salvadoran President Francisco Morazán defeated Honduran-Nicaraguan invaders at

Espíritu Santo (6 April), then faced a renewed invasion under Francisco Ferrera. Just north of San Salvador at San Pedro Perulapán, Ferrera was beaten and withdrew to Nicaragua. As a result, Morazán soon invaded **Guatemala** while another Salvadoran army in Honduras won at **Soledad** (25 September 1839).

San Pedro Sula I 1919 I Honduran Civil War

When former President Francisco Bertrand tried to install his brother-in-law Nazario Soriano after a disputed election, Rafael López Gutiérrez raised rebellion at Danlí, while General Vicente Tosta advanced on San Pedro Sula. After a weeklong battle, with heavy civilian losses, the US intervened. Bertrand and Soriano fled into exile and López Gutiérrez was elected (September 1919).

San Petru I 1611 I Balkan National Wars

Gabriel Bathory of Transylvania invaded Wallachia and Prince Radu Serban was forced to withdraw into Moldavia. An effective counter-attack then saw him to defeat Bathory at San Petru, near Brasov in northwest Transylvania. Turkish forces had meantime invaded Wallachia and installed the loyal Radu Mihnea. Radu Serban went into exile in Austria (September 1611).

San River I 1914 I World War I (Eastern Front)
    See **San**

San Roque I 1829 I Argentine Civil Wars

Shortly after part of General Juan Galo Lavalle's Unitarist force was defeated at **Vizcacheras**, his Federalist ally General José Maria Paz marched into Córdoba against Juan Bautista Bustos. Paz secured a decisive victory at San Roque, just west of Córdoba, and won again at **La Tablada**. However, Lavalle himself was defeated a few days later at **Puente de Márquez** (22 April 1829).

San Saba | 1839 | Cherokee Indian Wars

Pursuing Cherokees on the Colorado after their defeat at the **Neches** (16 July), Texans under General Ed Burleson intercepted a small group of survivors under Chief Egg and John Bowle (son of Chief Bowle killed at the Neches) near the mouth of the San Saba River. Egg and Bowle were among the few killed, with the others captured, ending war against the Cherokee in Texas (25 December 1839).

San Salvador | 1863 | Central American National Wars

Driven out of El Salvador at **Coatepeque** in February, President José Rafael Carrera of Guatemala invaded again with Nicaraguan support to capture Santa Ana (3 July), while General Vicente Cerna besieged President Gerardo Barrios in San Salvador. Barrios finally capitulated and fled into exile and Carrera installed Francisco Dueñas as President of El Salvador (July–29 October 1863).

San Sebastian | 1813 | Napoleonic Wars (Peninsular Campaign)

Generals Sir Thomas Graham and Gabriel Mendizabal, advancing into the western Pyrenees after the great Allied victory at **Vitoria** (21 June), besieged the vital port of San Sebastian, defended by General Emmanuel Rey. After heavy losses in failed assaults and a costly French sortie (26 July), the city was stormed and sacked (31 August). The citadel fell a week later (25 June–8 September 1813).

San Sebastian | 1836 | 1st Carlist War

A fresh offensive against government forces at San Sebastian in Navarre saw 10,000 Carlists with artillery support attack the lines at nearby Pasajes, held by the British Legion under General Sir George de Lacy Evans. While the English and their Spanish allies suffered 500 casualties (including Evans slightly wounded), the Carlists were driven off at a cost of over 1,200 men (1 October 1836).

Santa Ana | 1871 | Central American National Wars

While Salvadorans invaded Honduras after **Pasaquina** (16 March), rebel Santiago Gonzáles, with Honduran aid, marched against the forces of Salvadoran President Francisco Dueñas at Santa Ana. Gonzáles won a decisive victory and assumed the Presidency. He ended hostilities against Honduras, but a year later overthrew President José María Medina of Honduras at **Comayagua** (10 April 1871).

Santa Ana Amatlan | 1865 | Mexican-French War

Colonel Ramón Mendez followed Imperial victory at **Tacámbaro** by securing another decisive victory at Santa Ana Amatlan, southwest of Urupuan. Liberal Generals José María Arteaga and Carlos Salazar were defeated and captured, then executed under the Imperial "Black Decree," along with three Colonels. Mendez himself was executed after the fall of **Querétaro** in May 1867 (13 October 1865).

Santa Clara | 1958 | Cuban Revolution

Having blunted a massive Batista campaign into the **Sierra Maestra** in July, rebel forces took the offensive and advanced onto the plains. While Santiago surrendered with little resistance, Ernesto Che Guevara fought the last major battle of the revolution to take Santa Clara. President Fulgencio Batista fled into exile next day and Fidel Castro entered Havana in triumph (28–31 December 1958).

Santa Cruz | 1899 | Philippine-American War

Recalled from the fall of **Malolos**, American General Henry W. Lawton led a reconnaissance in force southeast from Manila across Laguna de Bay, where he landed and captured the insurgent stronghold at Santa Cruz. He then marched inland and took several more towns before withdrawing, permitting most of the area to be soon retaken by Philippine General Juan Cailles (10 April 1899).

Santa Cruz de Rozales ▌ 1848 ▌ American-Mexican War

Despite a peace treaty being signed, American General Sterling Price, military Governor of Chihuahua, led an unauthorised expedition into the interior against Mexican commander General Angel Trias. Marching through Chihuahua 35 miles southeast to Santa Cruz de Rozales, Price defeated a force twice his size and captured Trias. It was the last action of the war (16 March 1848).

Santa Cruz de Tenerife ▌ 1657 ▌ Anglo-Spanish Wars

Spain's large West Indies fleet had arrived at Santa Cruz, Tenerife, when it was attacked by English Admirals Robert Blake and Richard Stayner. By evening, all 16 galleons had been burned, blown up or sunk at the cost of about 150 English casualties and no English ship lost. However, Blake was unable to enjoy his success, dying of fever just before his ship reached Plymouth (20 April 1657).

Santa Cruz de Tenerife ▌ 1797 ▌ French Revolutionary Wars (1st Coalition)

Following victory at **Cape St Vincent** (14 February), British Admiral Sir John Jervis rashly sent Admiral Horatio Nelson to capture the Manila treasure ship and the Spanish fortress at Santa Cruz de Tenerife in the Canary Islands, held by Governor Don Juan Gutiérrez. With insufficient men, Nelson's boats were driven off at heavy cost and he withdrew, losing his arm in the battle (21–24 July 1797).

Santa Cruz Islands ▌ 1942 ▌ World War II (Pacific)

Japanese Admiral Nobutake Kondo renewed action after battle in the **Eastern Solomons** in August, leading a massive combined force towards **Guadalcanal**. Met near Santa Cruz by Admiral Thomas Kinkaid, a classic long-range carrier duel saw severe loss of aircraft on both sides, but the Americans also had one carrier sunk and their only remaining flat-top was badly damaged (26 October 1942).

Santa Fé ▌ 1680 ▌ Pueblo Rising

Pueblo Indians in modern New Mexico under Popé rose against Spanish rule, killing many settlers and missionaries before launching a large-scale attack on Santa Fé. The Indians were driven off in successive assaults, though Governor Antonio de Otermin withdrew to El Paso, losing about 400 killed. Popé died in 1690 and by 1692 Don Diego de Vargas had retaken Santa Fé (15–17 August 1680).

Santa Fé de Bogotá ▌ 1813 ▌ Colombian War of Independence

In the wake of victory at **Ventaquemada**, Federalist forces from Tunja under Colonel Antonio Baraya soon marched on Bogotá against Antonio Nariño, Centralist Dictator of Cundinamarca. In battle at nearby Santa Fé, the Federalists were routed and fled, losing over 1,000 prisoners, including Governor Juan Niño. The United Provinces soon agreed to join a central government (9 January 1813).

Santa Fé de Bogotá ▌ 1814 ▌ Colombian War of Independence
See **Bogotá**

Santa Gertrudis ▌ 1866 ▌ Mexican-French War

General Rafael Olvera led an Imperial convoy of 1,800 men and 200 wagons from Matamaros towards Monterrey and was attacked at Santa Gertrudis, near Camargo, by almost 4,000 Republicans under General Mariano Escobedo. A disastrous defeat cost Olvera over 500 casualties, 1,000 prisoners, and the entire convoy. **Matamaros** itself soon surrendered (16 June 1866).

Santa Inés, Mexico ▌ 1863 ▌ Mexican-French War

During their siege of **Puebla**, the French launched a powerful dawn attack against fortifications at Santa Inés, held by General Felipe Berriozábal, supported by Generals Nicolás de Regules and Luis Ghilardi. One of the most important actions of the siege saw the Imperial troops driven off with 240 casualties and 200 prisoners. The Republicans also lost almost 200 killed (25 April 1863).

Santa Inés, Venezuela I 1859 I Venezuelan Federalist Revolt

Amid a chaotic Presidential succession, Federalist army officers opposed the central government and the rival forces met in battle at Santa Inés, southeast of Barinas. Federalist General Ezequiel Zamora secured a clear victory over the Constitutionalist army of General Pedro Ramos. However, the government regained the upper hand two months later at **Cople** (10 December 1859).

Santa Isabel, Coahuila I 1866 I Mexican-French War

While campaigning east of Torréon near Parras, a French-Mexican column under General Paul-Amable de Brian was attacked at Santa Isabel by over 1,000 Republican troops led by General Andrés Viesca, supported by Colonels Francisco Naranjo and Jerónimo Treviño. The Imperialist force was heavily defeated, losing all its guns and over 100 dead, including de Brian (1 March 1866).

Santa Isabel, Sonora I 1916 I Villa's Raids

With rebel leader Francisco (Pancho) Villa isolated after the Mexican Revolution, his ally Colonel Pablo López ambushed a train at Santa Isabel in Sonora, murdering American mining engineer Charles R. Watson and 16 others. López—later executed by government forces—claimed the massacre was ordered by Villa, who raided into the United States two months later at **Columbus** (10 January 1916).

Santa Lucia I 1848 I 1st Italian War of Independence

When King Charles Albert of Sardinia joined the War of Independence against Austria, he achieved an early victory at **Goito** (10 April). Following an indecisive skirmish at Pastrengo, however, he met the full force of Marshal Josef Radetzky's Austrians at Santa Lucia, east of Treviso, northwest of Venice. The King suffered a major defeat and lost again a few weeks later at **Curtatone** (6 May 1848).

Santa Marta I 1702 I War of the Spanish Succession

British Admiral John Benbow was cruising off Colombia when he met a superior French squadron under Admiral Jean-Baptiste Ducasseand. A running four-day action between Cartagena and Santa Marta saw Benbow badly wounded. His six captains were court-martialled for failing to provide support and two were executed. On 4 November, Benbow died of his wounds (20–24 August 1702).

Santa Marta I 1815 I Colombian War of Independence

See **Cartagena, Colombia**

Santander I 1812 I Napoleonic Wars (Peninsular Campaign)

On an offensive against the northern coast of Spain to relieve pressure on the Allied campaign around **Salamanca**, British Admiral Sir Home Popham seized several fortresses, then joined guerrilla leader Tomás Campillos attacking Santander, defended by French General Jean Dubreton. Reinforced by Spanish General Gabriel Mendizabal, Popham captured the vital port (22 July–3 August 1812).

Santander I 1937 I Spanish Civil War

Nationalist General Fidel Dávila captured the Basque capital of **Bilbao** (18 June), then turned west against Santander, held by poorly equipped troops under General Mariano Gamir Ulíbarri. Driven out by artillery and aerial bombardment, Ulíbarri flew to France, effectively ending organised Basque resistance and leaving **Gijon** as the last remaining Republican city in the north (14–25 August 1937).

Sant'Angelo I 998 I Later German Imperial Wars

When the patricius John Crescentius drove Pope Gregory V out of Rome and had John XVI appointed, Gregory appealed to his cousin Emperor Otto III of Germany, who led an army into

Italy. The anti-Pope was captured fleeing the city and was brutally mutilated, while Otto besieged Crescentius in the Castello Sant'Angelo. When the fortress fell by storm, Crescentius was executed and Gregory was restored.

Santarem I 1147 I Christian Reconquest of Portugal

At the head of a renewed offensive against the Muslims of central Portugal, King Alfonso I attacked the powerful fortified city of Santarem on the Tagus. In a brilliant night-time assault, his troops took the city by a surprise escalade of the walls. Santarem fell, followed by indiscriminate slaughter of the population (March 1147).

Santarem I 1834 I Miguelite Wars
See **Asseiceira**

Santa Rita de Morelos I 1840 I Mexican Federalist War

Five months after defeat at **Alcantra**, Mexican President Anastasio Bustamente sent General Mariano Arista against Federalist rebels under Antonio Canales Rosillon. After repulsing an advance on Monterrey, Arista pursued the Federalists to Santa Rita de Morelos, in Coahuilla, where Canales Rosillon was routed. His second in command, Antonio Zapata, was captured and executed (24–25 March 1840).

Santa Rosa, Entre Rios I 1870 I Argentine Civil Wars

Federalist General Ricardo López Jordán assassinated Governor Justo José Urquiza of Entre Rios and seized power (11 April 1870), after which President Domingo Faustino Sarmiento sent General Ignacio Rivas, who met the rebels at the arroyo of Santa Rosa in Entre Rios. Despite being outnumbered, Rivas secured a bloody victory and months later won again at **Ñaembé** (12 October 1870).

Santa Rosa, Honduras I 1863 I Central American National Wars

Driven out of El Salvador at **Coatepeque** (24 February), President José Rafael Carrera of Guatemala sent General Vicente Cerna into Honduras, supported by Nicaragua. Near Santa Rosa, Cerna won a decisive victory, which brought down President Victoriano Castellamios. The Allies recognised José María Medina and Carrera invaded El Salvador to besiege **San Salvador** (16 June 1863).

Santa Rosa, Mendoza I 1874 I Argentine Civil Wars

A rising against the election of President Nicolas Avellaneda saw troops from Mendoza under General José Miguel Arredondo defeat and kill government commander Colonel Amaro Catalán at Santa Rosa, southeast of Mendoza. In a second action, General Juilo Roca, though severely wounded, defeated and captured Arredondo, ending the rebellion (29 October & 7 December 1874).

Santa Rosa de Copán I 1856 I National (Filibuster) War

American adventurer William Walker effectively seized power in Nicaragua after capturing **Granada** (October 1855), then entered northern Costa Rica, where part of his Filibuster force under Colonel Louis Schlessinger reached Santa Rosa, north of Liberia. Costa Rican President Juan Rafael Mora stormed the Filibuster camp and the invaders fled back over the border to **Rivas** (20 March 1856).

Santa Rosa de Copán I 1919 I Sapoa Revolution

Exiles in Nicaragua, attempting to overthrow President Frederico Tinoco of Costa Rica, invaded across the Sapoa, where rebel leader Alfredo Volio Jiménez died in a skirmish. After defeat at Santa Rosa de Copán, north of Liberia, his successor Julio Acosta Garcia led the survivors back to Nicaragua. Soon afterwards, Tinoco's brother was murdered and he went into exile (8 May 1919).

Santa Rosa de Copán I 1955 I Costa Rican Civil War

Christian Socialist forces loyal to former President Rafael Calderón Guardia—ousted from government in Costa Rica after defeat at

Ochomogo in 1948—invaded from Nicaragua against Conservative President José María Figueres Ferrer. The counter-revolution was repulsed at Santa Rosa de Copán, north of Liberia, though Calderón was eventually permitted to return (11 January 1955).

Santa Rosa Island ▮ 1861 ▮ American Civil War (Lower Seaboard)

Early in the war in the south, Confederate forces under General Richard H. Anderson attacked Union troops on Santa Rosa Island, off Pensacola Bay, Florida. Although Anderson secured initial success against New York Zouaves under Colonel William Wilson, he was counter-attacked by Colonel Harvey Brown from Fort Pickens and had to withdraw to the mainland (9 October 1861).

Santa Vittoria ▮ 1702 ▮ War of the Spanish Succession

Louis Duke de Vendôme took command after Francois de Neufville Marshal Villeroi was captured at **Cremona** and advanced to relieve Mantua. Prince Eugène of Savoy ordered Imperial cavalry under General Annibale Visconti to shadow the French, but they were surprised and routed at Santa Vittoria. Eugène raised the siege of Mantua and pursued Vendôme south to **Luzzara** (26 July 1702).

Santiago ▮ 1809 ▮ Napoleonic Wars (Peninsular Campaign)

Spanish General Martin La Carrera marched on Santiago to support guerrilla leaders Pablo Morillo and Garcia del Barrio and the ill-armed Spanish force was met by French General Antoine-Louis Maucune on the nearby plain of Campo de la Estrella. Maucune's force was routed, with over 600 men lost, and he abandoned Santiago, withdrawing towards Corunna (22 May 1809).

Santiago Bay ▮ 1898 ▮ Spanish-American War

American forces which captured **San Juan Hill** outside **Santiago de Cuba** (1 July), threatened the Spanish fleet in Santiago Bay and

Admiral Pascual Cervera was ordered to attempt a breakout. Met by part of the American blockading squadron under Commodore Winfield S. Schley, Cervera lost all seven of his ships with terrible casualties. Santiago soon surrendered (3 July 1898).

Santiago de Cuba ▮ 1741 ▮ War of the Austrian Succession

English Admiral Edward Vernon followed his disaster at **Cartagena** in April by taking a large force against Santiago in Spanish Cuba. Troops under General Thomas Wentworth landed at Guantánamo Bay, where badly strained relations between army and navy broke down. When Wentworth refused to advance on Santiago, the expedition withdrew in utter failure (18 July–7 December 1741).

Santiago de Cuba ▮ 1898 ▮ Spanish-American War

With victory at **Las Guásimas**, American commander William R. Shafter advanced on the key city of Santiago de Cuba, where he soon captured the outer defences at **San Juan Hill**. Following total destruction of the Spanish fleet in **Santiago Bay**, General José Toral negotiated to surrender the city and also troops in outlying areas, virtually ending the war in Cuba (24 June–17 July 1898).

Santo Domingo ▮ 1586 ▮ Drake's Caribbean Raid

On a large-scale English raid into the Caribbean, Admiral Sir Francis Drake took about 30 ships against Santo Domingo City in Hispaniola (modern Dominican Republic). Finding the once-prosperous Spanish city greatly reduced, Drake took his revenge by burning most of the buildings before the citizens paid a ransom to save the rest. He then sailed south to **Cartagena** (January 1586).

Santo Domingo ▮ 1655 ▮ Anglo-Spanish Wars

Cromwellian England despatched Admiral Sir William Penn to the West Indies, where he landed more than 7,000 troops under

Colonel Robert Venables on Spanish Santo Domingo (modern Dominican Republic). The British force was heavily defeated after a badly managed campaign and they re-embarked to move further west against **Jamaica** (13–25 April 1655).

Santo Domingo I 1802–1803 I Napoleonic Wars (Santo Domingo Rising)

Sent to Santo Domingo to suppress rebel Francois Toussaint l'Ouverture, French General Charles Leclerc suffered costly losses at **Crête-à-Perriot** (March 1802), then treacherously seized l'Ouverture. Leclerc died of fever and the rebel Jean Jacques Dessalines later seized **Port-au-Prince** and **Cap Francais**. When Fort St Nicolas fell (4 December 1803), he declared independent Haiti.

Santo Domingo I 1806 I Napoleonic Wars (4th Coalition)

When part of the French fleet from Brest under Admiral Corentin de Leissegues crossed the Atlantic, they were pursued by Admiral Sir John Duckworth, joined in the West Indies by Admiral Sir Alexander Cochrane. Attacked in Santo Domingo harbour (in modern Dominican Republic), all five French ships of the line were destroyed or captured. Only two frigates escaped (6 February 1806).

Santo Domingo I 1809 I Napoleonic Wars (5th Coalition)

With France ejected from western **Santo Domingo** (Haiti) in 1803, General Marie Louis Ferrand held out in neighbouring Spanish Santo Domingo until France and Spain were at war, then unwisely attacked Palo Hincado in El Seibo Province. Defeated by General Don Huan Sanchez, Ferrand killed himself. In July 1810, General Joseph Borquier surrendered after siege in Santo Domingo City (7 November 1809).

Santo Domingo I 1965 I Dominican Civil War

Left-wing forces tried to seize power in Dominica and civil war broke out with Conservatives under General Elias Wessin. Fearing supposed Communist influence, US President Lyndon Johnson sent 20,000 troops to intervene. Forty-seven Americans and perhaps 2,000 Dominicans were killed before Santo Domingo City was secured and a ceasefire was achieved (24 April–23 May 1965).

Santuario, Antioquia I 1829 I Colombian Civil Wars

Colonel José María Córdoba rebelled against the dictatorship of Simón Bolívar and seized the city of Medellín, then faced 900 veteran troops marching from Bogotá under General Daniel Florencio O'Leary. Southeast of Medellín at Santuario, Córdoba was defeated and killed, along with about 200 of his followers. The rebels were later pardoned and the province was pacified (17 October 1829).

Santuario, Cundinamarca I 1830 I Colombian Civil Wars

Rising against newly elected President Joaquín Mosquera, the largely Venezuelan Callao Batallion of Colonel José Florencio Jiménez marched on Bogotá and were met to the west at Santuario by government forces under Colonel Pedro Antonio García. Jiménez secured victory and occupied Bogotá for General Rafael Urdaneta, who then seized government (27 August 1830).

Sao del Indio I 1895 I 2nd Cuban War of Independence

When Spanish Colonel Francisco de Borja Canella marched southwest from Guantánamo to attack Cuban insurgent leader José Maceo, his brother Antonio Maceo joined him by forced march and intercepted the Spaniards on the Bacanao at Sao del Indio. A bloody 36-hour action saw the brothers defeat Canella, who burned his supply train and fled back to Guantánamo (31 August 1895).

Sao Mamede I 1128 I Portuguese War of Succession

Count Henry of Burgundy held Portugal through his wife Teresa, daughter of Alfonso VI of Castile, and at Henry's death his son Alfonso Henriques rebelled against his mother and her

Galician lover Ferdinand Peres. Teresa's Galician-Portuguese force was defeated at Sao Mamede, outside Guimaraes, and she died in exile. Alfonso later became King of independent Portugal (24 June 1128).

Sao Miguel ▮ 1583 ▮ Spanish-Portuguese War

After a failed attempt at **Terceira** to seize the Azores in support of Don Antonio de Crato's claim to the Spanish-held Portuguese throne, a larger Franco-Portuguese fleet under Aymard de Chaste was sent to the Azores to try again. Off Sao Miguel, the second attempt was also defeated by Spanish Admiral Alvaro de Bazán Marquess of Santa Cruz and Spain ruled the Azores as part of Portugal.

Sao Salvador ▮ 1574 ▮ Portuguese Colonial Wars in West Africa

When Jaga nomads overthrew King Alvaro of the Kongo (1568) and sacked his capital, Sao Salvador (modern Mbanza Kongo in northwest Angola), Portuguese musketeers were sent from Sao Tomé. After heavy fighting, the Portuguese recaptured Sao Salvador and reinstated Alvaro. In 1665, at **Ambuila**, the Portuguese finally overthrew Kongo, which once covered much of west central Africa.

Sao Vicente ▮ 1833 ▮ Miguelite Wars
See **Cape St Vincent**

Sapienza ▮ 1354 ▮ Venetian-Genoese Wars

Renewed warfare between Venice and Genoa saw Genoa achieve its greatest naval victory over Venice since **Curzola** (1298) in the Gulf of Sapienza, south of Methone in southwestern Greece. The Venetian fleet under Nicolo Pisani was almost completely destroyed by Genoese Admiral Pagano Doria. Pisani himself was among the thousands of prisoners taken to Genoa (3 November 1354).

Sappa Creek ▮ 1875 ▮ Red River Indian War

In the bloodiest action of the campaign, cavalry under Lieutenant Austin Henley pursued a band of Cheyenne to the Sappa Creek in northwestern Kansas (known to the Cheyenne as Dark Water Creek). Thirty escaped, but Henley's men shot down 19 warriors (including Chief Little Bull) and eight women and children, while two soldiers were also killed. The massacre ended the war (23 April 1875).

Sappony Church ▮ 1864 ▮ American Civil War (Eastern Theatre)

While raiding railways southwest of besieged **Petersburg**, Virginia, Union Generals James Wilson and Augustus V. Kautz were beaten at **Staunton River Bridge** and marched east towards Stoney Creek Depot. Met at Sappony Church by Confederate General Wade Hampton, returning from **Trevilian Station**, Wilson was routed and fled north towards **Reams Station** (28 June 1864).

Sapri ▮ 1857 ▮ Pisacane Rebellion

Carlo Pisacane attempted to renew revolution against the Kingdom of the Two Sicilies, landing with about 300 followers on the Coast of Campania, south of Naples. However, the brave yet foolhardy band were heavily defeated at Sapri, with Pisacane and many others killed. The struggle for Italian independence was not renewed for another two years (28 June 1857).

Saragarhi ▮ 1897 ▮ Great Frontier Rising

On Samana Ridge, south of the Khyber Pass, Afridi and Orakzai tribesmen attacked Forts Gulistan and Lockhart, as well as the tiny intervening Sarigarhi heliograph relay station, where 21 Sikhs under Havildar Isher Singh refused to surrender. Massively overwhelmed, they fought to the death. In a unique recognition, all 21 won Britain's highest gallantry award for Indian troops (12 September 1897).

Saragossa ▮ 1118 ▮ Early Christian Reconquest of Spain

King Alfonso I of Aragon—El Batallador, the Fighter—led a brilliant offensive against the Muslims of Spain, besieging the key city of Saragossa on the Ebro River. Its fall after seven months, followed by the capture of Tudela, encouraged renewed Muslim resistance, although Saragossa became capital of the Kingdom of Aragon (May–18 December 1118).

Saragossa I 1710 I War of the Spanish Succession

In the campaign to install Archduke Charles of Austria as King of Spain, General James Stanhope's Anglo-Austrian army advanced from their victory at **Almenar** (27 July) to challenge the Franco-Spanish army of Philip V under the walls of Saragossa. A one-sided rout cost Philip's army massive casualties and prisoners, as well as all their artillery (20 August 1710).

Saragossa (1st) I 1808 I Napoleonic Wars (Peninsular Campaign)

French General Charles Lefebvre-Desnouettes advanced down the Ebro River in northern Spain and besieged the strategic city of Saragossa, which held out for two months against a massive and bloody attack. Parts of the city were captured before the siege was lifted following French defeat at **Baylen**. Saragossa fell to a renewed siege later the same year (15 June–13 August 1808).

Saragossa (2nd) I 1808–1809 I Napoleonic Wars (Peninsular Campaign)

Four weeks after victory at **Tudela**, the French advanced down the Ebro to besiege Saragossa, defended by Spanish General José Palafox. Under successive command of Generals Bon Adrien Moncey, Édouard Mortier, Androche Junot and Jean Lannes, the siege and assaults cost over 50,000 Spanish lives by the time the ruined city was taken by storm (20 December 1808–20 February 1809).

Saragossa I 1937 I Spanish Civil War

In an effort to distract the offensive against **Santander**, Republican General Sebastián Pozas took 80,000 men from Catalonia into Aragon towards Saragossa. Though the small town of **Belchite** fell, Nationalist commander Miguel Ponte led a powerful defence and Saragossa was saved, as well as Huesca and Teruel, finally halting the Republican offensive (24 August–30 September 1937).

Sarajevo I 1878 I Austro-Turkish War in Bosnia

Determined to secure Bosnia-Herzogovina under the treaty which ended the Russo-Turkish War, Austria sent a large force under Baron Josef Philippovic von Philippsburg to oust the reluctant Turks. After a sharp campaign (said to have cost over 5,000 Austrian casualties), the capital Sarajevo was bombarded and taken by storm and the Turks eventually withdrew (19 August 1878).

Sarajevo I 1992–1996 I Bosnian War

With Bosnia torn apart by civil war, Serb forces besieged the capital Sarajevo, housing mainly Croats and Muslims. Shelling from nearby hills and the taking of UN hostages provoked NATO air-strikes and counter-attack by UN artillery, but the four-year siege was not lifted until peace talks ended the war. Sarajevo lost perhaps 10,000 killed and 50,000 wounded (6 April 1992–29 February 1996).

Sarandáporon I 1912 I 1st Balkan War

Prince Constantine of Greece supported his Balkan allies by invading Macedonia through Elasson to advance on Turks in the strategic pass at Sarandáporon, between the Kamvounia and Pieria Mountains. Attacking in heavy rain, Constantine routed the Turks and seized nearby Servia, then took Kozani and Veria before advancing on Thessalonica through **Jannitsa** (22 October 1912).

Sarandi I 1825 I Uruguayan War of Independence

When Uruguayan Juan Antonio Lavalleja and the "Thirty-Three Immortals" declared independence from Brazil, they recruited a Patriot army. North of Montevideo at Sarandi, Lavalleja decisively beat an Imperial force under Colonel Bentos Manuel Ribeiro. He then briefly annexed Uruguay to Argentina, which secured victory over Brazil in February 1827 at **Ituzaingó** (12 October 1825).

Saratoga, Cuba I 1896 I 2nd Cuban War of Independence

As rebel leader Máximo Gómez entered Camaguey Province in eastern Cuba, Spanish General Jimenez Castellanos marched out from Puerto Principe (modern Camaguey City) and was attacked at nearby Saratoga. Castellanos suffered heavy casualties and when Spanish reinforcements arrived, he retreated to Puerto Principe. Gómez was too exhausted to pursue (9–11 June 1896).

Saratoga, New York (1st) I 1777 I War of the American Revolution

Despite disastrous defeat at **Bennington** for his offensive from Canada (16 August), General John Burgoyne continued into New York State. South of Saratoga at Bemis Heights he was blocked by Americans under General Horatio Gates. A drawn action with very heavy fighting cost Burgoyne 600 men, but he held his position and fought again at the same site three weeks later (19 September 1777).

Saratoga, New York (2nd) I 1777 I War of the American Revolution

British General John Burgoyne became isolated in his failed offensive from Canada when he was checked at Bemis Heights, west of Saratoga. After three weeks, he renewed his attack on General Horatio Gates. Despite the courage of General Simon Fraser, who was mortally wounded, Burgoyne was defeated by General Benedict Arnold and surrendered ten days later (7 October 1777).

Saraun I 1858 I Indian Mutiny
See **Chanda, Uttar Pradesh**

Sarbinowo I 1758 I Seven Years War (Europe)
See **Zorndorf**

Sardarapat I 1918 I World War I (Caucasus Front)

Following the collapse of Tsarist Russia, Turkish forces crossed the pre-war Russian border to seize Kars and advance on the Armenian capital of Erivan. In a much-celebrated action at Sardarapat, Armenian Generals Movses Silikian and Tovmas Nazarbekian routed General Ferid Vehip Pasha. Independence was declared that day, though the Turks struck back at **Baku** (28 May 1918).

Sardinia I 1708 I War of the Spanish Succession

An Anglo-Dutch fleet under Admiral Sir John Leake launched a fresh offensive in the central Mediterranean, sailing from Barcelona for Sardinia. When Spanish Viceroy the Conde de San Antonio hesitated to surrender, the capital Cagliari was shelled. The island capitulated next day and Leake sent his deputy Admiral Sir Edward Whitaker against **Minorca** (1–2 August 1708).

Sardis I 546 BC I Persian-Lydian War

Soon after losing disastrously to Cyrus II the Great of Persia at **Pteria** and **Thymbria**, King Croesus of Lydia was besieged in his capital at Sardis, near Salihli in modern western Turkey, which fell by storm after 14 days. Though Croesus was well treated by Cyrus, the rapid destruction of the seemingly powerful Kingdom of Lydia heightened the Persian threat to Greek cities on the Aegean.

Sargana I 591 I Byzantine-Persian Wars
See **Ganzak**

Sarhu I 1619 I Manchu Conquest of China

Threatened in the north by rising Manchu power under Nurhachi, Ming General Yang Hao took a massive army into Liaodong (southern Manchuria). He then unwisely divided his force and General Du Song prematurely advanced on the Manchu. Ambushed at Sarhu, Du Song fled. The Ming and their Korean allies were defeated again next day further east at **Siyanggiayan** (14 April 1619).

Sari Bair I 1915 I World War I (Gallipoli)

British commander Sir Ian Hamilton resolved to break the Gallipoli deadlock and ordered a broad attack on the strategic Sari Bair Ridge. Aided by a diversion in the south at **Lone Pine** and a fresh landing in the north at **Suvla Bay**, British forces advanced at Hill Q and **Chunuk Bair**. Mustafa Kemal counter-attacked in force and the offensive failed with bloody losses (6–10 August 1915).

Sarikamish I 1914–1915 I World War I (Caucasus Front)

Determined to capture the Russian Caucasus, Turkish War Minister Enver Pasha led 90,000 men towards Kars and was met in bitter winter conditions at Sarikamish (now in Turkey) by the army of Viceroy Illarian Vorontsov under General Aleksandr Myshlaevsky. The Turks were destroyed by battle and frostbite and fewer than 20,000 returned to **Erzurum** (25 December 1914–4 January 1915).

Sar-i-Pul I 1501 I Mughal-Uzbek Wars

The teenage Mughal Babur led a new advance on **Samarkand** and retook the city by surprise, where he again faced a large Uzbek army under Muhammad Shaybani Khan. At Sar-i-Pul, in northern Afghanistan near the Band-i-Amir, Babur's General Kasim Beg allowed his advance units to be surrounded. After suffering a decisive defeat Babur was once more forced to withdraw (April 1501).

Sarjahan I 1029 I Eastern Muslim Dynastic Wars

Near the end of his reign, Mahmud of Ghazni sent his son Masud into Persia against Ibrahim ibn Marzuban, known as Salar, who withdrew to the fortress of Sarjahan, 60 miles northeast of Isfahan. Supported by Salar's rival Marzubin ibn Hasan, Masud destroyed Salar in battle nearby, then went on to capture Hamadan and Isfahan, securing central Persia for Ghazni (13 September 1029).

Sark I 1448 I Anglo-Scottish Border Wars

After Sir Henry Percy Earl of Northumberland invaded Scotland and burned Dunbar in May 1448, the Scots burned his family castles at Alnwick and Warkworth. Henry VI then gave him troops for a fresh invasion. However, at the River Sark, near Gretna on the Solway Firth, Northumberland was defeated by Scots under Hugh Douglas Earl of Ormond and taken prisoner (23 October 1448).

Sarkany I 1848 I Hungarian Revolutionary War

See **Mór**

Sarmada I 1119 I Crusader-Muslim Wars

See **Antioch, Syria**

Sarmi I 1944 I World War II (Pacific)

American forces on the north coast of New Guinea quickly took **Wakde**, but General Edwin Patrick (later General Franklin Sibert) faced prolonged defence on the nearby mainland around Sarmi under General Hachiro Tagami. Although Lone Tree Hill was taken after heavy losses (24 June), the Americans finally abandoned the Sarmi area after losing over 600 killed (17 May–September 1944).

Sarmizegethusa I 102 I 1st Dacian War

When peace talks failed in 101 after the inconclusive battle at **Tapae**, Roman Emperor Trajan launched a fresh offensive against Decebalus of Dacia (largely modern Romania). After progessively capturing the Mulbach fortresses, Trajan besieged the Dacian capital at Sarmizegethusa (modern Varhély). Decebalus capitulated to save his city and made peace, while Trajan took the honorific Dacicus.

Sarmizegethusa I 105 I 2nd Dacian War

Decebalus of Dacia once more resumed war against Rome and Emperor Trajan crossed the Danube, where he routed the Dacian army outside the capital Sarmizegethusa (modern Varhély). Decebalus fled to the north but was eventually surrounded and killed himself, ending the war. Rome then annexed and settled Dacia, which largely comprised the area of modern Romania.

Sarnal | 1572 | Mughal Conquest of Northern India

Emperor Akbar defeated Sultan Muzaffar II of Gujarat at **Ahmadabad** (2 September), then turned south against the Mirza. When Ibrahim Husain Mirza withdrew from Baroda, Akbar intercepted him at Sarnal on the Mahi and, with a dangerously small force of horsemen, won a decisive victory. Akbar captured Surat (11 January 1573) to complete his conquest of Gujarat (24 December 1572).

Sarnus | 553 | Gothic War in Italy
See **Mount Lactarius**

Sarsa | 1704 | Mughal-Sikh Wars

Despite promising Guru Gobind Singh safe passage after the siege of **Anandpur**, Mughal General Wazir Khan pursued the survivors. At Shahi Tibbi, Jiwan Singh was killed in a rearguard action. The Sikhs were then destroyed while crossing the Sarsa, with the Guru's two younger sons captured and later murdered. Gobind was defeated next day at **Chamkaur** (21 December 1704).

Sarum | 552 | Anglo-Saxon Conquest of Britain
See **Searobyrg**

Sarus | 625 | Byzantine-Persian Wars

Despite his victory at **Arcesh**, Byzantine Emperor Heraclius was pursued west across the Euphrates into Cilicia by a Sassanian Persian army under Shahbaraz. But at the Sarus (modern Seyhan) River, Heraclius won a sharp action and disengaged north to Caesarea. Shahbaraz was then ordered west to support the Avars against **Constantinople**, where the Persian advance suffered a costly repulse.

Sarvantikar | 1266 | Later Crusader-Muslim Wars

After defeating Mongol invaders at **Ain Jalut** in 1260, the Mamluk Sultan Baibars sent commander Qalawun through the Amanus Mountains into Cilicia against Hethum II of Armenia. A decisive battle with the King's sons and Templar knights at Sarvantikar saw Prince Thoros of Armenia killed and his brother Leo captured. The Muslims then ravaged Cilicia before attacking **Antioch** (24 August 1266).

Sasbach | 1675 | 3rd Dutch War

Within six months of his victories at **Mühlhausen** and **Turckheim**, French Marshal Henri de Turenne manoeuvred east of the Rhine to prevent Prince Raimondo Montecuccoli's Imperial army relieving Strasbourg. However, Turenne was killed by a cannonball while preparing to attack at Sasbach, near Buhl, and Montecuccoli drove the demoralised French back across the Rhine (27 July 1675).

Saseno | 1264 | Venetian-Genoese Wars

With the Venetian navy misled into attacking Tyre, Genoese Admiral Simone Grillo ambushed the annual Venetian trade convoy to the Levant, commanded by Michele Dauro, as it left the Adriatic. Near the island of Saseno, in the Otranto Channel, the escort was defeated and the entire merchant fleet was captured. Venice was avenged two years later off **Trapani** (14 August 1264).

Sasowy Rog | 1633 | Polish-Tatar Wars

Nine years after beating Tatars at **Martynow**, Polish Hetman Stanislas Koniecpolski marched south against a fresh Tatar invasion of Podlia in southwest Ukraine under Abaza Mehmed, the Ruthenian-born Pasha of Vidin. The Hetman surprised and routed the Tatars in camp at Sasowy Rog on the Pruth. But he failed to pursue and within months the Tatars advanced again on **Kamieniec** (July 1633).

Sassiah | 1857 | Indian Mutiny
See **Shahganj**

Sassoferrato I 295 BC I 3rd Samnite War
See **Sentinum**

Sas van Gent I 1644 I Netherlands War of Independence
Frederick Henry of Orange was determined to secure the southern Netherlands and besieged Sas van Gent, west of Antwerp. When the Dutch drove off Spanish forces under the Marquis de Tor de Laguna and stormed the outer defences, Governor Andrés de Prada capitulated. The following year, the Stadtholder further consolidated his gains by capturing nearby **Hulst** (27 July–5 September 1644).

Satara I 1690 I Mughal-Maratha Wars
With Mughal forces campaigning in central India, General Sharza Khan (later Rustum Khan) was marching to besiege Satara, south of Poona, when advance units led by his son Ghalib were attacked by Maratha Generals Santaji Ghorpade and Dhanaji Jadhav. When Sharza Khan advanced to his son's aid, both were captured in a Mughal defeat which cost 1,500 men (4 June 1690).

Satara I 1699–1700 I Mughal-Maratha Wars
In a renewed offensive against the Marathas of central India, Mughal Emperor Aurangzeb sent a large army against the powerful fortress of Satara, south of Poona. Despite repeated assaults by the Maratha field army under Dhanaji Jadhav, Mughal forces destroyed large sections of the walls with giant mines and garrison commander Subhanji surrendered (December 1699–21 April 1700).

Sathinungulum I 1790 I 3rd British-Mysore War
After British forces in southern India captured Coimbatore, Colonel John Floyd advanced on the Gajalhatti Pass, where Tipu Sultan made a brilliant surprise descent. Floyd lost his guns and over 500 men in a heavy assault near Sathinungulum. However, the death of Tipu's General Burhan-ud-din delayed the Mysorean

advance and the survivors escaped back to Coimbatore (13 September 1790).

Sattelberg I 1943 I World War II (Pacific)
See **Huon Peninsula**

Satus I 1856 I Yakima Indian Wars
Yakima Chief Kamiakin continued resisting white expansion in southern Washington despite defeat at **Union Gap** (October 1855) and attacked five companies under Colonel Thomas R. Cornelius on the Satus, near the Oregon state line. While caught unawares, Cornelius managed to escape south to Fort Dalles with few casualties. Kamiakin won again in 1858 at **Pine Creek** (9 April 1856).

Sauce Grande I 1840 I Argentine Civil Wars
Recovering from defeat at **Yerua** and **Cagancha** in late 1839, Federalist General Pascual Echague, Governor of Entre Rios, supporting Dictator Manuel de Rosas, met Unitarist Juan Galo Lavalle at Sauce Grande, east of Bahia Blanca. Lavalle was decisively beaten and driven back across the Parana. His anti-Rosas forces soon lost again at **Quebracho Herrado** and **Famaillá** (16 July 1840).

Sauchieburn I 1488 I Scottish Barons' Rebellion
In rebellion against James III in support of the King's 15-year-old son, Scottish nobles led by Patrick Lord Hailes, Alexander Lord Home and Andrew Lord Gray marched towards Stirling. At nearby Sauchieburn they defeated the outnumbered Loyalist army. The King was killed in mysterious circumstances while fleeing and his treacherous son became James IV (11 June 1488).

Saucourt I 881 I Viking Raids on France
Vikings who invaded the Low countries won a brutal victory in Saxony at **Ebsdorf**, but the following year they met a large army under Louis III of the West Franks, at Saucourt, on the Somme in Ponthieu. The teenage King Louis won a brilliant victory, which checked the Norse

threat, but he died a year later in a riding accident. The Vikings soon regrouped to besiege **Paris** (3 August 881).

Saugor | 1680 | Mughal-Berad Wars
See **Sagar**

Saugor | 1858 | Indian Mutiny
See **Sagar**

Saule | 1236 | Early Wars of the Teutonic Knights
See **Siauliai**

Saumur | 1793 | French Revolutionary Wars (Vendée War)
Following early rebel success in the counter-revolution in western France at **Thouars** and **Fontenay**, the Royalist rising reached a high-point with victory at Saumur, on the Loire southeast of Angers, defended by Republican General Louis Berthier. Royalist rebels led by Jacques Cathelineau captured the town, along with massive stores of supplies and arms, including 50 cannon (9 June 1793).

Saunshi | 1777 | Maratha-Mysore Wars
Haidar Ali of Mysore recovered from loss at **Chinkurli** (1771) to regain Coorg and Malabar, previously lost to the Marathas, then sent a force under Mohamed Ali across the Tungabhadra in southern India. Near Dharwar at Saunshi, Patwardhan Chief Konher Rao was defeated and killed and Padurang Rao was captured. As a result, many local Chiefs soon submitted to Haidar (8 January 1777).

Sauroren | 1813 | Napoleonic Wars (Peninsular Campaign)
See **Sorauren**

Savage's Station | 1862 | American Civil War (Eastern Theatre)
In the fourth of the **Seven Days' Battles**, east of Richmond, Virginia, Confederate General John B. Magruder, despite losses at **Garnett's and Golding's Farms**, attacked the Union rearguard withdrawing from **Gaines' Mill**. At Savage's Station, Union General Edwin Sumner lost about 1,500 casualties and abandoned 2,500 wounded as he withdrew across **White Oak Swamp** (29 June 1862).

Savandrug | 1755 | War Against Malabar Pirates
While campaigning against the pirate Chief Tulaji Angria, active on India's Malabar Coast between Bombay and Goa, Commodore Sir William James of the Bombay Marine joined Maratha land forces to attack and capture the pirate base at Savandrug (modern Savandurg). Savandrug was then handed to the Marathas and Angria was defeated again a year later at **Gheria** (2 April 1755).

Savandrug | 1791 | 3rd British-Mysore War
When Tipu Sultan of Mysore renewed war against Britain, Governor-General Charles Earl Cornwallis took **Bangalore** (21 March) and **Nandi Drug** (17 October), then sent Colonel James Stuart (1741–1815) against Savandrug, southwest of Bangalore. After two days of bombardment, the mountain fortress fell by assault, setting up the campaign against **Seringapatam** (21 December 1791).

Savannah | 1778 | War of the American Revolution
Colonel Archibald Campbell led a fresh British offensive in the south, landing near Savannah, Georgia, to advance on the city, supported by Captain Sir James Baird. American General Robert Howe attempted to defend Savannah with outnumbered militia but was badly defeated. He withdrew with heavy losses and Campbell seized many ships in the harbour (29 December 1778).

Savannah | 1779 | War of the American Revolution
Attempting to take the offensive in the south, American General Benjamin Lincoln and 4,500 troops under French Admiral Charles-Hector Comte d'Estaing besieged Savannah, Georgia, held by General Augustine Prevost. After suffering very heavy losses in a rash assault

(9 October), d'Estaing sailed for France and Lincoln had to withdraw towards **Charleston** (3 September–28 October 1779).

Savannah I 1781 I War of the American Revolution
    See **Charleston, South Carolina**

Savannah I 1864 I American Civil War (Western Theatre)
    See **Fort McAllister**

Savanur I 1756 I Maratha Rebellions
    Maratha General Muzaffar Khan Gardi rebelled against Peshwa Balaji Rao and sought an alliance with the Nawab of Savanur, in western India. In common cause against the rebel, the Peshwa and Nizam Salabat Jang of Hyderabad besieged Savanur and subjected it to a bombardment by western artillery. Muzaffar Khan fled and the Nawab surrendered (March–18 May 1756).

Savar I 1809 I Napoleonic Wars (Russo-Swedish War)
    After occupying Swedish Finland in the wake of decisive victory at **Oravais** (September 1808), Russian General Nikolai Kamenski pursued the retreating Swedes north around the Gulf of Bothnia into Sweden. At Savar, near Umea, in the bloodiest action of the campaign, Kamenski forced Swedish General Gustav Wachtmeister to withdraw and Sweden finally made peace (19 August 1809).

Save I 388 I Later Roman Military Civil Wars
    See **Siscia**

Savenay I 1793 I French Revolutionary Wars (Vendée War)
    Sent to suppress the Vendée Rebellion in western France, Republican General Jean-Baptiste Kléber and his veterans beat the Royalist rebels at **Cholet** and **Le Mans** in late 1793, then marched against them at Savenay, a village northwest of Nantes. A final brutal battle saw the counter-revolution virtually annihilated, though the Roy-

alist cause lingered for several years (23 December 1793).

Saverne I 1525 I German Peasants' War
    See **Zabern**

Savo Island I 1942 I World War II (Pacific)
    Responding to American landings on **Guadalcanal** and **Tulagi**, Admiral Gunichi Mikawa's cruiser squadron surprised the Allied covering force of Admiral Victor Crutchley at night near Savo Island. Within half an hour, one Australian and three American heavy cruisers were sunk with heavy loss of life. Mikawa retired unscathed, but lost a cruiser to submarine attack next day (8–9 August 1942).

Savona I 1795 I French Revolutionary Wars (1st Coalition)
    See **Genoa**

Savra I 1385 I Ottoman Conquest of the Balkans
    Sultan Murad I took advantage of an internal struggle between Prince Balsha II of Albania and his former ally Charles Thopia, sending the Ottoman army under Pasha Hayredin, who attacked the massively outnumbered Albanians on the Plain of Savra, on the left bank of the Devoll. Balsha was defeated and killed and the Turks effectively gained control of Albania (November 1385).

Saw I 238 BC I Truceless War
    While former mercenaries continued to besiege Carthage, Hamilcar Barca and his Numidian ally Naravas surrounded the mercenaries at a location referred to as the Saw, probably south of Carthage. Rebel leaders Spendius and Autaritus were seized when they tried to negotiate and their army was destroyed, with perhaps 40,000 killed. The Carthaginians then attacked the rebel camp at **Tunis**.

Saxa Rubra I 312 I Roman Wars of Succession
    See **Milvian Bridge**

Sayler's Creek I 1865 I American Civil War (Eastern Theatre)

As General Robert E. Lee's defeated Confederates retreated west from **Petersburg**, Virginia, part of his force under Generals Richard S. Ewell and John B. Gordon was attacked by General Philip Sheridan near Deatonsville at Sayler's Creek. Ewell and most of his force surrendered after hard fighting and Gordon led the survivors towards **High Bridge** on the Appomattox (6 April 1865).

Sbeitla I 647 I Muslim Conquest of North Africa
See **Sufetula**

Scapa Flow I 1939 I World War II (War at Sea)

One of Germany's most famous submarine exploits occurred in the first days of the war when Captain Günther Prien took *U-47* into Scapa Flow, the Royal Navy base in the Orkneys. The battleship *Royal Oak* was sunk with more than 830 men killed and Prien became the first U-boat commander to win the Knights Cross. He was lost with *U-47* in March 1941 (3 September 1939).

Scarborough I 1914 I World War I (War at Sea)

Four months after German failure off **Helgoland**, Admiral Fritz von Hipper took the initiative and led five battle cruisers, with light cruisers and destroyers, against England's east coast. Scarborough was bombarded, with considerable damage and 15 civilians killed, while Whitby and Hartlepool were also shelled. A month later, another German raid was intercepted on **Dogger Bank** (16 December 1914).

Scarpe I 1918 I World War I (Western Front)

On the northern flank of the Allied offensive east from **Arras**, British and Canadians under General Henry Horne advanced rapidly along the Scarpe River towards Douai. After the Allies took the key fortified town of Monchy, the retreating Germans resisted strongly at Bullecourt

before it finally fell. Horne then moved south to support the main attack towards **Bapaume** (26–31 August 1918).

Scarperia I 1351 I Florentine-Milanese Wars

At the start of a campaign by Milan to expand its power in northern Italy, Giovanni Visconti sent Giovanni Oleggio into Florentine-ruled Tuscany, where he was stalled by the heroic defence of the town and fortress of Scarperia, in the Mugello Hills, northeast of Florence. After a 55-day siege, a Florentine relief force under Salvestro de Medici defeated Oleggio and forced the invaders to withdraw.

Scarpheia I 191 BC I Roman-Syrian War
See **Thermopylae**

Scarpheia I 146 BC I Roman-Achaean War

With Rome distracted by war against Carthage, the Achaean League of Greek city-states tried to counteract growing Roman domination of Greece. The advancing allies under Diaeus and Critolaus were driven back from Heraclea, then were attacked at Scarpheia, east of Thermopylae, by Romans led by Quintus Caecilius Metellus. The Achaeans were routed, with Critolaus missing, presumed killed.

Scearston I 1016 I Danish Conquest of England
See **Sherston**

Sceaux I 1870 I Franco-Prussian War
See **Chatillon-sous-Bagneux**

Schaenzel I 1794 I French Revolutionary Wars (1st Coalition)
See **Platzberg**

***Scharnhorst* I 1943 I World War II (War at Sea)**
See **North Cape**

**Scheldt Estuary I 1944 I World War II
(Western Europe)**

Despite the fall of **Antwerp**, powerful German forces blocked the Scheldt Estuary, 55 miles downstream. Very heavy fighting saw Canadian General Guy Simonds seize the southern shore at **Breskens** and the South Beveland Isthmus before attacking the fortress of Walcheren, held by General Wilhelm Daser. The Allies lost over 12,000 casualties to open the river (1 October–8 November 1944).

**Schellenberg I 1599 I Balkan
National Wars**
See **Selimbar**

**Schellenberg I 1704 I War of the
Spanish Succession**
See **Donauwörth**

Schenectady I 1690 I King William's War

As part of King William's War—the American phase of the War of the Grand Alliance—a Canadian-Indian force under Nicolas d'Ailleboust de Manthet and Jacques le Moyne de Saint Hélène attacked Schenectady, New York. During a night raid, they killed 60 and returned to Montreal with 25 prisoners and massive plunder. Other French forces marched on **Salmon Falls** (8 February 1690).

Scheveningen I 1653 I 1st Dutch War

Following his losses at the **Gabbard Bank** (15 June), Dutch Admiral Maarten Tromp broke through the ensuing English blockade of the Dutch Coast and was killed in battle off Scheveningen, near the Hague. English Admiral George Monck drove the Dutch back to Texel with ten ships lost to his eight and claimed the hard-fought victory. The following year the Dutch sought peace (10 August 1653).

**Schladming I 1526 I German
Peasants' War**

With peasant rebellion spreading into Austria, Archbishop Mathhaus Lang of Salzburg called on veteran General Sigismund von Dietrichstein, whose Bohemians ravaged Styria before being routed by peasants under Michael Geismaier at Schladming, east of Bischofshofen. Dietrichstein and 40 officers were executed and war continued until 1527 when Geismaier was assassinated (3 July 1526).

**Schleitz I 1806 I Napoleonic Wars
(4th Coalition)**

As Napoleon Bonaparte's army converged on Prussia, Marshal Jean Baptiste Bernadotte advanced between the Saal and Elster to defeat a Prussian force under Count Bogislav Tauenzien west of Plauen at Schleitz. Although only a small action with just 400 Prussian casualties, it was a serious blow to Prussian morale and a prelude to the twin defeats at **Auerstadt** and **Jena** (9 October 1806).

Schlettstadt I 1870 I Franco-Prussian War

German commander Karl August Werder captured **Strasbourg** (28 September), then ordered General Hermann von Schmeling south along the Rhine against Schlettstadt (French Sélestat). The fortress capitulated following a heavy bombardment, yielding 2,400 prisoners and 120 guns. Von Schmeling then took his siege-train further south against **Neu-Breisach** (20–24 October 1870).

**Schliengen I 1796 I French Revolutionary
Wars (1st Coalition)**

Defeated by Archduke Charles of Austria close to the Rhine at **Emmendingen** (19 October), French General Jean Victor Moreau sent part of his force back across the river, then withdrew south as far as Schliengen, where he attempted to make a stand. Driven back by a powerful Austrian attack, Moreau finally withdrew across the Rhine over the next two days at **Huningue** (24 October 1796).

**Schlusselberg I 1702 I 2nd "Great"
Northern War**
See **Noteborg**

**Schmidt I 1945 I World War II
(Western Europe)**
See **Hürtgen Forest**

**Schnee Eifel ▮ 1944 ▮ World War II
(Western Europe)**

General Walther Lucht opened the German advance into the **Ardennes**, assaulting the Schnee Eifel Ridge, just inside the German border, occupied by inexperienced American troops under General Alan W. Jones. They were overwhelmed with 8,000 captured—the worst American surrender of the European war—and the Germans advanced into Belgium towards **St Vith** (16–20 December 1944).

**Schonchin Flow ▮ 1873 ▮ Modoc
Indian War**

During fighting against the Modoc in the Lava Beds of northern California, Captain Evan Thomas and Lieutenant Thomas Wright led a 68-man patrol to the Schonchin Flow, where they were ambushed by Captain Jack (Kintpuash) and Scarfaced Charley. Thomas, Wright and 23 others were killed and the war continued until the second assault in the **Lava Beds** (26 April 1873).

Schooneveld ▮ 1673 ▮ 3rd Dutch War

Prince Rupert and French Admiral Jean d'Estrées prepared for an Anglo-French invasion of the Netherlands by attacking the Dutch fleet in the Schooneveld at the mouth of the Scheldt. Admiral Mihiel de Ruyter counter-attacked with favourable winds and drove the Allies off, sinking many French ships. A second battle six days later was indecisive yet ended the planned invasion (7 & 14 June 1673).

**Schuinshoogte ▮ 1881 ▮ 1st Anglo-
Boer War**

See **Ingogo**

Schwaderloch ▮ 1499 ▮ Swabian War

In their final struggle for freedom, the Swiss cantons marched against the Habsburg cities of the Swabian League and two miles from Constance at Schwaderloch, they defeated a much larger German force. Further Swiss victories over the next few months at **Frastenz**, **Calven** and **Dornach** eventually forced Emperor Max-imilian to grant them virtual independence (11 April 1499).

**Schwechat ▮ 1848 ▮ Hungarian
Revolutionary War**

After Hungarian revolutionaries declared independence from Habsburg rule, over 20,000 Hungarians under General Johann Moga and Colonel Artur Gorgey marched to support a workers' rising in **Vienna**. Outside the city at Schwechat, Count Joseph Jellacic and Prince Adolph Auersperg repulsed the Hungarian militia with heavy losses. Vienna fell a few days later (30 October 1848).

**Schwedaung ▮ 1942 ▮ World War II
(Burma-India)**

See **Prome**

**Schweidnitz ▮ 1642 ▮ Thirty Years War
(Franco-Habsburg War)**

Marshal Lennart Torstensson took command of the Swedish army after its victory at **Wolfenbüttel** and the following year led a fresh advance into Silesia against a Saxon army on the Bystrzyca, southwest of Breslau at Schweidnitz. The Saxons were heavily defeated—with a massive loss of guns—and Torstensson then seized the city and marched into Moravia towards **Olmütz** (3 June 1642).

**Schweidnitz ▮ 1757 ▮ Seven Years War
(Europe)**

While campaigning in Saxony at **Rossbach**, Frederick II of Prussia left his brother Duke August-Wilhelm of Bevern to hold Silesia, where Austrian General Franz Leopold Nadasdy besieged Schweidnitz. When the Duke of Bevern was defeated nearby, the fortress fell after seven weeks yielding 7,000 prisoners. The Austrians then concentrated for battle days later at **Breslau** (11 November 1758).

**Schweidnitz ▮ 1762 ▮ Seven Years War
(Europe)**

See **Reichenbach, Poland**

Schweinfurt | 1943 | World War II (Western Europe)

In a daylight raid on the German ball-bearing industry at Schweinfurt in Bavaria, 291 American bombers were escorted only part of the way and suffered terrible losses to German fighters. The war's costliest air attack (Black Thursday) saw over 600 men killed in 64 bombers shot down and 138 damaged. Such raids ended until long-range fighter escort became available (14 October 1943).

Schweinschadel | 1866 | Seven Weeks War

Sent to oppose the Prussian invasion of Bohemia, Austrian General Tassilo Festetics arrived too late to save Königinhof (captured after defeat at **Soor**) then met General Karl Friedrich von Steinmetz north of Josefstadt marching west from victory at **Skalitz**. After a three-hour cannonade at Schweinschadel with 800 prisoners lost, Festetics fell back on the fortress at Josefstadt (29 June 1866).

Schwetz | 1462 | Thirteen Years War
See **Puck**

Sciari Sciat | 1911 | Italo-Turkish War
See **Sidi El Henni**

Scilly Isles | 1781 | War of the American Revolution

British Admiral Sir William Hotham was escorting a convoy with treasure seized at **St Eustatius** with just two ships of the line and three frigates, when he was intercepted west of the Scilly Isles by a strong squadron under Admiral Toussaint-Guillaume de la Motte-Picquet. Hotham wisely dispersed his heavily outnumbered convoy and the French recaptured most of the treasure (2 May 1781).

Scimitar Hill | 1915 | World War I (Gallipoli)

After replacing the incompetent Sir Henry Stopford at **Suvla Bay**, General Beauvoir de Lisle launched the last major offensive on the Gallipoli front towards Scimitar Hill. Despite a diversionary attack further south at **Hill 60**, the British assault against strong Turkish defences cost over 5,000 casualties for no gain. In December the Allies evacuated Suvla Bay (21 August 1915).

Scotitas | 199 BC | Spartan-Achaean Wars

With Sparta recovering from defeat at **Mantinea** (207 BC), new ruler Nabis led a fresh offensive into northern Laconia, where he was attacked near the Tegean border at Scotitas by Achaean forces under Philopoemen of Megalopolis, now Praetor of Achaea. Nabis suffered a bloody defeat and a temporary truce followed until he resumed the war and was defeated at **Argos** and **Mount Barbosthene**.

Scutari | 1474 | Venetian-Turkish Wars

Sultan Mehmed II renewed his war against Venetian Albania, sending 80,000 men under Hadim Suleiman Pasha against Scutari (modern Shkoder), held by Antonio Loredan. Although massive bombardment demolished the walls, high earthworks remained and a Turkish assault was repulsed with 7,000 dead. Suleiman withdrew on false reports of Venetian reinforcements (15 July–28 August 1474).

Scutari | 1478–1479 | Venetian-Turkish Wars

Four years after a failed campaign against Albania, Sultan Mehmed II concluded his war against Venice's trading colonies by launching a renewed assault against Scutari (modern Shkoder). Nearby **Krujë** was captured, but Scutari's garrison held out against siege until Venice sued for peace, yielding Scutari and other Adriatic possesssions to the Turks (22 June 1478–25 January 1479).

Scutari | 1912–1913 | 1st Balkan War

When Montenegro advanced into Albania towards Scutari, poor strategy and delay allowed the city to be reinforced before it came under siege. King Nicholas of Montenegro took command and made costly assaults before Essad

Pasha finally surrendered. The Great Powers later forced Nicholas to give up the prize which had cost almost 10,000 Montenegrin lives (23 October 1912–23 April 1913).

Seacroft Moor | 1643 | British Civil Wars

To cover the Parliamentary withdrawal from Selby to Leeds by Ferdinando Lord Fairfax, his son Sir Thomas Fairfax assaulted **Tadcaster**, near York. While withdrawing across Bramham Moor to Seacroft Moor, Sir Thomas was attacked in force and was heavily defeated by Royalist cavalry under George Lord Goring, losing 200 killed and 800 prisoners (30 March 1643).

Searobyrg | 552 | Anglo-Saxon Conquest of Britain

After inheriting Wessex from his father Cerdic, Cynric of the West Saxons advanced the borders of the kingdom to the west and inflicted a sharp defeat on the Britons at Searobyrg (Old Sarum), just north of modern Salisbury. The expansion of Wessex continued with further victories over the next 25 years at **Beranbyrg**, **Bedcanford** and **Deorham**.

Sebastia | 1070 | Byzantine-Turkish Wars

When Byzantine Emperor Romanus IV attempted to drive the Turks out of Anatolia, part of his army under Manuel Comnenus was attacked at Sebastia by a Turkish force under Er-Sighun, son of Yusuf Inal and a rebel kinsman of the Great Seljuk Alp Arslan. The Byzantines suffered a costly defeat, after which Turkish forces sacked Chonae. In August 1071 Alp Arslan himself seized **Manzikert**.

Sebastopol | 1854–1855 | Crimean War

See **Sevastopol**

Sebastopolis | 692 | Early Byzantine-Muslim Wars

Following a treaty violation by Emperor Justinian II, Umayyad Caliph Abd-al-Malik sent troops under his brother Mohamed into Byzantine Armenia and the armies met west of Sebastia at Sebastopolis (modern Sulusaray).

When the Emperor appeared to secure initial success, his Slav troops under Nebulus changed sides and he was routed, effectively delivering Armenia to the Arabs.

Seccandun | 757 | Anglo-Saxon Territorial Wars

Facing rebellion by the nobleman Beornred, King Aethelbald of Mercia was defeated and deposed at Seccandun (modern Seckington), east of Tamworth, Warwickshire. Aethelbald was either killed in the battle or murdered soon afterwards, possibly by his own bodyguard. However, the usurper Beornred enjoyed only a very brief reign before being overthrown by Aethelbald's kinsman, Offa.

Secchia | 1734 | War of the Polish Succession

Joseph Lothar Count von Königsegg regrouped the Austrian army after defeat at **Parma** (29 June) and led a surprise dawn attack across the Secchia, southeast of Mantua, against Marshal Francois-Marie Broglie. The French were driven back, losing 3,000 prisoners, before Marshal François de Coigny restored order and counter-attacked a few days later at **Guastalla** (15 September 1734).

Secessionville | 1862 | American Civil War (Lower Seaboard)

A fresh advance against the defences of **Charleston Harbour**, South Carolina, saw Union General Henry W. Benham attack Fort Lamar, at Secessionville on James Island, bravely defended by General Nathan G. Evans and Colonel Thomas G. Lamar. Driven off from costly frontal assaults, Benham was forced to withdraw. He was later relieved of command and demoted (16 June 1862).

Seckington | 757 | Anglo-Saxon Territorial Wars

See **Seccandun**

Secundrabagh | 1857 | Indian Mutiny

See **Sikander Bagh**

Sedan I 1870 I Franco-Prussian War

When Napoleon III was trapped at Sedan by Prussian armies under General Helmuth von Moltke and Prince Friedrich Wilhelm, General Auguste Ducrot suffered a decisive defeat, losing 17,000 casualties and 20,000 prisoners. One of France's worst military disasters saw General Emmanuel Wimpffen surrender 82,000 men. Napoleon himself was captured and soon abdicated (1 September 1870).

Sedd-el-Bahr I 1915 I World War I (Gallipoli)
See **Helles**

Sedgemoor I 1685 I Monmouth Rebellion

Rebelling against his Catholic uncle King James II of England, James Duke of Monmouth raised a Protestant revolt in the west, comprising largely miners and peasants. At Sedgemoor, near Bridgewater in Somerset, he was crushed by General Louis Duras Earl of Feversham and John Churchill. Monmouth was beheaded and over 1,000 rebels were executed or transported (6 July 1685).

Sediman I 1798 I French Revolutionary Wars (Middle East)

Napoleon Bonaparte routed General Murad Bey at the Battle of the **Pyramids** in July but soon became concerned about the Mamluk leader's presence on the Upper Nile and sent General Louis Desaix. At Sediman, 75 miles south of Cairo on the Bahr Yusuf, Desaix's infantry routed the Egyptians. A further victory in February 1799 at **Aswan** destroyed the Mamluk army (7 October 1798).

Seedasser I 1799 I 4th British-Mysore War
See **Sidassir**

Seekonk I 1676 I King Philip's War

In war against Wampanoag Chief Metacomet—known by American colonists as King Philip—his Narrangansett ally Canonchet escaped the defeat at the **Great Swamp Fight** and three months later had his revenge ambushing

Captain Michael Pierce near Seekonk, east of Providence, Rhode Island. Pierce and 40 militia were killed, but Canonchet was soon captured and executed (26 March 1676).

Segesvár I 1849 I Hungarian Revolutionary War

With Austria driven out of Hungary after **Hatvan** and **Waitzen** in April, Russia intervened to help. Following victory at **Pered** (21 June), Russian General Ivan Paskievich joined up with new Austrian commander Julius von Haynau to beat Hungarian General Josef Bem in Transylvania at Segesvár (modern Sighisoara). Bem withdrew west for the decisive battle at **Temesvár** (31 July 1849).

Segeswald I 757 I Anglo-Saxon Territorial Wars
See **Seccandun**

Segoyuela I 713 I Muslim Conquest of Spain

A Muslim army under Tarik ibn Ziyad advancing towards central Spain against the Christian Visigoths received reinforcements from Musa ibn Nusair, Arab Governor of the Maghreb (North Africa) and achieved a massive victory at Segoyuela, in Salamanca Province. Coming after similar defeats at **Guadalete** and **Ecija**, the battle effectively ended the Visigothic Kingdom in Spain (September 713).

Sehested I 1813 I Napoleonic Wars (War of Liberation)

Denmark was attacked in Holstein by Germans, Russians and Swedes led by former French Marshal Jean Baptiste Bernadotte (now Crown Prince of Sweden). Danish troops under Frederick of Hesse achieved a remarkable victory at Sehested, west of Kiel. However, Denmark lacked support in subsequent peace talks and was forced to cede Norway to Sweden (10 December 1813).

Seine I 1416 I Hundred Years War
See **Harfleur**

Sekigahara ∎ 1600 ∎ Japan's Era of the Warring States

After Japanese ruler Toyotomi Hideyoshi died in 1598, his leading General Tokugawa Ieyasu rejected the six-year-old heir Hideyori and fought Loyalist commander Ishida Mitsunari at Sekigahara, east of Lake Biwa. In one of Japan's greatest battles, Mitsunari and his allies were routed and Ieyasu founded the 250-year Tokugawa Shogunate. Hideyori retired to **Osaka Castle** (20 September 1600).

Sekou ∎ 1821 ∎ Greek War of Independence

Following a terrible rout in Romania at **Dragasani**, Greek leader Georgakis Olympios and the Albanian Yannis Farmakis tried to reach Russia and became surrounded in the monastery at Sekou, west of Jassy. After a brief siege, Georgakis blew himself up to avoid capture. Farmakis and his officers surrendered on condition of amnesty, but were tortured and executed (September–4 October 1821).

Se La ∎ 1962 ∎ Sino-Indian War

In the wake of Chinese victory at the **Namka Chu** in northeast India (20 October), the border war eased for diplomatic manoeuvring and India reinforced the forward position at Se La. When the Chinese attacked again in force, Brigadier Hoshiar Singh initially held them off and inflicted costly losses. He was finally overwhelmed and the invaders drove south on **Bomdila** (16 November 1962).

Selby ∎ 1644 ∎ British Civil Wars

As Ferdinando Lord Fairfax and his son Sir Thomas led a Parliamentary army into Yorkshire, Royalist commander William Cavendish Earl of Newcastle sent Sir John Belasyse to meet the invaders. Belasyse was routed south of York at Selby, with heavy losses in men and guns, and the Royalists in the north were forced back on **York** (11 April 1644).

Sele ∎ 212 BC ∎ 2nd Punic War

See **Silarus**

Sele ∎ 71 BC ∎ 3rd Servile War

See **Silarus**

Selimbar ∎ 1599 ∎ Balkan National Wars

Prince Michael of Wallachia resolved to unite the Romanians and (with Habsburg consent) invaded southern Transylvania against Prince Andreas Bathory. Michael defeated General Gaspar Kornis at Selimbar, near Hermannstadt (modern Sibiu), then proclaimed himself Prince of Transylvania. He seized Moldavia after victory in May 1600 at **Khotin** (28 October 1599).

Selinus ∎ 409 BC ∎ Carthaginian-Syracusan Wars

Determined to avenge his grandfather's defeat and death at **Himera** in 480 BC, Carthaginian commander Hannibal led a fresh invasion of Sicily, landing in the southwest to attack Selinus. A relief force from Syracuse under Diocles arrived too late and the city was taken by storm after a brief siege. It was then put to the sack and Hannibal moved north against **Himera**.

Sellasia ∎ 222 BC ∎ Cleomenic War

With the northern Peloponnese threatened by Cleomenes III of Sparta after victory in 226 BC at **Hecatombaeum**, Antigonus III of Macedon marched south with 10,000 men and gathering about 18,000 local troops. North of Sparta at Sellasia, Cleomenes was outnumbered and crushed. He fled to Egypt and Antigonus dominated much of the Peloponnese through the Achaean League (July 222 BC).

Selle ∎ 1918 ∎ World War I (Western Front)

Outflanking the Germans in the north at **Courtrai**, the main Allied offensive further south continued through **Le Cateau** across the Selle, led by British Generals Sir Henry Rawlinson and Julian Byng and French under General Marie Debeney. Defensive positions along the river were stormed and Valenciennes was captured as the Germans fell back on the **Sambre** (17–25 October 1918).

**Selma I 1865 I American Civil War
(Western Theatre)**

As the war approached its end, Union General James H. Wilson led a large-scale cavalry raid into Alabama, advancing on Confederate Selma, defended by Generals Nathan B. Forrest and Richard Taylor. A bold assault by Wilson took the city by storm. He also captured Montgomery, then entered Georgia to take Columbia and Macon before peace brought a conclusion to hostilities (2 April 1865).

**Selsey I 477 I Anglo-Saxon Conquest
of Britain**

See **Cymensore**

**Selwood I 1016 I Danish Conquest
of England**

See **Penselwood**

**Semen I 1818 I Venezuelan War
of Independence**

Patriot leader Simón Bolívar advancing from victory at **Calabozo** (12 February) pursued Spanish Pablo Morillo into Guárico and they met at Semen, near La Puerta, north of San Juan de los Morros. Bolívar was routed in a bloody action with 800 men killed and 400 captured, but recovered at **Queseras del Medio**. Severely wounded, Morillo was created Marquis de La Puerta (16 March 1818).

**Semendria I 1439 I Turkish-
Hungarian Wars**

Sultan Murad II invaded Serbia, where Despot George Brankovic left his sons Gregor and Stefan to hold the strategic fortress of Semendria (modern Smederevo). While Albert I of Hungary took an army to the Danube, he failed to provide aid and the starving garrison surrendered, with the Brankovic brothers captured and later blinded. Murad returned to Edirne and the next year besieged **Belgrade**.

**Semendria I 1441 I Turkish-
Hungarian Wars**

See **Császáhalom**

**Semigallia I 1626 I 2nd Polish-
Swedish War**

See **Wallhof**

**Seminara I 1495 I Italian War of
Charles VIII**

After Charles VIII of France invaded Italy to claim Naples, Spanish reinforcements under Gonsalvo de Cordoba landed in Calabria and the armies met at Seminara, northeast of Reggio. The Spanish were beaten by a smaller French force under General Bernard Stuart Seigneur d'Aubigny, though Cordoba's victory a year later at **Aversa** drove France temporarily out of Italy (28 June 1495).

**Seminara I 1503 I Italian War of
Louis XII**

While the end of the war between France and Spain over Naples focused on the siege of **Barletta** and battle at **Cerignola**, French General Bernard Stuart Seigneur d'Aubigny was campaigning independently in Calabria. However, northeast of Reggio at Seminara (site of his victory in 1495), he lost badly just a few days before the decisive French defeat at Cerignola (21 April 1503).

Sempach I 1386 I Habsburg-Swiss Wars

When Swiss cities joined the South German Swabian League against King Wenceslas and the House of Habsburg, Leopold III of Austria and his commander Johann von Ochenstein took an army into Switzerland. At Sempach, near Lucerne, outnumbered Swiss pikemen killed Leopold and destroyed his knights fighting dismounted. A further defeat at **Nafels** in April 1388 ended the war (9 July 1386).

**Sendaigawa I 1587 I Japan's Era of the
Warring States**

Toyotomi Hideyoshi intervened in Kyushu to repulse Satsuma forces, advancing down the west coast while his half-brother Hidenaga won in the east at **Takashiro**. Attempting to block him at the Sendaigawa near Oguchi with a massively outnumbered Satsuma army, Niiro Tadamoto was heavily defeated (reputedly spared in single combat) and withdrew south to **Kagoshima** (6 June 1587).

Seneffe I 1674 I 3rd Dutch War

On campaign against the Allies in the Dutch Republic, Louis II de Bourdon Prince of Condé attacked Spanish, German and Dutch under William of Orange marching to invade France. An indecisive struggle around Seneffe, near Nivelle, cost both sides heavy losses. Although the Allies could not be dislodged, their invasion was thwarted and Condé claimed the strategic gain (11 August 1674).

Senegal I 1758 I Seven Years War (West Africa)

At war with the French in West Africa, Britain sent six ships under Captain Henry Marsh, who sailed to the Senegal River with 200 Marines. Port Louis fell after hard fighting, yielding 230 prisoners and 92 guns as well as gold and ivory, although the squadron was insufficient to capture nearby **Gorée**. At the end of the war, Britain retained Senegal (23–30 April 1758).

Senegal I 1804 I Napoleonic Wars (3rd Coalition)

See **Gorée**

Senekal I 1900 I 2nd Anglo-Boer War

See **Biddulphsberg**

Senigallia I 551 I Gothic War in Italy

See **Sinigaglia**

Senlac I 1066 I Norman Conquest of Britain

See **Hastings, England**

Sennheim I 1638 I Thirty Years War (Franco-Habsburg War)

In a fresh attempt to save **Breisach**, besieged by Bernard of Saxe-Weimar after victory at **Rheinfelden** and **Wittenweier**, an Imperial force under Duke Charles of Lorraine advanced on the Rhine from the west. They were intercepted and destroyed at Sennheim (French

Cernay) outside Mühlhausen by Duke Bernard, who resumed his siege and starved Breisach into surrender (15 October 1638).

Senova I 1878 I Russo-Turkish Wars

Defending the strategic **Shipka Pass** through the Balkan Mountains, the Russian garrison received reinforcements from the fall of **Plevna** and General Mikhail Skobelev attacked the camp of Vessil Pasha two miles south at Senova near Kazanlik. Vessil was routed, losing 4,000 casualties and 26,000 prisoners. After the fall of **Plovdiv** Turkey sued for peace (8–9 January 1878).

Sens I 356 I Alemannic Invasion of Roman Gaul

Roman commander Flavius Claudius Julianus was sharply defeated near **Rheims**, yet restored his military reputation later that year at Sens in central Gaul. Attacked in his winter quarters by a large body of Alemanni tribesmen, Julianus led a courageous monthlong defence until the Germans were driven off and had no choice but to withdraw.

Sens I 886–887 I Viking Raids on France

Following the long Viking siege of **Paris**— which ended in 886 when Norse leader Sinric was paid off by King Charles III the Fat—Sinric took his army against the city of Sens, southeast of Paris. An heroic defence saw the city hold out against siege for six months before the Norsemen were finally driven off and withdrew.

Senta I 1697 I Later Turkish-Habsburg Wars

See **Zenta**

Sentinum I 295 BC I 3rd Samnite War

Recovering after **Camerinum**, Romans under Fabius Maximus Rullianus and Decius Mus quickly attacked Samnite commander Gellius Egnatius and his allies further north at Sentinum (modern Sassoferrato). Despite heavy Roman losses (including Decius killed), Egnatius was defeated and killed. Gauls and Etruscans made peace, but the Samnites fought on until beaten in 293 BC at **Aquilonia**.

Sentry Hill I 1864 I 2nd New Zealand War

Encouraged by success at **Te Ahuahu** (6 April), about 200 warriors of the religio-military Hauhau led by Hepanaia Kapewhiti attacked Sentry Hill (Te Morere), east of New Plymouth, held by 75 regulars under Captain William Shortt. Believing themselves immune to bullets, about 50 Hauhau were killed in a frontal assault (including Kapewhiti himself) before the rest were driven off (30 April 1864).

Seoni I 1818 I 3rd British-Maratha War

With the Maratha army destroyed at **Ashti** in February, Peshwa Baji Rao II was driven northeast by General Sir John Doveton (1768–1847) and ran into Colonel Sir John Worthington Adams at Seoni. Baji Rao was routed and fled, abandoning his guns and stores. He withdrew west to Asirgargh to start the negotiations, which led to his eventual exile and British annexation of the Maratha territory.

Seoul I 1592 I Japanese Invasion of Korea

See **Chongju**

Seoul (1st) I 1950 I Korean War

At the start of the war, North Koreans stormed across the border and the main force advanced on Seoul, where South Korean General Chae Byong Duk was completely outmanoeuvred. His premature demolition of bridges on the Han cost men and equipment and ended any hope of resistance. General Lee Kwon Mu took the city in three days then attacked across the **Han** (25–28 June 1950).

Seoul (2nd) I 1950 I Korean War

After landing at **Inchon**, General Edward Almond raced east towards Seoul and took Yongdung-po (22 September). However, his Marines met costly losses failing to storm the Han before being joined by Army General Walton Walker from the **Pusan Perimeter**. Seoul was taken after further fighting and the

Americans and South Koreans moved north on **Pyongyang** (18–28 September 1950).

Seoul I 1951 I Korean War

With Seoul lost (4 January) after defeat at the **Chongchon**, General Matthew Ridgeway checked the Communist offensive at **Chipyong** (15 February), retook territory south of the Han in Operation Killer, then began Operation Ripper. After heavy fighting, the Allies retook Seoul (14 March), followed by Hongchon and Chunchon, and the Chinese fell back through Munsan (7–31 March 1951).

Sepeia I 494 BC I Spartan-Argive Wars

King Cleomenes was determined to expand Spartan power and took a large and well-organised force against Argos in the eastern Peloponnese. In a bloody and decisive action at Sepeia, near Tiryns at the head of the Gulf of Argolis, the Argive army was utterly destroyed, though Cleomenes wisely spared the capital Argos. Victory virtually confirmed Spartan supremacy in southern Greece.

Seria I 1962 I Brunei Rebellion

When Indonesian-backed rebels began a revolt in Brunei, Gurkhas secured the capital, **Brunei** Town, and British regulars under Colonel William McHardy were airlifted from Singapore to retake the important oil town of Seria, 50 miles to the southwest. Landing under fire at the main airfield, the Highlanders stormed Seria without loss and freed oil company hostages (10–12 December 1962).

Seringapatam I 1792 I 3rd British-Mysore War

When Tipu Sultan of Mysore renewed war against Britain, Governor-General Charles Earl Cornwallis captured **Bangalore**, then advanced against the Mysorean capital at Seringapatam (modern Srirangapatnam). After a full-scale siege, which cost Tipu over 4,000 men and all his guns, the Maharaja ended the war, ceding half his territory to Britain (15–16 February 1792).

Seringapatam I 1799 I 4th British-Mysore War

Tipu Sultan of Mysore once again resumed war with Britain and General George Harris brushed his army aside at **Malavalli**, then advanced on Seringapatam (modern Srirangapatnam). General David Baird stormed the fortress after bombardment breached the walls and Tipu died in the assault. The attack ended the war, finally securing southern India for Britain (6 April–4 May 1799).

Seringham I 1752 I 2nd Carnatic War

Driven back from **Trichinopoly** in southeast India, Nawab Chanda Sahib of Arcot and French Colonel Jacques Law withdrew to siege by Major Stringer Lawrence at nearby Seringham (modern Srirangam). Facing disaster, Law negotiated safe surrender for the Nawab, then surrendered 3,000 men and 40 guns. Chanda Sahib was later murdered by his Tanjorean captors (10 April–13 June 1752).

Seritsa I 1501 I 1st Muscovite-Lithuanian War

Beaten by Duke Ivan III of Moscow at the **Vedrosha** (July 1500), Alexander of Lithuania and Poland secured aid from the Livonian Order, whose Master Walther von Plettenberg threatened Pskov. Ivan sent Prince Daniil Penkov, with Ivan Gorbaty of Pskov, but at the Seritsa, near Isborsk, the Russian army was destroyed by artillery and fled. Russia was soon avenged at **Helmed** (27 August 1501).

Serravalle I 1544 I 4th Habsburg-Valois War

Following his defeat at **Ceresole**, south of Turin in April, Imperial commander Alfonso d'Avalos Marquis del Vasto attacked a large body of Italians marching from the east to reinforce Francis de Bourbon Prince d'Enghien. The mercenaries under Marshal Piero Strozzi were heavily defeated at Serravalle Libarna, near Novi Ligure, with a large number taken prisoner (2 June 1544).

Sesia I 1524 I 1st Habsburg-Valois War

Two years after Francis I of France was driven from Lombardy at **Bicocca**, he sent Admiral William de Bonnivet, who took Milan but was repulsed at **Rebecco** by Imperial commander Fernando d'Avalos Marquis of Pescara. On the Sesia near Romagnano, northwest of Novara, the retreating French were routed, with Bonnivet wounded and Chevalier Pierre Terrail de Bayard killed (30 April 1524).

Seskar I 1790 I 2nd Russo-Swedish War
See **Kronstadt Bay**

Seta I 1184 I Gempei War
See **Uji**

Settat I 1908 I French Colonial Wars in North Africa

With the Moroccan siege of Casablanca driven off by action at **Taddert**, new French commander General Albert d'Amade took 2,500 men three days south against Moulai Hafid at Settat. An over-managed drill-book assault allowed the Moroccans to escape, although 40 were killed in the pursuit. D'Amade withdrew and tried again a week later at **Wadi M'Koun** (15 January 1908).

Sevastopol I 1854–1855 I Crimean War

The Anglo-French forces of General Fitzroy Somerset Lord Raglan and General Francois Canrobert advanced across the **Alma** and besieged the fortress of Sevastopol, brilliantly defended by General Frants Todleben. With a final relief attempt repulsed at the **Chernaya**, and the storming of the **Malakov**, Russia withdrew, effectively ending the war (28 September 1854–9 September 1855).

Sevastopol I 1914 I World War I (War at Sea)

Without any declaration of war, the German-manned Turkish cruisers *Goeben* (Yavuz) and *Breslau* (Midilli) led a Turkish squadron against Russian ports in the Black Sea. Admiral Wilhelm Souchon in *Goeben* bombarded Sevastopol, while other ships attacked Odessa and No-vorossisk. Russia responded by declaring war and soon fought back off **Cape Sarych** (29 October 1914).

Sevastopol I 1941–1942 I World War II (Eastern Front)

General Erich von Manstein broke into the Crimean Peninsula at **Perekop** and advanced on the great fortified naval base at Sevastopol, held by General Ivan Petrov. After a failed initial assault, the Germans went to clear **Kerch,** then returned to reduce Sevastopol (7 June). It fell after a 250-day siege with 90,000 captured. Manstein was made a Field Marshal (30 October 1941–3 July 1942).

Sevastopol I 1944 I World War II (Eastern Front)

As Russian forces invaded the Crimea through **Perekop** and **Kerch**, the German Seventeenth Army under General Erwin Jaenecke fell back on Sevastopol, where Russians attacked behind heavy artillery. Although many escaped by sea before the fortress fell, the Germans lost perhaps 50,000 men killed or captured at Sevastopol, or in a final stand at nearby Cape Khersonessky (7–9 May 1944).

Seven Days' Battles I 1862 I American Civil War (Eastern Theatre)

After advancing through Virginia from **Yorktown**, Union commander George B. McClellan fought a weeklong series of battles east and south of Richmond, which led to his withdrawal and the end of the Peninsula campaign. The battles were at **Oak Grove, Beaver Dam Creek, Garnett's and Golding's Farms, Savage's Station, White Oak Swamp** and **Malvern Hill** (25 June–1 July 1862).

Sevenoaks I 1450 I Cade's Rebellion

Rebelling over land grievances, the men of Kent marched on London led by Jack Cade, an Irish-born former soldier. South of the capital at Sevenoaks, the insurgents beat a heavily outnumbered Royalist army, killing commander Sir Humphrey Stafford. The rebels then entered the capital and were defeated at **London Bridge**. The rebellion soon collapsed with many leaders executed (18 June 1450).

Seven Pines I 1862 I American Civil War (Eastern Theatre)

Union commander George B. McClellan advancing along the Virginia Peninsula was met east of Richmond at Seven Pines by General Joseph E. Johnston (who was wounded and succeeded by General Gustavus W. Smith). Despite almost 6,000 Union and 8,000 Confederate casualties, both sides claimed victory, though McClellan withdrew through the **Seven Days' Battles** (31 May–1 June 1862).

Seven Springs I 1862 I American Civil War (Eastern Theatre)

See **White Hall**

Seventythree Easting I 1991 I 1st Gulf War

See **Wadi al-Batin**

Severndroog I 1755 I War Against Malabar Pirates

See **Savandrug**

Severndroog I 1791 I 3rd British-Mysore War

See **Savandrug**

Seville I 1248 I Early Christian Reconquest of Spain

Ferdinand III of Castile captured **Cordova** from the Moors (1236) and advanced down the Guadalquivir River to besiege Seville, defended by Arab General Muhammed ibn al-Akhmar. The garrison held out until Ferdinand sent ships to blockade supplies arriving along the river and the city was starved into surrender. The fall of Seville left the Moors in Spain with little beyond Granada.

Sewell's Point ∎ 1861 ∎ American Civil War (Eastern Theatre)

Within weeks of war starting at **Fort Sumter**, two Union gunboats under Lieutenant Daniel L. Braine blockading Chesapeake Bay engaged the Confederate Battery at Sewell's Point, just north of Norfolk, commanded by General Walter Gwynn. The gunboats were driven off after indecisive action and a fresh assault was attempted ten days later at **Aquia Creek** (18–19 May 1861).

Shabatz ∎ 1476 ∎ Turkish-Hungarian Wars
See **Sabac**

Shabatz ∎ 1521 ∎ Turkish-Hungarian Wars
See **Sabac**

Shabatz ∎ 1806 ∎ 1st Serbian Rising
See **Misar**

Shabatz ∎ 1914 ∎ World War I (Balkan Front)
See **Sabac**

Shabkadr ∎ 1897 ∎ Great Frontier Rising

Soon after Pathan tribesmen inspired by Mullah Sadullah were driven off from a siege at **Malakand**, further south and just 15 miles from Peshawar itself, a reported 5,000 Mohmand tribesmen from the west attacked the Border Police fort at Shabkadr. A column from Peshawar under Colonel (later Sir) John Woon dispersed the rebels with a flank attack by Bengal Lancers (7 August 1897).

Shaggy Ridge ∎ 1943–1944 ∎ World War II (Pacific)

General George Vasey's 7th Australian Division, advancing up the Markham-Ramu Valley in New Guinea, confronted Japanese forces of the Eighteenth Army entrenched on a massive feature in the Finisterre Mountains which the Australians called Shaggy Ridge. A slogging three-month fight finally cleared the last Japa-

nese defenders and the advance continued (October 1943–January 1944).

Shahdadpur ∎ 1843 ∎ British Conquest of Sind

In an opportunistic war against the Baluchi Amirs of Sind (in modern Pakistan), British General Sir Charles Napier routed a massive Baluchi force under Sher Muhammad near **Miani** (17 February), then captured his capital at Mirpur and sent Major John Jacob to pursue the Amir into the Sind desert. The Lion of Mirpur was finally defeated at Shahdadpur and fled across the Indus (14 June 1843).

Shahganj ∎ 1857 ∎ Indian Mutiny

With rebel forces approaching Agra, Brigadier Thomas Polwhele marched six miles from the city to meet his opponents at Shahganj. While his troops fought courageously in a badly handled action, their ammunition had been destroyed during a needless delay under artillery fire. Heavily outnumbered, Polwhele was forced to retreat to **Agra** and was later relieved of command (5 July 1857).

Shahi Tibbi ∎ 1704 ∎ Mughal-Sikh Wars
See **Sarsa**

Shaho ∎ 1900 ∎ Russo-Chinese War

Russian General Fleisher was reinforced after victory in southern Manchuria at **Haicheng** (12 August) and advanced west towards Niezhuang, while commander General Deian Ivanovich Subotich marched direct to Shaho, north of Anshan, held by over 50,000 Chinese. An artillery duel and sharp fighting forced the Chinese to withdraw north through **Liaoyang** (27 September 1900).

Shaho ∎ 1904 ∎ Russo-Japanese War

Withdrawing north into Manchuria from **Liaoyang** (3 September), Russian General Aleksei Kuropatkin turned on Marshal Iwao Oyama's pursuing Japanese south of **Mukden** (modern Shenyang) at Shaho. Heavy fighting along an extended front cost about 40,000 Russian and 16,000 Japanese casualties before winter conditions forced both sides to dig in behind barbed wire (7–16 October 1904).

Shahrabad I 1117 I Eastern Muslim Dynastic Wars

See **Ghazni**

Shahr Rey I 1194 I Wars of the Great Seljuk Sultanate

When Toghril III—last of the Great Seljuk Sultans of Iran—attempted to reassert his influence, the Caliph called for help from Sultan Tekish of Khwarezm. In battle at Shahr Rey, south of Tehran, Toghril was defeated and killed—reportedly when he accidentally hit his own horse with his mace and fell. As a result, much of western Persian was lost to the Khwarezmian Empire.

Shaiba I 1915 I World War I (Mesopotamia)

Turkish forces driven out of Basra after defeat at **Sahil** in November 1914 later tried to retake the city near the mouth of the Euphrates. Advancing on Basra, they were blocked by the small British garrison west of the city at Shaiba. A three-day defence saw the Turks driven off after heavy losses on both sides. General Sir John Nixon then advanced upriver against **Amara** (12–14 April 1915).

Shakargarh I 1971 I 3rd Indo-Pakistan War

Indian General Khem Karan Singh responded to a Pakistani invasion through **Chhamb** by launching a massive counter-offensive further south to pinch off the strategic Shakargarh Salient, west of Pathankot. The largest armoured battle of the war saw heavy losses in men and tanks on both sides, but Pakistan was badly defeated with 45 tanks destroyed and had to sue for peace (8–16 December 1971).

Shakarkhelda I 1724 I Mughal-Hyderabad War

Four years after victory over Imperial armies at **Ratanpur** and **Balapur**, the ambitious Nizam-ul-Mulk and his commander Iwaz Khan defeated and killed Mabariz Khan, Mughal Governor of Patna, at Shakarkhelda (modern Fathkelda), northeast of Aurangabad. Nizam was pardoned by Emperor Muhammad Shah and eventually became independent ruler of Hyderabad (11 October 1724).

Shalateng I 1947 I 1st Indo-Pakistan War

As Pakistan-backed Muslim tribesmen stormed into Indian Kashmir through **Uri**, they paused to loot. The Maharaja of Kashmir appealed to India, which sent forces under Brigadier Lionel Protip "Bogie" Sen to reinforce Srinigar. The rampaging tribesmen were routed at nearby Shalateng and the capital was saved. Sen's Indian regulars soon advanced to retake Baramula and **Uri** (7 November 1947).

Shamkhor I 1826 I Russo-Persian Wars

When Persia invaded Russian Azerbaijan, Amir Khan of Erivan captured Yelizavetpol, then faced a much smaller Russian force under General Valerian Gregorevich Madatov further west at the Shamkhor River. Superior Russian artillery led to a Persian rout, after which Madatov occupied **Yelizavetpol**. Ten days later he helped defeat the main Persian army (3 September 1826).

Shamsabad I 1858 I Indian Mutiny

Threatened by a large rebel force which had crossed the Ganges just 12 miles upstream of his base at Fateghar, General Sir Colin Campbell sent Brigadier Adrian Hope northwest on an overnight march. A surprise attack at the village of Sutia, just outside Shamsabad, saw Hope inflict a heavy defeat. The rebels fled back across the Ganges, abandoning four guns (27 January 1858).

Shangani I 1893 I Matabele War

Major Patrick Forbes led a British column into Matabeleland (in modern Zimbabwe) against the great King Lobengula and crossed the Shangani River, where his camp was attacked by about 5,000 Matabele under Manonda and Mjaan. Routed by cannon and Maxim guns, Manonda hanged himself in shame. Forbes then advanced through **Bembesi** towards Bulawayo (25 October 1893).

Shangani Incident | 1893 | Matabele War

As the great Matabele King Lobengula fled north from Bulawayo after defeat at **Bembesi**, Major Patrick Forbes in pursuit sent a small patrol under Major Allan Wilson, which stumbled into the main Matalebe army and was trapped by the flooded Shangani. In a legendary heroic stand, the 35 troopers were all killed. Lobengula continued his flight and later died of fever (4 December 1893).

Shangdang | 1945 | 3rd Chinese Revolutionary Civil War

During Chinese peace negotiations after World War II, over 35,000 Nationalists under warlord Yan Xishan invaded southeast Shanxi and occupied Tunliu, Lucheng and Xiangyuan in the Shangdang area, north of Changzhi. Attacked by Communist General Liu Bocheng, the Kuomintang were decisively defeated. Liu moved east to meet another incursion at **Handan** (15 October 1945).

Shanggao | 1941 | Sino-Japanese War

On a fresh offensive into northern Jiangxi, Japanese advanced southwest from **Nanchang** along the Xin Jiang towards Shanggao. The Chinese 19th Army under General Luo Zhuoyin fought a bloody defence east of the city. After heavy fighting and a threatened encirclement, the Japanese had to withdraw. The next enemy offensive was further west against **Changsha** (22–25 March 1941).

Shanghai | 1860 | Taiping Rebellion

Having driven off the Imperial siege of **Nanjing** in May, Taiping commander Hong Rengan and General Li Xuicheng advanced east towards the great international city of Shanghai. Following action to the west at **Songjiang** and **Qingpu**, Hong attempted to occupy the city but was attacked by "neutral" French and British troops and withdrew after four days (18–21 August 1860).

Shanghai | 1862 | Taiping Rebellion

Taiping commander Li Xiucheng secured **Hangzhou**, then days later attacked Shanghai, held by British Admiral James Hope, French Admiral Léopold Protet and irregulars under American Frederick T. Ward (later reinforced by Imperial General Li Hongzhang). After months of bloody fighting, Tan Shaoguang's final assault failed and the Taiping withdrew (7 January–30 August 1862).

Shanghai | 1927 | 1st Chinese Revolutionary Civil War

Turning north after capturing **Hangzhou**, Nationalist commander Bai Chongxi and General Xue Yeu attacked Shanghai, held for the northern warlord Sun Zhuanfang by Bi Shu Cheng. After Admiral Yang Shu Zhang declared for the Kuomintang, the city fell by storm and **Nanjing**, further west, fell two days later. Bi Shu Cheng fled but was captured and executed (18–22 March 1927).

Shanghai | 1932 | Shanghai Incident

In response to a boycott and anti-Japanese riots in Shanghai, a Japanese army of 70,000 landed to attack the great Chinese city. Supported by devastating air and naval firepower, they crushed the local garrison. A League of Nations ceasefire was eventually signed and the Japanese withdrew after China agreed to end the boycott (29 January–4 March 1932).

Shanghai | 1937 | Sino-Japanese War

While Japanese forces in northern China advanced from **Beijing** towards **Taiyuan**, another offensive began on the central coast, where up to 200,000 men were thrown against Shanghai. Chinese commander Chang Fakui fought a prolonged defence before he was eventually overwhelmed by numbers and withdrew west towards **Nanjing** (13 August–11 November 1937).

Shangkao | 1941 | Sino-Japanese War
See **Shanggao**

Shangqiu l 757 l An Lushan Rebellion
See **Suiyang**

Shanhaiguan l 1644 l Manchu Conquest of China

When rebel leader Li Zicheng captured **Beijing** and overthrew the Ming Dynasty, Ming General Wu Sangui invited his enemy Manchu Prince Dorgon to come to his aid. In a massive battle at the Great Wall at Shanhaiguan, Li's forces suffered a terrible defeat and withdrew towards **Tongguan**. Dorgon seized Beijing and the new Manchu (Qing) Dynasty reigned until 1912 (27 May 1644).

Shanhaiguan l 1924 l 2nd Zhili-Fengtian War

As warlords fought for northern China, Zhili leader Kao Kun in Beijing sent Generals Wu Beifu and Feng Yuxiang east to Shanhaiguan against Zhang Zuolin of Manchuria (whose army had been repulsed at **Changxindian**). After costly fighting, Feng changed sides and returned to overthrow Kao by coup (22 October), giving Zhang control of Beijing (October 1924).

Shanhaiguan l 1945 l 3rd Chinese Revolutionary Civil War

With World War II newly over, Nationalist Chinese entered Soviet-occupied **Manchuria** and met Communist Chinese at the Liao River, where severe fighting developed around Shanhaiguan Pass at the seaward end of the Great Wall. Attacking with tanks, the Nationalists broke through and reached as far as Jinzhou before an American-imposed ceasefire (10–16 November 1945).

Shao-Hsing l 1359 l Rise of the Ming Dynasty
See **Shaoxing**

Shaoxing l 1359 l Rise of the Ming Dynasty

Amid warlord rivalry during the decline of the Yuan Dynasty, Zhang Shicheng of Wu seized Shaoxing, southeast of Hangzhou, where his General Lu Chen soon faced a large Ming army under Hu Dahai. The epic siege of Shaoxing saw months of bitter fighting among flooded levees before losses and disease forced the Ming to withdraw. Zhang Shicheng was finally overcome in 1367 at **Suzhou**.

Sharashett l 1911 l Italo-Turkish War
See **Sidi El Henni**

Sharkiyan l 1008 l Eastern Muslim Dynastic Wars
See **Balkh**

Sharm el-Sheikh l 1956 l Arab-Israeli Sinai War
See **Straits of Tiran**

Sharon l 1918 l World War I (Middle East)
See **Megiddo**

Sharpsburg l 1862 l American Civil War (Eastern Theatre)
See **Antietam**

Sharqat l 1918 l World War I (Mesopotamia)

The war was almost over when Anglo-Indian commander Sir William Marshall determined to secure the Upper Tigris and sent General Sir Alexander Cobbe against Ismail Haqqi Bey north of **Baghdad** around Sharqat. Very heavy action forced about 18,000 Turks to surrender and Mosul was occupied. Commander Ali Ihsan Pasha signed a local armistice to end the conflict (26–29 October 1918).

Sharur l 1501 l Persian-Turkoman Wars

At war with the Turkomans of the south Caucasus, Sheikh Ismail of Ardabil in northern Iran marched into the Araxes Valley in pursuit of Sultan Alwand of the Ak Koyunlu (White Sheep) Turkoman confederacy. At Sharur, Alwand was routed and fled. Ismail then captured Tabriz and two years later he advanced to completely destroy the Turkomans at **Hamadan** (August 1501).

**Sharwa | 1019 | Muslim Conquest
of Northern India**

Mahmud of Ghazni led his army from Afghanistan into India, advancing through Kanauj
against Raja Chandar Ray of Sharwa, who abandoned his capital and took to the forest. Mahmud
pursued him and dealt out a terrible defeat. He
then sacked Sharwa and seized a massive plunder,
including gold, silver and reputedly over 50,000
slaves and 350 elephants (6 January 1019).

Shayuan | 537 | Wei Dynastic Wars

With the north China kingdom of Wei divided, Gao Huan of Eastern Wei led a failed
advance west. A few months later he invaded
again with a force claimed to be well over
100,000-strong. The outnumbered Western Wei
army under Yuwen Tai ambushed the invaders
at Shayuan, inflicting massive losses. A Western
counter-offensive the following year was halted
at **Heqiao** (19 November 537).

Sheerness | 1667 | 2nd Dutch War
See **Medway**

Sheikan | 1883 | British-Sudan Wars
See **El Obeid**

**Sheikhabad | 1866 | Later Afghan
War of Succession**

In a war of succession following the death of
Dost Muhammad, Amir Sher Ali marched from
Kandahar to recover **Kabul**, seized by his brother
Azim Khan and nephew Abdur Rahman (son of
Afzal Khan). Despite commanding 15,000 troops,
the Amir was heavily defeated 30 miles south of
Kabul at Sheikhabad. Azim Khan and Afzal Khan
were proclaimed joint rulers (9 May 1866).

**Sheik Sa'ad | 1916 | World War I
(Mesopotamia)**

As British forces led by Sir Fenton Aylmer
advanced up the Tigris to relieve besieged **Kut-
al-Amara**, the Meerut Division under General
Sir George Younghusband was sent forward
to attack the Turks 20 miles downstream from
Kut at Sheik Sa'ad. The outnumbered and ill-
equipped British lost 4,000 men in a futile assault, though the Turks withdrew upstream to the
Wadi (7 January 1916).

**Shelon | 1471 | Muscovite Wars
of Expansion**

Determined to crush pro-Lithuanian Novgorod, Duke Ivan III of Moscow sent a converging force under the command of Prince
Daniil Dimitrievich Kholmsky, supported by the
army of Pskov. The larger Novgorod army was
routed in a decisive action southwest of Novgorod at the Shelon, with a claimed 12,000 killed. The Muscovites soon won again at the
Shilenga (14 July 1471).

**Shenhe | 395 | Wars of the Sixteen
Kingdoms Era**

When the Xianbei leader Taowu established
the Kingdom of Wei in northern China, his
southern neighbour Murong Chui of Later Yan
sent his son Murong Bao against him. At
Shenhe, near Horinger in Inner Mongolia, the
Yan army was utterly routed. After Murong
Chui died the following year, Taowu gradually
conquered Yan, capturing the cities of Zhong-
shan and Ye (December 395).

**Shenyang | 1621 | Manchu Conquest
of China**

Manchu commander Nurhachi destroyed an
Imperial army in Manchuria in 1619 at **Sarhu**,
Siyanggiayan and **Niumaozhai**, then attacked
the well-fortified city of Shenyang. The Ming
garrison marched out to meet him but were cut
off and badly defeated. Nurhachi seized the city
as his capital and renamed it Mukden. Five years
later he advanced into China itself and was repulsed at **Ningyuan**.

Shenyang | 1905 | Russo-Japanese War
See **Mukden**

Shenyang | 1931 | Manchuria Incident
See **Mukden**

**Shenyang | 1946 | 3rd Chinese
Revolutionary Civil War**
See **Mukden**

Shenyang | 1948 | 3rd Chinese Revolutionary Civil War
See **Mukden**

Shepherdstown | 1862 | American Civil War (Eastern Theatre)
General Robert E. Lee's Confederate army was withdrawing south from **Antietam**, Maryland, when his rearguard under Generals William N. Pendleton and Ambrose P. Hill attacked General Fitz-John Porter at Boteler's Ford on the Potomac near Shepherdstown, West Virginia. Porter was defeated, but failure to pursue cost General George B. McClellan his army command (19–20 September 1862).

Sheria | 1917 | World War I (Middle East)
Within days of destroying the Turkish left flank at **Beersheba**, British commander Sir Edmund Allenby ordered a naval bombardment of the western end of the Turkish line at Gaza, then struck from the east through Sheria to cut off their retreat. Following a costly defeat at Sheria, the Turks evacuated Gaza and withdrew north through **El Mughar** towards **Jerusalem** (6 November 1917).

Sheriffmuir | 1715 | Jacobite Rebellion (The Fifteen)
Rising in support of James Stuart—the Old Pretender—John Erskine Earl of Mar led a Jacobite army to Sheriffmuir, near Dunblane north of Stirling, against a much smaller Hanoverian force under Archibald Campbell Duke of Argyle. Both sides lost about 500 men in an indecisive action and a Jacobite defeat the same day at **Preston** made Mar flee to France (13 November 1715).

Sherpur, India | 1760 | Seven Years War (India)
Emperor Shah Alam II and General Kamgar Khan launched a new invasion of Bengal, where they defeated Raja Ramnarain at **Masumpur**. Two weeks later, they faced a large British-Indian army under Major John Caillaud and Miran, son of Nawab Mir Jafar of Bengal. The Emperor

was routed in a sharp action southeast of Patna at Sherpur and withdrew south to Bihar city (22 February 1760).

Sherpur, Afghanistan | 1879 | 2nd British-Afghan War
When British General Sir Frederick Roberts occupied Kabul after victory at **Charasia**, he was besieged by about 100,000 Afghan tribesmen under Mohammed Jan. At nearby Sherpur cantonment, Roberts repulsed repeated attacks, then counter-attacked for a decisive victory. Former Amir Yakub Khan's cousin, Abdur Rahman, was then made Amir (11–23 December 1879).

Sherston | 1016 | Danish Conquest of England
Shortly after succeeding his father Aethelred as King of Wessex, Edmund Ironside defeated Knut, son of the great Sweyn Forkbeard of Denmark, at **Penselwood**. The Danish and Saxon armies then met again in an inconclusive engagement at Sherston (formerly Scearston), near Malmesbury, Wiltshire. The decisive battle at **Ashingdon** later that year completed the Danish conquest of England.

Shevardino | 1812 | Napoleonic Wars (Russian Campaign)
As the French army advanced into Russia past **Smolensk**, Generals Jean Dominique Complans and Josef Poniatowski led about 35,000 men against the Shevardino redoubt, held by Prince Gorchakov II. Fierce fighting and heavy bombardment cost about 8,000 men on either side before the outnumbered Russians were ordered to withdraw to nearby **Borodino** (5 September 1812).

Shijo Nawate | 1348 | War of the Japanese Emperors
With victory at **Minatogawa** and the heroic death of Kusunoki Masashige (1336), Ashikaga Takauji created a rival court at Kyoto, provoking years of warfare. Eventually, Ashikaga Generals Ko Moronao and Ko Moroyasu attacked Emperor Go-Murukami at Yoshino. A bloody disaster at nearby Shijo Nawate saw Imperial

champion Kusunoki Masatsura defeated and killed (4 February 1348).

Shilenga | 1471 | Muscovite Wars of Expansion

Two weeks after a crushing victory over Novgorod at the **Shelon**, another Muscovite army under General Boris Slepts attacking in the north was met by Novgorod's commander Prince Vasili Shuiski at the Shilenga, where Slepts won a second decisive victory. Within a few years Duke Ivan III of Moscow captured Novgorod itself (1478) and annexed much of the land of the Dvina (27 July 1472).

Shiloh | 1862 | American Civil War (Western Theatre)

Union commander Ulysses S. Grant secured western Kentucky at **Fort Donelson**, then advanced up the Tennessee and was surprised at Shiloh by Confederate General Albert S. Johnston. In one of the war's bloodiest actions, Grant counter-attacked for a costly victory. With Johnston killed, General Pierre G. T. Beauregard led the retreat south into Mississippi to **Corinth** (6–7 April 1862).

Shimabara | 1584 | Japan's Era of the Warring States
See **Okita Nawate**

Shimbra-Kure | 1529 | Adal-Ethiopian War

When Ahmad ibn Ibrahim (Ahmad Grañ) became leader of the Muslim Somali state of Adal, he declared war against Ethiopia. After bloody campaigning, he met Emperor Lebna-Dengel (David II) in battle at Shimbra-Kure, where the Imperial army was decisively defeated. Ibrahim subjugated much of Christian Ethiopia before he was finally halted at **Wayna Daga** (16 October 1529).

Shimoga | 1791 | 3rd British-Mysore War

Nizam Ali of Hyderabad joined Britain in renewed war against Tipu Sultan of Mysore by supporting Maratha General Parashuram Bhau and Captain John Little invading Bednur Province against an 8,000-strong force under Tipu's cousin Muhammad Raza (the Binky Nabob). The Mysoreans were routed near Shimoga, losing their guns and baggage, and Bhau took the city (3 January 1791).

Shimonoseki | 1864 | Shimonoseki War

Soon after Choshu failed to seize **Kyoto**, British, Dutch and French warships under Admirals Sir Augustus Kuper and Jean-Louis Jaurès attacked the Choshu port of Shimonoseki, commanding the Strait between Kyushu and Honshu in southern Japan. A massive bombardment and capture of the shore battery forced Mori Motonori to open the Strait to western trade with Yokohama (5–8 September 1864).

Shinowara | 1183 | Gempei War

Pursued south towards Kyoto after a disastrous defeat at **Kurikara**, Taira Komemori was caught just days later at Shinowara by the victorious army of Minamoto Yoshinaka, now joined by his uncle Yukiie. Komemori was once again routed and fled to Kyoto. The Taira evacuated the capital, taking the boy-Emperor Antoku, then withdrew west, where they defended **Mizushima** (12 June 1183).

Shipka Pass | 1877 | Russo-Turkish Wars

Determined to hold the Shipka Pass in the Balkan Mountains, to prevent Turkish aid to **Plevna**, Russian forces faced a massive attack by Suleiman Pasha. When General Feodor Radetzky arrived with reinforcements, the Turks were repulsed with terrible losses on both sides. Russia held the pass for five months with further victories at **Mount St Nicholas** and **Senova** (20–27 August 1877).

Shirakawa | 1156 | Hogen War

During a disputed succession in Japan, Fujiwara Yorinaga and Minamoto Tameyoshi tried to restore former Emperor Sutoku against Emperor

Go-Shirakawa. Attacking at night, Taira Kiyomori and Minamoto Yoshitomo stormed the rebel stronghold at Shirakawa Palace, just northeast of Kyoto. Yorinaga and Tameyoshi were killed and Sutoku was exiled, ending the attempted coup (29 July 1156).

Shiraz ∎ 1393 ∎ Conquests of Tamerlane

The Turko-Mongol Tamerlane marched into Persia after victory over the Golden Horde at **Kunduzcha** (June 1391) and attacked Shah Mansur, who had rebelled against Mongol rule imposed when Tamerlane overthrew a previous Shah in 1387. On the Plain of Patila near his capital at Shiraz, in modern southern Iran, Mansur was defeated and killed and the Muzaffarid Dynasty came to an end.

Shiraz ∎ 1730 ∎ Persian-Afghan Wars

See **Zarghan**

Shiraz ∎ 1758 ∎ Persian Wars of Succession

With Isfahan recaptured after victory over Azad Khan Afghan at **Urmiya** (July 1757), Mohammad Hasan Khan of Qajar marched to besiege Shiraz, held by the Regent Karim Khan Zand and his brilliant General Shaykh Ali Khan. Having suffered heavy losses to sorties and attacks in the rear by Afghans and Uzbeks, Mohammad Hasan withdrew. He was defeated early the next year at **Ashraf**.

Shiraz ∎ 1780–1781 ∎ Persian Wars of Succession

During the war of succession following the murder of the usurper Zaki Khan of Persia, his nephew Ali Murad laid siege to his uncle Sadiq Khan, who had returned from **Basra** and occupied Shiraz. The city fell by treachery after eight months, following which Ali Murad murdered his uncle. His family then took the throne and moved the capital to Isfahan (August 1780–February 1781).

Shirbarghan ∎ 1646 ∎ Mughal-Uzbek Wars

See **Balkh**

Shire ∎ 1936 ∎ 2nd Italo-Ethiopian War

In a third offensive to secure northern Ethiopia after **Amba Aradam** and **Tembien**, Marshal Pietro Badoglio sent General Pietro Maravigna west from Aksum to attack Ras Imru at Shire (modern Ednaselassie). The Italians were stalled in hard fighting before massive artillery fire drove Ras Imru south across the Takkaze, with hundreds killed by pursuing aircraft (29 February–2 March 1936).

Shiroyama ∎ 1877 ∎ Satsuma Rebellion

Rebel Japanese Marshal Saigo Takamori was driven back from **Kumamoto** to **Kagoshima** in southern Kyushu, where he found himself surrounded on land and sea by Imperial forces. A bloody last stand at Shiroyama, overlooking Kagoshima Bay, saw many of his supporters die in a final suicidal charge. The great General committed seppuku, ending Japan's last civil war (24 September 1877).

Shirts ∎ 1544 ∎ Scottish Clan Wars

The "Battle of the Shirts" climaxed a long feud between the MacDonalds of Ranald and the Frasers, who fought to annihilation at Laggan on Loch Lochy. Fighting in shirts after removing their plaids because of the heat, both sides suffered terrible casualties in hand-to-hand combat. Lord Lovat and 300 Frasers were killed, including his heir, leaving the MacDonalds to claim victory (3 July 1544).

Shizugatake ∎ 1583 ∎ Japan's Era of the Warring States

When Toyotomi Hideyoshi seized power after the death of Oda Nobunaga, he was opposed by Oda's son Nobutaka and Shibata Katsuie of Echizen, who sent Sakuma Morimasa to besiege the mountain fortress of Shizugatake (near modern Kinomoto). Hideyoshi routed Morimasa, after which Katsuie and Nobutaka committed suicide.

He then fought Oda Nobuo at **Nagakute** (11 June 1583).

Shoal Creek I 1861 I American Civil War (Trans-Mississippi)

Pursued through **Round Mountain** and **Chusto-Talasah**, pro-Union Creeks and Seminoles under Chief Opothleyaholo were attacked on Shoal Creek (Chustenalah) in northeast Okalahoma by Confederate Colonels James McIntosh and Douglas H. Cooper. In a decisive defeat, the Indians quickly ran out of ammunition and fled north into Kansas, posing no further threat (26 December 1861).

Sholapur I 1818 I 3rd British-Maratha War

Fleeing after destruction of the Maratha army at **Ashti** and **Seoni**, Peshwa Baji Rao II's troops under Chief Gompat Rao made a stand near Sholapur, southeast of Bombay. British General Theophilus Pritzler routed the Marathas, killing over 1,000, and the fortress surrendered five days later. Within weeks the British then turned against the forts at **Chanda** and **Malegaon** (10 May 1818).

Sholinghur I 1781 I 2nd British-Mysore War

Weeks after heavy defeats at **Porto Novo** and **Pollilore**, Haidar Ali of Mysore and his son Tipu Sultan tried to block General Sir Eyre Coote advancing to relieve the siege of Vellore. A one-sided disaster northwest of Vellore at Sholinghur cost the Mysorean army terrible casualties, yet within six months Tipu was successful at **Kumbakonam** and **Cuddalore** (27 September 1781).

Shrewsbury I 50 I Roman Conquest of Britain

See **Caer Caradoc**

Shrewsbury I 1403 I Percy's Rebellion

A large-scale rebellion against Henry IV of England saw Sir Henry Percy (Hotspur) and Scots under Archibald Earl of Douglas enter Cheshire against Henry, Prince of Wales. At Hateley Field, near Shrewsbury, they instead encountered the King and his full army. Douglas was captured and Hotspur was killed. His father the Earl of Northumberland fought on until 1408 at **Bramham Moor** (21 July 1403).

Shrubs I 1712 I 2nd Villmergen War

See **Bremgarten**

Shuangduiji I 1948 I 3rd Chinese Revolutionary Civil War

Reeling before the Communist **Huaihai** offensive, Nationalist General Huang Wei and 125,000 men advancing on besieged Xuzhou were trapped to the southwest at Shuangduiji between Generals Chen Yi and Liu Bocheng. A relief army from Xuzhou was stopped at **Chenguanzhuang**, after which Huang's army was annihilated and he was captured (23 November–15 December 1948).

Shubra Khit I 1798 I French Revolutionary Wars (Middle East)

Napoleon Bonaparte invaded Egypt to seize **Alexandria** (2 July), then advanced up the Nile from Rosetta. At Shubra Khit, his small flotilla engaged a larger group of heavily manned Mamluk vessels. During an indecisive struggle, French artillery on the bank sank the Mamluk flagship. The survivors afloat and ashore then fled south towards the **Pyramids** (13 July 1798).

Shumen I 1774 I Catherine the Great's 1st Turkish War

See **Kozludzha**

Shumla I 377 I 5th Gothic War

See **Marcianopolis**

Shumla I 1774 I Catherine the Great's 1st Turkish War

See **Kozludzha**

Shupiyan I 1819 I Afghan-Sikh Wars

A year after the fall of **Multan**, Sikh leader Ranjit Singh led a Punjabi army into Kashmir and sent Misr Dewan Chand and Prince Kharak Singh against Shupiyan, south of Srinigar, held by Jabbar Khan, brother of Governor Azim Khan. With his Afghan troops hard hit by artillery, Jabbar Khan escaped badly wounded. Srinigar was occupied next day and Ranjit secured Kashmir (3 July 1819).

Shusha I 1795 I Persian-Georgian War

As part of the campaign to expand his northern lands, Aga Mohammad Khan of Persia led his army to the Araxes, where he attacked Shusha, defended by Ibrahim Khan of Qarabagh. Ibrahim surrendered after a sharp siege and agreed to pay tribute, while Aga Mohammad Khan marched into Christian Georgia against **Tiflis** (8 July–9 August 1795).

Shusha I 1826 I Russo-Persian Wars

Persian Prince Abbas Mirza renewed war against Russia and besieged the frontier fortress of Shusha, bravely held by Colonel Iosif Antonovich Reut and 1,800 men. The delay allowed commander Alexei Ermolov to prepare a counter-attack and, following Persian defeat at the **Shamkhor**, Abbas Mirza left Shusha to meet the Russians a week later at **Yelizavetpol** (July–5 September 1826).

Shwegyin I 1942 I World War II (Burma-India)

Concluding the British retreat from **Burma**, General William Slim fell back through Kyaukse and Monywa and his rearguard was surprised at Shwegyin, on the upper Chindwin near Kalewa. Despite inflicting unexpectedly high casualties on General Shozo Sakurai, the British had to destroy their tanks and guns and withdraw into India to begin the terrible march to **Imphal** (9–11 May 1942).

Sialkot I 1761 I Indian Campaigns of Ahmad Shah

Ahmad Shah Durrani returned to Afghanistan following victory at **Panipat** in January, then sent Nur-ud-din Khan and 12,000 Afghans to punish the Sikhs for attacking his army as it was crossing the Punjab. Repulsed at the Chenab by Charat Singh, Nur-ud-din withdrew under siege to Sialkot, northeast of Lahore. He eventually fled in disguise and his army was starved into surrender (August 1761).

Sialkot I 1763 I Indian Campaigns of Ahmad Shah

After another invasion of the Punjab, General Ahmad Shah Durrani returned to Kabul and left Kabuli Mal as Governor in Lahore, where he came under increasing Sikh pressure. In battle at Sialkot, northeast of Lahore, Charhut Singh Sukerchakia defeated Afghan forces under General Jahan Khan and besieged Lahore to impose terms. This provoked a fresh Afghan invasion (November 1763).

Sialkot I 1965 I 2nd Indo-Pakistan War

Two days after her offensive towards **Lahore**, India opened a new front further north towards Sialkot to cut communications with the capital. Large-scale armored actions southeast of Sialkot around **Chawinda**, **Phillora** and **Buttar Dograndi** saw both sides suffer heavy losses. With no sign of any breakthrough, the combatants agreed to accept a UN ceasefire (8–22 September 1965).

Sian I 1949 I 3rd Chinese Revolutionary Civil War
See **Xi'an**

Siauliai I 1236 I Early Wars of the Teutonic Knights

The German Sword Brethren and Crusaders from Holstein advanced from Livonia into Lithuania to meet Duke Mindaugus and the Samogitian leader Vykintas. Trapped on soft ground at Siauliai, the knights were destroyed with Master Volquin killed. The survivors were absorbed into the Livonian Order and German expansion east was soon checked at **Lake Peipus** (22 September 1236).

Sibir I 1582 I Russian Conquest of Siberia
See **Kashlyk**

Sibiu I 1599 I Balkan National Wars
See **Selimbar**

Sibiu I 1916 I Turkish-Hungarian Wars
See **Hermannstadt**

**Sibiu I 1916 I World War I
(Balkan Front)**
See **Hermannstadt**

**Sibuyan Sea I 1944 I World War II
(Pacific)**
Admiral Takeo Kurita was heading east
through the Philippines towards **Leyte Gulf**
when he was attacked in the Sibuyan Sea by
aircraft from Admiral Marc Mitscher's Task
Force. Despite losing a carrier to land-based air
attack, Mitscher sank the giant battleship *Mu-
sashi* and damaged the other Japanese battleships. Kurita withdrew to regroup then attacked
off **Samar** (23–24 October 1944).

**Sicilian Vespers I 1282 I War of the
Sicilian Vespers**
Less than 20 years after Charles of Anjou
killed King Manfred and seized Sicily and Naples, a popular rising was triggered when a
French soldier reportedly insulted a young bride
walking to Vespers near Palermo. In the resulting uprising—the Sicilian Vespers—thousands
of French soldiers and their families died and
Sicily was claimed by Manfred's son-in-law,
Pedro III of Aragon (30 March 1282).

**Sicily I 1943 I World War II
(Southern Europe)**
After victory in **Tunisia**, 180,000 Allied
troops landed in southern Sicily in one of the
largest amphibious operations of the war. There
was costly fighting at **Gela**, **Catania** and
Troina, before **Palermo** and **Messina** were
captured to secure the island. However, 100,000
Axis troops escaped to the Italian mainland,
along with 10,000 vehicles and about 50 tanks (9
July–17 August 1943).

Sidassir I 1799 I 4th British-Mysore War
Tipu Sultan of Mysore renewed war with
Britain in southern India and Generals George
Harris and James Stuart (1741–1815) threatened
his capital at **Seringapatam**. West of Mysore

near Piriyapatna at Sidassir (modern Siddeswara), Colonel John Montresor's vanguard was
surrounded. But they were relieved by Stuart
after a courageous overnight stand and the advance continued (6 March 1799).

**Siddeswara I 1799 I 4th British-
Mysore War**
See **Sidassir**

Side I 190 BC I Roman-Syrian War
See **Eurymedon**

**Sidi Abd-el-Jelil I 1912 I Italo-
Turkish War**
See **Zanzur (1st)**

**Sidi Barrani I 1940 I World War II
(Northern Africa)**
When Italy entered the war, Marshal Rudolfo
Graziani invaded Egypt from Libya and set up
fortified positions south from Sidi Barrani.
General Richard O'Connor outflanked and routed General Mario Berti's Italians, capturing
over 40,000 men plus tanks and guns. He then
invaded Libya at **Bardia**, while other forces
went to Eritrea and beat the Italians at **Agordat**
(9–12 December 1940).

**Sidi Ben Othman I 1912 I French Colonial
Wars in North Africa**
In response to Sultan Mulai Hafid abdicating
at **Fez**, the pretender El Hiba seized Marakesh
(18 August). French Colonel Charles Mangin
arrived with 5,000 men and El Hiba rashly
marched north and attacked a French square at
nearby Sidi Ben Othman. Cannon, machine-
guns and modern rifles killed over 2,000 Moroccans before they withdrew and Marakesh was
secured (6 September 1912).

Sidi Bilal I 1912 I Italo-Turkish War
See **Zanzur (2nd)**

**Sidi Bou Zid I 1943 I World War II
(Northern Africa)**
See **Faid Pass**

Sidi El Henni (1st) **|** 1911 **|** Italo-Turkish War

On a determined offensive against Italian-held **Tripoli**, a large Turko-Arab force assaulted positions east of the city, mainly around Sidi El Henni. Two Italian companies were virtually destroyed before General Guglielmo Pecori-Giraldi sent reinforcements. Very hard fighting saw the line eventually stabilised before a renewed attack days later around **Sidi Mesri** (23 October 1911).

Sidi El Henni (2nd) **|** 1911 **|** Italo-Turkish War

See **Sidi Mesri (2nd)**

Sidi Mesri (1st) **|** 1911 **|** Italo-Turkish War

Three days after intense fighting east of Tripoli around **Sidi El Henni**, the Turko-Arab army renewed its offensive in a dawn attack along an extended line, with the heaviest fighting around Sidi Mesri. While the Turks were eventually driven off, the two actions cost the Italians over 400 killed and they withdrew their line for better defence before counter-attacking a month later (26 October 1911).

Sidi Mesri (2nd) **|** 1911 **|** Italo-Turkish War

Having absorbed Turko-Arab attacks east of Tripoli around **Sidi El Henni** and **Sidi Mesri**, well-reinforced Italian General Felice de Chaurand launched a massive counter-attack over the same ground. Supported by artillery and naval bombardment, the Italians retook Sidi Mesri after heavy fighting and also Sidi El Henni. They then advanced south towards **Ain Zara** (26 November 1911).

Sidi Nsir **|** 1943 **|** World War II (Northern Africa)

As German forces in southern Tunisia struck at **Kasserine**, Colonel Rudolph Lang in the north advanced on Beja. The full weight of his assault fell on Colonel Charles Newnham and a small British force dug in at Sidi Nsir, who managed to disable up to 40 German tanks. While almost the entire unit became casualties, their delaying action helped ensure Lang's defeat at **Hunt's Gap** (26 February 1943).

Sidi Rezegh **|** 1941 **|** World War II (Northern Africa)

Six months after British failure at **Sollum-Halfaya** to relieve **Tobruk**, new commander Sir Claude Auchinleck sent General Sir Alan Cunningham on a fresh offensive around Sidi Rezegh. Despite Italian resistance at Bir Gubi and a powerful German counter-attack, General Erwin Rommel had to abandon Cyrenaica. He soon struck back at **Mersa Brega** (18 November–7 December 1941).

Sidi Sliman **|** 1915 **|** French Colonial Wars in North Africa

In renewed campaigning against the Zaia of central Morocco six months after disaster at **El Herri**, Colonel Noel Garnier-Duplessis marched southwest from **Khenifra** and was attacked at Sidi Sliman near Kasbah Tadla by up to 4,000 tribesmen. The Berbers lost 300 killed and 400 wounded in two days of heavy fighting, but continued to attack French convoys around Khenifra (15–16 May 1915).

Sidon **|** 1110 **|** Crusader-Muslim Wars

Baldwin I of Jerusalem captured the Mediterranean ports of **Acre**, **Tripoli** and **Beirut**, then used the arrival of the so-called "Norwegian Crusade" under King Sigurd I to attack Sidon (modern Saida, Lebanon). Supported at sea by Venetian ships under Doge Ordelafo Falieri, Baldwin besieged Sidon for two months against strong resistance before forcing its surrender (19 October–4 December 1110).

Sidon **|** 1196 **|** 4th Crusade

A year after the fall of Joppa to the Ayyubid Sultan al-Adil Saif al-Din, German Crusaders marched north from Acre and challenged the Sultan's army between Tyre and Sidon (modern Saida). Led by the Duke of Saxony, the so-called "German Crusade" inflicted a massive defeat, which led the Muslims to abandon most of the key cities on the Palestine Coast, including Joppa and Sidon.

Sidonia Ghat ∎ 1858 ∎ Indian Mutiny
See **Banki**

Siedlce ∎ 1831 ∎ Polish Rebellion
Gathering support after victory at **Wawer**, Polish rebel General Jan Skrzynecki reorganised his army and at Iganie, near Siedlce east of Warsaw, soon gained another bloody win over Russian forces. Fearing the main Russian army under Field Marshal Hans von Diebitsch, the cautious Skrzynecki failed to follow up. By September the rebels had lost at **Ostrolenka** and **Warsaw** (10 April 1831).

Siegfried Line ∎ 1944–1945 ∎ World War II (Western Europe)
Facing the Siegfried Line (West Wall) along Germany's western border, the Allies failed an attempted end-run in the north at **Arnhem** and there was very costly combat at **Aachen**, **Nancy**, **Metz**, and in the **Hürtgen Forest**. The Germans counter-attacked in the **Ardennes** and **Alsace** before being driven back in continued fighting for the **Rhineland** (17 September 1944–9 February 1945).

Siena ∎ 1554–1555 ∎ 5th Habsburg-Valois War
Amid resistance to Imperial oppression, Siena held out against attack by Cosmo Duke of Florence and a long siege by Gian Medecino Marquis of Marignano. After defeating a relief army at **Marciano** (August 1554), Medecino resumed the siege and Marshal Blaise de Montluc's French garrison were eventually starved into surrender, ending the Republic (27 January 1554–April 1555).

Sierck ∎ 1643 ∎ Thirty Years War (Franco-Habsburg War)
The 22-year-old Louis II Duke d'Enghien succeeded in his bloody siege of **Thionville**, then days later took his French troops northeast against the Spanish-held town of Sierck, which commanded the southern approaches to Lux-

embourg. The small town on the Moselle fell just a few days later and d'Enghien went on to drive the Germans back across the Rhine (August 1643).

Sierra Chica ∎ 1855 ∎ Argentine Civil Wars
When Indians of the pampas under the Chief Juan Calfucurá raided settlements in eastern Argentina, they were met at Sierra Chica, northeast of Olavarría, by a national army under Colonel Bartolomé Mitre. A bloody action forced the government troops to withdraw northeast to Azul, though in 1858 Calfucurá suffered a costly defeat at **Pigüé** (31 May 1855).

Sierra Maestra ∎ 1958 ∎ Cuban Revolution
Determined to crush the revolution of Fidel Castro, President Fulgencio Batista sent General Eugenio Cantillo, with massive superiority in numbers and equipment, against the rebel stronghold in the Sierra Maestra. The prolonged campaign saw bitter fighting and heavy losses on both sides before the rebels finally won at El Jigüe (11 July) and assumed the offensive (May–July 1958).

Sierra Negra ∎ 1794 ∎ French Revolutionary Wars (1st Coalition)
See **Figueras**

Sieveshausen ∎ 1553 ∎ War of the German Reformation
Maurice of Saxony helped Emperor Charles V defeat the Protestant Schmalkaldic League at **Mühlberg** (1547), then sided with Henry II of France against the Emperor and joined a Protestant coalition against Margrave Albert II Alcibiades of Brandenburg. Maurice's Saxons defeated Albert in bloody battle at Sieveshausen, near Hanover, though Maurice was fatally wounded (9 July 1553).

Siffin ∎ 657 ∎ Muslim Civil Wars
When Governor Mu'awiya of Syria raised a revolt aided by Amr ibn al-As, conqueror of Egypt, Caliph Ali invaded Syria with a large

army. A long and inconclusive battle was fought at Siffin, on the west bank of the Euphrates near Rakka. Mu'awiya became the first Umayyad Caliph after Ali's assassination in 661, splitting Islam between Sunni and Shi'ite Muslims (26–27 July 657).

Sighisoara ▍ 1849 ▍ Hungarian Revolutionary War

See **Segesvár**

Sigurds ▍ 1918 ▍ Finnish War of Independence

With Whites checked east of **Helsinki** at **Porvoo** (12 February), Red commander Ali Aaltonen sent 3,000 men west from the capital against a small White force at Sigurds in Kirkkonummi. The Whites broke out after terrible damage by artillery and were pursued. While about 150 escaped, almost 500 surrendered to Swedish negotiators and were taken prisoner to Helsinki (23–25 February 1918).

Sihayo's Kraal ▍ 1879 ▍ Anglo-Zulu War

On the first day of the war, as British commander Lord Frederick Chelmsford crossed the Buffalo River into Zululand at **Rorke's Drift**, his centre column under Colonel Richard Glyn met a Zulu force at nearby Sihayo's Kraal under Sihayo's son Nkhumbi. A sharp action saw 16 Zulus killed, including Nkhumbi, and the British advanced to the fateful campsite at **Isandhlwana** (12 January 1879).

Siikajoki ▍ 1808 ▍ Napoleonic Wars (Russo-Swedish War)

Swedish commander Wilhelm Klingspor retreated north before the Russian invasion of Finland and was replaced by General Karl Johann Adlercreutz, who made an heroic stand at the Siikajoki River, south of Oulu. The Swedes repulsed Russian General Jacob Kulneff to secure a remarkable victory and began a summer counter-offensive through **Revolax** and **Nykarleby** (18 April 1808).

Sikandarabad ▍ 1760 ▍ Indian Campaigns of Ahmad Shah

As Afghans moved into the decaying Mughal Empire, Ahmed Shah Durrani killed Maratha Chief Dattaji Sindhia at **Barari Ghat**, then pursued his nephew Jankoji Sindhia, who joined with the Maratha Mulhar Rao Holkar. At Sikandarabad, southeast of Delhi, the Marathas were surprised and defeated by Afghan General Jahan Khan though they later managed to take Delhi (4 March 1760).

Sikander Bagh ▍ 1857 ▍ Indian Mutiny

A large force of Highlanders and Indians under General Sir Colin Campbell, marching to relieve the British besieged at **Lucknow** attacked the Sikander Bagh, a heavily defended position just outside the city. When the walls were breached by artillery, the building was taken in hand-to-hand fighting, with almost 2,000 Sepoys killed. Campbell lost 500 killed and wounded (16 November 1857).

Sikar ▍ 1859 ▍ Indian Mutiny

Pursued by forces under General Sir Robert Napier after defeat at **Dausa** (14 January), rebel leader Tantia Topi was surprised and routed at Sikar, northwest of Jaipur, by Colonel John Holmes. About 600 disheartened rebels surrendered to the Raja of Bikanir and Tantia fled into the jungle. He was later betrayed to Napier by his former ally Man Singh of Narwar and was hanged (21 January 1859).

Sikasso ▍ 1887–1888 ▍ Franco-Mandingo Wars

Mandingo leader Samory Touré led a renewed offensive on the Ivory Coast, attacking Sikasso, in modern Mali, held by King Tieba of Kénédougou, who called for French aid. Samory was forced to withdraw after a long failed siege—which reportedly cost him 10,000 men and most of his horses—and Tieba signed a friendly treaty with France, further isolating the Mandingo (April 1887–August 1888).

Sikasso I 1898 I Franco-Mandingo Wars

Determined to finally secure the Ivory Coast from Mandingo leader Samory Touré, Colonel René Audéoud attacked Sikasso in modern Mali, where King Babemba Traore had renounced the former friendship with France. Two weeks of bombardment smashed the city's massive walls and the King committed suicide to avoid capture. Samory himself was soon taken at **Guélémou** (1 May 1898).

Silang I 1897 I Philippines War of Independence

On fresh offensive south of Manila, Spanish Governor Camilo de Polaveija and General José Lachambre advanced through **Zapote Bridge** against General Vito Belarmino at Silang, where Belarmino had to withdraw after an heroic defence. A failed counter-attack by Emilio Aguinaldo and Artemio Ricarte forced the Filipinos to continue falling back to **Dasmariñas** (16–19 February 1897).

Silao I 1860 I Mexican War of the Reform

Despite securing victory at **Guadalajara**, President Miguel Miramón faced a revitalised Liberal force under Generals Jesús González Ortega and Ignacio Zaragoza. Near Guadalajara at Silao, Miramón unwisely met a much larger army and was utterly routed, losing all his artillery and 2,000 prisoners, including General Tomás Mejía. Ortega soon won again at **Calderón** (10 August 1860).

Silarus I 212 BC I 2nd Punic War

While withdrawing from **Capua** towards Tarentum, the Carthaginian General Hannibal was blocked at the Silarus (modern Sele) by Marcus Centenius Penula, who unwisely attacked with a force comprising at least half unreliable local levies. Surrounded by the Carthaginians, Penula was killed and his force was all but destroyed. A few days later, Hannibal beat another Roman force at **Herdonea**.

Silarus I 71 BC I 3rd Servile War

After beating three Roman armies, former gladiator Spartacus was trapped in the "toe" of Italy by Marcus Licinius Crassus. His army of escaped slaves broke though to the north, but was blocked by freshly arrived Legions under Marcus Lucullus on the River Silarus in Lucania. Spartacus was defeated and killed and up to 6,000 of his followers were crucified along the Appian Way from Capua to Rome.

Silchester I 296 I Roman Military Civil Wars

When Marcus Carausius, Roman Tyrant of Britain, was murdered and deposed by his Chief Minister Allectus, Emperor Constantius and his Praetorian Prefect Asclepiodotus took a force to Britain. In battle near Silchester in Hampshire, Asclepiodotus killed Allectus and defeated his largely mercenary army to re-establish Imperial control.

Silipa I 206 BC I 2nd Punic War
See **Ilipa**

Silistria I 971 I Byzantine-Russian Wars
See **Dorostalon**

Silistria I 1773 I Catherine the Great's 1st Turkish War

General Pyotr Rumyantsev led a major Russian offensive against the Turks on the Danube, where he advanced near the key city of Silistria. Despite a successful diversionary attack 20 miles upstream at **Turtukai**, Rumyantsev was repulsed with heavy losses. He was forced to withdraw across the river and **Hirsov** became Russia's only remaining position on the southern bank (17 June 1773).

Silistria I 1809 I Russo-Turkish Wars

Russians under Prince Pyotr Bagration renewed warfare on the Danube, capturing several key positions before reaching Silistria, where they were defeated by the Grand Vizier Yusuf Pasha with the loss of 10,000 men. Although General Count Alexander Langeron managed to hold off the Turkish advance, the Russians withdrew across the Danube and Bagration was replaced (26 September 1809).

Silistria I 1810 I Russo-Turkish Wars

After a costly repulse on the Danube at Silistria in 1809, Russian commander Prince Pyotr Bagration was replaced by General Nikolai Kamenski (son of Count Mikhail), who returned to the Danube in the spring and sent General Count Alexander Langeron to besiege Silistria. The city fell to Langeron after just seven days and Kamenski advanced to capture Giurgiu and **Ruschuk** (12 June 1810).

Silistria I 1854 I Crimean War

Despite Russian defeat at **Oltenitza** in late 1853, Marshal Ivan Paskevich crossed the Lower Danube and besieged Silistria, bravely defended by Mussa Pasha (and after his death by Captain James Butler and Lieutenant Charles Nasmyth). Following the Anglo-French landing at Varna, and a final failed assault on Silistria, the Russians withdrew upstream towards **Giurgiu** (4 May–23 June 1854).

Silkaatsnek I 1900 I 2nd Anglo-Boer War
See **Zilikats Nek**

Silver Creek, Missouri I 1862 I American Civil War (Trans-Mississippi)
See **Roan's Tan Yard**

Silver Creek, Oregon I 1878 I Bannock Indian War

Bannock Indians crossed into Oregon after defeat at **Battle Creek** (8 June) and joined the Paiute in the Steen Mountains, where they were attacked in camp at Silver Creek, near modern Riley, by Captain Reuben Bernard. Withdrawing to nearby bluffs, the Indians held a strong position until nightfall, but their camp and supplies were destroyed. Reuben soon won again at **Birch Creek** (23 June 1878).

Simancas, Valladolid I 939 I Christian-Muslim Wars in Spain

After leading a successful offensive into central Spain, Emir Abd ar-Rahman of Cordova was challenged by a large army under Ramiro II of Leon and was heavily defeated at Simancas, near Valladolid. Abd-ar-Rahman was beaten again in retreat to the south at Alhandega (modern Fresno Alhandiga), where Muslim commander Najda was killed. The Emir narrowly escaped with his life.

Simancas Barracks, Asturias I 1936 I Spanish Civil War
See **Gijon**

Simbirsk I 1670 I Cossack Rebellion

Don Cossack leader Stenka Razin led a large-scale peasant uprising on the Volga, where he seized Tsaritsyn and later besieged Simbirsk (modern Ulyanovsk). Tsar Alexis sent an Imperial force under Prince Yuri Baryatinsky and Razin's large but ill-equipped army was routed in a decisive action at Simbirsk. Razin fled to the Don but was soon captured and executed in Moscow (October 1670).

Simbirsk I 1918 I Russian Civil War
See **Samara**

Siming I 1285 I Mongol Wars of Kubilai Khan

Despite a check at **Champa** (1283), Kubilai Khan sent a large army under his son Toghon and General Sodu to secure Annam (in Northern Vietnam). The Mongols achieved initial success before being driven out by a counter-offensive under General Tran Hung Dao. Near the Yunnan border at Siming, Sodu was massively defeated and killed. A renewed invasion in 1288 was destroyed at **Bach Dang**.

Simmon's Bluff I 1862 I American Civil War (Lower Seaboard)

A few days after the costly repulse at **Secessionville**, guarding Charleston Harbour, South Carolina, a Union raiding party under Lieutenant Alexander C. Rhind landed at Simmon's Bluff, on the east side of Young's Island in Wadmelaw Sound. Confederate forces under Colonel James McCullough were defeated and scattered before the raiders returned to their ships (21 June 1862).

Sindkhed I 1757 I Later Mughal-Maratha Wars

In renewed war against Hyderabad, Maratha Peshwa Balaji Rao sent his teenage son Viswas Rao and veteran General Dattaji Sindhi to besiege Sindkhed near Jalna, held by the renegade Ramchandra Jadhav. A relief force under Nizam Ali and Ibrahim Gardi Khan reached Sindkhed, where they were routed in a terrible four-day battle. Nizam Ali sued for peace (12–16 December 1757).

Singapore I 1942 I World War II (Pacific)

Following the disastrous effort to defend the Peninsula of **Malaya**, British forces under General Arthur Percival withdrew to Singapore. After heavy shelling, General Tomoyuki Yamashita's army stormed the island and Percival was forced to surrender. Britain's worst military defeat saw perhaps 80,000 soldiers captured. More than 12,000 died in captivity (31 January–15 February 1942).

Singara I 348 I Early Byzantine-Persian Wars

Shapur II of Sassanid Persia crossed the Tigris into Mesopotamia and took position near the Roman frontier city of Singara (modern Sinjar, northern Iraq). The Roman army, under personal command of Emperor Constantius, advanced in the heat of the day and drove the Persians back towards their camp. The Persians counter-attacked then withdrew, but Shapur eventually took the city in 360.

Singaraja I 1846 I Dutch Conquest of Bali

Under the pretext of punishing the looting of shipwrecks, 3,000 Dutch colonial troops invaded northern Bali and attacked a claimed 50,000 poorly armed men in Buleleng. A one-sided disaster at Singaraja saw up to 400 Balinese killed and the Royal Palace destroyed. The Raja of Buleleng submitted until fresh resistance was raised two years later at **Jagaraga** (June 1846).

Singhasari I 1293 I Mongol Wars of Kubilai Khan

To avenge the attack on a Mongol envoy, Kubilai Khan sent General Shibi and 20,000 men against King Kertanagara of Singhasari in eastern Java. However, the King was killed by local rebel Jayakatwang of Kediri and the Mongols helped his son-in-law Prince Vijaya defeat and kill the usurper. Vijaya then ambushed and defeated the Mongols, who withdrew with nothing achieved.

Sinhgarh I 1670 I Mughal-Maratha Wars

The great Maratha Shivaji renewed war against the Mughals, attacking the powerful fort of Sinhgarh, guarding the southern approaches to Poona. With the fortress inaccessible to artillery fire, Shivaji sent his champion, Tanaji Malusre, who scaled the walls at night. Terrible fighting saw Tanaji and Mughal commander Uday Bhan Rathor both killed before the fortress was taken (4 February 1670).

Sinigaglia I 551 I Gothic War in Italy

A Goth fleet built by Totila for his invasion of Sicily was supporting a siege of Ancona on Italy's east coast, when it was attacked by Emperor Justinian's ships north of Ancona off Sinigaglia (modern Senigallia). Lacking experience at sea, the Goths were heavily defeated by Byzantine Admiral Artabanes and had to raise the siege, effectively ending their naval operations in the Adriatic.

Sinkat I 1884 I British-Sudan Wars

When an approaching relief force was routed by the Dervish army at **El Teb**, in eastern Sudan (4 February), the courageous commander of besieged Sinkat, Mohammad Tewfik, refused to surrender but spiked his guns and tried to evacuate his garrison and their families. After less than a mile, they were overwhelmed and massacred. Nearby **Tokar** surrendered two weeks later (8 February 1884).

Sinnigallia I 551 I Gothic War in Italy
See **Sinigaglia**

Sinope I 1853 I Crimean War

Near the start of the war, Russian Admiral Paul Nakhimov attacked Sinope Harbour on the Black Sea, where Osman Pasha commanded nine frigates and three corvettes. With Russia using newly invented naval shells against wooden hulls, the Turkish fleet was utterly destroyed. Over 4,000 died, including Osam fatally wounded. Only one steamer escaped in the smoke (30 November 1853).

Sinpaul I 1575 I Balkan National Wars

When Hungary supported Gaspar Bekes claiming the throne of Transylvania, Prince Stephen Bathory of Transylvania took a substantial force against the Habsburg pretender and, with Turkish aid, defeated him at Sinpaul (Kereloszentpal). Gaspar escaped, though Stephen executed many of his followers. On the strength of his victory, Stephen was elected King of Poland (8 July 1575).

Sinsheim I 1674 I 3rd Dutch War

After the French conquest of Franche-Comte, Louis XIV sent Marshal Henri de Turenne across the Rhine at Philippsburg into Alsace, where he burned much of the Palatinate. Southeast of Heidelberg at Sinsheim, he defeated an Imperial army led by Duke Charles of Lorraine and Count Aeneas Silvia Caprara before advancing along the Rhine to Strasbourg and **Enzheim** (16 June 1674).

Sinuiju I 1951 I Korean War

One of the largest American air-strikes against a single target saw 48 B-29 bombers with 80 jet escorts attack the Sinuiju Bridge on the Yalu River. In a large-scale response, MiG fighters shot down three bombers, the heaviest American losses to date, and the bridge remained standing. Following the costly raid on **Namsi** in October, B-29s were withdrawn from daylight operations (12 April 1951).

Sipe-Sipe I 1815 I Argentine War of Independence

Argentine General José Rondeau was adancing into Spanish Upper Peru (modern Bolivia), when he was beaten at **Venta y Media** and a month later suffered decisive defeat at Sipe-Sipe, southwest of Cochabamba. Victory for General Joaquín de la Pezuela consolidated local Spanish rule and he became Viceroy of Peru. Rondeau was replaced by General Manuel Belgrano (26–28 November 1815).

Siping I 1946 I 3rd Chinese Revolutionary Civil War

Nationalist advance units driving into Manchuria from **Mukden** (modern Shenyang) reached the railway city of Siping (Szepingkau), where they were repulsed by well-entrenched Communist forces. Heavily reinforced and equipped with tanks, Nationalist General Sun Liren launched a massive assault and fierce fighting drove the Communists beyond **Changchun** (17 March & 21 April–19 May 1946).

Siping I 1947 I 3rd Chinese Revolutionary Civil War

At the height of the Communist offensive on the **Songhua** in Manchuria, General Lin Biao seized the strategic railway city of Siping (Szepingkau) and two Nationalist armies were rushed north. Simultaneous attacks from Changchun, Jilin and Mukden (modern Shenyang) under General Chen Mingren forced Lin to abandon Siping, though he soon struck back at **Liaoshi** (16 June–2 July 1947).

Siping I 1948 I 3rd Chinese Revolutionary Civil War

Communist General Lin Biao inflicted costly losses in southwest Manchuria in the **Liaoshi** Corridor, then launched a fresh offensive north of Mukden (modern Shenyang). Heavy fighting saw the Nationalists abandon Jilin (9 March) and Lin captured Siping (Szepingkau) to cut the railway and further isolate **Changchun**. It fell later in the year in the **Liaoshen** offensive (February–13 March 1948).

Sirhind I 1555 I Mughal Conquest of Northern India

Taking advantage of a disputed succession in the Afghan Suri Empire, the former Mughal

Emperor Humayun returned to northern India. At Sirhind in eastern Punjab, his teenage son Akbar and General Bairam Khan crushed the Afghan-Turk force of Sikander Shah. Humayun recaptured **Delhi** though died soon after, leaving Akbar to secure the empire in late 1556 at **Panipat** (22 June 1555).

Sirhind ▮ 1710 ▮ Mughal-Sikh Wars

Sikh leader Banda Singh Bahadur's ragged peasant army succeeded in an attack on the Mughal city of **Samana**, then besieged Sirhind, in the Punjab, defended by a large and well-armed force under the Subedar Wazir Khan. Outside the city at Chhappar Chiri, the Sikhs defeated and killed Wazir Khan and massacred his army. They then stormed and sacked Sirhind (22 May 1710).

Sirhind ▮ 1748 ▮ Indian Campaigns of Ahmad Shah
See **Manupur**

Siris River ▮ 280 BC ▮ Pyrrhic War
See **Heraclea, Lucania**

Sirmium ▮ 441 ▮ Hun Invasion of the Roman Empire

During his campaign against the Eastern Roman Empire along the Danube, Attila the Hun captured Margus and Singidunum (Belgrade). Perhaps the worst Roman loss was the attack on the strategic city of Sirmium (modern Sremska Mitrovica) on the Sava. Sirmium was destroyed, with its citizens enslaved. A new invasion two years later took Attila to the walls of **Constantinople**.

Sirmium ▮ 580–582 ▮ Byzantine-Balkan Wars

In a threat to the Byzantine Empire's northern border, Avars under the Khan Baian besieged Sirmium (modern Sremska Mitrovica), then withdrew when Justin II agreed to pay an annual tribute (574). A fresh advance by Baian again besieged the city, which was starved into surrender after two years. The Avars dominated the

northern Balkans until Byzantine victory in 601 at **Viminacium**.

Sironj ▮ 1631 ▮ Mughal-Ahmadnagar Wars

When Mughal commander Khan Jahan Lodi threatened to make an alliance with Nizam Shah II of Ahmadnagar, Emperor Shahjahan declared war. Near Sironj, north of Bhopal, the rebel rearguard was attacked by Bikramajit of Bundelkhand and Khan Jahan's Lieutenant, Darya Khan, was defeated and killed. The rebel commander himself was soon killed near **Kalinjar** (11 January 1631).

Sirsa ▮ 1858 ▮ Indian Mutiny

Despite a costly debacle at **Ruiya** (15 April), General Robert Walpole pursued the rebels 40 miles north to Sirsa, on the Ramganga near Aliganj covering Fatehpur. Exercising greater care, Walpole used his artillery better, but delay sending in his cavalry meant heavy fighting before the rebels were driven out with 300 dead. Most escaped before he captured their camp at Aliganj (22 April 1858).

Sirte ▮ 1941 ▮ World War II (War at Sea)

While escorting an essential fuel-tanker from Alexandria to **Malta**, British Admiral Philip Vian's cruiser squadron and destroyers met a much larger Italian fleet under Admiral Angelo Iachino, also on escort duty, in the Gulf of Sirte. An indecisive exchange saw the British suffer some damage before the Italians broke off at nightfall. Both sides claimed victory (17 December 1941).

Sirte ▮ 1942 ▮ World War II (War at Sea)

Determined to prevent desperately needed supplies reaching **Malta**, Italian Admiral Angelo Iachino with a battleship, three cruisers and destroyers attacked Admiral Philip Vian's cruiser and destroyer escort in the Gulf of Sirte. While the Italians were driven off at the cost of two destroyers to either side, most of the convoy was subsequently lost to German bombers (22 March 1942).

Sis | 1605 | Turko-Persian Wars
See **Sufiyan**

Slsak | 1593 | Turkish-Habsburg Wars
See **Sissek**

Siscia | 34 BC | Wars of the Second Triumvirate
At war with the fierce tribes of the Balkans, Octavian (later Emperor Augustus Caesar) captured the Iapudae capital at **Metulum**. Later that year he marched east against Siscia (modern Sissek), at the confluence of the Sava and Kupa in modern Croatia. Besieged by land and from the two rivers, Siscia fell after a month and Octavian returned in triumph to Rome.

Siscia | 388 | Later Roman Military Civil Wars
When Magnus Clemens Maximus declared himself Emperor in Britain in 383 and marched into Italy to displace young Valentinian II, Theodosius, Emperor in the East, advanced into the Balkans. He routed the usurper's army under Andragathius on the Sava at Siscia (modern Sissek) near Zagreb, then defeated the usurper's brother at Poetovio and pursued Maximus to **Aquileia**.

Sishui | 621 | Rise of the Tang Dynasty
See **Hulao**

Siska | 1593 | Turkish-Habsburg Wars
See **Sissek**

Sissek | 1593 | Turkish-Habsburg Wars
Hasan Pasha, the Ottoman military Governor of Bosnia, raiding into Croatia found himself facing a large Imperial force led by Michael of Wallachia and Sigismund Bathory of Transylvania outside Sissek, on the Kupa and Save Rivers. Hasan was killed in a terrible defeat. Grand Vizier Sinan Pasha was later sent to avenge the loss and in October he laid siege to **Veszprem** (20 June 1593).

Sisters Creek | 1844 | Comanche Indian Wars
See **Walker's Creek**

Sit | 1238 | Mongol Conquest of Russia
On campaigning in Russia, the Mongols Batu (grandson of Genghis Khan) and Subetai invaded the Princedom of Vladimir-Suzdal and destroyed **Moscow** and **Vladimir**. They then marched north to the Sit River, where Grand Prince Yuri of Vladimir-Suzdal was defeated and killed by General Burundai. However, spring thaw saved Novgorod and the Mongols marched south towards **Kiev** (4 March 1238).

Sitibaldi | 1817 | 3rd British-Maratha War
Raja Appa Sahib of Nagpur took advantage of renewed war between the British and Peshwa Baji Rao II to attack the local British garrison, who withdrew to the nearby fortress of Sitibaldi. Colonel Hopeton Scott's tiny force withstood the Marathas until they were driven off by Bengal cavalry under Captain Charles Fitzgerald. The Raja was routed a month later at **Nagpur** (26 November 1817).

Sitka Ghat | 1859 | Indian Mutiny
See **Rapti**

Sitoli | 1815 | British-Gurkha War
See **Almorah**

Sittang | 1826 | 1st British-Burmese War
While British General Sir Archibald Campbell advanced up the Irriwaddy from **Rangoon**, a smaller force moved 50 miles down the Sittang from Shwegyin against the stockade at Sittang, east of Pegu. An initial attack was repulsed, with commander Colonel Edmund Conry killed, before a costly second assault under Colonel Hercules Pepper took the stockade by storm (7 & 11 January 1826).

Sittang | 1942 | World War II (Burma-India)
Japanese commander Shojiro Iida crossed the **Bilin**, then next day sent his key divisions

towards the Sittang, where British General John Smyth prematurely destroyed the bridge, leaving 5,000 men and nearly all his heavy equipment on the Japanese side of the river. The survivors then fell back to through **Pegu**. Smyth's much-debated disaster sealed the fate of Rangoon (22–23 February 1942).

Sivas ▌ 72 BC ▌ 3rd Mithridatic War
See **Cabira**

Sivas ▌ 1070 ▌ Byzantine-Turkish Wars
See **Sebastia**

Siwa ▌ 1917 ▌ World War I (Middle East)
Despite the pro-Turkish Senussi Bedouin losing at **Agagia** (February 1916), rebel Chieftain Sayyid Ahmed attacked towns west of the Suez Canal before withdrawing to the remote Siwa Oasis. In a brilliant expedition south from Salum, General Henry Hodgson led armoured cars across the desert to surprise and beat the Senussi. Sayyid fled to Constantinople on a German submarine (4 February 1917).

Siyanggiayan ▌ 1619 ▌ Manchu Conquest of China
Marching into Manchuria against the rising power of Manchu leader Nurhachi, Ming commander Yang Hao's troops were defeated at **Sarhu**. The following day, further east at Siyanggiayan, Nurhachi attacked another divided Ming force under General Ma Lin. Once again, the Chinese were routed and fled and the Manchu advanced southeast towards **Niumaozhai** (15 April 1619).

Skaggerak ▌ 1916 ▌ World War I (War at Sea)
See **Jutland**

Skalice ▌ 1424 ▌ Hussite Wars
Amid an armistice in the brutal doctrinal war among Bohemian Hussites, Jan Zizka led an offensive against Royalist Barons led by Lord John Mestecky of Opocno and Puta of Castolovice. Marching north from Hradec Králové, Zizka inflicted a terrible defeat at Skalice (Ska-

litz), near Jaromer. He then resumed his factional war with decisive victory in June at **Malesov** (6 January 1424).

Skalitz ▌ 1866 ▌ Seven Weeks War
While Prussian Crown Prince Friedrich Wilhelm invaded Austrian Bohemia through **Trautenau**, he sent General Karl Friedrich von Steinmetz to drive General Wilhelm Ramming out of **Nachod**. Von Steinmetz attacked Ramming again further west at Skalitz, capturing 4,000 prisoners and heavy guns, then secured a further victory the following day at **Schweinschadel** (28 June 1866).

Skardu ▌ 1948 ▌ 1st Indo-Pakistan War
Opening the war in northern Kashmir, Pakistani regulars and Pathan tribesmen seized Gilgit and Major Ehsan Khan advanced up the Indus Valley to besiege Skardu, defended by Indian Colonel Sher Jang Thapa. After holding out for six months against overwhelming odds, Thapa was starved into surrender. Further south, the invaders failed to take **Leh** (12 February–14 August 1948).

Skeleton Cave ▌ 1872 ▌ Apache Indian Wars
On campaign against hostile Apache in the Tonto Basin of central Arizona, General George Crook sent Captains William Brown and James Burns against a hostile band under Chuntz at Skeleton Cave, on the Salt River west of the modern Roosevelt Dam. Of 100 Apache in the cave, 76 were killed, including many women and children, and Chuntz took refuge on **Turret Butte** (26 December 1872).

Skenesboro ▌ 1777 ▌ War of the American Revolution
See **Fort Anne**

Skoriatino ▌ 1436 ▌ Wars of Russian Succession
After being overthrown by his uncle Yuri Dimitrievich (who died soon afterwards), Grand Prince Vasili II of Moscow returned to oust his cousin Vasili Kosoi, who was defeated at the

River Kotorosl (1435). In a second, decisive defeat at Skoriatino, near Rostov, Kosoi was captured and later blinded. Vasili ruled again until 1445, when he was defeated and captured by the Mongols at **Suzdal**.

Skull Cave I 1872 I Apache Indian Wars
  See **Skeleton Cave**

Slaak I 1631 I Netherlands War of Independence
  Frederick Henry of Orange learned that a 35-strong Spanish fleet under Count John of Nassau had set sail from Antwerp and he despatched just 12 ships to intercept the Spaniards. In a remarkable action on the Slaak near Tholen, outnumbered Dutch Admiral Marinus van Valckenisse attacked and took or sank the entire Spanish fleet, capturing a reported 4,000 prisoners (13 September 1631).

Slankamen I 1691 I Later Turkish-Habsburg Wars
  Despite Turkish defeats at **Vienna**, **Harkany** and **Belgrade**, Grand Vizier Fazil Mustafa Pasha took a major force to reconquer Transylvania, Bulgaria and Serbia and recaptured **Belgrade**. A new Imperial army under Louis of Baden marched down the Danube and, at Slankamen northwest of Belgrade, defeated and killed Mustafa, securing Transylvania for the Habsburgs (19 August 1691).

Slash Church I 1862 I American Civil War (Eastern Theatre)
  See **Hanover Court House**

Slim Buttes I 1876 I Sioux Indian Wars
  Pursuing the Sioux after defeat at **Little Big Horn** (26 June), General George Crook sent Captain Anson Mills against the Teton camp at Slim Buttes, just south of modern Reva in western South Dakota. Chief American Horse was defeated and died of wounds after being captured. The campaign to destroy the Sioux piecemeal continued in November at **Crazy Woman Creek** (9 September 1876).

Slim River I 1942 I World War II (Pacific)
  After British losses at **Jitra** and **Kampar** in western Malaya, General Sir Lewis Heath tried to hold positions at the Slim River. Attacking with tanks, General Takuro Matsui inflicted a decisive defeat with about 500 killed and 3,200 prisoners. The Japanese also captured Slim River Bridge and huge quantities of supplies. The shattered survivors continued the retreat into Johore (7 January 1942).

Slioch I 1307 I Rise of Robert the Bruce
  Robert the Bruce and a force of about 700 men were campaigning in northeast Scotland when they were intercepted at Slioch, just east of Huntly, by the English ally John Comyn Earl of Buchan. With Bruce seriously ill, his brother Edward repulsed two heavy assaults to enable them to reach nearby Strathbogie. Buchan was routed a few months later at **Inverurie** (25 & 31 December 1307).

Sliven I 1829 I Russo-Turkish Wars
  Advancing against the Turks after victory at **Varna** (October 1828), Russian General Count Hans von Diebitsch led his troops across the Balkan Mountains and defeated a major Turkish force west of Burgas at Sliven. Diebitsch received the honorific Zabalkansky to recognise his remarkable mountain crossing and the victory which opened the way to the capture of **Adrianople** (12 August 1829).

Slivnitza I 1885 I Serbo-Bulgarian War
  King Milan IV of Serbia marched into newly independent Bulgaria in a dispute over eastern Rumelia, capturing many strongpoints and driving the Bulgarians back across the Dragoman Pass. Near Sofia at Slivnitza, Prince Alexander (Battenberg) of Bulgaria and General Stefan Stambolov halted the invaders, then drove them back into Serbia to defeat at **Pirot** (17–19 November 1885).

Slobodyszcze I 1660 I Russo-Polish Wars
  In a planned co-ordinated attack on Lvov, Russian commander Vasili P. Sheremetev was defeated at **Liubar**, while his Cossack ally Yuri

Chmielnicki delayed. Chmielnicki was then attacked and defeated to the southeast at Slobodyszcze by Polish General Jerzy Lubomirski. The Cossack commander made a separate peace with the Poles, who then advanced on Sheremetev at **Chudnov**.

Slobodzeya ┃ 1811 ┃ Russo-Turkish Wars
  See **Ruschuk**

Slonihodrek ┃ 1655 ┃ Russo-Polish Wars
  See **Lvov**

Sluys ┃ 1340 ┃ Hundred Years War
  At the start of the Hundred Years War, Edward III of England took a large fleet, commanded by Robert de Morley, to attack Philip VI's ships near Sluys on the River Zwin. Trapped in confined waters, the French ships, reinforced by Genoese galleys, were destroyed with terrible slaughter. The dead included French Admiral Hugh Quieret, reputedly killed while trying to surrender (24 June 1340).

Sluys ┃ 1587 ┃ Anglo-Spanish Wars
  A few weeks after the great English raid on **Cadiz**, Alessandro Farnese Duke of Parma laid siege to the English and Dutch garrison in the port of Sluys. Robert Dudley Earl of Leicester failed in repeated attempts to relieve the port and was recalled after Sluys capitulated. Only Leicester's influence with Elizabeth I saved him from charges of incompetence (29 May–30 July 1587).

Sluys ┃ 1603 ┃ Netherlands War of Independence
  During the Dutch blockade of Sluys, Spanish galleys under Admiral Frederigo Spinola made a foray from the port and were attacked by Dutch ships under Vice-Admiral Joost de Moor. In calm conditions, the oared Spanish vessels caused heavy damage, though Spinola was killed by a cannonball. Threatened by Dutch reinforcements from Flushing, his ships withdrew to Sluys (26 May 1603).

Sluys ┃ 1604 ┃ Netherlands War of Independence
  Prince Maurice of Orange was attempting to relieve the long Spanish siege of **Ostend**, when he took an army into Flanders against Sluys (modern Sluis). After driving off Don Louis de Velasco (May 1604), he besieged the garrison under Aurelio Spinola, nephew of the Spanish Netherlands commander. Sluys was finally starved into surrender, though too late to save Ostend (19 May–19 August 1604).

Smala ┃ 1843 ┃ French Conquest of Algeria
  Campaigning to complete the conquest of western Algeria, France forced Arab warrior Abd-el-Kader into the mountains following defeat at **Mascara** (1835). New commander Marshal Thomas Bugeaud gradually drove the Arabs into the desert. At Smala, a column under Henri d'Aumale Duke of Orleans dispersed Kader's forces. He withdrew into Morocco and later fought at **Isly** (10 May 1843).

Smara ┃ 1976 ┃ Western Sahara Wars
  When Morocco and Mauritania partitioned Western Sahara, Moroccan forces seized the northern city of Smara, east of El Ayoun, where they soon came under assault by Polisario guerrillas. Heavy fighting saw high yet hotly disputed losses on both sides, including Moroccan commander Colonel Driss Harti killed. Hundreds of Saharawis were able to flee to Algeria (6 October 1976).

Smederevo ┃ 1439 ┃ Turkish-Hungarian Wars
  See **Semendria**

Smerwick Massacre ┃ 1580 ┃ Geraldine Rebellion
  See **Fort del Or**

Smithfield ┃ 1864 ┃ American Civil War (Eastern Theatre)
  As Union General Philip Sheridan again advanced into the Shenandoah Valley towards **Winchester**, part of his force under General

Wesley Merritt was attacked to the northeast at Smithfield, West Virginia. An inconclusive action cost Confederate General Jubal A. Early greater losses before Merritt fell back east towards Charlestown. Early also retired (29 August 1864).

Smolensk | 1502 | 1st Muscovite-Lithuanian War

A new attempt to seize Smolensk after failure to exploit victory at **Mstislavl** (November 1501) saw Duke Ivan III of Moscow send a large force under his son Dimitri. Failed assaults and the bloody action at **Lake Smolino** forced Dimitri to lift his siege, though Alexander of Poland soon sued for peace. While Alexander retained Smolensk, Ivan secured most of eastern Lithuania (August–October 1502).

Smolensk | 1512–1514 | 2nd Muscovite-Lithuanian War

After Russian failure at Smolensk in 1502, Basil III of Moscow renewed war in Lithuania, where his advance on Smolensk was repulsed by Polish-Lithuanian commander Konstantine Ostrozhsky (December 1512). Duke Basil was driven off again in September 1513 after a six-week siege of the city, but on a third attempt, the Muscovites seized Smolensk and held it, despite defeat at **Orsha** (June 1514).

Smolensk | 1609–1611 | Russian Time of Troubles

King Sigismund III of Poland invaded Russia to claim the throne and besieged the powerful city of Smolensk, defended by Mikhail Shein. A Russian-Swedish relief army was defeated at **Klushino** (4 July 1610) and Sigismund advanced to capture **Moscow**. However, the siege of Smolensk continued and the city was largely in ruins when it fell after almost two years (26 September 1609–13 June 1611).

Smolensk | 1632–1634 | Russo-Polish "War of Smolensk"

Determined to regain Smolensk, Tsar Michael sent General Mikhail Shein, who had defended the city 20 years earlier. After 11 months of siege, Shein was defeated by a relief force under Ladislav IV of Poland (September 1633). The Russians were surrounded and finally had to surrender. Peace was restored and Shein was executed for failure (September 1632–25 February 1634).

Smolensk | 1654 | Russo-Polish Wars

Tsar Alexius opened a new war against Poland, leading a huge force into Lithuania, supported by General Yakov K. Cherkassy and 20,000 Cossacks under Ivan Zolotarenko. He besieged Smolensk and after disaster at **Szepiele** (24 August) the Polish-Lithuanian garrison surrendered. A Polish counter-offensive in the south in January was checked at **Okhmatov** (2 July–23 September 1654).

Smolensk | 1812 | Napoleonic Wars (Russian Campaign)

As he advanced into Russia, Napoleon Bonaparte marched east from Vitebsk to meet Russians Prince Pyotr Bagration and General Mikhail Barclay de Tolly moving forward to defend Smolensk. A hard-fought battle outside the city saw the Russian army eventually repulsed. By the time Smolensk was taken after a costly assault, Barclay had fired the city and escaped (17 August 1812).

Smolensk | 1941 | World War II (Eastern Front)

Days after destroying the Russian pockets at **Bialystok** and **Minsk**, Marshal Fedor von Bock raced east to encircle Marshal Symeon Timoshenko at Smolensk. Over 300,000 men, 3,200 tanks and 3,100 guns were captured, though many Soviet divisions escaped. The over-stretched Germans halted, turning south towards **Kiev**, which fatally delayed their advance on **Moscow** (10 July–5 August 1941).

Smolensk | 1943 | World War II (Eastern Front)

At the northern end of the Soviet offensive on the **Dnieper**, over a million Russians under Generals Andrei Yeremenko and Vasili Sokolovsky advanced along a 250-mile front towards

Smolensk, held by Army Group Centre under Marshal Gunther von Kluge. Three German armies were destroyed and Smolensk fell before the line stabilised west of the city (7 August–25 September 1943).

Smoliantsy I 1812 I Napoleonic Wars (Russian Campaign)

French forces under Marshal Claude Victor on the retreat from **Moscow** were attacked west of Smolensk by Russian Prince Ludwig Wittgenstein near Smoliantsy (modern Smolyany). Victor managed to withdraw north after a sharp action, but he was defeated again a week later as he attempted to fall back on the Dvina at **Vitebsk** (1 November 1812).

Smyrna I 1344 I Later Crusader-Muslim Wars

In response to raids on shipping by the Emir Omar of Aydin, a fleet involving Venice, Cyprus, the Papacy and the Knights Hospitallier of Rhodes attacked Smyrna (modern Izmir, Turkey). Omar was defeated at sea off his port and Smyrna was captured and held by the Knights of St John for 60 years until they were driven out by Tamerlane's Tatar conquest of Anatolia (October 1344).

Smyrna I 1402 I Conquests of Tamerlane

The Turko-Mongol Tamerlane destroyed the Ottoman army at **Angora** and marched against the Christian stronghold of Smyrna (modern Izmir, Turkey), where the Knights of St John had resisted repeated Ottoman attack. The port city fell by storm after a two-week siege and the nearby Genoese Islands of Chios and Lesbos quickly submitted to the conqueror, who then returned to Samarkand.

Smyrna I 1922 I 2nd Greco-Turkish War

In the days after victory at **Afyon**, Turkish commander Mustafa Kemal pursued the Greeks to Smyrna (modern Izmir), where they had landed in May 1919 as agents for the World War I allies. Smyrna fell by assault, with Greece driven out of Turkey amid terrible massacres and destruction. Kemal became President of the new Turkish Republic, taking the name Ataturk (9–11 September 1922).

Snicker's Ferry I 1864 I American Civil War (Eastern Theatre)

Confederate General Jubal A. Early was repulsed outside Washington, D.C. at **Fort Stevens** (12 July) and withdrew to the Shenandoah Valley, pursued by General Horatio G. Wright. At Snicker's Ferry near Berryville, Virginia, Confederate General Robert E. Rodes routed the Union vanguard of Colonel Joseph Thoburn. Early's force soon lost again further west at **Stephenson's Depot** (17–18 July 1864).

Snipe I 1942 I World War II (Northern Africa)

See **Kidney Ridge**

Snowshoes I 1758 I Seven Years War (North America)

On a long-range winter patrol west of Lake George, New York, Major Robert Rogers ambushed a small Indian force led by Oliver Morel de la Durantaye, west of Bald Mountain. He was then surprised by French marines and Canadian militia under Jean-Baptiste de de Langy. In battle on snowshoes, "Rogers Rangers" were routed with 125 killed and fled to Fort Edwards (13 March 1758).

Snyder's Bluff I 1863 I American Civil War (Western Theatre)

As a diversion from the Union offensive south of Vicksburg, Mississippi, at **Port Gibson**, General William T. Sherman sent Captain K. Randolph Breese and General Francis P. Blair against Confederate batteries at Snyder's Bluff to the north, defended by General Louis Hébert. They withdrew after an effective demonstration and **Vicksburg** was soon besieged (29 April–1 May 1863).

Sobota I 1655 I 1st Northern War

Charles X of Sweden and General Arvid Wittenberg advanced into Poland through **Ujscie** to meet the Polish Royal army at Sobota. A two-day running battle saw King John II Casimir driven off and three days later Charles X marched east to capture Warsaw. He then turned southwest again to join Wittenberg for a decisive action against the Poles two weeks later at **Opoczno** (23–24 August 1655).

Sobraon I 1846 I 1st British-Sikh War

With the Sikh invasion of British East Punjab repulsed at **Mudki** and **Ferozeshah**, the Sikhs were thrown back to decisive defeat on the Sutlej River at **Aliwal**. Two weeks later they were attacked by General Sir Hugh Gough in a strong position at Sobraon. Fighting with their backs to the river, Ranjur Singh's army was heavily defeated, bringing the war to an end (10 February 1846).

Socabaya I 1836 I Bolivian-Peruvian War

After invading Peru to win at **Yanacocha** (August 1835), President Andrés Santa Cruz of Bolivia advanced north towards Lima, where General Felipe Santiago Salaverry marched out to meet him at Socabaya, near Arequipa. Salaverry was routed and then executed and Santa Cruz forced a confederation with Peru, which was eventually overthrown in 1839 at **Yungay** (7 February 1836).

Soconusco I 1498–1500 I Aztec Wars of Conquest

At the greatest extent of Aztec conquest, Ahuitzotl personally led a force 800 miles southeast to Soconusco (near the modern Mexico-Guatemala border), where a bold series of actions secured the main towns of the region. When Ahuitzotl died a few years later, his nephew Motecuhzoma II faced rebellion in distant Soconusco (Xoconochco) before he was overwhelmed by the Spanish Conquest.

Soczawa I 1676 I Turkish Invasion of the Ukraine

At war with Turk and Tatar invaders of the Polish Ukraine, John III Sobieski was rejoined by the Lithuanians, who deserted him at **Zloczow** (August 1675). North of the Dniester at Soczawa (modern Sokhachevka, near Vinnitsa), he again routed Ibrahim Shetan. The Turks fell back on Kamieniec, their last fortress in Poland, before their final repulse later that year at **Zurawno** (May 1676).

Sofia I 981 I Byzantine Wars of Tsar Samuel
    See **Mount Haemus**

Sogdiana I 36 BC I Wars of the Former Han
    See **Kangju**

Sogdian Rock I 327 BC I Conquests of Alexander the Great

Alexander the Great beat the Scythians at the **Jaxartes** (329 BC), then advanced into Sogdiana (modern Uzbekistan), where he attacked the stronghold at Sogdian Rock in the Hissar Range, held by Ariamazes. When a small unit scaled the precipitous fortress, the garrison surrendered. Alexander married Roxane, daughter of Oxyartes of Sogdia, and soon advanced into India after taking **Aornos**.

Sohanpur I 1857 I Indian Mutiny

On a campaign north of the Gaghara, a mixed force under British Colonel Francis Rowcroft was reinforced by a second Gurkha regiment before meeting a much larger rebel army at Sohanpur, at the mouth of the Little Gandak. The rebels were very heavily defeated, effectively securing the Sarun District, and they withdrew northwest through further defeat at **Gorakhpur** (26 December 1857).

Sohr I 1745 I War of the Austrian Succession
    See **Soor**

So-i Ford I 1852 I Taiping Rebellion
    See **Suo'yi Ford**

Soissons I 486 I Fall of the Western Roman Empire

At the head of his first major campaign, Clovis, King of the Franks, marched south to Soissons on the Aisne River and routed Syagrius, last Roman commander in Gaul. The decisive battle extended Frankish territory to the Loire and helped establish the Merovingian Dynasty. Syagrius fled to the Visigoths, who subsequently handed him over to Clovis for execution.

Soissons | 719 | Rise of Charles Martel

Charles Martel of Austrasia beat his rival Neustrians at **Ambleve** (716) and **Vincy** (717), but was not able to fully consolidate Frankish expansion until two years later when he defeated Raginfrid, Neustrian Mayor of the Palace, at Soissons. Following this victory, Charles assumed the title of Mayor under King Childeric II. Charles was King in all but name of the revitalized Frankish Empire.

Soissons | 923 | Franco-Norman Wars

Rivalry for the throne of France saw Robert (formerly Rollo) Marquess of Neustria (brother of the late King Odo) oppose the German-sponsored Charles III "the Simple," the illegitimate son of Louis II. Charles was routed in battle at Soissons, near the Aisne, though Robert I was killed in the fighting and his Norman son-in-law, Rudolf Duke of Burgundy, was crowned King (15 June 923).

Soissons | 1814 | Napoleonic Wars (French Campaign)

While Prussian General Gebhard von Blucher was held up northeast of Paris at the **Ourcq**, further north on the Aisne, Soissons was besieged by 45,000 men under General Friedrich von Bulow and Baron Ferdinand von Winzingerode. The French-Polish garrison of General Baron Jean Moreau was persuaded to surrender prematurely and Blucher crossed the Aisne (3 March 1814).

Soissons | 1870 | Franco-Prussian War

Grand Duke Friedrich Franz II of Mecklenburg marched south from **Sedan** to capture **Toul** (23 September), then took his Prussian army and siege train northwest against Soissons. The city had to surrender following three weeks of investment and a four-day bombardment. The Germans then moved their strategic railway terminus forward from Chateau Thierry (28 September–16 October 1870).

Sokoto | 1903 | British Conquest of Northern Nigeria

When British forces seized the great north Nigerian city of **Kano** (3 February), General George Kemball took command of the Royal West African Frontier Force and marched northwest, via **Rawiya**, on Sokoto. Confronted by a powerful Fulani army, his machine-guns and artillery inflicted terrible casualties. Sultan Attahiru had to abandon his capital and flee north towards **Burmi** (15 March 1903).

Solachon | 586 | Byzantine-Persian Wars

After years of indecisive warfare, Byzantine Emperor Maurice sent his brother-in-law Philippicus into Mesopotamia against Persian commander Kardarigan and his colleague Mebodes. At Solachon, near Dara, the Persians were defeated and Rome campaigned east of the Tigris. The Roman recovery faltered when the eastern army mutinied in 588, but the Romans still won later that year at **Martyropolis**.

Soldier Spring | 1868 | Canadian River Expedition

A month after the massacre at the **Washita**, another army column under Major Andrew Evans attacked a Comanche-Kiowa camp about 30 miles further south at Soldier Spring, near the Wichita Mountains in the west of modern Oklahoma. The camp was destroyed and shortly afterwards a Comanche-Kiowa reservation was established in Indian Territory near Fort Sills (25 December 1868).

Sole Bay | 1672 | 3rd Dutch War

Dutch Admiral Mihiel du Ruyter opened the war by attacking an Anglo-French fleet off Southwold in Suffolk. With French Admiral Jean d'Estrées forced out of the battle, de Ruyter concentrated on the English under James Duke of York. De Ruyter finally had to retreat, though only after heavy Allied losses, including Edward Montagu Earl of Sandwich drowned (7 June 1672).

Soledad I 1839 I Central American National Wars

Salvadoran General José Trinidad Cabañas invaded Honduras and seized **Tegucicalpa** (6 September), then faced newly appointed President José Francisco Zelaya and General Nicolas Espinoza just outside the capital at nearby Soledad. Zelaya's troops were heavily defeated and he sought aid from Nicaragua to help him overcome Cabañas in January 1840 at **El Potrero** (13 November 1839).

Solferino I 1796 I French Revolutionary Wars (1st Coalition)
  See **Castiglione**

Solferino I 1859 I 2nd Italian War of Independence

Following Austria's defeat at **Magenta** (4 June), Emperor Franz Josef took personal command against Victor Emmanuel II of Piedmont and his ally Napoleon III. In a bloody battle at Solferino, near Castiglione, Napoleon and Marshal Marie MacMahon routed General Franz von Schlick (who was saved only by General Ludwig von Benedck's rearguard). Austria then ceded Lombardy (24 June 1859).

Solicinium I 368 I Alemannic Invasion of Roman Gaul

Two years after his army inflicted a costly defeat on the rebellious Alemanni at **Chalons**, Emperor Valentinian personally led a renewed offensive across the Rhine. He won an even greater victory over the Alemanni at Solicinium, an uncertain site identified as possibly either Sulz am Neckar or Schwetzingen in Baden-Württemberg.

Sollum-Halfaya I 1941 I World War II (Northern Africa)

Under political pressure to relieve besieged **Tobruk**, British commander Sir Archibald Wavell sent General Sir Henry Beresford-Pierse on a counter-offensive between Sollum and Halfaya. A major armoured action saw the British heavily repulsed with the loss of 100 out of 180 tanks. Wavell was replaced and a new

attempt succeeded six months later at **Sidi Rezegh** (15–17 June 1941).

Solomon Forks I 1857 I Cheyenne Indian War

In response to raids along the Smoky Hill Trail in central Kansas, Colonel Edwin Sumner and 300 cavalry met 300 Cheyenne in battle array on the Solomon Forks of the Kansas River. The Indians were dispersed by the reputed only sabre charge of the Indian Wars, though casualties were light on both sides. Next day Sumner destroyed the nearby Cheyenne village of 171 lodges (29 July 1857).

Solomon Islands I 1942 I World War II (Pacific)

Seven naval actions in the Solomons around embattled **Guadalcanal** are claimed to have turned the tide in the Pacific War. After American losses at **Savo Island**, **Eastern Solomons** and **Cape Esperance**, new Admiral William Halsey took the initiative at **Santa Cruz**, then won twice at **Guadalcanal** and at **Tassafaronga** to secure command of the sea (9 August–30 November 1942).

Solomon Islands I 1943–1944 I World War II (Pacific)

Five months after bloody victory at **Guadalcanal**, Allied forces advanced west to secure the central Solomons, with the key fighting to secure **New Georgia**, **Vella Lavella**, the **Treasury Islands** and **Bougainville**. Action on land was supported at sea at **Kula Gulf**, **Kolombangara**, **Vella Gulf**, **Vella Lavella**, **Empress Augusta Bay** and **Cape St George** (July 1943–March 1944).

Solonitsa I 1596 I Cossack-Polish Wars
  See **Lubny**

Solothurn I 1318 I Habsburg Wars of Succession

Despite his terrible defeat at **Morgarten** in 1315, Duke Leopold of Austria (brother of Emperor Frederick) returned to attack Swiss Burgundian towns, which united against the

Habsburgs. Leopold and a large army besieged Solothurn, south of Basel on the Aare, but when severe flooding destroyed his camp and siege works, the Duke withdrew after ten weeks to avoid further loss.

**Soltsy ❙ 1941 ❙ World War II
(Eastern Front)**

While Marshal Wilhelm von Leeb advanced towards Leningrad, Panzer General Erich von Manstein's mobile units approaching Shirmsk on Lake Ilmen were surprised by General Vasilii Morozov around Soltsy. The Panzer Corps was driven back about 25 miles by the reputed first Soviet counter-attack, claimed to have created time to improve defences at **Leningrad** (14–17 July 1941).

**Solway Moss ❙ 1542 ❙ Anglo-Scottish
Royal Wars**

James V of Scotland was encouraged by victory at **Hadden Rig** in August and sent 10,000 men under Oliver Sinclair of Pitcairns to invade Northumberland, where they were blocked near the Esk at Solway Moss by the smaller force of Sir Thomas Wharton. While casualties were light, many Scots were captured, including Sinclair. A few weeks later, James was dead of despair (25 November 1542).

**Solygeia ❙ 425 BC ❙ Great
Peloponnesian War**

Weeks after victory at **Pylos-Sphacteria** in southwest Greece, Athenian commander Nicias attempted a similar landing in Corinth at Solygeia, at the head of the Saronic Gulf, where he was attacked by a Corinthian force before he could establish a strong position. Stubborn fighting won the Athenians a hollow victory, before Nicias withdrew northeast to Crommyon (September 425 BC).

**Sombrero, Mexico ❙ 1817 ❙ Mexican
Wars of Independence**

Spanish adventurer Francisco Javier Mina landed in Mexico, where he failed in an advance on Leon and his forces were besieged at Sombrero, north of Leon, by Royalist Marshal

Pascual Liñan. After heavy bombardment, American Colonel Bradburn led an evacuation at night and Liñan murdered the wounded left behind. Mina was soon captured at **Venadito** and executed (30 July–19 August 1817).

**Sombrero, Venezuela ❙ 1818 ❙
Venezuelan War of Independence**

Having eluded the Revolutionary army of Simón Bolívar following defeat at **Calabozo**, on the Guárico in central Venezuela, Spanish commander Pablo Morillo withdrew upstream and days later took a defensive position to the northeast at El Sombrero. Bolívar's pursuing force was driven off in a sharp action with 100 men lost and Morillo turned northwest towards **Valencia** (17 February 1818).

**Somerset Court House ❙ 1777 ❙ War of
the American Revolution**

When British General Charles Earl Cornwallis sent a large foraging party to capture flour from a store on the Millstone River, New Jersey, they were met at nearby Somerset Court House by 400 recruits under Colonel Philemon Dickinson. The untrained Americans fought unexpectedly well to drive off the British, capturing 40 wagons and 100 draft horses (20 January 1777).

**Somerton ❙ 733 ❙ Anglo-Saxon Territorial
Wars**

As he fought to expand the power of Mercia, King Aethelbald marched into Wessex and defeated King Aethelheard to secure Somerton, near the River Parrett in Somerset. The victory effectively ended the war with Wessex and made Aethelbald ruler of the kingdom beyond Selwood until his defeat by the West Saxons 20 years later at **Burford**.

**Somme ❙ 1916 ❙ World War I
(Western Front)**

The main Allied offensive in 1916 was the bloody campaign along the Somme, which cost about 420,000 British, 200,000 French and perhaps 500,000 German casualties before winter closed in. Principal actions were at **Albert**, **Bazentin**, **Delville Wood**, **Pozières**,

Guillemont, **Flers-Courcelette**, **Morval**, **Thiepval**, **Transloy** and **Ancre** (1 July–18 November 1916).

Somme I 1918 I World War I (Western Front)

When German commander Erich von Ludendorff launched a massive offensive on the Somme, General Julian Byng fell back, then held Arras against General Oscar von Below. Further south, Generals Georg von der Marwitz and Oscar von Hutier advanced 40 miles against General Hubert Gough before the offensive ended and was switched north to the **Lys** (21 March–5 April 1918).

Somnath I 1026 I Muslim Conquest of Northern India

On campaign from Afghanistan, the Muslim Mahmud of Ghazni secured most of the Punjab after successive victories near **Peshawar** (1001, 1006 and 1008) and later marched to the Gujarat coast against the Hindu Holy city of Somnath (modern Dwarka). The defence was smashed—with a reported 50,000 Indians killed—and Mahmud sacked and looted the city's famous temple (January 1026).

Somorrostro (1st) I 1874 I 2nd Carlist War

Republican commander Marshal Francisco Serrano was determined to raise the siege of **Bilbao** by the Pretender Don Carlos VII and sent General Domingo Moriones with a reported 20,000 men. At nearby Somorrostro, despite a courageous assault by General Fernando Primo de Rivera, Moriones was driven back by General Nicolás Ollo and lost 1,200 men (24–25 February 1874).

Somorrostro (2nd) I 1874 I 2nd Carlist War

In a renewed attempt to raise the siege of **Bilbao** by Don Carlos VII, Republican commander Marshal Francisco Serrano himself arrived with 27,000 men and 70 cannon. However, the Carlist General Joaquín Elío, with just 17,000 men, once again drove off the attack at nearby Somorrostro. It was another six weeks before Serrano managed to relieve Bilbao (25 March 1874).

Somosierra I 1808 I Napoleonic Wars (Peninsular Campaign)

Advancing south through the eastern Guadarrama Mountains towards Madrid, Napoleon Bonaparte was blocked by mixed Spanish units under General José San Juan in defensive positions at the Somosierra Pass. After repulsing a suicidal charge by Polish cavalry, the Spaniards fired just a few volleys then fled, leaving Bonaparte to enter Madrid without further fighting (30 November 1808).

Somosierra I 1936 I Spanish Civil War

Nationalist General Emilio Mola was determined to hold the Guadarrama Mountains north of **Madrid** and sent Colonel José Gistau (later Colonel García Escámez) to secure the key eastern pass of Somosierra. Near-suicidal attacks drove the Republicans out and the rebels held Somosierra—and also the western pass at **Alto de León**—until the end of the war (20–25 July 1936).

Soncino I 1431 I Venetian-Milanese Wars

Despite signing a treaty in 1428 to end the war with Florence and Venice, Milan soon resumed military raids, provoking an invasion by a Venetian-Florentine army under Francesco Bussone Count Carmagnola. Near the Po at Soncino, Carmagnola was disastrously defeated by Sforza of Milan. He lost again a few days later in a great naval battle on the Po near **Cremona** (6 June 1431).

Songhua I 1114 I Jurchen Invasion of Northern China

When Wanyan Aguda united the Jurchen against the Liao Dynasty in Manchuria, Emperor Tianzuo sent a large force under Xiao Si Xian, who was surprised and routed at the Songhua (Sungari) River. Aguda declared himself Emperor of a new Jin (Chin) Dynasty and finally seized Beijing. Tianzuo was eventually captured and in 1127 Aguda's son defeated the Northern Song at **Kaifeng**.

Songhua (1st) ▌ 1947 ▌ 3rd Chinese Revolutionary Civil War

Communist General Lin Biao took the initiative in Manchuria, launching three offensives south across the Songhua (Sungari). All three advances secured initial success and threatened Changchun and Jilin, before eventually being driven back by Nationalist General Pan Yugun. The actions cost Lin very heavy losses, though he was soon reinforced and struck again (6 January–10 March 1947).

Songhua (2nd) ▌ 1947 ▌ 3rd Chinese Revolutionary Civil War

Despite previous failure, Communist General Lin Biao in Manchuria was reinforced by General Lu Zhengcao and once again attacked across the Songhua (Sungari) with over 250,000 men. He isolated **Changchun**, Jilin and **Siping** (Szepingkau) and inflicted massive losses before new Nationalist commander General Sun Liren was reinforced and stabilised the front (4 May–10 July 1947).

Songhwan ▌ 1894 ▌ Sino-Japanese War

With a puppet government installed in Seoul, Japanese General Yoshimasa Oshima marched north against Chinese commander Yeh-chi-chao at Asan, who took a defensive position northeast at Songhwan. Encouraged by naval success at **Phung-tao**, Oshima stormed Songhwan and captured Asan in Japan's first foreign battle for 300 years. Yeh fled north to **Pyongyang** (29 July 1894).

Songjiang ▌ 1860 ▌ Taiping Rebellion

As Taiping commander Li Xiucheng marched east towards **Shanghai**, his General Lu Shunde captured Songjiang (Sungkiang) to the southwest (1 July), where he was attacked by foreign troops under American Colonel Frederick T. Ward. After an initial repulse, Ward captured Songjiang, supported by Imperial General Li Hengsong, then marched north against **Qingpu** (16 July 1860).

Song Ngan ▌ 1966 ▌ Vietnam War

When North Vietnamese General Nguyen Vang led 10,000 men across the DMZ into Quang Tri, Americans and South Vietnamese under General Lowell English launched a massive attack (Operation Hastings) around the Song Ngan Valley, northwest of Dong Ha. The Allies suffered costly initial losses before the invaders were dispersed with more than 800 killed (15 July–3 August 1966).

Songpan ▌ 641 ▌ Tang Imperial Wars

See **Sungqu**

Songshan ▌ 1944 ▌ World War II (China)

Chinese General Zhong Bin crossed the **Salween** in Yunnan and besieged the mountain fortress at Songshan, northeast of **Longling**. Major Keijiro Kanemitsu's 1,200-strong garrison resisted fiercely, despite the explosion of two massive mines. Only 20 Japanese survived when the "Gibraltar of the Burma Road" eventually fell at the cost of 7,600 Chinese lives (15 June–September 1944).

Son Tay ▌ 1883 ▌ Sino-French War

Following French defeat at **Hanoi**, General Alexandre Bouet campaigned west towards Son Tay and was repulsed by Chinese Black Flag leader Liu Yongfu (15 August & 1 September). Admiral Amédée Courbet then took command in Tonkin and a bloody action saw 400 French casualties and over 1,000 Chinese killed before Son Tay was finally taken by storm (14–16 December 1883).

Son Tay ▌ 1970 ▌ Vietnam War

A dramatic attempt to rescue American POWs saw US Rangers led by Colonel Arthur Simons fly by helicopter from Thailand to Son Tay prison, 25 miles north of Hanoi, under cover of diversionary air-raids. While they killed guards at the camp and troops at a military school where they landed accidentally, the prisoners had been moved and the Americans left empty-handed (21 November 1970).

Sontius I 489 I Goth Invasion of Italy

Theodoric the Ostrogoth was encouraged by the Eastern Roman Emperor Zeno to march across the Alps into Italy, where he attacked the German ruler Odoacer in a powerful position on the Sontius (modern Izonzo) River, near the ruins of the city of Aquileia. Odoacer suffered a sharp defeat and fell back through **Verona** to **Ravenna** (28 August 489).

Soochow I 475–473 BC I Wars of China's Spring and Autumn Era

See **Suzhou**

Soochow I 1366–1367 I Rise of the Ming Dynasty

See **Suzhou**

Soochow I 1863 I Taiping Rebellion

See **Suzhou**

Soor I 1745 I War of the Austrian Succession

Despite defeat at **Hohenfriedberg** (4 June), Prince Charles of Lorraine pursued Frederick II of Prussia into Silesia and faced an unexpected Prussian attack at Soor, near Prausnitz, north of Breslau. A tactically brilliant action enabled Frederick to overwhelm the Austrians, inflicting over 8,000 casualties. Austria recovered for an advance on Berlin, halted in November at **Hennersdorf** (30 September 1745).

Soor I 1866 I Seven Weeks War

When Prussian Crown Prince Friedrich Wilhelm and General Adolf von Bonin invaded Austrian Bohemia, Baron Ludwig von Gablenz fell back from **Trautenau** and set a strong artillery line near Soor, west of Burkersdorf. While Prussian advance units under General Konstantin von Alvensleben suffered heavy losses, Gablenz had to withdraw. Königinhof fell next day (28 June 1866).

Sooty I 1763 I Bengal War

See **Gheria, Bengal**

Sorauren I 1813 I Napoleonic Wars (Peninsular Campaign)

During the weeklong "Battles of the Pyrenees," Allied forces attempting to prevent French Marshal Nicolas Soult relieving the siege of **Pamplona** fell back from **Roncesvalles** and days later took up position at Sorauren. In two separate engagements, Arthur Wellesley Lord Wellington destroyed Soult's offensive and drove his defeated army back to France (28 & 30 July 1813).

Sorpresa I 1927 I Chaco War

As Bolivia advanced fortified positions into the disputed Chaco Boreal towards Paraguay, a Paraguayan patrol was attacked near the small Bolivian fortress of Sorpresa, close to the Rio Pilcomayo, where Paraguayan Lieutenant Adolfo Rojas Silva was killed. Argentina then intervened to secure a temporary truce, broken in December 1928 by an incident at **Vanguardia** (26 February 1927).

Soto La Marina I 1817 I Mexican Wars of Independence

After landing on the east coast of Mexico (15 April), Spanish adventurer Francisco Javier Mina took Soto La Marina, in Tamaulipas, then marched inland to raise a peasant revolt, leaving Major José Sardá in command. Bombarded by a Royalist force under General Joaquin Aredondo, the small rebel garrison at Soto La Marina was forced to surrender. Many later died in captivity (11–15 June 1817).

Souchez I 1915 I World War I (Western Front)

See **Artois (1st)**

Souk-Ahras I 1958 I Algerian War

As part of the Battle of the **Frontier**, along the sealed border between Tunisia and Algeria, the largest action of the war developed around Souk-Ahras when up to 900 ALN insurgents tried to breach the Morice Line. After six days of fierce fighting, the survivors retreated into Tunisia, leaving over 500 dead and 100 captured. France lost 38 killed and 35 wounded (28 April–3 May 1958).

Sound I 1658 I 1st Northern War

Dutch Admiral Jacob Opdam van Wassaener, intervening to aid Denmark against Charles X of Sweden, tried to prevent Sweden closing the waterway between the Kattegat and Baltic. The bloody Battle of The Sound saw Admiral Cornelius Witte de With killed and his ship sunk. However, Count Karl Gustav Wrangel was beaten, with five ships lost, and Copenhagen was relieved (29 October 1658).

Sourton Down I 1643 I British Civil Wars

As Parliamentary forces resumed the offensive in the west after defeat in January at **Braddock Down**, James Chudleigh's Puritans lost to Sir Ralph Hopton at **Launceston**, but ambushed the Royalists crossing Sourton Down, near Okehampton, Devon. Chudleigh seized over 1,000 muskets and also captured Hopton's orders to advance into Somerset. This led to battle at **Stratton** (25 April 1643).

South Beveland I 1944 I World War II (Western Europe)

See **Scheldt Estuary**

South Foreland I 1217 I 1st English Barons' War

Supported by English Barons against King John, Crown Prince Louis of France landed in England and besieged **Dover** Castle, held by Hubert de Burgh. After forcing Louis into a costly blockade, de Burgh defeated a large French supply fleet under Eustace the Monk, off South Foreland near Sandwich. The Prince (later Louis VIII) abandoned the siege and the rebellion waned (24 August 1217).

South Georgia I 1982 I Falklands War

A British carrier task force under Admiral John "Sandy" Woodward opened the campaign by attacking South Georgia, where an Argentine landing party had earlier precipitated the war. Advancing through heavy seas from Ascension, the British badly damaged an Argentine submarine and seized the island without loss. It was a minor military gain yet a significant political victory (24–25 April 1982).

South Mills I 1862 I American Civil War (Eastern Theatre)

Union General Ambrose E. Burnside campaigned against the North Carolina coast, where he captured **New Bern**, then sent General Jesse L. Reno north to destroy the Dismal Swamp Canal and cut Confederate access to Albermarle Sound. Intercepted by Colonel Ambrose R. Wright, northwest of Camden near South Mills, Reno had to withdraw and abandoned his objective (19 April 1862).

South Mountain I 1862 I American Civil War (Eastern Theatre)

Crossing the Potomac into Maryland after victory at **Bull Run**, Confederate commander Robert E. Lee soon came under attack at South Mountain by General George B. McClellan's Union army advancing from the east. After beating the Confederates at key passes, including Crampton's Gap, McClellan hesitated, allowing Lee to concentrate further west at **Antietam** (14 September 1862).

Southwark I 1450 I Cade's Rebellion

See **London Bridge**

Southwold Bay I 1672 I 3rd Dutch War

See **Sole Bay**

Souville I 1916 I World War I (Western Front)

Despite failure northeast of **Verdun** at **Fleury** (1 July), General Konstantin Schmidt von Knobelsdorf attacked again from **Vaux** towards Souville. German troops managed to secure some outer fortifications before they were eventually driven off by stubborn French defence under General Charles Mangin. A third attack was launched days later further north through **Fleury** (11–15 July 1916).

Soyang I 1951 I Korean War

See **No Name Line**

Spalmadori ∣ 1695 ∣ Venetian-Turkish Wars

When Venetian Captain-General Antonio Zeno captured **Chios** from the Turks in September 1694, Grand Admiral Amjazadé Hussein Pasha was sent to recover the island, off western Turkey. Two naval battles off the nearby Spalmadori Islands saw both sides suffer heavy losses, but Zeno was badly defeated and abandoned Chios. He was arrested for failure and died in prison (9 & 19 February 1695).

Spanish Armada ∣ 1588 ∣ Anglo-Spanish Wars

In one of Europe's most decisive naval actions, the 124-ship Spanish Armada commanded by Admiral Alonso Perez Duke of Medina Sidonia was defeated in the English Channel by Thomas Lord Howard and Sir Francis Drake, with no English ships lost. Storms then completed the destruction of Spain's fleet and King Philip II's planned invasion of England was abandoned (21–30 July 1588).

Spanish Fork Canyon ∣ 1863 ∣ Ute Indian Wars

Determined to protect settlers and the overland mail, about 200 California cavalry under Colonel George S. Evans attacked the Ute at Spanish Fork Canyon, south of Provo in central Utah. Coming just months after the Shoshone were routed at **Bear River**, the Ute were defeated. Their Chiefs soon signed a treaty with Colonel Patrick Connor and Governor James Doty (15 April 1863).

Spanish Fort ∣ 1865 ∣ American Civil War (Western Theatre)

On expedition east from New Orleans, Union General Edward R. S. Canby led an assault on Mobile Bay where, aided by General Frederick Steele, he besieged strategic Spanish Fort, Alabama, opposite Mobile. Defeated and cut off, garrison commander General Randall L. Gibson and most of his force escaped. Canby then marched north to complete the siege of **Blakely** (27 March–8 April 1865).

Spartolus ∣ 429 BC ∣ Great Peloponnesian War

Soon after taking **Potidaea**, Athens tried to extend control further north in Chalcidice and sent 2,000 hoplites and 200 cavalry under Xenophon, Hestiodorus and Phanomachus, to take over the city of Spartolus. However, when nearby Olynthus sent reinforcements, the Athenians were routed outside Spartolus, with their Generals and 430 men killed. The survivors withdrew to Potidaea (May 429 BC).

Speicher ∣ 1403 ∣ Habsburg-Swiss Wars

When the people of Appenzell in northeast Switzerland rose against their Habsburg Lord—Abbot Cuno of St Gall—they faced a large force of armoured cavalry and infantry raised from the Imperial cities of Swabia. Aided by men of Schwyz and Glarus, the Appenzellers routed the Germans at Speicher, near St Gall. Two years later, they beat an Austrian Imperial army at **Stoss** (15 May 1403).

Spercheios ∣ 996 ∣ Byzantine Wars of Tsar Samuel

Amid continuing war between Byzantium and Bulgaria, Tsar Samuel of Bulgaria invaded Greece, then found his way home blocked by the Byzantine General Nicephorus Uranus. The Byzantine army attacked Samuel's camp at the Spercheios River, near Thermopylae, crushing the invaders. A fresh Bulgarian offensive 20 years later was destroyed at **Balathista**.

Speyer ∣ 1703 ∣ War of the Spanish Succession

Marshal Count Camille de Tallard captured the Rhine city of **Breisach** (6 September), then advanced north into the Palatinate against Speyer, 12 miles from Ludwigshafen. In a disastrous defeat, Austrian commander Prince Frederick of Hesse-Cassel was surprised and captured. The French then retook **Landau**, 15 miles to the southwest, which had been lost a year earlier (13 November 1703).

Speyer ▌ 1792 ▌ French Revolutionary Wars (1st Coalition)

A week after the "Cannonade of **Valmy**" drove the Prussian invaders out of France, advance French units under General Adam Philippe Custine reached the Rhine and quickly captured the Austrian strongpoint at Speyer, south of Ludwigshaven. French forces managed to hold the town until the Prussian offensive in July 1794 (30 September 1792).

Sphakteria ▌ 425 BC ▌ Great Peloponnesian War

See **Pylos-Sphacteria**

Sphakteria ▌ 1825 ▌ Greek War of Independence

With **Navarino** holding out against Turkish-Egyptian siege, Hussein Bey Djertili, conqueror of **Kasos**, led 3,000 men against nearby Sphakteria, off Pylos Bay. The strategic island was taken at bayonet-point in a brilliant assault, with 350 Greeks killed and 200 captured, and Pylos fell three days later. Hussein Bey died the following year in the failed attack outside Missolonghi at **Klissova** (8 May 1825).

Spicheren ▌ 1870 ▌ Franco-Prussian War

French forward units were advancing through **Saarbrucken**, when General Charles Auguste Frossard came under attack to the southwest near Forbach at Spicheren by Generals Karl Steinmetz and August von Goeben. Despite initial superiority in numbers, French hesitancy led to defeat. Frossard fell back towards **Metz** to join other forces beaten the same day at **Wörth** (6 August 1870).

Spin Baldak ▌ 1919 ▌ 3rd British-Afghan War

Amir Amanullah of Afghanistan crossed his eastern border into India near **Bagh** (11 May) and, in response, British General Richard Wapshare invaded southern Afghanistan, attacking the border town of Spin Baldak, southeast of Kandahar. The fortress fell after six hours of shelling, with about 350 Afghan casualties among the garrison of 600. Fighting in the south effectively ended (27 May 1919).

Spion Kop ▌ 1900 ▌ 2nd Anglo-Boer War

Five weeks after disaster at **Colenso**, British General Sir Redvers Buller made another attempt to relieve **Ladysmith**, besieged by Louis Botha. While General Sir Charles Warren achieved initial success attacking a Boer position on a ridge to the southwest at Spion Kop, it turned into disaster and Buller withdrew with over 1,000 casualties. He soon tried again at **Vaal Kranz** (23–24 January 1900).

Spirit Lake ▌ 1857 ▌ Sioux Indian Wars

When the white trader Henry Lott killed a Sioux Chief and his family (1854), his kinsman Inkpadutah swore revenge and later attacked the small settlement of Spirit Lake in northwest Iowa. His band killed 38 settlers and carried off four women, of whom only two survived. Pursuing troops from Fort Ridgely failed to catch Inkpadutah and he died in exile in Canada in 1861 (8–12 March 1857).

Spithead ▌ 1545 ▌ French War of Henry VIII

After English forces had captured **Boulogne**, French Mareschal Claude d'Annebault took an invasion fleet against England. However, following an indecisive action against Admiral John Dudley Lord Lisle off Spithead (in which *Mary Rose* foundered with heavy loss of life), the French withdrew. Peace the following year saw France recognise the English conquest of Boulogne (18–19 July 1545).

Spitzbergen ▌ 1943 ▌ World War II (Northern Europe)

Determined to destroy the Norwegian weather station on the Arctic Island of Spitzbergen, the German battleships *Tirpitz* and *Scharnhorst* and nine destroyers under Admiral Erich Bey bombarded Barentsburg township, then landed and seized the garrison. It was noted as the only occasion *Tirpitz* fired on any enemy. *Scharnhorst* was sunk three months later off **North Cape** (8 September 1943).

Split Rock I 1776 I War of the American Revolution
See **Valcour Island**

Spokane Plain I 1858 I Yakima Indian Wars

With Indians in eastern Washington resisting removal to reservations, Colonel George Wright won at **Four Lakes**, then days later met the united tribes on nearby Spokane Plain. The Coer d'Alanes, Spokanes and Palouses were decisively defeated, though Kamiakin of the Yakima escaped. His nephew Qualchin was hanged and his brother Owhi was shot escaping, ending the war (5 September 1858).

Spotsylvania Court House I 1864 I American Civil War (Eastern Theatre)

Union commander Ulysses S. Grant continued his offensive in Virginia, moving south from the action in the **Wilderness** to attack General Robert E. Lee's defensive position next day at Spotsylvania Court House. After some of the heaviest fighting of the war—with 18,000 Union and 12,000 Confederate casualties—Grant disengaged and continued south to the **North Anna** (8–21 May 1864).

Springfield, Massachusetts I 1787 I Shays' Rebellion

A rebellion in Massachusetts against taxes and debt saw former army officer Daniel Shays lead a force against the Federal armory at Springfield. Without waiting for reinforcements, militia General William Shepard attacked and dispersed Shays' men. Two days later Federal troops under General Benjamin Lincoln defeated a separate force under Luke Day, son of a wealthy Springfield family (25–27 January 1787).

Springfield, Missouri I 1861 I American Civil War (Trans-Mississippi)

Determined to secure Missouri, Union commander John C. Frémont took a large force from St Louis against the southwest of the state. In a brilliant cavalry action outside Springfield, his vanguard under Major James Zagonyi routed Confederate militia led by Colonel James Frazier and captured the town. However, Frémont was soon dismissed for his previous failure at **Lexington** (25 October 1861).

Springfield, Missouri I 1863 I American Civil War (Trans-Mississippi)

A month after a Confederate repulse in northwest Arkansas at **Prairie Grove**, General John S. Marmaduke led an expedition towards Springfield, across the border in Missouri, defended by a scratch Union force under General Egbert B. Brown. While Brown was badly wounded, the Union militia held firm against repeated attacks and Marmaduke withdrew east towards **Hartville** (8 January 1863).

Springfield, New Jersey I 1780 I War of the American Revolution

British General Wilhelm Knyphausen led an offensive into New Jersey, advancing towards Springfield, where he was halted (7 June) by General Nathanael Greene. After receiving reinforcements, Knyphausen advanced again in force and burned much of Springfield. He was eventually repulsed by Greene and General William Maxwell and withdrew to Staten Island (23 June 1780).

Spring Hill I 1864 I American Civil War (Western Theatre)

Confederate commander John B. Hood was marching through Tennessee towards **Nashville** when he met Union General John M. Schofield at **Columbia**. Supported by General Nathan B. Forrest's cavalry, Hood tried to outflank Schofield further north at Spring Hill. However, the attempt was driven off and the two armies continued north to the bloody action at **Franklin** (29 November 1864).

Springs of Cresson I 1187 I 3rd Crusade
See **Cresson**

Spurs I 1302 I Franco-Flemish Wars
See **Courtrai**

Spurs I 1513 I War of the Holy League
See **Guinegate**

Srebrenica ▎ 1993–1995 ▎ Bosnian War

As Serbian forces swept northeast Bosnia, perhaps 50,000 Muslim refugees crowded into Srebrenica, which became the first UN-declared "safe haven." As Bosnian General Radko Mladic advanced to take the besieged city, promised NATO air-strikes were cancelled and Dutch peacekeepers failed to prevent thousands of men and boys being taken away and killed (March 1993–11 July 1995).

Sremska Mitrovica ▎ 441 ▎ Hun Invasion of the Roman Empire
See **Sirmium**

Sremska Mitrovica ▎ 580–582 ▎ Byzantine-Balkan Wars
See **Sirmium**

Srinigar ▎ 1947 ▎ 1st Indo-Pakistan War
See **Shalateng**

Sripurambiyan ▎ 880 ▎ Later Indian Dynastic Wars

Varaguna II won Pandya's throne at **Madura** (862), but near Kumbakonam at Sripurambiyan, he was defeated and killed by Prithvipati of West Ganga and Aditya of Chola, fighting for their overlord, Aparajita of Pallava. (Prithvipati was killed in the battle.) Pandya virtually disappeared, but Pallava was also eclipsed when Aditya overthrew his lord Aparajita in 893 and Imperial power passed to Chola.

Srirangam ▎ 1752 ▎ 2nd Carnatic War
See **Seringham**

Srirangapatnam ▎ 1792 ▎ 3rd British-Mysore War
See **Seringapatam**

Srirangapatnam ▎ 1799 ▎ 4th British-Mysore War
See **Seringapatam**

Ssu-ming ▎ 1285 ▎ Mongol Wars of Kubilai Khan
See **Siming**

Ssupingchieh ▎ 1946 ▎ 3rd Chinese Revolutionary Civil War
See **Siping**

Ssu shui ▎ 621 ▎ Rise of the Tang Dynasty
See **Hulao**

Stadt ▎ 1900 ▎ 2nd Anglo-Boer War

During the siege of **Mafeking**, Boer commander Jacobus "Koos" Snyman authorised an assault by Cornet Sarel Eloff, who broke into an outlying position to the southwest, known as the Stadt (held mainly by Baralong auxiliaries) and captured Colonel Charles O. Hore. Major Alexander Godley led a sharp counter-attack and Eloff surrendered, with 60 casualties and 100 captured (12 May 1900).

Stadtlohn ▎ 1623 ▎ Thirty Years War (Palatinate War)

Christian of Brunswick attempted to revive the Protestant cause in Lower Saxony, but was attacked by a massive Catholic army under Johan Tserclaes Count Tilly. Withdrawing towards the Netherlands, Christian made a stand at Stadtlohn in Munster, where his army was destroyed. Frederick V, Palatine of the Rhine soon made peace with Emperor Ferdinand II (6 August 1623).

Staffarda ▎ 1690 ▎ War of the Grand Alliance

As they advanced into Italian Savoy, the French army of Louis XIV led by General Nicolas Catinat met Victor Amadeus Duke of Savoy at Staffarda, south of Pinerolo near Turin. During a decisive one-sided engagement, Catinat inflicted heavy casualties and captured 10 of 11 Italian guns. Victory enabled the French to secure Savoy and they went on to capture much of Piedmont (18 August 1690).

Stainmore ▎ 954 ▎ Viking Wars in Britain

In the confused struggle for Northumbria between Saxon and Viking forces following **Brunanburh**, a Saxon army defeated and killed Norwegian claimant Erik Bloodaxe in a decisive battle at Stainmore, near Edendale, Westmoreland. The rival Danish claimant Olaf Sihtricsson was driven to Ireland and Eadred of Wessex finally ended Norse rule of northern England.

Stalingrad | 1942–1943 | World War II (Eastern Front)

Having reached Stalingrad (modern Volgagrad), General Friedrich von Paulus was halted by General Vasilii Chuikov and trapped by massive encircling counter-attacks. After a failed relief effort at **Kotelnikovo**, Paulus surrendered. One of history's bloodiest battles cost 800,000 Germans and over one million Russians killed, arguably deciding the war in Europe (24 August 1942–2 February 1943).

Stalluponen | 1914 | World War I (Eastern Front)

The first major action in the east took place when German Corps commander Herman von Francois led an unauthorised attack on General Pavel Rennenkampf entering East Prussia. Francois checked the Russian army at Stalluponen (modern Nesterov) and took 3,000 prisoners. He then fell back west to **Gumbinnen** to support the main German counter-offensive (17 August 1914).

Stalowicz | 1771 | Polish Rebellion

After Polish defeat at **Lanskroun** (10 May), Hetman Michael Oginski of Lithuania took command against Russia and established a defensive position with 5,000 men at Stalowicz, in northeast Poland. In a brilliant night action, he was attacked in the rear and routed by General Alexander Suvorov. Oginski fled to Prussia and his Nationalist army virtually ceased to exist (23 September 1771).

Stamford Bridge | 1066 | Norwegian Invasion of England

Facing an invasion of Northumbria by Harald Hadrada of Norway, Harold II of England had to rush north after English defeat at **Fulford** (20 September). East of York at Stamford Bridge on the Derwent, Harold killed the Norwegian King and his own renegade brother Tostig. However, the costly victory fatally damaged Harold's

strength against the Norman invasion at **Hastings** (25 September 1066).

Stamford Hill | 1643 | British Civil Wars
See **Stratton**

Standard | 1138 | Anglo-Scottish Territorial Wars

David I of Scotland took advantage of a period of instability in England to cross the border and capture **Clitheroe** (10 June) before advancing towards Northallerton against an English army led by Archbishop Thurston of York. In the Battle of the Standard—named for relics of English Saints borne into the fray—King David suffered a terrible defeat and withdrew north (22 August 1138).

Stangebjerg | 1028 | Norwegian Wars of Succession

Threatened by Olaf II Haraldsson of Norway and Anund Jakob of Sweden, Knut II, King of Denmark and England, defeated their combined fleets at **Helgeaa**. Two years later, Knut inflicted an even more decisive naval defeat off Stangebjerg, in East Scania. Olaf then fled into exile in Kiev and Knut seized the throne of Norway. Olaf returned in 1030 and was killed at **Stiklestad**.

Stangebro | 1598 | Swedish War of Succession

After John III of Sweden died, war broke out between his Lutheran brother Duke Charles and Catholic son Sigismund III of Poland, who invaded Sweden. In fighting at Stangebro, near Linkoping, Sigismund was decisively defeated and withdrew. The Duke later became King Charles IX, upholding Lutheranism in Sweden, but he was beaten in Livonia at **Kirkholm** in 1605 (25 September 1598).

Stanilesti | 1711 | Russian Invasion of Moldavia

When Turkey declared war on Russia in support of Charles XII of Sweden, Tsar Peter I unwisely invaded Turkish Moldavia with 40,000 men and was surrounded on the Pruth near Stanilesti by 200,000 Turks under Grand Vizier

Baltaji Mehmet. After heavy casualties in three days' fighting, the Tsar was unexpectedly offered terms. He withdrew after agreeing to abandon Azov (9–12 July 1711).

Stanislau I 1917 I World War I (Eastern Front)

As the southern element of the **Kerensky Offensive**, General Lavr Kornilov attacked around Stanislau (modern Ivano-Frankovsk) against Austrian General Karl Tersztyánsky and broke through to seize Kalusz and Halisz. With German victory further north around **Tarnopol**, a counter-attack retook Stanislau, Czernowitz and all of Galicia, driving Kornilov back to the Zbrucz (6–24 July 1917).

Stanley I 1982 I Falklands War

After establishing a bridgehead on East Falkland at **San Carlos** (26 May), British forces advanced east across the island towards Stanley. Very heavy fighting west of the capital— including **Mount Longdon** and **Mount Tumbledown**—crushed Argentine resistance. General Mario Menendez in Stanley surrendered to General Jeremy Moore, effectively ending the 72-day war (14 June 1982).

Stanleyville I 1964 I Congolese Civil War

During rebellion in eastern Congo, leftists under Gaston Sumialot seized Stanleyville (modern Kisangani) and over 1,000 white hostages (4 August). Prime Minister Moise Tshombe's mercenary army advanced behind 600 Belgian paratroops flown in on American aircraft and Stanleyville was retaken, with about 150 hostages killed. The rebellion was then crushed (24–27 November 1964).

Staraya Ryazan I 1237 I Mongol Conquest of Russia

See **Ryazan**

Stara Zagora I 1877 I Russo-Turkish Wars

Soon after Russians crossed the Danube at **Svistov**, Turkish commander Suleiman Pasha found his way north through the Balkans blocked at the small town of Stara Zagora by Bulgarians led by General Nikolai Gregorivich Stoletov and Russian General Osip Gourko. Heroic defence by the small garrison delayed the Turks and enabled the Russians to fortify the **Shipka Pass** (31 July 1877).

Starlite I 1965 I Vietnam War

See **Chu Lai**

Staten Island I 1777 I War of the American Revolution

General George Washington attacked the British in New York, sending General John Sullivan to land on Staten Island, where he burned facilities at Decker's Ferry then marched towards Richmond. However, General John Campbell had recently been reinforced by Commander General Sir Henry Clinton and the Americans were repulsed, losing a large number of prisoners (21–22 August 1777).

Staunton River Bridge I 1864 I American Civil War (Eastern Theatre)

While raiding southwest of **Petersburg**, Union Generals James Wilson and Augustus V. Kautz were blocked at Staunton River Bridge, outside Randolph, Virginia, by a scratch force under Captain Benjamin Farinholt. Wilson was driven off by the pursuing Confederate cavalry of General William H. F. Lee and withdrew east through **Sappony Church** (25 June 1864).

Stavropol I 1918 I Russian Civil War

Defeated mid-year at **Torgovaya** and **Ekaterinodar**, and with General Ivan Sorokin executed after a failed coup, disorganised Red forces in the Kuban attempted to hold Stavropol against victorious White commander Anton Denikin. With the city surrounded, the Reds fought a bloody breakout, leaving behind 2,500 dead and 4,000 wounded. Stavropol quickly fell (4–15 November 1918).

Stavuchany I 1739 I Austro-Russian-Turkish War

Despite an earlier repulse at **Bender** (1738), Russian Marshal Count Burkhard Christoph von

Münnich gathered fresh forces to advance into Moldavia. On the Dniester near Khotin at Stavuchany he routed a much larger Turkish army under Grand Vizier Al-Haji Mohammed and next day captured Khotin. However, Austria soon abandoned her ally and Russia had to make peace (17 August 1739).

Steenkirk I 1692 I War of the Grand Alliance

William III of England and Holland, commanding the Allied army in Flanders, failed to drive off the French siege of Namur and manoeuvred for some months before attacking French Marshal Duke Francois Henri of Luxembourg, near the coast at Steenkirk. William was repulsed with heavy losses and 12 months later he was defeated again at **Neerwinden** (3 August 1692).

Steen Mountain I 1878 I Bannock Indian War

See **Silver Creek, Oregon**

Steenwijk I 1580–1581 I Netherlands War of Independence

Turning against William of Orange, Georges van Lalaing—Count Rennenberg and Stadtholder of Groningen—declared for Spain and took a force against Steenwijk, held by Johann van de Korpput and 19-year-old William Louis of Nassau. The siege was broken after four months and Rennenberg withdrew. He died a few months later after defeat at **Kollum** (18 October 1580–23 February 1581).

Steenwijk I 1592 I Netherlands War of Independence

Instead of relying on siege and starvation, Prince Maurice of Orange turned a powerful bombardment on the fortress of Steenwijk. Using his troops to dig siege positions under the direction of engineers Joost Mattheus and Jacob Kemp, Maurice fired over 29,000 rounds from 50 guns and the Spanish garrison of 1,000 under Antonio Coquel surrendered (28 May–3 June 1592).

Stefaniana I 1344 I Serbian Imperial Wars

While Stephan Dushan was expanding Serbian power into Macedonia, a Turkish naval force of the Emir of Smyrna was beaten at sea by the Venetians and came ashore near Salonika in northern Greece to return home by land. They were pursued by mailed Serbian cavalry led by Gregory Preljub and at nearby Stefaniana the 3,000 Turks turned and routed Preljub's horsemen (May 1344).

Steinau I 1633 I Thirty Years War (Swedish War)

Imperial General Albrecht von Wallenstein was determined to extend his personal power and advanced against the Swedes in Silesia, where he attacked Steinau, on the Oder. He captured the city and about 6,000 prisoners, including veteran Count Matthias Thurn, but he controversially released Thurn without ransom. In February 1634 Wallenstein was murdered by his own officers (13 October 1633).

Steinkirk I 1692 I War of the Grand Alliance

See **Steenkirk**

Stephenson's Depot I 1864 I American Civil War (Eastern Theatre)

As Confederate General Jubal A. Early retreated into the Shenandoah Valley from **Fort Stevens**, near Washington, D.C., part of his force under General Stephen D. Ramseur was attacked at Stephenson's Depot, just north of Winchester, Virginia, by Union General William W. Averell. Ramseur was badly beaten and Early withdrew. But he soon struck back at **Kernstown** (20 July 1864).

Steppes I 1391 I Conquests of Tamerlane

See **Kunduzcha**

Steptoe Butte I 1858 I Yakima Indian Wars

See **Pine Creek**

Stiklestad I 1030 I Norwegian Wars of Succession

Driven into exile after losing at **Stangebjerg** in 1028, Olaf II Haraldsson tried to regain the throne of Norway from Knut II of Denmark. While Knut was campaigning in England, Olaf landed near Trondheim, supported by Anund Jakob of Sweden. However, he was defeated and killed at Stiklestad by Norwegian and Danish forces. Olaf was later canonised as Patron Saint of Norway (29 July 1030).

Stillfried I 1278 I Bohemian Wars
See **Marchfeld**

Stillman's Run I 1832 I Black Hawk Indian War
See **Rock River**

Stillwater I 1777 I War of the American Revolution
See **Saratoga, New York**

Stilo I 982 I Later German Imperial Wars
See **Cotrone**

Stirling I 1297 I William Wallace Revolt

Edward I of England declared himself King of Scotland after victory at **Dunbar** (April 1296), then faced rebellion by William Wallace and sent an army under John de Warenne Earl of Surrey. Crossing Stirling Bridge over the Forth near Cambuskenneth, Surrey's vanguard was routed. Wallace swept across southeastern Scotland before meeting defeat in 1298 at **Falkirk** (11 September 1297).

Stirling I 1304 I William Wallace Revolt

Facing a new offensive by Edward I, launched at **Happrew** in March, Scottish rebel leaders (except Sir William Wallace) submitted and Sir William Oliphant held out in Stirling. But the powerful fortress was forced to surrender after three months of siege under personal direction of the King. The capture and execution of Wallace a year later checked the rebellion (22 April–24 July 1304).

Stirling I 1313–1314 I Rise of Robert the Bruce

As Scotland secured her border areas following victory at **Loudon Hill** in 1307, Edward Bruce besieged the powerful English fortress of Stirling, then unwisely permitted Governor Sir Philip Mowbray a truce, which allowed Edward II to send a massive relief army. However, the English were heavily defeated at nearby **Bannockburn**. Stirling surrendered next day (25 June 1314).

Stirling I 1745–1746 I Jacobite Rebellion (The Forty-Five)

Charles Stuart—Bonnie Prince Charlie—was driven back to Scotland after a failed invasion of England and used French artillery to besiege Stirling, defended by General William Blakeney. An English relief attempt was defeated at **Falkirk**, though the siege was lifted when the Duke William of Cumberland arrived. He beat the Highlanders in April at **Culloden** (December 1745–1 February 1746).

Stirling's Plantation I 1863 I American Civil War (Lower Seaboard)

Two months after defeating a Union force in western Louisiana near Donaldsonville at **Cox's Plantation**, Confederate General Thomas Green was reinforced and attacked General Napoleon J. T. Dana further south at Stirling's Plantation, near Fordoche on the Atchafayala. Green secured a sharp victory before escaping, but the defeat had little strategic impact on the Union (29 September 1863).

Stochod I 1916 I World War I (Eastern Front)

In the second phase of the **Brusilov Offensive** after failure at **Baranovitchi**, Russian General Aleksei Evert attacked along the Stochod towards Kovel, with General Aleksei Kaledin further south. Austrian General Karl Tersztyánsky and the German Georg von der Marwitz stopped the Russians east of Kovel. The offensive also petered out at **Brzezany** (6 July–3 August 1916).

Stockach I 1799 I French Revolutionary Wars (2nd Coalition)

Responding to an Austrian advance into Germany, French General Jean-Baptiste Jourdan crossed the Rhine and, after defeat at **Ostrach**, met Archduke Charles south of Danube at Stockach, near the head of Lake Constance. A bloody and decisive battle cost the Austrians greater casualties, yet they broke up the French offensive and drove Jourdan back to the Rhine (25 March 1799).

Stockach I 1800 I French Revolutionary Wars (2nd Coalition)

During a major French offensive across the Rhine northwest of Lake Constance, while General Jean Victor Moreau was defeating Austrian General Paul Kray in the Black Forest at **Engen**, his right wing under General Claude-Jacques Lecourbe pursued the Austrian rearguard east to Stockach. The Austrians were defeated the same day at heavy cost in prisoners and stores (3 May 1800).

Stoke I 1487 I Simnel's Rebellion

At the end of the War of the Roses, Yorkist forces supported Lambert Simnel, claiming to be Edward Earl of Warwick, son of the murdered Duke of Clarence. Aided in battle by John de la Pole Earl of Lincoln and Francis Lord Lovell, Simnel was routed at Stoke by Henry VII. Lincoln was killed, Lovell disappeared and the pretender was captured and disgraced, ending the rising (16 June 1487).

Stollhofen I 1707 I War of the Spanish Succession

Marshal Claude Villars moved onto the offensive after French disaster in the Netherlands at **Ramillies** (May 1706) and advanced against the defensive line from Stollhofen to the Rhine north of Strasbourg, defended by new Imperial commander Margrave Charles-Ernest of Bayreuth. Villars seized the fortifications by a brilliant night attack, then overran much of southwest Germany (22 May 1707).

Stone Houses I 1837 I Kichai Indian War

In pursuit of Kichai Indians raiding along the Colorado River in Texas, a detachment of 18 Texas Rangers under Lieutenant A. B. van Benthuysen met about 150 Indians outside Windthorst, east of modern Archer City. In bloody action near a rock formation known as the Stone Houses, ten of the Rangers died before the survivors managed to escape to the Sabine River (10 November 1837).

Stones River I 1862–1863 I American Civil War (Western Theatre)

Confederate General Braxton Bragg recovered from defeat at **Perryville** and advanced to Murfreesboro, Tennessee, against General William S. Rosecrans, marching southeast from Nashville. Heavy fighting outside Murfreesboro at Stones River cost Rosecrans more men, but Bragg had to withdraw south. In June Bragg lost again at **Hoover's Gap** (31 December 1862–2 January 1863).

Stoney Creek I 1813 I War of 1812

Withdrawing west along Lake Ontario after being driven out of **Fort George** on the Niagara, British General John Vincent was belatedly pursued by the inexperienced American Generals William Winder and John Chandler. Leading a surprise counter-attack at Stoney Creek, Colonel John Harvey routed and captured Winder and Chandler. Vincent then advanced back to the Niagara (6 June 1813).

Stoney Creek Depot I 1864 I American Civil War (Eastern Theatre)
See **Sappony Church**

Stonington I 1637 I Pequot Indian War
See **Mystic**

Stonington I 1814 I War of 1812
Sent to New Brunswick to enforce local allegiance, Admiral Sir Thomas Hardy secured Moose Island (11 July) then sailed south to bombard Stonington, Connecticut, east of Long Island Sound, held by Captain Jeremiah Holmes. After a barrage of shells and Congreve rockets,

Hardy withdrew with minor damage from shore batteries. The British later attacked **Hampden**, Maine (10–12 August 1814).

Stono Ferry I **1779** I **War of the American Revolution**

The approach of American General Benjamin Lincoln forced General Augustine Prevost to abandon his attack on **Charleston**, South Carolina, and the British commander left a rearguard under Colonel John Maitland at nearby Stono Ferry. Attacking the strongly defended position, Lincoln was repulsed with heavy losses before Maitland withdrew west towards **Savannah** (20 June 1779).

Stony Lake I **1863** I **Sioux Indian Wars**

General Henry Hastings Sibley, advancing into North Dakota in pursuit of Santee and Teton Sioux under Inkpaduta, defeated the Indians at **Big Mound** and **Dead Buffalo Lake**, then after two days came under attack at Stony Lake, in modern Burleigh County. The largest of the actions saw the Indians driven off and they were defeated again six weeks later at **Whitestone Hill** (28 July 1863).

Stony Point I **1779** I **War of the American Revolution**

When Colonel Henry Johnson captured Stony Point on the Hudson near West Point (31 May), American General Anthony Wayne counterattacked and the British garrison surrendered after heavy fighting and about 100 casualties. Threatened by reinforcements under General Sir Henry Clinton, the Americans withdrew two days later. They attacked again next month at **Paulus Hook** (16 July 1779).

Storkyro I **1714** I **2nd "Great" Northern War**

General Karl Gustav Armfelt took over the defence of Swedish Finland from the incompetent General Georg Lybecker and was repulsed by the Russians at Tammerfors (6 October 1713) before making a courageous stand near Vasa at Storkyro (modern Isokyro). However, Armfelt's inexperienced and outnumbered force was de-stroyed and by year's end Finland had fallen (13 March 1714).

Stormberg I **1899** I **2nd Anglo-Boer War**

Supporting a broad British offensive, General Sir William Gatacre moved against a Boer advance from Queenstown and was ambushed near Stormberg by Commandant Jan Hendrik Olivier. In the first disaster of "Black Week," Gatacre lost about 700 casualties and over 600 men captured. The second failure occurred next day to the northwest at **Magersfontein** (10 December 1899).

Stoss I **1405** I **Habsburg-Swiss Wars**

After defeat at **Speicher** in northeast Switzerland (May 1403), the Habsburg Abbot Cuno of St Gall sought aid from Duke Frederick IV of Austria to suppress rebellion in Appenzell. Near Stoss, south of Lake Constance, rebels under Rudolf of Werdenberg destroyed the advancing Imperial army from the heights above. Frederick withdrew and Appenzell joined the Swiss League (17 June 1405).

Stow I **1646** I **British Civil Wars**

The final battle of the First Civil War after Royalist defeat at **Naseby** (June 1645) saw a 1,500-strong Welsh force under Sir Jacob Astley attacked at Stow-on-the Wold, west of Oxford, by Parliamentary forces under Sir Thomas Morgan and Sir William Brereton. Astley was crushed and soon afterwards King Charles I surrendered to imprisonment and eventual execution (21 March 1646).

Stracathro I **1130** I **Scottish Dynastic War**

King David I of Scotland was absent in England when his Constable Edward, son of Siward Beorn, faced a rebellion by Angus MacHeth of Moray and his brother Malcolm. Angus was defeated and killed at Stracathro, on the North Esk near Brechin, along with a reported 4,000 Moraymen. Four years later Malcolm MacHeth was betrayed and imprisoned.

Strachowa I **1423** I **Hussite Wars**

See **Strachuv**

Strachuv **I** 1423 **I** Hussite Wars

As a doctrinal civil war broke out among the Hussites of Bohemia, the Taborite leader Jan Zizka ousted Jetrich of Miletinek, Governor of Hradec Králové, whose brother Divis Borek marched from **Kromeriz** to lead the men of Prague and the Utraquist faction. While the Praguers were routed just southwest of Hradec Králové at Strachuv Dvur, they were soon avenged at **Tynec** (4 August 1423).

Straits of Tiran **I** 1956 **I** Arab-Israeli Sinai War

When Egypt blocked the Straits of Tiran, Israel launched a pre-emptive war in the Sinai at **Abu Ageila,** then Colonel Avraham Yoffe drove south along the Gulf of Aqaba towards Sharm el-Sheik, held by Colonel Raif Mahfouz Zaki. Joined by Colonel Ariel Sharon from **Mitla Pass,** Yoffe took the fortress to secure the strategic strait and a ceasefire began next day (2–5 November 1956).

Stralsund **I** 1184 **I** Danish Wars of Expansion

Despite victory in 1168 at **Arkona,** Waldemar I of Denmark faced continued attacks by Wendish pirates and Duke Boguslaw of Pomerania led a large fleet to regain the island of Rügen, held by Danish vassal Prince Jaromir. Battle in fog off nearby Stralsund saw a brilliant victory for Waldemar's counselor Bishop Absalon, which effectively ended Pomeranian seapower.

Stralsund **I** 1628 **I** Thirty Years War (Saxon-Danish War)

Catholic forces pursuing Christian IV of Denmark to the Baltic after his loss at **Lutter am Barenberg** (1626) seized Stade, Rostock and Rügen and General Hans von Arnim besieged Stralsund. Imperial commander Albrecht von Wallenstein soon reinforced the siege, but Stralsund held out. Wallenstein eventually withdrew and beat King Christian a month later near **Wolgast** (13 May–5 August 1628).

Stralsund **I** 1714–1715 **I** 2nd "Great" Northern War

Five years after his disastrous defeat at **Poltava** Charles XII of Sweden returned from exile in Turkey and tried to defend the port of Stralsund, in Swedish Pomerania, against siege by Danish and German forces. Heavily repulsed from an attempt to recapture nearby Rügen Island, Charles escaped by boat. Shortly afterwards the ruined city surrendered (November 1714–22 December 1715).

Stralsund **I** 1807 **I** Napoleonic Wars (4th Coalition)

Sent against the Swedish Baltic port of Stralsund, defended by General Jean Henri Essen Governor of Pomerania, French Marshal Édouard Mortier secured the siege, then left to attack Kolberg. Following a powerful German sortie in early April, Mortier returned and reimposed the siege. An armistice was agreed and in September Stralsund was handed to France (30 January–29 April 1807).

Stralsund **I** 1809 **I** Napoleonic Wars (5th Coalition)

In a Prussian rising against French rule, Major Ferdinand von Schill's Hussars fought their way north from Berlin through Mecklenberg and seized the Baltic city of Stralsund, where they were attacked by Dutch and Westphalian troops. Von Schill died in a vicious street battle and his men were imprisoned, while his officers were tried and shot on Napoleon Bonaparte's orders (31 May 1809).

Strasbourg **I** 357 **I** Alemannic Invasion of Roman Gaul

See **Argentoratum**

Strasbourg **I** 1870 **I** Franco-Prussian War

As the French withdrew in disorder after defeat at **Wörth,** Prussian General Karl August von Werder was sent south to recapture Strasbourg, seized by Louis XIV in 1681. Commander Jean Jacques Uhrich held out against siege through heavy bombardment before surrendering almost 18,000 men. Peace in 1871 saw

the city finally restored to Germany (13 August–
28 September 1870).

**Strathbogie I 1058 I Scottish War
of Succession**
See **Essie**

Strathfleet I 1453 I MacDonald Rebellion
Determined to renew the rebellion checked at
Inverlochy (1431), John MacDonald Lord of
the Isles took 500 men into Sutherland, where he
was beaten with terrible losses at Strathfleet,
north of Dornoch, by John Earl of Sutherland.
MacDonald came to terms with the King and
relinquished his Earldom, but in 1480 he was
defeated at the Battle of **Bloody Bay** by his own
illegitimate son Angus Og.

Stratton I 1643 I British Civil Wars
Henry Grey Earl of Stamford was resolved to
prevent Royalist General Sir Ralph Hopton entering Somerset and marched into Cornwall to
occupy defensive works (later called Stamford
Hill) at Stratton, near Bude. While Hopton was
heavily repulsed, a failed counter-attack by
James Chudleigh led to a Parliamentary surrender, yielding 1,700 prisoners and massive stores
(16 May 1643).

Strela I 1184 I Danish Wars of Expansion
See **Stralsund**

**Striegau I 1745 I War of the Austrian
Succession**
See **Hohenfriedberg**

Stromboli I 1676 I 3rd Dutch War
When Sicilians rebelled against Spanish rule,
France sent troops to garrison **Messina** and a
supply convoy under the Marquis Abraham
Duquesne was met near the Lipari Islands off
Stromboli by a Dutch fleet under Michiel de
Ruyter. Although the outcome was indecisive,
de Ruyter's ships inflicted greater damage. The
French lost four ships and failed to renew battle
next day (8 January 1676).

Stronghold I 1873 I Modoc Indian War
See **Lava Beds**

**Strymon I 1185 I 2nd Byzantine-
Sicilian War**
Leading a fresh offensive against the Byzantine Empire, William II "The Good" of Sicily
captured Dyrrhachium and Thessalonica, then
advanced on Constantinople, where he was
ambushed and defeated to the west at the Strymon by Alexius Branas for Emperor Isaac II.
Two months later, Branas beat the Norman fleet
off Greece at **Demetritsa**, halting the Norman
offensive (7 September 1185).

**Strypa I 1915–1916 I World War I
(Eastern Front)**
The first major Russian offensive since the
routs of 1915 saw Generals Dmitry Shcherbachev
and Platon Lechitskii advance on the Bessarabian
front near the Strypa. After initial success against
Austro-Hungarian commander General Karl
Pflanzer-Batlin, the offensive stalled with perhaps
50,000 casualties. The massive **Brusilov Offensive** followed in June (24 December 1915–10
January 1916).

Stuhm I 1629 I 2nd Polish-Swedish War
See **Sztum**

**Stura I 1822 I Greek War
of Independence**
In search of glory in eastern Greece, Elias
Mavromichales (son of Greek leader Petros) and
the Montenegrin Vassos attacked Stura, the
magazine and grain-store for Karystos, in
southeast Euboea. When Omer Bey arrived with
reinforcements, young Mavromichales was defeated and killed. Omer Bey secured his supplies
before withdrawing to Karystos (24 January
1822).

Styr I 1916 I World War I (Eastern Front)
Near the start of the second phase of the **Brusilov Offensive**, Russian General Leonid Lesh
attacked along the Styr north of Lutsk, smashing a
salient near Kolki and advancing through Mane-
vici towards **Kovel**. Austro-German commander

Alexander Linsingen ordered his army group to withdraw, then sent reinforcements to help a rally on the **Stochod** halt the Russians (4–7 July 1916).

Styrsudden ▮ 1790 ▮ 2nd Russo-Swedish War
See **Kronstadt Bay**

Suan ▮ 1761 ▮ Seven Years War (India)
A third abortive advance into Bengal saw Mughal Emperor Shah Alam II and his French General Jean Law try to besiege Patna, defended by Major John Carnac and the troops of Nawab Mir Jafar of Bengal. Just west of Bihar City at Suan, the Imperial army was routed and Law was overpowered and captured. The Emperor was later allowed to retire to Oudh (15 January 1761).

Subachoque ▮ 1861 ▮ Colombian Civil Wars
Twelve months after being checked at **Manizales**, rebel General Tomás Cipriano de Mosquera resumed the war against the government of Mariano Ospina and marched towards Bogotá. Just to the northwest at Subachoque, he met and decisively defeated the government force of General Joaquin Paris. In July, Mosquera won again at **Bogotá** itself and resumed the Presidency (25 April 1861).

Sucat ▮ 1899 ▮ Philippine-American War
American commander Elwell S. Otis faced fresh insurgent activity in southern Luzon and sent General Henry W. Lawton, supported by Generals Lloyd Wheaton and Samuel Ovenshine. Met at Sucat by Generals Artemio Ricarte and Mariano Noriel, the Americans suffered a humilating defeat and had to withdraw. However, Lawton attacked again three days later at the **Zapote** (10 June 1899).

Sucro ▮ 75 BC ▮ Sertorian War
On the offensive against rebel Quintus Sertorius in Spain, Roman commander Gnaeus Pompey won at the **Turia** then soon advanced on Sertorius at the Sucro (modern Jucar). Pompey's left wing under Lucius Afranius met some

success in a premature attack before Pompey was wounded and badly defeated. However, with Quintus Metellus Pius approaching, Sertorius withdrew next day.

Suddasain ▮ 1848 ▮ 2nd British-Sikh War
See **Sadusam**

Sudomer ▮ 1420 ▮ Hussite Wars
Hussite leader Jan Zizka marching south from Prague towards his fortified position at Tabor was attacked by Catholic Royalists at Sudomer (modern Sudomerice). Despite costly Taborite losses—including Lord Benek of Skala killed—the Barons were heavily defeated. Within months Zizka had won again at **Porici** and against King Sigismund himself at **Vitkov Hill** (25 March 1420).

Suenske Sound ▮ 1790 ▮ 2nd Russo-Swedish War
See **Svenskund**

Suessa ▮ 339 BC ▮ Latin War
Determined to resist the Roman conquest of central Italy, the Legions of Latium took the field with Capuan allies against an army led by the Consuls Manlius Torquatus and Decius Mus. The Latins were repulsed with heavy losses near the foot of Rocca Monfina, at Suessa, although Decius died on the battlefield. The war was virtually over and Latium was absorbed under Roman control.

Suez Canal ▮ 1915 ▮ World War I (Middle East)
Advancing on the Suez Canal in hope of triggering a Muslim rising in Egypt, Turkish commander Ahmed Djemal Pasha led 25,000 men across the Sinai. Met at the canal around Ismailia by mainly Indian troops under General Alexander Wilson, Djemal was repulsed with over 1,000 men lost and returned to Beersheba. Turkey's next major advance was checked at **Romani** (3 February 1915).

Suez Canal (1st) ▌ 1973 ▌ Arab-Israeli Yom Kippur War

After massive bombardment, Egyptian General Sa'ad el Din Shazli launched a brilliant surprise assault across the Suez Canal towards the Bar-Lev defensive line, inflicting terrible losses in men, tanks and aircraft. Israel suffered further costly losses in a disastrous counter-attack by Generals Ariel Sharon and Avraham Adan and Egypt soon captured the Bar-Lev Line (6–8 October 1973).

Suez Canal (2nd) ▌ 1973 ▌ Arab-Israeli Yom Kippur War

From bridgeheads east of the Suez Canal, Egyptian General Sa'ad el Din Shazli launched a huge offensive east against Israeli forces under General Shmuel Gonen. One of history's largest armoured actions saw about 2,000 tanks in combat. However, the Egyptian effort was dispersed along a 100-mile front and they were fought to a standstill, with up to 260 tanks lost (14 October 1973).

Suez Canal (3rd) ▌ 1973 ▌ Arab-Israeli Yom Kippur War

Israeli Generals Ariel Sharon and Avraham Adan blunted Egypt's last advance into the Sinai, then assumed the offensive against Arab bridgeheads east of the Suez Canal. After severe fighting at **Chinese Farm**, Israeli forces surrounded key Egyptian units and stormed across the canal to threaten major cities on the West Bank. Egypt quickly accepted a ceasefire (15–22 October 1973).

Sufetula ▌ 647 ▌ Muslim Conquest of North Africa

Marching west from Egypt with a substantial army, General Abdullah ibn Saad besieged Tripoli, then faced a relief force from Carthage under Gregory, Byzantine Governor of North Africa. A prolonged battle at Sufetula (modern Sbeitla) saw Gregory defeated and killed (reputedly by Abdullah, son of the great warrior Zubayr). General Abdullah returned to Alexandria with massive booty.

Suffolk ▌ 1863 ▌ American Civil War (Eastern Theatre)

Confederate General James Longstreet resumed the offensive in southern Virginia, besieging the Union garrison at Suffolk under General John J. Peach. General Samuel G. French occupied nearby Fort Huger but was driven out by a Union counter-attack. After Confederate failure in North Carolina at **Washington** (20 April), Longstreet was recalled to **Fredericksburg** (11 April–4 May 1863).

Sufiyan ▌ 1605 ▌ Turko-Persian Wars

After Shah Abbas of Persia had advanced into Turkish Azerbaijan and recovered key cities including **Tabriz**, **Erivan** and Kars, he marched north again to meet a large-scale counter-offensive by teenage Sultan Ahmed I. At Sufiyan, northeast of Lake Urmiya, the Turkish army under Cighalzade Sinan Pasha was destroyed. Eventual peace yielded much land to Persia (9 September 1605).

Sugar Loaf Rock ▌ 1753 ▌ 2nd Carnatic War

See **Trichinopoly (3rd)**

Suipacha ▌ 1810 ▌ Argentine War of Independence

The first Argentine Patriot victory over Spain saw General Antonio González Balcarce and Juan José Castelli recover from loss at **Cotagaita** (27 October) to rout a Spanish force at Suipacha, near Tupiza in the southwest of modern Bolivia. Royalist Generals Vicente Nieto and José de Cordoba and Intendente Paulo Sanz were captured and shot, but the Patriots soon lost at **Huaqui** (7 November 1810).

Suiyang ▌ 757 ▌ An Lushan Rebellion

The rebel An Lushan captured **Luoyang** and **Chang'an**, then sent a large force under Yin Ziji into Henan, where Zhang Xun determined to hold Suiyang (near modern Shangqiu). After an epic 122-day siege, with relief just three days away, the starving survivors surrendered and Zhang Xun was executed. Meanwhile, the

Tang counter-offensive had begun at **Xiangji** (February–24 November 757).

Sulechow I 1759 I Seven Years War (Europe)
See **Kay**

Suleimaniya I 1987 I Iraq-Iran War
Despite failure in the south around **Basra**, Iran renewed its effort in Iraqi Kurdistan with a broad offensive around Suleimaniya. Along with its Kurdish allies, Iran threatened Mawat in the north, took the strategic heights near Suleimaniya itself and the city of Arabit to the south. Iraq responded with chemical attacks on Kurdish villages and the atrocity at **Halabja** in March 1988 (April–June 1987).

Sullivan's Island I 1776 I War of the American Revolution
See **Fort Sullivan**

Sultanpur I 1858 I Indian Mutiny
See **Badshahganj**

Sulusaray I 692 I Early Byzantine-Muslim Wars
See **Sebastopolis**

Sumbilla I 1813 I Napoleonic Wars (Peninsular Campaign)
During the weeklong "Battles of the Pyrenees," British General Sir Lowry Cole pursued the defeated French after **Sorauren** and on the Bidassoa at Sumbilla two days later, he caught up with French units under General Bertrand Clausel. A sharp action forced Clausel's men to withdraw and continue their retreat towards France (1 August 1813).

Summa I 1940 I Russo-Finnish War
See **Mannerheim Line**

Summit Point I 1864 I American Civil War (Eastern Theatre)
When Union General Philip Sheridan moved south from the Potomac into the Shenandoah near Charlestown, he was attacked to the southwest at Summit Point, West Virginia, by converging Confederate Generals Jubal A. Early and Richard H. Anderson. Although fighting was inconclusive, Sheridan suffered more casualties and withdrew north to Harper's Ferry (21 August 1864).

Summit Springs I 1869 I Cheyenne-Arapaho Indian War
The southern Cheyenne attempted to march from northern Texas to join their tribal brethren in Wyoming and were intercepted in northeast Colorado at Summit Springs by cavalry under Major Eugene Carr. A surprise attack on the Indian camp saw more than 50 killed (including Chief Tall Bull) and another 177 captured, effectively destroying the southern Cheyenne (11 July 1869).

Sumter I 1861 I American Civil War (Lower Seaboard)
See **Fort Sumter**

Sunchon I 1598 I Japanese Invasion of Korea
As the Japanese withdrew to a few key fortresses in southern Korea, the great commander Konishi Yukinaga was blockaded at Sunchon by a Korean-Chinese fleet under Chen Lin and troops led by Liu Ting. After failing to bribe his besiegers, a Japanese victory at **Sachon** allowed Konishi to break the blockade. However, he was soon defeated at sea off **Noryang** (19 October–6 December 1598).

Sunda Strait I 1942 I World War II (Pacific)
The day after disaster in the **Java Sea**, the Allied cruisers *Perth* and *Houston* attacked Japanese transports in the Sunda Strait, between Java and Sumatra. However, they were sunk by Admiral Takeo Kurita. Late that night, the damaged cruiser *Exeter* and two destroyers were also sunk by Kurita. Only four US destroyers escaped from Java, which fell a week later (28 February–1 March 1942).

Sundays ❙ 1802 ❙ 3rd Cape Frontier War

A renewed offensive along the Sundays River in eastern Cape Province after failure in February at **Roodewal** saw commandant Tjaart van der Walt join Hendrik Janse van Rensberg. In two months they killed 200 Xhosa and recovered 13,000 cattle, but when van der Walt was killed at Baviaanskloof the war soon ended. The Xhosa later agreed not to cross the Zuurveld (June–August 1802).

Sungari ❙ 1114 ❙ Jurchen Invasion of Northern China
See **Songhua**

Sungari ❙ 1947 ❙ 3rd Chinese Revolutionary Civil War
See **Songhua**

Sung-chou ❙ 641 ❙ Tang Imperial Wars
See **Sungqu**

Sungkiang ❙ 1860 ❙ Taiping Rebellion
See **Songjiang**

Sungqu ❙ 641 ❙ Tang Imperial Wars

The great Tibetan leader Srong-brtsan-sgampo united his country into a strong confederation, then took a huge army against Imperial China and besieged Sungqu (modern Songpan) in northwestern Sichuan. Tang Emperor Taizong sent a massive force which defeated and drove off the invaders. However, he then made peace, sealed by giving his niece in marriage to the Tibetan King.

Sungshan ❙ 1944 ❙ World War II (China)
See **Songshan**

Sunomata ❙ 1181 ❙ Gempei War

New commander Taira Munemori recovered from a rout at **Fujigawa** (November 1180) to march east from Kyoto against Minamoto Yukiie, who was advancing to support his victorious nephew Yoritomo. Attacking across the Sunomata, near modern Nagoya, Yukiie suffered terrible defeat, losing perhaps 400 dead.

Two years later, he joined the Minamoto victory at **Shinowara** (25 April 1181).

Suntel Hill ❙ 782 ❙ Wars of Charlemagne

Saxon rebels under Chief Widikund rose against Frankish authority and defeated an army sent by Charlemagne, King of the Franks, at Suntel Hill, near modern Hanover in Lower Saxony. The defeat provoked a terrible slaughter of Saxon prisoners by the Franks, which ensured continuing support for the rebellion.

Suoi Tre ❙ 1967 ❙ Vietnam War

After earlier falling back before an Allied sweep in the **Iron Triangle**, northwest of Saigon, Viet Cong and North Vietnamese stood firm against a new US and South Vietnamese offensive further north. Heaviest fighting was at Suoi Tre, where the Communists counterattacked in force. Operation Junction City ended when the Communists withdrew into Cambodia (22 February–14 May 1967).

Suomussalmi ❙ 1939 ❙ Russo-Finnish War

On the offensive in central Finland, two Russian divisions converged on Suomussalmi and General Andrei Zelentsov took the village. He then came under sustained attack by Finnish Generals Wiljo Tuompo and Hjalmar Siilasvuo. The Russian 163rd Division was completely destroyed, with Zelentsov killed and the Finns turned against a second Russian force on the **Raate Road** (7–28 December 1939).

Suo'yi Ford ❙ 1852 ❙ Taiping Rebellion

Marching north through Guangxi, the Taiping army was ambushed just north of **Quanzhou** at the strategic Suo'yi Ford by a small Imperial force under Zhiang Zhongyuan. Heavy fighting saw a large number of rebels burned in boats or drowned, but Zhiang had too few troops for decisive victory and the battered Taiping entered Hunan. A few months later, they attacked **Changsha** (10 June 1852).

Supa ❙ 1596 ❙ Mughal-Ahmadnagar Wars

When Mughal forces withdrew from the siege of **Ahmadnagar**, the Bahadur Nizam Shah unwisely sent his army under Soheil Khan in pursuit into Berar. Mughal allies Raja Ali Khan of Kandeish and the Hindu Raja Ram Chundur were defeated on the Godaveri at Supa. However, the next day Soheil's Deccan army was beaten by the outnumbered Mughal Khan Khanan (27–28 December 1596).

Sur I 1820 I Anglo-Arab Wars

After Britain captured **Ras al-Khaimah** in the Persian Gulf (December 1819), Captain Thomas Perronet Thompson joined Sultan Saiyid Said of Muscat in a rash expedition against the Banu Bu Ali in Oman. The Allies were heavily repulsed near Sur, though the defeat was avenged early the next year at **Balad Bani Bu Ali**. Thompson was tried and reprimanded for his rash attack (9 November 1820).

Surabaya I 1942 I World War II (Pacific)
See **Java Sea**

Surabaya I 1945 I Indonesian War of Independence

British-Indian forces supporting Dutch reoccupation of Indonesia after Japanese surrender landed in Jakarta and advanced on Surabaya. When General Aubertin Mallaby was killed while negotiating with Nationalists, a counterattack under General Robert Mansergh took Surabaya in the bloodiest battle of the war. The last British troops left Indonesia a year later (10–19 November 1945).

Surat I 1664 I Mughal-Maratha Wars

Maratha warlord Shivaji followed an audacious raid on **Poona** (April 1663) by advancing against the key Mughal port of Surat, north of Bombay. When Governor Inayat-ulla Khan tried to assassinate him, Shivaji subjected the city to two days of destruction before withdrawing to meet an approaching Mughal army at **Purandar**. He returned in 1670 to sack the city again (8–9 January 1664).

Surat I 1670 I Mughal-Maratha Wars

On a second raid against the wealthy Mughal port of Surat, north of Bombay, the great Maratha Shivaji learned it had only a weak garrison after the death of its Governor and attacked with a force of 15,000 horsemen. With three days of pillage, Shivaji completed the destruction he had started six years earlier, then withdrew to meet an approaching Mughal army at **Dindori** (3–6 October 1670).

Surigao Strait I 1944 I World War II (Pacific)

While one Japanese naval force was being checked in the central Philippines' **Sibuyan Sea**, further south Admirals Shoji Nishimura and Kiyohide Shima joined to break through the Surigao Strait into **Leyte Gulf**. In the last classic battleship line-action, American Admiral Jesse Oldendorf sank two Japanese battleships, a cruiser and three destroyers and halted Japan's advance (24–25 October 1944).

Surinam I 1800 I French Revolutionary Wars (2nd Coalition)

To punish the occupation of Holland by Revolutionary France, a British force under Admiral Lord Hugh Seymour (Commander in Chief in Jamaica) and General Sir Thomas Trigge was sent to capture the Dutch colony of Surinam on the northeastern coast of South America. The colony fell with little resistance and was returned to the Dutch in 1802 (August 1800).

Surinam I 1804 I Napoleonic Wars (3rd Coalition)

In recognition of the renewed French occupation of Holland, Britain once again sent a force to occupy the Dutch South American colony of Surinam, which had been returned in 1802. Commodore Samuel Hood (1722–1814) and General Sir Charles Green landed at the Surinam River and just three days of fighting saw the colony fall. It was held until the end of the war (25–28 April 1804).

Surveyors' Fight I 1838 I Kickapoo Indian Wars
See **Battle Creek, Texas**

Susangerd | 1980 | Iraq-Iran War

As Iraqi forces entered Khuzestan, they took undefended Susangerd (28 September) but left no garrison and it was retaken by Iran. After being repulsed at Dezful and **Ahwaz** in October, Iraq returned to launch a massive assault on the city yet failed, despite huge superiority in men and armour. Iran held the strategic salient at Susangerd and later launched its own offensive (13–21 November 1980).

Susangerd | 1981 | Iraq-Iran War

Having halted Iraqi invaders at **Ahwaz** and **Susangerd** in late 1980, Iran launched a poorly co-ordinated armoured counter-offensive south from Susangerd to relieve besieged **Abadan**. Advancing deep into Iraq's positions, the Iranians were attacked on three sides and withdrew after losing over 100 tanks. Iraq also suffered heavy losses though it was able to recover or replace its tanks (6–8 January 1981).

Sutherland Station | 1865 | American Civil War (Eastern Theatre)

Union General Nelson A. Miles marched north towards the Appomattox River, west of Petersburg, Virginia, where he attacked and defeated Confederate forces under Generals Henry Heth and Cadmus Wilcox on the Southside Railroad at Sutherland Station. The Union victory cut the last rail supply route to besieged **Petersburg**, which was evacuated later that night (2 April 1865).

Suthul | 109 BC | Jugurthine War

When King Jugurtha of Numidia attacked Roman interests in North Africa, General Aulus Albinus took a large army against his fortress at Suthul, near Calama (modern Guelma) in northeastern Algeria. Aulus suffered a humiliating defeat and his army of 40,000 was reputedly forced to "pass under the yoke" before being allowed to withdraw. Rome was avenged a year later at the **Muthul**.

Sutia | 1858 | Indian Mutiny
See **Shamsabad**

Suvla Bay | 1915 | World War I (Gallipoli)

Determined to break the Gallipoli deadlock, British General Sir Frederick Stopford was sent north with 20,000 troops to Suvla Bay. However, his force failed to advance quickly enough and reinforced Turkish units met and contained the fresh landing. Stopford was dismissed and, after subsequent failure at **Scimitar Hill**, Suvla was evacuated 18–20 December (6–10 August 1915).

Suwayda | 1925 | Druze Rebellion

Druze Sultan al-Atrash rose against France's Mandate in Syria and routed a column at **Kafr**, then besieged the southeastern town of Suwayda. A relief column was destroyed at **Mazraa**, but new French commander General Maurice Gamelin broke through the siege. Desperately short of supplies, the French destroyed much of the town and withdrew to **Damascus** (21 July–24 September 1925).

Suwayda | 1926 | Druze Rebellion

On the offensive against Druze rebellion in southern Syria, French General Charles Andréa marched from Azra with Legionnaires and Tunisians to retake the key town of Suwayda, abandoned to rebels the previous September. Suwayda fell by assault with costly losses on both sides. Following a failed rising in **Damascus**, Druze Sultan al-Atrash soon fled to Jordan (25 April 1926).

Suzdal | 1445 | Russian-Mongol Wars

When Mongol Khan Ulug-Mahmed raided into Russia, Prince Vasili II of Moscow marched out and attacked the Khan at Suzdal, where Vasili was defeated and captured. After being ransomed and released, he was overthrown and blinded by his cousin Shemiaka (to avenge the blinding of his brother Kosoi by Vasili after **Skoriatino**). Shemiaka was eventually poisoned and Vasili restored.

Suzhou **I** 475–473 BC **I** Wars of China's Spring and Autumn Era

In the struggle between Wu and Yeu for the fertile Yangzi Delta, King Goujian of Yeu defeated neighbouring Wu at the **Lizhe** (478 BC), then gathered a large army and invaded Wu to invest the capital at Suzhou (Soochow). After a three-year siege, the city fell and King Fuchai hanged himself. Wu was then incorporated into Yeu, which was in turn overwhelmed by Chu 140 years later.

Suzhou **I** 1366–1367 **I** Rise of the Ming Dynasty

Having defeated the Han at **Poyang Lake**, Ming commander Zhu Yuanzhang took a large army into Wu, where he besieged and took Huzhou and Hangzhou. Ming General Xu Da then besieged the city of Suzhou, held by Wu leader Zhang Shicheng. When Suzhou finally fell, Zhu had conquered all his main rivals and established the Ming Dynasty, which ruled until 1644 (27 December 1366–1 October 1367).

Suzhou **I** 1863 **I** Taiping Rebellion

On campaign west from **Shanghai**, Imperial commander Li Hongzhang besieged Suzhou and seized surrounding towns. Facing defeat, Taiping General Li Xuicheng withdrew, but Tan Shaoguang refused to surrender and was killed by a Taiping peace faction. Li Hongzhang seized the city, killing the traitors and their followers, then advanced on **Changzhou** (22 August–6 December 1863).

Sveaborg **I** 1808 **I** Napoleonic Wars (Russo-Swedish War)

Shortly after the Russian invasion of Swedish Finland, Russian Count Jan van Suchtelen besieged the fortress of Sveaborg, outside Helsinki harbour. But the Swedish army under General Wilhelm Klingspor had already retreated north. After minimal fighting, commandant Admiral Karl Kronstedt shamefully surrendered the most powerful bastion in all Finland (3 May 1808).

Sveaborg **I** 1855 **I** Crimean War

In a sidelight to war against Russia in the Crimea, Anglo-French forces in the Baltic under Admirals Sir Richard Dundas and Charles Penaud unsuccessfully blockaded Kronstadt, then bombarded the fortress of Sveaborg, off Helsinki harbour. After causing some damage and 56 casualties, the Allies withdrew. The focus of their attention then returned to the Black Sea (9–11 August 1855).

Svendborg **I** 1535 **I** Danish Counts' War
See **Bornholm**

Svenskund **I** 1789 **I** 2nd Russo-Swedish War

On the same day that the Swedish army under Gustav III was defeated at **Fredriksham**, on the Gulf of Finland east of Helsinki, Swedish Admiral Karl Ehrensward met Russian forces under Prince Charles Nassau-Siegen nearby on the Svenskund (Russian Rochensalm). The Swedish flotilla withdrew after heavy losses and Ehrensward lost again a week later off **Hogfors** (24 August 1789).

Svenskund **I** 1790 **I** 2nd Russo-Swedish War

After inflicting heavy losses on the Swedish fleet escaping from **Vyborg Bay**, Russian Prince Charles Nassau-Siegen rashly attacked the Swedish ships on the nearby Svenskund, commanded by King Gustav III and Colonel Carl Cronstedt. A one-sided disaster cost the Russians more than 50 ships and massive casualties. However, Sweden quickly made peace without any gain (9–10 July 1790).

Sverdlovsk **I** 1918 **I** Russian Civil War
See **Ekaterinburg**

Svetigrad **I** 1448 **I** Albanian-Turkish Wars

Ottoman Sultan Murad II invaded Albania to besiege Svetigrad (Kodjadjik), then advanced against **Krujë**. Albanian commander George Kastriote Skanderbeg broke off his siege of Venetian **Danj**, but before he could relieve

Svetigrad, the Turks cut off its water and forced the city to surrender. The Turks were then defeated at **Dibra** before victory in October at **Kossovo** (June–August 1448).

Svistov I 1877 I Russo-Turkish Wars

Shortly after war was declared, Russian Grand Duke Nicholas advanced into northern Bulgaria and launched a surprise attack across the Danube at Svistov, opposite Zimnicea. The Turkish fortress fell to General Mikhail Skobelev and the Russians turned upstream towards **Nicopolis** before marching south against the key stronghold at **Plevna** (26–27 June 1877).

Svolde I 1000 I Scandinavian National Wars

Olaf I Tryggvason seized Norway's throne in 995 and was sailing to claim land in Pomerania when he was attacked southeast of Rügen near Svolde by Sweyn Forkbeard of Denmark, Norwegian Prince Eric Jarl and Olaf Skutkonung of Sweden. A semi-legendary naval battle saw Tryggvason defeated and apparently drowned. Norway was then divided between Sweden and Denmark (9 September 1000).

Swalde I 1000 I Scandinavian National Wars
See **Svolde**

Swally Roads I 1612 I Anglo-Portuguese Colonial Wars

At the mouth of the Tapti River, off Swally north of Bombay, the British galleon *Red Dragon* (Captain Thomas Best) and the pinnace *Osiande*, drove off four Portuguese galleons, marking the real beginning of Britain in India. A Portuguese attack on another British squadron in the Swally Roads was repulsed three years later (20 January 1615) by Captain Nicholas Dowton (29 November 1612).

Swansea I 1675 I King Philip's War

In bloody resistance against white settlement, Chief Metacomet of the Wampanoag—known by the colonists as King Philip—attacked the small town of Swansea, in southeast Massachusetts,

south of Plymouth. The town was abandoned after about ten settlers were killed and it was burned by the Indians, triggering a bitter war in Massachusetts and Rhode Island (24 June 1675).

Swiecin I 1462 I Thirteen Years War
See **Puck**

Swift Creek I 1864 I American Civil War (Eastern Theatre)

Campaigning north of Confederate Petersburg, Virginia, General Benjamin Butler destroyed rail track at **Port Walthall Junction**, then fought an inconclusive action against General Pierre G. T. Beauregard just to the west at Swift Creek. Instead of crossing the Appomattox to outflank the Confederates, Butler withdrew. Days later he advanced again towards **Drewry's Bluff** (9 May 1864).

Sword Beach I 1944 I World War II (Western Europe)
See **D-Day**

Sybota I 433 BC I Corinthian-Corcyrean War

Two years after victory off **Leucimne**, Corcyra (modern Corfu) faced a new offensive by Corinth and a large action was fought at sea south of Corcyra off Sybota. The Corinthian fleet inflicted heavy losses but withdrew when a small Athenian squadron arrived to support Corcyra, allowing both sides to claim victory. Another Athenian check at **Potidaea** triggered the Second Peloponnesian War.

Sycamore Creek I 1832 I Black Hawk Indian War
See **Rock River**

Syllaeum I 677 I Early Byzantine-Muslim Wars

Despite defeat on land at **Amorium** (669), Caliph Mu'awiya established a presence in the Sea of Marmara at Cyzicus and began a blockade of Constantinople (672). However, Arab ships taking troops to reinforce the siege were heavily defeated at Syllaeum, including the first reported use of "Greek Fire." Defeat at sea forced withdrawal of the siege and eased the Arab threat to Eastern Europe.

Syme I 411 BC I Great Peloponnesian War

With Sparta's navy campaigning along the coast of Asia Minor at **Chios** and **Miletus**, Spartan commander Astyochos was sent to defend Knidos and attacked Athenian Admiral Charminos off Syme, northwest of Rhodes. In Sparta's first naval victory of the renewed war, Charminos was defeated, with six ships lost. Athens won later that year at **Cynossema** (January 411 BC).

Syni Vody I 1362 I Russian-Mongol Wars

At the height of Lithuanian power, Grand Duke Algirdas (Olgierd) marched east against the Golden Horde of the Mongols on the Syniukha in the Ukraine. In the so-called Battle of Blue Water at Syni Vody (possibly near Torgovitsa east of Uman), Mongol expansion was finally checked and Algirdas then seized Kiev. In 1380 Mongols on the Don were destroyed at **Kulikovo**.

Syracuse I 415 BC I Great Peloponnesian War

Leading a massive expedition—reputedly comprising 260 ships and 27,000 men—Athenian General Nicias sailed for Sicily to attack the city-state of Syracuse. Nicias advanced against the fortified position at Olympieum, just west of the city, and defeated the Syracusan army in the field. However, he decided not to risk a siege of the city itself and withdrew up the coast to Catana.

Syracuse I 414–413 BC I Great Peloponnesian War

Athenian commander Nicias beat Syracusan forces outside the city and later led a fresh advance from Catana to besiege Syracuse, prompting Sparta to send reinforcements under Gylippus. A new Athenian force sent under Demosthenes tried to encircle Syracuse by occupying the Heights of Epipolae, but they were defeated in a confused night battle (May 414–September 413 BC).

Syracuse I 396 BC I 1st Dionysian War

Ten years after campaigning against the Greeks in Sicily to capture **Acragas**, Carthaginian General Himilco returned to recapture the island city of **Motya** from Dionysius the Elder, Tyrant of Syracuse, then marched against Syracuse itself. With his troops weakened by plague, Himilco could not resist a counter-attack by Dionysius. He was utterly defeated and later committed suicide.

Syracuse I 311–307 BC I Agathoclean War

Beaten by Carthaginians at the **Himera River** (June 311 BC), Agathocles of Syracuse withdrew under siege to his capital in eastern Sicily. Leading a counter-invasion against **Carthage**, Agathocles left his brother Antander in command. Carthaginian commander Hamilcar was later killed outside Syracuse. However, with defeat in Africa and rebellion in Sicily, Agathocles returned and made peace.

Syracuse I 213–212 BC I 2nd Punic War

Syracuse declared for Carthage and Rome sent Marcus Claudius Marcellus to Sicily, where he seized **Leontini** but failed to take Syracuse by storm. A two-year siege captured outer defences and, when fever struck the Syracusan army, killing its commander Hippocrates, Marcellus gained the rest of city through treachery. His troops led a destructive rampage, including killing the great mathematician Archimedes,

Syracuse I 827–828 I Byzantine-Muslim Wars

At the start of the Muslim conquest of Byzantine Sicily, Asad ibn al-Furat landed from North Africa with 10,000 men to capture Mazara, then marched east against Syracuse. During a yearlong siege, a great pestilence killed thousands of Arabs, including Asad. Threatened by reinforcements arriving from Constantinople, the survivors burned their ships and withdrew overland west to Mazara.

Syracuse | 877–878 | Byzantine-Muslim Wars

Fifty years after an initial repulse at Syracuse, the Arab invaders of Sicily had seized most of the island, including **Palermo** and **Messina**. Djafar ibn Muhammad al-Tamini then led a large force to seize the great eastern city. Following a long siege, with no aid from the Emperor, Syracuse was starved into surrender. The fall of **Taormina** in 902 secured Muslim control of Sicily (August 877–21 May 878).

Syracuse | 1085 | Norman Conquest of Southern Italy

Norman victory in the north at **Palermo** in 1072 secured most of Sicily, though the Muslim champion Benavert (Ibn Abbad) continued war in the east of the island, attacking Catania and Calabria. Determined to crush resistance, Count Roger I of Sicily besieged Syracuse and Benavert was killed in battle for the port. The fall of Noti in 1091 completed the 30-year conquest of the island (25 May 1085).

Syracuse | 1676 | 3rd Dutch War
See **Augusta, Sicily**

Syracuse Harbour | 413 BC | Great Peloponnesian War

Having failed to blockade Syracuse by land, Athenians under Nicias and Demosthenes tried to break out of Great Harbour, where their fleet was stationed. But a decisive action against the combined Corinthian and Syracusan fleets saw the Athenian ships overwhelmed. Nicias and Demosthenes tried to retire overland but they were routed at the Assinarus and both were executed (September 413 BC).

Syr Darya | 329 BC | Conquests of Alexander the Great
See **Jaxartes**

Syr Darya | 1389 | Conquests of Tamerlane

While the Turko-Mongol Tamerlane campaigned in Persia, his rebellious former protégé Toktamish, Mongol Khan of the Golden Horde, crossed the Oxus to threaten Samarkand in Uzbeskistan. Pursued north to the Syr Darya River, Toktamish's rearguard suffered a terrible defeat at the hands of Tamerlane. The great conqueror beat him again three years later at **Kunduzcha** and finally at the **Terek** in 1395.

Syria | 1941 | World War II (Middle East)

With a pro-British government restored in **Iraq**, General Henry Wilson and Free French commander Paul Legentilhomme took a large force into Vichy Syria and **Lebanon**. There was sharp action before Damascus fell (21 June), but fighting continued at **Palmyra** before Vichy General Henri Dentz surrendered. Most of his troops returned home rather than join the Allies (8 June–14 July 1941).

Syriam | 1613 | Burmese Dynastic Wars

King Anaukpetlun resolved to restore control in Lower Burma and besieged the key port of Syriam, held since the fall of **Pegu** in 1599 by Portuguese adventurer Felipe de Brito, who had alienated his former Mon allies by looting and enforced conversions. With de Brito defeated, then executed by impalement, the Portuguese garrison was expelled and Anaukpetlun consolidated his kingdom.

Szalankemen | 1691 | Later Turkish-Habsburg Wars
See **Slankamen**

Szczara | 1920 | Russo-Polish War

Russian forces routed northeast of **Warsaw** on the **Nieman** retreated south and east under Generals Dimitri Shuvaev and Avgust Kork. They were attacked days later on the Szczara by Polish General Franciszek Krajowski and Byelorussian Cossack commander Stanislau Balakhovich. The Red Army suffered further terrible losses and within days Russia sued for peace (27–28 September 1920).

**Szczekociny I 1794 I War of the
2nd Polish Partition**

In renewed Polish insurrection, the Russian garrison of Warsaw was bloodily expelled and Frederick William III of Prussia took his army into Poland. Commander Tadeusz Kosciuszko met the Prussians at Rawka village, near Szczekociny north of Cracow, where he was utterly crushed and retired to defend **Warsaw**. Although Cracow fell, Warsaw held out until the Prussians withdrew (6 June 1794).

**Szentgotthard I 1664 I Later Turkish-
Habsburg Wars**
See **St Gotthard**

Szentkiraly I 1451 I Hungarian Civil War

During a struggle for power in Hungary, Regent Janos Hunyadi took a force to besiege the northern fortress of Szentkiraly, near Lucenec in southern Slovakia, headquarters of General Jan Jiskraz of Brandysa. Jiskraz arrived and heavily defeated Hunyadi, though the Regent eventually neutralised his opponent. A truce was arranged the following year (10 August–7 September 1451).

Szepiele I 1654 I Russo-Polish Wars

While Tsar Alexius besieged **Smolensk**, Prince Aleksei Trubetskoi's Southern Army captured Roslavl (June) and Msistlavl (July), then attacked Lithuanian Prince Janusz Radziwill at Szepiele, northwest of Minsk in Belarus. The Lithuanians and their Polish allies were heavily defeated and Smolensk soon fell before Trubetskoi was recalled to help meet a Swedish invasion (24 August 1654).

**Szepingkau I 1946 I 3rd Chinese
Revolutionary Civil War**
See **Siping**

**Szigetvar I 1566 I Turkish-
Habsburg Wars**

When Turks under the elderly Sultan Suleiman I and Grand Vizier Sokollu Mehmet invaded Hungary, their advance in the southwest was blocked by the stubborn fortress at Szigetvar, held by Count Miklos Zrinyi. Szigetvar fell when Zrinyi and his entire garrison died in an heroic last charge. However, the Sultan had died two days earlier and his army withdrew (5 August–8 September 1566).

Sztum I 1629 I 2nd Polish-Swedish War

After failing to prevent Imperial General George von Arnim reinforcing Polish commander Stanislas Koniecpolski, Gustavus Adolphus of Sweden withdrew his outnumbered army through Marienwerder and was routed by Polish cavalry at nearby Sztum. The King narrowly escaped before withdrawing nine miles north to Marienburg. He soon made peace with Poland (27 June 1629).

**Szylow I 1241 I Mongol Conquest
of Europe**
See **Cracow**

T

Tabora **|** 1916 **|** World War I
(African Colonial Theatre)

In support of the British offensive in German East Africa towards **Morogoro**, Belgian commander Charles Tombeur advanced from the Congo and attacked German General Kurt Wahle in a well-entrenched position at the strategic railway city of Tabora. After large-scale fighting, Wahle and Governor Heinrich Schnee withdrew south through **Iringa** (19 September 1916).

Tabriz **|** 1585 **|** Turko-Persian Wars

At the head of a massive army, Grand Vizier Osman Pasha invaded Azerbaijan against Persian Prince Hamza Mirza. Despite previous Turkish defeat near **Khoi** (1584) Osman captured Tabriz, which remained 20 years in Turkish hands. However, Osman died soon afterwards, and Cighalzada Sinan Pasha led a costly retreat to Erzurum. Hamza was assassinated the following year (23 September 1585).

Tabriz **|** 1603 **|** Turko-Persian Wars

Shah Abbas of Persia regained Herat and the Khorasan from the Uzbeks, then determined to march into the south Caucasus to recover territory lost to the Turks. After a long siege he recaptured Tabriz, then over the following year retook Erivan, Shirwan and Kars. Two years later a Turkish counter-offensive towards Tabriz was defeated at **Sufiyan** (21 October 1603).

Tabriz **|** 1724–1725 **|** Turko-Persian War

When Turkish forces had captured **Erivan**, Kopruluzadeh Abdallah Pasha marched into Azerbaijan against the heavily defended city of Tabriz. A Persian army was beaten at Tabriz, but after the defeat of a massive Turkish supply convoy the invaders withdrew. The following year they returned with an even larger force and Tabriz finally fell. Both sides were said to have lost at least 20,000 men.

Tacámbaro (1st) **|** 1865 **|** Mexican-French War

Colonel Charles-Marie de Potier attempted to block Mexican General Nicolás de Regules advancing towards Morelia and sent Belgian Major Constant Tydgadt to hold Tacámbaro, east of Uruapan. The massively outnumbered Belgians were routed, with Tydgadt fatally wounded, and 200 survivors surrendered. De Potier later pursued and defeated de Regules (11 & 23 April 1865).

Tacámbaro (2nd) **|** 1865 **|** Mexican-French War

Determined to avenge defeat months earlier, Imperial commander Baron Alfred von de Smissen, supported by Zouaves under Colonel Justin Clinchant and Mexicans led by Colonel Ramón Méndez, lured Republican General José María Arteaga into action near Tacámbaro. Arteaga was decisively defeated with heavy losses and he soon lost again at **Santa Ana Amatlan** (11 July 1865).

Tacaña **|** 1871 **|** Central American National Wars

Fifteen months after a false start at **Palencia**, Liberal Revolution began in Guatemala against

President Vicente Cerna and a handful of rebels crossing from Mexico were attacked in the mountains at Tacaña by Captain Antonio Búcaro. Comparing themselves to the Spartans at **Thermopylae**, they beat the government force. Cerna was soon overthrown at **San Lucas Sacatepéquez** (2 April 1871).

Tacauri ▮ 1811 ▮ Paraguayan War of Independence

Near the start of her war against Spain, Argentina sent General Manuel Belgrano to incorporate Paraguay. Defeated by militia Colonel Manuel Atanasio Cavañas at **Cerro Porteño** (15 January), Belgrano met him again in the far south of the country at Tacauri. Cavañas secured another decisive victory, followed by armistice and eventual Paraguayan independence from Argentina (9 March 1811).

Tachau ▮ 1427 ▮ Hussite Wars
See **Tachov**

Tachov ▮ 1427 ▮ Hussite Wars

Despite Imperial defeat at **Aussig** (1426), a huge Catholic force under English Cardinal Henry Beaufort marched into Hussite Bohemia against Taborite leader Prokob the Bald, fresh from victory at **Zwettl**. The German Crusade reached Tachov (German Tachau), west of Pilsen, but fled in disorder before Prokob and the Praguers. There was no fresh crusade until **Domazlice** (4–11 August 1427).

Tacines ▮ 1814 ▮ Colombian War of Independence

Four months after capturing Popayán with victory at **Calibio**, Colombian General Antonio Nariño and Colonel José María Cabal marched south against the Spanish invaders at Pasto. Blocked at Tacines by Marshal Melchor Aymerich, Nariño defeated the Royalists. But when he attempted to seize Pasto, his army was driven off in confusion and the survivors struggled back to Popayán (9 May 1814).

Tacna ▮ 1880 ▮ War of the Pacific

After landing on the Peruvian coast, 10,000 Chileans under General Manuel Baquedano won at **Los Angeles** (22 March) then met the Peruvian-Bolivian allies led by General Narciso Campero at Alto de la Alianza, outside Tacna. Following costly fighting, with 2,000 Chilean and 3,000 Peruvian casualties, the Peruvians withdrew to make a stand against the invaders at **Arica** (26 May 1880).

Tacuarembó ▮ 1820 ▮ Brazilian Occupation of Uruguay

General José Gervasio Artigas tried to establish his authority in the north of modern Uruguay, where he came under attack by Portuguese forces from Brazil. His army under General Andrés Latorre was destroyed by Jose de Castlelo Branco Conde da Figueira in battle at the Tacuarembó Chico, leading to Brazilian occupation of the country. Artigas died in exile in Paraguay (22 January 1820).

Tacubaya ▮ 1859 ▮ Mexican War of the Reform

The Liberal army under Santos Degollado, marching towards Mexico City, was attacked at nearby Tacubaya by Reactionary Generals Leonardo Márquez and Tomás Mejía. Degollado suffered a terrible defeat, with massive losses in men and arms and was pursued through Chapultepec. Márquez slaughtered the wounded and prisoners, becoming known as the Tiger of Tacubaya (11 April 1859).

Tadcaster ▮ 1642 ▮ British Civil Wars

With Leeds captured, Parliamentary forces under Ferdinando Lord Fairfax and his son Sir Thomas advanced to Tadcaster, near York, where they were attacked by William Cavendish Earl of Newcastle. While the Royalists were driven off, Fairfax withdrew to Selby due to lack of ammunition. Earl Newcastle's Cavaliers occupied Tadcaster the next day (6 December 1642).

**Taddert ∎ 1907 ∎ French Colonial Wars
in North Africa**

Moroccan Chief Madoni el Glaoui had **Casablanca** under siege when General Antoine Drude led 2,000 foot and 300 cavalry against his camp eight miles away at Taddert. A slow textbook attack forced the Moroccans to withdraw but Drude failed to secure decisive victory. Although he was soon replaced, the French failed again in January 1908 at **Settat** and **Wadi M'Koun** (12 September 1907).

Taegu ∎ 1950 ∎ Korean War
See **Naktong Bulge**

Taejon ∎ 1950 ∎ Korean War

Storming south from **Seoul**, North Korean forces smashed through American defences at the **Kum**, then advanced to outflank the city of Taejon, held by General William Dean. Newly arrived anti-tank rockets helped slow the Communist advance, but the outnumbered Americans finally had to abandon Taejon. Dean was captured in the withdrawal towards the **Pusan Perimeter** (19–20 July 1950).

**Tafalla ∎ 1813 ∎ Napoleonic Wars
(Peninsular Campaign)**
See **Tiebas**

**Tafileh ∎ 1918 ∎ World War I
(Middle East)**

In a rare set-piece battle during the Arab Revolt, Prince Feisal's brother Zeid seized Tafileh, a market town south of the Dead Sea, and prepared it against Turkish counter-attack. The ensuing action saw a 900-strong Turkish force routed, with a reported 400 killed and 200 captured. Major T. E. Lawrence was promoted to Lieutenant Colonel for planning the victory (16 & 23 January 1918).

**Taghit ∎ 1903 ∎ French Colonial Wars
in North Africa**

On a fresh offensive in western Algeria near the Moroccan border, tribes united under Mulai Amar marched south from Béchar against Taghit, held by Captain Adolphe Susbielle.

Checked by cannon and rifle fire with about 200 killed, the Moroccans eventually withdrew as reinforcements arrived. A week later they destroyed a supply column at **El Moungar** (17–26 August 1903).

Taginae ∎ 552 ∎ Gothic War in Italy

Emperor Justinian launched a decisive offensive to recover Italy from the Ostrogoths, sending General Narses with a large army to defeat Totila. In a mountain valley in the Apennines at Taginae, near modern Gubbio, north of Perugia, the outnumbered Goths were routed, with Totila among the dead. A final battle in 553 on **Mount Lactarius**, south of Naples, ended the power of the Ostrogoths.

**Tagliacozzo ∎ 1268 ∎ Angevin Conquest
of the Two Sicilies**

Two years after Manfred of the Two Sicilies was killed at **Benevento**, his 16-year-old nephew, Emperor Conradin, invaded southern Italy to reclaim the Kingdom from Charles I of Anjou. Near the Salto River at Tagliacozzo, Conradin and his commander, Duke Frederick of Austria, were routed. Charles had them both executed, ending the Hohenstaufen Dynasty (23 August 1268).

**Tagliamento ∎ 1797 ∎ French
Revolutionary Wars (1st Coalition)**

In a delaying action intended to halt Napoleon Bonaparte's advance into northeast Italy after his capture of **Mantua**, Archduke Charles of Austria spread his troops behind the Tagliamento River, from Latisana in the south to Gemona in the north. However, the French advance smashed through his centre near Codroipo and the Austrians withdrew east through Palmanova (16 March 1797).

**Tagliamento ∎ 1805 ∎ Napoleonic Wars
(3rd Coalition)**

With Napoleon Bonaparte campaigning in Austria, Marshal André Masséna fought Archduke Charles in northern Italy at **Caldiero**, then attacked the Austrians at Tagliamento, where Masséna's Germans were forced back in a hard-fought action. However, when French reinforcements threatened to cut him off, Charles retired at night and later withdrew across the Alps (12 November 1805).

Taguanes I 1813 I Venezuelan War of Independence

Advancing from San Carlos towards Caracas, Revolutionary leader Simón Bolívar set out to intercept 1,200 of General Juan Domingo Monteverde's troops withdrawing towards Puerto Cabello under Colonel Julián Izquierdo. Bolívar defeated and killed Izquierdo in a night cavalry attack at Taguanes, southwest of Valencia, then marched in triumph into Valencia and Caracas (31 July 1813).

Tagus I 220 BC I 2nd Punic War

Carthaginian General Hannibal Barca campaigning in central Spain was cut off at the Tagus by an estimated 100,000 local tribesmen from the Tagus north to the Durius (modern Duero). Crossing the Tagus at night by a secret ford, Hannibal attacked the barbarians and inflicted a terrible defeat with massive slaughter. Soon afterwards he triggered war against Rome by attacking the city of **Saguntum**.

Tahir I 1877 I Russo-Turkish Wars

Attempting to prevent Russian General Arzas Artemevich Tergukasov reinforcing the siege of **Kars**, Ahmed Mukhtar, Turkish commander in the Caucasus, ordered Mehmet Pasha to defend the village of Tahir in the Eleskirt Valley. Mehmet was heavily repulsed and killed and, after a costly failed counter-attack by Ahmed Mukhtar, the Turks withdew towards **Erzurum** (16 & 21 June 1877).

Tahkahokuty I 1864 I Sioux Indian Wars
See **Killdeer Mountain**

Tahuda I 683 I Muslim Conquest of North Africa
See **Biskra**

Taierzhuang I 1938 I Sino-Japanese War

As Japanese forces converged on **Xuzhou**, Chinese commander Chiang Kai-shek sent Li Zongren northeast towards Taierzhuang, in southern Shandong on the railway from Jinan. A much-heralded victory saw two Japanese divisions besieged and virtually destroyed before heavy Japanese reinforcements arrived. Xuzhou was later abandoned (31 March–7 April 1938).

Taif I 1916 I World War I (Middle East)

After the relatively easy capture of **Yanbu** for the Arab Revolt, Prince Abdullah took 5,000 men against Taif, southeast of Mecca, where a 3,000-strong garrison held out in the fort. Shelling by Egyptian and captured Turkish guns caused heavy damage, but Abdullah did not attack. With no hope of aid the Turks surrendered, yielding large quantities of guns and stores (16 July–22 September 1916).

Taif I 1924 I Saudi-Hashemite Wars

When Sharif Hussein in Jeddah presumptuously proclaimed himself Caliph, Abd al-Aziz (Ibn Saud) of Nejd sent 3,000 Ikhwan warriors under Khalid ibn Lu'ay and Sultan ibn Bijad against Taif, defended by Hussein's son Ali. The much larger Hashemite army eventually abandoned Taif and Aziz captured Mecca to the north (13 October). The following year he took **Medina** (1–5 September 1924).

Taillebourg I 1242 I Anglo-French Wars

In support of local barons against Louis IX of France, led by Hugh de Lusignan Comte de la Marche, Henry III of England landed his army on the Bay of Biscay to regain Angevin land lost by his father, King John. Henry was defeated at Taillebourg, near the Charente River, southeast of Rochefort. A further defeat at **Saintes** next day forced him back to English-held Gascony (21 July 1242).

Taipingshan I 1895 I Sino-Japanese War

A continued Japanese offensive in southern Manchuria saw Generals Motoharu Yamaji and Maresuke Nogi advance from **Kaiping** against Chinese commander Song Qing at Taipingshan, southwest of beleaguered **Haicheng**. The Chinese were driven out of their entrenchments with costly losses to heavy artillery fire and withdrew northwest towards **Yingkou** (21–31 February 1895).

Taiyuan I 577 I Wei Dynastic Wars

Concluding the long struggle for northern China, Emperor Wu of Northern Zhou (Western Wei) seized **Pingyang**, and advanced up the Fen River to Taiyuan against Emperor Gao Wei of Northern Qi (Eastern Wei). Outside Taiyuan, Wu defeated the army of Qi then took the city by storm. Gao Wei fled and was later killed. Wu then unified northern China under what soon became the Sui Dynasty.

Taiyuan I 1937 I Sino-Japanese War

Driving southwest from **Beijing**, Japan's Guandong Army shrugged off a costly flank attack at **Pingsingguan** (25 September) and advanced on Taiyuan. Chiang Kai-shek's Nationalist forces attempted a forward defence, but after prolonged fighting to the north and east, the walled city fell by storm with heavy loss of life. The Chinese then withdrew west (September–8 November 1937).

Taiyuan I 1949 I 3rd Chinese Revolutionary Civil War

Two months after the fall of **Beijing**, Communist Generals Nie Rongzhen and Xu Xiangqian in northern China renewed the attack on Taiyuan in Shanxi, under siege since July 1948. Local warlord Yan Xishan flew to Nanjing, supposedly to seek help, but did not return. His starving garrison under General Hosaku Imamura was overwhelmed in a bloody final assault (March–24 April 1949).

Takamatsu I 1582 I Japan's Era of the Warring States

Campaigning against the Mori in the west, Oda Nobunaga sent Toyotomi Hideyoshi, who took **Kozuki** and besieged Takamatsu (outside modern Okayama), held for the Mori by Shimizu Muneharu. Hideyoshi diverted the Ashimori River to flood the fortress and Muneharu committed seppuku. Hideyoshi then marched to **Yamazaki** against the retainer who had killed Nobunaga (June 1582).

Takashima I 1281 I Mongol Wars of Kubilai Khan

See **Hakata Bay**

Takashiro I 1587 I Japan's Era of the Warring States

Japanese ruler Toyotomi Hideyoshi intervened in northern Kyushu to repulse Satsuma forces, sending his half-brother Hashiba Hidenaga through **Toshimitsu** to besiege Takashiro in Hyuga, held by Yamada Shinsuke Arinoba. The fortress fell when a Satsuma relief force under Shimazu Iehisa was heavily repulsed. Hidenaga then marched south to join his brother attacking **Kagoshima** (24 May 1587).

Takkolam I 949 I Later Indian Dynastic Wars

Parantaka of Chola annexed Tondaimandalam, where the Banas and Viadumbas appealed to Krishna III of Rashtrakuta. With his brother-in-law, Butuga II of Western Ganga, Krishna won a decisive battle at Takkolam, near Arakkonam. The Cholas were routed, with Crown Prince Rajaditya killed. Chola lost Tondaimandalam and also Madura, but remained a major power in southern India.

Takoon I 1823 I Cape Frontier Wars

The warrior-Queen Ma-Ntatisi and her son Sikonyela led a force of perhaps 40,000 Mantatees towards the Orange River to threaten Griquatown, west of Kimberley. Met at Takoon, near Lattakoo, by about 100 men under Griqua leaders Andries Waterboer and Adam Kok, the Mantatees were defeated with heavy losses, saving the northern border of the young Cape Colony (June 1823).

Taku Forts I 1858 I 2nd Opium War

See **Dagu Forts**

Taku Forts I 1859 I 2nd Opium War

See **Dagu Forts**

Taku Forts I 1860 I 2nd Opium War
See **Dagu Forts**

Taku Forts I 1900 I Boxer Rebellion
See **Dagu Forts**

**Talakad I 1116 I Later Indian
Dynastic Wars**
The Hoysala King Vishnuvardhana determined to recover Gangavadi (modern Mysore
State), which had been seized by the Chola. At
Talakad, east of Mysore, his General Gangaraja
won a brutal battle and Vishnuvardhana started
the great temple of Belur to celebrate victory
over the Chola Dynasty. But despite prolonged
warfare he was never able to overthrow the hegemony of the Chalukya.

Talana Hill I 1899 I 2nd Anglo-Boer War
When Boers invaded Natal and shelled General Sir William Penn Symons at Dundee, he
attacked Lucas Meyer on nearby Talana Hill and
drove the Boers off in a bloody action. The
British suffered about 500 casualties, including
Symons killed. With Dundee still under fire from
Mpati Hill, General James Yule withdrew
southwest through **Rietfontein** to **Ladysmith**
(20 October 1899).

Talas I 751 I Tang Imperial Wars
As Tang Imperial forces advanced west into
Transoxania, they were confronted in modern
Kyrgyzstan by a Turkish-Arab Muslim force
under Ziyad ibn-Salih. At the Talas River,
northeast of Tashkent, in the only major battle
between Chinese and Arab armies, Tang General
Gao Xianzhi was defeated, halting Chinese expansion and securing Central Asia for Islam's
sphere of influence.

**Talavera de la Reina I 1809 I Napoleonic
Wars (Peninsular Campaign)**
British General Sir Arthur Wellesley ad-
vanced along the Tagus from Portugal to support
Spanish troops under General Gregorio Cuesta
and reached Talavera de la Reina, southwest of
Madrid, where the Allies beat a large French
army led by King Joseph Napoleon and Marshal

Claude Victor. Threatened in the north by
Marshal Nicolas Soult, Wellesley eventually fell
back to Portugal (28 July 1809).

**Talavera de la Reina I 1936 I Spanish
Civil War**
With **Badajoz** secured in August, the Nationalist army advanced on **Madrid**, and government forces tried to defend Talavera de la
Reina, the last major city southwest of the capital. Heavy fighting saw rebel Colonel Carlos
Asenio surround and seize the city. Further
Nationalist forces then repulsed a Republican
counter-attack before the advance continued
through **Chapinería** (2–3 September 1936).

**Talcahuano I 1818 I Chilean War
of Independence**
Attempting to reinforce Spanish-ruled Chile
after defeat at the **Maipú** (5 April), Cadiz sent
the frigate *María Isabel* and 11 transports with
2,000 troops and supplies, which were attacked
at Talcahuano, just north of Concepción, by
Chilean squadron commander Manuel Blanco
Encalada. A decisive action saw all but one of
the transports taken and the captured frigate
entered Chilean service (26 October 1818).

**Talegaon I 1779 I 1st British-
Maratha War**
See **Wargaom**

Taleh I 1920 I Wars of the Mad Mullah
Determined to finally crush Muhammad
Abdullah Hassan of Somaliland, a major British
force captured northern Dervish forts including
Baran and **Galiabur**, then pursued the Mullah
south and bombed him at Taleh (Taleex). The
stronghold was captured by Captain Alan Gibbs
of the Camel Corps. The Mullah escaped but
soon died of influenza and the war ended (9
February 1920).

**Tali-lhantala I 1944 I World War II
(Northern Europe)**
See **lhantala**

Talikota ▌ 1565 ▌ Wars of the Deccan Sultanates

Despite rivalry between the Deccan Sultanates, Ali Adil Shah of Bijapur, Husain Nizam Shah of Ahmadnagar, Ali Barid Shah of Bidar and Ibrahim Qutb Shah of Golconda temporarily united against Rama Raya of Vijayanagar. After a massive battle on the Krishna near Talikota, Rama Raya was executed and his capital was destroyed, effectively ending the 200-year Hindu Empire (23 January 1565).

Ta-ling-ho ▌ 1631 ▌ Manchu Conquest of China

See **Dalinghe**

Talladega ▌ 1813 ▌ Creek Indian War

At war with the Creek following a massacre at **Fort Mims**, American General Andrew Jackson struck back at **Littafatchee** and **Tallaseehatchee**, then took over 2,000 men against Indians at Talladega, east of Birmingham, Alabama. More than 500 Creek were killed for minimal American losses, followed by another massacre at **Hillabee**, then a much bigger action at **Horseshoe Bend** (9 November 1813).

Tallaseehatchee ▌ 1813 ▌ Creek Indian War

Two months after disaster at **Fort Mims**, General Andrew Jackson destroyed **Littafatchee**, then sent 1,000 Tennessee militia under General John Coffee against the Creek at Tallaseehatchee, in modern Calhoun County, Alabama. A dawn attack saw the troops kill 186 men and capture 84 women and children for just five Americans killed. The General claimed no man escaped alive (3 November 1813).

Tallinn ▌ 1219 ▌ Danish Wars of Expansion

See **Reval**

Tallinn ▌ 1343 ▌ Wars of the Teutonic Knights

See **Reval**

Tallinn ▌ 1570–1571 ▌ Livonian War

See **Reval**

Tallinn ▌ 1790 ▌ 2nd Russo-Swedish War

See **Reval**

Tallinn ▌ 1919 ▌ Estonian War of Independence

When German forces withdrew from Estonia after World War I, the Red Army invaded (22 November 1918), seizing much of the country and threatening Tallinn. A bold counter-attack near the capital saw General Johan Laidoner defeat the Russians and within two months he had driven them out of Estonia. In June he turned to defeat a German threat from Latvia at **Cesis** (7 January 1919).

Talmay ▌ 1870 ▌ Franco-Prussian War

See **Gray**

Talneer ▌ 1818 ▌ 3rd British-Maratha War

Moving to take possession of Talneer, ceded by Maratha Chieftain Mulhar Rao Holkar of Indore, British forces came under fire from the largely Arab mercenary garrison, which declined to surrender. British General Thomas Hislop stormed the fortress, on the Tapti southwest of Indore, then hanged the Maratha Governor and put the garrison of 300 to the sword (27 February 1818).

Tamai ▌ 1884 ▌ British-Sudan Wars

Generals Sir Gerald Graham and Sir Redvers Buller routed a Mahdist force at **El Teb** to relieve **Tokar**, then marched inland from the Red Sea port of Suakin against Dervish commander Osman Digna at Tamai. The Mahdists "broke a British square" in bloody fighting but were eventually driven off with great slaughter. However, Graham's force was withdrawn to Cairo (13 March 1884).

Tamames ▌ 1809 ▌ Napoleonic Wars (Peninsular Campaign)

Spanish General Lorenzo Duke del Parque marching north towards Salamanca reached Tamames, northeast of Ciudad Rodrigo, where he soundly defeated General Jean-Gabriel Marchand, commanding for Marshal Michel Ney. While the poorly managed French fled, abandoning Salamanca, Parque withdrew from the city two weeks later in the face of a counter-offensive (18 October 1809).

Tamaron I 1037 I Spanish Territorial Wars

In the Spanish territorial war following the death of Sancho the Great of Navarre, his son Ferdinand I of Castile marched against his brother-in-law, the 19-year-old King Bermudo III of Leon. Bermudo was defeated and killed at Tamaron, on the Carrion River east of Leon, and the crown of Leon was absorbed into the Kingdom of Castile (4 September 1037).

Tamatave I 1811 I Napoleonic Wars (5th Coalition)
See **Foule Point**

Tamatave I 1845 I French Conquest of Madagascar

When new Queen Ranavalona I of Madagascar began to threaten Christians and foreigners, two French warships and one British bombarded Tamatave. While a joint landing party then seized an outer battery, the main fortress proved too strong and they had to withdraw with over 80 casualties. Madagascar was isolated from Europe until new King Radama II readmitted foreigners (15 June 1845).

Tamatave I 1883 I French Conquest of Madagascar

On a renewed offensive against Madagascar, French Admiral Pierre-Joseph Pierre occupied Majunga (May) then sailed to the east coast, where he bombarded and captured Tamatave. Pierre died soon afterwards. Following two years of further intermittent fighting, France signed a Treaty of Protectorate to secure Diego Suarez and territory in northern Madagascar (June 1883).

Tammerfors I 1714 I 2nd "Great" Northern War
See **Storkyro**

Tammerfors I 1918 I Finnish War of Independence
See **Tampere**

Tampa I 1862 I American Civil War (Lower Seaboard)

A bold action against Tampa, on the west coast of Florida, saw a Union gunboat under Captain Andrew J. Drake demand the surrender of the town. Drake opened fire when Captain John W. Pearson of the local Osceola Rangers refused to yield, but after two days of unsuccessful intermittent shelling, the Union force had little choice except to withdraw (3 June–1 July 1862).

Tampere I 1918 I Finnish War of Independence

White commander Carl Gustav Mannerheim led a massive offensive in southwest Finland, launching a converging attack on Tampere, defended by Hugo Salmela. Heavy bombardment saw the city taken by storm at the cost of 600 Whites killed. However, the decisive action also saw the Reds lose 2,000 killed and 11,000 captured, with further losses at **Helsinki** and **Vyborg** (3–5 April 1918).

Tampico I 1829 I Spanish Invasion of Mexico

Five years after creation of the Mexican Republic, 3,000 Spanish troops from Havana under General Isidro Barradas seized Tampico. Sailing north from Veracruz with 2,500 men, General Antonio de Santa Anna routed the invaders on the nearby Panuco and the Spanish expedition to recover Mexico surrendered. Santa Anna was proclaimed hero of Tampico (29 July–11 September 1829).

Tampico I 1839 I Mexican Federalist War

When Federalists rose against Mexican President Anastasio Bustamente, General José Urrea fled north from defeat at **Acajete** (3 May) to join General Ignacio Escalada under siege at Tampico by Centralist General Mariano Arista. Heavily outnumbered, Escalada was forced to capitulate. The loss of the Gulf coast port was a major blow to the Federalist cause (26 May–4 June 1839).

Tamsui ∎ 1884 ∎ Sino-French War
  See **Tanshui**

Tanagra ∎ 457 BC ∎ 1st Peloponnesian War
  Facing the threat of a military alliance between Sparta and Thebes, Athenian commander Myronides marched into Boeotia and met a combined force at Tanagra, east of Thebes. After heavy losses on both sides, Athens was defeated when Thessalian cavalry deserted. Despite the victory, Sparta was not able to prevent Athens seizing control of Thebes just two months later at **Oenophyta**.

Tanagra ∎ 426 BC ∎ Great Peloponnesian War
  After a failed expedition against Melos with 60 ships, Athenian commander Nicias landed in Boeotia with 2,000 Hoplites and advanced on Tanagra to support the field army under Hipponicus and Eurymedon marching north from Athens. The main Boeotian army escaped the trap, but at Tanagra the Athenians defeated the Tanagrans (along with some Thebans) then returned to Athens.

Tananarive ∎ 1895 ∎ French Conquest of Madagascar
  General Jacques Duchesne, advancing into Madagascar through **Tsarasoatra** and **Andriba**, suffered terrible losses from malaria, and led a selected party forward against the capital Tananarive. Queen Ranavalona III surrendered after a brief bombardment, and was later exiled. Securing the whole country had cost France more than 6,000 lives, all but a handful lost to disease (30 September 1895).

Tanga ∎ 1914 ∎ World War I (African Colonial Theatre)
  A disastrous expedition to German East Africa began when 8,000 Anglo-Indian troops under Colonel Arthur Aitken landed near Tanga (in modern Tanzania). Colonel Paul von Lettow-Vorbeck and about 1,000 men routed the British

in a confused action, during which swarms of bees attacked both sides. Aitken withdrew with over 800 casualties and was dismissed (4 November 1914).

Tanghangpo ∎ 1592 ∎ Japanese Invasion of Korea
  Korean Admiral Yi Sun-shin assaulted the main Japanese fleet in the islands off southern Korea, inflicted costly losses at **Sachon** and **Tangpo**, before attacking 26 Japanese ships off Tanghangpo Bay, west of Pusan. Lured into pursuit, the Japanese commander was defeated and killed, and Yi's triple victory was complete, costing a total of 72 Japanese ships destroyed (13 July 1592).

Tangier ∎ 1437 ∎ Portuguese Colonial Wars in North Africa
  Twenty-two years after Portugal captured **Ceuta**, on the African side of the Strait of Gibraltar, King Duarte I sent his brothers Henry and Ferdinand against nearby Tangier. The siege was disastrously defeated by Governor Salat ben Salat, who accepted Portuguese surrender in return for Ceuta. Ferdinand was held for ransom and died in captivity when Ceuta was not handed over (September–October 1437).

Tangier ∎ 1471 ∎ Portuguese Colonial Wars in North Africa
  See **Arsilah**

Tangpo ∎ 1592 ∎ Japanese Invasion of Korea
  As the main Japanese fleet arrived west of **Pusan**, Korean Admiral Yi Sun-shin inflicted a costly defeat off **Sachon**. Three days later he attacked 21 Japanese ships at Tangpo, off the Hansan Strait. During a decisive action in narrow waters, Admiral Kurushima Michiyuki was defeated and killed. Yi then sailed north to complete his triple victory at **Tanghangpo** (11 July 1592).

Tangumdae ∎ 1592 ∎ Japanese Invasion of Korea
  See **Chongju**

Tanizahua I 1821 I Ecuadorian War of Independence

Determined to avenge defeat at **Huachi** in late 1820, Patriot Colonel José Garcia marched southwest on Royalist Guaranda, west of Riobambo. A few miles away at Tanizahua, he was ambushed and routed by Royalists under Francisco Xavier Benavides, losing over 500 killed or captured. Garcia was executed, but within a year the Patriots were avenged at **Yaguachi** and **Huachi** (3 January 1821).

Tanjore I 1758 I Seven Years War (India)

French Governor General Comte Thomas Lally captured British **Fort St. David**, on India's southeast coast, then marched inland to besiege Tanjore (modern Thanjavur). However, he lacked sufficient ammunition for his guns. When Admiral Ann-Antoine d'Aché was repulsed in battle off **Negapatam** (3 August), Lally abandoned the siege and returned to the coast (18 July–10 August 1758).

Tannenberg I 1410 I Later Wars of the Teutonic Knights

On a massive offensive against the Teutonic Order, Ladislav II of Poland and Grand Duke Witold of Lithuania met the German knights in a decisive and bloody action between Tannenberg and Grunwald in East Prussia. Grand Master Ulrich von Jungingen was killed, along with half his army, but the Order's capital at Marienburg held out against siege until the allies withdrew (15 July 1410).

Tannenberg I 1914 I World War I (Eastern Front)

Marching into eastern Pussia through **Orlau-Frankenau**, Russian General Aleksander Samsonov advanced on Paul von Hindenburg near Tannenberg (Grunwald, Poland). Samsonov committed suicide after losing 125,000 men and 400 guns to a double envelopment. Hindenburg then turned north to destroy another Russian army at the **Masurian Lakes** (26–31 August 1914).

Tanshui I 1884 I Sino-French War

While French forces blockaded **Chilung** in northern Taiwan to support the war against China in Vietnam, Admiral Sébastien Lespès sailed against the port of Tanshui (Tamsui), 20 miles west, where the river mouth was well protected by a barrage of sunken ships. Lespès landed 600 men but had to withdraw after heavy fighting. The French then established a naval blockade (2 October 1884).

Tanta I 1768 I Mamluk Wars

Mamluk leader Ali Bey returned from exile in Upper Egypt to secure Cairo from his rivals Khalil Bey and Husayn Bey Kashkash (October 1767), then sent General Abu'l-Dhahab northwest to besiege the rebels at Tanta. Khalil and Kashkash were eventually defeated and killed— reportedly while trying to surrender—and Ali Bey continued to assert independence from the Ottomans (May 1768).

Tan-Tan I 1979 I Western Sahara Wars

With Algerian aid, Polisario guerillas from Western Sahara opened a new offensive into southern Morocco, where they overwhelmed the garrison to fight their way into the strategic coastal town of Tan-Tan. The rebels destroyed military installations and the power station before withdrawing. Moroccan field commander Colonel Abdelaziz Bennani was dismissed (28 January 1979).

Taormina I 902 I Byzantine-Muslim Wars

In order to complete the Muslim seizure of Sicily, largely secured with the fall of **Syracuse** in 878, Sultan Ibrahim II abdicated in favour of his son Abdallah to take personal control of operations on the island. The city of Taormina, on the east coast at the foot of Mount Etna, was the main last Byzantine stronghold, and its fall effectively concluded the 80-year conquest of Sicily (1 August 902).

Taos I 1847 I American-Mexican War
See **Pueblo de Taos**

Tapae ∎ 86 ∎ Domitian's Dacian War

Decebalus of Dacia invaded Roman Moesia (roughly Bulgaria), where he killed Governor Oppius Sabinius. Emperor Domitian then sent a large force under his Prefect of the Praetorian Guards, Cornelius Fuscus, who used a bridge of boats to cross the Danube into Dacia itself. In a disastrous defeat near the Dacian capital at Tapae, Fuscus was killed along with up to two entire Legions.

Tapae ∎ 88 ∎ Domitian's Dacian War

Two years after a Roman disaster in Dacia at Tapae, Emperor Domitian sent a fresh army against Decebalus of Dacia, who was threatening Roman Moesia. Veteran Roman commander Tettius Julianus led his Legions across the Danube and routed Decebalus at Tapae, on the plain of Caransebes in modern Romania. However, Rome was threatened by other enemies and agreed to make peace.

Tapae ∎ 101 ∎ 1st Dacian War

Fifteen years after his previous defeat, Decebalus of Dacia renewed war against Rome, and Emperor Trajan crossed the Danube to secure Tibiscum. He then met the Dacian army near Tapae, in modern Romania. After very heavy fighting both sides withdrew to winter quarters. However, peace talks failed and the following year Trajan attacked again for victory near the capital **Sarmizegethusa**.

Tappan Zee ∎ 1781 ∎ War of the American Revolution

In a demonstration of British naval power, a small flotilla under Captain Hyde Parker in the frigate *Phoenix* broke through American defences on the Hudson and sailed upriver to the Tappan Zee, north of Irvington. Colonel Benjamin Tupper failed in an assault on the flotilla (3 August) and, after another unsuccessful attack, Parker ran the gauntlet back down the Hudson (12 July–18 August 1781).

Tapti ∎ 1428 ∎ Malwa-Bahmani Wars
See **Kherla**

Tara ∎ 980 ∎ Later Viking Raids on Britain

Following expulsion from Northumbria after **Stainmore** (954), Olaf Sihtricsson returned to Ireland and led the Danes of Dublin in a long campaign against the native Kings. A decisive battle at Tara, near the Boyne, saw Olaf's heir Reginald defeated and killed by Malachy II. Olaf went into exile, ending the Norse Kingdom of Dublin (apart from a Danish rising in 1014 at **Clontarf**).

Tara ∎ 1798 ∎ Irish Rebellion

At the start of the rebellion in Ireland, about 4,000 rebels gathered at the historic meeting place on Tara Hill, in County Meath, were attacked by 400 Fencibles led by Captain Blanche, supported by a six pounder. The rebels were driven out of their position with about 350 dead, against reported Loyalist losses of just 13 killed and 28 wounded (26 May 1798).

Tarain ∎ 1191 ∎ Later Muslim Conquest of Northern India
See **Taraori**

Tarain ∎ 1216 ∎ Wars of the Delhi Sultanate
See **Taraori**

Tarakan ∎ 1945 ∎ World War II (Pacific)

Following heavy bombardment, Australians under General George Wootten landed on Tarakan Island, off northeast **Borneo**, with its vital airfield and oilfields. The garrison of about 2,000 Japanese fought a bitter defence before being finally driven out with flamethrowers and napalm. The battle cost 240 Australians, and about ten Americans killed and up to 1,600 Japanese dead (1 May–14 June 1945).

Taranto ∎ 1501–1502 ∎ Italian War of Louis XII

After France and Spain had agreed to divide up Naples, Louis XII of France re-invaded northern Italy and Spanish General Gonsalvo de Cordoba besieged Taranto, held by Ferdinand, son of Ferdinand II of Naples. Taranto was captured when Cordoba took ships overland to attack the city from a lake in the rear and Spain and France resumed their war (August 1501–March 1502).

Taranto I 1940 I World War II (War at Sea)

A brilliant coup which presaged **Pearl Harbour** saw Swordfish torpedo bi-planes from the British aircraft carrier *Illustrious* (Admiral Arthur Lyster) attack the Italian fleet at anchor in Taranto. At the cost of just two aircraft shot down, the British sank three battleships and a heavy cruiser. Within six months, all losses except one battleship had been refloated and repaired (11 November 1940).

Taraori I 1191 I Later Muslim Conquest of Northern India

Muhammad of Ghor led a major expedition from the Punjab to the Upper Ganges, where his Muslim-Afghan force met a Hindu army under Raja Prithvaraja of Delhi. At Taraori, near Thanesar on the Saraswati River, north of Ahmadabad, Muhammad was wounded and heavily defeated. He returned a year later and was avenged by victory in another battle near the same location.

Taraori I 1192 I Later Muslim Conquest of Northern India

On a second expedition from the Punjab to the Upper Ganges, the Muslim-Afghan forces of Muhammad of Ghor returned to Taraori, near Thanesar on the Saraswati River north of Ahmadabad. Reversing the previous year's defeat, the Muslim archers defeated Hindu commander Raja Prithvaraja of Delhi, who was captured and executed. Muhammad then took Delhi and the rest of northern India.

Taraori I 1216 I Wars of the Delhi Sultanate

Driven out of Ghazni by Ala-ud-Din Muhammad of Ghor, the Afghan Tajuddin Yildoz marched into India and seized Lahore from Qabacha Nasiruddin, Governor of Sind, then faced an army under Sultan Iltutmish of Delhi. At Taraori, north of Ahmadabad, Yildoz was heavily defeated and taken prisoner by Iltutmish.

He was then sent to Badaun and put to death (25 January 1216).

Tarapacá I 1879 I War of the Pacific

A week after Chilean forces captured Iquique near **San Francisco**, 2,000 men under Colonel Luis Arteaga advancing inland against Tarapacá were intercepted at night by a much larger Peruvian army led by General Juan Buendía. Arteaga had unwisely divided his force and suffered a disastrous defeat, losing almost 700 casualties before being forced to withdraw to Tamarugal (27 November 1879).

Tarascan Frontier I 1478 I Aztec Wars of Conquest

As the Aztec Empire expanded, Emperor Axayacatl then took a reported 24,000 men west against the rival Tarascans, based around Lake Pátzcuaro in Michoacán. In a series of battles along the Tarascan frontier, Axayacatl found himself badly outnumbered and lost perhaps 20,000 men before returning to Tenochtitlan. It was one of the worst defeats of an Aztec army before the Spanish Conquest.

Tarawa I 1943 I World War II (Pacific)

Admiral Henry Hill and General Julian Smith attacked Tarawa, in the **Gilbert Islands**, where the largest island Betio was fiercely defended by 4,800 Japanese under Admiral Shibasaki Keiji. The Americans took the atoll, killing the entire garrison, though losses of 1,000 killed and 2,000 wounded made it one of the bloodiest actions for its size in American history (20–24 November 1943).

Tarbes I 1814 I Napoleonic Wars (Peninsular Campaign)

Withdrawing weeks after defeat north of the Pyrenees at **Orthez**, French Marshal Nicolas Soult faced Arthur Wellesley Lord Wellington advancing from **Aire**, reinforced by Sir William Beresford from Bordeaux and fresh Spanish troops under General Manuel Freire. Soult fought a desperate rearguard action at Tarbes, on the Upper Adour, then escaped towards **Toulouse** (20 March 1814).

**Targu Jiu ❙ 1916 ❙ World War I
(Balkan Front)**

Despite defeat in southern Transylvania at **Hermannstadt** (29 September), Romanians held the key Carpathian passes and General Erich von Falkenhayn sent his Germans west against the Vulcan Pass. While an initial attack was repulsed, a second reinforced assault broke through to Targu Jiu and the Germans advanced through Craiova towards **Bucharest** (23–27 October & 11–15 November 1916).

**Tarifa ❙ 1340 ❙ Later Christian
Reconquest of Spain**
See **Rio Salado**

**Tarifa ❙ 1811–1812 ❙ Napoleonic Wars
(Peninsular Campaign)**

In an unwise mid-winter campaign, French Marshal Nicolas Soult sent General Jean Francois Leval against the fortress of Tarifa, west of Gibraltar, defended by British Colonel John Skerrett and Spanish General Francisco Copons. Bogged down by mud, and facing disease and inadequate ammunition, Leval withdrew after losing over 500 men (20 December 1811–4 January 1812).

**Tarnopol ❙ 1917 ❙ World War I
(Eastern Front)**

With Russia's **Kerensky Offensive** halted southeast of Lemberg (Lvov) around **Brzezany**, Austro-German forces under effective command of General Max Hofmann launched a massive counter-offensive towards General Ivan Erdeli around Tarnopol. The strategic railway city fell in two days, fatally exposing Russia's left flank, and the entire Eastern Front collapsed (19–21 July 1917).

**Tarnopol ❙ 1944 ❙ World War II
(Eastern Front)**

After driving the Germans out of **Kamenets Podolsk**, southeast of Lvov, the First Ukrainians of Marshal Georgi Zhukov advanced north to besiege German forces in the key city of Tarnopol. Many men were lost in an attempted breakout and commander General Egon von Neidorff was killed in very heavy fighting before the city fell. **Lvov** was taken three months later (23 March–15 April 1944).

**Tarnow ❙ 1915 ❙ World War I
(Eastern Front)**
See **Gorlice-Tarnow**

**Tarontin ❙ 1812 ❙ Napoleonic Wars
(Russian Campaign)**

In advance of the French retreat from Moscow, Napoleon Bonaparte sent Marshal Joachim Murat probing towards the southwest, where he met Prince Mikhail Kutuzov at Tarontin, just west of Vinkovo. Murat's cavalry was ambushed by Russian artillery, and suffered heavy casualties, but Murat remained in the area until French defeats at **Vinkovo** and **Maloyaroslavetz** (6 October 1812).

**Tarq ❙ 1002 ❙ Eastern Muslim
Dynastic Wars**

Mahmud of Ghazni marched into the Seistan region on the Eastern Iran border, where he attacked Khalaf ibn Ahmad, who was facing a rebellion of nobles after murdering his son. Besieged at the fortress of Tarq, Khalaf suffered a terrible defeat and surrendered. Mahmud left General Habib Qinji in command but had to return a year later to **Uk** to complete his conquest (November 1002).

Tarq ❙ 1051 ❙ Seljuk Wars of Expansion

Determined to counter Seljuk expansion into eastern Iran, Ghaznavid General Toghril (Qiwan al Daula) besieged Tarq. A Seljuk relief force under Bighu and Abu l'Fadl was repulsed and commander Hilal Daraqi died defending Tarq. However, Toghril could not capture the fortress and withdrew. In 1052 he briefly usurped the throne of Ghazni, but was assassinated (10 November–23 December 1051).

Tarqui ❙ 1829 ❙ Peruvian-Colombian War

When President José de Lamar of Peru invaded Ecuador to annexe Guayaquil, the country was defended by outnumbered Colombian Marshal Antonio José de Sucre. Following a costly Peruvian defeat south of Cuenca at Tarqui, near Giron, de Lamar withdrew. After signing peace he was overthrown by Agustín Gamarra. Sucre was assassinated the following year (28 February 1829).

Tarracina I 314 BC I 2nd Samnite War

On an offensive south of Rome, Samnite forces attacked the powerful coastal fortress of Tarracina (modern Terracina), midway between Rome and Naples near Caudium. Very heavy fighting saw the Samnites repulsed in a courageous defence by Caius Sulpicius Longus, supported by Peotelius, and the strategic citadel was saved.

Tarraco I 218 BC I 2nd Punic War

Despite Carthaginian invasion of Italy for victory at the **Ticinus** and **Trebbia**, General Publius Scipio led two Legions on a counteroffensive into Spain. Marching south to Tarraco (modern Tarragona) Scipio defeated Carthaginian commander Hanno and his local auxiliaries. Hanno and local Chief Andobales were captured and Rome secured northeast Spain as far as the **Ebro River**.

Tarraco I 422 I Roman-Vandal Wars

Campaigning in eastern Spain, the Vandal King Gunderic defeated the Suevi, then met Roman commander Flavius Castinus near Tarraco (modern Tarragona). Following desertion by their Visigoth allies, the Roman army suffered a devastating defeat and the Vandals became masters of Spain. After Gunderic's death a few years later his brother Gaiseric built a kingdom in North Africa.

Tarragona I 1811 I Napoleonic Wars (Peninsular Campaign)

General Louis Suchet left Marshal Jacques Macdonald besieging **Figueras** and invested the strategic Catalan seaport of Tarragona, defended by Spanish General Juan Contreras. The fall of the city effectively secured French control of the entire Catalan seacoast. Suchet was created a Marshal in recognition as he moved on to the siege of **Valencia** (4 May–28 June 1811).

Tarragona I 1813 I Napoleonic Wars (Peninsular Campaign)

Ordered into action to divert Marshal Louis Suchet in Valencia, General Sir John Murray led an incompetent amphibious landing in Catalonia to besiege French-held Tarragona. Despite strong support from Spanish General Francisco Copon, when Murray was threatened by Suchet he withdrew to Alicante, abandoning his guns and stores. He was later court-martialled (3–12 June 1813).

Tarrant's Tavern I 1781 I War of the American Revolution

British commander Charles Earl Cornwallis advanced into North Carolina from victory at **Cowan's Ford**, then the same day sent Tory cavalry Colonel Banastre Tarleton ten miles ahead against rebels at **Tarrant's Tavern**. Repaying his recent terrible defeat at **Cowpens**, Tarleton dispersed the rebel militia and the British continued north towards **Guildford Courthouse** (1 February 1781).

Tarshiha I 1948 I Israeli War of Independence

Days after Arabs attacked **Manara**, Jewish commander Moshe Carmel led a converging offensive against the Lebanese enclave inside Galilee. Heavy fighting saw success in the east at Safad, but a Jewish column, with Druze support, was repulsed with costly losses in the west at Tarshiha. After heavy bombing the town fell by assault, followed by a ceasefire in the north (28–30 October 1948).

Tarsus I 965 I Later Byzantine-Muslim Wars

Determined to drive the Muslims from Asia Minor, Emperor Nicephorus II Phocas captured **Adana** (964) then marched east to besiege the key fortress of Tarsus in Cilicia, held for Sayf ad-Dawla, Emir of Aleppo. The city fell and became Christian once again after Muslim residents abandoned the defence and fled into Syria, where Nicephorus soon captured **Antioch** and **Aleppo** (16 August 965).

Tarsus | 1097 | 1st Crusade

Detaching themselves from the main Crusader advance towards **Antioch, Syria**, Tancred (cousin of Bohemund of Taranto) and Baldwin (brother of Godfrey of Bouillon) took a small force and drove south to the coast of Cilicia. They captured the city of Tarsus after hard fighting, then quarrelled over its possession and Baldwin departed to establish his own Principality at **Edessa** (September 1097).

Tarvis | 1797 | French Revolutionary Wars (1st Coalition)

Napoleon Bonaparte smashed the Austrians in northern Italy, then despatched General André Masséna to cut off their withdrawal through the Carnic Alps at Tarvis. Although Masséna reached the pass first he was repulsed by an Austrian advance force under General Adam Bajalich. However, Masséna routed the Austrians in the decisive battle next day at **Malborghetto** (22 March 1797).

Ta-shih-ch'iao | 1904 | Russo-Japanese War

See **Dashiqiao**

Tashkent | 1365 | Conquests of Tamerlane

On campaign against the Mongol Emirs Tamerlane and Husayn, Khan Ilyas Khoja of Mughalistan marched west to the Syr Darya River and the armies met near Tashkent in Uzbekistan. After a violent storm turned the battlefield into mud, Tamerlane and his brother-in-law Husayn fled, leaving a reported 10,000 dead. Ilyas Khoja then advanced to a failed siege of Samarkand.

Tashkent | 1865 | Russian Conquest of Central Asia

At the start of a new offensive into Central Asia, 2,000 Russians under Colonel Mikhail Chernyaev marched on the key city of Tashkent in the Khanate of Bokhara. The city fell after a sharp action and later became capital of the new territory of Russian Turkestan. Within ten years the Russians had captured **Bokhara** itself and seized the Khanates of **Khiva** and **Khokand** (17 May 1865).

Tashkessan | 1878 | Russo-Turkish Wars

Covering the Turkish withdrawal down the Maritsa Valley from **Plovdiv** to Adrianople, just 2,000 men under Valentine Baker (a disgraced British officer in Turkish service) made a stand at Tashkessan, near Kharmanli. The gallant rearguard held off Russian General Ossip Gourko for ten hours, allowing Shakir Pasha to withdraw, but Baker lost half of his men (1 January 1878).

Tash Kupri | 1885 | Russo-Afghan War

See **Penjdeh**

Tassafaronga | 1942 | World War II (Pacific)

Admiral Raizo Tanaka used destroyers as transports in a final attempt to reinforce **Guadalcanal** where he was met after midnight by a cruiser squadron under Admiral Carleton Wright. Tanaka's torpedoes sank one American cruiser and badly damaged three others for the loss of one Japanese destroyer. However, his landing was repulsed (30 November–1 December 1942).

Tatarahama | 1336 | Ashikaga Rebellion

Driven out of Honshu after defeat at **Kyoto** in February, rebel Samurai leader Ashikaga Takauji gathered support for his opposition to Emperor Go-Daigo, then attacked the Imperialist Kikuchi clan under Kikuchi Taketoshi at Tatarahama, near Hakata. The Ashikaga allies secured a decisive victory and Takauji returned to Honshu in July for his greatest battle at the **Minatogawa** (14 April 1336).

Tatayiba | 1867 | War of the Triple Alliance

Campaigning from besieged **Humaitá** in southwest Paraguay, General Bernadino Caballero's Paraguayans were ambushed about three miles away at Tatayiba by a large Brazilian force under Marshal Luíz Alves de Lima Marquis de Caxias. Caballero was badly beaten and driven back, losing about 500 men on a desperate fighting withdrawal to the protection of the fortress (21 October 1867).

Tatishchevo I 1774 I Pugachev Rebellion
Cossack rebel Emelyan Pugachev had besieged the Ural city of **Orenburg** for six months when General Pyotr Mikhailovich Golitsyn arrived with a relief army of 6,500 men and 25 guns to attack the larger rebel force defending nearby Tatishchevo. When the undisciplined rebels were destroyed, with 2,500 killed and 4,000 more captured, Pugachev fled and the siege collapsed (22 March 1774).

Ta-Tung Mountains I 1852 I Taiping Rebellion
See **Dadong Mountains**

Tauberbischofsheim I 1866 I Seven Weeks War
Following Prussian victory at **Aschaffenburg**, General Erwin von Manteuffel led the advance southeast towards the Tauber, where General Karl von Wrangel attacked Tauberbischofsheim, held by Würtembergers under General Oskar Hardegg. Driven off by artillery fire, Hardegg withdrew northeast through **Gerchsheim** to **Würzburg**. Meanwhile, other Prussians advanced through **Werbach** (24 July 1866).

Tauffes I 1799 I French Revolutionary Wars (2nd Coalition)
French General Jean-Joseph Dessoles advancing towards Switzerland met Austrian General Johann Loudon, who was trying to prevent him joining Claude-Jacques Lecourbe's Rhine army. In the Italian Alps near the Swiss border at Tauffes, Dessoles routed the Austrians, inflicting almost 6,000 casualties and 4,000 prisoners. He entered Glurns next day before joining Lecourbe (25 March 1799).

Taunton I 1645 I British Civil Wars
Fresh from defending **Lyme**, Parliamentary Colonel Robert Blake captured Taunton in Somerset (8 July 1644) and later faced a siege by George Lord Goring. A small reinforcement under Colonel Ralph Weldon broke in (May) and Blake held out until the Royalists withdrew to meet an approaching force under Sir Thomas Fairfax and were defeated at **Langport** (11 March–4 July 1645).

Tauris I 47 BC I Wars of the First Triumvirate
Despite Pompey's great defeat at **Pharsalus** (48 BC), Pompeian Admiral Marcus Octavius besieged the Adriatic city of Epidauris (modern Cavtat near Dubrovnik) held by Quintus Cornificus. With a much smaller fleet, Caesarian Admiral Publius Vatinius boldly attacked Octavius near Tauris (modern Scedro). Octavius was defeated and driven out of the Adriatic and Epidauris was relieved.

Tauromenium I 133 BC I 1st Servile War
After local failure to suppress a large-scale slave rebellion in Sicily—led by Eunus the Syrian and a Cilician named Cleon—Rome despatched veteran Publius Rupilius, who besieged the coastal city of Tauromenium (modern Taormina). After desperate resistance, the starving city fell by treachery. Prisoners were tortured to death and Rupilius turned to attack the main rebel stronghold at **Enna**.

Tauromenium I 36 BC I Wars of the Second Triumvirate
Two days after an indecisive clash with Agrippa at sea off **Mylae**, Sextus Pompeius (Pompey the Younger) slipped through the Straits of Messina and ambushed the remainder of Octavian's fleet off the Sicilian east coast city of Tauromenium (modern Taormina). While Sextus destroyed more than 50 rival ships, his victory was reversed two weeks later at **Naulochus** (15 August 36 BC).

Taus I 1431 I Hussite Wars
See **Domazlice**

Taveta I 1916 I World War I (African Colonial Theatre)
See **Salaita**

Tawurgah I 761 I Berber Rebellion

Continuing the rebellion against Arab rule, the Berber Abu al-Khattab extended control over Tripolitania, Tunisia and eastern Algeria, then defeated Arab armies at Surt (759) and Maghamadas (760). But at Tawurgah, east of Tripoli, Arab General Ibn al Ash'ath decisively defeated and killed al-Khattab and about 12,000 of his followers. Arab rule was then gradually restored (June 761).

Tayasal I 1697 I Spanish-Itzá War
See **Nojpeten**

Tayeizan I 1868 I War of the Meiji Restoration
See **Ueno**

Tay Ket I 1285 I Mongol Wars of Kubilai Khan
See **Siming**

Taylor's Bridge I 1864 I American Civil War (Eastern Theatre)
See **North Anna**

Ta-yüan I 102 BC I Wars of the Former Han
See **Dayuan**

Tblisi I 1795 I Persian-Georgian War
See **Tiflis**

Tcherkovna I 1829 I Russo-Turkish Wars
See **Kulevcha**

Tchermen I 1371 I Ottoman Conquest of the Balkans
See **Maritza**

Tchernaya I 1855 I Crimean War
See **Chernaya**

Tchernigov I 1078 I Russian Dynastic Wars
See **Nezhatina Niva**

Tchernigov I 1094 I Russian Dynastic Wars
See **Chernigov**

Tchesme I 1770 I Catherine the Great's 1st Turkish War
See **Chesme**

Tczew I 1627 I 2nd Polish-Swedish War

Gustavus Adolphus of Sweden supported his siege of **Danzig** in Polish Prussia by capturing nearby **Kasemark**, then attacking Polish commander Stanislas Koniecpolski south of Danzig at Tczew (German Dirschau). In a two-day battle the Swedish cavalry were at first brilliantly successful, before Gustavus was wounded and withdrew. Two years later he was defeated at **Sztum** (7–8 August 1627).

Te Ahuahu, Bay of Islands I 1845 I 1st New Zealand War

After the costly action at **Puketutu**, in New Zealand's far north, Hone Heke withdrew to nearby Te Ahuahu, which was seized during his absence by the pro-government Chief Te Taonui, who was then joined by Tamati Waka Nene. Heke attempted to recover the position but he was heavily repulsed and wounded in a fierce action, then withdrew to join Kaiwiti at **Ohaewai** (12 June 1845).

Te Ahuahu, Taranaki I 1864 I 2nd New Zealand War

Sent south from New Plymouth to destroy crops of the religio-military Hauhau leader Te Ua Hamene, Captain Thomas W. J. Lloyd, with soldiers and military settlers, was attacked by Te Ua at Te Ahuahu, near Oakura. The British suffered seven killed and 12 wounded before reaching Oakura. The unfortunate Lloyd's severed head was dried and became a Hauhau religious icon (6 April 1864).

Te-an I 1206–1207 I Jin-Song Wars
See **De'an**

Teanum I 90 BC I Roman Social War

The Marsi and Samnites of central Italy fighting Rome over citizenship defeated and killed Rutilius Lupus on the **Tolenus**, then confronted his co-Consul Lucius Julius Caesar further south in the Volturno Valley near Teanum. Caesar, who was attempting to relieve the siege of Aesernia, was badly beaten by Marius Egnatius but was soon reinforced and won further down the valley near **Acerrae**.

Te Arei I 1861 I 2nd New Zealand War

On campaign against Wiremu Kingi's Ngatiawa on the Waitara, northeast of New Plymouth after **Mahoetai**, General Thomas Pratt captured the fortified sites at Matarikoriko (28 December) and Huirangi (23 January) before attacking the powerful camp at Te Arei. After British sapping and costly fighting the Maoris surrendered to end the war, but Kingi escaped (2 February–18 March 1861).

Tearless Battle I 368 BC I Wars of the Greek City-States

See **Midea**

Tebaga Gap I 1943 I World War II (Northern Africa)

See **Mareth Line**

Tebicauri I 1868 I War of the Triple Alliance

With the fall of **Humaitá**, in southwest Paraguay, Brazilian commander Jose Joaquim de Andrade Neves marched northeast against Paraguayans on the Rio Tebicauri under Colonel Gorgônio Rojas, earlier defeated at **Nhembucu**. Rojas was defeated and captured in heavy fighting, with 170 Paraguayans killed. Andrade Neves continued advancing north and was killed at **Ita Ybate** (28 August 1868).

Tébourba I 1942 I World War II (Northern Africa)

British General Kenneth Anderson advancing into Tunisia from **Algiers** reached as far as Tébourba, 20 miles west of Tunis, where his forces stalled under sustained counter-attack by newly

arrived German tanks. Very heavy fighting forced the British to withdraw southwest along the Medjerda Valley, where a new advance in December failed at **Longstop Hill** (27 November–4 December 1942).

Tecoac I 1876 I Diaz Revolt in Mexico

Ending a confused war, Porfirio Diaz recovered from defeat at **Icamole**, and met Federal General Ignacio Alatorre at Tecoac, north of Huamantla. While Diaz was initially repulsed, General Manuel Gonzalez arrived to help secure a decisive victory, taking over 3,000 prisoners. President Sebastián Lerdo de Tejada fled into exile and Diaz dominated Mexico until 1911 (16 November 1876).

Tegea I 473 BC I Arcadian War

After supporting Sparta against Persia at **Plataea** (479 BC), the cities of Arcadia (in the central Peloponnese) began to resist their former ally and the main city-state Tegea joined with Argos. In battle at Tegea, Sparta achieved a narrow victory but could not repress the Arcadian cities, most of which united to meet the Spartans again in 417 BC at **Dipaea** (uncertain date c 473 BC).

Tegucicalpa I 1839 I Central American National Wars

After repulsing Honduran-Nicaraguan invaders at **Espiritu Santo** in April, Salvadoran General José Trinidad Cabañas invaded Honduras and took Comayagua (28 August) then marched on Tegucicalpa, where he defeated forces of President José Maria Bustillo to seize the capital. In November at nearby **Soledad** he routed a counter-attack by new President José Francisco Zelaya (6 September 1839).

Tegucicalpa I 1894 I Central American National Wars

When President José Santos Zelaya of Nicaragua intervened in Honduras to support Liberal rebel Policarpo Bonilla, Honduran President Domingo Vásquez was defeated at **Choluteca** and fell back under siege to his capital Tegucicalpa. Some sharp fighting forced Vásquez to capitulate and he went into exile. Bonilla became President and in return he helped support Zelaya (22 February 1894).

Tegucicalpa ▍ 1924 ▍ Honduran Civil War
Following an indecisive election, Tiburcio Carías raised rebellion against President Rafael López Gutiérrez, supported by Vicente Tosta and Gregoria Ferrera who advanced on Tegucicalpa. President López Gutiérrez was killed early in the siege, which caused terrible losses. The United States then intervened and Carías ally Miguel Paz Baraona later became President (9 March–28 April 1924).

Tegyra ▍ 375 BC ▍ Wars of the Greek City-States
When the Theban army assumed the offensive against Spartans occupying Boeotia, they were repulsed at Orchamenus, then met a much larger Spartan force further northeast at Tegyra, north of Lake Copais. In a bold action, the Theban "Sacred Band" under Pelopidas inflicted heavy casualties to secure a significant victory. Theban prestige was greatly increased, crowned in 371 BC by victory at **Leuctra**.

Te Kohia ▍ 1860 ▍ 2nd New Zealand War
See **Waitara**

Tel Afar ▍ 1920 ▍ Iraqi Revolt
Just weeks after Britain secured a mandate in Iraq, Arab insurgents advanced towards Mosul, north of Baghdad, and attacked the nearby small British post at Tel Afar. The first act of the revolt saw the garrison destroyed, along with an incoming armoured car column. A force under Colonel George Sarel retook the post four days later, helping slow fighting in the north (5 June 1920).

Telamon ▍ 225 BC ▍ Gallic Wars in Italy
Responding to Roman expansion, Insubrian Gauls from north Italy campaigned to the south with victories at **Faesulae** and **Clusium**. Later in the year at Telamon (modern Talamone), they were trapped between Lucius Aemelius Papus advancing from Arminium and Gaius Atilius

Regulus marching south from Pisa. A decisive action saw the Gallic army virtually destroyed, but Regulus was killed.

Tel Azaziat ▍ 1967 ▍ Arab-Israeli Six Day War
See **Golan Heights**

Tel-Danith ▍ 1115 ▍ Crusader-Muslim Wars
In the last Great Seljuk invasion of northern Syria, Sultan Mohammed sent Bursuq ibn Bursuq of Hamadan towards Aleppo with a large army. After capturing Hama, Bursuq advanced down the Orontes and was surprised at Tel-Danith, southwest of Aleppo, by Crusaders under Roger, Prince of Antioch. The Seljuk army was destroyed and the invasion dispersed (14 September 1115).

Tel el Aqqaqir ▍ 1942 ▍ World War II (Northern Africa)
See **Kidney Ridge**

Tel el Ful ▍ 1917 ▍ World War I (Middle East)
Just two weeks after **Jerusalem** fell to Sir Edmund Allenby, Turkish forces under General Erich von Falkenhayn regrouped and counterattacked north of the city around Beitunia Ridge and on the Nablus Road at Tel el Ful. Heavy fighting saw the night assault driven off with about 1,500 casualties on either side and the Turks fell back on **Jericho** for the winter (26–27 December 1917).

Tel-el-Kebir ▍ 1882 ▍ Arabi's Egyptian Rebellion
Generals Sir Garnet Wolseley and Sir Gerald Graham advanced west into Egypt against rebel war Minister Arabi Pasha, pushing on through **Kassassin** to Tel-el-Kebir, northeast of Cairo. The Egyptian army was driven out at bayonet-point by a surprise dawn attack, losing all its guns. The rebellion was crushed and the victor was created Baron Wolseley of Cairo (12 September 1882).

Tel-el-Mahuta ▮ 1882 ▮ Arabi's Egyptian Rebellion
See **Tel-el-Maskhuta**

Tel-el-Maskhuta ▮ 1882 ▮ Arabi's Egyptian Rebellion
When War Minister Arabi Pasha attempted to assert Egyptian sovereignty, a British force under General Sir Garnet Wolseley landed at the canal and Egyptian forces tried to block them at Tel-el-Maskhuta (modern Abu Suweir), west of Ismailia. Advance units led by General Sir Gerald Graham swept the Egyptians aside and Wolseley continued through **Kassassin** to **Tel-el-Kebir** (24 August 1882).

Tel el Sheria ▮ 1917 ▮ World War I (Middle East)
See **Sheria**

Tel-el-Zataar ▮ 1976 ▮ Lebanon Civil War
As civil war began in Lebanon, Syria feared growing Palestinian influence and sent over 20,000 men and 500 tanks to support Christian militias. While the Palestinian refugee camp at Jisr al-Basha fell within a week, severe fighting developed for the larger camp at Tel-el-Zataar. After a five-week siege it fell by storm with perhaps 3,000 guerrillas killed and the conflict died down (22 June–12 August 1976).

Tel Faher ▮ 1967 ▮ Arab-Israeli Six Day War
See **Golan Heights**

Telissu ▮ 1904 ▮ Russo-Japanese War
See **Delisi**

Tellaru ▮ 830 ▮ Later Indian Dynastic Wars
As the Kingdoms of southern India struggled for supremacy, Nandivarman II of Pallava stood firm against the tide of aggression by Pandya. In a decisive battle at Tellaru, near modern Wandiwash in northern Arcot, Nandivarman secured a bloody victory over Srimara of Pandya. The great dynastic rivalry continued until Srimara

was killed by Pallava forces in 860 at **Arisil** (disputed date c 830).

Tembien (1st) ▮ 1936 ▮ 2nd Italo-Ethiopian War
With Ethiopians halted at **Dembeguina**, Marshal Pietro Badoglio launched an offensive west into the Tembien. The heaviest fighting was against Ras Seyoum near Warieu Pass, where General Filippo Diamanti suffered costly losses before the garrison was relieved. Ras Seyoum eventually had to withdraw and Badoglio attacked south towards **Amba Aradam** (20–24 January 1936).

Tembien (2nd) ▮ 1936 ▮ 2nd Italo-Ethiopian War
Following victory south of Makale at **Amba Aradam**, Marshal Pietro Badoglio sent his 2nd Corps west into the Tembien against Ras Kassa and Ras Seyoum. Following hard fighting around the strategic Warieu Pass, about 200,000 Ethiopians escaped south towards **Maychew**, leaving perhaps 8,000 dead and wounded. Badoglio then turned against Ras Imru at **Shire** (27–29 February 1936).

Temesvár ▮ 1514 ▮ Transylvanian Peasant War
When Bishop Tomas Bakócz of Esztergom preached a peasant crusade against the Turks, it became a popular uprising under Gyorgy Dózsa, who attacked the nobility in Hungary and Transylvania. While besieging Temesvár (modern Timisaora in western Romania) the peasant army was destroyed by John Zapolya, Governor of Transylvania. Dózsa was later brutally tortured to death (15 July 1514).

Temesvár ▮ 1552 ▮ Turkish-Habsburg Wars
On a fresh offensive in the central Balkans, Turkish forces under Kara Ahmed laid siege to the key Hungarian city of Temesvár (modern Timisaora in Romania), heroically defended by Stephan Losonczy. The city fell after a month-long siege and Kara Ahmed joined with the Pasha of Buda to capture Szolnok before their

campaign stalled in September at the fortress of **Eger** (27 July 1552).

Temesvár I 1716 I Austro-Turkish War

After inflicting a terrible defeat on Turkey on the Danube at **Peterwardein**, Austrian Field Marshal Prince Eugène of Savoy took advantage of the resulting disorder to besiege Temesvár (Timisoara), the last remaining Ottoman fortress in Hungary. It was captured after six weeks and the following year, Eugène marched into the Balkans against **Belgrade** (1 September–14 October 1716).

Temesvár I 1849 I Hungarian Revolutionary War

With Austria driven out of Hungary by Revolutionary forces, Russia intervened. After victory at **Segesvár**, Generals Ivan Paskievich and Julius von Haynau marched to relieve the three-month Hungarian siege of Temesvár (Timisoara, Romania). Hungarian General Henry Dembinksi was routed, losing 6,000 prisoners, and two days later General Artur Gorgey surrendered the army (9 August 1849).

Temple Bar I 1554 I Wyatt's Rebellion

When Sir Thomas Wyatt led a rebellion triggered by Queen Mary's plan to marry the Catholic Philip II of Spain, his forces were defeated at **Wrotham Heath** in Kent before Wyatt led perhaps 3,000 men from Rochester into London. After skirmishing and a failed assault on Ludgate, the rebels were cornered and defeated at Temple Bar. Wyatt and about 100 rebels were executed (8 February 1554).

Tempsford I 918 I Viking Wars in Britain

Edward the Elder of Wessex defeated the Danes of Northumbria at **Tettenhall** (910) and **Wednesfield** (911), then joined his widowed sister Aethelflaed of Mercia against the Danes of the East Midlands and East Anglia. At Tempsford, near Bedford, Edward defeated and killed Guthrum II, securing East Anglia for Wessex. When Aethelflaed died, Edward added Mercia to his kingdom.

Tenaru I 1942 I World War II (Pacific)

When Americans landed on **Guadalcanal** and secured the vital airfield, about 800 elite troops led by Colonel Kiyono Ichiki prematurely attacked in the east at the Tenaru (Ilu) River against Marines under Colonel Edwin Pollock. Only 130 Japanese survived the suicidal assault and Ichiki later committed seppuku. The next major Japanese attack was in September at **Bloody Ridge** (21–22 August 1942).

Tenchbrai I 1106 I Norman Dynastic Wars

See **Tinchebrai**

Tendra I 1790 I Catherine the Great's 2nd Turkish War

After an indecisive action east of Crimea at **Yenikale**, Russian Admiral Fedor Fedrorovich Ushakov and Turkish Vice-Admiral Said Bey met west of the Crimea off Tendra. The Turks were driven off and next day Ushakov attempted to seize two damaged vessels, including the Turkish flagship. However, the flagship blew up after surrendering, killing her crew (27–28 August 1790).

Tenedos I 85 BC I 1st Mithridatic War

With Pontic forces defeated in Greece at **Orchomenus** and in Asia Minor at **Miletopolis**, Roman commander Lucius Licinius Lucullus raised support in Cyprus and Rhodes and off Tenedos, guarding the Dardanelles, he decisively beat the Pontic fleet under Admiral Neoptolemus. Victory at sea opened the way for Lucius Sulla to invade Asia Minor and Mithridates VI of Pontus sued for peace.

Tenerife, Canary Islands I 1657 I Anglo-Spanish Wars

See **Santa Cruz de Tenerife**

Tenerife, Canary Islands I 1797 I French Revolutionary Wars (1st Coalition)

See **Santa Cruz de Tenerife**

Tenerife, Colombia I 1820 I Colombian War of Independence

With Colombian independence assured by victory at **Boyacá**, Patriot infantry led by Colonel José María Córdoba and seven ships under Hermógenes Maza attacked Spanish forces still holding Tenerife, on the Magdalena just north of Plato. Nine out of 11 Spanish ships were captured or destroyed in a brilliant action and the Royalists withdrew northwest to **Cartagena** (27 June 1820).

Tengchong I 1944 I World War II (China)

As Chinese crossed the **Salween** in Yunnan, the northern force under General Hou Kuizhang advanced on the walled city of Tengchong, on the road to **Myitkyina**. After heavy American air attack and prolonged siege, Tengchong finally fell to massive assault and hand to hand fighting. The Chinese then moved south to support the attack on **Longling** (26 July–14 September 1944).

Te Ngutu-o-te-manu I 1868 I 2nd New Zealand War

Campaigning against the religio-military Hauhau in southern Taranaki, Colonel Thomas McDonnell was repulsed at Te Ngutu by the warrior Titokowaru. A second attack saw McDonnell repulsed with 50 casualties, including the famous Forest Ranger Gustavus von Tempsky killed. Titokowaru later defeated another force sent against him at **Moturoa** (21 August & 7 September 1868).

Tenochtitlan I 1520 I Spanish Conquest of Mexico

After reaching the Aztec capital of Tenochtitlan (modern Mexico City) in November 1519, Conquistador Hernán Cortés held Emperor Motecuhzoma a virtual hostage and pillaged his wealth. But resistance by the Emperor's cousin Cuauhtemoc—the Noche Triste—began after Motecuhzoma was killed. Cortés was expelled with over 600 dead but turned on his pursuers at **Otumba** (30 June 1520).

Tenochtitlan I 1521 I Spanish Conquest of Mexico

Heavily reinforced after being bloodily expelled from the Aztec capital of Tenochtitlan, Spanish Conquistador Hernán Cortés besieged and stormed the city, on an island in a lake. Cortés then destroyed much of Tenochtitlan and rebuilt it as Mexico City. The last Aztec Emperor Cuauhtemoc was captured later that year and was killed in 1522 en route to Honduras (26 May–13 August 1521).

Te Porere I 1869 I 2nd New Zealand War

As the hunt continued for the Hauhau rebel Te Kooti after his raid on **Mohaka** in April, he was attacked in a fortified position at Te Porere, in New Zealand's central North Island near Tongariro, by Captain William McDonnell and Maoris under Major Kepa Te Rangihiwinui. Sharp fighting cost the British four dead, but 37 Hauhau were killed and Te Kooti withdrew towards **Rotorua** (3 October 1869).

Te Ranga I 1864 I 2nd New Zealand War

In a renewed threat to Tauranga after his moral victory at **Gate Pa**, Rawiri Puhirake started to dig in at Te Ranga, just four miles away. Determined to avenge the previous loss, Colonel Henry Greer took a large force and, in heavy fighting with three Victoria Crosses won, Rawiri and over 70 Maoris were killed. The local chiefs soon surrendered, ending fighting in the Bay of Plenty (21 June 1864).

Terceira I 1582 I Spanish-Portuguese War

Two years after Spain seized the Portuguese throne at **Alcántara**, French ships under Filippo Strozzi sailed to the Azores to support a Portuguese rebellion in favour of Don Antonio de Crato against Phillip II of Spain. Off the island of Terceira, Spanish Admiral Alvaro de Bazán Marquess of Santa Cruz defeated the French and occupied the islands. Santa Cruz won again next year off **Sao Miguel**.

Terceira I 1583 I Spanish-Portuguese War

See **Sao Miguel**

Terek ∎ 1263 ∎ Mongol Dynastic Wars

Battle in Azerbaijan near **Kuba** between Il-Khan Hulegu of Iran and Berke Khan of the Golden Horde—grandsons of Genghis Khan—saw Berke beaten, then rashly pursued further north to the Terek by Hulegu's son Abaqa. Although Abaqa was heavily defeated on the frozen river, Berke continued withdrawing. Hulegu secured his Khanate by crushing King Davit V of Georgia (13 January 1263).

Terek ∎ 1395 ∎ Conquests of Tamerlane

The Turko-Mongol Tamerlane beat Toktamish, Khan of the Golden Horde, at the **Syr Darya** (1389) and **Kunduzcha** (1391), then attacked his former protégé in the northern Caucausus at the Terek, west of the Caspian. Toktamish suffered a decisive defeat and fled to the Ukraine while Tamerlane sacked his capital at Sarai and placed a puppet ruler over the once mighty Golden Horde (April 1395).

Tergoes ∎ 1572 ∎ Netherlands War of Independence

See **Goes**

Terjan ∎ 1472 ∎ Ottoman-Turkoman War

When Uzun Hassan of the White Sheep Turkomans advanced from Azerbaijan into Anatolia and destroyed Tokat, Ottoman Sultan Mehmed II took a large army east towards Erzurum, where his right wing under Hassan Murad Pasha impulsively attacked at Terjan (Tercan). The Imperial favourite was ambushed and killed and Mehmed withdrew. He soon destroyed Uzun Hassan at **Erzincan**.

Termoli ∎ 1943 ∎ World War II (Southern Europe)

British General Sir Bernard Montgomery raced north along Italy's Adriatic coast to seize **Foggia**, then advanced on strong defences at Termoli, just north of the Biferno. A commando assault (Brigadier John Durnford-Slater) took the port from the sea, but the British had to repulse a brutal German counter-attack. Montgomery next attacked towards the **Sangro** (3–7 October 1943).

Terschelling ∎ 1666 ∎ 2nd Dutch War

See **Vlie**

Tertry ∎ 687 ∎ Frankish Civil Wars

In a civil war, which effectively began the establishment of France, Pepin II of Austrasia invaded Neustria and defeated Thierry III and his Mayor, Berthar, at Tertry on the River Somme near Péronne. Thierry was taken prisoner and Berthar was killed by his own supporters. The battle ended the power of the Merovingian royal house and marked the beginning of what became the Carolingian Dynasty.

Teruel ∎ 1937–1938 ∎ Spanish Civil War

Despite a failed Republican offensive west of Madrid towards **Brunete**, Generals Leopoldo Menéndez and Hernández Sarabía marched east and seized Teruel from Colonel Rey d'Harcourt. Nationalist Generals José Varela and Antonio Aranda besieged then took the city, while the Republicans withdrew with crippling losses in men and equipment (15 December 1937–20 February 1938).

Teschen ∎ 1919 ∎ Polish-Czech War

Disputing the post-war border between Poland and Czechoslovakia, Czech Colonel Josef Snejdarek marched into coal-rich Teschen in eastern Silesia and drove out a weak Polish force. An armistice signed by Polish General Franciczek Latinik ended the seven-day war and Czechoslovakia secured Teschen. It was seized again by Poland in 1938 but returned in 1945 (23–30 January 1919).

Tescua ∎ 1841 ∎ Colombian War of Supreme Commanders

On campaign against rebels in the north, General Tomás Cipriano de Mosquera for the government, supported by Colonel Joaquín Barriga, won at **Aratoca** in January then attacked General Francisco Carmona at Tescua, in Norte de Santander. A major success against the rebels saw Carmona decisively defeated, with final government victory in September in the north at **Ocaña** (1 April 1841).

Testry I 687 I Frankish Civil Wars
See **Tertry**

Tet Offensive I 1968 I Vietnam War
After diversionary attacks such as **Khe Sanh, Con Thien, Dak To** and **Loc Ninh**, Communist forces launched the Tet Offensive against over 100 towns and cities, including bloody fighting in **Hue**, **Saigon** and **Dong Ha**. The surprise offensive was finally defeated with decisive losses, though its shocking impact helped weaken America's will to continue the war (30 January–29 February 1968).

Tétouan I 1860 I Spanish-Moroccan War
See **Tetuán**

Tettenhall I 910 I Viking Wars in Britain
As a result of the Danes of Northumbria attacking King Acthclred of Saxon Mercia, his brother-in-law Edward of Wessex (son of Alfred the Great) marched into modern Staffordshire and routed the Danes near modern Wolverhampton at Tettenhall. The victory extended Wessex to the Humber and is regarded as beginning the Saxon reconquest of Danish England (6 August 910).

Tetuán I 1860 I Spanish-Moroccan War
When Moroccan forces raided Spanish possessions in North Africa, Marshal Leopoldo O'Donnell invaded against the newly throned Sultan Sidi Muhammed. Advancing south from **Castillejos**, the Spanish won a decisive victory near Tetuán, east of Tangier, then seized the city. O'Donnell was created Duke of Tetuán and won again in March at the **Guad-el-Ras** (4 February 1860).

Teugen I 1809 I Napoleonic Wars (5th Coalition)
See **Hausen**

Teutoburgwald I 9 AD I Rome's Germanic Wars
Consul Publius Quintilius Varus was fighting the Germanic tribes east of the Rhine and took three legions into the Teutoburg Forest, traditionally outside Detmold, but probably near Osnabruck. Ambushed and routed by Arminius of the Cherusci, Varus committed suicide to avoid capture, and the surviving troops and camp-followers were all slaughtered. It was Rome's greatest defeat in Europe.

Tewkesbury I 1471 I Wars of the Roses
Arriving too late to prevent Lancastrian defeat at **Barnet**, Margaret of Anjou and Prince Edward landed at Weymouth to rally their cause. However, north of Gloucester at Tewkesbury, their army under Edmund Beaufort Duke of Somerset was decisively defeated by Edward IV. Somerset and the young Prince were killed and Henry VI's death in captivity secured Edward's throne (4 May 1471).

Texel I 1653 I 1st Dutch War
See **Scheveningen**

Texel I 1673 I 3rd Dutch War
Renewing the invasion repulsed at **Schooneveld** in June, the Anglo-French fleet of Prince Rupert and Admiral Jean d'Estrées met the smaller Dutch fleet off Texel. As in battle at **Sole Bay** (June 1672), Admiral Mihiel de Ruyter isolated the French and attacked the English ships, inflicting heavy casualties. While no ships were lost, de Ruyter had effectively defeated the invasion (21 August 1673).

Texel I 1795 I French Revolutionary Wars (1st Coalition)
In the course of brilliant mid-winter invasion of Holland, French General Charles Pichegru surprised part of the Dutch fleet frozen at anchor near the island of Texel. In an extraordinary assault across the frozen Zuyder Zee with cavalry and horse-artillery, Lieutenant Colonel Louis-Joseph La Hure captured the 14 ships and Holland became a French satellite (22–23 January 1795).

Texel I 1797 I French Revolutionary Wars (Irish Rising)
See **Camperdown**

Textri I 687 I Frankish Civil Wars
See **Tertry**

Tezin ∎ 1841 ∎ 1st British-Afghan War

Sent east from Kabul to force the passes and secure communication with Peshawar, General Sir Robert Sale stormed the Khurd Kabul (12 October), then heavily defeated an Afghan force on the Heights of Tezin. After forcing the Pass at Jagdalak and taking the fortress of Mamu Khel from Mir Afzal Khan, he reached **Jalalabad** and held it for six months (22 October 1841).

Tezin ∎ 1842 ∎ 1st British-Afghan War

General Sir George Pollock's Army of Retribution marched into Afghanistan to avenge the murder of British soldiers and civilians from **Kabul** in January. They captured **Jagdalak** (8 September) then advanced through the Khyber against Akbar Khan and about 16,000 Afghans at Tezin, near Khurd Kabul. The Afghans were routed and Pollock entered Kabul two days later (13 September 1842).

Thabraca ∎ 398 ∎ Gildo's Rebellion

See **Theveste**

Thakhek ∎ 1946 ∎ French Indo-China War

As French forces retook northern Laos from Nationalist Chinese who had accepted Japan's surrender, the Lao Issara (Free Lao) movement under Prince Souphanouvong determined to resist at Thakhek. Attacking behind air-strikes, the French stormed the town with perhaps 1,000 civilians and soldiers killed. Souphanouvong was badly injured and went into exile in Thailand (17–21 March 1946).

Thal ∎ 1919 ∎ 3rd British-Afghan War

In his attack on British India, Amir Amanullah of Afghanistan sent General Nadir Khan and a large mixed force into the Kurram Valley against Thal, held by about 800 militia. The Afghans shelled Thal with 20 Krupp guns, but were dispersed by a relief force under General Reginald Dyer, whose actions at **Amritsar** had provoked outrage. A truce quickly followed (28 May–1 June 1919).

Thala ∎ 107 BC ∎ Jugurthine War

Caecilius Metellus defeated King Jugurtha of Numida at the **Muthul** (108 BC) then led a bold expedition across the desert against the stronghold and treasury at Thala, in modern Tunisia. Attempting to ambush the Romans, Jugurtha and his General Bomilcar were badly beaten. Jugurtha fled to his father-in-law, Bocchus of Mauretania, and they were defeated the following year near **Cirta**.

Thalner ∎ 1818 ∎ 3rd British-Maratha War

See **Talneer**

Thames ∎ 1813 ∎ War of 1812

American General William Harrison invaded Upper Canada after British withdrawal from **Detroit**, pursuing General Henry Proctor up the Thames through Chatham to Moraviantown. Dispirited and lacking ammunition, Proctor's British-Indian force was routed with heavy casualties, including the great Tecumseh killed. Harrison did not pursue further and returned to Detroit (5 October 1813).

Thana ∎ 1738 ∎ Portuguese-Maratha War

During the epic Maratha siege of the Portuguese island fortress of **Bassein**, near Bombay, the Portuguese garrison made a last heroic attempt to recapture the strategic fortification at nearby Thana, which had fallen a year earlier (26 March 1737). Although Portuguese commander Pedro de Mello was killed in the failed assault, Bassein held out for a further 12 months (27 February 1738).

Thana ∎ 1774 ∎ 1st British-Maratha War

Attacking the former Portuguese island colony of Salsette, north of Bombay, a large British force under General Robert Gordon besieged the fortress town of Thana, held by Maratha Anand Rao Ram Bivalkar. With a Maratha relief force approaching from Poona, Colonel William Cockburn led a decisive assault to capture the fort and with it the island (12–28 December 1774).

Thaneswar ∎ 1011 ∎ Muslim Conquest of Northern India

On campaign against the Hindus of Northern India, the Afghan ruler Mahmud of Ghazni marched against the temple city of Thaneswar and found his way blocked at the nearby Sutlej by Raja Ram of Dera. Despite suffering the greater losses, Mahmud drove off Raja Ram, then seized and sacked Thaneswar. He withdrew before the Raja of Delhi could send troops to protect his city.

Thanet I 851 I Viking Raids on Britain

Following decisive defeat at **Aclea**, Danish invaders withdrew to the island of Thanet in the Thames Estuary, where they faced a powerful attack from the men of Kent and Sussex led by Ealchere of Wessex (victor of **Sandwich**) and Ealdorman Huda. Both Saxon leaders were killed in a decisive defeat and the Danish position on Thanet marked the start of enduring Viking settlement in the south.

Thang Long I 1258 I Mongol Wars of Kubilai Khan

Kubilai Khan secured southwest China then ordered General Uriangkatai into Vietnam, where he seized and razed the capital Thang Long (later Hanoi). However, Vietnamese King Tran Thai Tong led a counter-offensive, and in battle at nearby Dong Bo Dau, the Mongols were badly defeated and withdrew. A renewed Mongol invasion thirty years later was destroyed at **Bach Dang** (17 January 1258).

Thang Long I 1789 I Vietnamese Civil War

When Nguyen Hue led a rebellion against Vietnam's declining Le Dynasty, the weak King Chien Tong called for Chinese aid and 200,000 Qing (Ching) troops invaded and occupied Thang Long (later Hanoi). Proclaiming himself Emperor Quang Trung, Nguyen marched north with a massive force and attacked at Lunar New Year. The Qing army was routed and fled and Quang made peace with China.

Thang Long I 1802 I Vietnamese Civil War

After the Tay Son defeated a Chinese army to secure Vietnam, civil war soon ensued and Prince Nguyen Anh, with French military aid, began to reconquer the country. Ending three years of war, he finally attacked Thang Long (later Hanoi) and overthrew the remnant Tay Son forces. He made himself Emperor Gia Long, reviving the Nguyen Dynasty, and moved the capital to Hué (July 1802).

Thapsus I 46 BC I Wars of the First Triumvirate

Julius Caesar was reinforced after defeating the Pompeians in Tunisia at **Ruspina** in January and marched on Metellus Scipio at Thapsus, near modern Teboulba. Attacking before Scipio could be supported by King Juba of Numidia, Caesar won a decisive victory. Juba and Scipio were later killed, while Gnaeus Pompey and Titus Labienus fled to Spain and defeat at **Munda** (6 February 46 BC).

Thasos I 465–463 BC I Wars of the Delian League

Alarmed at growing Athenian power, the rich Aegean island of Thasos, just off the coast of Thrace, rose in revolt and seceded from the Delian League. Returning from victory at **Eurymedon**, Cimon of Athens defeated the Thasian navy, then blockaded the island by land and sea. Thasos yielded after two years, and was forced to demolish its walls and surrender its once-powerful fleet.

Thebes I 335 BC I Conquests of Alexander the Great

With Alexander the Great falsely reported killed in the Balkans, the central Greek city of Thebes rose against its Macedonian masters. Returning by forced march, Alexander overcame fierce resistance to storm the city then let his auxiliaries loose on an orgy of slaughter. As punishment and an example to others, Alexander ordered Thebes demolished and the citizens enslaved (September 335 BC).

Thedonisi Island I 1788 I Catherine the Great's 2nd Turkish War

Despite defeat off the **Liman**, on the Dnieper, Turkish Admiral Hassan el Ghasi attacked Russian commander Charles Nassau-Siegen, now reinforced by Admiral Mark Voynovich.

After initial Turkish success, a counter-attack by Commodore Fyodor Ushakov's vanguard routed the Kapudan Pasha, who withdrew his fleet. Besieged **Ochakov** fell to land assault five months later (3 July 1788).

Thermopylae I 480 BC I Greco-Persian Wars

Determined to avenge the rout at **Marathon** in 490 BC, King Xerxes of Persia sent a fresh land invasion of Greece. An heroic action saw Spartan King Leonides and about 5,000 men attempt to hold the defile at Thermopylae but they were outflanked. The King and his 300-strong rearguard were all killed. Xerxes then occupied Athens, but soon withdrew after naval defeat off **Salamis** (August 480 BC).

Thermopylae I 191 BC I Roman-Syrian War

When Rome drove Macedonia out of Greece at **Cynoscephalae** (197 BC) Antiochus III of Syria invaded Greece to support Aetolia and captured Thessaly. Intervening again, Rome sent an army under Marcus Porcius Cato and Marcus Acilius Glabrio, which routed Antiochus at Thermopylae. He abandoned his adventure in Greece and left for Asia Minor, where he was beaten next year at **Magnesia**.

Thermopylae I 1821 I Greek War of Independence

Campaigning in the north, Athanasios Diakos and the Bishop of Salona-Essaias captured Levadia (25 April). But in heavy fighting near Thermopylae at the Bridge of Alamana they failed to halt a Turkish force under Omer Vrioni. Diakos and the Bishop were defeated and executed and Vrioni captured and burned Levadia. He then advanced on Athens to relieve the **Acropolis** (5 May 1821).

Therouanne I 1513 I War of the Holy League
See **Guinegate**

Thessalonica I 586 I Byzantine-Balkan Wars

Following sweeping Avar raids along the Danube Valley to the Black Sea, Slav tribes moved across Thrace towards Constantinople and south into the Greek peninsula, where they threatened Thessalonica, second city of the Balkans. Their attempted surprise was reputedly revealed by the city's patron saint, Demetrius, who drove the assailants from the ramparts (September 586).

Thessalonica I 615 I Byzantine-Balkan Wars

With Byzantium occupied by war with Persia, Avars and Slavs recaptured Roman land south of the Danubian border and a large Slav force advanced on Thessalonica, attempting to capture the city by attack from the sea. Saint Demetrius was again credited with securing the salvation of his citizens, when the Slav assault ended in chaotic failure with their leader Chatzon taken prisoner.

Thessalonica I 618 I Byzantine-Balkan Wars

In yet another attack on Thessalonica, Slav forces were this time supported by the mighty Avars who supplied their awesome siege machines. The city held out for 33 days, with Archbishop John touring the ramparts to raise morale. Divine intervention by Saint Demetrius reputedly persuaded the Avars to withdraw. Their failure at **Constantinople** in 626 led to the rapid decline of Avar power.

Thessalonica I 1043 I Later Byzantine Military Rebellions
See **Ostrovo**

Thessalonica I 1224 I Latin-Epirote War

In support of Byzantine Nicaea against the Latin Emperors in Constantinople, Theodore Ducas of Epirus invaded the vassal Kingdom of Thessaly, in north and central Greece, held by Demetrius of Montferrat. Thessalonica was captured following a long siege, ending 20 years of Latin rule. The ambitious Theodore was proclaimed Emperor but was soon overthrown at **Klokotnitsa**.

Thessalonica I 1264 I 3rd Latin-Byzantine Imperial War

Following the Byzantine restoration in **Constantinople**, Emperor Michael VIII determined to beat Michael II of Epirus, who had been part of the alliance against him at **Pelagonia** (1259). After an army under Alexius Strategopoulos was repulsed, a fresh force led by the Emperor's brother John Paleologus secured decisive victory at Thessalonica and Michael II recognised Byzantine suzerainty.

Thessalonica I 1430 I Venetian-Turkish Wars
See **Salonika**

Thessalonica I 1912 I 1st Balkan War
See **Jannitsa**

Thessalonica I 1915–1918 I World War I (Balkan Front)
See **Salonika**

Thessaly I 353 BC I 3rd Sacred War

When Thessalians invited Philip of Macedon to help them against Pherae, he first defeated Phayllus of Phocis then faced Phayllus' brother, Onomarchus. At an unknown site in Thessaly, Onomarchus lured the Macedonians into a valley and routed them with artillery on surrounding hills. Philip was fortunate to escape, though he returned the next year to defeat the Phocians at **Pagasae**.

Thetford I 870 I Viking Wars in Britain
See **Hoxne**

Theveste I 398 I Gildo's Rebellion

When Roman General Gildo, son of King Nubel of Mauretania, rose against Western Emperor Honorius, his brother Mascezel fled to Italy, where Stilicho gave him 5,000 veterans. Landing in Numidia, Mascezel marched inland, and near Theveste (modern Tebessa, Algeria) routed his

brother when most of his army deserted. Gildo fled to Thabraca on the coast, where he was captured and committed suicide.

Thielt I 1128 I War of Flemish Succession

Amid war for succession in Flanders, William Clito, appointed by his father Duke Robert of Normandy, attacked his rival Theodoric of Alsace (Dietrich von Elsass) at Thielt, northeast of modern Roeselare. A decisive action saw Theodoric's forces badly defeated and William became Count of Flanders. A month later William was killed during a siege further west at **Alost** (21 June 1128).

Thiepval I 1916 I World War I (Western Front)

Recovering from losses around **Flers-Courcelette** during the Battle of the **Somme**, General Sir Henry Rawlinson attacked east from Pozières towards **Morval** and north towards Thiepval, which was quickly captured. The British then advanced onto Thiepval Ridge. While much of the strategic ridge was captured, it remained the scene of fighting for some time (26–28 September 1916).

Thionville I 1639 I Thirty Years War (Franco-Habsburg War)

Advancing into the Spanish Netherlands, French forces under Isaac Manassès Marquis de Feuquière besieged Thionville (German Diedenhofen) on the Moselle northwest of Metz, where they were heavily defeated by General Ottavio Piccolomini. The captured Feuquière died of wounds in captivity after failed ransom negotiations while Piccolomini was created Duke of Amalfi (28 June 1639).

Thionville I 1643 I Thirty Years War (Franco-Habsburg War)

Just weeks after destroying Spain's famous infantry at **Rocroi**, 22-year-old Louis II Duke d'Enghien took his French army southeast against Thionville (German Diedenhofen) on the Moselle northwest of Metz. The city fell after heroic resistance and d'Enghien quickly went on to capture **Sierck** before advancing as far as Luxemburg itself (14 June–10 August 1643).

Thionville I 1870 I Franco-Prussian War

Campaigning to the north after the fall of **Metz**, General Edwin von Manteuffel sent the German 7th Division under General Heinrich Adolf von Zastrow against the stubborn fortress of Thionville, which had already been bombarded and partly invested. The fortress capitulated in flames after four days of heavy fighting, yielding a reported 2,000 prisoners (20–24 November 1870).

Thirty I 1351 I Hundred Years War

Amid skirmishes between English and French in Brittany, Jean de Beaumanoir Governor of Josselin challenged Captain John Bramborough at Ploermel to meet with thirty knights each at Mi-Voie, midway between the castles, and fight to the death. The "Battle of the Thirty" saw Bramborough among nine Englishmen killed and his wounded survivors conceded the combat (27 March 1351).

Thompson's Station I 1863 I American Civil War (Western Theatre)

Leading a disastrous Union offensive from Nashville, Tennessee, Colonel John Coburn marched south through Franklin and was attacked at nearby Thompson's Station by Confederate forces under General Earl Van Dorn. Underestimating the Confederate strength, Coburn was utterly routed and had to surrender, along with most of his officers and about 1,200 men (5 March 1863).

Thonotosassa I 1836 I 2nd Seminole Indian War

Following American defeat at the **Withlacoochee**, Colonels William Chisholm and William Foster were sent to decommission Fort Alabama, on the Hillsborough, just outside Tampa. Attacked by Seminole at nearby Thonotosassa Creek, they suffered five dead and 25 wounded before driving the Indians off with a bayonet charge. The site was later rebuilt and renamed Fort Foster (27 April 1836).

Thorn I 1703 I 2nd "Great" Northern War

Charles XII of Sweden defeated a large Saxon army at **Pultusk** (21 April) and marched north against the powerful fortress of Thorn (modern Torun) on the Vistula, held by adherents of Augustus II, Elector of Saxony and King of Poland. Thorn fell after a long siege—which reputedly cost Charles fewer than 50 men—effectively completing his control of Poland (May–22 September 1703).

Thornton's Ambush I 1846 I American-Mexican War

As General Zachary Taylor advanced towards the Rio Grande to open the war, General Anastasio Torrejón serving under General Mariano Arista crossed the river and ambushed an American patrol northwest of modern Brownsville. After losing 20 men, Captain Seth Thornton was captured along with 70 survivors. However, Arista was soon repulsed at nearby **Fort Texas** (25 April 1846).

Thoroughfare Gap I 1862 I American Civil War (Eastern Theatre)

Confederate commander Robert E. Lee crossed the Bull Run Mountains towards the Union army north of Manassas, where part of his force under General James Longstreet stormed Thoroughfare Gap, west of Haymarket, Virginia. In a minor but vital skirmish, Union General James B. Ricketts failed to hold the strategic pass, opening Lee's access to vital battlefield at **Bull Run** (28 August 1862).

Thouars I 1793 I French Revolutionary Wars (Vendée War)

In the wake of early rebel success for the counter-revolution in western France, Republican forces determined to defend Thouars on the River Thouet in the east. Bitter fighting forced Colonel Pierre Quentineau to surrender the town to Royalist leader Henri de la Rochejaquelein, yielding the Vendéeans an enormous booty of cannon, muskets, and 5,000 prisoners (5 May 1793).

Three Emperors I 1805 I Napoleonic Wars (3rd Coalition)
See **Austerlitz**

Three Hundred I 547 BC I Spartan-Argive Wars
See **Champions**

Three Kings I 1578 I Portuguese-Moroccan War
See **Alcazarquivir**

Three Peaks I 1880 I Apache Indian Wars
See **Tres Castillos**

Three Rivers I 1776 I War of the American Revolution
See **Trois Rivières**

Throg's Neck I 1776 I War of the American Revolution
British General William Howe attempted to by-pass General George Washington's defence of New York City at **Harlem Heights**, on Manhattan Island, by landing a force at Throg's Neck, north of Long Island Sound. Howe was delayed by a courageous defence from American riflemen under Colonel Edward Hands, but he was soon reinforced and advanced on **Pell's Point** (12 October 1776).

Thuan-An I 1883 I French Conquest of Indo-China
See **Hue**

Thukela I 1838 I Boer-Zulu War
See **Tugela**

Thukela Heights I 1900 I 2nd Anglo-Boer War
See **Tugela Heights**

Thymbria I 546 BC I Persian-Lydian War
Facing a massive invasion by Cyrus II the Great of Persia after defeat at **Pteria**, King Croesus of Lydia drew up his army on the Plain of Thymbria, outside his capital at **Sardis**, in the west of modern Turkey. Despite the resistance of experienced troops sent by his ally, Amasis of Egypt, Croesus was utterly defeated and his army fled to siege behind the walls of the Lydian capital.

Thyrea I 547 BC I Spartan-Argive Wars
See **Champions**

Tiagar I 1790 I 3rd British-Mysore War
Tipu Sultan of Mysore renewed war against Britain in southern India and marched north from Trichinopoly to attack the fortress of Tiagar, 30 miles south of Trinomalee, defended by a stubborn garrison under Captain William Flint. Tipu gave up after heavy losses in failed assaults and crossed the river to sack the defenceless town of Trinomalee (December 1790).

Tianjin (1st) I 1900 I Boxer Rebellion
When foreign ships seized the **Dagu Forts** at the mouth of the Bei He, anti-foreign Boxers besieged the well-defended international settlement upstream at Tianjin (Tientsin). After a weeklong attack, 2,000 British, American and Russian troops arrived from Dagu to break the Chinese lines. The Boxers withdrew three days later after a lucky Allied shell destroyed their arsenal (17–27 June 1900).

Tianjin (2nd) I 1900 I Boxer Rebellion
Reinforced in the foreign settlement at Tianjin (Tientsin), a 5,000-strong multi-national force attacked anti-foreign Boxers in the native city. Following heavy bombardment, Tianjin was taken by storm with 800 Allied casualties, mainly Japanese, and perhaps 5,000 Boxers. Imperial Viceroy Yu Lu killed himself in disgrace and a fresh relief force soon set out for besieged **Beijing** (13–14 July 1900).

Tianjin I 1925 I Guo Songling's Revolt
Manchurian warlord Zhang Zuolin secured northern China at **Shanhaiguan** (October 1924), then drove former ally Feng Yuxiang out of Beijing before facing a rebellion by General Guo Songling, aided by Feng. Southeast of Beijing at Tianjin (Tientsin) Feng's army under Zhang Zhizhang beat Manchurian General Li Jinglin,

but Guo was quickly routed at **Xinmintun** (9–23 December 1925).

Tianjin I 1926 I Guo Songling's Revolt

Facing revolt by his General Guo Songling and rival warlord Feng Yuxiang, the Manchurian Zhang Zuolin killed Guo at **Xinmintun** (December 1925), then sent Li Jinglin and Chang Zongchang to recover Tianjin (Tientsin) southeast of Beijing. Heavy fighting forced Feng's ally Lu Zhonglin to abandon the city, and within weeks Zhang had recovered **Beijing** (February–21 March 1926).

Tianjin I 1937 I Sino-Japanese War
See **Beijing**

Tianjin I 1949 I 3rd Chinese Revolutionary Civil War

Just weeks after the **Liaoshen** offensive in Manchuria, Communist General Lin Biao joined General Nie Rongzhen in northern China for the huge Beijing-Tianjin offensive. A furious assault saw the besieged city of Tianjin taken by storm, with 130,000 Nationalist troops routed and General Chen Changjie captured. The ring then closed around **Beijing** (14–15 January 1949).

Tianzhuangtai I 1895 I Sino-Japanese War
See **Yingkou**

Tiberias I 1187 I 3rd Crusade
See **Hattin**

Tiberias I 1948 I Israeli War of Independence

Before the expiry of the UN mandate in Palestine, Zionist forces launched a "pre-war" to optimise their position at independence. The first major town to fall to the Jews was Tiberias in eastern Galilee, which was attacked and seized by a Haganah brigade. The Arab population fled to Transjordan and Jewish commander Ygal Allon turned north against **Safad** (18 April 1948).

Tibi I 1848 I 2nd British-Sikh War
See **Sadusam**

Ticinum I 271 I Roman-Alemannic Wars
See **Pavia**

Ticinum I 569–572 I Lombard Invasion of Italy
See **Pavia**

Ticinus I 218 BC I 2nd Punic War

Carthaginian Hannibal Barca crossed the Alps from Gaul to surprise a Roman army under Scipio the Elder at the junction of the Ticinus and Po Rivers. Attempting to pull back across the Ticinus after a cavalry skirmish, the outnumbered Romans suffered heavy casualties, and Scipio was seriously wounded. Hannibal won another decisive victory in December at the **Trebbia** (November 218 BC).

Ticonderoga I 1758 I Seven Years War (North America)
See **Fort Ticonderoga**

Ticonderoga I 1775 I War of the American Revolution
See **Fort Ticonderoga**

Tiebas I 1813 I Napoleonic Wars (Peninsular Campaign)

Using British-supplied siege guns, Spanish guerrilla General Francisco Espoz y Mina besieged Tafalla, just 30 miles from Pamplona in the western Pyrenees. A large French relief force marching south towards Tafalla under General Louis Abbé, Governor of Navarre, was defeated at Tiebas (10 February). Tafalla itself surrendered next day (9–11 February 1813).

Tientsin I 1900 I Boxer Rebellion
See **Tianjin**

Tientsin I 1925 I Guo Songling's Revolt
See **Tianjin**

Tientsin I 1926 I Guo Songling's Revolt
See **Tianjin**

Tientsin I 1937 I Sino-Japanese War
See **Beijing**

**Tientsin I 1949 I 3rd Chinese
Revolutionary Civil War**
  See **Tianjin**

**Tierra Blanca I 1913 I Mexican
Revolution**
  Francisco (Pancho) Villa was repulsed at
Chihuahua but days later circled north to capture **Ciudad Juárez** before marching south
again. Thirty miles north of Chihuahua, on the
sandy plains of the Tierra Blanca, he decisively
defeated a large Federal army. Chihuahua was
then evacuated and Generals Pascual Orozco
and José Inez Salazar withdrew northeast to
Ojinaga (23–25 November 1913).

Tieshan I 630 I Tang Imperial Wars
  See **Iron Mountain, China**

Tiflis I 1795 I Persian-Georgian War
  Determined to expand his northern lands, Aga
Mohammad Khan of Persia seized **Shusha** (9
August) then led 40,000 men against Christian
Tiflis (modern Tblisi). Heraclius (Erekle) of
Georgia unwisely met the invaders outside Tiflis
and his heavily outnumbered army was de-
stroyed. Aga Mohammad then sacked and en-
slaved Tiflis but was assassinated two years later
(10 September 1795).

Tigra I 1858 I Indian Mutiny
  See **Jaunpur**

**Tigranocerta I 69 BC I
3rd Mithridatic War**
  Roman Lucius Licinius Lucullus secured
Pontus at **Cabira** (72 BC) then invaded Armenia
in pursuit of Mithridates VI of Pontus who had
fled to his son-in-law Tigranes. Lucullus besieged Tigranocerta on the Tigris, then met a
relief army under Tigranes. Though massively
outnumbered, Lucullus achieved a brilliant victory and won again the following year at **Ar-
taxata** (6 October 69 BC).

**Tigris River I 363 I Later Roman-
Persian Wars**
  See **Ctesiphon**

Tikal I 562 I "Star" Wars
  During the classic period of warfare between
the cities of the Mayan lowlands, with battles
planned by the position of the stars, the great
capital Tikal (in modern Guatemala) was attacked by Caracol to the southeast, aided by
Calakmul to the north. King Wak Chan K'awiil
of Tikal was defeated and killed and the kingdom was eclipsed for over a century until **Calakmul** in 695.

Tikrit I 2003 I 2nd Gulf War
  As coalition forces converged on Baghdad,
American troops further north closed in and,
from 5 April, virtually besieged Tikrit, birth-
place and power base of Iraqi President Saddam
Hussein. After the fall of **Baghdad**, Saddam's
last stronghold was taken by storm to effectively
conclude the initial phase of the war. On 1 May
US President George W. Bush declared an end
to "major combat" (13–14 April 2003).

**Tila Pass I 1899 I Philippine-
American War**
  See **Tirad Pass**

**Tillis Farm I 1856 I 3rd Seminole
Indian War**
  When Seminole forces attacked the farm of
Willoughby Tillis, on the Peace River south of
Barlow (14 June) Florida militia were sent in
response from nearby Fort Meade. Although five
soldiers were killed in fierce fighting, the Indians
also suffered costly casualties, including Chief
Oscen Tustenuggee killed. This was effectively
the last substantial action of the war (16 June
1856).

Tillyangus I 1571 I Huntly Rebellion
  Renewing Catholic rebellion following abdi-
cation by Mary Queen of Scots, Sir Adam
Gordon, brother of George Earl of Huntly, used
a family quarrel to march against the Forbes clan
at Tillyangus in Aberdeenshire. The outnumbered Forbes were defeated, with about 120
killed (including "Black Arthur," son of the 7th
Lord). The feud soon continued at **Craibstane**
(10 October 1571).

Timbuktu I 1468 I Wars of the Songhai Empire

When Sonni Ali took control of the state of Songhai, on the middle reaches of the Niger River, he led an aggressive campaign of expansion, driving the Tuareg from the strategic city of Timbuktu, which they had occupied since 1433. Sonni drove north and built a great West African Empire, but soon after his death (1492) his son was deposed at **Anfao**.

Timimoun I 1901 I French Colonial Wars in North Africa

While General Armand Servière marched south from Timimoun, the west Algerian town was attacked by 1,500 Moroccan Berbers. Major René Reibell and 160 Legionnaires fought a bold defence then routed the Berbers at a nearby oasis, using dynamite in place of cannon. The Moroccans withdrew with over 150 killed and were intercepted by Servière at **Charouine** (18 February 1901).

Timisoara I 1514 I Transylvanian Peasant War
    See **Temesvár**

Timisoara I 1552 I Turkish-Habsburg Wars
    See **Temesvár**

Timisoara I 1716 I Austro-Turkish War
    See **Temesvár**

Timisoara I 1849 I Hungarian Revolutionary War
    See **Temesvár**

Tinaja de las Palmas I 1880 I Apache Indian Wars

As Apache Chief Victorio re-entered Texas he was met at Tinaja de las Palmas, a water-hole in the Quitman Canyon south of modern Sierra Blanca, by Buffalo Soldiers under Colonel Benjamin Grierson. With just 24 men against perhaps 150 Indians, Grierson's black troopers held off the Apache until relief arrived. Victorio

was repulsed again days later at **Rattlesnake Springs** (30 July 1880).

Tinaquillo I 1813 I Venezuelan War of Independence
    See **Taguanes**

Tinchebrai I 1106 I Norman Dynastic Wars

Henry I succeeded his father William the Conqueror to the throne of England, but soon faced rebellion at home by his brother, Duke Robert of Normandy. Crossing the channel, Henry defeated Robert near Tinchebrai, a castle north of Domfront held by the dissident Count Robert of Mortain. Henry then held his brother prisoner for life and reunited Normandy and England (28 September 1106).

Tindouf I 1963 I Western Sahara Wars

While claiming the Western Sahara, Morocco invaded the nearby mineral-rich Tindouf region in newly independent Algeria. Moroccan troops nearly took Tindouf town itself before being repulsed in sharp fighting. Algerian air-strikes on northern Morocco further helped end the brief border war which cost perhaps 300 killed on both aides. Fighting resumed 12 years later at **Amgala** (October 1963).

Tinghai I 1840 I 1st Opium War
    See **Dinghai**

Tingsiqiao I 1926 I 1st Chinese Revolutionary Civil War

Campaigning towards **Wuchang**, Nationalist commander Chiang Kai-shek took **Pingjiang**, then drove north and seized **Tingsiqiao** (Tingszekiao). Northern General Wu Beifu sent a massive counter-offensive under Maqi and the city changed hands several times in brutal fighting before he withdrew. Wu himself was defeated next day further east at **Hesheng** (26–29 August 1926).

Tingszekiao I 1926 I 1st Chinese Revolutionary Civil War
    See **Tingsiqiao**

Tingzu I 1926 I 1st Chinese Revolutionary Civil War

General Chiang Kai-shek opened the Nationalist offensive against the warlords of northern China by advancing northeast from **Changsha** through **Pingjiang**. He then sent Zhang Fakui racing for the key Tingzu bridge southeast of Wuchang. Threatened by a bold circling movement, warlord General Wu Beifu was beaten and withdrew north to **Hesheng** (26 August 1926).

Tinian I 1944 I World War II (Pacific)

Two weeks after bloody fighting secured **Saipan**, in the northern **Mariana Islands**, American Generals Harry Schmidt and Thomas Watson landed on nearby Tinian, held by about 9,500 Japanese under Admiral Kakuji Kakuda and Colonel Keishi Ogata. While the island's vital airfields were secured in about a week, it took three months to mop up the last resistance (24 July–1 August 1944).

Tintwa Inyoni I 1899 I 2nd Anglo-Boer War

See **Rietfontein**

Tippecanoe I 1811 I Tecumseh's Confederacy

When the Shawnee Chief Tecumseh organised a confederacy against white expansion, General William Henry Harrison led 1,000 men to Tippecanoe Creek near Lafayette, Indiana. Attacked by Tecumseh's brother Tenskwatawa, Harrison secured an indecisive victory and destroyed nearby "Prophetstown." Tecumseh later supported the British in the War of 1812 (7 November 1811).

Tipperary I 1922 I Irish Civil War

A week after government forces captured rebel **Waterford**, other government units further west under commander Jerry Ryan advanced from Thurley towards Republican troops at Tipperary. Following heavy action just to the east at the town of Golden, Tipperary fell next day and the Republican survivors retired to help defend Carrick-on-Suir, east of **Clonmel** (29–30 July 1922).

Tippermuir I 1644 I British Civil Wars

Following the debacle on **Marston Moor** (2 July) Charles I sent James Graham Marquis of Montrose to Scotland to lead Scots and Irish Royalists against non-conformist Covenanters under David Wemyss Earl of Elcho. At Tippermuir, near Perth, Elcho's much larger force was routed with over 2,000 killed. Within weeks Montrose went on to capture Perth and **Aberdeen** (1 September 1644).

Tirad Pass I 1899 I Philippine-American War

Pursuing Revolutionary President Emilio Aguinaldo along the west coast of Luzon, American Major Peyton C. March and 900 men attacked his rearguard of just 60 men under 24-year-old General Gregorio del Pilar on Mount Tirad, southeast of **Vigan** near Candon. All but seven of the rearguard were killed, including the "Boy-General," but Aguinaldo was able to escape to the north (2 December 1899).

Tiran I 1956 I Arab-Israeli Sinai War

See **Straits of Tiran**

Tirano I 1620 I Swiss-Milanese Wars

Urged on by Spanish Milan, Italian Catholics in the Valtellina Valley on the Upper Adda rose against Switzerland and Bern and Zurich sent forces to protect local Protestants. At Tirano the Cantons were heavily defeated by Spanish regulars and it was almost 20 years before the valley—providing access between Habsburg Austria and Milan—was returned to Swiss sovereignty.

Tirapegui I 1836 I 1st Carlist War

Recovering from a repulse at **Zubiri**, northeast of Pamplona, Spanish Carlists resumed their assault on the French Foreign Legion garrison at nearby Larrasoaña. During an indecisive five-hour action on the overlooking heights of Tirapegui, Legion Colonel Joseph Bernelle inflicted costly losses on a greatly superior Carlist force but eventually had to withdraw into Larrasoaña (25 April 1836).

Tirawari I 1191 I Later Muslim Conquest of Northern India
  See **Taraori**

Tirawari I 1216 I Wars of the Delhi Sultanate
  See **Taraori**

Tirgovist I 1595 I Wallachian-Turkish War
  Ottoman Grand Vizier Sinan Pasha advancing into Romania against Prince Michael the Brave of Wallachia was defeated at **Calugareni** (23 August). He gathered fresh forces to attack Bucharest, then marched northwest and captured Tirgovist. After a brief siege Sinan was driven out by Prince Michael, who pursued the Turks to the Danube and inflicted a costly defeat at **Giurgiu** (October 1595).

Tirlement I 1914 I World War I (Western Front)
  As German troops swept into Belgium and attacked **Liège**, further west General Alexander von Kluck advanced on Brussels. East of the capital near Tirlement (Tienen) a hastily-assembled Belgian force tried to block the invaders but was overwhelmed. Brussels was occupied without resistance next day and King Albert and his survivors withdrew north towards **Antwerp** (18–19 August 1914).

Tiruchirapalli I 1740 I Later Mughal-Maratha Wars
  See **Trichinopoly**

Tiruchirapalli I 1751–1752 I 2nd Carnatic War
  See **Trichinopoly**

Tiruchirapalli I 1757 I Seven Years War (India)
  See **Trichinopoly**

Tiruvadi I 1677 I Bijapur-Maratha Wars
  Campaigning in southeast India, Maratha King Shivaji left part of his army to besiege **Vellore** and pursued Pathan General Sher Khan Lodi to Tiruvadi, west of Cuddalore, where he unwisely challenged the Marathas in the field. Sher Khan Lodi was heavily defeated and made terms (5 July), paying a massive ransom and granting Shivaji all his territory in Bijapur (26 June 1677).

Tiruvadi I 1750 I 2nd Carnatic War
  French Colonel Louis d'Auteil advanced inland from Pondicherry to establish a position on the Poonaiyar at Tiruvadi, where he defeated a force under Captain John Cope and Muhammad Ali, the British-supported Nawab of Arcot. When Cope withdrew d'Auteil again attacked and routed Muhammad Ali, who fled after losing more than 1,000 men (30 July & 1 September 1750).

Tiruvadi I 1753 I 2nd Carnatic War
  Attacking British communications in southeast India, French Colonel Maissin and 2,000 Marathas under Morari Rao besieged Tiruvadi on the Poonaiyar. Reinforcements under Major Stringer Lawrence were repulsed (12 April) and after Lawrence was sent to **Trichinopoly**, a bold sortie from Tiruvadi was completely destroyed. The British garrison then surrendered (14 January–5 May 1753).

Tishomingo Creek I 1864 I American Civil War (Western Theatre)
  See **Brice's Cross Roads**

Tisza I 601 I Byzantine-Balkan Wars
  See **Viminacium**

Tisza (1st) I 1919 I Hungarian-Romanian War
  Determined to prevent Bolshevik Hungary recapturing Transylvania, Romanian forces began a broad offensive east of the Tisza and the key cities of Debrecen and Gyula fell (23–24 April) after heavy Hungarian losses. Hungarian Colonel Károly Kratochvil's division surrendered at Nyírbátor and surviving forces withdrew across the Tisza, stabilising the eastern front (16–26 April 1919).

Tisza (2nd) ▌ 1919 ▌ Hungarian-Romanian War

Hungary's Communist leader Béla Kun withdrew from Slovakia after defeat at **Nove Zamky**, then launched a fresh offensive in the east across the Tisza. His Red Army captured Szolnok, but a week later Kun faced a powerful Romanian counter-attack along the Tisza. The Hungarian army was repulsed along a broad front and the Romanians advanced on **Budapest** (2–27 July 1919).

Tit ▌ 1902 ▌ French Colonial Wars in North Africa

On a reprisal raid south from **In Salah** against the Taureg of southeast Algeria, Lieutenant Gaston Cottonest and 130 men, mainly Arab, came under attack at Tit, northwest of Tamanrasset. The Taureg were eventually repulsed with 93 killed for just 13 casualties in the outnumbered patrol. Taureg power was badly damaged and in 1905 Moussa ag Amastane sued for peace (7 May 1902).

Tizin ▌ 1105 ▌ Crusader-Muslim Wars
See **Artah**

Tizzi Azza ▌ 1922 ▌ Spanish-Rif War

Despite Spanish disaster in Morocco at **Anual** (July 1921) General Ricardo Burguete ordered a new advance from Melilla against the Riffian rebel Abd el Krim. Attacked south of Anual at Tizzi Azza, the Spanish Legion lost almost 2,000 casualties in heavy fighting and the offensive was halted. However, further rebel attacks were repulsed in December and the following June (1–2 November 1922).

Tizzi Azza ▌ 1923 ▌ Spanish-Rif War

Determined the repel the Spanish offensive in Morocco, Rif leader Abd el Krim launched a renewed assault against the Legion outpost at Tizzi Azza, southwest of Melilla. His army was driven off with heavy losses, although Spanish commander Colonel Rafael Valenzuela was killed leading a charge. Peace talks failed and at the end of 1924 the Rif destroyed a Spanish army at **Chaouen** (5 June 1923).

Tjiledug ▌ 1752 ▌ Later Dutch Wars in the East Indies

In support of Ratu Sjarifa of Bantam, in northwest Java, Dutch forces under Colonel Willem von Ossenberch attacked the rebel Kjahi Tapa, who had met with considerable early success and threatened Batavia itself. The Dutch secured a decisive victory at Tjiledug, southeast of Cheribon, then entered Bantam, effectively ending the independence of the Sultanate (13 July 1752).

Toba-Fushimi ▌ 1868 ▌ War of the Meiji Restoration
See **Fushimi**

Tobago ▌ 1793 ▌ French Revolutionary Wars (1st Coalition)

While campaigning against French territory in the West Indies, a British squadron under Admiral Sir John Laforey arrived at Tobago from Bridgetown, Barbados. A 500-strong landing force stormed the town's fort and took the island in less than a day with minimal casualties. Tobago changed hands again several times during the course of the war (14 April 1793).

Tobitschau ▌ 1866 ▌ Seven Weeks War

Crown Prince Karl Wilhelm of Prussia advanced towards Vienna after victory at **Königgratz** (3 July) and attacked Tobitschau, just east of modern Prostejov in eastern Bohemia, held by Austrian General Lothar Rothkirch. After very courageous resistance and an attempted counter-attack, the Austrians were forced to withdraw north to Olmütz, losing 500 casualties and 500 prisoners (16 July 1866).

Tobol ▌ 1919 ▌ Russian Civil War

Defeated in the Urals at **Zlatoust, Ekaterinburg** and **Chelyabinsk**, White commander Admiral Aleksandr Kolchak withdrew to the Tobol, where he made a bold stand against the advancing Red Army of General Mikhail Tukhachevski. Despite initial success, Kolchak was crushed in a renewed offensive and fled east towards **Omsk**, abandoning the city of Petropavlosk (August–October 1919).

Tobruk (1st) I 1941 I World War II (Northern Africa)

After taking **Bardia** in Libya, General Richard O'Connor raced west to attack Tobruk. Following intense air and naval bombardment, British forces stormed the strategic port, capturing huge quantities of stores and 25,000 prisoners, including General Petassi Manella. O'Connor then crossed the desert via **Mechili** to intercept the retreating Italians at **Beda Fomm** (6–22 January 1941).

Tobruk (2nd) I 1941 I World War II (Northern Africa)

Axis General Erwin Rommel advanced into Cyrenaica from **El Agheila** and took Benghazi and Derna, then faced stubborn British resistance at the strategic port of Tobruk. After some costly failed assaults, Rommel turned to drive off a relief force at **Sollum-Halfaya** and Tobruk remained under blockade until after the Allied counter-offensive at **Sidi Rezegh** (10 April–8 December 1941).

Tobruk I 1942 I World War II (Northern Africa)

Having destroyed the defensive line at **Gazala**, German commander Erwin Rommel attacked the garrison left behind at Tobruk, where the defensive perimeter had deteriorated badly. When Axis forces attacked behind a massive artillery and aerial bombardment, South African General Hendrik Klopper surrendered 33,000 men and Rommel raced east towards **El Alamein** (18–21 June 1942).

Tocuyito I 1899 I Venezuelan Civil Wars

Renewing resistance to President Ignacio Andrade, begun at **Mata Carmelera**, Cipriano Castro's "Revolution of Liberal Restoration" secured much of the country. In a final effort General Diego Bautista Ferrer gathered 5,500 men at Valencia, but at nearby Tocuyito he was routed with over 1,000 casualties. The army then started peace talks and Castro became President (14 September 1899).

Tofrek I 1885 I British-Sudan Wars

General Sir Gerald Graham tried to open the road from the Red Sea west to the Nile, beating the Dervishes at **Hashin** before sending General Sir John McNeill VC south to establish a stockade at Tofrek. Surprised by a large Dervish force, McNeill lost almost 300 casualties before his opponents were repulsed with perhaps 2,000 killed. Whitehall then ordered Graham to withdraw (22 March 1885).

Togbao I 1899 I French Conquest of Chad
See **Niellim**

Tohopeka I 1814 I Creek Indian War
See **Horseshoe Bend**

Tohyang-san I 1593 I Japanese Invasion of Korea
See **Haengju**

Tokar I 1883 I British-Sudan Wars

In an effort to relieve the Mahdist siege of Tokar in eastern Sudan, Governor Suleiman Pasha Niyazi sent a force under Mahmud Tahir inland from the Red Sea port of Trinkitat. Advancing towards Tokar, they were routed by a Dervish force led by Abdullah ibn Hamed—with Lynedoch Moncrieff, British consul at Suakin killed—and the survivors fled back to Suakin (4 November 1883).

Tokar I 1891 I British-Sudan Wars

Determined to capture Tokar, in eastern Sudan, Colonel Sir Charles Holled-Smith, Governor of Suakin, advanced inland from Trinkitat against Mahdist commander Osman Digna's camp at nearby Afatit. Osman surprised the outnumbered Anglo-Egyptian force but was eventually defeated. Holled-Smith secured Tokar and Osman withdrew to the Atbara (19 February 1891).

Tokay I 1527 I Turkish-Habsburg Wars

Following his victory at **Mohacs** (August 1526) Sultan Suleiman I withdrew from Hungary leaving the Transylvanian John Zapolya to rule in his name. Ferdinand of Habsburg recovered most of the country, then in the north-east at Tokay decisively defeated Zapolya. In order to aid his vassal, Suleiman then launched a fresh invasion, culminating in the siege of **Vienna** (26 September 1527).

Tokyo I 1868 I War of the Meiji Restoration
See **Ueno**

Tolbiacum I 496 I Frankish-Alemannic War
See **Zulpich**

Toledo, Paraguay I 1933 I Chaco War
While trying to distract Bolivia's attack on **Nanawa** in the Chaco Boreal, Paraguayan Colonel Juan Ayala attacked the Bolivians at Corrales, south of Mariscal Estigarribia, but was himself besieged at nearby Toledo. After a prolonged and bloody assault, the mutinous Bolivians were driven off with 2,000 casualties, including 700 killed, and fled towards Camacho (16 February–11 March 1933).

Toledo, Spain I 1084–1085 I Early Christian Reconquest of Spain
Alfonso VI of Castile took advantage of disunity among the rulers of Islamic Spain to seize the tributary city of Toledo, which fell after a prolonged siege. He then made it his capital, extending the Christian border to the Tagus. However, the Muslims sought military aid from the Almoravids of Morocco and in October 1086 Alfonso was badly defeated at **Zallaka** (1084–6 May 1085).

Toledo, Spain I 1936 I Spanish Civil War
See **Alcazar**

Tolentino I 1815 I Napoleonic Wars (The Hundred Days)
Prematurely declaring war after Napoleon Bonaparte's return from Elbe, King Joachim I of Naples (Marshal Murat) led a Neapolitan army against Austria and was routed by General Vincenz Bianchi at **Ferrara**, then again in central Italy near Macerata at Tolentino, losing all his guns. The Austrians could now move against Bonaparte and Murat returned to France in disgrace (3 May 1815).

Tolenus I 90 BC I Roman Social War
With the Marsi of central Italy fighting Rome after a failed bid for citizenship, Consul Rutilius Lupus marched against them on the Tolenus, north of Carsioli. Attacked by a large force under Vettius Scato, Lupus was defeated and killed, with perhaps 8,000 men lost. Roman commander Gaius Marius quickly counter-attacked downstream and Scato withdrew with costly losses (11 June 90 BC).

Tolhuis I 1672 I 3rd Dutch War
Louis XIV of France and Louis II de Bourbon Prince of Condé invaded Holland with a massive army and advanced down the Rhine. In a sharp action against Field Marshal Paul Wirtz they forced the river on the Dutch border at Tolhuis (modern Lobith) then seized **Nijmegen** and much of the central Dutch Republic. However, they could not manage to capture Amsterdam (12 June 1672).

Tololing I 1999 I Kargil War
When Pakistani regulars and Mujahaden fighters occupied strategic heights in Indian Kashmir, India counter-attacked in force, with heaviest fighting for 16,000 foot Tololing, overlooking Das and the Srinigar-Leh highway. After initial costly failure, large-scale artillery was introduced and the position was taken by brutal assault. Nearby heights fell and the Pakistanis withdrew (22 May–13 June 1999).

Tolomé I 1832 I Mexican Civil Wars
Rebelling in support of Gómez Pedraza against President Anatasio Bustamente, General Antonio de Santa Anna, Governor of Veracruz, met an advancing government army under Generals José Maria Calderón and José Antonio Facio northwest of Veracruz at Tolomé. Santa Anna's outnumbered force suffered a decisive defeat and fell back under siege to **Veracruz** (5 March 1832).

Tolosa, Andalucía I 1212 I Early Christian Reconquest of Spain
See **Las Navas de Tolosa**

Tolosa, Basque Country I 1813 I Napoleonic Wars (Peninsular Campaign)
Five days after the great Allied victory at **Vitoria**, a mixed British-Portuguese-Spanish army advancing into northern Spain under General Sir Thomas Graham encountered French General Maximilien Foy attempting to hold the crossroads city of Tolosa, southwest of San Sebastián. Despite confused and indecisive fighting, Foy held off the attack and was able to retreat into France (26 June 1813).

Tolosa, France I 439 I Goth Invasion of the Roman Empire
See **Toulouse**

Tolosa, France I 458 I Goth Invasion of the Roman Empire
See **Toulouse**

Tolosa, France I 721 I Goth Muslim Invasion of France
See **Toulouse**

Toluca I 1860 I Mexican War of the Reform
Reversing the government defeat at **Calderón** (10 November) President Miguel Miramón and General Miguel Negrete marched west from Mexico City and surprised a Liberal force under Generals Felipe Berriozábal and Santos Degollado at Toluca. While Miramón secured a sharp victory, it was only a brief reprieve and his army was crushed two weeks later at **Calpulalpam** (8 December 1860).

Tolvajärvi I 1939 I Russo-Finnish War
While Russia's main invasion of Finland assaulted the **Mannerheim Line**, General Nikolai Beljajev advanced with 20,000 men further north around Tolvajärvi. General Woldemar Hägglund and Colonel Paavo Talvela drove the Russians off in very heavy fighting and inflicted terrible losses. The invaders meantime suffered even worse casualties around **Suomussalmi** (1–23 December 1939).

Tom's Brook I 1864 I American Civil War (Eastern Theatre)
As Union commander Philip Sheridan withdrew along Virginia's Shenandoah Valley after victory at **Fisher's Hill** (22 September) he sent General Albert T. Torbert against pursuing Confederate Generals Thomas L. Rosser and Lunsford L. Lomax. At Tom's Brook, five miles south of Strasburg, Torbert's cavalry won a sharp victory and the rebels fled south towards Woodstock (9 October 1864).

Tonamiyama I 1183 I Gempei War
See **Kurikara**

Tondibi I 1591 I Moroccan-Songhai War
With the West African Songhai Empire threatening his southern border, Ahmad al-Mansur of Morocco sent 4,000 cavalry and musketeers across the Sahara under Spanish mercenary Judar Pasha. At Tondibi, northwest of Lake Chad, the primitively armed troops of Songhai suffered a terrible defeat. Judar went on to sack Gao and Timbuktu, after which Songhai never fully recovered (12 March 1591).

Tongguan I 756 I An Lushan Rebellion
See **Chang'an**

Tongguan I 1645 I Manchu Conquest of China
Manchu forces helped Ming General Wu Sangui beat rebel Li Zicheng at **Shanhaiguan** before taking Beijing for themselves. Manchu Prince Dodo and General Wu later pursued the rebels into Shaanxi where bloody fighting at Tongguan Pass, east of Xi'an, cost Li's army very heavy losses, including commander Ma Shiyao captured. Li himself was killed later that year (7–8 February 1645).

Tongnae I 1592 I Japanese Invasion of Korea
At the start of Toyotomi Hideyoshi's invasion of Korea, Konishi Yukinaga and So Yoshitomo

secured **Pusan**, then advanced inland against the powerful fortress at Tongnae, courageously defended by 20,000 men under Song Sang-hyun. However, the fortress was stormed, with about 5,000 killed including Song. Japanese forces then advanced through **Sangju** and **Chongju** to Seoul (24 May 1592).

Tongos I 1882 I War of the Pacific

A few days after Chilean forces destroyed the Peruvian hamlet of Nahiumpuqio, southeast of Huancayo, and massacred the people, they were attacked just to the east at Tongos by Huancavelica guerrillas under Domingo Huaripata and Custodio Damián. The Chileans suffered heavy losses and, as an act of revenge, the heads of the slain were displayed on pikes at nearby Izcuchaca (28 March 1882).

Tongres I 57 BC I Rome's Later Gallic Wars

See **Aduatuca**

Tongue I 1865 I Cheyenne-Arapaho Indian War

General Patrick Connor and a force of 250 soldiers and 80 Pawnee Scouts marched out of Fort Laramie against the Arapaho in northern Wyoming and attacked Black Bear at the upper Tongue on the Wyoming-Montana border near modern Ranchester. With their camp overrun and burned, the Arapaho were forced to withdraw, losing 64 warriors and several hundred ponies (29 August 1865).

Tonning I 1713 I 2nd "Great" Northern War

Encouraged by Swedish disaster at **Poltava** in 1709, Frederick IV of Denmark and Augustus II Elector of Saxony invaded Swedish territory in northern Germany. Rallying after defeat at **Gadebusch** (December 1712) the Allies attacked Swedish General Magnus Stenbock at Tonning in Holstein. Stenbock was defeated and forced to capitulate, leaving the Allies to besiege **Stralsund** (16 May 1713).

Toppenish I 1855 I Yakima Indian Wars

Resisting land-hungry miners, Yakima warriors in southern Washington State under Kamiakin killed an Indian Agent then met troops under Major Granville Haller at the Toppenish, near Fort Simcoe. Haller was at first successful, but when Indian reinforcements arrived, he slipped away at night with eight killed and seven wounded. Kamiakin lost weeks later at **Union Gap** (6–8 October 1855).

Tora Bora I 2001 I Afghanistan War

With the fall of the Taliban regime at **Kandahar**, Afghan militia, supported by British and American Special Forces, closed in on perhaps 1,000 Al Qaeda fighters in the Tora Bora Mountains, south of Jalalabad. After heavy ground attack and unprecedented aerial bombing, the besieged survivors fled their devastated cave complex, leaving many killed and wounded (December 2001).

Torata I 1823 I Peruvian War of Independence

On a fresh advance in Peru, Patriot forces led by General Rudecindo Alvarado captured Moquegua then attacked Royalists under Gerónimo Valdez to the northeast at Torata. Leading a rash frontal assault, Alvarado was routed by Spanish cavalry under General José Canterac. With his ammunition exhausted, Alvarado was forced to withdraw, leaving about 400 casualties (19 January 1823).

Torbat-i-Jam I 1528 I Persian-Uzbek Wars

The Uzbek Ubaid Khan defeated Persia and its Mongol allies in 1512 at **Kul-i-Malik** and **Ghujduwan**, then entered western Afghanistan to besiege **Herat**. But he had to withdraw after an Uzbek loss at **Damghan**. Between Herat and Meshed at Torbat-i-Jam, Ubaid was intercepted by Persian Shah Tahmasp and, after heavy losses on both sides, he was wounded and left the field (26 September 1528).

Torbat-i-Jam I 1751 I Persian-Afghan Wars

Amid political confusion following the death of Nadir Shah of Persia, Mir Alum Khan of

Seistan seized government from Nadir's 14-year-old grandson Shah Rukh and marched southeast from Meshed to recapture **Herat**. En route at Torbat-i-Jam he was routed by Timur Shah, son of Afghan ruler Ahmad Shah Durrani. Ahmad then captured Meshed and restored Shah Rukh under his suzerainty.

Torch ▮ 1942 ▮ World War II (Northern Africa)

With Axis forces retreating across Libya after defeat at **El Alamein**, over 100,000 Anglo-American troops under General Dwight D. Eisenhower invaded Vichy Northwest Africa in the amphibious operation codenamed Torch. After landings at **Algiers, Oran** and **Casablanca**, some heavy fighting secured a ceasefire and the Allies advanced into **Tunisia** (8–17 November 1942).

Torches ▮ 1583 ▮ Turko-Persian Wars
See **Vilasa**

Tordesillas ▮ 1812 ▮ Napoleonic Wars (Peninsular Campaign)

While withdrawing from his failed siege of **Burgos** (21 October) Arthur Wellesley Lord Wellington lost at **Venta del Pozo** and **Villa Muriel** before his rearguard tried to hold a position on the Duoro at Tordesillas, southwest of Valladolid. However, they were beaten by French advance units under General Maximilien Foy and Wellington continued his retreat towards Portugal (29 October 1812).

Torfou ▮ 1793 ▮ French Revolutionary Wars (Vendée War)

Days after defeating Royalist rebel leader Francois-Athanase Charette south of the Loire at **Montaigu**, Republican General Jean-Baptiste Kléber pursued him to nearby Torfou and was routed in a brilliant rebel counter-attack. Kléber skillfully disengaged and withdrew northwest pursued by Charles Bonchamp towards **Pallet**, while Charette returned west to recapture Montaigu (19 September 1793).

Torgau ▮ 1760 ▮ Seven Years War (Europe)

Frederick II of Prussia was marching towards Berlin after cutting his way out of **Liegnitz** (15 August) when he turned to attack Austrian Marshal Leopold von Daun south of the capital at Torgau. The Austrians were driven across the Elbe in a disorganised action which continued into the night. It was Frederick's bloodiest victory and both sides withdrew to winter quarters (3 November 1760).

Torgovaya ▮ 1918 ▮ Russian Civil War

On the offensive in the Kuban, White commander Anton Denikin marched against Red General Boris Dumenko at Torgovaya. The respected White General Sergei Markov was killed leading his troops at the capture of nearby Shablievskaya Station, but Torgovaya was taken by storm. Denikin himself then advanced on a Red Brigade at **Belaya Glina** (25 June 1918).

Torgovaya ▮ 1920 ▮ Russian Civil War

As General Symeon Budenny invaded the Kuban east of **Rostov**, White General Aleksandr Pavlov led a counter-offensive to Torgovaya, which fell after he routed General Boris Dumenko's Red cavalry. After hard fighting in bitter cold along the Egorlyk, including the largest cavalry action of the war, Pavlov abandoned his guns and fell back on **Novorossisk** (14 February–2 March 1920).

Torinomi ▮ 1057 ▮ Earlier Nine Years War

When the Abe Clan of Mutsu Province in northeast Japan rose against the Imperial Court, Imperial Governor Minamoto Yoriyoshi attacked the rebels at the Torinomi Stockade, north of modern Hiraizumi in Iwate. Clan leader Abe Yoritoki was defeated and killed, but his son Sadato recovered to check the Imperial forces the following year at **Kawasaki**.

Torna ▮ 1704 ▮ Mughal-Maratha Wars

Emperor Aurangzeb captured the Maratha fortress of **Raigargh** southwest of Poona then quickly sent Muhammad Amin Khan and Tarbiyat Khan against nearby Torna. After a brief siege the Mughals stormed Torna by escalade and forced the garrison to surrender. The victory completed capture of the principal Maratha forts, although most were soon recaptured (23 February–10 March 1704).

Tornavento I 1636 I Thirty Years War (Franco-Habsburg War)

As a French-Savoyard army under Duke Victor Amadeus and Marshal Charles de Crequi campaigned in northern Italy, they were attacked on the Ticino, west of Milan at Tornavento, by Spanish Governor Diego Felipe de Guzmán Marquis de Leganés. The Spaniards were forced to retreat after fierce fighting and suffered another loss the following year at **Monte Baldo** (23 June 1636).

Toro I 1476 I Portuguese-Castilian Wars

Following the death of Henry IV of Castile, many nobles supported his daughter Joanna against his sister Isabella, who married Ferdinand of Aragon and had herself declared Queen of Castile. Joanna's uncle Alfonso V of Portugal (who had married her by proxy) invaded Spain and was defeated at Toro, east of Zamora. Portugal made peace and Joanna retired to a convent.

Toronto I 1837 I Canadian Rebellion

With French-Canadian rebellion crushed at **St Denis**, Upper Canada Governor Francis Head faced an advance on Toronto by insurgents under William McKenzie seeking a provisional government independent of Britain. A volley by Sheriff William Jarvis repulsed the rebels and they were dispersed two days later at nearby Montgomery's Tavern. McKenzie fled to the United States (5 December 1837).

Torrence's Tavern I 1781 I War of the American Revolution

See **Tarrant's Tavern**

Torréon I 1913 I Mexican Revolution

Entering Mexico from Texas, Francisco (Pancho) Villa created the División del Norte and attacked Torréon, which fell by storm after a 24-hour action, yielding vast supplies of arms, ammunition and railway rolling-stock. After executing the Federal officers, Villa left a small garrison and marched on **Chihuahua**, though Torréon was soon retaken by government forces (1 October 1913).

Torréon I 1914 I Mexican Revolution

After taking **Chihuahua** in December 1913, Francisco (Pancho) Villa led a large force against Torréon in central Mexico. The city, which he had won and lost the previous year, was now defended by veteran Federal General José Refugio Velasco. Villa lost heavy casualties in some of the hardest fighting of the revolution before the Federals escaped in a sudden duststorm (26 March–3 April 1914).

Torres Vedras I 1810 I Napoleonic Wars (Peninsular Campaign)

British General Arthur Wellesley Lord Wellington fell back from his bloody victory at **Bussaco** in central Portugal (27 September) and occupied the powerful defensive lines of Torres Vedras outside Lisbon. French Marshal André Masséna probed the sophisticated complex of defences but could make no impact and after a month the French started back to Spain (10 October–14 November 1810).

Torrington I 1646 I British Civil Wars

Bringing an end to the war in the west, Parliamentary commander Sir Thomas Fairfax captured Dartmouth (18 January) then pursued Sir Ralph Hopton into North Devon. Hopton's Cornish infantry were heavily defeated at Torrington, near Barnstaple, and he later signed a separate surrender a week before the Royalist cause was finally crushed in March at **Stow** (16 February 1646).

Tortona I 1155 I Frederick's 1st Expedition to Italy

Emperor Frederick Barbarossa marched into northern Italy with a large army and attempted to weaken Milan by ravaging her allies such as Asti and Chiari. He then besieged the unfortunate city of Tortona, east of Alessandria, which held out for two months against a bloody siege until forced by lack of water to surrender. Tortona was then burned to the ground (February–April 1195).

Tortosa | 1148 | Early Christian Reconquest of Spain

A renewed Christian offensive in eastern Spain saw Ramon Berenguer IV of Aragon launch a major attack against Tortosa at the mouth of the Ebro, aided by Count William of Montpellier, Genoese troops and European Crusaders fresh from capturing Lisbon. The city fell after a six-month siege, completing Christian control of the whole Ebro basin (July–December 1148).

Tortosa | 1810–1811 | Napoleonic Wars (Peninsular Campaign)

Six months after the siege and capture of **Lérida**, Marshal Louis Suchet marched into Catalonia to besiege Tortosa on the Ebro, defended by General Miguel Lili e Idiáquez Conde de Alacha. Tortosa was subjected to extreme shelling and, with the capture of the bastion of San Pedro, Alacha surrendered the city. Suchet then advanced to the siege of **Tarragona** (19 December 1810–2 February 1811).

Torun | 1703 | 2nd "Great" Northern War
See **Thorn**

Tory Island | 1798 | French Revolutionary Wars (Irish Rising)
See **Donegal Bay**

Toshimitsu | 1587 | Japan's Era of the Warring States

The Shimazu brothers Yoshihiro and Iehisa led a Satsuma invasion of northeast Kyushu to besiege Toshimitsu and threaten Funai (modern Oita) where Otomo Yoshimune sought aid from Toyotomi Hideyoshi. He sent Sengoku Hidehisa and Chosokabe Motochika from Shikoku, who were routed near Toshimitsu at the Hetsugigawa, but the Satsuma withdrew to **Takashiro** (January 1587).

Toski | 1889 | British-Sudan Wars

Flushed with victory over Abyssinia at **Gallabat** (9 March) about 8,000 Mahdists under Emir Wad el-Najumi invaded Egypt, where they were met at Toski, north of Wadi Halfa, by an Egyptian army led by the Sirdar Sir Francis Grenfell, supported by cavalry under Colonel Herbert Kitchener. Najumi was killed in a complete rout with most of his army killed or captured (3 August 1889).

Tot-dong | 1426 | Sino-Vietnamese War

Besieged at **Dong-do** (later Hanoi) by Vietnamese commander Le Loi and General Nguyen Trai, Ming Chinese General Wang Tong rashly attempted a counter-offensive, against the advice of Commissioner Chen Qia. At nearby Tot-dong the Chinese were routed, with Chen Qia fatally wounded. After further defeat at **Chi Lang** (1427) China withdrew from Vietnam (5–6 December 1426).

Totopotomoy Creek | 1864 | American Civil War (Eastern Theatre)

Union commander Ulysses S. Grant was advancing south from the **North Anna** across the Pamunkey towards Richmond, Virginia, when he was blocked northeast of the Confederate capital at Totopotomoy Creek by General Robert E. Lee. After inconclusive manoeuvring and about 1,000 men lost on either side, both armies moved further south to meet again at **Cold Harbour** (28–30 May 1864).

Toul | 1870 | Franco-Prussian War

Advancing west from **Strasbourg**, German forces attacked Toul, commanding the vital rail line to Paris. After failure to take it by assault, the fortress was besieged. When Friedrich Franz II of Mecklenburg arrived from **Sedan** with reinforcements and siege guns, Toul was forced to capitulate. The Grand Duke then marched northwest against **Soissons** (17 August–23 September 1870).

Toulon | 1707 | War of the Spanish Succession

With the French driven out of Italy after **Turin** (September 1706) Prince Eugène and Victor

Amadeus II of Savoy marched west towards Toulon, defended by Marshal Count René de Tessé. Despite a naval blockade by Sir Clowdesley Shovell, and eight French ships scuttled, the siege and assault failed and the Allies withdrew. Shovell drowned in a shipwreck on the way home (15 July–10 August 1707).

Toulon I 1744 I War of the Austrian Succession

Admirals Claude-Élisée La Bruyère and José Navarro led their ships out of Toulon and were intercepted by British Admirals Thomas Matthews and Richard Lestock. In a badly handled action the French and Spanish ships inflicted the greater damage and broke the English blockade. Matthews was court-martialled and cashiered while Lestock was controversially acquitted (21 February 1744).

Toulon I 1793 I French Revolutionary Wars (1st Coalition)

Supporting Royalists in Toulon, British Admiral Sir Alexander Hood and Admiral Juan de Langara of Spain seized the port and landed a force under Sir Henry Phipps. After General Jacques Dugommier besieged Toulon and Colonel Napoleon Bonaparte captured strategic forts, the Allies evacuated, taking or destroying much of the French fleet (27 August–19 December 1793).

Toulon I 1944 I World War II (Western Europe)

When Allied forces invaded southern France along the **Riviera**, Free French commander Jean de Lattre de Tassigny ordered General Edgar de Larminant west along the coast against the key port of Toulon. The strong German garrison resisted in bloody street-by-street fighting, but with the French closing in on **Marseilles** to the west, 17,000 men finally surrendered (20–28 August 1944).

Toulouse I 439 I Goth Invasion of the Roman Empire

Over-confident after the siege of **Narbonne** (437) Roman General Litorius led his largely Hun army against the Goth capital at Tolosa (modern Toulouse). In the war's decisive battle, the Goth King Theodoric attacked the Roman camp, causing heavy casualties, including Litorius captured and executed. However, Goth losses were also heavy and Theodoric made peace with Governor Avitus.

Toulouse I 458 I Goth Invasion of the Roman Empire

The Western Emperor Majorian led an epic mid-winter expedition over the Alps, taking a large army from Italy into Gaul to restore Roman authority after chaos at the end of Avitus' reign. He defeated the Visigoth Theodoric II near his capital at Toulouse, then secured his co-operation against the Suevi in Spain. However, fighting later resumed and Theodoric's army was finally routed at **Orleans** in 463.

Toulouse I 721 I Muslim Invasion of France

Having conquered Spain, Muslim Arabs crossed the Pyrenees into Aquitaine where Sama ibn Malik, the Arab Viceroy of Spain, besieged Toulouse. Attacked by a relief army under Eudo Duke of Aquitaine, Sama was heavily defeated and killed. The victory marked the first major setback to the Arab invasion of Western Europe. Eudo also helped repulse a second expedition ten years later at **Tours**.

Toulouse I 1218 I Anglo-French Wars

After Simon de Montfort's defeat of the Albigensians at **Muret**, the Anglo-Norman knight was granted land belonging to Raymond IV of Toulouse, who had supported the heretics. Raymond reoccupied Toulouse in 1217, where he was besieged by de Montfort. Simon was killed in the fighting and his son Amaury later conceded the disputed land to King Louis VIII (25 June 1218).

Toulouse I 1799 I French Revolutionary Wars (2nd Coalition)

With the Royalist cause gaining renewed support in southwestern France, a large Royalist force, with English and Spanish support, advanced on Republican Toulouse. Heavy fighting outside the city and on the nearby Pech David

Hill saw the rebels badly defeated with perhaps 400 killed and 800 captured. The survivors were then crushed to the southwest at **Montréjeau** (7–9 August 1799).

Toulouse I 1814 I Napoleonic Wars (Peninsular Campaign)

Marshal Nicolas Soult was withdrawing after defeat at **Orthez** (27 February) when he turned to defend the French city of Toulouse against Arthur Wellesley Lord Wellington. Soult threw back a costly attack by Spanish General Manuel Freire but was driven out by General Sir William Beresford. Only after the battle did the combatants learn Napoleon Bonaparte had already abdicated (10 April 1814).

Toumorong I 1966 I Vietnam War

North Vietnamese regulars opened a monsoon season offensive into the central Highlands of Kontum, advancing around the isolated mountain outpost at Toumorong. Aided by massive bombing, US airborne forces counter-attacked (Operation Hawthorne) to raise the siege and virtually annihilate an enemy regiment. The action was claimed as some of the hardest fighting of the war (5–7 June 1966).

Toungoo I 1942 I World War II (Burma-India)

While Japanese forces occupied Rangoon, General Hiroshi Takeuchi drove north towards Mandalay and met Chinese coming down the Burma Road, who tried to halt the invaders at Toungoo. Despite courageous defence by General Tai Anlan's 200th Brigade, the Chinese were driven off towards **Lashio** with heavy losses. Further west, the British lost **Prome** (26–30 March 1942).

Tourane I 1858 I French Conquest of Indo-China

See **Danang**

Tourcoing I 1794 I French Revolutionary Wars (1st Coalition)

Invading from Belgium, the Austrian-British-Hanoverian army of Friedrich Josias Prince of Saxe-Coburg met the French at Tourcoing, northeast of Lille, led by Generals Charles Pichegru and Joseph Souham. After the Allied army divided into columns, the centre advanced and was cut to pieces. Prince Friedrich was forced to withdraw and the French went on to take **Charleroi** (18 May 1794).

Tournai I 1214 I Anglo-French Wars

See **Bouvines**

Tournai I 1340 I Hundred Years War

Following his great naval victory at **Sluys** (24 June) Edward III of England landed in Flanders and marched to support the siege of Tournai, held by Gaston II Count of Foix against Jacob van Artevelde and his Flemish artisan army. The siege cost both sides heavy losses and when Philip VI of France approached with a large force the rival kings made a brief truce (29 July–24 September 1340).

Tournai I 1581 I Netherlands War of Independence

Repulsed from an attack on Cambrai, Spanish Viceroy Alexander Farnese, later Duke of Parma, turned against Tournai, courageously defended in the absence of her husband by Marie van Lalaing, Princess of Espinoy. She negotiated an honourable capitulation after a two-month siege and the citizens were levied a ransom to save the city from sack (1 October–29 November 1581).

Tournai I 1709 I War of the Spanish Succession

Following failed peace talks after the fall of **Lille**, John Churchill Duke of Marlborough and Prince Eugène of Savoy marched east to besiege Tournai, defended by Louis de Hautefort, Marquis de Surville. French Marshal Claude Villars was unable to relieve the fortress and, after it was forced to surrender, the Allies marched southeast against Villars at **Mons** (28 June–3 September 1709).

Tournai I 1794 I French Revolutionary Wars (1st Coalition)

French General Charles Pichegru failed to follow up his victory at **Tourcoing** in Belgium, permitting the Austrian-British-Hanoverian Allies to reform on the Scheldte. In an indecisive battle five days later at Tournai, east of Lille, despite success around **Pont-à-Chin**, both sides disengaged with heavy casualties and the Allies were forced to continue withdrawing north (22 May 1794).

Tours I 732 I Muslim Invasion of France

The Arab governor Abd-ar-Rahman invaded France from Spain to win at **Bordeaux** before being confronted near the Vienne, between Tours and Poitiers, by Eudo Duke of Aquitaine and a Frankish army under Charles Martel. An historic victory which halted the tide of Islam in western Europe saw Abd-ar-Rahman killed. Charles was given the name Martel—The Hammer (October 732).

Towcester I 61 I Roman Conquest of Britain
See **Boudicca**

Towton I 1461 I Wars of the Roses

Despite victory at **St Albans**, Henry VI and Margaret of Anjou returned to Lancashire, pursued by Edward Duke of York and Richard Neville Earl of Warwick. After defeat at **Ferrybridge**, the Lancastrians were routed next day at Towton, near Tadcaster, in the bloodiest battle of the war. Henry and Queen Margaret fled to Scotland and York took the throne as Edward IV (29 March 1461).

Toyotomi Castle I 1614–1615 I Japan's Era of the Warring States
See **Osaka Castle**

Trading Post I 1864 I American Civil War (Trans-Mississippi)
See **Marais des Cygnes**

Trafalgar I 1805 I Napoleonic Wars (3rd Coalition)

One of Britain's most important naval victories saw Admiral Lord Horatio Nelson lead his fleet to intercept and destroy the French-Spanish fleet under Admiral Pierre Villeneuve off Cape Trafalgar, west of Gibraltar. Without any ships lost, the British sank or captured 18 rival vessels and inflicted about 14,000 casualties. However, Nelson was fatally wounded by a French sniper (21 October 1805).

Trajan's Gate I 986 I Byzantine Wars of Tsar Samuel

After marching into Bulgaria against the newly established Tsar Samuel, the Byzantine Emperor Basil II failed in a poorly managed siege of Sardica (modern Sofia) and was attacked as he withdrew southeast through Trajan's Gate, a mountain pass beyond Ikhtiman. The Imperial army was heavily defeated, losing valuable baggage, and Basil was lucky to escape with his life (17 August 986).

Tra-khe I 605 I Sino-Vietnamese Wars

Sent to restore Chinese authority in rebellious Vietnam, General Liu Fang secured Annam in the north with victory at **Giao-chao**, then marched south into Champa, where he defeated King Sambhuvarman's army and looted his capital at Tra-khe (near modern Danang). The King agreed to maintain tribute to China but on the way home Liu Fang died in an epidemic which struck his army.

Traktir Bridge I 1855 I Crimean War
See **Chernaya**

Trancheron I 1648 I Thirty Years War (Franco-Habsburg War)

French Marshals Charles de la Porte Duke de la Meilleraie and Cesar de Choiscul du Plessis-Praslin captured **Piombino** and **Porto Longone**, then concluded war in northern Italy by advancing against the Spanish army entrenched at Trancheron, between Cremona and the Oglio. Luis Benavides Marquis de Caracéna was heavily defeated, then shut up in the ruins of Cremona (30 June 1648).

Transloy Ridges I 1916 I World War I (Western Front)

Days after success on the **Somme** at **Morval** and **Thiepval**, British General Sir Henry

Rawlinson attacked on a broad front along the Albert-Bapaume Road. The Battle of the Transloy Ridges saw Eaucourt and Le Sars captured, lost to German counter-attack, then taken again. The French took Sailly before the action ground to a halt in terrible cold and mud (1–18 October 1916).

Tranter's Creek | 1862 | American Civil War (Eastern Theatre)

As part of his expedition against the Carolina coast, Union General Ambrose E. Burnside sent Colonel Francis A. Osborn from Washington, on the Pamlico River in North Carolina, west along the Grenville Road towards Pactolus. In action at nearby Tranter's Creek, Osborne defeated and killed Confederate Colonel George B. Singletary, then returned to Washington (5 June 1862).

Trapani | 249 BC | 1st Punic War
    See **Drepanum**

Trapani | 1266 | Venetian-Genoese Wars

Venetian Admiral Jacopo Dandolo resolved to avenge losses at **Saseno** (1264) and pursued Genoa's fleet to Trapani, in western Sicily, where Admiral Lanfranco Borborino unwisely decided to chain and defend his ships rather than meet the Venetians at sea. Dandolo captured all 27 Genoese galleys, reinforcing Venetian naval supremacy. Borborino was tried for cowardice (23 June 1266).

Trasimeno | 217 BC | 2nd Punic War
    See **Lake Trasimene**

Trautenau | 1866 | Seven Weeks War

While Prussian Prince Friedrich Karl invaded Austrian Bohemia through **Liebenau** and **Podol**, Crown Prince Friedrich Wilhelm and General Adolf von Bonin invaded towards Trautenau (modern Trutnov) northeast of **Königgratz**. Although the invaders were initially driven back, Austrians under Baron Ludwig von Gablenz suffered far greater losses and fell back through **Soor** (27 June 1866).

Travancore | 1789 | 3rd British-Mysore War

Tipu Sultan of Mysore was dissatisfied with the peace of 1784 and sought French aid to renew war. The trigger was a dispute over Cochin in which Tipu attacked the British protectorate of Travancore. He was driven off with costly losses and France provided no real help in the ensuing war. When it ended at **Seringapatam** (February 1792) Tipu lost half his kingdom (29 December 1789).

Treasury Islands | 1943 | World War II (Pacific)

New Zealanders under Brigadier Robert Row helped secure **Vella Lavella** (5 October) then moved west to the Treasury Islands for their first opposed landing since **Gallipoli** 1915. While Stirling fell quickly, sharp fighting on Mono caused the New Zealanders 40 killed and 140 wounded, as well as 40 American casualties. All but eight of the 200 Japanese garrison died (27 October–1 November 1943).

Trebbia | 218 BC | 2nd Punic War

Driven back from defeat at the **Ticinus** by Hannibal's Carthaginians, a Roman army took up position on the Trebbia River, near Placentia (modern Piacenza). Reinforced by Gauls from the Po Valley, Hannibal enticed Consul Sempronius Longus to attack in a snowstorm. A total rout saw the Romans destroyed, with many drowned trying to escape across the icy river (December 218 BC).

Trebbia | 1799 | French Revolutionary Wars (2nd Coalition)

Marching north through the Apennines to reinforce General Jean Victor Moreau, General Jacques Macdonald found himself facing a massive Austrian-Russian army under General Alexander Suvorov, who was determined to keep the two French forces apart. A hard-fought battle on the Trebbia, saw Macdonald heavily defeated with massive losses in casualties and prisoners (17–19 June 1799).

**Trebizond I 1916 I World War I
(Caucasus Front)**

While Russian forces stormed across the Caucasus through **Erzurum**, General V. P. Lyakhov led a subsidiary advance along the Black Sea through Rize (7 March). Aided by naval bombardment from Admiral Andrei Ebergard, the Russians stormed the supply port at Trebizond, driving out the Turks and Germans. Lyakhov then turned south to aid the attack on **Bayburt** (17–18 April 1916).

Trembowla I 1657 I Transylvanian-Polish War

Prince George Rákóczi II of Transylvania captured **Warsaw** in an attempt to seize the Polish throne (23 July) but was then abandoned by his Swedish and Cossack allies and his humiliating retreat was intercepted in the Ukraine by Crimean Tatars. At Trembowla (modern Terebovlya) southeast of Ternopol he suffered a crushing defeat, with his commander Janos Kemény captured (31 July 1657).

Trembowla I 1675 I Turkish Invasion of the Ukraine

After Turkish and Tatar forces invaded the Polish Ukraine, Trembowla (modern Terebovlya), southeast of Ternopol, held out—according to legend—when the Polish commander's wife threatened to kill herself if her husband surrendered. Following his victory further west at **Zloczow** (24 August) John Sobieski III of Poland relieved the fortress, whose defence became a byword for heroism.

Trench I 627 I Campaigns of the Prophet Mohammed
See **Medina**

Trenchin I 1708 I Rákóczi Rebellion

Recovering from defeat at **Zsibó** in 1705, Prince Ferenc II Rákóczi of Transylvania continued rebellion against Austria and attempted to advance into Bohemia. Near the Moravian border at Trenchin, on the Vah River, Rákóczi's superior force was utterly destroyed by Field Marshal Siegbert Heister. However, the rebellion dragged on until 1711 when Rákóczi fled to Poland (4 August 1708).

Trent I 679 I Anglo-Saxon Territorial Wars

In the final great battle between Mercia and Northumbria, Aethelred of Mercia marched against Ecgfrith of Northumbria, who had defeated his brother Wulfhere at **Biedenheafde** (674) and seized the disputed Kingdom of Lindsey. Ecgfrith was heavily defeated near the River Trent and Lindsey was recovered. In 685 the Northumbrian King was killed fighting the Picts at **Dunnichen Moss**.

Trentino Offensive I 1916 I World War I (Italian Front)
See **Asiago**

Trenton I 1776 I War of the American Revolution

American General George Washington retreated through New Jersey after defeat at **White Plains** (28 October) then resolved to regain the initiative and crossed the Delaware in a snowstorm to attack Trenton. Washington routed the Hessian garrison, which lost almost 1,000 captured and 20 dead (including Colonel Johann Rall). He soon won again at **Princeton** (26 December 1776).

Trepa I 1809 I Napoleonic Wars (Peninsular Campaign)

As French Marshal Nicolas Soult invaded Portugal, Spanish General Pedro La Romana withdrew along the northern border towards Puebla de Sanabria. At Trepa, east of Verin near Osono, his rearguard under General Nicolas Mahy was attacked by General Jean-Baptiste Franceschi, who killed 300 and took over 600 prisoners. However, La Romana's main army got away (6 March 1809).

Trepani I 1266 I Venetian-Genoese Wars
See **Trapani**

Tre Ponti ∎ 1859 ∎ 2nd Italian War of Independence

On campaign in northern Italy, Giuseppe Garibaldi won at **Varese** and **San Fermo** before the Italian army command sent him on an almost suicidal mission against the Austrians at Lonato. Garibaldi's advance units under General Stefan Turr were heavily repulsed southeast of Brescia at Tre Ponti, near Castenedolo, but Austrian defeat at **Solferino** soon ended the war (15 June 1859).

Tres Castillos ∎ 1880 ∎ Apache Indian Wars

The Apache Chief Victorio was driven back into northern Mexico from **Rattlesnake Springs** and reached the Chihuahua desert, where he was attacked at Tres Castillos by 350 Mexicans and Tarahumara Indians under Colonel Joaquin Terrazas. Victorio and about 80 Apache were killed, and 68 men, women and children captured, but the veteran Nana escaped to join Geronimo (15 October 1880).

Treschina ∎ 1794 ∎ War of the 2nd Polish Partition
See **Brest-Litovsk**

Trevilian Station ∎ 1864 ∎ American Civil War (Eastern Theatre)

As Union commander Ulysses S. Grant withdrew from **Cold Harbour** towards **Petersburg**, he sent General Philip Sheridan raiding into the Confederate rear. In a bloody cavalry action about 50 miles northwest of Richmond at Trevilian Station, Virginia, Sheridan was repulsed by Confederate General Wade Hampton. He then withdrew through **St Mary's Church** to the James (11–12 June 1864).

Treviño ∎ 1875 ∎ 2nd Carlist War

The Spanish Republican commander General Jenardo de Quesada was advancing on the key city of Vitoria, in Navarre, when he sent General Juan Tello to attack the Carlist lines just to the southwest at Treviño. The newly appointed Carlist leader General José Pérula was heavily defeated and withdrew. Soon afterwards Quesada entered Vitoria in triumph (7 July 1875).

Triangle Hill ∎ 1952 ∎ Korean War

With peace talks stalled, American General James van Fleet launched a limited offensive north of Kumho against Triangle Hill (plus nearby Jane Russell Hill and Pike's Peak). However, United Nations and South Korean troops were halted by unexpectedly strong Communist resistance. The failed offensive cost perhaps 9,000 Allied and 19,000 Chinese casualties (14 October–5 November 1952).

Tricameron ∎ 533 ∎ Vandal War in Africa

Fleeing from the fall of **Carthage**, Vandal King Gelimer took up position 20 miles away at Tricameron, where he was reinforced by his brother Tzazo, returned from the conquest of Sardinia. But the combined Vandal force was routed by the Roman cavalry of General Belisarius, with Gelimer captured and Tzazo killed, effectively ending the Vandal occupation of North Africa (December 533).

Trichinopoly ∎ 1740–1741 ∎ Later Mughal-Maratha Wars

Maratha General Raghuji Bhonsle invaded southeast India to kill Nawab Dost Ali Khan of Arcot at **Damalcherry** (May 1740) then besieged the Nawab's son-in-law Chanda Sahib at Trichinopoly (Tiruchirapalli). When Chanda Sahib's brother Bada Sahib was killed trying to relieve the siege, Chanda was starved into surrender and the Marathas secured Arcot (December 1740–14 March 1741).

Trichinopoly ∎ 1743 ∎ Later Mughal-Maratha Wars

Determined to intervene in a disputed succession in the Carnatic, Nizam-ul-Mulk of Hyderabad set out with a very large force against the Marathas and, after capturing Arcot, laid siege to Trichinopoly (modern Tiruchirapalli). After five months, Maratha Murari Rao Ghorpade agreed to evacuate the Carnatic and the Nizam appointed Anwar-ud-Din as Nawab (March–21 August 1743).

Trichinopoly | 1751–1752 |
2nd Carnatic War

Driven south from defeat at **Volkondah** (20 July) British and Indian troops under Captain Rudolph Gingens and Muhammad Ali of Arcot were besieged at Trichinopoly (modern Tiruchirapalli) by Nawab Chanda Sahib and Colonel Jacques Law. Trichinopoly was eventually relieved by British Major Stringer Lawrence, who then beat the besiegers at nearby **Seringham** (July 1751–10 April 1752).

Trichinopoly (1st) | 1753 |
2nd Carnatic War

French Governor General Joseph Dupleix resolved to retake Trichinopoly (modern Tiruchirapalli) in southeast India and sent Colonel Astruc to besiege Captain John Dalton's garrison. However, at nearby Golden Rock, reinforcements under Major Stringer Lawrence saw field guns and infantry defeat French-led native cavalry. Astruc was replaced in command (7 July 1753).

Trichinopoly (2nd) | 1753 |
2nd Carnatic War

After a previous failed attempt to retake Trichinopoly (modern Tiruchirapalli) in southeast India, French Governor General Joseph Dupleix sent Colonel Brenier against Major Stringer Lawrence, who had received 5,000 Tanjorean reinforcements. Advancing to Weyconda, west of the fortress, Brenier was heavily defeated by Lawrence and was removed from command (18 August 1753).

Trichinopoly (3rd) | 1753 |
2nd Carnatic War

In a third attempt to retake Trichinopoly (modern Tiruchirapalli) in southeast India, French Colonel Astruc was restored to command and led a powerful assault from the south near Sugar Loaf Rock. He was again heavily defeated and was taken prisoner by the garrison under Major Stringer Lawrence. The French eventually withdrew in August 1754 and the war ended (2 October 1753).

Trichinopoly | 1757 | Seven Years
War (India)

When France resumed war in southeast India, Colonel Louis d'Auteil took 4,000 men against Trichinopoly (modern Tiruchirapalli) defended by British Captain Joseph Smith with a handful of Europeans and fewer than 2,000 Sepoys. With a small relief column under Captain John Caillaud approaching, d'Auteil withdrew to Pondicherry and he lost his command (14–25 May 1757).

Triesen | 1499 | Swabian War

At the beginning of their final struggle for freedom, the Swiss cantons marched against the Habsburg cities of the Swabian League and entered the Vorarlberg, where they routed a Swabian army at Triesen, in modern Lichtenstein. The Swiss then went on to burn Vaduz and ten days later defeated a major German force at **Hard** (9 February 1499).

Trifanum | 339 BC | Latin War
See **Suessa**

Trikalur | 1782 | 2nd British-
Mysore War

Colonel Thomas Humberston was campaigning on the Malabar coast of southwest India when he advanced inland against Mysorean General Mukhdum Ali, brother-in-law of Haidar Ali of Mysore. Despite massive numerical superiority, Mukhdum Ali was heavily defeated and killed at Trikalur. The Marathas were eventually repulsed in November at the **Paniani** (3 April 1782).

Trikorpha | 1825 | Greek War
of Independence

When the Egyptian-Turkish army of Ibrahim Pasha was checked at **Lerna**, Greek General Theodoros Kolokotronis attempted to advance on Tripolitza, securing the nearby heights at Trikorpha. Personally leading an attack, Ibrahim defeated the Greeks, who lost about 200 killed. After further Greek losses in heavy skirmishing, Ibrahim eventually withdrew towards **Missolonghi** (6 July 1825).

Trimmu Ghat ▌ **1857** ▌ **Indian Mutiny**

While British forces besieged rebel-held **Delhi**, General John Nicholson was sent in pursuit of Sialkot mutineers. Advancing through Gurdaspur, he intercepted the rebels crossing the Ravi nine miles away at Trimmu Ghat. Despite heavy losses to grape and shrapnel, the mutineers remained on a mid-river island, where they were attacked again four days later and destroyed (12 and 16 July 1857).

Trincomalee ▌ **1639** ▌ **Later Portuguese Colonial Wars in Asia**

A year after the Portuguese were disastrously defeated at **Gannoruwa**, Dutch forces joined with the Kingdom of Kandy in central Ceylon and captured the east coast Portuguese trading city of Trincomalee. The Dutch handed Trincomalee and Batticaloa to the Kandyans, but later captured and kept Galle and Negombo. They eventually seized the entire country in 1656 after the fall of **Colombo**.

Trincomalee ▌ **1759** ▌ **Seven Years War (India)**

See **Pondicherry**

Trincomalee ▌ **1782** ▌ **War of the American Revolution**

In the fourth of five indecisive naval actions off the east coast of India, British Admiral Edward Hughes appeared off Trincomalee in Ceylon just after it had fallen to French Admiral Pierre André Suffren. Following a poorly managed engagement, with the French flagship heavily damaged, Hughes withdrew and the fleets met again nine months later off **Cuddalore** (3 September 1782).

Trincomalee ▌ **1795** ▌ **French Revolutionary Wars (1st Coalition)**

After Napoleon Bonaparte's forces occupied the Netherlands, British forces under Admiral Peter Rainier, Commander in Chief of the East India Station, and Colonel James Stuart (1741–1815) of the Madras Army invaded Dutch Ceylon (modern Sri Lanka) and captured Trincomalee. They then moved around the coast by sea to attack the capital, **Colombo** (25 August 1795).

Trincomalee ▌ **1942** ▌ **World War II (Indian Ocean)**

When Admiral Chuichi Nagumo attacked **Colombo** in **Ceylon** (modern Sri Lanka) Admiral Sir James Somerville cleared the other key naval base at Trincomalee. Carrier planes damaged the docks and the British lost 11 fighters plus five bombers sent against the attacking fleet. Japanese aircraft then pursued the scattered British ships, sinking the old carrier *Hermes* and four other vessels (9 April 1942).

Trinidad, Mexico ▌ **1915** ▌ **Mexican Revolution**

Francisco (Pancho) Villa turned on his former ally President Venustiano Carranza and suffered a terrible defeat at **Celaya** in central Mexico (15 April) then withdrew northwest to Trinidad, where General Álvaro Obregón began a broad battle of attrition. Attempting to attack the Constitutionalists' rear at Leon, Villa was routed and continued falling back on **Aguascalientes** (29 April–5 June 1915).

Trinidad, West Indies ▌ **1797** ▌ **French Revolutionary Wars (1st Coalition)**

Advancing against the West Indian island of Trinidad, British Admiral Sir Henry Harvey and General Sir Ralph Abercromby defeated the Spanish garrison and Abercromby's Spanish-speaking Aide, Colonel Thomas Picton, was left in command as Governor. At the peace of 1801, partly at the request of the Spanish residents, the island remained a British possession (16–17 February 1797).

Trinkitat ▌ **1884** ▌ **British-Sudan Wars**

See **El Teb**

Trinomalee ▌ **1767** ▌ **1st British-Mysore War**

Driven back by Haidar Ali of Mysore following defeat at **Chengam** Colonel Joseph Smith met the Maharaja and Nizam Ali of Hyderabad at Trinomalee (modern Tiruvannamalai), inland from

Pondicherry. Smith secured a decisive victory against massive odds with fewer than 100 casualties. The Nizam made peace and Haidar Ali marched against **Ambur** (26 September 1767).

Triple Offensive I 1915 I World War I (Eastern Front)

German commander Erich von Ludendorf was determined to crush Russia's armies on the eastern front and launched his massive Triple Offensive, in the north through **Kovno** towards **Vilna** and **Dvinsk**, in the centre through **Warsaw** and in south through **Brest-Litovsk**. The "Great Retreat" cost the Russians two million casualties before the front stabilised (29 June–26 September 1915).

Tripole I 1093 I Russian Dynastic Wars

Facing invasion by Kipchak Turk (Cuman) horsemen of the northern Steppe, Grand Prince Sviatopolk of Kiev and his cousins Vladimir and Rostislav—sons of former Grand Prince Vsevolod—met their enemy at Tripole (modern Tripolye) near Kiev. The Russians were routed, with Rostislav killed, and Sviatopolk sued for peace, later marrying a daughter of the Kipchak Khan (23 May 1093).

Tripoli, Lebanon I 1102 I Crusader-Muslim Wars

Marching south from Tortosa (modern Tartus) Raymond of Saint-Gilles Count of Toulouse advanced on the key fortress of Tripoli, held by Emir Fakhr al-Mulk, supported by troops from Homs and Damascus. Battle outside the city saw the larger Muslim army defeated with terrible losses. However, Raymond had insufficient men to attack Tripoli itself and he eventually withdrew.

Tripoli, Lebanon I 1109 I Crusader-Muslim Wars

King Baldwin I of Jerusalem raised a large army for a major Crusader offensive against the powerful port of Tripoli, supported by Bertrand of Toulouse and Tancred of Antioch. Fatimid Egyptian Governor Sharaf ad-Daulah surrendered after weeks of heavy assault, and Bertrand

(illegitimate son of the great Crusader Raymond of Toulouse) became Governor of Tripoli (6 March–12 July 1109).

Tripoli, Lebanon I 1289 I Later Crusader-Muslim Wars

Years of campaigning against Crusaders culminated when Mamluk Sultan Qalawun finally gathered his Egyptian-Syrian army for a decisive assault against the powerful fortress of Tripoli. After a massive bombardment the Muslims stormed the city and massacred the population. Tripoli was then razed to the ground and the Mamluks soon turned against at **Acre** (25 March–27 April 1289).

Tripoli, Libya I 647 I Muslim Conquest of North Africa

See **Sufetula**

Tripoli, Libya I 1510 I Spanish Colonial Wars in North Africa

Continuing his offensive in North Africa after capturing **Bougie**, Spanish commander Pedro Navarro took his fleet from Sicily against Tripoli (modern Tarabulus, Libya). After capturing the city, Navarro reportedly destroyed many of its buildings and killed or enslaved much of the population. In 1524, Spain gave Tripoli to the Knights of St John, who lost it in 1551 to Ottoman forces (26 July 1510).

Tripoli, Libya I 1551 I Turkish Imperial Wars

Expanding Ottoman territory in North Africa, Kapudan Sinan Pasha and the Corsair Turghud Re'is (Dragut) attacked strategic Tripoli, held with difficulty by the Knights of St John from their base in Malta. Tripoli was taken, but the two victors fell out, contributing to their failed attack on the main objective, Malta. In 1560 Turghud was more successful against **Djerba**, off Tripoli (15 August 1551).

Tripoli, Libya I 1728 I Franco-Barbary Wars

Determined to exact reparation from the Barbary pirates, French Admiral Nicola de

Grandpré took six ships of the line and three bomb ketches against Peshwa Ahmad Karamanli of Tripoli. After inflicting a massive bombardment, shortage of water and ammunition forced Grandpré to withdraw. A French blockade the following January persuaded the Peshwa to accept terms (20–26 July 1728).

Tripoli, Libya I 1803 I Tripolitan War

During America's war against North African piracy, the frigate *Philadelphia* (Captain William Bainbridge) ran aground in Tripoli harbour trying to preserve her blockade. Attacked by Algerine gunboats, Bainbridge and 307 crew surrendered, though their captured ship was destroyed in a later raid. The crew were finally released when war ended in 1805 after the fall of **Derna** (31 October 1803).

Tripoli, Libya (1st) I 1804 I Tripolitan War

In a brilliant raid on Tripoli during the war against North African piracy, American Lieutenant Stephen Decatur and 74 volunteers disguised as Arabs entered port on a captured Tripolitan ketch, renamed *Intrepid*, and burned the captured American ship *Philadelphia* to deny her to the pirates. Decatur escaped without a man lost, but *Intrepid* was later sunk on a second raid (16 February 1804).

Tripoli, Libya (2nd) I 1804 I Tripolitan War

Following weeks of bombardment by American Admiral Edward Preble, Lieutenants Stephen Decatur and Richard Somers entered Tripoli harbour in shallow-draft gunboats and seized three pirate craft (3 August). But in a subsequent failed assault, Somers and his crew were killed when the fireship *Intrepid* blew up prematurely. The Americans then resumed a passive blockade (1 September 1804).

Tripoli, Libya I 1911 I Italo-Turkish War

At the start of Italy's invasion of Libya, Tripoli refused to surrender to Admiral Luigi Faravelli and his fleet shelled the outlying fortresses (3 October). A landing party under Captain Umberto Cagni then seized the city and held it until the main force arrived five days later. While Tobruk and Derna in Cyrenaica quickly fell, the Italians faced stronger resistance at **Benghazi** (5 October 1911).

Tripolis I 1821 I Greek War of Independence

See **Tripolitza**

Tripolitza I 1821 I Greek War of Independence

After taking **Monemvasia** and **Navarino**, Demitrius Ipsilantis and Theodoros Kolokotrones besieged Tripolitza in central Peloponnesia, holding out despite Turkish defeat at **Valtesti**. When the Albanian garrison negotiated to withdraw, the starving city had to surrender and the ensuing destruction saw 8,000 citizens massacred. The Turks were avenged in June 1822 at **Chios** (May–8 October 1821).

Trippstadt I 1794 I French Revolutionary Wars (1st Coalition)

The day after French success southeast of Kaiserslautern at **Platzberg**, Generals Claude Michaud and Alexandre Taponier attacked the Prussian camp to the south at Trippstadt. A brutal 19-hour action saw Michaud capture large quantities of guns, munitions and stores and kill 4,500 Prussians at the cost of 2,000 French dead. Three days later the French took **Kaiserslautern** (14 July 1794).

Tristan de Cunha I 1815 I War of 1812

A remarkable action in the South Atlantic off Tristan de Cunha saw the British sloop *Penguin* (Commander James Dickinson) encounter the American sloop *Hornet* (Captain James Biddle). Despite heavy damage Dickinson was killed attempting to ram *Hornet* and *Penguin* was captured. However, peace had already been signed and this was the last action of the war (23 March 1815).

Trnovo I 1218 I Bulgarian Imperial Wars

With Tsar Boril of Bulgaria weakened by warfare, his cousin Ivan Asen raised rebellion in the north. Assisted by Russian troops he laid siege to the capital Trnovo (modern Veliko Tarnovo) then took the city by storm. When Boril was captured his eyes were put out and his cousin seized the throne as Ivan II, leading the Second Bulgarian Empire to its greatest triumphs.

Trocadera I 1823 I Franco-Spanish War

French under Louis Duke of Angouleme intervened in the Spanish Liberal revolution to support Ferdinand VII and invaded to seize Madrid. Driven back to Cadiz, rebel General Rafael del Riego was badly defeated at the Trocadera Forts, outside the city. When Cadiz fell to the French a month later (23 September), Ferdinand was restored to power and del Riego was executed (31 August 1823).

Troia I 1462 I Aragon's Conquest of Naples

Twenty years after René of Anjou was driven out of Italy following defeat at **Naples** by Alfonso V of Aragon, the Barons of Naples rose in revolt against Alfonso's son Ferdinand and sought aid from René's son, Jean of Lorraine. At Troia, southwest of Foggia, the Barons suffered a bloody defeat and Jean returned to Provence, curbing French claims on Naples (18 August 1462).

Troina I 1943 I World War II (Southern Europe)

American General George Patton secured **Palermo** in western Sicily then turned his forces east along the coast and inland through Nicosia towards the mountain town of Troina, west of Mount Etna. It took five days of intense and costly combat before General Terry Allen secured Troina and General Eberhart Rodt fell back through Cerami towards **Messina** (31 July–4 August 1943).

Trois Rivières I 1776 I War of the American Revolution

Recovering from a failed attack on **Quebec** (1 January) American forces in Montreal under Generals John Sullivan and William Thompson attempted a fresh advance down the St Lawr-

ence. But British General John Burgoyne, recently arrived from England, defeated Thompson at Trois Rivières. Sullivan then abandoned the invasion of Canada and retreated to **Lake Champlain** (8 June 1776).

Troisville I 1794 I French Revolutionary Wars (1st Coalition)

See **Beaumont-en-Cambresis**

Trompettersdrift I 1793 I 2nd Cape Frontier War

When Xhosa under Ndlambe again entered the Zuurveld in eastern Cape Province, they were met by a Dutch commando under Landdrost Honoratus C. D. Maynier, who won a series of actions along the Fish River, including a notable victory at Trompettersdrift where 40 Xhosa were killed. However, Maynier could not force the Xhosa to withdraw and he accepted peace on 8 October 1793.

Trondheim I 1940 I World War II (Northern Europe)

See **Andalsnes**

Trouillas I 1793 I French Revolutionary Wars (1st Coalition)

Responding to an invasion of France by a Spanish army under Don Antonio Ricardos, Governor of Catalonia, French General Lucien Dagobert attempted to march on the Spanish at Pontiella. At Trouillas, south of Perpignan, Dagobert was repulsed with over 3,000 casualties. However, Ricardos thought the French were about to be reinforced and he withdrew to **Boulou** (21 September 1793).

Troy I 1184 BC I Trojan War

The Trojan Prince Paris led a raid on Greece and in response Greek leader Agamemnon landed an army on Asia Minor to seize the city of Troy. At the end of a semi-legendary ten-year siege the city fell by storm, or perhaps by the mythic stratagem of the "Wooden Horse." King Priam was killed and Troy was destroyed, effectively ending the Trojan State (trad date 1184 BC).

Troyes | 1814 | Napoleonic Wars (French Campaign)

As Napoleon Bonaparte campaigned east of Paris against the Allies, General Gebhard von Blucher moved forward to occupy Merv (22 February) while Prince Karl Philipp Schwarzenberg left General Karl von Wrede to defend Troyes. After driving off two heavy attacks, von Wrede withdrew and Bonaparte occupied Troyes, while Schwarzenberg fell back on **Arcis** (23–24 February 1814).

Truckee | 1860 | Pyramid Lake Indian War

When Paiute in western Nevada attacked a pony express station where two Indian girls were abducted and raped, over 100 miners and other volunteers set out under Major William M. Ormsby. But Ormsby was ambushed by Paiute under Numaga on the Truckee, just south of Pyramid Lake, and suffered about 46 killed. The Indians were soon pursued to **Pinnacle Mountain** (May 1860).

Trujillo | 1860 | National (Filibuster) War

The American William Walker was driven out of Nicaragua by the Central American allies at **Rivas** (May 1857) and he toured the United States before attempting a comeback in Honduras. His small Filibuster force landed and seized the fortress at Trujillo but no allies rallied to him. Walker eventually surrendered to the British Navy, which handed him to Honduras for execution (6 August 1860).

Truk | 1944 | World War II (Pacific)

To cover the invasion of **Eniwetok**, American Admiral Marc Mitscher led a massive carrier and battleship strike against Truk, the Japanese "Gibraltar of the Pacific." While Japan's capital ships had been withdrawn following early reconnaissance, the raid sank 150,000 tons of Japanese shipping—including two cruisers and four destroyers—and destroyed about 270 aircraft (16–17 February 1944).

Trzcianka | 1629 | 2nd Polish-Swedish War

See **Sztum**

Ts'ai-chou | 817 | Later Tang Imperial Wars

See **Caizhou**

Ts'ai-shih | 1161 | Jin-Song Wars

See **Caishi**

Ts'ao-ho-kou | 1894 | Sino-Japanese War

See **Caohekou**

Tsarasoatra | 1895 | French Conquest of Madagascar

When Madagascar's Hova government refused to recognise French suzerainty, General Jacques Duchesne landed a large force at Majunga and marched southeast towards the central plateau. General Rainianjalahy and 5,000 well-entrenched troops attempted to block the French at Tsarasoatra but they were driven out with heavy losses and Duchesne continued towards **Andriba** (29 June 1895).

Tsaritsyn | 1774 | Pugachev Rebellion

Cossack rebel Emelyan Pugachev recovered from costly defeats at **Tatishchevo** and **Kazan** to advance down the Volga towards Tsaritsyn (modern Volgograd) but was driven off by heavy artillery fire. Four days later his rebel force was destroyed by Colonel Ivan Michelson, aided by Don Cossacks and the city garrison. Pugachev fled and was subsequently captured and executed (21–25 August 1774).

Tsaritsyn | 1919 | Russian Civil War

As part of White commander Anton Denikin's offensive from the Kuban, General Pyotr Wrangel advanced through **Velikoknyazheskaya** on Tsaritsyn (later Stalingrad and Volgograd) which resisted attack in late 1918. Although Wrangel's assault was driven off by General Aleksandr Yegorov, a second attempt took the city by storm and the offensive continued (12–13 & 29 June 1919).

Tseng Jong I 1962 I Sino-Indian War

At the start of armed border confrontation in disputed northeast India (Arunachal Pradesh), an ill-advised Indian patrol of just 50 men advanced towards the invading Chinese on the Thag La Ridge. Near the village of Tseng Jong the Indians were routed by a battalion-size Chinese force. Both sides lost about 30 casualties and the Rajputs fell back to the **Namka Chu** River (10 October 1962).

Tshaneni I 1884 I Zulu Civil War

When Zulu King Cetshwayo died after escaping the defeat at **Ondini**, his 16-year-old son Dinuzulu promised the Boers land to support his uSuthu against Zibebhu of the Mandlakazi. At Tshaneni, 6,000 uSuthu and 200 Boers destroyed the Mandlakazi and Zibebhu fled. When British annexed Zululand two years later Dinuzulu started a rebellion at **Ceza** and utterly routed Zibebhu at **Ivuna** (5 June 1884).

Tsinan I 1928 I 2nd Chinese Revolutionary Civil War
    See **Jinan**

Tsinan I 1948 I 3rd Chinese Revolutionary Civil War
    See **Jinan**

Tsingpu I 1860 I Taiping Rebellion
    See **Qingpu**

Tsingtao I 1914 I World War I (Far East)
    See **Qingdao**

Tsitsihar I 1900 I Russo-Chinese War
    See **Qiqihar**

Tsorona I 1999 I Ethiopian-Eritrean War

Two weeks after breaking through Eritrean defences around **Badme**, over-confident Ethiopian forces attempted a frontal assault against entrenched positions to the southwest around Tsorona, near Zelambessa. Reportedly advancing behind human waves sent over minefields, the Ethiopians suffered terrible losses and had to pull back, though fighting continued for months (16–18 March 1999).

Tsung-chou I 771 BC I Wars of the Western Zhou
    See **Zongzhou**

Tsushima I 1905 I Russo-Japanese War

In one of history's most decisive naval battles, Russia's Baltic fleet under Admiral Zinovi Rozhdestvenski steamed 17,000 miles to the Far East and arrived after the land war was effectively over. In Tsushima Strait, between Japan and Korea, Japanese Admiral Heihachiro Togo utterly annihilated the Russian fleet—including all eight battleships destroyed—and the war ended (27–28 May 1905).

Tubberneering I 1798 I Irish Rebellion

Sent south from Gorey to reinforce Loyalist General William Loftus at Ballycanew, Colonel Lambert Walpole (Aide to the Viceroy Earl Camden) impulsively took a shortcut through the hills and was ambushed in the pass at Tubberneering by rebels under Father John Murphy. Colonel Walpole fell in the first volley and the survivors fled to Gorey, which fell to the rebels the same day (4 June 1798).

Tucannon I 1848 I Cayuse Indian War

Advancing into southeast Washington State against Cayuse who had murdered Dr **Whitman**, Colonel Cornelius Gilliam reached an Indian camp on the Tucannon and started rounding up cattle. Heavily attacked by Cayuse allies, the Palouse, Gilliam fought a running two-day withdrawal. However, soon afterwards he was accidentally killed and the war was virtually over (14–15 March 1848).

Tucapel I 1553 I Spanish Conquest of Chile

After invading Chile in 1541 and founding Santiago, Pedro de Valdivia returned as Governor and tried to extend Spanish influence south of the Bio Bio River where he met fierce resistance by Araucanians under Chief Caupolicán.

The warrior Lautaro attacked and defeated Valdivia at Tucapel and Valdivia was executed a month later. Lautaro soon won again at **Marigüeñu** (26 December 1553).

Tucumán ▌ 1812 ▌ Argentine War of Independence

Sent to command the Patriot army in Upper Peru after its terrible defeat at **Huaqui** (June 1811) General Manuel Belgrano withdrew through **Río Piedras**, then determined, against government orders, to hold Argentina's northwestern provinces. At Tucumán Belgrano won an unexpected victory, which bought time as defeated Spanish General Pío Tristán withdrew north to Salta (24 September 1812).

Tudela (1st) ▌ 1808 ▌ Napoleonic Wars (Peninsular Campaign)

At the start of Bonaparte's campaign in Spain, Spanish General José Palafox sent his brother Luis Marquis of Lazan along the Ebro from Saragossa to meet the advancing army of General Charles Lefebvre-Desnouettes. Lazan's recruits were routed at Tudela and, after sacking the town, the French advanced to further victories at Mallen and Alagon before besieging **Saragossa** (8 June 1808).

Tudela (2nd) ▌ 1808 ▌ Napoleonic Wars (Peninsular Campaign)

Within days of victory in northern Spain at **Gamonal**, **Espinosa** and **Reynosa**, Napoleon Bonaparte turned against the Spanish Army of the Centre under Generals Francisco Castanos and José Palafox. Smashing his way overextended Spanish lines on the Ebro at Tudela, French Marshal Jean Lannes inflicted heavy casualties and opened the way to **Saragossa** (23 November 1808).

Tug Argan ▌ 1940 ▌ World War II (Northern Africa)

Soon after Italy joined the war, General Guglielmo Nasi entered British Somaliland, where newly arrived General Alfred Godwin-Austin attempted to hold the strategic mountain pass at Tug Argan. Heavy fighting saw the massively outnumbered defenders forced to retreat and the British then abandoned the capital Berbera and evacuated by sea to Aden (11–16 August 1940).

Tugela ▌ 1838 ▌ Boer-Zulu War

Days after Boer defeat at **Italeni**, a handful of whites and 800 Zulus were ambushed near the mouth of the Tugela by Nongalaza, leading the Zulu army of Mpande, brother of King Dingane. The whites suffered terrible losses, including leaders John Cane, Robert Biggar and John Stubbs killed, and Mpande then sacked Durban. The Boers were avenged in December at **Blood River** (17 April 1838).

Tugela ▌ 1856 ▌ Zulu Wars of Succession
See **Ndondakusuka**

Tugela Heights ▌ 1900 ▌ 2nd Anglo-Boer War

In a final attempt to relieve Ladysmith, after failure at **Colenso, Spion Kop** and **Vaal Kranz**, British General Sir Redvers Buller led a determined assault on the Heights of Tugela to the south. After hard fighting—which climaxed with a British attack on Pieter's Hill and cost about 2,200 British and 230 Boer casualties—Louis Botha withdrew and Ladysmith was relieved (14–28 February 1900).

Tukaroi ▌ 1575 ▌ Mughal Conquest of Northern India

Mughal Emperor Akbar completed the conquest of Gujarat at **Ahmadabad** (1572) then marched east against Daud Khan, the rebellious young Afghan ruler of Bengal. After Akbar returned to Delhi his commander Munim Khan defeated Daud at Tukaroi, near Mughulmari, then accepted a lenient peace. Daud rebelled again and had to be defeated a year later at **Rajmahal** (3 March 1575).

Tukra ▌ 1575 ▌ Mughal Conquest of Northern India
See **Tukaroi**

Tulagi (1st) | 1942 | World War II (Pacific)

As a Japanese invasion headed for Port Moresby in **Papua**, Admiral Kiyohide Shima took a secondary force to set up a seaplane base on Tulagi, in the Solomons. Attacked next day by aircraft from Admiral Frank Fletcher's carrier *Yorktown,* the Japanese lost a destroyer and three smaller ships sunk. The Americans then turned to meet the main force days later in the **Coral Sea** (3–4 May 1942).

Tulagi (2nd) | 1942 | World War II (Pacific)

In support of the major offensive in the Solomons against **Guadalcanal,** American Marines under General William Rupertus landed on Tulagi, just 25 miles to the north, where Japanese forces resisted fiercely around the seaplane base on the nearby islets of Tanambogo and Gavutu. Tulagi was then secured and became a naval base to support the fighting around Guadalcanal (7–9 August 1942).

Tulcán | 1862 | Ecuador-Colombia War

When President Gabriel García Moreno of Ecuador declared war on Colombia over a border dispute, he marched to the border with a largely untrained army and was cut off near Tulcán by Colombian General Julio Arboledo. García Moreno was defeated and captured, then sued for peace. War resumed late in 1863 and Ecuador was routed at **Cuaspud** (31 July 1862).

Tumen River | 1938 | Russo-Japanese Border Wars
See **Changfukeng**

Tumu | 1449 | Ming Imperial Wars

When Oirat Mongols under Esen Khan expanded into northwestern China, Imperial eunuch Wang Zhen rashly persuaded Emperor Zhengtong to advance against the invaders. After reaching Dadong, the panicked Ming army withdrew and was surrounded then routed at Tumu Fortress, near Huailai, with Wang killed. The Emperor himself was captured but later released and restored (8 September 1449).

Tumunui | 1870 | 2nd New Zealand War
See **Waikorowhiti**

Tumusla | 1825 | Bolivian War of Independence

Despite defeat for Spanish Royalists at **Ayacucho** in late 1824, General Pedro Antonio Olañeta and a remaining force of Royalists held out in Upper Peru where Simon Bolívar sent Colombian Marshal Antonio José de Sucre. Outside the mountain city of Potosí at Tumusla, Olañeta was defeated and killed. Bolivia was declared an independent Republic with Sucre as President (1 April 1825).

Tunga | 1787 | Mughal-Maratha War of Ismail Beg
See **Lalsot**

Tung-kuan | 756 | An Lushan Rebellion
See **Chang'an**

Tunis | 255 BC | 1st Punic War

The Carthaginians were heavily defeated by a Roman army at **Adys**, near Carthage, then invited Spartan General Xanthippus to reorganise their army. In return battle the following year against Atilius Regulus outside the walls of Carthage, not far from Tunis, the revitalised Carthaginians defeated and captured Regulus. The demoralised survivors were rescued by ship and Rome was driven from Africa.

Tunis | 238 BC | Truceless War

When former mercenaries rose in revolt against Carthage they suffered a terrible loss at the **Saw** and Carthaginian Generals Hannibal and Hamilcar Barca besieged their main camp at Tunis (Tunes). However, rebel leader Mathos led a bold counter-offensive, and Hannibal was captured and executed. Defeat forced Hamilcar to withdraw, but Mathos himself was soon finally beaten at **Leptis**.

Tunis | 1533 | Turkish Imperial Wars

Sailing from Constantinople with 80 galleys and 8,000 troops, Turkish Admiral Khair-ed-din Barbarossa appeared before Tunis where Mulei

Hassan attempted a brief defence, then fled. The Turks put the city to the sack and later defeated Mulei Hassan at Kairouan to secure Tunisia. However, the Tunisian King was restored after two years by Emperor Charles V (18 August 1533).

Tunis I 1535 I Turkish-Habsburg Wars
Responding to Muslim attacks on Christian shipping, Emperor Charles V led Admiral Andrea Doria and Count Max of Eberstein against the naval base of Tunis, where he defeated Turkish Admiral Khair-ed-din Barbarossa. Charles released over 2,000 Christian slaves and restored King Mulei Hassan, but war at home deferred his advance against **Algiers** (20 June–21 July 1535).

Tunis I 1943 I World War II (North Africa)
See **Bizerte-Tunis**

Tunisia I 1942–1943 I World War II (Northern Africa)
Squeezed between Allied armies advancing from Libya after **El Alamein** and from Algeria after **Torch**, Axis forces in Tunisia were reinforced from Sicily and took the offensive at **Tébourba**, **Kasserine** and **Médenine**. The Allies struck back at **Mareth Line, El Guettar** and **Bizerte-Tunis**, and the Axis finally surrendered 250,000 men to end the campaign (November 1942–13 May 1943).

Tupelo I 1864 I American Civil War (Western Theatre)
Confederate General Nathan B. Forrest raided Union railways in Mississippi where he defeated a pursuing force at **Brice's Cross Roads** then sent General Stephen D. Lee against another pursuing force under General Andrew J Smith. A heavy defeat further south at Tupelo cost Lee over 1,000 men, yet Forrest was able to regroup and a month later he attacked **Memphis** (14–15 July 1864).

Tupium I 1869 I War of the Triple Alliance
During fighting in the Cordillera Province, east of the Paraguay River, Brazilian Brigadier José Antônio Correia da Câmara attacked a Paraguayan detachment under Colonel Manuel Galeano at Tupium, on the Rio Aguarai-Guacu. The Paraguayans were heavily defeated with 500 men lost. A further 300, mainly young boys, were captured at the nearby fortress of Santa Cruz (30 May 1869).

Turabah I 1919 I Saudi-Hashemite Wars
With World War I over, Sharif Hussein sent his son Abd Allah and 5,000 men east from Mecca to seize the city of Turabah and threaten the Nejd. Emir Abd al-Aziz (Ibn Saud) of Riyadh sent 1,100 Ikhwan warriors under Ibn Bijad, who attacked Turabah at dawn. The Hashemite army was destroyed, but Aziz turned against the Rashid at **Hail** before advancing on **Mecca** (26 May 1919).

Turbigo I 1859 I 2nd Italian War of Independence
Intervening to support King Victor Emmanuel II of Piedmont against Austria, French Marshal Marie MacMahon advanced through Novara and seized the bridge on the Ticino at Turbigo. An inadequate Austrian blocking force under Marshal Franz Freiherr von Cordon was swept aside and MacMahon marched southeast to join Napoleon III for victory next day at **Magenta** (3 June 1859).

Turckheim I 1675 I 3rd Dutch War
French Marshal Henri de Turenne advanced along the Rhine in mid-1674 to beat Imperial forces at **Sinsheim** and **Enzheim** before driving into Alsace against a large army under Frederick William Elector of Brandenburg and the Austrian Count Raimondo Montecuccoli. The Allies were defeated at Turckheim, near Colmar, and the Elector withdrew into Brandenburg (5 January 1675).

Turfan I 1877 I Xinjiang Rebellion
See **Turpan**

Turia I 75 BC I Sertorian War
Recovering from disaster at **Lauron** (76 BC) Rome's commander in Spain, Gnaeus Pompey, resumed the offensive against rebel Quintus Sertorius and advanced south to the Turia

(modern Guadalaviar) to meet Gaius Herrenius and Marcus Perpenna. The Sertorian lieutenants were routed, losing perhaps 10,000 killed (including Herrenius) and Pompey pursued Perpenna south to the Sucro.

Turin I 312 I Roman Wars of Succession

Emperor Constantine advanced from Gaul into Italy against rival Emperor Maxentius and met his first substantial opposing force west of Turin. While Constantine's army initially fell back before a heavy cavalry attack, his infantry prevailed and the Maxentian army was driven back to Turin, which prepared for a siege but then surrendered. Constantine then marched on to victory at **Verona**.

Turin I 1640 I Thirty Years War (Franco-Habsburg War)

After beating Diego Felipe de Guzmán Marquis of Leganés at **Casale** (29 April), French commander Henri Comte d'Harcourt advanced on Turin to besiege Thomas of Savoy, who had invested the French garrison in the citadel. Harcourt was in turn besieged by a reinforced Spanish army under Leganés, but Harcourt eventually secured a bloody victory and took the city (July–17 September 1640).

Turin I 1706 I War of the Spanish Succession

With Imperial forces driven out of central Lombardy at **Calcinato** (19 April) Philippe II Duke d'Orleans and Marshal Ferdinand de Marsin besieged Turin, held by Victor Amadeus II, who escaped to join Prince Eugène of Savoy with a relief force. In a brilliant attack Eugène killed Marshal Marsin and destroyed his besieging army, driving the French out of Italy (26 May–7 September 1706).

Turin I 1799 I French Revolutionary Wars (2nd Coalition)

Following the fall of Milan after **Cassano** (27 April) Russian General Alexander Suvorov's advance guard under Baron Philip von Vukassovitch led a surprise attack on Turin, driving General Jean Victor Moreau into the city's cit-adel, abandoning a reported 300 guns and 60,000 muskets. Moreau later withdrew over the mountains towards Genoa and the citadel fell on 20 June (27 May 1799).

Turna Dag I 1515 I Turko-Persian War in Anatolia

Ottoman Sultan Selim I secured eastern Anatolia with victory over Shah Ismail I of Persia at **Chaldiran** (August 1514) then took a force against the Persian vassal Ala al-Dawlah of the Principality of Dulgadir. At Turna Dag, Selim defeated and killed Ala al-Dawlah in a decisive victory, which secured Cilicia and left the Sultan free to turn against the Mamluks in 1516 at **Marj-Dabik** (13 June 1515).

Turnau I 1866 I Seven Weeks War
See **Liebenau**

Turnham Green I 1642 I British Civil Wars

The advance on London by King Charles I was delayed at **Brentford** and next day he faced Parliamentary commander Robert Devereux Earl of Essex and 24,000 London Militia in battle order on Turnham Green near Putney. A daylong confrontation saw only scattered shots fired and the "battle" ended when the outnumbered Royalists withdrew and London was saved (13 November 1642).

Turnhout I 1597 I Netherlands War of Independence

Facing continued success by Prince Maurice of Orange, Spanish Viceroy Count Ernst von Mansfeld sent Count Jean de Rie of Varas to invade Holland. Overtaken at Turnhout, northeast of Antwerp, the Spaniards were destroyed by Dutch cavalry under Maurice himself, losing thousands killed (including Count Jean) and hundreds taken prisoner for minimal Dutch loss (24 January 1597).

Turnhout I 1789 I Brabantine Rebellion

Jean-Francois Vonck led a rising against Austria in the Netherlands to declare Belgian Brabant independent after which Colonel Jean-

Andre van de Meersch routed an Austrian force at Turnhout, northeast of Antwerp. While the Belgians went on to capture Flanders, Austrian authority was quickly restored, though Brabant was soon conquered by Revolutionary France (24 October 1789).

Turpan ▮ 1877 ▮ Xinjiang Rebellion

When Yakub Beg of Khokand established the Muslim Khanate of Kashgari in western China, a massive Imperial army under Qing General Zuo Zongtang recaptured **Ürümqi** then attacked the rebel in his capital to the southeast at Turpan. Turpan was seized after heavy fighting and Yakub Beg committed suicide, ending the rising. China then established the Province of Xinjiang (16 May 1877).

Turret Butte ▮ 1873 ▮ Apache Indian Wars

Pursuing hostile Apache after victory at **Skeleton Cave**, General George Crook sent Major George Randall against Chuntz and Delshay at Turret Butte, west of the Verde River, near modern Cordes Junction, Arizona. Randall led a brilliant night ascent of the inaccessible position to surprise and rout the Indian camp. Most Apache soon surrendered and ended the war (27 March 1873).

Turtukai (1st) ▮ 1773 ▮ Catherine the Great's 1st Turkish War

While Russians threatened Ruschuk on the Danube, further downstream near Oltenitsa General Alexander Suvorov attacked Bim Pasha's garrison at Turtukai (modern Tutrakan). Suvorov destroyed the fortress and killed 1,500 in a brilliant assault before retiring with 15 guns and 50 boats. The Turks later reoccupied the position and Suvorov had to take it again (10 May 1773).

Turtukai (2nd) ▮ 1773 ▮ Catherine the Great's 1st Turkish War

General Alexander Suvorov destroyed the Turkish Danube fort at Turtukai (modern Tutrakan), then attacked again a month later to divert from an offensive by General Pyotr Rumyantsev downstream at **Silistria**. A bloody night-time assault saw Turtukai commander Sari Mehmet Pasha defeated and killed. But the at-

tack at Silistria failed and Suvorov had to withdraw (17 June 1773).

Turtukai ▮ 1774 ▮ Catherine the Great's 1st Turkish War

In a fresh Russian offensive on the Danube, while the main army marched against the Turks at Kozludzha and Silistria, General Ivan Saltikov took 10,000 men towards Ruschuk and met a superior Turkish force at Turtukai (modern Tutrakan). On the same day Suvorov won at **Kozludzha**, Saltikov defeated Assan Bey to once again secure victory at Turtukai and peace soon followed (9 June 1774).

Tushki ▮ 1889 ▮ British-Sudan Wars
See **Toski**

Tutora ▮ 1620 ▮ Polish-Turkish Wars
See **Cecora**

Tutrakan ▮ 1916 ▮ World War I (Balkan Front)

When Romanians marched north into Transylvania, General August von Mackensen attacked in the south with a mixed German-Bulgarian-Turkish force. The powerful Danube fortress at Tutrakan (formerly Turtukai) boasted that it would be "Romania's Verdun" but fell after a brief siege. Mackensen took Silistria two days later then continued east towards **Constanta** (4–6 September 1916).

Tuttlingen ▮ 1643 ▮ Thirty Years War (Franco-Habsburg War)

On the day Jean-Baptiste Guébriant died from wounds after taking **Rottweil** in Swabia, the Weimar army under his successor Josias von Rantzau was attacked a few miles to the southeast at Tuttlingen by Imperial Generals Franz von Mercy and Johann von Werth. Von Rantzau was defeated and captured, after which Rottweil was lost and the Germans withdrew into Alsace (24 November 1643).

Tuyen-Quang ▮ 1885 ▮ Sino-French War

Following victory in northern Vietnam (Tonkin) at **Bac Ninh**, the French secured

Tuyen-Quang northwest of Hanoi (1 June 1884) where a 400-strong garrison was later besieged by perhaps 20,000 Chinese troops. By the time General Oscar de Négrier's relief force finally defeated the besiegers at nearby Hoa-Moc, the heroic garrison had lost 23 killed and 126 wounded (23 January–3 March 1885).

Tuy Hoa I 1966 I Vietnam War

Determined to protect the rice crop in coastal Phu Yen, American, South Vietnamese and Korean forces began a large search and destroy mission (Operation Van Buren) against Viet Cong and North Vietnamese regulars in the Tuy Hoa Valley. Severe fighting saw the Allies secure the area then move north to join the larger offensive on the Plain of **Bon Son** (19 January–21 February 1966).

Tuyutí I 1866 I War of the Triple Alliance

Three weeks after victory at **Estero Bellaco**, Argentine, Brazilian and Uruguayan forces under General Bartolomé Mitre entered southwest Paraguay against President Francisco Solano López at Paso de Patria south of Tuyutí, between the Parana and Paraguay. While suicidal attacks by López inflicted 8,500 Allied casualties, he lost over 20,000 men and had to fall back north on **Humaitá** (24 May 1866).

Tuyutí I 1867 I War of the Triple Alliance

Attempting to relieve **Humaitá** in southwest Paraguay, President Francisco Solano López of Paraguay sent General Vicente Barrios and 8,000 men against the Allied siege base at nearby Tuyutí. Brazilian General Manuel Marques de Sousa was driven out and the camp was looted, but Argentine Colonel Manuel Hornos counter-attacked and Barrios withdrew with heavy losses (3 November 1867).

Tweebosch I 1902 I 2nd Anglo-Boer War

Jacobus de la Rey resumed his offensive in the western Transvaal, destroying a British column at **Yzer Spruit** (24 February) then attacking 1,200 men and four guns under General Lord Paul Methuen at Tweebosch, southwest of Lichtenburg. The column was virtually de-

stroyed in Britain's worst defeat for two years and Methuen became the only British General captured in the war (7 March 1902).

Tweefontein I 1900 I 2nd Anglo-Boer War
See **Boshof**

Tweefontein I 1901 I 2nd Anglo-Boer War

As Britain built blockhouses to entrap Boer commandos, General Christiaan de Wet led 700 Boers against the blockhouse line under construction near Tweefontein, 25 miles east of General Sir Leslie Rundle's headquarters at Bethlehem. Attacking on Christmas Day at nearby Groenkop, de Wet surprised and routed a force of Yeomanry, killing Major George A. Williams (25 December 1901).

Two Palms I 1912 I Italo-Turkish War

Following months of relative inactivity in Cyrenaica, about 6,000 Turks and Arabs outside **Benghazi** attacked through the oasis at Two Palms. Recovering from surprise, Italian Generals Ottavio Briccola and Giovanni Ameglia counter-attacked and the attackers were driven out by a brutal bayonet charge. The costly action effectively ended fighting around Benghazi (12 March 1912).

Twt Hill I 1463 I Wars of the Roses

Edward IV secured the English crown at **Towton** (March 1461) and later sent William Earl of Herbert against Lancastrian forces holding out in Wales. After capturing Pembroke Castle, Herbert met Jasper Tudor Earl of Pembroke and Henry Holland Duke of Exeter near Canaervon at a location called Twt Hill. The Welsh were beaten and remaining Lancastrian strongholds quickly fell (16 October 1463).

Tynec I 1423 I Hussite Wars

In doctrinal war among Bohemian Hussites, Jan Zizka secured victory for the Taborite faction at **Strachuv** but was soon besieged at Caslav by Praguers and Lord Hasek of Waldstein, who intercepted a relief force from Hradec Králové under Zizka's ally Matthew Lupák. On the Elbe at Tynec, upstream of Kolin, Lupák was defeated and killed, though the siege of Caslav was raised (22 August 1423).

Tyre ❙ 332 BC ❙ Conquests of Alexander the Great

On his way to conquer Egypt after victory at **Issus** (333 BC) Alexander the Great attacked the city of Tyre, half a mile off the Phoenician coast. In one of the most complex sieges of ancient times, Alexander built a causeway to the island fortress. Smashing through formidable walls by land and sea, he fell on Tyre and slaughtered the population, then marched on to **Gaza** (January–August 332 BC).

Tyre ❙ 315–314 BC ❙ Wars of the Diadochi

In war between the successors of Alexander the Great, Antigonus secured Persia at **Gabiene**, then invaded Syria against Ptolemy, who left a strong garrison at Tyre before withdrawing to Egypt. The powerful city held out against siege for 13 months before falling to Antigonus. He then sailed west to campaign in Asia Minor, leaving his son Demetrius Poliorcetes to govern Syria from **Gaza**.

Tyre ❙ 1110–1111 ❙ Crusader-Muslim Wars

King Baldwin I of Jerusalem captured most major cities in Palestine then attacked the key port of Tyre, where the Fatimid Egyptian garrison resisted assault by huge stones and battering rams and destroyed Crusader siege towers with incendiaries. A large Turkish relief army under Toghtekin arrived from Damascus and helped drive off the siege after four months (29 November 1110–10 April 1111).

Tyre ❙ 1124 ❙ Crusader-Muslim Wars

After Crusader failure to seize the port of Tyre in 1111, Gormond, Patriarch of Jerusalem, renewed the attack on this remaining Muslim stronghold. Blockaded by Venetian ships and facing continuous assault by land the Tyrian garrison held out against the siege until two relief attempts from Damascus were driven back.

The city was then forced to surrender (15 February–7 July 1124).

Tyre ❙ 1187 ❙ 3rd Crusade

Following Crusader disaster at **Hattin** (4 July) Kurdish-Muslim conqueror Saladin retook most major cities of the Holy Land, including **Jerusalem**. However, he was thwarted by the fortress port of Tyre to which many Crusader nobles had escaped. Led by Conrad of Montferrat, the garrison drove off an attack in July and a two-month siege in November–December, saving both the city and the kingdom.

Tyrnavos ❙ 1897 ❙ 1st Greco-Turkish War
See **Mati**

Tzarevlatz ❙ 1712 ❙ Ottoman Invasions of Montenegro
See **Podgoritza**

Tzeki ❙ 1862 ❙ Taiping Rebellion

American adventurer Frederick T. Ward helped save **Shanghai** from Taiping attack in 1860 then created the "Ever Victorious Army" of western-armed and led Chinese irregulars. When Huang Chengzhong and Fan Ruceng seized Tzeki (modern Cicheng) just northwest of Ningbo, the EVA drove the Taiping out, though Ward was fatally wounded in the assault (18–21 September 1862).

Tzirallum ❙ 313 ❙ Roman Wars of Succession

In war between Emperors, Constantine in Rome made peace with Valerius Licinius, who could then turn his efforts in the east against his rival Galerius Maximinus Daia. Maximinus had crossed the Bosphorus into Europe, but was heavily defeated at Tzirallum, south of Adrianople in modern Bulgaria. Licinius then pursued Maximinus into Asia Minor, where he apparently took poison (30 April 313).

Tzurulum ❙ 313 ❙ Roman Wars of Succession
See **Tzirallum**

U

Ualual ▌ 1935 ▌ 2nd Italo-Ethiopian War
See **Walwal**

Uckerath ▌ 1796 ▌ French Revolutionary Wars (1st Coalition)
As French General Jean-Baptiste Jourdan withdrew down the east bank of the Rhine after defeat at **Wetzlar**, days later General Jean-Baptiste Kléber's outnumbered force made a stand against Austrian General Paul Kray east of Bonn at Uckerath. After heavy losses on both sides, Kléber drove the Austrians off, but Kray also claimed victory because the French continued their retreat (19 June 1796).

Uclés ▌ 1108 ▌ Early Christian Reconquest of Spain
In a renewed Muslim offensive towards Toledo, a huge army under Tamin ibn Yusuf, brother of the Emir Ali ibn Yusuf, attacked Uclés, 80 miles to the east. While the town fell on 27 May, the citadel held out and a relief army from Leon was destroyed outside the city two days later. Among the dead was Sancho Alfonsez, natural son and heir to King Alfonso VI of Leon (29 May 1108).

Uclés ▌ 1809 ▌ Napoleonic Wars (Peninsular Campaign)
Recovering after defeat at **Tudela** (November 1808), units of the Spanish Army of the Centre under General Francisco Venegas advanced on Madrid. In a one-sided rout southeast of the capital at Uclés, French Marshal Claude Victor destroyed the Spanish force and captured many prisoners and guns. The survivors fled and Victor turned to the invasion of Portugal (13 January 1809).

Udayagiri ▌ 1513–1514 ▌ Vijayanagar-Gajapati War
Krishnadeva Raya of Vijayanagar secured his northern borders then sent forces east to besiege the powerful hill fortress of Udayagiri, in modern Nellore, held by Tirumala Rautaraya for his nephew King Pratapudra Gajapati of Orissa. After many failed assaults, Krishnadeva took command to defeat a relief army under Pratapudra and seized the fortress by storm (January 1513–9 June 1514).

Udaynala ▌ 1763 ▌ Bengal War
British Major Thomas Adams defeated Mir Kasim, deposed Nawab of Bengal, near **Gheria** (2 August), then took his mixed force against a strongly defended gorge on the Ganges at Udaynala, just downstream of Rajmahal. Turning the Bengali position, Adams took it by storm, inflicting heavy losses in killed or drowned, then captured Monghyr and advanced towards **Patna** (5 September 1763).

Udgir ▌ 1760 ▌ Seven Years War (India)
At the height of Maratha power in northern India, Sadashiv Bhao, cousin of Peshwa Balaji Baji Rao, marched east against Nizam Salabat Jang of Hyderabad. In a crushing victory at Udgir, northwest of Hyderabad, the Nizam's army was utterly defeated, but the Marathas were forced to turn north against an Afghan

force, which had just defeated them in Punjab at **Barari Ghat** (3 February 1760).

Ueno ▌ 1868 ▌ War of the Meiji Restoration

After the defeat of former Tokugawa Shogun Yoshinobu at **Fushimi**, Prince Arisugawa Taruhito's Imperial army occupied Edo (soon to be renamed Tokyo), yet faced continued resistance by pro-Shogunate Shogitai rebels holding out in the city's Ueno temple district. Imperial General Omura Masujiro decisively routed the rebels, who fled north towards **Goryokaku** (4 July 1868).

Ufa ▌ 1773–1774 ▌ Pugachev Rebellion

In support of the Cossack leader Emelyan Pugachev, his able lieutenant Zarubin Chika led 12,000 rebels against the Russian city of Ufa, on the Belaya. The bloody attack was driven off and Chika settled down to a siege. But after five months, he was routed by a large relief force under Colonel Ivan Michelson. Chika was captured and the siege ended (November 1773–24 March 1774).

Ufa ▌ 1918 ▌ Russian Civil War

While White forces advanced into the Urals and stormed the key city of **Perm**, Red troops to the south crossed the Volga and seized Ufa, which had fallen to the Czech Legion (23 June). White commander Admiral Aleksandr Kolchak sent General Mikhail Khanzhin south to try and retake Ufa, but he was driven off and the city held firm until Kolchak's Spring Offensive (31 December 1918).

Ufa (1st) ▌ 1919 ▌ Russian Civil War

When spring arrived in the Urals, White commander Admiral Aleksandr Kolchak in **Perm** sent General Mikhail Khanzhin and 140,000 men into southern Russia, where Ufa was reportedly defended by fewer than 10,000 Red soldiers. Although the city fell by storm after cruel Red losses, the retreating Red Army soon regrouped and launched a brilliant counter-offensive (13 March 1919).

Ufa (2nd) ▌ 1919 ▌ Russian Civil War

With Red forces defeated in the Urals at Perm and Ufa, commander Mikhail Tukhachevski launched a bold counter-offensive and General Mikhail Frunze advanced through Buguruslan and Bugulma towards the key city of Ufa, which fell after heavy fighting. With the capture of **Perm**, the Red offensive continued east through **Zlatoust**, **Ekaterinburg** and **Chelyabinsk** (9 June 1919).

Ugbine ▌ 1897 ▌ British Conquest of Nigeria

When Lieutenant James Phillips of Britain's Niger protectorate led an impulsive move against King Oba of Benin, his force of ten British officers and 200 Africans was ambushed southwest of Benin City at Ugbine by Oba's son-in-law Chief Ologbosheri. Phillips and eight officers were killed along with many of their troops. A punitive expedition the following month razed **Benin** (4 January 1897).

Ugra ▌ 1480 ▌ Russian-Mongol Wars

Mongol leader Ahmed Khan was checked at **Aleksin** (1472), but advanced on Moscow and was confronted at the Ugra by massive Russian forces under Ivan Ivanonich (son of the Tsar). An initial assault was repulsed and, with his capital at Sarai attacked by Russian allies, Ahmed withdrew and was later assassinated. The "stand" is said to have ended Mongol rule (8 October–11 November 1480).

Uhud ▌ 625 ▌ Campaigns of the Prophet Mohammed
See **Ohud**

Uiju ▌ 1904 ▌ Russo-Japanese War
See **Yalu**

Uji ▌ 1184 ▌ Gempei War

Minamoto Yoshinaka seized Kyoto after victory at **Shinowara** (June 1183), then attacked former Emperor Go-Shirakawa at **Hojuji**, provoking his cousin Yoritomo to send his brothers against the rebel. Minamoto Yoshitsune routed

Yoshinaka east of Kyoto at Uji, while Noriyori crossed the Uji at nearby Seta. The brothers thus secured Kyoto and pursued Yoshinaka to **Awazu** (February 1184).

Ujigawa ▪ 1180 ▪ Gempei War

At the start of the war against Japan's ruling Taira clan, Prince Mochihito (son of retired Emperor Go-Shirakawa) joined with Minamoto Yorimasa in an attempted coup in Kyoto. Battle east of the capital at Ujigawa saw Taira Kiyomori rout the rebels, with Mochihito killed and Yorimasa permitted to commit seppuku. Minamoto forces soon lost again at **Ishibashiyama** (20 June 1180).

Ujjain ▪ 1801 ▪ Maratha Territorial Wars

Determined to avenge the murder of a kinsman, Jaswant Rao Holkar of Indore invaded the territory of Daulat Rao Sindhia of Gwalior and was held off at Satwas by Major John Brownrigg. However, Holkar then routed Sindhia's army under Colonel George Hessing at Ujjain and put the city to the sack. In October, Holkar was in turn defeated by Sindhia further south at **Indore** (2 July 1801).

Ujscie ▪ 1655 ▪ 1st Northern War

At the start of Sweden's invasion of Poland, General Arvid Wittenberg advanced on a large force of irregulars near Ujscie, north of Poznan, under Krystof Opalinksi of Poznan. After minor skirmishing, the local Polish leadership disgracefully surrendered their army and the rich western province. Charles X soon defeated the Polish Royal army to the southeast at **Sobota** (15 July 1655).

Uk ▪ 1003 ▪ Eastern Muslim Dynastic Wars

Returning to the Seistan region of eastern Iran after previous victory at **Tarq**, Mahmud of Ghazni attacked rebellious nobles near the eastern border at Uk (modern Ark). Supported by his son Nasr and General Altuntash, Mahmud destroyed a powerful sortie, then took the fortress by storm and killed most of the garrison. He then appointed Nasr as Governor of Seistan (15 October 1003).

Ukmerge ▪ 1435 ▪ Later Wars of the Teutonic Knights
See **Wilkomierz**

Ulan Butong ▪ 1690 ▪ Chinese-Mongol Wars

When Galdan of the Zunghar Mongols expanded east and threatened to establish a Russian alliance on China's northern border, the Kangxi Emperor led a large Qing army north, but illness forced his return before the principal battle at Ulan Butong. After indecisive action, Qing General Arni allowed Galdan to withdraw, but the Emperor later returned to the offensive at **Jaomodo** (3 September 1690).

Ulla ▪ 1564 ▪ Livonian War
See **Chashniki**

Ullais ▪ 633 ▪ Muslim Conquest of Iraq

Muslim conqueror Khalid ibn al-Walid advancing into Persian-ruled Mesopotamia through victory at **Hafir**, **Mazar** and **Walaja**, met non-Muslim Arab tribes under Abdul Aswad and Persian commander Jaban at Ullais, near modern Samawah, northwest of Basra. After inflicting a massive defeat, Khalid reportedly beheaded all his prisoners (the "River of Blood") then captured **Hira** (May 633).

Ulm ▪ 1376 ▪ War of the Swabian League

Southern German cities of the Swabian League joined together to oppose the efforts of German King Charles IV to secure the succession of his son Wenceslas and Charles took his army against the key city of Ulm on the Danube. The King was forced to withdraw after a six-week siege and the Imperial forces were defeated again a year later at **Reutlingen**.

Ulm ▪ 1800 ▪ French Revolutionary Wars (2nd Coalition)
See **Höchstädt**

Ulm ∎ 1805 ∎ Napoleonic Wars
(3rd Coalition)

Napoleon Bonaparte's Grand Army crossed the Rhine in massive force and swung south to the Danube to cut off the Austrian invasion of Bavaria, encircling General Karl Mack von Leiberich at Ulm, southeast of Stuttgart. When breakouts failed at **Gunzburg** and **Elchingen**, Mack surrendered 30,000 men and 65 guns. He was court-martialled and imprisoned (20 October 1805).

Ulsan ∎ 1598 ∎ Japanese Invasion of Korea

Pursuing the Japanese south from **Chiksan**, Chinese commander Yang Hao besieged Ulsan, northeast of Pusan, held by Kato Kiyomasa. A massive Chinese-Korean assault nearly took the fortress by storm before the starving Japanese were finally relieved by Hachisuka Iemasa and Kuroda Yoshitaka. The Chinese withdrew and in October attacked further west at **Sachon** (January–February 1598).

Ulsan ∎ 1904 ∎ Russo-Japanese War

Four days after Russian defeat in the **Yellow Sea**, three Russian cruisers under Admiral Nikolai (von) Essen met Admiral Hikonojo Kamimura and four cruisers in the Japan Sea off Ulsan. Attacking out of the rising sun, Kamimura sank the cruiser *Rurik*, while *Rossiya* and *Gromoboi* were driven back to Vladivostok with heavy damage and casualties, giving Japan command of the sea (14 August 1904).

Ulu Muar ∎ 1445 ∎ Thai-Malacca War

When Sultan Muzaffar Shah of Melaka (modern Malacca) refused to pay allegiance to the Thai kingdom of Ayutthaya, a large Thai army marched overland under Awi Chakra. The Thais were met and routed at Ulu Muar, where great leadership was shown by Tun Perak of Klang. Tun Perak was appointed Bendahara (Chief Minister) and in 1456 he led a brilliant victory over the Thais at **Batu Pahat**.

Ulundi ∎ 1879 ∎ Anglo-Zulu War

Following British victory at **Khambula** in March, commander Lord Frederick Chelmsford took the offensive against King Cetshwayo and advanced on the royal Kraal at Ulundi, north of the White Mfolozi River. A decisive action cost the British 100 men for about 1,500 Zulus killed, effectively eclipsing Zulu power. Cetshwayo was captured and Zululand became part of Natal (4 July 1879).

Umachiri ∎ 1815 ∎ Peruvian War
of Independence

Indian Chief Mateo Pumacahua led a rising at Cuzco and seized Arequipa in late 1814 after victory at **Apacheta**. But he withdrew before the advance of Spanish General Juan Ramirez de Orosco, who pursued him to Umachiri, just west of Ayaviri. Pumacahua's ill-armed multitude was routed, with over 1,000 Indians killed, and the 77-year-old Chief was hanged, crushing his rebellion (11 March 1815).

Uman ∎ 1941 ∎ World War II
(Eastern Front)

As German forces advanced into the Ukraine, Panzer General Ewald von Kliest joined with the Seventeenth Army to isolate 20 Russian divisions under General Ivan Tyulenev south of Kiev at Uman. Severe fighting saw some Russians break out, but the pocket was crushed, yielding 100,000 prisoners, 300 tanks and 100 guns. The Germans then turned to reduce **Kiev** (16 July–8 August 1941).

Uman ∎ 1944 ∎ World War II
(Eastern Front)

With the **Korsun** Pocket west of the Dnieper crushed, Marshal Ivan Konev sent a massive fresh offensive west from Zvenigorodka towards Uman and from Kirovograd towards Novoukrainka against German Army Group South. Marshal Erich von Manstein committed and lost his last reserves of men and tanks and was dismissed when the Germans fell back towards Romania (4–10 March 1944).

Um Diwaykarat ∎ 1899 ∎ British-
Sudan Wars

In the final act of the war against the Khalifa Abdullah-al-Taaishi after his decisive defeat at

Omdurman, a British force under Sir Reginald Wingate tracked him down more than a year later 250 miles to the south on the upper reaches of the White Nile at Um Diwaykarat, near modern Kosti. The remnant of his Dervish army was defeated and the Khalifa was killed (24 November 1899).

Umm-at-Tubal I 1915 I World War I (Mesopotamia)

Anglo-Indian General Charles Townshend retreated south along the Tigris from **Ctesiphon** (25 November) and rested for two days at Aziziyah before facing a persistent Turkish dawn attack downriver at Umm-at-Tubal. The bloody rearguard action cost 700 Turkish and 500 British casualties before Townshend reached **Kut-al-Amara**, where he unwisely remained under siege (1 December 1915).

Umm Qasr I 2003 I 2nd Gulf War

At the start of the war, British marines established a bridgehead on the Al Faw Peninsula, then joined American forces advancing on Umm Qasr, Iraq's only deep water port, which fell after tanks and helicopters overcame stiff resistance. The first humanitarian aid ship arrived three days later, while British forces contained **Basra** and the Americans moved north towards **Nasiriya** (21–25 March 2003).

Umm Urdhumah I 1929 I Ikhwan Rebellion

Despite defeat at **Sabila**, the Ikhwan brotherhood of central Arabia fought on against Abd al-Aziz (Ibn Saud) of Nejd, who sent Abd al-Azizi Ibn Musa'id to defend the oasis of Umm Urdhumah against Azaiyiz, son of Faisal al-Dawish. Driven off with terrible losses, the rebels died of thirst in the desert. Al-Dawish later surrendered and Aziz created the Kingdom of Saudi Arabia (August 1929).

Umrani I 1673 I Bijapur-Maratha Wars

Bahlol Khan of Bijapur took a large force to recover **Panhala** fortress near Kolhapur (which had fallen on 6 March) and the Maratha warlord Shivaji sent Pratap Rao Gujar to intercept him at Umrani, 35 miles west of Bijapur. After a day-long battle, with heavy losses on both sides, Bahlol Khan's Afghans held firm and Pratap Rao unwisely permitted him to withdraw (April 1673).

Umuahia I 1969 I Biafran War

While Biafran rebel forces launched a surprise counter-offensive towards Owerri, further east Nigerian Colonel Ibrahim Haruna followed air attacks with an assault on Umuahia, which had become Biafran capital after the fall of **Enugu**. Umuahia fell after heavy fighting, but the Federal success was overshadowed by the rebel capture of **Owerri** three days later (January–22 April 1969).

Unao I 1857 I Indian Mutiny
   See **Unnao**

Unayzah I 1904 I Saudi-Rashidi Wars

Determined to aid the Rashid of central Arabia against Emir Abd al-Aziz (Ibn Saud) of Riyadh, Turkey sent 2,400 men who met the Saudi army at Unayzah, between Hail and Riyadh. Abd al-Aziz suffered heavy losses to Turkish artillery before withdrawing, but Unayzah tribesmen killed many Turks when they stopped to loot. Abd al-Aziz later struck back at **Bukairiya** in July (15 June 1904).

Undwanala I 1763 I Bengal War
   See **Udaynala**

Union Gap I 1855 I Yakima Indian Wars

Resisting white expansion in southern Washington State, Yakima Chief Kamiakin defeated a small force at the **Toppenish** (8 October) then faced 350 regulars under Major Gabriel Rains and 400 Oregon volunteers led by Colonel James Willis Nesmith. At Union Gap, just south of modern Yakima, Kamiakin was decisively defeated but struck back six months later at the **Satus** (30 October 1855).

Union Mill I 1862 I American Civil War (Eastern Theatre)
   See **Kettle Run**

United States vs *Macedonian* ▮ 1812 ▮ War
of 1812
   See **Madeira**

Unnao ▮ 1857 ▮ Indian Mutiny
   General Sir Henry Havelock relieved **Cawnpore** (16 July), then marched east across the
Ganges towards besieged **Lucknow** and met the
rebels eight miles away in a strong defensive
position at Unnao. A bold assault by Havelock's
heavily outnumbered, but better armed, force
drove the rebels out with more than 300 killed.
He then marched to further action the same day
at **Bashiratganj** (29 July 1857).

Unsan ▮ 1950 ▮ Korean War
   After securing **Pyongyang**, the Allies lunged
forward towards the Yalu. North of Unsan, invading Chinese forces checked South Korean
General Sun Yup Paik then opened an offensive
against Paik and American General Frank Mil-
burn. Threatened with encirclement, the Allies
were repulsed with very heavy losses and fell
back towards the **Chongchon** (1–6 November
1950).

Unstrut ▮ 1075 ▮ German Civil Wars
   Facing large-scale revolt by Saxon nobles in
1073, German Emperor Henry IV was initially
forced into a humiliating peace. However, he
eventually raised a large new army for the decisive battle on the Unstrut River near Langensalza. In a classic clash of mounted knights,
there were heavy losses on both sides before
Henry triumphed and reasserted Imperial authority in Saxony (9 June 1075).

**Upperville ▮ 1863 ▮ American Civil War
(Eastern Theatre)**
   As Confederate commander Robert E. Lee
invaded the north, General Alfred Pleasonton
assaulted his flank at **Middleburg**, southwest of
Leesburg, Virginia, then attacked Generals
Wade Hampton and Beverly Robertson at
nearby **Upperville**. The Confederates fell back,
but General James "Jeb" Stuart defended Ash-
by's Gap as Lee crossed the Potomac towards
Gettysburg (21 June 1863).

**Upsala ▮ 1160 ▮ Swedish Wars
of Succession**
   Swedish King Eric Jedvardsson established
Christianity in Sweden, then faced rebellion by
non-Christian nobles who sought aid from the
King of Denmark, who sent his son Prince
Magnus. The Danish army under Magnus defeated and killed Eric near Upsala, though they
were eventually repulsed. Eric was later canonised as Patron Saint of Sweden (18 May 1160).

**Urbigas ▮ 456 ▮ Goth Invasion of the
Roman Empire**
   See **Orbigo**

Uri ▮ 1947 ▮ 1st Indo-Pakistan War
   Supported by Pakistan, Muslim tribesmen invaded Indian Kashmir, storming the border town
of Muzzafarabad before advancing on the key
city of Uri. Kashmir Chief of Staff Brigadier
Rajinder Singh rushed in with reinforcements
but was killed leading a stubborn defence. When
Uri fell, the tribesmen advanced to take Baramula and the road was open to **Srinigar** (23–24
October 1947).

**Urica ▮ 1814 ▮ Venezuelan War
of Independence**
   With a Venezuelan rebel army destroyed at
Aragua de Barcelona, Spanish forces under
José Tomás Boves and Tomás Morales met and
defeated another Patriot force under General
José Félix Ribas in the northeast at Urica, near
Cumaná. Boves was fatally wounded but Mo-
rales, avenging defeat at **La Victoria**, pursued
and captured Ribas, who was later executed (5
December 1814).

**Urmiya ▮ 1757 ▮ Persian Wars
of Succession**
   Mohammad Hasan Khan of Qajar routed
Azad Khan Afghan of Azerbaijan in winter at
Lahijan (10 February) then captured Tabriz and
marched west to besiege Urmiya (modern Orumiyeh), held for Azad by Yusef Khan. Azad
approached to relieve the siege and was routed
when his allies changed sides. Urmiya quickly

surrendered and Mohammad Hasan went on to retake Isfahan (July 1757).

Urmiya I 1762–1763 I Persian Wars of Succession

In the concluding struggle for control of Persia, Regent Karim Khan Zand defeated his rival Fath Ali Afshar at **Qara Chaman** (June 1762) then besieged him at Urmiya (modern Orumiyeh), west of Lake Urmiya. Terrible winter conditions forced Fath Ali to surrender, finally securing western Persia for Karim. Fath Ali was pardoned, but later executed (24 July 1762–20 February 1763).

Uruguayana I 1865 I War of the Triple Alliance

Early in his offensive war, Paraguayan Dictator Francisco Solano López was defeated on the Uruguay at **Yatay** and Colonel Antonio de la Cruz Estigarribia was besieged across the river at Uruguayana, in modern Brazil's southwest. About 6,000 men were forced to surrender to Brazilian General Manuel Marques de Sousa and the invaders withdrew to **Humaitá** (18 September 1865).

Ürümqi I 1876 I Xinjiang Rebellion

When Yakub Beg of Khokand marched into western China and established the Muslim Khanate of Kashgari, the Qing Emperor, distracted by the Taiping Rebellion, eventually sent General Zuo Zongtang to restore order. At the head of a massive army, Zuo defeated the rebels to seize Ürümqi. In May 1877 he defeated Yakub Beg again to the southeast at **Turpan** (17 August 1876).

Urzu I 1880 I 2nd British-Afghan War

While marching from Kandahar in southern Afghanistan to support General Sir Frederick Roberts in Kabul, General Sir Donald Stewart beat a force of Afghan Ghilzais near Ghazni at **Ahmad Khel** (19 April). After reaching Ghazni, he and General Sir Charles Palliser attacked the Afghans just to the southeast at Urzu, inflicting further heavy losses before continuing to Kabul (23 April 1880).

Usagre I 1811 I Napoleonic Wars (Peninsular Campaign)

Marshal Nicolas Soult was withdrawing after failing to relieve **Badajoz** and halted at Llerena to send General Marie Latour-Mauberge's cavalry northwest to repulse the Allied advance. In one of the campaign's major cavalry victories, General Sir William Lumley—leading British, Spanish and Portuguese cavalry—ambushed and routed the French fording a river at Usagre (25 May 1811).

Ushant I 1778 I War of the American Revolution

In the first naval action since France joined the war, the British Channel Fleet under Admiral Augustus Keppel met Admiral Louis Comte d'Orvilliers west of Ushant, off Brittany, where the fleets simply exchanged broadsides then withdrew. While Keppel blamed his rear division under Admiral Hugh Palliser for failing to support him, both were court-martialled though acquitted (27 July 1778).

Ushant I 1781 I War of the American Revolution

Departing Brest for the West Indies, a French convoy escorted by Admiral Luc-Urbain Comte de Guichen was intercepted in the Bay of Biscay, southwest of Ushant, by a much smaller British force under Admiral Richard Kempenfelt. With the escort to leeward, Kempenfelt attacked the merchantmen, seizing 15. He took a further five as the stragglers fled to Brest (12 December 1781).

Ushant I 1794 I French Revolutionary Wars (1st Coalition)
See **First of June**

Ushant I 1795 I French Revolutionary Wars (1st Coalition)

British Admiral William Cornwallis was cruising off Ushant with just eight ships when he met the thirty-strong French fleet of Admiral Louis-Thomas Villaret de Joyeuse. Although Cornwallis suffered some damage, clever manoeuvring enabled him to escape without loss. Cornwallis was thanked by both British Houses of Parliament, while Villaret was accused of excessive timidity (17 June 1795).

Ussuri River ∎ 1938 ∎ Russo-Japanese Border Wars
    See **Changfukeng**

Usti nad Labem ∎ 1426 ∎ Hussite Wars
    See **Aussig**

Utah Beach ∎ 1944 ∎ World War II (Western Europe)
    See **Normandy**

Utica (1st) ∎ 240 BC ∎ Truceless War
    During peace between the First and Second Punic Wars, mercenaries of Carthage rose in revolt and besieged cities, including Utica, in modern Tunisia. Hanno took a large force from Carthage, with a reputed 100 elephants, and relieved the siege. However, he failed to secure victory and was overwhelmed by a rebel counter-attack. The Carthaginians had to withdraw but soon struck back at the **Bagradas**.

Utica (2nd) ∎ 240 BC ∎ Truceless War
    See **Bagradas**

Utica (1st) ∎ 203 BC ∎ 2nd Punic War
    While Roman General Publius Scipio the Younger was besieging the Carthaginian city of Utica, in modern Tunisia, Gaius Laelius and deposed Numidian Prince Masinissa launched a surprise night-time attack on the nearby camp of Syphax, King of Numidia. With the Numidian camp set on fire amid massive destruction, the main Carthaginian army of Hasdrubal Gisco was forced to withdraw.

Utica (2nd) ∎ 203 BC ∎ 2nd Punic War
    After Carthage and her Numidian allies had been defeated on land in Tunisia at the **Bagradas** and near Utica, Carthage soon sent a fleet to attack the Romans besieging Utica. Avoiding a full naval action at sea, Roman General Publius Scipio the Younger (later Africanus) drew his unprepared fleet close to shore. Although six Roman vessels were lost, the Carthaginians were driven off.

Utica ∎ 49 BC ∎ Wars of the First Triumvirate
    Julius Caesar was occupied against Pompeian forces at **Ilerda** in Spain and sent Gaius Curio to North Africa, where he advanced on Publius Atius Varus at Utica, in modern Tunisia. Rashly choosing to fight outside the city, Varus was badly beaten and withdrew under siege. However, after Curio was defeated by Pompeian ally Juba of Numidia at the **Bagradas**, the siege of Utica was abandoned.

Utoy Creek ∎ 1864 ∎ American Civil War (Western Theatre)
    Determined to cut supplies to the Confederate army in **Atlanta**, Georgia, after a previous attempt at **Ezra Church**, Union commander William T. Sherman sent General John M. Schofield further west towards Utoy Creek. A prolonged action saw Schofield repulsed by Generals William B. Bate and William J. Hardee, but he then established a new entrenched position (5–7 August 1864).

Utus ∎ 447 ∎ Hun Invasion of the Roman Empire
    With **Constantinople** hit by an earthquake, Attila the Hun led a large new invasion, supported by Ardaric of the Gepids and Goths under Valamer. Emperor Theodosius sent an army under the German Arnegisclus, who was defeated and killed at the Utus (Vid), south of the Danube. Attila then sacked Marcianopolis, but he too had suffered heavy losses and withdrew to the Hungarian plain.

Ututlán ∎ 1524 ∎ Spanish Conquest of Guatemala
    Conquistador Pedro de Alvarado invaded Guatemala and killed King Tecún Umán of Quiché at **Quetzaltenango**, then marched northeast towards his fortified capital at Ututlán (Gumarcaj) near modern Santa Cruz del Quiché. After an initial repulse, Alvarado and his Cakchiquel Indian allies returned to besiege then burn the city, securing the kingdom in a matter of months (April 1524).

V

**Vaagso ▌ 1941 ▌ World War II
(Northern Europe)**

While a diversionary force attacked **Lofoten**, 600 British commandos and Norwegians under Brigadier Charles Haydon attacked Vaagso and nearby Malloy, off Norway's coast near Trondheim. While German facilities and nine ships were destroyed, the raiders lost 19 killed, including Norwegian Major Martin Linge. The attack made Germany divert troops to defend Norway (27 December 1941).

**Vaalgras ▌ 1905 ▌ German Colonial
Wars in Africa**

Continuing guerrilla war in the south of German Southwest Africa after defeat at **Naris**, 80-year-old Nama leader Hendrik Witbooi was pursued by new German commander Lothar von Trotha. Attacking a German convoy at Vaalgras, near Keetmanshoop, Witbooi was fatally wounded and the Nama began to surrender. The war effectively ended the next year at **Van Rooisvlei** (29 October 1905).

**Vaal Kranz ▌ 1900 ▌ 2nd Anglo-
Boer War**

In a third attempt to relieve besieged **Ladysmith**, after failure at **Colenso** and **Spion Kop**, General Sir Redvers Buller again crossed the Tugela and seized Vaal Kranz to the southwest. However, Boers under Louis Botha counterattacked and Buller eventually withdrew, losing about 350 killed and 300 wounded. Days later he succeeded in a renewed assault at **Tugela Heights** (5–7 February 1900).

**Vác ▌ 1849 ▌ Hungarian
Revolutionary War**

See **Waitzen**

**Vaila ▌ 1509 ▌ War of the League of
Cambrai**

See **Agnadello**

**Vajreshwari ▌ 1780 ▌ 1st British-
Maratha War**

See **Doogaur**

**Valcour Island ▌ 1776 ▌ War of the
American Revolution**

With America's invasion of Canada repulsed at **Quebec** and **Trois Rivières**, General Benedict Arnold built a makeshift fleet to halt Britain's counter-offensive along Lake Champlain. Near Valcour Island, then off Split Rock, the British fleet of General Sir Guy Carleton won decisive victory. However, the delay convinced Carleton to end his advance and return to Canada (11–13 October 1776).

**Val-de-Junquera ▌ 920 ▌ Christian-
Muslim Wars in Spain**

Two years after King Ordono II of Leon beat Abd-ar-Rahman III at **San Esteban de Gormaz**, a fresh Muslim army was sent under General al-Nasir. Ordono and King Sancho I of Navarre were routed at Val-de-Junquera (modern Antzuola), near San Sebastian, with survivors killed at nearby Muez. Ordono blamed defeat on defection by four Counts of Castile and had them executed (25 July 920).

Valdevez I 1140 I Portuguese-Castilian Wars

See **Arcos de Valdevez**

Valdivia I 1820 I Chilean War of Independence

Chilean Admiral Lord Thomas Cochrane was repulsed in Peru at **Callao** (September 1819) then led a tiny force in a surprise attack on Valdivia, in southern Chile, the best-fortified port in Spanish South America. After the town suffered terrible damage by bombardment, the Royalists were defeated and fled, losing Spain its last major possession on the South Chilean mainland (3–4 February 1820).

Valdres I 1940 I World War II (Northern Europe)

While German invaders advanced northwest from **Oslo** towards Trondheim, Norwegian troops fought a bitter defence in the southwestern Valdres district, west of Bergen, around Bagn. Although Major Halfdan Haneborg-Hansen tied up considerable German forces, failure of the Allied advance from **Andalsnes** left the outnumbered Norwegians no choice but to capitulate (14 April–2 May 1940).

Valea Alba I 1476 I Moldavian-Turkish War

Stephen the Great of Moldavia defeated the Turks at **Rakhova** (January 1475), then faced a renewed Ottoman invasion. In battle in the Valea Alba, near the Danube at Rasbeoni, east of Baltatesti, the Turks won, despite massive losses, and proceeded to ravage Wallachia. After they withdrew, Stephen restored his cousin Vlad the Impaler, but his prestige was greatly diminished (17 July 1476).

Valencia, Alcántara I 1705 I War of the Spanish Succession

In a fresh offensive from Portugal into Spain, an Anglo-Dutch and Portuguese army under Henri de Massue Earl of Ruvigny and Baron Nicolas Fagel besieged French-held Valencia d'Alcántara, which was taken by storm after artillery beached the walls. Although the garri-

son of 700 capitulated, the town was sacked before the Allies marched southeast to seize Albuquerque (3–8 May 1705).

Valencia, Alcántara I 1762 I Seven Years War (Europe)

With Spain threatening Portugal in support of France, Britain sent reinforcements to aid the Portuguese. In a pre-emptive attack on the Spanish border town of Valencia d'Alcántara, General John Burgoyne surprised the invasion supply base, capturing a large quantity of arms and ammunition. Two months later he defeated the Spanish again at **Vila Velha** (27 August 1762).

Valencia, Valencia I 1093–1094 I Early Christian Reconquest of Spain

When Ibn Jahhuf overthrew and murdered Qadir of Valencia, Rodrigo Diaz de Bivar—El Cid—an ally of Qadir, took the east coast Muslim city by storm and Jahhuf was put to death. El Cid then held Valencia as independent ruler until his death in 1099. His widow Ximena initially defended Valencia, then burned the city before abandoning it to the Muslims (July 1093–15 June 1094).

Valencia, Valencia I 1808 I Napoleonic Wars (Peninsular Campaign)

Marshal Bon Adrien Moncey was sent to suppress Spanish insurrection in Catalonia and met initial success at the **Cabrillas**. However, he was heroically repulsed at the walls of Valencia by raw levies under Antonio Osorio Count of Cervellon. When two bloody assaults cost more than 1,000 men, Moncey realised he could not succeed without siege guns and withdrew to Madrid (27–28 June 1808).

Valencia, Valencia I 1811–1812 I Napoleonic Wars (Peninsular Campaign)

Two months after victory at **Sagunto**, French Marshal Louis Suchet drove defeated Spanish General Joachim Blake south into siege at Valencia. Facing a terrible bombardment, Blake's disheartened force surrendered and the captured city yielded Suchet a massive prize of prisoners, guns and stores. Suchet was later created Duke of **Albufera** (26 December 1811–9 January 1812).

Valencia, Valencia I 1938 I Spanish Civil War

Nationalist forces campaigned down Spain's eastern coast through **Castellón de la Plana** and advanced on Valencia. But strong resistance from well-prepared defences, and losses suffered during the four-month Aragon offensive, meant they could not take the city. The Republicans soon counter-attacked towards the **Ebro** and Valencia was not taken until the closing days of the war (July 1938).

Valencia, Venezuela (1st) I 1814 I Venezuelan War of Independence

While Patriot leader Simón Bolívar defended **San Mateo**, he ordered Colonel Rafael Urdaneta and just 280 men to hold Valencia against 4,000 Royalists under Spanish Colonels José Ceballos and Sebastián de le Cazada. When Bolívar himself arrived with reinforcements, the Royalist siege force withdrew. In June Bolívar was defeated further east at **La Puerta** (13 March–3 April 1814).

Valencia, Venezuela (2nd) I 1814 I Venezuelan War of Independence

Following his crushing victory at **La Puerta**, Spanish leader José Tomás Boves marched west to renew the siege of Valencia, defended by a massively outnumbered Patriot force under General Juan de Escalona. When Escalona capitulated in return for safe conduct, Boves treacherously killed many of the garrison. Boves himself was mortally wounded six months later at **Urica** (19 June–9 July 1814).

Valencia, Venezuela I 1818 I Venezuelan War of Independence

See **Semen**

Valenciennes I 1006–1007 I Revolt of Baldwin of Flanders

Count Baldwin IV of Flanders responded to Imperial expansion by capturing Ghent. He then secured Valenciennes, provoking war with his overlord, Robert of Burgundy, and King Henry II of Germany, who jointly failed to dislodge him. The King then made a fresh assault alone and forced Baldwin to surrender Valenciennes. He later pardoned the Count and granted him both cities.

Valenciennes I 1566–1567 I Netherlands War of Independence

As a prelude to full war, Governor Philip de Noircarmes of Hainault led Spanish forces against rebellious Calvinists in Valenciennes. The siege continued while Regent Margaret of Parma negotiated with William of Orange, until a 36-hour bombardment forced its surrender. This was followed by collapse of the rebellion and start of the Eighty Years Netherlands War (December 1566–March 1567).

Valenciennes I 1656 I Franco-Spanish War

Amid renewed fighting in northern France, Spanish-held Valenciennes, southeast of Lilles, was besieged by French Marshal Henri de Turenne. A relief army under the great French soldier Louis II de Bourbon Prince of Condé (in Spanish service), aided by Don John of Austria, arrived just as the city was about to surrender. They routed Turenne and drove off the siege (18 May–16 July 1656).

Valenciennes I 1793 I French Revolutionary Wars (1st Coalition)

After Marquis August Dampierre was killed at **Condé-sur-l'Escaut** (8 May) the demoralised French Army of the North was given to General Adam Philippe Custine, who was beaten at Famars, near Valenciennes, southeast of Lille, by Friedrich Josias Prince of Saxe-Coburg (21–23 May). Custine was guillotined and Valenciennes fell to the Duke of York after a two-month siege (23 May–28 July 1793).

Val-ès-Dunes I 1047 I Rise of William of Normandy

Amid continuing dynastic struggles in France, Duke William of Normandy (later William the Conqueror) was supported by Henry I of France against rebellious nobles, led by Guy Lord of Vernon and Brienne. The nobles were routed at Val-ès-Dunes, near Caen, but Henry eventually turned against the ambitious William. In 1054 the King suffered a terrible defeat at **Mortemer** (June 1047).

Valetta I 1798–1800 I French Revolutionary Wars (1st Coalition)

Following Napoleon Bonaparte's capture of **Malta** in June 1798 (en route to invade Egypt) British Admiral Sir Alexander Ball was despatched in October to recover the island. Landing with a small force of marines, supported by Maltese militia, Ball quickly drove General Claude-Henri Vaubois back to siege in Valetta, which finally succumbed to starvation (September 1798–5 September 1800).

Val Gudina I 1709 I War of the Spanish Succession

Portuguese commander Fernando Mascarenhas Marquis de Fronteira determined on a final offensive to prevent French forces under Alexandre Marquis de Bay destroying the harvest in the south. English leader Henri de Massue Earl of Ruvigny had urged caution, and at Val Gudina, on the Caia northwest of Badajoz, he and Fronteira were beaten back to the Guadiana (17 May 1709).

Valievo I 1737 I Austro-Russian-Turkish War

See **Valjevo**

Valjevo I 1737 I Austro-Russian-Turkish War

Austrian Marshal Count Friedrich von Seckendorff supported Russia against Turkey in the Balkans, advancing from **Nish** into Bosnia, where a Turkish counter-attack had repulsed Austrians at **Banyaluka** (4 August). Seckendorff suffered a major defeat at Valjevo, southwest of Belgrade. A further loss a year later at **Kroszka** persuaded Austria to abandon her ally and make a separate peace.

Valjouan I 1814 I Napoleonic Wars (French Campaign)

See **Mortmant**

Valladolid I 1813 I Mexican Wars of Independence

Despite the death of Miguel Hidalgo after **Calderón**, Mexican rebellion continued under José María Morelos, who captured a number of cities. After his defeat at **Cuautla** (May 1812), Morelos rashly attacked Valladolid and was badly beaten by Royalists Ciriaco de Llano and Agustin de Iturbide. The rising lost momentum and Morelos was eventually captured and executed (23 December 1813).

Valls I 1809 I Napoleonic Wars (Peninsular Campaign)

Advancing from Tarragona to attack General Laurent Gouvion Saint-Cyr around Barcelona, General Teodoro Reding's Spanish force fought a confused campaign of manoeuvre before the two armies met near Valls, north of Tarragona, where the Spaniards were crushed and lost their guns. With Reding mortally wounded, the survivors fell back on Tarragona (25 February 1809).

Valls I 1811 I Napoleonic Wars (Peninsular Campaign)

See **Pla**

Valmaseda I 1808 I Napoleonic Wars (Peninsular Campaign)

Spanish General Joachim Blake, withdrawing west from **Bilbao**, was impetuously pursued from **Pancorbo** by Marshal Claude Victor. At Valmaseda, French General Eugène Villatte unexpectedly faced Blake and massive Spanish reinforcements sent by General Pedro La Romana. He was heavily repulsed before Victor came up and drove Blake towards defeat at **Espinosa** (5 November 1808).

Valmont I 1416 I Hundred Years War

On campaign northeast from Harfleur, Thomas Beaufort Earl of Dorset and 1,000 men were blocked by about 4,000 Gascons under Bernard of Armagnac Constable of France, east of Fé-camp at Valmont. Fighting off an attack, Dorset slipped away in the night and next day, near Etretat, defeated part of Armagnac's army under Marshal Louis de Loigny and made it back to **Harfleur** (March 1416).

Valmy I 1792 I French Revolutionary Wars (1st Coalition)

After capturing **Longwy** and **Verdun**, Karl Wilhelm Ferdinand Duke of Brunswick advanced slowly towards Paris. At Valmy, north-east of Chalons, his Prussians and Austrians faced French veterans under Generals Charles-Francois Dumouriez and Francois Kellerman and were repulsed by accurate artillery fire. Brunswick withdrew to the Rhine, abandoning his prizes (20 September 1792).

Valparaiso I 1814 I War of 1812

At the end of a successful cruise off the Pacific coast of South America, the American frigate *Essex* (Captain David Porter) was blockaded in neutral Valparaiso, Chile, by the British frigate *Phoebe* (Captain James Hillyar) and sloop *Cherub* (Commander Tudor Tucker). Attempting to break out to sea, *Essex* was badly damaged with heavy casualties and surrendered (28 March 1814).

Valparaiso I 1866 I Peruvian-Spanish War

When Chile supported Peru in war with Spain, Imperial Commodore Casto Mendez-Nuñez blockaded Chilean ports and, with British and American squadrons insisting on neutrality, he attacked virtually unprotected Valparaiso harbour. A massive bombardment destroyed shore facilities and over 30 merchant ships. The Spanish fleet then sailed against **Callao** in Peru (31 March 1866).

Valpovo I 1537 I Turkish-Habsburg Wars

While Sultan Suleiman besieged **Corfu**, a large Imperial army advanced into Croatia. After being driven off from a siege at Osijek it was destroyed by a Turkish force on the Drava near Valpovo. A reported 20,000 Austrians and Hungarians were killed, including Generals Ludwig Lodron and Paul Bakicz, while commander Johann Katzianer fled and was later murdered (2 December 1537).

Valtesti I 1821 I Greek War of Independence

Ottoman General Kurshid Pasha met rising nationalism in Greece by reinforcing **Tripolitza**, then led 5,000 men against about 3,000 Greeks in a strong defensive position to the southwest at Valtesti. The Turks were repulsed in heavy fighting, losing 400 killed and large quantities of military supplies in the pursuit. The Greeks lost 150 killed in their first major victory of the war (24 May 1821).

Valtierra I 1110 I Early Christian Reconquest of Spain

At a time of consistent Muslim success against the Christians of northeastern Spain, King Alfonso I of Aragon—El Batallador, the fighter—secured a welcome victory at Valtierra, north of Tudela. While the battle itself was not particularly significant, it was strategically important in costing the life of the important Muslim ruler al-Mustain of Saragossa (January 1110).

Valutino I 1812 I Napoleonic Wars (Russian Campaign)

Two days after capturing **Smolensk**, Napoleon Bonaparte's advance units under Marshal Michel Ney attempted to trap the Russian rearguard led by General Mikhail Barclay de Tolly further east between Valutino-Gora and Lubina. Although both sides suffered heavy losses, hesitation by Marshal Andoche Junot allowed Barclay to escape and continue his withdrawal (19 August 1812).

Valverde I 1862 I American Civil War (Trans-Mississippi)

Confederate General Henry Hopkins Sibley, with Colonel Thomas J. Green, campaigned into New Mexico, where he advanced towards Fort

Craig and was met just to the north at Valverde by a mixed force under Colonel Edward R. S. Canby. Despite costly losses in a bloody action, Sibley forced the larger Union force to retire and pushed on north to capture Santa Fe (21 February 1862).

Van Buren ∎ 1966 ∎ Vietnam War
See **Tuy Hoa**

Vanguardia ∎ 1928 ∎ Chaco War
As tension continued in the disputed Chaco Boreal following the incident at **Sorpresa** in early 1927, Paraguayan Major Rafael Franco led an unauthorised attack on the fortress at Vanguardia, north of Bahia Negra, held by Bolivian Colonel Victorino Gutiérrez. Franco was dismissed and Paraguay was forced to accept a humiliating truce until hostilities broke out four years later (5 December 1928).

Vaniyambadi ∎ 1767 ∎ 1st British-Mysore War
Colonel Joseph Smith repulsed Haidar Ali of Mysore at **Ambur**, then chased him to Vaniyambadi, on the Palar, southwest of Vellore, where Haidar Ali turned on his pursuers. During an indecisive action, his son Tipu Sultan's cavalry attacked the rearguard of the British force, which was forced to pull back with heavy losses. However, Haidar Ali also had to withdraw (December 1767).

Van Rooisvlei ∎ 1906 ∎ German Colonial Wars in Africa
Nama leader Jakob Morenga continued guerrilla war in German Southwest Africa after Hendrik Witbooi's death near **Vaalgras** (October 1905) and was finally attacked in camp at Van Rooisvlei, just inside British South Africa, by a German column under Captain Bech. The Nama lost 23 killed and three days later Morenga surrendered to the British, ending the so-called Herero War (4 May 1906).

Van Thuong ∎ 1965 ∎ Vietnam War
See **Chu Lai**

Vaprio ∎ 1799 ∎ French Revolutionary Wars (2nd Coalition)
See **Cassano**

Varaville ∎ 1058 ∎ Rise of William of Normandy
Henry I of France was concerned at the rise of Duke William of Normany and, after a failure at **Mortemer** (1054), he and Geoffrey of Anjou again entered Normandy. As they crossed the Dives at its mouth near Varaville, William attacked and inflicted a bloody defeat, with many drowned when the bridge collapsed. Henry withdrew and made peace while William went on to seize England at **Hastings**.

Varberg ∎ 1565 ∎ Nordic Seven Years War
On campaign into Danish Halland, Erik XIV of Sweden captured Varberg, supported by artillery under his brother Charles. Very heavy fighting against Danish commander Daniel Rantzau saw parts of the port change hands, But with discipline breaking down, Rantzau withdrew after a costly final assault. Days later he met Swedish reinforcements at **Axtorna** (28 August–18 October 1565).

Varberg ∎ 1569 ∎ Nordic Seven Years War
When John III of Sweden resumed hostilities, Danish commander Daniel Rantzau led a fresh offensive and besieged Varberg, where he and his successor Frans Brockenhausen were both killed. Frederick II of Denmark then stormed Varberg, killing garrison commander Bo Birgersson Grip. War soon ended with Denmark agreeing to withdraw all claim on Sweden (October–4 December 1569).

Vardar ∎ 1915 ∎ World War I (Balkan Front)
Intervening to support Serbia against German-Bulgarian invasion, Anglo-French forces landed at **Salonika** and advanced north into the Vardar Valley under General Maurice Sarrail. The key city of Strumica changed hands several times before a powerful Bulgarian counter-attack drove the Allies back to Greece, defeating the

British at **Kosturino** (15 October–15 December 1915)

Vardar ∎ 1918 ∎ World War I (Balkan Front)

After years of stalemate in **Salonika**, new Allied commander Louis Franchet d'Esperey launched a massive offensive along the Vardar Valley through **Dobro Polje** against Bulgarian General Nikola Zhekov. While British forces in the east were checked near **Doiran**, the British, French, Serb, Italian and Greek Allies broke through and Bulgaria sued for peace (15–26 September 1918).

Varese ∎ 1859 ∎ 2nd Italian War of Independence

Giuseppe Garibaldi was campaigning against Austria in northern Italy, east of Lake Maggiore, when he led 3,000 irregulars against Varese, held by Marshal Karl von Urban. The Austrians withdrew after fierce fighting and were driven out when they tried to dig in at nearby Malnate. While Garibaldi won again at **San Fermo** and **Tre Ponti**, his campaign produced little strategic benefit (26 May 1859).

Varna ∎ 1444 ∎ Turkish-Hungarian Wars

Encouraged by Pope Eugenius IV, Ladislas III of Poland and Hungary led the "Crusade of Varna" against the Turks in the Balkans. On the Black Sea Coast, near Varna, the 20-year-old King was defeated and killed by Sultan Murad II, who then reconquered Serbia and Wallachia. The Hungarian commander Janos Hunyadi escaped and was killed in 1448 at **Kossovo** (10 November 1444).

Varna ∎ 1828 ∎ Russo-Turkish Wars

Russian Prince Alexander Menshikov crossed the Danube in support of Greek independence and despatched General Count Hans von Diebitsch to besiege the Black Sea port of Varna, held by 20,000 Turkish troops. Powerful sorties by the garrison were repulsed on 7 and 21 August and the city was eventually taken by storm (5 August–11 October 1828).

Varvarin ∎ 1810 ∎ 1st Serbian Rising

On a fresh campaign in Serbia after the costly defence of **Nish** in May 1809, Khurshid Pasha and an Ottoman army of 30,000 advanced against Kara George and 3,000 Serbians to the northwest at Varvarin. Irish-born Russian General Joseph O'Rourke arrived just in time to help defeat Kurshid. Another victory at **Loznitza** a month later drove the Turks out of Serbia (8 September 1810).

Vasa ∎ 1808 ∎ Napoleonic Wars (Russo-Swedish War)

Supporting the Swedish summer offensive down the west coast of Finland from **Siikajoki**, Swedish General Johan Bergenstrahle landed against General Nikolai Demidoff's Russian invaders at Vasa. The main Swedish army was unable to send aid from nearby **Nykarleby** and the outnumbered Swedes evacuated by sea. The port was recaptured for Sweden a few days later (25–26 June 1808).

Vasai ∎ 1780 ∎ 1st British-Maratha War
See **Bassein, India**

Vasaq ∎ 1442 ∎ Turkish-Hungarian Wars

To avenge Turkey's defeat at **Hermannstadt**, Ottoman Sultan Murad II sent Governor Sehabeddin of Rumelia into Transylvania with a massive army against the outnumbered Hungarians of Janos Hunyadi. In the Ialomita Valley at Vasaq the Turks suffered an even worse defeat, with a reported 20,000 casualties. They lost again the next year at **Nish** (6 September 1442).

Vasilika ∎ 1821 ∎ Greek War of Independence

As 5,000 Ottoman troops under three Pashas advanced south to support Omer Vrioni at the **Acropolis**, they were blocked at Vasilika by Greeks under Nikitas Nikitaras, later reinforced by Odysseus Androutsos. Ambushed at nearby Mount Oeta, the Turks lost 800 men and withdrew. With his reinforcements defeated and **Tripolitza** lost (8 October), Vrioni abandoned Athens (4 September 1821).

aslui | 1475 | Moldavian-Turkish War
See **Rakhova**

Vassy | 1562 | 1st French War of Religion
More a massacre than a battle, this strategic incident occurred when the Catholic Francis Duke of Guise, claiming a violation of limited rights granted to Protestant Huguenots by Queen Catherine de Medici, allowed his men to attack worshippers in church at Vassy, near Condé sur Noireau, Normandy. About 60 unarmed Huguenots were killed, triggering the First French War of Religion (1 March 1562).

Vatapi | 642 | Indian Dynastic Wars
To avenge the defeat of his father Mahendra at **Kanchi** (610), Narasimhavarman of Pallava took a large army against Pulakesin II of Chalukya. With General Paranjothi, Narasimha won a decisive battle near the Chalukya capital Vatapi (modern Badami). Pulakesin was killed in the fighting and Vatapi was occupied until his son Vikramaditya drove Pallava out in 655 and struck back at **Kanchi**.

Vauchamps | 1814 | Napoleonic Wars (French Campaign)
In a brilliant five-day campaign east of Paris against General Gebhard von Blucher's Army of Silesia, Napoleon Bonaparte won at **Champaubert**, **Montmirail** and **Chateau-Thierry**, then defeated Blucher's vanguard further east between Janvilliers and Vauchamps. The Russians and Prussians withdrew in tatters and Bonaparte was able to turn against the Austrians (14 February 1814).

Vaught's Hill | 1863 | American Civil War (Western Theatre)
Two weeks after the Union rout south of Nashville, Tennessee, at **Thompson's Station**, Colonel Albert S. Hall led a Union Brigade northeast from Murfreesboro and met Confederate General John H. Morgan at Vaught's Hill, near Milton, southeast of Nashville. Hall repulsed the Confederates and, with Union reinforcements marching from Murfreesboro, Morgan withdrew (20 March 1863).

Vaux (1st) | 1916 | World War I (Western Front)
While German forces attacked northwest of **Verdun** around **Le Mort-Homme**, General Konstantin Schmidt von Knobelsdorf in the east attacked the powerful fort at Vaux. Intense fighting with shocking losses on both sides forced Major Sylvain Raynal to surrender the fortress. After a failed French counter-attack, General Philippe Nivelle had to withdraw (8 March–7 June 1916).

Vaux (2nd) | 1916 | World War I (Western Front)
A counter-attack by General Robert Nivelle retook the fortress of **Douaumont** (24 October) then turned against Vaux. After costly losses in an initial assault, the French bombarded the fortress for six days and forced its surrender. German commander Erich von Ludendorff began to withdraw his army and action around **Louvement** ended the battle of **Verdun** (25 October–3 November 1916).

Vaxholm | 1612 | War of Kalmar
Christian IV of Denmark became stalled on land after seizing **Alvsborg** (24 May), so took a large fleet against the fortress of Vaxholm, outside Stockholm, where a massive Danish bombardment damaged the fortress and the nearby Swedish fleet. But Vaxholm held out and, with winter approaching, Christian withdrew and made peace with King Gustavus Adolphus (August–4 September 1612).

Vedrosha | 1500 | 1st Muscovite-Lithuanian War
Determined to secure Lithuania, Duke Ivan III of Moscow sent Daniil Shchenya, whose army met Lithuanian commander Prince Konstantine Ostrozhsky on the banks of the Vedrosha, west of Dorogbuzh. An extraordinarily bloody action saw virtually the entire Lithuanian army killed or captured, with Ostrozhsky himself taken prisoner. Russia won again next year at **Mstislavl** (14 July 1500).

Vega ▌ 1319 ▌ Later Christian Reconquest of Spain

In an ill-considered expedition against Muslim Granada, Prince Peter and Prince John of Castile—Regents for the infant Alfonso XI—took an inadequate force close to Granada itself. After some initial success they suffered a terrible defeat to the west at Vega. Both Peter and John were killed and King Ismail of Granada was encouraged to take the offensive against the Christians.

Vegkop ▌ 1836 ▌ Boer-Matabele War

As Boers moved into Orange River Valley, a party under Andries Potgieter and Sarel Cilliers was attacked at Vegkop, southeast of modern Heilbron, by 5,000 of Mzilikazi's Matabele under Mkhalipi. Potgieter's brother Nicolaas died in a terrible fight before the Matabele were driven off after costly losses, taking the trekkers' stock. Potgieter was soon avenged at **Mosega** (19 October 1836).

Veglaer ▌ 1838 ▌ Boer-Zulu War

Having taken part in the Boer defeat at **Italeni**, Jacobus Potgieter and Hans de Lang led the courageous defence of Veglaer lager, close to the Tugela River near modern Estcourt, where they were attacked by a reported ten regiments of Zulus. The Zulus were driven off after heavy fighting (though they captured the trekkers' cattle). They were routed in December at **Blood River** (13 August 1838).

Veii ▌ 405–396 BC ▌ Roman-Etruscan Wars

Twenty years after taking Estruscan **Fidenae**, Rome began a prolonged campaign against their major rival city of Veii, just a few miles away up the Tiber. Following a siege claimed to have lasted ten years, Marcus Furius Camillus took Veii by storm, then looted and destroyed the city. After recovering from defeat by invading Gauls at the **Allia**, Rome gradually subsumed the remaining cities of Etruria.

Velasco ▌ 1832 ▌ Texan Wars of Independence

Attempting to reinforce Texan patriots at **Anahuac**, a citizen force of over 100 led by John Austin and Henry Brown was blocked by Mexican Colonel Domingo de Ugartechea at Fort Velasco, at the mouth of the Brazos River. In a fierce action, supported by the Texan schooner *Brazoria*, both sides lost about 20 casualties. Ugartechea then surrendered and was returned to Mexico (26 June 1832).

Velbuzhde ▌ 1330 ▌ Serbian Imperial Wars

Stephan Dechanski (Urosh III) expanded the power of Serbia and invaded Bulgaria against his former brother-in-law Tsar Mikhail Shishman, who was defeated and killed in battle at Velbuzhde (modern Kustendil), southwest of Sofia. The Serbian victory was largely due to the bravery of Serbian Crown Prince Stephan Dushan, who beat the Byzantines in 1355 at **Adrianople** (28 July 1330).

Velencze ▌ 1848 ▌ Hungarian Revolutionary War
See **Pakozd**

Velestino (1st) ▌ 1897 ▌ 1st Greco-Turkish War

Ottoman commander Edhem Pasha advanced into Thessaly through victory at **Mati** (23 April) to seize Larissa from the fleeing Greeks and sent Mahmud Bey southeast towards the strategic railway junction at Velestino, held by heavily outnumbered Greeks under Colonel Konstantinos Smolenskis. After a disastrous cavalry charge and over 1,200 casualties, the Turks fell back (30 April 1897).

Velestino (2nd) ▌ 1897 ▌ 1st Greco-Turkish War

Advancing south into Thessaly, Ottoman commander Edhem Pasha was repulsed at Velestino and a week later sent Hakki Pasha on a second attack. In a two-day action, with heavy artillery fire from both sides, Turkish infantry assaults were driven off. With ammunition low and possible outflanking at **Pharsalus**, Greek Colonel Konstantinos Smolenskis withdrew east to Volo (5–6 May 1897).

**Velez-Malaga I 1704 I War of the
Spanish Succession**
See **Malaga**

Velikie Luki I 1580 I Livonian War

King Stephen Bathory of Poland resolved to
cut off Moscow's campaign against Livonia and
captured **Polotsk**. The following year he took a
fresh expedition deeper into Russian territory,
where he and commander Jan Zamoyski attacked Velikie Luki. In a brutal siege the fortified city was taken by storm and plundered.
Bathory led his final expedition in 1581 against
Pskov (4 September 1580).

**Velikoknyazheskaya I 1919 I Russian
Civil War**

As part of General Anton Denikin's great
White offensive in the Kuban, General Pyotr
Wrangel's South Caucasian Army crossed the
Manych from Torgovaya and advanced on the
Reds at Velikoknyazheskaya, east of Rostov.
Heavy fighting saw Wrangel capture the town,
along with 15,000 prisoners and 55 guns. He
then continued northeast towards **Tsaritsyn** (17
May 1919).

Vella Gulf I 1943 I World War II (Pacific)

A new attempt to reinforce the Japanese garrison on Kolombangara, west of **New Georgia**,
saw Captain Kaju Sugiura surprised to the west
in Vella Gulf by six destroyers under Commander Frederick Moosbrugger. Unlike previous actions at **Kula Gulf** and **Kolombangara**,
three out of four Japanese destroyers were sunk
with no American loss (6–7 August 1943).

**Vella Lavella—Land I 1943 I
World War II (Pacific)**

While Allied forces secured **New Georgia**,
American Admiral Theodore Wilkinson bypassed neighbouring Kolombangara and landed
further west on Vella Lavella. After initial success, some Japanese reinforcements arrived and
fighting was renewed. New Zealanders under
General Harold Barrowclough later took over
and successfully cleared the island (15 August–5
October 1943).

**Vella Lavella—Naval I 1943 I
World War II (Pacific)**

As the Japanese evacuated Vella Lavella, west
of **New Georgia**, the screening force led by
Admiral Matsuji Ijuin was intercepted by destroyers under Captain Frank Walker. A fierce
night action saw the Americans outnumbered
and outmanoeuvred with two destroyers sunk.
Although one Japanese destroyer was also sunk
the evacuation was successfully completed (6–7
October 1943).

**Velletri I 1744 I War of the Austrian
Succession**

Austrian Prince Johann George Christian von
Lobkowitz advancing south against the Spanish
kingdom of Naples was met southeast of Rome
at Velletri by a Spanish and Neapolitan army
under Charles IV of Sicily and General Count
Juan de Gages. The Austrians were checked
in an indecisive action and they withdrew north
to support Charles Emmanuel at **Cuneo** (11
August 1744).

**Velletri I 1849 I 1st Italian War of
Independence**

Sent to intercept Neapolitan troops advancing
to support the French siege of Republican Rome,
Giuseppe Garibaldi and about 2,000 men met
the Bourbon force at Velletri, southeast of
Rome. As at nearby **Palestrina** earlier, the numerically superior Neapolitans were driven off,
but Garibaldi did not follow up his victory and
Rome itself was eventually force to capitulate
(19 May 1849).

**Vellinghausen I 1761 I Seven Years
War (Europe)**

Four months after victory at **Gruneberg**, a
French army under Marshals Charles Soubise
and Victor-Francois Broglie invaded Westphalia. At Vellinghausen, southeast of Hamm,
Broglie was driven off by Prussian Marshal
Duke Ferdinand of Brunswick. The following
day Soubise and Broglie were defeated when
they failed to co-operate and were driven back to
the Rhine (15–16 July 1761).

Vellore I 1677–1678 I Bijapur-Maratha Wars

Maratha King Shivaji campaigned against Bijapur in southeast India, where he attacked the strong fortress of Vellore, then pursued Mughal commander Sher Khan Lodi to **Tiruvadi**, leaving Narahari Rudra and 7,000 men to maintain the siege. Garrison commander Abdullah Khan finally surrendered Vellore after losing 2,000 men through starvation and disease (23 May 1677–22 July 1678).

Vellore I 1806 I Vellore Mutiny

When Sir John Cradock in Madras ordered Indian troops to remove beards, turbans and other religious symbols, 1,500 sepoys attacked the British barracks at Vellore. Colonel Rollo Gillespie arrived from nearby Arcot with loyal troops and crushed the mutiny. About 130 British troops and 400 mutineers died and Cradock and Governor General Lord William Bentinck were recalled (10 July 1806).

Vellur I 917 I Later Indian Dynastic Wars

After the death of Aditya of Chola (907), his son Parantaka extended the empire, waging war against Rajasimha II of Pandya. Rajasimha sought aid from Kassapa V of Ceylon, who sent an army under his son the Sakkasenapati, but at Vellur (modern Vellore) Parantaka defeated the combined force. Parantaka later drove Rajasimha from Madura and claimed Ceylon, but was checked in 949 at **Takkolam**.

Venadito I 1817 I Mexican Wars of Independence

While Mexican Royalists besieged a rebel army at **Los Remedios** in Guanajuato, rebel leader Francisco Javier Mina campaigned in the field against Marshal Pascual Liñán's communication lines. But Mina was defeated and captured by Colonel Francisco de Orrantía at Venadito, near Silao. The Spanish adventurer was executed a few days later and his rising was effectively over (27 October 1817).

Vences I 1847 I Argentine Civil Wars
See **Rincón de Vences**

Vengi I 830 I Later Indian Dynastic Wars

Govinda III of Rashtrakuta drove Vijayaditya II of Eastern Chalukya out of Vengi, between the Godaveri and Krishna Rivers. Vijayaditya later regained the city and began a revolt (817), which drove Govinda's teenage son Amoghavarsha off the throne. Aided by Karkka of Gujarat, Amoghavarsha regained control and at Vengi inflicted a crushing defeat. In 850 he won again at **Vingavelli**.

Venice I 1310 I Tiepolo's Rebellion

Opposed to the increasingly oligarchic Venetian Grand Council, Baiamonte Tiepolo and Marco Querini conspired to storm the palace of Doge Pietro Gradenigo and overthrow his government. When word leaked the plotters attacked prematurely and were crushed in the streets. Querini was executed, but Tiepolo managed to escape. A secret Council of Ten was created to protect the Republic (15 June 1310).

Venice I 1849 I Italian Wars of Independence

With Austria driven out of Milan, Daniele Manin declared a Republic in Venice (26 March 1848) which a year later held out against siege by Marshal Josef Radetzky despite Piedmontese defeat at **Novara**. Following a terrible bombardment and rampant cholera, the starving city was forced to capitulate. Manin was exiled and Austria regained control in Italy (20 July–22 August 1849).

Venta del Pozo I 1812 I Napoleonic Wars (Peninsular Campaign)

As Arthur Wellesley Lord Wellington withdrew from a failed siege of **Burgos**, his rearguard under General Sir Stapleton Cotton, with Brigadier George Anson and General Eberhardt von Bock, was attacked at Venta del Pozo by French Generals Jean-Baptiste Curto and Joseph Boyer. The Allies suffered a sharp defeat and continued through Villadrigo towards Portugal (23 October 1812).

Venta de Urroz I 1813 I Napoleonic Wars (Peninsular Campaign)
See **Buenza**

Ventaquemada I 1812 I Colombian War of Independence

Dictator Antonio Nariño secured Cundina-marca then took 1,500 men to try and seize Tunja, held by Federalist Governor Juan Niño and Colonel Antonio Baraya. Just south of Tunja at Ventaquemada, Nariño was met and routed by Federalist Brigadier Joaquín Ricaurte. Nariño then withdrew south towards Bogotá, which he defended at **Santa Fé** (2 December 1813).

Venta y Media I 1815 I Argentine War of Independence

Advancing from victory at **Puesto del Már-quez** in northern Argentine (17 April), the van-guard of General José Rondeau's Patriot Army of the North under General Martin Rodríguez was attacked by General Joaquín de la Pezuela at Venta y Media, near Oruro, in western Bolivia. The Royalists inflicted a decisive defeat and Rondeau lost again a month later further north at **Sipe-Sipe** (21 October 1815).

Venusia I 208 BC I 2nd Punic War

With the war in Italy stalling, Consuls Titus Crispinus and Marcus Marcellus marched to support the siege of Locri in central Italy and Hannibal ambushed the Romans near the camp at Venusia (modern Venosa), north of Potenza. In sharp fighting, Crispinus was mortally wounded and Marcellus was killed outright, depriving Rome of one of its most effective Generals.

Vera (1st) I 1813 I Napoleonic Wars (Peninsular Campaign)

A co-ordinated effort to relieve the Allied siege of San Sebastian on the Spanish north coast saw French Marshal Nicolas Soult cross the **Bidassoa** near **San Marcial**, while General Bertrand Clausel advanced further upriver. De-feated by Allied General William Inglis, Clausel fought his way back across the river at Vera. **San Sebastian** town fell by storm the same day (31 August 1813).

Vera (2nd) I 1813 I Napoleonic Wars (Peninsular Campaign)

While Arthur Wellesley Lord Wellington forced his way across the estuary of the **Bidassoa** in northeastern Spain, other Allied forces ad-vanced the same day further upstream towards the key bridge at Vera. Spanish General Francisco Longa and British General Sir James Kempt overwhelmed the defence of General Nicolas-Francois Conroux, who retreated north (7 October 1813).

Veracruz I 1832 I Mexican Civil Wars

General Antonio de Santa Anna, opposing the government of President Anatasio Bustamente, was defeated at **Tolomé** and fell back to nearby Veracruz, which he held with 2,500 men and over 100 guns against Federal General José Maria Calderón. After losing perhaps 1,000 men, mainly to disease, Calderón retired to Jalapa. In Sep-tember Bustamente won at **Gallinero** (12 April–13 May 1832).

Veracruz I 1838 I Pastry War
See **San Juan de Ulúa**

Veracruz I 1847 I American-Mexican War

In a bold amphibious assault on Mexico's east coast, American General Winfield Scott and Commodore David Conner landed unopposed near Veracruz. After a five-day land and naval bombardment, General Juan Morales surren-dered the city and the great fortress of San Juan de Ulúa. Scott then began his epic advance in-land through **Cerro Gordo** to **Mexico City** (9–27 March 1847).

Veracruz I 1859 I Mexican War of the Reform

Conservative President Miguel Miramón led a fresh offensive against the Liberal forces of Benito Juarez to recapture Guanajuato then marched to besiege the Juarista capital at Vera-cruz. With his army driven off by yellow fever, Miramón had to return to Mexico City, where the Conservative cause was soon boosted by a great victory over the Liberals at **Tacubaya** (1–29 March 1859).

Veracruz I 1860 I Mexican War of the Reform

Resuming the offensive in eastern Mexico, Conservative President Miguel Miramón took a force against the Liberal city of Veracruz, held for Benito Juarez by General Ramon Iglesias. While Veracruz was heavily bombarded, it suffered little damage and Miramón was forced to withdraw to Mexico City. He was more successful a few weeks later at **Guadalajara** (5–21 March 1860).

Veracruz Incident I 1914 I Mexican Revolution

A few days after Mexican forces seized American sailors for allegedly going ashore at Tampico without permission, American Marines under Colonel John Lejeune seized Veracruz on reports that the German ship *Ypiranga* was landing arms for President Victoriano Huerta. About 200 Mexicans died attempting to resist the Marines and Huerta soon fled into exile (21 April 1914).

Verbitza I 811 I Byzantine-Bulgarian Wars

Emperor Nicephorus I launched a large-scale offensive against the Bulgar Khan Krum and burned the Bulgar capital Pliska (modern Plioskov) before being ambushed at nearby Verbitza. Trapped by wooden pallisades erected at each end of the steep pass, the Byzantine army was annihilated, with Nicephorus himself killed. Krum won again two years later at **Versinikia** (26 July 811).

Vercellae I 101 BC I Rome's Gallic Wars

After Cimbri from Jutland defeated Quintus Lutatius Catulus in Italy on the **Adige**, he was reinforced by Gaius Marius, fresh from victory in Gaul at **Aquae Sextiae**. East of Turin at Vercellae, the invaders were crushed and King Boiorix was killed. With thousands massacred and women and children enslaved, the Cimbri

were annihilated, ending the Germanic threat to Italy (30 July 101 BC).

Vercelli I 218 BC I 2nd Punic War
See **Ticinus**

Verdun I 1792 I French Revolutionary Wars (1st Coalition)

As war started, Prussians and Austrians under Karl Wilhelm Ferdinand Duke of Brunswick stormed the border to besiege then bombard Verdun. Colonel Nicolas Beaurepaire vehemently opposed surrender, but under suspicious circumstances was reported to have shot himself. Verdun capitulated, though was retaken (14 October) after Brunswick's defeat at **Valmy** (29 August–2 September 1792).

Verdun I 1870 I Franco-Prussian War

German forces moving west from **Metz** confronted the stategic fortress at **Verdun**, garrisoned by about 7,000 men under Baron Guerin de Waldersbach. Heavy attacks by field artillery were repulsed (24 August & 8 September) before General Wilhelm von Gayl brought up siege guns for a full investment from 13 October. Verdun was soon forced to capitulate (24 August–7 November 1870).

Verdun I 1916 I World War I (Western Front)

In the reputed bloodiest battle then known, German forces attacked Verdun, seizing and then losing **Le Mort-Homme** and **Fleury** and the fortresses of **Douaumont**, **Vaux** and **Souville**. This ultimate battle of attrition cost 542,000 French and 434,000 German casualties for no strategic gain before the Germans eventually fell back to their starting line (21 February–18 December 1916).

Verdun I 1917 I World War I (Western Front)

New commander Henri Petain rebuilt after disaster at the **Aisne** (April–May) and launched a relieving campaign north from Verdun to reaffirm the French offensive and support the

British at **Ypres**. Advancing east and west of the Meuse, the French secured extensive ground and over 10,000 prisoners, recovering most of the key defensive positions lost in early 1916 (20–28 August 1917).

Vergt | 1562 | 1st French War of Religion

Following the massacre of Protestants at **Vassy** (1 March), Huguenots led by Louis I de Bourbon Prince of Condé seized many cities before a setback at Vergt, south of Perigueux, where they were badly defeated by the Gascon Marshal Blaise de Monluc on behalf of Catholic commander Francis Duke of Guise. The battle largely ended Protestant Huguenot power in the Guyenne (9 October 1562).

Vermillion Bayou | 1863 | American Civil War (Lower Seaboard)

Union commander Nathaniel P. Banks continued his offensive in western Louisiana through victory at **Fort Bisland** and **Irish Bend**, ordering General Cuvier Grover northwest in pursuit of General Richard Taylor at Vermillion Bayou, near Vermillionville. Despite initial success, the Confederates were driven off by Union artillery and fell back north towards Opelousas (17 April 1863).

Verneuil | 1424 | Hundred Years War

A year after defeat at **Cravant**, Dauphin Charles VII of France sent a Franco-Scottish army into English Normandy, where it was routed at Verneuil, east of Paris, by John Duke of Bedford's outnumbered English longbowmen. Archibald Earl of Douglas and John Stewart Earl of Buchan (Constable of France) were killed, while Duke Jean of Alencon was captured (17 August 1424).

Verona | 249 | Roman Military Civil Wars

When Gaius Trajanus Decius successfully put down a rebellion on the Danube, Roman Emperor Philip I appointed his General to take command in the area, where the troops promptly elected him Emperor. Philip gathered his army to punish the usurper but was defeated and killed near Verona in northern Italy. Decius was formally recognised as Emperor.

Verona | 312 | Roman Wars of Succession

Emperor Constantine advanced through northern Italy against his rival Emperor Maxentius to win near **Turin** then defeat the powerful General Pompeianus Ruricius at Brescia and drive him back to siege in Verona. Ruricius broke out to bring reinforcements but was killed when his relief force was destroyed. Verona surrendered and Constantine marched to seize Rome at the **Milvian Bridge**.

Verona | 403 | Goth Invasion of the Roman Empire

The Goth leader Alaric withdrew from a bloody battle at **Pollentia**, but the following year renewed his offensive in Italy and attempted to besiege Verona. Attacked nearby by the Roman-Vandal General Flavius Stilicho, Alaric again suffered a decisive defeat yet withdrew east in good order. He concluded a treaty with Stilicho and was later appointed to hold Illyricum for Emperor Honorius.

Verona | 489 | Goth Invasion of Italy

Driven back from defeat on the **Sontius** (Isonzo) River in northern Italy (28 August), Odoacer, the first Germanic ruler of Italy, prepared to defend Verona against the invasion of Theodoric the Ostrogoth. Fighting near Verona, Odoacer suffered another defeat at the hands of the Ostrogoths and was forced back to his capital at **Ravenna** (30 September 489).

Verona | 1799 | French Revolutionary Wars (2nd Coalition)

With France defeated in Germany at **Ostrach** and **Stockach**, Generals Barthélemy Schérer and Jean Victor Moreau attempted a broad offensive against Austrian General Paul Kray in Italy, crossing the Adige north of Verona at Pastrengo, while General Joseph Montrichard marched south to Legnano. Their dispersed forces were driven back at heavy cost and lost again at **Magnano** (26 March 1799).

Versinikia I 813 I Byzantine-Bulgarian Wars

After terrible Byzantine defeat at **Verbitza** (811), new Emperor Michael marched west to meet a fresh offensive by the Bulgar Khan Krum. A confused battle at Versinikia, northwest of Adrianople, saw Byzantine General Leo the Armenian desert the field and Krum won a bloody victory to take Adrianople. Leo was acclaimed Emperor and soon made peace with Krum's son Omortag (22 June 813).

Vertieres I 1803 I Napoleonic Wars (Santo Domingo Rising)

Black revolutionary Jean Jacques Dessalines seized **Port-au-Prince** (17 October) then turned north against the remaining French under General Donatien Rochambeau at Cap Francais (modern Cap Haitien). An heroic assault by rebel leader Francois Capois on nearby Fort Vertieres was repulsed, but Rochambeau surrendered Cap Francais next day and independent Haiti was soon declared (18 November 1803).

Verulamium I 54 BC I Roman Invasion of Britain
See **Wheathampstead**

Verulamium I 61 I Roman Conquest of Britain
See **Boudicca**

Veseris I 339 BC I Latin War
See **Suessa**

Vesontio I 1674 I 3rd Dutch War
See **Besançon**

Vesuvius I 339 BC I Latin War
See **Suessa**

Veszprem I 1593 I Turkish-Habsburg Wars

Grand Vizier Sinan Pasha invaded Hungary to avenge the Ottoman defeat at **Sissek** (20 June), taking a large force which laid siege to the Imperial fortress of Veszprem, southwest of Buda. Although the town fell after just three days, the approach of winter ended Sinan's campaign and his elite Janissary infantry insisted on returning to Belgrade (10–13 October 1593).

Veurne I 1297 I Franco-Flemish Wars
See **Furnes**

Vézeronce I 524 I Burgundian-Frankish War

Renewing the Frankish war against Burgundy, suspended after **Avignon** (500), Clodomir of Orleans (son of Clovis) captured and later murdered King Sigismund, then invaded with his half-brother Theodoric. Sigismund's brother Godomar was defeated in battle near Vienne at Vézeronce but Clodomir was killed in the pursuit. Burgundy was finally extinguished in 532 at **Autun** (25 June 524).

Viana I 1067 I War of the Three Sanchos

While a war of succession was under way in Castile, King Sancho II of Castile attacked his cousin King Sancho IV of Navarre, who turned for aid to another cousin, King Sancho I of Aragon. At Viana, in Navarre north of Logroño, the Allies routed the Castilian army and the war ended with nothing achieved. Next year Sancho II defeated his brother Alfonso VI of Leon at **Lantada** (September 1067).

Viasma I 1812 I Napoleonic Wars (Russian Campaign)
See **Vyazma**

Vibo I 48 BC I Wars of the First Triumvirate

Pompeian Admiral Gaius Cassius Longinus destroyed Julius Caesar's ships at **Messana** and months later attacked another Caesarian fleet under Sulpicius Rufus off Vibo (modern Vibo Valentia), on the "toe" of Italy. This time, the Pompeians were driven off without heavy loss to either side. Cassius withdrew his fleet after news arrived of Caesar's great victory on 9 August at **Pharsalus**.

Viborg I 1157 I Danish War of Succession
See **Grathe Heath**

Viborg ▮ 1710 ▮ 2nd "Great" Northern War
See **Vyborg**

Viborg ▮ 1918 ▮ Finnish War of Independence
See **Vyborg**

Vic-de-Bigorre ▮ 1814 ▮ Napoleonic Wars (Peninsular Campaign)
With the Allied army delayed by flooded rivers from pursuing the French after their defeat north of the Pyrenees at **Aire** (2 March), the right wing under General Sir Thomas Picton advanced against General Jean Baptiste d'Erlon at Vic-de-Bigorre, ten miles north of Tarbes on the Upper Adour. The French were driven out and the Allies advanced next day to capture **Tarbes** (19 March 1814).

Vicenza ▮ 1513 ▮ War of the Holy League
Raymond of Cardona, Spanish Viceroy of Naples, recovered from defeat at **Ravenna** (April 1512) to invade Venetia and, west of Venice near Vicenza, he met the Venetian army of Bartolomeo d'Alviano. While Cardona's cavalry had heavy losses, his infantry under Fernando d'Avalos Marquis of Pescara won a decisive victory, repeated in 1524–1525 at **Rebecco**, **Sesia** and **Pavia** (7 October 1513).

Vicenza ▮ 1848 ▮ 1st Italian War of Independence
Advancing from victory at **Curtatone** (29 May), Austrian Marshal Josef Radetzky approached the Lombardy city of Vicenza, where King Charles Albert of Sardinia had positioned the Italian Allies behind powerful defences. However, Vicenza came under heavy fire when a jaeger battalion captured the nearby fortress of Monte Berico and General Giacomo Durando capitulated (11 June 1848).

Vich ▮ 1810 ▮ Napoleonic Wars (Peninsular Campaign)
Just weeks after French forces took **Gerona** in Catalonia, French General Joseph Souham marched along the Ter Valley against surrounding Spanish insurgents. North of Barce-

lona at Vich, Souham was surprised by Spanish General Henry O'Donnell, who caused heavy casualties—including Souham who was badly wounded. However, O'Donnell was eventually driven off (20 February 1810).

Vicksburg ▮ 1863 ▮ American Civil War (Western Theatre)
Union commander Ulysses S. Grant closed in on Vicksburg, Mississippi, winning to the east at **Jackson** and **Champion Hill** before launching his assault on the Confederate river stronghold. After prolonged siege and bombardment, Confederate General John C Pemberton surrendered almost 30,000 men. The fall of **Port Hudson** a few days later secured the Mississippi (18 May–4 July 1863).

Victoria de la Tunas ▮ 1897 ▮ 2nd Cuban War of Independence
Continuing the war in eastern Cuba following rebel disaster at **Punta Brava**, Calixto Garcia took almost 1,000 insurgents against Victoria de la Tunas, held by Spanish Colonel José Civera. After seizing the town, Garcia bombarded then captured the forts, along with about 400 prisoners. Bayamo and Holguin also fell and America later intervened to seize the country (28–30 August 1897).

Vid ▮ 447 ▮ Hun Invasion of the Roman Empire
See **Utus**

Vidin ▮ 1366 ▮ Ottoman Conquest of the Balkans
Louis I of Hungary recovered from defeat by the Ottomans at the **Maritza** (1363) to wage war on Christian heretics led by Prince Stratsimir of Western Bulgaria. A sharp campaign on the Danube saw Louis capture Vidin and imprison Stratsimir, then forcibly convert his people to orthodoxy. With Ottoman aid Stratsimir threw the invaders out in 1369, but Louis recaptured Vidin a year later.

Vienna ▮ 1485 ▮ Hungarian National Wars
Campaigning against Emperor Frederick III, Matthias I Corvinus of Hungary besieged and

captured Vienna, making it his Royal seat of government. His so-called Black Army then helped him to secure Carinthia and Styria. However, when Matthias died in Vienna five years later, the city reverted to the empire and his weak successor Ladislas VI saw Hungary's power rapidly fade.

Vienna I 1529 I Turkish-Habsburg Wars

Sultan Suleiman I led a fresh invasion across the Danube to capture **Buda** (8 September) before besieging Vienna, held by Count Philip of Austria with Count Nicolas of Salm and Marshal Wilhelm von Roggendorf. After a failed attack by land and from the river—and with winter approaching—Suleiman executed his prisoners and withdrew (22 September–15 October 1529).

Vienna I 1683 I Later Turkish-Habsburg Wars

As Grand Vizier Kara Mustafa advanced up the Danube the Emperor fled Vienna, leaving Governor Count Rudiger von Starhemberg to hold the city against siege. After two months, John III Sobieski of Poland and Charles V of Lorraine arrived and destroyed the besieging army in mountains to the south at Kahlenberg. The Turks fled and the West was saved (13 July–12 September 1683).

Vienna I 1809 I Napoleonic Wars (5th Coalition)

In relentless pursuit after victory on the Danube east of Linz at **Ebelsberg** (3 May), Napoleon Bonaparte drove the defeated Austrians under Baron Johann Hiller to Vienna, where Archduke Maximilian refused to surrender. The Austrian capital fell after two days of intermittent bombardment, but not before most of Hiller's troops had withdrawn east over the Danube (10–13 May 1809).

Vienna I 1848 I Hungarian Revolutionary War

Inspired by Revolutionary fervour, workers in Vienna rose against the empire and were besieged by Habsburg Field Marshal Alfred Windischgratz, fresh from suppressing rebellion in Prague. Vienna was heavily shelled and, after a Hungarian relief army was repulsed at **Schwechat**, further bombardment and street fighting forced the city's surrender (26 October–2 November 1848).

Vienna I 1945 I World War II (Eastern Front)

Following a failed German offensive at **Lake Balaton** in Hungary, the survivors withdrew towards Vienna and Soviet Marshal Rodion Malinovksy entered Austria from the southeast. Despite Panzer reinforcements, Vienna fell after heavy fighting and German Army Group South was isolated east of the city. General Lothar Rendulic finally surrendered his force on 8 May (6–13 April 1945).

Vienne I 411 I Later Roman Wars of Succession

When usurper Flavius Claudius Constantinus claimed recognition as joint Roman Emperor in Gaul, his son Constans was besieged on the Rhone south of Lyons at Vienne by their former General Gerontius, who had now deserted to the cause of Emperor Honorius. After much of his army deserted to Gerontius, Constans was defeated and put to death. His father was defeated and executed at **Arles**.

Vienne I 500 I Burgundian-Frankish War

Gundobald of Burgundy was defeated at **Dijon** by Clovis, King of the Franks, then turned on his own brother, Godegisil, who had treacherously supported the invaders. Clovis made no attempt to assist his former ally when Gundobald besieged and defeated Godegisil at Vienne, on the Rhone south of Lyons. Gundobald executed his brother and took control of all Burgundy.

Vientiane I 1574 I Burmese-Laotian Wars

With the Laotian Kingdom of Lan Xang disorganised after the death of King Sethathirat, King Bayinnaung of Burma invaded against Regent Saesurin (Sene Soulinthara). Following capture of the capital Vientiane (Vien Chan), Burma ruled Laos through vassal Kings (including Saesurin). The country later lapsed into anarchy until Laotian control was restored in 1637 by the great Souligna Vongsa.

Vientiane ∎ 1827 ∎ Siamese-Laotian Wars
See **Nong Bua Lamphu**

Vientiane ∎ 1960 ∎ Laotian Civil War
When army Captain Kong Le staged a coup (9 August) and neutralist Prime Minister Prince Souvanna Phouma tried to make peace with the Communist Pathet Lao, Rightist General Phoumi Nosavan advanced on Vientiane, supported by Colonel Kouprasith Abhay inside the city. Three days of fighting secured the capital and Kong Le withdrew north into the Plain of Jars (13–16 December 1960).

Viervoet ∎ 1851 ∎ 8th Cape Frontier War
British Resident Major Henry Warden tried to enforce order in the Orange River Sovereignty (later Orange Free State) and took a small force, supported by African allies, against the Basotho Chief Moshoeshoe. At Viervoet, near Modderspoort, Warden suffered a sharp defeat at the hands of the Chief's sons. However, Moshoeshoe was beaten next year further east at **Berea Mountain** (30 June 1851).

Vigan ∎ 1899 ∎ Philippine-American War
Attempting to cut off President Emilio Aguinaldo's retreat through western Luzon, American Colonel James Parker landed at Vigan, where he was attacked a week later by 400 men under General Manuel Tiñio. Heavily outnumbered, Parker repulsed the night assault. Next day General Samuel B. M. Young advanced to drive Tiñio out of Tagudin, northwest of **Tirad Pass** (3–4 September 1899).

Vigirima ∎ 1813 ∎ Venezuelan War of Independence
Spanish commander Juan Domingo Monteverde followed up Royalist success over Republicans near **Barquisimeto** in western Venezuela (10 November) by sending Colonel José Miguel Salomón to threaten Barcelona. Patriot leader Simón Bolívar marched out to meet the advancing Royalists, securing victory at Vigirima. He won even more decisively next week at **Araure** (25 November 1813).

Vigla ∎ 1897 ∎ 1st Greco-Turkish War
After Turkey's invasion of Thessaly was checked in the east at **Nezeros**, Crown Prince Constantine of Greece received reinforcements at Larissa and advanced on Edhem Pasha at Vigla, near the Maluna Pass. The Greek infantry secured outer Turkish entrenchments following heavy artillery bombardment, but there was no final assault and the forces met again near **Mati** (20 April 1897).

Vigo ∎ 1719 ∎ War of the Quadruple Alliance
In response to Spain's attack on Britain at **Glenshiel**, British Admiral James Mighella landed 4,000 men under Sir Richard Temple Viscount Cobham at Vigo in Galicia. After bombardment of Fort San Sebastian the citadel surrendered and nearby Pontevedra was also taken. The expedition withdrew with seven prizes and massive quantities of guns and ammunition (29 September–10 October 1719).

Vigo Bay ∎ 1702 ∎ War of the Spanish Succession
Returning from failure at **Cadiz** (15 September), Admiral Sir George Rooke attacked the Spanish treasure fleet, unloading at Vigo Bay under Francois de Rousselet Marquis de Chateaurenault. While Dutch troops led by James Butler Duke of Ormonde seized the forts, Admiral Thomas Hopsonn stormed the port, where every Franco-Spanish ship was taken or destroyed (12 October 1702).

Viipuri ∎ 1918 ∎ Finnish War of Independence
See **Vyborg**

Vijaya ∎ 1471 ∎ Vietnamese-Cham War
With China expelled from northern Vietnam at **Dong-do** (1427), the greatest Emperor of Vietnam's Le Dynasty, Le Thanh Tong, resolved to subjugate the neighbouring state of Champa, along the coast of southern Vietnam.

The capital Vijaya (near modern Quy Nhon) was seized by a massive assault and the population was massacred, effectively ending Champa as an independent kingdom.

Vijayanagar I 1406 I Vijayanagar-Bahmani Wars

Just eight years after King Harihara II of Vijayanagar was defeated at the **Krishna**, his son King Deva Raya renewed war against the Bahmanids, whose Sultan Firuz Shah immediately attacked the city of Vijayanagar. Despite being repulsed and wounded, Firuz ravaged the countryside and Deva Raya had to accept a humiliating peace, yielding the strategic fortress of Bankapur.

Vilafranca del Penedès I 1810 I Napoleonic Wars (Peninsular Campaign)

Following his attack on French troops at **Vich**, Spanish General Henry O'Donnell maintained pressure on French communication lines in Barcelona by sending General Juan Caro against Vilafranca del Penedès, west of Barcelona. A strong French infantry unit was virtually destroyed, with the survivors captured. Nearby **Manresa** fell a week later (30 March 1810).

Vilande I 731 I Indian Dynastic Wars

Amid ongoing war between the rival kingdoms of southern India, Crown Prince Vikramaditya of Chalukya joined with King Sripurusha of Ganga against Pallava. In battle at Vilande, Paramesvaravarman II was defeated and his capital Kanchi was occupied. A few years later, Vikramaditya invaded again (740) and defeated the new King Nandivarman to once more seize Kanchi.

Vilasa I 1583 I Turko-Persian Wars

Ottoman Sultan Murad III faced a renewed effort by Persia's Safavids to recover the Caucasus and despatched a massive army under Osman Pasha, which crushed the Crimean rebels and their Persian supporters on the banks of the Samur, near Vilasa. The engagement—known as the Battle of the Torches because it continued day and night—secured Ottoman rule in the Caucasus (7–11 May 1583).

Vila Velha I 1762 I Seven Years War (Europe)

With Spain threatening Portugal, Britain sent reinforcements under General John Burgoyne, who took the Spanish base at **Valencia, Alcántara** (27 August) then marched against forces preparing to cross the Tagus into Alentejo. In a night attack on the entrenched Spanish cavalry camp at Vila Velha de Rodao, Burgoyne inflicted heavy casualties, effectively ending the campaign (5 October 1762).

Vilcapugio I 1813 I Argentine War of Independence

Patriot General Manuel Belgrano won brilliant victories over the Spanish at **Tucumán** and **Salta**, then marched north into modern Bolivia, where he met a revitalised Royalist army under General Joaquín de la Pezuela at Vilcapugio, near Potosi. Belgrano was disastrously defeated in a bloody action, losing most of his guns and equipment, and was soon beaten again at **Ayohuma** (1 October 1813).

Viljandi I 1560 I Livonian War
See **Fellin**

Villach I 1492 I Turkish-Hungarian Wars

After Ottoman Sultan Bayazid II was repulsed from an attempt to surprise Belgrade, some of his forces raided into Croatia and Carinthia in southern Austria, where they were attacked near Villach, west of Klagenfurt, by a large Christian army. The Turks suffered a decisive defeat, with a reported 10,000 killed and 7,000 captured, while 15,000 Christian prisoners were said to have been saved.

Villafranca de Oria I 1813 I Napoleonic Wars (Peninsular Campaign)

As French General Maximilien Foy withdrew towards Tolosa after defeat at **Vitoria** (21 June), his rearguard under General Antoine-Louis Maucune delayed the Allies near Villafranca de Oria. Attacked by Spanish advance units under

Colonel Francisco Longa, Maucune lost about 200 men before breaking off the engagement and withdrawing northeast to **Tolosa** (24 June 1813).

Villafranca de Oria I 1835 I
1st Carlist War

Carlist commander Tomás Zumalacárregui continued his offensive against Spanish Regent Maria Cristina in Navarre, where he besieged Villafranca de Oria, southwest of Tolosa. After Liberal aid was driven off at **Larrainzar** and **Descarga**, Villafranca fell, yielding a massive prize of arms. The Carlists quickly took Durango, Tolosa and Vergara and advanced on **Bilbao** (May–3 June 1835).

Villagarcia I 1810 I Napoleonic Wars
(Peninsular Campaign)

Faced by a fresh Spanish offensive in Andalusia, French Marshal Nicolas Soult sent General Jean-Baptiste Girard towards the passes of the Morena to meet General Pedro La Romana. Severely underestimating the forces against him, La Romana accepted battle at Villagarcia de la Torre, near Llerena. He was driven back with heavy losses, withdrawing towards Zafra (11 August 1810).

Villagarcia I 1812 I Napoleonic Wars
(Peninsular Campaign)

When the Allies captured **Badajoz**, British cavalry led by General Sir Stapleton Cotton pursued the French Army corps of General Jean Baptiste Drouet Count D'Erlon. Southeast of Badajoz at Villagarcia, Cotton caught up with the French rearguard under General Henri-Dominique Lallemand, who took a defensive position but lost badly and was driven back on Llerena (11 April 1812).

Village Creek I 1841 I Cherokee
Indian Wars

General Edward H. Tarrant retaliated against Indian raids on settlements in the new Republic of Texas, leading about 70 volunteers against Cherokee, Caddo and other tribes in the Village Creek settlements close to modern Fort Worth.

Although Texan casualties were light for a reported 12 Indians killed, the outnumbered militia were driven off and withdrew (24 May 1841).

Villa Glori I 1867 I Garibaldi's Second
March on Rome

Taking advantage of war between Italy and Austria, Giuseppe Garibaldi renewed his support for insurgency in Rome and sent 70 men up the Tiber with arms. At Villa Glori, Enrico Cairoli was attacked and killed by French Zouaves. Most of his supporters were also killed or captured and his brother Giovanni died of wounds. Garibaldi was defeated a week later at **Mentana** (27 October 1867).

Villalar I 1521 I Comuneros Uprising

On campaign against the Comuneros popular rising in Castile, the Royalist army of Charles I of Spain destroyed the rebels at Villalar, near Toro on the Duoro River. Comuneros leaders Juan de Padilla and Juan Bravo were executed while Antonio de Acuna, rebel Bishop of Zamora, fled. Toledo held out briefly under Padilla's widow before the entire rising collapsed (23 April 1521).

Villa Muriel I 1812 I Napoleonic Wars
(Peninsular Campaign)

As Arthur Wellesley Lord Wellington withdrew from his failed siege of **Burgos**, his rearguard was defeated at **Venta del Pozo** then again two days later on the Carrion at Villa Muriel, by French Generals Antoine-Louis Maucune and Maximilien Foy. Wellington hastened back and retook Villa Muriel, but the position was turned and he resumed his withdrawal (25 October 1812).

Villar de Puerco I 1810 I Napoleonic Wars
(Peninsular Campaign)

See **Barquilla**

Villarreal de Alava I 1936 I Spanish
Civil War

When Basque forces launched an attempt to retake the northern Spanish city of Vitoria, they came under massive Nationalist attack just to the north at Villarreal de Alava. Heavy fighting saw the only major Basque offensive of the war driven off with severe losses. Six months later the Nationalists attacked and seized the Basque capital at **Bilbao** (30 November–5 December 1936).

Villa Velha I 1762 I Seven Years War (Europe)
See **Vila Velha**

Villaviciosa I 1665 I Spanish-Portuguese Wars
See **Montes Claros**

Villaviciosa I 1710 I War of the Spanish Succession
After an Anglo-Austrian army captured Madrid, they were driven out by French General Louis Duke de Vendôme. The day after he defeated the Allied rearguard at **Brihuega**, Vendôme attacked the main force under Guido von Starhemberg at Villaviciosa, northeast of Guadalajara. The Austrians inflicted heavy French losses but had to continue their withdrawal (10 December 1710).

Villazón I 1934 I Chaco War
Following Bolivia's victory over Paraguay in the Chaco Boreal at **Cañada-Strongest** (24 May), General Enrique Peñaranda sent Colonel David Toro to encircle the Paraguayans near Villazón. Despite huge numerical superiority, Toro's partial victory produced only 400 prisoners and 50 trucks captured. Most of the Paraguayans escaped south towards **Cañada el Carmen** (7–11 November 1934).

Villeré's Plantation I 1814 I War of 1812
British Colonel William Thornton advanced up the Mississippi from **Lake Borgne** and captured the plantation of Jacques Villeré, where he was attacked by American Generals Andrew Jackson and John Coffee, supported by two ships. Reinforced by General John Keane, the British drove off the attack, losing almost 300 casualties. Jackson withdrew to **New Orleans** (23 December 1814).

Villers-Bretonneaux I 1870 I Franco-Prussian War
See **Amiens**

Villers-en-Cauchies I 1794 I French Revolutionary Wars (1st Coalition)
During a French attempt to relieve **Landrécies**, besieged by Frederick Augustus Duke of York, a small British-Austrian cavalry unit under Major-General Karl Ott inflicted costly losses on a much larger force of French infantry and artillery east of Cambrai at Villers-en-Cauchies. Another cavalry action at **Beaumont** helped drive off the relief army and led to the fall of Landrécies (24 April 1794).

Villersexel I 1871 I Franco-Prussian War
French commander Charles-Denis Bourbaki was advancing up the Ognon Valley to relieve besieged **Belfort**, when he was intercepted to the southwest at the small town of Villersexel by German forces under General Karl August von Werder. The Germans withdrew after fierce fighting, but a week later Bourbaki was routed at **Héricourt** and Belfort remained under siege (9 January 1871).

Villiers I 1870 I Franco-Prussian War
The so-called Great Sortie from besieged **Paris** saw General Auguste Alexandre Ducrot lead a large force southeast across the Marne towards the Württemburg division at Villiers and Champigny. After costly losses on both sides, a counter-attack by Prince Albert of Saxony repulsed the French. Similar sorties were attempted at **Le Bourget** and **Mont Valerian** (29 November–3 December 1870).

Villmanstrand I 1741 I 1st Russo-Swedish War
See **Willmanstrand**

Villmergen I 1656 I 1st Villmergen War
During resumed religious warfare in Switzerland, the Protestant forces of Berne under Sigismund von Erlach were ambushed at Villmergen, west of Zurich, by an army from Lucerne and

other Catholic Cantons under Christopher Pfyffer. The men from Zurich and Berne were heavily defeated—with almost 1,000 dead—and a troubled peace was established (24 January 1656).

Villmergen ▪ 1712 ▪ 2nd Villmergen War

Almost 60 years after Catholic victory west of Zurich at Villmergen, religious warfare in Switzerland resumed and Ackermann of Unterwalden took 12,000 men against Protestant Berne and Zurich. Once again, the decisive battle was fought near Villmergen. Ackermann was defeated, with over 2,000 killed, and the Catholic Cantons were forced to yield territory (25 July 1712).

Vilmanstrand ▪ 1741 ▪ 1st Russo-Swedish War
See **Willmanstrand**

Vilna ▪ 1658 ▪ Russo-Polish Wars
See **Werki**

Vilna ▪ 1794 ▪ War of the 2nd Polish Partition

As Poland rose in a fresh insurrection against Russia, the Lithuanian city of Vilna turned against its Russian occupiers. The garrison was successfully driven out in a powerful midnight attack by troops under Colonel Jakob Jasinski, supported by a large number of civilians. But by 12 August the Russians had recaptured the Lithuanian capital (22 April 1794).

Vilna ▪ 1915 ▪ World War I (Eastern Front)

On the northern flank of Germany's **Triple Offensive**, General Hermann von Eichhorn advanced through **Kovno** and **Grodno** against General Aleksei Evert around the key city of Vilna. A frontal assault cost Eichhorn 50,000 men over two weeks, before he circled to take Vilna in the flank. However, the offensive soon ground to a halt and ended a week later (8–18 September 1915).

Vilna (1st) ▪ 1919 ▪ Lithuanian War of Independence

Revolutionary Russia's capitulation to Germany at Brest-Litovsk ceded Lithuania. But shortly after Germany's defeat, the Bolsheviks determined to regain control. Russian forces seized Vilna and the Lithuanian government evacuated to Kaunas. A few months afterwards, Poland drove the Red Army out of Vilna, helping trigger the Russo-Polish War (5 January 1919).

Vilna (2nd) ▪ 1919 ▪ Russo-Polish War

Early in Poland's war against Russia in the eastern Marchland, new Polish commander Josef Pilsudski advanced on Vilna, supported by General Stanislaw Szeptycki. Heavy fighting saw the Soviet troops defeated and driven out. Following a failed Russian counter-attack, the front largely stabilised until a fresh Polish offensive to the southeast around **Minsk** (16–19 April 1919).

Vilna ▪ 1920 ▪ Russo-Polish War

As the war ended, Polish commander Josef Pilsudski was determined to regain Vilna against international opinion and he condoned a fictional "mutiny" by General Lucjan Zeligowski, who led his Lithuanian-Byelorussian Division on a surprise raid. After a skirmish at Jaszuny, Zeligowski took Vilna by coup, creating an "independent state" until the city voted to join Poland (9 October 1920).

Vilna ▪ 1944 ▪ World War II (Eastern Front)

With the fall of **Minsk**, Soviet Generals Ivan Bagramyan and Ivan Chernyakovsky converged on Vilna, where the new commander of Army Group Centre, Marshal Walther Model, attempted large-scale counter-attacks. However, the Lithuanian capital fell, with about 15,000 Germans killed. The Russians then drove west to take Kaunus and north through Dvinsk towards **Riga** (8–13 July 1944).

Vilnius ▪ 1794 ▪ War of the 2nd Polish Partition
See **Vilna**

Vilppula I 1918 I Finnish War of Independence

Russian Colonel Mikhail Svetchnikov launched an offensive in southwest Finland, where he attacked White forces under Colonel Martin Wetzer around Vilppula. With both sides reinforced during the action, Svetchnikov was eventually checked further to the west near Ruovesi and the Vilppula front was established. A week later the Russians attacked again through **Ruovesi** (2–13 February 1918).

Viluma I 1815 I Argentine War of Independence

See **Sipe-Sipe**

Vimeiro I 1808 I Napoleonic Wars (Peninsular Campaign)

When British troops landed in Portugal, they repulsed a French delaying action at **Rolica**. Four days later General Sir Arthur Wellesley, with Portuguese support, smashed an attack by General Androche Junot north of Lisbon at Vimeiro. However, British commander Sir Harry Burrard forbade pursuit and amazingly agreed to evacuate the defeated French in British ships (21 August 1808).

Viminacium I 601 I Byzantine-Balkan Wars

After several campaigns to stabilise the Danube frontier, Emperor Maurice sent General Priscus to confront the Avars under Khan Baian in their homeland, north of the Danube. A series of engagements in the Tisza Valley saw Priscus defeat the Avars, including a major victory at Viminacium (modern Kostalac, Serbia). The death of Maurice in a coup (602) helped secure a temporary peace.

Vimy (1st) I 1915 I World War I (Western Front)

See **Artois (1st)**

Vimy (2nd) I 1915 I World War I (Western Front)

See **Artois (2nd)**

Vimy I 1917 I World War I (Western Front)

See **Arras**

Vinaroz I 1938 I Spanish Civil War

Continuing the offensive on the Ebro, which had begun at **Belchite**, Nationalist forces seized Lerida (3 April) and reached the coast at Vinaroz, between Barcelona and Valencia. The strategic town was taken by General Camilo Alonso Vega, effectively dividing Republican Catalonia in two. Vega then turned south to join the advance towards **Castellón de la Plana** (15 April 1938).

Vincennes I 1779 I War of the American Revolution

As American frontiersman George Rogers Clark campaigned in Illinois, British Governor Henry Hamilton marched southwest from Detroit and reoccupied Vincennes, on the Wabash in Indiana (17 December 1778), where he was later besieged by Clark. With failing support from his French and Indian garrison, Hamilton surrendered and Clark retained his conquests (25 February 1779).

Vincy I 717 I Rise of Charles Martel

After defeating the Neustrians at **Ambleve** (716), Charles Martel of Austrasia consolidated his authority over the Kingdom of the Franks by beating the Neustrians again at Vincy, near Cambrai, where King Childeric of Neustria was routed. Charles lacked sufficient forces to seize Paris and withdrew to Cologne. Two years later he secured northern France with victory at **Soissons** (21 March 717).

Vinegar Hill, Idaho I 1879 I Sheepeater War

Campaigning in the Salmon River Mountains of Idaho against Bannock and Shoshoni (known as Sheepeaters), Lieutenant Henry Catley was ambushed at Vinegar Hill, near the middle Fork of the Salmon. Catley's patrol disgracefully abandoned their baggage and fled. But after a brief campaign in rough country, General Oliver Howard forced the Sheepeaters to surrender (29 July 1879).

**Vinegar Hill, Ireland I 1798 I
Irish Rebellion**

The final major battle of the Irish Rebellion saw a large Loyalist force under General Sir Gerard Lake attack the rebel army of Father John Murphy on Vinegar Hill, near Enniscorthy, 14 miles north of Wexford. With no protection against heavy shellfire, the rebels were destroyed, with an estimated 4,000 killed. French reinforcements landed in August, but too late (21 June 1798).

**Vingavelli I 850 I Later Indian
Dynastic Wars**

In one of the great dynastic rivalries of medieval India, Amoghavarsha of Rashtrakuta fought a prolonged campaign against the Eastern Chalukya, who he had defeated in 830 at **Vengi**. The decisive battle eventually took place at Vingavelli, where Amoghavarsha routed Vijayaditya III. Within a few years the Eastern Chalukya had acknowledged the supremacy of Rashtrakuta.

Vingeanne I 1870 I Franco-Prussian War
See **Gray**

**Vinh Yen I 1951 I French Indo-
China War**

Viet Minh General Vo Nguyen Giap opened his offensive into the **Red River Delta**, advancing on Vinh Yen, northwest of Hanoi and taking outlying positions. French commander Jean de Lattre de Tassigny flew in with reinforcements to take control and human wave attacks were driven off by firepower and napalm. Giap withdrew with 5,000 killed and many wounded (13–17 January 1951).

**Vinkovce I 316 I Roman Wars
of Succession**
See **Cibalae**

**Vinkovo I 1812 I Napoleonic Wars
(Russian Campaign)**

The day before Napoleon Bonaparte began retreating from Moscow, Prince Mikhail Kutuzov sent General Vasilii Orlov-Denisov probing towards Vinkovo, southwest of the capital. After

French General Francois Sébastiani suffered a sharp loss, Marshal Joachim Murat was wounded repelling the Russians. Days later the French were defeated at **Maloyaroslavetz** (18 October 1812).

Vionville I 1870 I Franco-Prussian War
See **Mars-la-Tour**

**Vipurii I 1944 I World War II
(Northern Europe)**
See **Vyborg**

**Virgen I 1855 I National
(Filibuster) War**
See **La Virgen**

**Virgin Bay I 1855 I National
(Filibuster) War**
See **La Virgen**

Virginia I 1812 I War of 1812

In a classic broadside action off the coast of Virginia, the British sloop *Frolic* (Commander Thomas Whinyates) on convoy escort north of Bermuda was attacked by the American sloop *Wasp* (Captain Jacob Jones). *Frolic* suffered very heavy damage and casualties, but *Wasp* was also badly damaged. Later that day she was forced to surrender to the British warship *Poictiers* (18 October 1812).

**Virginia Capes I 1781 I War of the
American Revolution**
See **Chesapeake Capes**

**Virginius Incident I 1873 I 1st Cuban
War of Independence**

While carrying war materials for Cuban rebels, the blockade runner *Virginius*, illegally flying the American flag, was seized off Jamaica by the Spanish gunship *Tornado*. British and Americans (including Captain Joseph Fry) were among 53 passengers and crew executed before the sloop *Niobe* intervened. Spain later paid compensation to Britain and America to avoid war (31 October 1873).

**Virta bro I 1808 I Napoleonic Wars
(Russo-Swedish War)**

Falling back before a reinforced Russian invasion of Finland, Swedish General Karl Adlercreutz was decisively defeated at **Oravais** and
retreated north to the Swedish border. At the
bridge at Virta (modern Iisalmi), General Johan
August Sandels held off Russian General Nikolai Tutschkoff, but the Russians later invaded
Sweden itself for victory in August 1809 at
Savar (27 October 1808).

**Virton I 1914 I World War I
(Western Front)**

See **Ardennes**

**Vis I 1866 I 3rd Italian War
of Independence**

See **Lissa**

**Visby I 1361 I Wars of the
Hanseatic League**

King Valdemar IV Atterdag of Denmark landed on the west coast of Gotland with a reported
70 ships and 2,500 men and repulsed Gotland
peasants at Masterby. Three days later he
butchered the peasant army outside the walls of
Visby and the city yielded without a siege.
Danish victory a year later off **Helsingborg**
confirmed the beginning of the decline of Gotland (27 July 1361).

**Visingso I 1167 I Swedish Wars
of Succession**

After Prince Magnus of Denmark killed
Swedish King Eric—the Saint—near **Upsala**
(1160), the Danish army was eventually repulsed by Eric's rival and successor Charles VII.
However, Eric's son Knut later returned to
Sweden with a Norwegian army and in battle
near Visingso, on Lake Vattern, Charles was
defeated and executed. Knut Eriksson was then
recognised as King.

**Vistula I 1914 I World War I
(Eastern Front)**

See **Warsaw (1st)**

Vistula I 1920 I Russo-Polish War

See **Warsaw**

**Vistula-Oder I 1945 I World War II
(Eastern Front)**

Opening a stunning offensive across the Vistula, four Russian armies smashed through
German defences along a 300-mile front. In little
over two weeks, they advanced 350 miles to the
Oder, just 40 miles from **Berlin**, to secure Poland and part of Czechoslovakia. The Germans
lost over 500,000 casualties, with large forces
trapped at **Poznan** and **Breslau** (12–31 January
1945).

**Vitebsk I 1812 I Napoleonic Wars
(Russian Campaign)**

During his advance into Russia, Napoleon
Bonaparte had captured Vitebsk on the Dvina
after victory at **Ostrowno** (26 July). But his plan
to withdraw through Vitebsk on his retreat from
Moscow ended when Prince Ludwig Wittgenstein defeated Marshal Claude Victor and seized
the city. The loss forced Bonaparte to withdraw
along the more exposed southerly route (7 November 1812).

**Vitebsk I 1944 I World War II
(Eastern Front)**

At the start of the Russian offensive into **Belorussia**, Generals Ivan Bagramyan and Ivan
Chernyakovsky converged on Vitebsk and
encircled five German divisions under General
Georg-Hans Reinhardt. All rescue attempts
failed and the city fell after bloody fighting with
20,000 Germans killed and 10,000 captured.
Further heavy losses followed at **Mogilev** and
Bobruysk (23–27 June 1944).

**Vithalwadi I 1780 I 1st British-
Maratha War**

See **Kalyan**

Vitkov Hill I 1420 I Hussite Wars

Determined to seize Bohemia, despite Imperial defeats at **Sudomer** and **Porici**, Sigismund
of Hungary laid siege to Prague. At nearby
Vitkov Hill he attempted to drive off the great

Hussite leader Jan Zizka and suffered a decisive defeat. (The battlesite was renamed Zizkov in honour of Zizka.) Sigismund withdrew until his renewed offensive later that year, repulsed at **Vysehrad** (14 July 1420).

Vitoria ▐ 1813 ▐ Napoleonic Wars (Peninsular Campaign)

On his final Spanish offensive, Arthur Wellesley Lord Wellington drove King Joseph Bonaparte from Madrid and met Bonaparte and Marshal Jean-Baptiste Jourdan north of the Ebro at Vitoria. The large English-Portuguese-Spanish army won their most decisive battle, then seized vast treasure and supplies as the French abandoned central Spain (21 June 1813).

Vitsi ▐ 1949 ▐ Greek Civil War

Opening the final campaign against Communist forces in northern Greece, Marshal Alexandros Papagos feinted towards Grammos, then launched a huge offensive against about 7,000 men under Nikos Zakhariadis around Vitsi, south of **Florina**. After bloody fighting, the massively outnumbered insurgents escaped west to Albania or south to help defend **Grammos** (10–16 August 1949).

Vittorio Veneto ▐ 1918 ▐ World War I (Italian Front)

New Italian commander Armando Diaz resolved to avenge defeat a year before at **Caporetto** and began a massive offensive from the **Piave** towards Vittorio Veneto, aided by French General Jean Graziani and British General Frederick Lambert Earl of Cavan. Austrians under Archduke Josef and Svetozar Boroevic were destroyed and Austria quickly sued for peace (24 October–4 November 1918).

Vizcacheras ▐ 1829 ▐ Argentine Civil Wars

General Juan Galo Lavalle seized power with victory at **Navarro** in December 1828, then faced substantial Federalist forces under Estanislao López of Santa Fe. Part of Lavalle's army was beaten by irregular Federalist cavalry at Vizcacheras, near the Salado River, with German Colonel Frederic Rauche killed. Lavalle's main force was soon defeated at **Puente de Márquez** (28 March 1829).

Vlaardingen ▐ 1018 ▐ German Civil Wars

When Count Dirk II of Frisia overstepped his authority raising taxes, Emperor Henry II sent a force under Duke Godfrey of Lotharingen and the Bishop of Utrecht against his fortress at Vlaardingen, west of modern Rotterdam. Panicking in swampy conditions, the Imperial army was cut to pieces, with perhaps 900 killed. Despite such losses, the Emperor soon made peace with his vassal (29 July 1018).

Vladar ▐ 1421 ▐ Hussite Wars

Despite the Imperial repulse at **Zatec** (2 October), German cities in Bohemia sent forces against the Hussite Jan Zizka, who was pursued northeast by Henry of Plauen, a great Lord of Pilsen. When Zizka's badly outnumbered force made a stand on the Vladar, near Zlutice, Plauen suffered very heavy losses in costly frontal assaults before Zizka broke out at night and escaped to Zatec (November 1421).

Vladimir ▐ 1238 ▐ Mongol Conquest of Russia

The Mongol Batu (grandson of Genghis Khan) and his General Subetai campaigned in Russia, where they destroyed **Ryazan** and **Moscow**, then marched east and besieged Vladimir, the capital of Vladimir-Suzdal. Grand Duke Yuri had left the city, which was taken and burned, and his family was put to death. The following month Duke Yuri himself was defeated at the **Sit** River (3–8 February 1238).

Vlakfontein ▐ 1901 ▐ 2nd Anglo-Boer War

On a drive in the western Transvaal searching for Boer arms, British General Henry Dixon marched west from Naauwpoort with 1,200 men and camped at Vlakfontein, where Boers under Jan Kemp attacked and routed a patrol. In a massive counter-attack, the Boers were driven off after very heavy fighting. But Dixon's position was untenable and he withdrew to Naauwpoort (30 May 1901).

Vlie I 1666 I 2nd Dutch War

English commander George Monck defeated the Dutch fleet off **North Foreland** (5 August) then despatched Admiral Sir Robert Holmes to raid the Dutch coast, where he attacked the Waddenzee anchorage off Vlie and Terschelling. In an action which became known as "Holmes' Bonfire," he burned 160 Dutch merchantmen with cargoes alone valued at one million pounds sterling (20 August 1666).

Vlotho I 1638 I Thirty Years War (Franco-Habsburg War)

Following Allied victory near **Breisach**, the 23-year-old Elector Palatinate Karl Ludwig boldly attempted to recover his patrimony with Swedish encouragement and English money. However, his small army was routed at Vlotho, on the Weser near Herford, by Imperial General Melchior Hatzfeld. The Elector narrowly escaped though his brother Prince Rupert was captured (7 October 1638).

Vogelinseck I 1403 I Habsburg-Swiss Wars

See **Speicher**

Volkerschlacht I 1813 I Napoleonic Wars (War of Liberation)

See **Leipzig**

Volkondah I 1751 I 2nd Carnatic War

Sent with reinforcements for Nawab Muhammad Ali of Arcot, British and Indian troops under Swiss-born Captain Rudolph Gingens came under attack at Volkondah, north of the Coleroon River. Heavily defeated by a greatly superior French-Indian force under Nawab Chanda Sahib and Colonel Louis d'Auteil, Gingens was driven back to siege at **Trichinopoly** (19–20 July 1751).

Volo I 352 BC I 3rd Sacred War

See **Pagasae**

Volta I 1848 I 1st Italian War of Independence

See **Custozza**

Volturno I 554 I Gothic War in Italy

See **Casilinum**

Volturno I 1860 I 2nd Italian War of Independence

Giuseppe Garibaldi was marching north from Naples when he was attacked in a strong position at the Volturno, outside Capua, by the Neapolitan army of Francis II under General Giosuè Ritucci. Aided by Piedmontese, fresh from victory at **Castelfidardo**, Garibaldi drove off the Bourbon forces with heavy losses on both sides. He then captured Capua and advanced on **Gaeta** (1–2 October 1860).

Volturno I 1943 I World War II (Southern Europe)

Advancing up western Italy from **Salerno**, Anglo-American forces under General Mark Clark secured **Naples** then faced 35,000 Germans led by General Heinrich von Vietinghoff determined to hold the Volturno River. Very heavy fighting saw the Germans withdraw north to the **Gustav Line** and the exhausted Allies were forced to pause before renewing their advance (13–18 October 1943).

Vönnu I 1919 I Estonian War of Independence

See **Cesis**

Voronezh I 1919 I Russian Civil War

As General Anton Denikin's White Army swept north towards Moscow, Red commander Symeon Budenny was driven out of Voronezh by General Vladimir Sidorin (6 October). **Orel** also fell, but the Red Army soon countered with a massive flank attack. General Andrei Shkuro was left to cover a bloody retreat as the Whites fled south to the **Don Basin** (25 September–24 October 1919).

Voronezh I 1942 I World War II (Eastern Front)

With the Russian winter offensive halted at **Kharkov**, Panzer General Herman Hoth opened the second German offensive north towards Voronezh. After heavy resistance, Voronezh was taken from General Filip Golikov and a bridgehead was established on the Don. However, the German advance was halted and Hoth moved south through **Rostov** towards the **Caucasus** (28 June–5 July 1942).

Vorskla ▮ 1399 ▮ Conquests of Tamerlane

Fleeing from defeat at the **Terek** by the Turko-Mongol Tamerlane, Toktamish (former Khan of the Golden Horde) gained support from Grand Duke Witold (Vytautus) of Lithuania, who invaded the Ukraine with a force of Lithuanians, Poles and Teutonic knights. At the Vorskla, a tributary of the Dnieper, Tamerlane's General Edigu attacked and destroyed Witold's army (12 August 1399).

Vougle ▮ 507 ▮ Visigothic-Frankish Wars
See **Vouillé**

Vouillé ▮ 507 ▮ Visigothic-Frankish Wars

On the pretext of religious persecution, Clovis, the Catholic King of the Salian Franks, and his Burgundian allies, brought on a major battle against Alaric II, King of the Arian Christian Visigoths in Gaul. Alaric was routed at Vouillé, near Poitiers, then killed in the subsequent pursuit, reputedly at the hands of Clovis himself. The defeat ended Visigothic rule in Gaul and they retreated into Spain.

Voulon ▮ 507 ▮ Visigothic-Frankish Wars
See **Vouillé**

Vozha ▮ 1378 ▮ Russian-Mongol Wars

Grand Prince Dimitri of Moscow was determined to challenge Mongol rule and attacked settlements along the Volga. He then faced a counter-attack by Mongol leader Maimai, who sent a force under General Begich. On the Vozha, a tributary of the Oka, the Russians secured a decisive victory, which led directly to Dimitri's great victory two years later at **Kulikovo** (10 August 1378).

Vrachori ▮ 1821 ▮ Greek War of Independence

Early in the war, a large force of Greeks, mainly Armatoli militia, attacked Vrachori (modern Agrinion) north of Missolonghi, with its large population of Jews and Muslims. The garrison of about 600 Albanian mercenaries under Nourka negotiated their own safe withdrawal (after looting the town) before the Greeks entered Vrachori and massacred the Jews and Turks (9 June 1821).

Vryheid ▮ 1900 ▮ 2nd Anglo-Boer War

In a new Boer offensive in the eastern Transvaal, Louis Botha led 1,100 men in a night attack on Vryheid, south of Piet Retief, garrisoned by 900 under Colonel John M. Gawne. In heavy fighting at nearby Lancaster Hill, the British lost about 60 casualties (including Gawne fatally wounded), but the Boers were eventually driven off and Botha turned north to **Belfast** (11–12 December 1900).

Vucji Do ▮ 1876 ▮ Serbo-Turkish War

To support Christians in Bosnia-Herzogovina against Turkey, Montenegrans under Prince Nicholas invaded and defeated the Turks in a number of engagements, most notably, the bloody action at Vucji Do, near Cetinje, where Turkish commander Ahmed Mukhta Pasha was decisively defeated. However, Montenegro's Serb allies were less successful against the Turks at **Alexinatz** (18 July 1876).

Vuelte de Obligada ▮ 1845 ▮ Argentine-Uruguayan War

Concerned by Argentina's intervention in Uruguay and siege of **Montevideo**, Anglo-French ships under Admiral Sir Charles Hotham entered the Parana River, blocked at Vuelte de Obligada, north of San Pedro, by General Lucio Norberto Mansilla. Despite brilliant defence, with Mansilla wounded, the Allies broke through but did not affect the siege of Montevideo (18–20 November 1845).

Vukovar ▮ 1991 ▮ Croatian War

When Croatia broke away from Yugoslavia, the Yugoslav army and Serb paramilitary invaded and besieged Vukovar, where 1,800 police and volunteers led by Mile Dedakovic held out against General Mile Mrksic and 50,000 troops with tanks and artillery. The "Croatian Stalingrad" fell with awful destruction and killings and a ceasefire came six weeks later (24 August–19 November 1991).

Vulcan Pass I 1916 I World War I (Balkan Front)
See **Targu Jiu**

Vuoksi River I 1944 I World War II (Northern Europe)
See **Vuosalmi**

Vuosalmi I 1944 I World War II (Northern Europe)
Despite terrible losses around **Ihantala** in Karelia, Soviet forces attempted to turn the Finnish left and crossed the Vuoksi River. However, they suffered severe casualties in bitter fighting around Vuosalmi and along the Äyräpää Ridge and were forced back onto the defensive. A final Russian offensive in southeast Finland next month was repulsed further north at **Ilomantsi** (4–11 July 1944).

Vyazma I 1812 I Napoleonic Wars (Russian Campaign)
Russian Prince Mikhail Kutuzov harassed Napoleon Bonaparte's retreat from Moscow, attacking Prince Eugène de Beauharnais and Marshal Louis Davout at Fiodoroivksoy, near Vyazma, between Moscow and Smolensk. While General Mikhail Miloradovich failed in an attempt to cut off the rear of the retreating army, the French suffered further heavy losses (3 November 1812).

Vyazma I 1941 I World War II (Eastern Front)
As Germany resumed the offensive toward Moscow, Panzer General Herman Hoth was joined by General Erich Hoepner advancing to trap six Soviet armies around Vyazma. The pocket was crushed in a double battle with the encirclement further south at **Bryasnk**. The Germans

reached to within 25 miles of the capital before the Russians counter-attacked west from **Moscow** (2–14 October 1941).

Vyborg I 1710 I 2nd "Great" Northern War
Tsar Peter I destroyed the Swedish army at **Poltava** (July 1709) then sent Admiral Fedor Apraxin to besiege Vyborg, at the head of the Gulf of Finland. The siege stalled until the spring thaw enabled the Russian fleet to bring more troops and fire power. Peter was present when the garrison of 4,000 surrendered, finally securing the approaches to St Petersburg (February–13 June 1710).

Vyborg I 1918 I Finnish War of Independence
Weeks after a local White victory in eastern Karelia at **Rautu**, commander General Ernst Löfström determined on a final offensive against the Red Army further west at the key city of Vyborg (inside modern Russia). With a brilliant envelopment and siege, the Whites took Vyborg by storm, capturing about 12,000 Red troops. War soon ended with Finland independent (23–29 April 1918).

Vyborg I 1941 I World War II (Northern Europe)
See **Karelia**

Vyborg I 1944 I World War II (Northern Europe)
Soviet forces broke the German siege of **Leningrad**, then turned on Finland in the so-called Continuation War and 24 divisions invaded the Karelian Isthmus. With the Mannerheim Line pierced, the city of Vyborg was taken after a short battle and the Finns fell back northeast to defend **Ihantala**. Fighting for strategic islands in Vyborg Bay continued until mid-July (10–20 June 1944).

Vyborg Bay I 1790 I Russo-Swedish War
Swedish Duke Charles of Sodermanland was blockaded in Vyborg Bay in the Gulf of Finland by Russian Admiral Paul Tchitchakov and

Prince Charles Nassau-Siegen, but drove off a Russian attack and led a remarkable dash to the open sea. While both sides lost ships in a confused action, the Swedes suffered heavier losses before escaping for the decisive action on the **Svenskund** (2–3 July 1790).

Vysehrad I 1420 I Hussite Wars

Hussites from Prague continued the war against Sigismund of Hungary after victory at **Vitkov** (14 July) with Hynek Krusina besieging the nearby fortress of Vysehrad, held by Czech and German Royalists under Lord Vsembera of Boskovice. A large force led by Sigismund arrived too late to save the starving garrison from surrender and he was heavily defeated next day (1 November 1420).

Vysokov I 1866 I Seven Weeks War
See **Nachod**

W

Wabash ❙ 1791 ❙ Little Turtle's War
　See **St Clair's Defeat**

**Wachau ❙ 1813 ❙ Napoleonic Wars
(War of Liberation)**
　Opening the three-day Battle of **Leipzig**, a brutal action was fought east of the city around the village of Wachau, where Russians under Prince Eugene of Württemberg attacked French Marshal Claude Victor. With Napoleon Bonaparte's personal intervention, the French eventually repulsed the Allied assault, but the overall battle of Leipzig was a resounding French defeat (16 October 1813).

**Wadi ❙ 1916 ❙ World War I
(Mesopotamia)**
　A week after a disastrous repulse at **Sheik Sa'ad**, General Sir Fenton Aylmer's Anglo-Indian force advancing up the Tigris to relieve **Kut-al-Amara** attacked again a few miles further upstream against Turkish positions in a steep valley known as the Wadi. Heavy fighting cost over 1,600 British casualties, though the Turks still held the nearby strategic defile at **Hanna** (13 January 1916).

**Wadi Akarit ❙ 1943 ❙ World War II
(Northern Africa)**
　General Sir Bernard Montgomery breached the **Mareth Line** in southern Tunisia before pushing on to Gabès, where General Giovanni Messe tried to hold a defensive line at the Wadi Akarit. In the reputed last set-piece battle of the campaign, Montgomery took over 7,000 Axis prisoners. He then joined up with Americans

from **Gafsa** and drove on through Enfidaville to **Tunis** (6 April 1943).

**Wadi al-Arabah ❙ 634 ❙ Muslim
Conquest of Syria**
　Marching north into Palestine, Muslim General Amr ibn al-As defeated a Byzantine force at Dathin, between Aila and Gaza, while in the Wadi al-Arabah, south of the Dead Sea, Yazib ibn abi Sofian defeated and killed Sergius, Patrician of Caesarea. Facing renewed Byzantine resistance, Caliph Abu Bekr recalled Khalid ibn al-Walid from Mesopotamia for victory at **Ajnadin** (4 February 634).

Wadi al-Batin ❙ 1991 ❙ 1st Gulf War
　As part of the final 100-hour ground offensive against Iraq, American General Frederick Franks and British General Rupert Smith drove deep into Iraq, then swung east to cut off the elite Republican Guard around Wadi al-Batin. In some of the fiercest fighting of the war, the claimed largest tank battle since World War II saw Iraq routed. The war ended next day (26–27 February 1991).

**Wadi al-Makhazin ❙ 1578 ❙ Portuguese-
Moroccan War**
　See **Alcazarquivir**

**Wadi Bekka ❙ 711 ❙ Muslim Conquest
of Spain**
　See **Guadalete**

Wadi Chelif ❙ 740 ❙ Berber Rebellion
　See **El Asnam**

**Wadi Isly I 1844 I French Conquest
of Algeria**
  See **Isly**

**Wadi Kiss I 1907 I French Colonial
Wars in North Africa**
  Beni Snassen tribesmen campaigning in
northeast Morocco raided into Algeria and attacked a French column at Wadi Kiss, on the
border, just inland from Port Say. A week later
over 4,000 advancing Moroccans suffered a
terrible defeat in the Wadi Kiss and were repulsed at Port Say. The Beni Snassen were
crushed and General Louis Lyautey levied a
heavy fine (29 November 1907).

**Wadi M'Koun I 1908 I French Colonial
Wars in North Africa**
  General Albert d'Amade followed indecisive
action east of Casablanca at **Settat** by leading
2,000 men circling north against Wadi M'Koun,
while a second force marched east through Ber
Rechid. The attempted pincer movement was a
complete failure, with the southern column
forced to fight off a heavy ambush. D'Amade
suffered another costly loss a month later at
R'Fakha (21 January 1908).

Wadi Salit I 742 I Berber Rebellion
  Facing Berber revolt in southern Spain,
Umayyad Governor Abd al-Malik ibn Katan
invited in the Syrian Baldj ibn Bishr, who had
lost to the Berbers at **Bakdura** in Morocco.
Baldj defeated the main Berber force besieging
Toledo at Wadi Salit, on the River Tagus, but he
then overthrew Abd al-Malik and had himself
appointed Governor. This was confirmed by his
victory in August at **Aqua Portora**.

Wadi Sebou I 741 I Berber Rebellion
  See **Bakdura**

**Wadi Zem Zem I 1943 I World War II
(Northern Africa)**
  See **Buerat**

Waerenga I 1865 I 2nd New Zealand War
  Pursuing the religio-military Hauhau on New
Zealand's east coa ' ' " J: es Fraser, with
Captain Charles Westrupp's Forest Rangers and
Maori allies, won at **Hungahungatoroa**, then
attacked a strong position at Waerenga-a-Hika,
on the Waikonu. A bloody seven-day siege saw
100 Hauhau killed before over 400 surrendered,
securing a brief halt to fighting in Poverty Bay
(November 1865).

Wafangtien I 1904 I Russo-Japanese War
  See **Delisi**

**Wager's Action I 1708 I War of the
Spanish Succession**
  See **Cartagena, Colombia**

Wagingera I 1705 I Mughal-Berad Wars
  Emperor Aurangzeb captured the last major
Maratha fortress at **Torna** (June 1704) then
turned against Wagingera, capital of the Berad
tribesmen who had withstood the Mughals at
Sagar (1680). Chief Pidia Nayak held out
against huge odds for three months before
evacuating the city at night. The elderly Emperor
returned exhausted to Ahmadnagar and died
soon after (19 February–8 May 1705).

**Wagon Box Fight I 1867 I Red
Cloud's War**
  With inadequate resources to attack **Fort Phil
Kearney**, south of modern Sheridan, Wyoming,
1,500 Sioux and Cheyenne under Red Cloud
attacked 32 soldiers and workmen under Captain
James Powell at a woodcutting camp just west of
the fort. Shielded behind loaded log wagons,
Powell's men, armed with repeating rifles, beat
off six attacks, inflicting very heavy Indian losses (2 August 1867).

Wagon Hill I 1900 I 2nd Anglo-Boer War
  During the Boer siege of **Ladysmith**, commandant Cornelis de Villiers led an uncharac-
teristic frontal assault on a ridge to the south,
known as the Platrand, defended by General
Sir Ian Hamilton. One of the war's bloodiest

actions—around Wagon Hill and Caesar's Camp—saw the Boers eventually repulsed, with up to 800 casualties, including de Villiers killed (6 January 1900).

Wagram I 1809 I Napoleonic Wars (5th Coalition)

Napoleon Bonaparte suffered a costly loss near Vienna at **Aspern-Essling**, then concentrated a large force on the mid-river island of Lobau before crossing the Danube against Archduke Charles of Austria at Wagram. A massive battle with very heavy casualties on both sides saw Charles defeated when Archduke John arrived too late with reserves. Austria then sued for peace (6 July 1809).

Wahlstadt I 1241 I Mongol Invasion of Europe
See **Liegnitz**

Wahoo Swamp I 1836 I 2nd Seminole Indian War

On a fresh offensive in Florida, General Richard Call led 2,500 men, including 750 Creeks, south from Fort Drane. After twice dispersing the Seminole in the Wahoo Swamp, near the **Withlacoochee** northeast of modern Dade City, Call met a large Seminole concentration and was forced to withdraw with very heavy losses, especially among his Creek allies (17, 18 & 21 November 1836).

Waiara I 1864 I 2nd New Zealand War
See **Mangapiko**

Waihand I 1006 I Muslim Conquest of Northern India

Invading Multan from Afghanistan, the Muslim Mahmud of Ghazni attacked the Carmathian heretic Sultan Abdul Fath Daud, who sought help from the Hindu Prince Anandpal. At Waihand, near Peshawar in modern Pakistan, Anandpal suffered a heavy defeat but met Mahmud at the same site two years later. After a brief siege of Multan, Sultan Daud accepted Orthodox Islam (March–April 1006).

Waihand I 1008 I Muslim Conquest of Northern India

Mahmud of Ghazni led a fresh campaign from Afghanistan into India and met a large Hindu force under Prince Anandpal at the same site as two years earlier. Mahmud's Muslims dispersed the Hindu war-elephants and inflicted a decisive defeat in battle at Waihand, near Peshawar in modern Pakistan. The Afghan's subsequent invasions ravaged much of northern India (31 December 1008).

Waikorowhiti I 1870 I 2nd New Zealand War

As the hunt for the Hauhau rebel Te Kooti continued in New Zealand's central North Island after defeat at **Te Porere**, he was attacked near Rotorua by Lieutenant Gilbert Mair and Arawa Maori allies. A running action near Waikorowhiti and Tumunui cost the Hauhau valuable supplies and about 20 killed. Te Kooti escaped but was a spent force and soon fled to the King Country (7 February 1870).

Waima Incident I 1893 I British Occupation of Sierra Leone

Threatened in northern Sierra Leone by Sofa warriors, British Colonel Alfred Ellis and Captain Edward Lendy marched out of Freetown. They were attacked at Waima by French under Lieutenant Gaston Maritz (who mistook them for the hostiles) with Maritz, Lendy and many troops killed. France paid compensation and a British Protectorate was later proclaimed (22 December 1893).

Wairau I 1843 I 1st New Zealand War

On disputed land at Wairau, on New Zealand's South Island, Maoris under Te Rauparaha and his nephew Te Rangihaeata exchanged fire with a survey party on the Tuamarina Stream. Six Maoris and 22 Europeans died, half of them killed after capture, including Resident Agent Captain Arthur Wakefield. The "Wairau Massacre" shocked the young colony and helped trigger war (17 June 1843).

Waireka I 1860 I 2nd New Zealand War

Five men were killed by Maoris south of New Plymouth at Omata and Colonel George Murray, with militia Captain Charles Brown, was sent into action at nearby Waireka. Although Murray prematurely withdrew, Captain Peter Cracroft (*Niger*) arrived to secure victory and New Zealand's first Victoria Cross was won. Fighting soon resumed at **Puketakauere** (28 March 1860).

Waitara I 1860 I 2nd New Zealand War

When hostile Maoris disputed a grant of land at Waitara, north of New Plymouth, martial law was declared and troops under Colonel Charles Gold, aided by local mounted militia, marched against the Ngatiawa Chief Hapurona at Te Kohia. Attacking with howitzers and a rocket tube, Gold forced Hapurona to withdraw, but trouble soon flared south of New Plymouth at **Waireka** (17 March 1860).

Waitzen I 1849 I Hungarian Revolutionary War

Hungarian General Janos Damjanics advanced to break the siege of **Komárom** and repulsed Austrian forces at Szolnok, then defeated and killed General Christian Goetz at Waitzen (modern Vác), north of Budapest. Komárom was relieved and, after being further driven back through **Nagy Sallo** (19 April), Austrian Field Marshal Alfred Windischgratz had to evacuate Hungary (10 April 1849).

Wakamatsu I 1868 I War of the Meiji Restoration

After securing central Japan and renaming the capital **Edo** as Tokyo, Imperial forces marched into northern Honshu to suppress continued resistance in pro-Tokugawa Aizu (modern Fukushima). Following widespread fighting and heavy losses, the great Aizu stronghold at Wakamatsu finally surrendered to Saigo Takamori, leaving only the rebels at **Goryokaku** (22 September 1868).

Wakde I 1944 I World War II (Pacific)

Just days after landings at **Hollandia** in northern New Guinea, American General Horace Fuller attacked further west at Wakde, which was fiercely defended by 800 Japanese. Brutal action saw all but four Japanese killed before the island was secured, at a cost of 40 American dead. Resistance was much more prolonged on the nearby mainland around **Sarmi** (17–21 May 1944).

Wake I 1941 I World War II (Pacific)

As war started, Admiral Sadamichi Kajioka attacked the American base on Wake Island, where he was driven off by artillery and aircraft with two destroyers lost. Reinforced by two carriers returning from **Pearl Harbour**, he attacked again and, despite courageous fighting by Major James Devereux's Marines, commander Winfield Cunningham had to surrender (8–23 December 1941).

Wakefield I 1460 I Wars of the Roses

Richard Duke of York was proclaimed heir after **Northampton** (10 July), but was besieged at Sandal Castle, near Wakefield, by Henry Percy Earl of Northampton and Henry Beaufort Duke of Somerset, loyal to Queen Margaret. York rashly sallied out and was among 2,000 killed, along with his son Edmund Earl of Rutland and commander Richard Neville Earl of Salisbury (30 December 1460).

Wakefield I 1643 I British Civil Wars

In an attempt to capture prisoners to exchange for those captured in his defeat on **Seacroft Moor**, Parliamentary General Sir Thomas Fairfax led a bold dawn attack on Wakefield, Yorkshire. Despite being unexpectedly outnumbered, Fairfax took the city and over 1,500 prisoners, including Royalist commander George Lord Goring (21 May 1643).

Walaja I 633 I Muslim Conquest of Iraq

Alarmed by defeat in Mesopotamia at **Hafir** and **Mazar**, the Persian Emperor sent fresh forces under Andarzaghar, supported by non-Muslim Arabs. Without waiting for Persian commander Bahram, Andarzaghar advanced to Walaja, on the eastern bank of the Euphrates, where Muslim General Khalid ibn al-Walid secured a brilliant victory. Khalid soon won again at **Ullais** (April 633).

Walcheren I 1574 I Netherlands War of Independence

Viceroy Don Luis de Requesens was triumphant on land, re-establishing Spanish supremacy in the Netherlands, and sent Colonel Julian Romero to relieve the long blockade of **Middelburg**. Off Walcheren near Reimerswaal, Dutch privateers known as "Sea Beggars" under Louis de Boisot routed the Spanish force, destroying nine warships. Middelburg soon had to surrender (29 January 1574).

Walcheren I 1809 I Napoleonic Wars (5th Coalition)

Attempting to divert Napoleon Bonaparte's attention away from Austria, 40,000 British troops under General Sir John Pitt Lord Chatham and Admiral Sir Richard Strachan landed on swampy Walcheren Island, guarding Antwerp. Nothing was achieved and malaria killed 4,000 and disabled 10,000 before the disastrous expedition was abandoned (30 July–23 December 1809).

Walcheren I 1944 I World War II (Western Europe)

See **Scheldt Estuary**

Walcourt I 1689 I War of the Grand Alliance

Amid renewed fighting in the Spanish Netherlands, French under the Dukes Louis d'Humières and Claude de Villars clashed at Walcourt, south of Charleroi, with a Spanish-German army led by Prince George Frederic of Waldeck, supported by the English Brigade of the Duke of Marlborough. The French were heavily defeated and d'Humières lost his command (25 August 1689).

Walker's Creek I 1844 I Comanche Indian Wars

Texas Rangers under Captain Jack Hays, pursuing the Comanche Yellow Wolf west from San Antonio, met a large Indian force near the Guadalupe River on the Pimta trail at Walker's Creek. Yellow Wolf and more than 20 Indians

were killed in a close action—said to be one of the first using the newly introduced revolvers—while the Rangers lost one killed and four wounded (9 June 1844).

Walkerton I 1864 I American Civil War (Eastern Theatre)

As Union General Judson Kilpatrick raided outside the Confederate capital at Richmond, Virginia, a detached brigade under Colonel Ulric Dahlgren was ambushed north near the Pamunkey at Walkerton by units of General Wade Hampton's Confederates under Lieutenant James Pollard. With Dahlgren killed and most of his men captured Kilpatrick withdrew to Yorktown (2 March 1864).

Wallhof I 1626 I 2nd Polish-Swedish War

Gustavus Adolphus of Sweden resumed war against Poland in Livonia, where he was threatened southeast of Riga by two armies under Generals Krystof Radziwill and Lew Sapieha. Arriving by forced marches before Radziwill could assist, Gustavus badly defeated Sapieha on the Plain of Semigallia near Wallhof, causing massive Polish casualties. He then invaded Prussia to besiege **Danzig** (7 January 1626).

Wallingford I 1153 I English Period of Anarchy

With the Empress Matilda defeated in a long dynastic dispute with her cousin King Stephen, her son Henry Plantagenet, the Count of Anjou, returned to England with 3,000 men and marched on the King at Wallingford, near Oxford. After a brief clash Stephen agreed to recognise Henry as his heir, ending "The Anarchy." When Stephen died a year later, Plantagenet became Henry II (January 1153).

Walnut Hills I 1862 I American Civil War (Western Theatre)

See **Chickasaw Bluffs**

Waltersdorf I 1807 I Napoleonic Wars (4th Coalition)

In a prelude to Napoleon Bonaparte's battle in eastern Prussia at **Eylau**, French Marshal Michel

Ney was sent southwest to Waltersdorf, near the Passarge, to prevent the Prussians of General Anton Lestocq linking up with the main Russian army. Lestocq's outnumbered force was defeated and his survivors arrived too late to affect the outcome at **Eylau** three days later (5 February 1807).

Walwal I 1934 I 2nd Italo-Ethiopian War

During a dispute on Ethiopia's border with Italian Somaliland, Captain Roberto Cimmaruta, with a force of mainly Somali irregulars, provoked a major clash at the important oasis of Walwal, 50 miles inside Ethiopia. The Italian force and Ethiopians under Kiferra Balcha both suffered casualties and Mussolini used the clash to justify an invasion of Ethiopia in 1935 through **Adowa** (5 December 1934).

Wanborough I 592 I Anglo-Saxon Territorial Wars

See **Wodnesbeorg**

Wanborough I 715 I Anglo-Saxon Territorial Wars

See **Wodnesbeorg**

Wandewash I 1760 I Seven Years War (India)

Encouraged by his defence of **Madras** against French Governor General Comte Thomas Lally, British Colonel Eyre Coote captured Wandewash, 60 miles to the southwest (29 November 1759), which was besieged by Lally two months later. Lally's Maratha cavalry deserted during this decisive battle and he was badly defeated. He then withdrew to siege and defeat at **Pondicherry** (22 January 1760).

Wanganui I 1847 I 1st New Zealand War

See **Rutland Stockade**

Wanting I 1944–1945 I World War II (China)

Chinese commander Wei Lihuang captured **Longling** across the **Salween**, then pursued the Japanese to the Burmese border, where General Yuzo Matsuyama determined to defend Want-

ing. Heavily attacked from all sides, the Japanese held out for 25 days before withdrawing to Namhkam. Within days, convoys were using the reopened Burma Road (27 December 1944–20 January 1945).

Warangal I 1309–1310 I Wars of the Delhi Sultanate

After failure in 1303 against the Kingdom of Kakatiya (Andhra Pradesh), Sultan Ala-ud-din sent a large army under Malik Kafur against the fortified city of Warangal. Twenty-five days of fighting secured the outer mud fortresses and, when the inner stone citadel came under siege, Prataparuda II sued for peace. Malik withdrew with massive treasure, but disputes over tribute led to further warfare.

Warangal I 1322–1323 I Wars of the Delhi Sultanate

Delhi conquered the Kingdom of Kakatiya in 1310, but disputes over unpaid tribute led to further fighting. Sultan Tughluk Shah I finally sent his son Muhammad against Warangal. False reports of a coup in Delhi led to Muhammad withdrawing, but he was soon reinforced and resumed the siege. After five months, Prataparuda II surrendered and died going into captivity, ending the Kakatiya Dynasty.

War Bonnet Creek I 1876 I Sioux Indian Wars

Attempting to join Sitting Bull after his great victory at **Little Big Horn**, about 1,000 Cheyenne in northwest Nebraska were intercepted at War Bonnet Creek, near modern Montrose, by Colonel Wesley Merritt, who had marched east from Fort Laramie. In a fierce battle—during which William F. Cody killed Yellow Hand—the Cheyenne were defeated and driven back (17 July 1876).

Warburg I 1760 I Seven Years War (Europe)

The Prussian-British army of Duke Ferdinand of Brunswick responded to a new French offensive towards Hanover by meeting Louis-Nicolas Felix Comte du Muy at Warburg, northwest of

Kassel. Supported by British cavalry under John Manners Marquis of Granby, Duke Ferdinand routed the French and drove them back to the Rhine, where they made a stand at **Kloster-Kamp** (31 July 1760).

Ware Bottom Church I 1864 I American Civil War (Eastern Theatre)

Four days after checking Union commander Benjamin F. Butler south of Richmond, Virginia, at **Drewry's Bluff**, Confederate General Pierre G. T. Beauregard attacked further south near Ware Bottom Church. The Union line stabilised when General Adalbert Ames was driven out of his forward position, though Butler remained "bottled up" on the James at Bermuda Hundred (20 May 1864).

Wareham I 876 I Viking Wars in Britain

Advancing southwest from Cambridge, the Danish King Guthrum led his Vikings across Wessex, where they defeated the garrison and captured the coastal port of Wareham, west of Bournemouth. King Alfred of Wessex paid them a tribute to leave the kingdom, but the Vikings escaped during the night towards Exeter. In 878 they returned to defeat Alfred at **Chippenham**.

Wargaom I 1779 I 1st British-Maratha War

A British column advancing from Bombay towards Poona under Colonel William Cockburn was surrounded and massively outnumbered between Talegaon and Wargaom by Marathas under Mahadji Sindhia of Gwalior and Tukaji Holkar of Indore. After suffering heavy losses, Cockburn obtained safe passage by agreeing to a truce, later repudiated by his superiors (13 January 1779).

Warka I 1656 I 1st Northern War

With Charles X of Sweden blockaded by Polish forces on the Vistula near **Sandomierz**, Margrave Frederick V of Baden marched with reinforcements to relieve the King. Frederick was intercepted at Warka, south of Warsaw, and badly beaten by Polish commander Stefan Czarniecki. Charles later managed to break out

from Sandomierz and retook **Warsaw** in July (28 March 1656).

Warmstadt I 1113 I German Civil Wars

Siegfried, Count-Palatine of the Rhine, rebelled against Emperor Henry V with support from Lothar of Saxony, Rudolf of the North Mark, Wiprecht of Groitsch and Ludwig of Thuringia. At Warmstadt, near Quedlinburg, north of the Harz, the rebels were crushed by Imperial General Hoyer of Mansfeld, with Count Siegfried killed. Rebellion soon flared again at **Andernach** and **Welfesholze**.

Warren's Action I 1798 I French Revolutionary Wars (Irish Rising)
See **Donegal Bay**

Warren Wagontrain Raid I 1871 I Kiowa Indian War
See **Salt Creek**

Warsaw I 1655 I 1st Northern War
See **Sobota**

Warsaw I 1656 I 1st Northern War

Following Swedish defeat at **Warka** (28 March), Swedish commander Arvid Wittenberg was eventually forced to surrender nearby Warsaw (21 June). Having meanwhile escaped from **Sandomierz**, Charles X of Sweden was reinforced by Brandenburgers under Georg von Derfflinger and attacked in force. Polish commander Stefan Czarniecki was defeated and Charles retook Warsaw (28–30 July 1656).

Warsaw I 1657 I Transylvanian-Polish War

Prince George Rákóczi II of Transylvania, with Swedish support and Cossacks under Anton Zhdanovich, tried to seize the Polish throne, taking and looting Cracow and Warsaw. However, when Sweden withdrew to fight Denmark (and his Cossacks mutinied) Rákóczi was forced into a humiliating surrender. Returning home, he was routed by Tatars at **Trembowla** (9 June–23 July 1657).

Warsaw (1st) ▌ 1794 ▌ War of the 2nd Polish Partition

Amid renewed Polish insurrection, a Warsaw cobbler named Jan Kalinski led a brutal Easter rising against the Russian garrison, who were pursued and slaughtered in the streets on Good Friday and driven out (17–18 April). Warsaw later withstood an unsuccessful two-month siege by King Frederick William III of Prussia and his Russian allies (2 July–9 September 1794).

Warsaw (2nd) ▌ 1794 ▌ War of the 2nd Polish Partition

See **Praga**

Warsaw ▌ 1831 ▌ Polish Rebellion

After costly losses in northeast Poland at **Ostrolenka**, Polish rebels under General Henryk Dembinksi withdrew to Warsaw, pursued by Russian Field Marshal Ivan Paskevich. The outnumbered Poles lost 9,000 men in a terrible two-day battle before the capital fell and the war ended. Paskevich became Viceroy and stamped out Polish nationalism (6–8 September 1831).

Warsaw (1st) ▌ 1914 ▌ World War I (Eastern Front)

With Austria driven out of eastern Poland around **Lemberg**, German commander Paul von Hindenberg and General August von Mackensen in the north marched on Warsaw. Russia's Nikolai Ivanov concentrated his forces under General Nikolai Ruzskii and heavy fighting forced the Germans to withdraw. Further south Austria was checked at the **San** (28 September– 17 October 1914).

Warsaw (2nd) ▌ 1914 ▌ World War I (Eastern Front)

Recovering from German losses on the **Nieman**, General August von Mackensen launched a fresh offensive into Poland and retook **Lodz** (6 December) then advanced on Warsaw. But desperate Russian defence and bitter cold stopped the Germans 30 miles west of the capital at the Bzura. Both sides entrenched for the winter until the New Year German attack at **Bolimov** (7–20 December 1914).

Warsaw ▌ 1915 ▌ World War I (Eastern Front)

As part of Germany's new **Triple Offensive**, General Max von Gallwitz advanced on the Polish Salient, where Grand Duke Nicolas withdrew from the **Bzura**, west of Warsaw. Under determined German attack, the Russians then abandoned the Polish capital and withdrew through **Vilna**, while further west Germany seized the fortress of **Nowo Georgiewsk** (4–5 August 1915).

Warsaw ▌ 1920 ▌ Russo-Polish War

Polish commander Josef Pilsudski was forced back to Warsaw by Russian victory on the **Berezina**, then he led a bold counter-offensive along the Vistula against General Mikhail Tukhachevski. Against all international expectation, Pilsudski won a stunning victory and Tukhachevski withdrew east towards the **Nieman** with crippling losses in men and equipment (16–25 August 1920).

Warsaw ▌ 1939 ▌ World War II (Western Europe)

Determined to crush **Poland**, German forces raced for Warsaw and launched a bloody land and air assault. A Polish counter-attack to the west at the **Bzura** eased the siege, but with ammunition exhausted and much of the capital in flames, General Juliuscz Rommel had to surrender the city and over 100,000 men. The last Polish resistance soon ended at **Hel** and **Kock** (9–28 September 1939).

Warsaw ▌ 1944 ▌ World War II (Eastern Front)

When Soviet forces reached the Vistula, General Tadeusz Bor-Komorovski's Polish Home Army rose against the German garrison of Warsaw and seized more than half the city. However, expected Soviet help did not come and the rising was brutally crushed by SS General Erich von dem Bach-Zelewski. Warsaw fell

(17 January) in the **Vistula-Oder** offensive
(1 August–2 October 1944).

**Wartenburg I 1813 I Napoleonic Wars
(War of Liberation)**

As Napoleon Bonaparte returned west of the
Elbe, General Gebhard von Blucher's Prussians
pursued him hard and units of the Prussian army
under General Hans Yorck forced the Elbe at
Wartenburg, south of Wittenberg. Yorck, later
created Graf von Wartenburg, drove off General
Henri Bertrand and the Allies continued their
advance on **Leipzig** (3 October 1813).

Washington, DC I 1814 I War of 1812
See **Bladensburg**

**Washington, New York I 1776 I War of
the American Revolution**
See **Fort Washington**

**Washington, North Carolina I 1863 I
American Civil War (Eastern Theatre)**

Confederate General Daniel H. Hill on campaign against the Union army in North Carolina
was repulsed near New Bern at **Fort Anderson**
(13–15 March) then moved north against the
Union garrison at Washington, in the Pamlico
Sound, defended by General George G. Foster.
However, Hill was unable to blockade the river
city and was eventually forced to withdraw (30
March–20 April 1863).

**Washita I 1868 I Cheyenne-Arapaho
Indian War**

Colonel George Custer marched into Indian
Territory and launched a dawn attack on Black
Kettle, camped under a flag of truce on the
Washita River, near modern Cheyenne, Oklahoma. Fighting back bravely, the Indians killed
16 soldiers, including Major Joel Elliot. However, Black Kettle and 100 others were killed,
with many more wounded and their families
captured (27 November 1868).

Wasp vs Avon I 1814 I War of 1812
See **Western Approaches (2nd)**

Wasp vs Frolic I 1812 I War of 1812
See **Virginia**

Wasp vs Reindeer I 1814 I War of 1812
See **Western Approaches (1st)**

**Waterberg I 1904 I German Colonial
Wars in Africa**

Taking command in German Southwest Africa
after humilation at **Oviumbo**, Colonel Lothar von
Trotha led about 4,000 well-equipped men
against the Herero rebels in the Waterberg
Mountains. The rebels were routed in a decisive
action and fled into the Omaheke Desert, where
they were hunted down and annihilated. Fewer
than 20,000 out of 80,000 Herero survived the
war (11–12 August 1904).

**Wateree Ferry I 1780 I War of the
American Revolution**

As American commander Horatio Gates pre-
pared to fight the British army at **Camden**,
South Carolina, guerrilla Colonel Thomas
Sumter sent Colonel Thomas Taylor against the
British rear at Wateree Ferry, just outside
Camden. The rebels defeated a small force under
Colonel Isaac Carey and seized 50 wagonloads
of supplies but were soon caught at **Fishing
Creek** (15 August 1780).

**Waterford I 1170 I Anglo-Norman
Conquest of Ireland**

After Norman adventurer Raymond Fitzgerald
"Le Gros" besieged the Viking Irish city of
Waterford and inflicted massive casualties repulsing an attack on his camp, he was reinforced
by Richard de Clare Earl of Pembroke "Strong-
bow" and the Irish leader Mac Murchada. Waterford was taken by storm and the Norman and
Irish allies then captured Dublin (May–25 August
1170).

Waterford I 1922 I Irish Civil War

While fighting continued in **Limerick**, government forces under General John Prout
advanced south from Kilkenny towards Waterford, held by Republican Colonel Pax Whelan.

Following heavy shelling, Prout's men stormed into the city, which fell with few casualties but very extensive damage. The Republicans then withdrew west towards **Clonmel** (18–21 July 1922).

Waterkloof ∎ 1851 ∎ 8th Cape Frontier War

General Sir Harry Smith was determined to secure the Waterkloof in the eastern Cape and sent Colonel John Fordyce with 450 Highlanders and 400 Mfengu levies against Chief Macomo's stronghold in the Amatolas. However, Fordyce was attacked on the steep mountain and driven off. Two months later, a much larger force drove Macomo out, though Fordyce was killed by a sniper (8 September 1851).

Waterloo ∎ 1815 ∎ Napoleonic Wars (The Hundred Days)

Climaxing the "Hundred Days" following his return from Elbe, Napoleon Bonaparte was defeated at Waterloo, south of Brussels. The British-Dutch army of Arthur Wellesley Duke of Wellington and General Gebhard von Blucher's Prussians achieved one of the major victories in western history and Bonaparte abdicated again, ending the Napoleonic Wars (18 June 1815).

Wattee-Goung ∎ 1825 ∎ 1st British-Burmese War

British General Sir Archibald Campbell defeated the Burmese at **Danubyu** (1 April) and moved up the Irriwaddy to captured Prome. After the failure of peace talks, Colonel Robert McDowell then advanced 16 miles northeast to the stockade at Wattee-Goung (Wettigan), held by Maha Nemyu. McDowell was killed in a heavy defeat and the British fell back on **Prome** (16 November 1825).

Wattignies ∎ 1793 ∎ French Revolutionary Wars (1st Coalition)

Attempting to repulse the Austrian siege of the French border fortress of Maubeuge, poorly trained French recruits under General Jean Baptiste Jourdan met the veterans of Prince Friedrich Josias of Saxe-Coburg over two days

at nearby Wattignies. After initial heavy French losses, the Austrians were driven off and the starving garrison of Maubeuge was relieved (15–16 October 1793).

Wauhatchie Station ∎ 1863 ∎ American Civil War (Western Theatre)

Determined to secure the western approaches to **Chattanooga**, Tennessee, Union General Joseph Hooker seized a bridgehead at Brown's Ferry then sent General John W. Geary south to secure Wauhatchie Station. Confederate General Micah Jenkins was repulsed in a hard-fought night action and Union forces in Chattanooga soon broke out to the east at **Missionary Ridge** (28–29 October 1863).

Wavre ∎ 1815 ∎ Napoleonic Wars (The Hundred Days)

Napoleon Bonaparte was determined to keep General Gebhard von Blucher's Prussians away from the main battle at **Waterloo**, south of Brussels, and sent his right ring under Marshal Emmanuel de Grouchy eight miles east to Wavre. However, the Prussian rearguard of General Johann Thielmann held Grouchy off and Blucher was able to march to Waterloo in time to seal victory (18 June 1815).

Wawer ∎ 1831 ∎ Polish Rebellion

After halting a Russian advance outside Warsaw at **Grochow** and **Praga**, Polish General Jan Skrznyecki crossed the Vistula at night and drove General Fedor Geismar's Sixth Corps from their positions at Wawer with over 10,000 casualties and also captured massive amounts of stores. Russian Marshal Hans von Diebitsch then ordered a withdrawal to **Siedlce** (31 March 1831).

Waxhaw ∎ 1780 ∎ War of the American Revolution

With the capture of **Charleston**, British cavalry Colonel Banastre Tarleton pursued approaching American reinforcements under Colonel Abraham Buford, who Tarleton had defeated at **Lanneau's Ferry**. Making a stand at Waxhaw, just inside North Carolina, Buford was brutally defeated and his wounded were bayonetted in what was ironically called "Tarleton's Quarter" (29 May 1780).

Wayna Daga | 1543 | Adal-Ethiopian War
Muslim leader Ahmad ibn Ibrahim (Ahmad Grañ) of the Somali state of Adal routed Ethiopia at **Shimbra-Kure** and secured the southern part of the country before new Emperor Galawdewus (Claudius) secured Portuguese aid and attacked the Muslims at Wayna Daga (Woina Daga) near Lake Tana. Ahmad was defeated and killed and the state of Adal was fatally weakened (21 February 1543).

Waynesboro, Virginia | 1865 | American Civil War (Eastern Theatre)
Concluding his campaign in the Shenandoah after victory at **Cedar Creek**, Union commander Philip Sheridan, with General George A. Custer, marched southeast from Staunton against General Jubal A. Early's Confederate remnant at Waynesboro, Virginia. Sheridan secured a one-sided victory, capturing guns, supplies and over 1,000 prisoners, though Early himself escaped (2 March 1865).

Waynesborough, Georgia | 1864 | American Civil War (Western Theatre)
As Union commander William T. Sherman marched through Georgia from Atlanta, his left wing under General H. Judson Kilpatrick withdrew from a costly action against Confederate General Joseph Wheeler at **Buck Head Creek**, then attacked him at Waynesborough. Wheeler fled north to Augusta after heavy fighting and within a week Sherman had reached **Savannah** (4 December 1864).

Wednesfield | 911 | Viking Wars in Britain
After Edward the Elder of Wessex defeated the Danes of Northumbria at **Tettenhall** and returned to Kent (August 910), the Danes broke the peace and Edward marched back to Staffordshire to defend his widowed sister Aethelflaed, the Lady of Mercia. At Wednesfield (Wodensfield) near Wolverhampton, Edward

defeated and killed the Danish Kings Halfdan and Ecwils.

Weenan | 1838 | Boer-Zulu War
See **Bloukranz**

Weihaiwei | 1895 | Sino-Japanese War
Marshal Iawo Oyama supported the Japanese offensive in southern Manchuria, landing on the Shandong Peninsula to attack Weihaiwei, which fell after two days of bitter fighting (31 January). The Chinese fleet in Weihaiwai Bay then came under attack by land as well as sea. With costly losses and no hope of aid, Admiral Ding Ruchang committed suicide and his fleet surrendered (2–12 February 1895).

Weinsberg | 1141 | German Civil Wars
When German King Lothair died, his son-in-law and heir, Henry the Proud, Duke of Saxony and Bavaria, was outmanoeuvred by Conrad Hohenstaufen—who was elected as Conrad III and immediately broke up Henry's lands. On Henry's death, his brother Welf reclaimed Bavaria, but at Weinsberg, near Heilbronn, Conrad defeated Welf and forced his surrender (December 1140).

Weinsberg | 1525 | German Peasants' War
Following peasant defeat at **Leipheim** (4 April), about 8,000 Franconian peasants under Jaecklein Rohrbach and Florian Geyer attacked Count Ludwig von Helfstein at Weinsberg, just east of Heilbronn. The castle was stormed and the "Weinsberg Massacre" saw the garrison slaughtered, with the Count and 17 other nobles executed. Heilbronn surrendered the same day (16 April 1525).

Weissenburg | 1870 | Franco-Prussian War
See **Wissembourg**

Weissenstein | 1604 | 1st Polish-Swedish War
As Swedish forces in Livonia were driven out by a Polish counter-offensive under Hetman Jan

Karol Chodkiewicz, General Arvid Stalarm lost the key city of **Dorpat**. He later unwisely attacked Chodkiewicz, southeast of Tallin near Weissenstein (modern Paide, Estonia) and the Swedes suffered a disastrous defeat. King Charles IX himself was beaten in 1605 at **Kirkholm** (15 September 1604).

Weisser Berg ▌ 1620 ▌ Thirty Years War (Bohemian War)
  See **White Mountain**

Wejh ▌ 1917 ▌ World War I (Middle East)
  Arab leader Prince Feisal was encouraged by his success at **Yanbu**, on the Red Sea. Shadowed by the British navy, he then took perhaps 11,000 men north along the coast against a 1,200-strong Turkish garrison at Wejh (al Wajh). Having landed forces from British ships just to the north of Wejh, Feisal secured the port. Later that year he marched further north against **Aqaba** (24 January 1917).

Weldon Railroad (1st) ▌ 1864 ▌ American Civil War (Eastern Theatre)
  See **Jerusalem Plank Road**

Weldon Railroad (2nd) ▌ 1864 ▌ American Civil War (Eastern Theatre)
  See **Globe Tavern**

Welfesholze ▌ 1115 ▌ German Civil Wars
  Renewing rebellion crushed at **Warmstadt** (1113), Saxon and Thuringian nobles rose against Emperor Henry V. Again led by Duke Lothar of Saxony, the rebels were better organised and, after defeating the King at **Andernach**, soon won again at Welfesholze, near Mansfeld in the eastern Harz. With the church against him and few supporters, Henry effectively abandoned his authority in Saxony.

Welika Pond ▌ 1836 ▌ 2nd Seminole Indian War
  At the start of the evacuation of **Fort Drane**, Florida, Captain William Maitland led a 60-man escort with 22 wagons of stores ten miles towards Fort Defiance, outside Micanopy. Just

short of his objective he was attacked at Welika Pond by 200 Seminole under Osceola. A sharp action cost Maitland five killed and six wounded before he was rescued by troops from Fort Defiance (19 July 1836).

Wells ▌ 1692 ▌ King William's War
  Encouraged by success against **York** in Maine, French Governor Joseph Robineau de Villebon sent his brother Rene and Abnaki Indians across Penebscot Bay to attack the settlement at Wells, on the coast southwest of Portland. However, the British led by Joseph Storer and militia Captain James Convers fought back strongly from well-fortified houses and the attack was driven off (9–10 June 1692).

Welshpool ▌ 1400 ▌ Glendower's Rebellion
  Owen Glendower (Owain Glynn Dwr) led a Welsh rebellion which destroyed the estates of the Anglo-Norman noble Reginald Lord Grey of Ruthin and captured several towns before facing 1,400 English levies led by Hugh Burnell on the Severn at Welshpool. Glendower was defeated and his estates forfeited, though his largely guerrilla campaign continued for many years (24 September 1400).

Wenden ▌ 1577 ▌ Livonian War
  Soon after failure at **Reval**, Tsar Ivan IV sent Magnus, his vassal King of Livonia, who captured Wenden (Cesis in Latvia). When Magnus promised protection against Russia he was arrested and Ivan attacked his men holding the citadel. After heavy bombardment, the garrison blew themselves up to avoid capture. Ivan then killed thousands of citizens in the so-called "Massacre of Wenden."

Wenden ▌ 1578 ▌ Livonian War
  At war with Russia over Livonia, Stephen Bathory of Poland had been occupied with the siege of **Danzig** and was unable to prevent the brutal capture of Wenden (modern Cesis in Latvia). The following year he sent a force of German cavalry, who surprised the city at night. The Russian garrison were caught unaware and

were slaughtered in revenge for the previous massacre (21 October 1578).

Wenden I 1919 I Estonian War of Independence
See **Cesis**

Wepener I 1900 I 2nd Anglo-Boer War
Continuing his raid in Orange Free State after victory at **Sannah's Post** and **Reddersburg**, Christiaan de Wet attacked 1,900 men, mainly pro-British Afrikaaners under Colonel Edmund Dalgety, at Wepener, southeast of Bloemfontein. Despite repeated assaults and 300 casualties, Dalgety held out and de Wet withdrew north as General Lord Frederick Roberts approached (9–25 April 1900).

Werbach I 1866 I Seven Weeks War
General Erwin von Manteuffel followed Prussian victory at **Aschaffenburg** by advancing southeast towards the Tauber, where General August von Goeben secured Hochhausen, then attacked the Bavarians at Werbach, west of Würzburg. Advancing breast deep across the Tauber, the Prussians secured Werbach then marched on through **Helmstadt** and **Gerchsheim** to **Würzburg** (24 July 1866).

Werben I 1631 I Thirty Years War (Swedish War)
Marching north along the Elbe after destroying **Magdeburg**, the starving Imperial army of Johan Tserclaes Count Tilly met the Swedish forces of Gustavus Adolphus near the junction with the Havel at Werben. In the face of a massive Swedish assault, Tilly lost a reported 6,000 casualties then withdrew through neutral Saxony towards Leipzig and eventual battle at **Breitenfeld** (22 July 1631).

Werki I 1658 I Russo-Polish Wars
While on campaign against Sweden in Latvia, Polish Hetman Wincenty Gosiewski was surprised outside Vilna at Werki by Russian Prince Yuri Dolgorukov. Gosiewski was heavily defeated and captured and the Russians sacked Vilna. However, a Cossack siege of Minsk forced Dolgorukov to withdraw. Another offensive into Lithuania in 1660 was repulsed at **Polonka** (21 October 1658).

Wertingen I 1805 I Napoleonic Wars (3rd Coalition)
Napoleon Bonaparte's Grand Army advanced across the Rhine in massive force and swung south to cut off the Austrian invasion of Bavaria under General Karl Mack von Leiberich. Northeast of **Ulm** at Wertingen, the advance guard of Marshals Joachim Murat and Jean Lannes destroyed an Austrian force. The French then continued south to threaten Mack with encirclement (8 October 1805).

Wesel I 1629 I Netherlands War of Independence
In a bold raid to support the Dutch siege of **Hertogenbosch**, Colonel Otto van Gendt (Heer van Dieden) took a small force east from Arnhem against the Spanish base at Wesel, north of Duisberg. Attacking at night, the Dutch seized the city, along with supplies and prisoners, including Governor Francisco Lozano, hastening the capitulation of Hertogenbosch (19 August 1629).

Wesel I 1945 I World War II (Western Europe)
Two days after American forces crossed the Rhine near Mainz, Allied commander Sir Bernard Montgomery launched over a million British, American, French and Canadian troops across the Rhine around Wesel. While there was sharp resistance at **Emmerich**, a bridgehead was established and the Americans swung south to surround the **Ruhr** Pocket (23 March 1945).

Weser I 16 I Rome's Germanic Wars
Roman General Julius Caesar Germanicus advanced into Germania, where he buried victims of the disaster at **Teutoburgwald** (9 AD) then attacked the Cherusci under Arminius. In open battle at a location known as Idistaviso, probably on the Weser near Minden, Germanicus won a decisive victory. However, he was

soon recalled and Rome failed to establish her authority beyond the Rhine.

Western Approaches (1st) I 1814 I War of 1812

The American sloop *Wasp* (Captain Johnston Blakeley) sank five vessels in the Western Approaches to the English Channel then met the British sloop *Reindeer* (Commander William Manners) in a famous action. After bloody losses on both sides, Manners was killed attempting to board the American ship and *Reindeer* was forced to surrender (28 June 1814).

Western Approaches (2nd) I 1814 I War of 1812

Refitted in France after action against *Reindeer*, the American sloop *Wasp* (Captain Johnston Blakeley) resumed raiding in the Western Approaches to the English Channel and was met at night by the British brig *Avon* (Commander James Arbuthnot), which was badly damaged and later sank. *Wasp* was driven off by other British ships and was lost without trace on the way home (1 September 1814).

Western Hubei I 1943 I World War II (China)

After a long pause since **Zhejiang** (August 1942), General Isamu Tokoyama led an offensive into Hubei to clear the upper Yangzi and threaten China's wartime capital at Chongqing. Advancing against the fortress at Shipai near Yichang, the Japanese were driven off by a large counter-offensive under General Chen Cheng and within weeks were back to the starting point (5 May–17 June 1943).

Westerplatte I 1939 I World War II (Western Europe)

War started when German battleships opened fire on the naval depot at Westerplatte, in Danzig harbour. An heroic defence against overwhelming naval and aerial bombardment and land attack came to symbolise Polish resistance. The action cost 15 Poles killed and perhaps 200 Germans before Major Henryk Sucharski surrendered to General Friedrich Eberhard (1–7 September 1939).

West Irian I 1962 I Dutch-Indonesian War

When Indonesia tried to seize West Irian (Netherlands New Guinea), two Dutch warships engaged four torpedo boats offshore, sinking one and damaging another with 50 killed, including Indonesia's Deputy Chief of Navy. Indonesia sent land forces and, facing international opposition, the Netherlands yielded the territory, incorporated into Indonesia in 1963 (15 January 1962).

West Point I 1862 I American Civil War (Eastern Theatre)
See **Eltham's Landing**

Westport I 1864 I American Civil War (Trans-Mississippi)

Confederate General Sterling Price crossed Missouri to seize **Independence** (11 August) then found himself between two Union armies southeast of Kansas City. Using one division to hold the **Big Blue River**, he turned west against Union commander Samuel R. Curtis at Westport. However, he was driven off in a large-scale action and turned south through **Marais des Cygnes** (23 October 1864).

West Scheldt I 1574 I Netherlands War of Independence
See **Walcheren**

West Wall I 1944–1945 I World War II (Western Europe)
See **Siegfried Line**

Wethersfield I 1637 I Pequot Indian War

Retaliating for the murderous colonial attack on **Block Island**, off southern New England, 200 Pequot Indians under Chief Sassacus attacked the town of Wethersfield, just south of Hartford, Connecticut, killing six men and three women. The attack led to a formal declaration of war at Hartford and resulted in the decisive attack on the Pequot six weeks later at **Mystic** (12 April 1637).

Wettigan I 1825 I 1st British-Burmese War
See **Wattee-Goung**

Wetzikon I 1799 I French Revolutionary Wars (2nd Coalition)
In a prelude to the First Battle of **Zurich**, French General Nicolas Soult was attacked and driven back at **Wetzikon**, east of the city, by Austrian General Franz von Jellachich. With the arrival next day of General André Masséna, the Austrians were repulsed with heavy losses on both sides. But over the coming days at Zurich, Masséna was forced to withdraw (2–3 June 1799).

Wetzlar I 1796 I French Revolutionary Wars (1st Coalition)
Two months after French General Jean-Baptiste Jourdan crossed the Rhine and defeated Archduke Charles Louis of Austria at **Altenkirchen**, he sent General Francois Lefebvre forward to cover the left flank and drive the Austrians out of Wetzlar. Lefebvre was repulsed when the Archduke arrived with reinforcements and Jourdan retired down the east bank of the Rhine (15 June 1796).

Wewak I 1944–1945 I World War II (Pacific)
Australian General Jack Stevens took over command at **Aitape** in New Guinea and led a slow offensive east against about 50,000 Japanese isolated at Wewak. Heavy fighting and costly losses on both sides forced General Hatazo Adachi to abandon Wewak and take his survivors into the mountains, where they held out until the end of the war (December 1944–11 May 1945).

Wexford I 1649 I British Civil Wars
On a campaign of destruction against Catholic-Royalist Ireland, Oliver Cromwell's New Model Army massacred the inhabitants of **Drogheda** (12 September) then advanced against Wexford on the Slaney. The town was taken by storm and sacked with further slaughter, prompting the surrender of other towns to avoid a similar fate (11 October 1649).

Weyconda I 1753 I 2nd Carnatic War
See **Trichinopoly (2nd)**

Wheathampstead I 54 BC I Roman Invasion of Britain
Julius Caesar returned to Britain with a larger force after a failed invasion at **Deal** and attacked confederated tribes under Cassivellaunus, King of the Catuvellauni. After scattered fighting, the Romans won a decisive action, probably at Wheathampstead near Verulamium (St Albans). When Cassivellaunus sued for peace the Romans left and did not return for almost 100 years (July–September 54 BC).

White Bird Canyon I 1877 I Nez Percé Indian War
Resisting relocation to a reservation, Nez Percé Chief Joseph attacked settlers in northern Idaho. General Oliver Howard sent cavalry Captain David Perry against Joseph's camp, on the Salmon River southeast of Grangeville, where the troopers were ambushed at White Bird Canyon, with 36 killed out of 100. Howard then led a much larger force to the **Clearwater River** (17 June 1877).

White City I 1944 I World War II (Burma-India)
See **Indaw**

White Hall I 1862 I American Civil War (Eastern Theatre)
On expedition deep into North Carolina from New Bern, Union General John G. Foster dispersed a Confederate force at **Kinston**. Two days later he met the Confederates further west on the Neuse at White Hall, where General Beverly Robertson tried to block his advance. Inconclusive action allowed Foster to continue advancing the few miles northwest towards **Goldsboro** (16 December 1862).

Whitehaven I 1778 I War of the American Revolution
American John Paul Jones in the Sloop *Ranger* sailed into Solway Firth and landed on England's west coast at Whitehaven, where he

spiked two batteries and burned several ships. He then landed on St Mary's Isle in an abortive attempt to kidnap the Earl of Selkirk. Though no blood was shed, Whitehaven was America's only attack on English soil and spread great alarm (22–23 April 1778).

White Horse Hill I 1952 I Korean War

While the Americans struggled at **Old Baldy**, South Koreans faced a massive Chinese assault on White Horse Hill, west of Chorwon, with a diversionary attack on the French at nearby Arrowhead. Some of the heaviest fighting of the war saw White Horse Hill reportedly change hands 20 times before the Chinese were repulsed. The invaders meantime succeeded at **Triangle Hill** (6–15 October 1952).

White Marsh I 1777 I War of the American Revolution

British General Sir William Howe defeated George Washington at **Brandywine** and **Germantown**, then advanced from Philadelphia to destroy the Continental Army. But after days of manoeuvring and small actions at White Marsh and Edge Hill, Howe failed to bring them to battle. He returned to base and Washington withdrew to winter quarters in Valley Forge (5–8 December 1777).

White Mountain I 1620 I Thirty Years War (Bohemian War)

When Protestant Bohemia elected Frederick V of the Rhine to rival Emperor Ferdinand II, Christian of Anhalt and Bethlen Gabor of Hungary faced a Catholic army under Johan Tserclaes Count Tilly and Charles-Bonaventure de Longueval Comte de Bucqoi. West of Prague at White Mountain the Protestants were routed. Prague was sacked and Frederick fled (8 November 1620).

White Oak Road I 1865 I American Civil War (Eastern Theatre)

Attacking Confederate defences southwest of besieged **Petersburg**, Virginia, General Gouverneur K. Warren advanced through **Lewis's Farm** against General Robert H. Anderson at the White Oak Road and was checked after heavy fighting. The Union was also checked the same day at **Dinwiddie Court House**, but won decisively next day at **Five Forks** (31 March 1865).

White Oaks I 1862 I American Civil War (Eastern Theatre)

See **Beaver Dam Creek**

White Oak Swamp I 1862 I American Civil War (Eastern Theatre)

As General Robert E. Lee pursued George B. McClellan's Union army through **Seven Days' Battles** to White Oak Swamp, southeast of Richmond, Virginia, the Union rearguard under General William Franklin delayed General Thomas "Stonewall" Jackson at White Oak Bridge. Two miles away near Glendale, the main force fought a bloody action then withdrew to **Malvern Hill** (30 June 1862).

White Plains I 1776 I War of the American Revolution

General George Washington conducted a fighting withdrawal north from New York City, from **Harlem Heights** to White Plains, on the Bronx River in New Jersey, where British General William Howe attempted an encirclement. While the Americans were driven out in heavy fighting, a storm delayed Howe's pursuit and Washington escaped to Connecticut (28 October 1776).

White River I 1879 I Ute Indian Wars

Nathan Meeker was Indian agent at the White River Agency, near modern Meeker, northwest Colorado, whose policy of assimilation provoked a war with the Ute under Jack (Nicaagat) and Colorow. When an army column was besieged at nearby **Red Canyon**, the Indians murdered Meeker and nine other white men and seized his wife, daughter and another woman (29 September 1879).

White Rock I 218 BC I 2nd Punic War

Crossing the Alps from Gaul, Carthaginian General Hannibal Barca routed the Allobroge at

Chevelu then advanced up the Isère, where he was attacked by other Barbarian tribesmen. Hannibal suffered costly losses east of Séez, near a promontory known as the White Rock, but continued over the Little St Bernard Pass into Italy for victory in November at the **Ticinus** (October 218 BC).

White Russia I 1944 I World War II (Eastern Front)
See **Belorussia**

Whitestone Hill I 1863 I Sioux Indian Wars
General Alfred Sully took command after victory at **Stony Lake** (28 July) pursuing Sioux Chief Inkapaduta to southern North Dakota, where he attacked and destroyed his camp at Whitestone Hill, near modern Merricourt. A very fierce action saw 20 soldiers and about 200 Sioux men, women and children killed. The Indians soon fought again at **Killdeer Mountain** (3 September 1863).

White Wing I 1966 I Vietnam War
See **Bon Son**

White Wolf Mountain I 207 I Wars of the Three Kingdoms
After victory over Yuan Shao at **Guandu** (200), warlord Cao Cao (Ts'ao Ts'ao) fought his sons and eventually pursued Yuan Shang and Yuan Xi northeast into Liaoning, where they allied themselves with Wuhuan leader Tadun. At White Wolf Mountain (Bailung Shan) the allies were routed. Tadun died in battle and the Yuan brothers were killed in exile, leaving Cao Cao unrivalled in northern China.

Whitman Massacre I 1847 I Cayuse Indian War
Angered by a measles outbreak, Cayuse under Tiloukaikt attacked the mission station of Dr Marcus Whitman at Waiilatpu, west of modern Walla Walla, in southeast Washington. Whitman, his wife Narcissa and 12 others were massacred and about 53 women and children were captured for ransom. The murders trig-

gered a war and Tiloukaikt and four others were eventually hanged (29 November 1847).

Wiazma I 1812 I Napoleonic Wars (Russian Campaign)
See **Vyazma**

Wiazma I 1941 I World War II (Eastern Front)
See **Vyazma**

Wibbandun I 568 I Anglo-Saxon Conquest of Britain
In a determined campaign to expand his kingdom northwest towards the Thames, Aethelbert, the Jute King of Kent, met Ceawlin of the West Saxons and his brother Cutha at Wibbandun (modern Wimbledon). Aethelbert was heavily defeated and the battle helped consolidate Ceawlin as undisputed ruler of Saxon Wessex.

Wichita Agency I 1862 I Kickapoo Indian Wars
As Civil War continued, pro-Union Kickapoo under Papequah attacked the Wichita Agency on Oklahoma's Washita River, where three white traders were killed and Indian Agent Matthew Leeper was terribly wounded. Next day the Kickapoo pursued the local Tonkawa and took over 100 scalps before returning north with massive booty and a large herd of captured horses (23–24 October 1862).

Wieselburg I 1096 I 1st Crusade
With European forces gathering for the First Crusade, Count Emich of Leisengen led a large force east from the Rhine, attacking Jews on the way. Refused passage through Hungary by King Coloman, the Crusaders besieged the fortress of Wieselburg, east of Amstetten in Austria, where they were destroyed in full battle by Hungarian troops. Some of the survivors later joined the main Crusade.

Wiesenthal I 1866 I Seven Weeks War
After defeating Hanover at **Langensalza**, Prussians invaded Bavaria and General August von Goeben sent General Karl von Wrangel east

from Dermbach against General Jakob von Hartmann at Wiesenthal. As at **Zella** earlier in the day, the Bavarians were driven off. The Prussians regrouped to advance on **Kissingen**, while Prince Alexander of Hesse fell back west on Frankfort (4 July 1866).

Wiesloch I 1622 I Thirty Years War (Palatinate War)

Supporting Frederick V Palatine of the Rhine against Emperor Ferdinand II, the Protestant mercenary Count Ernst von Mansfeld crossed the Rhine to prevent Johan Tserclaes Count Tilly of Bavaria joining forces with Spanish General Gonzalo Fernández de Cordoba. Tilly suffered a sharp defeat south of Heidelberg near Wiesloch, but joined Cordoba for victory at **Wimpfen** (27 April 1622).

Wigan I 1651 I British Civil Wars

As Charles II advanced into England after Royalist defeat at **Inverkeithing** (20 July), James Stanley Earl of Derby landed in Lincolnshire with reinforcements from the Isle of Man. However, his small cavalry force was beaten near Wigan by Puritan Colonel Robert Lilburne. Lord Derby escaped to fight at **Worcester** (3 September), after which he was court-martialled and shot (25 August 1651).

Wilderness I 1864 I American Civil War (Eastern Theatre)

At the start of his offensive against General Robert E. Lee in northern Virginia, Union commander Ulysses S. Grant launched a massive attack in the Wilderness, across the Rapidan west of Fredericksburg. Grant lost more men in a very hard-fought drawn action but did not retreat. Instead, he continued advancing south to resume the fight at **Spotsylvania Court House** (5–7 May 1864).

Wilhelmstahl I 1762 I Seven Years War (Europe)

With Russia out of the war, the Prussian-British army of Duke Ferdinand of Brunswick renewed its assault on the French in Hesse. At Wilhelmstahl, near Kassel, the French suffered a costly defeat,

concluded by the British cavalry of John Manners Marquis of Granby. Duke Ferdinand soon inflicted another defeat at **Lutterberg** and drove the French back across the Rhine (24 June 1762).

Wilkomierz I 1435 I Later Wars of the Teutonic Knights

Teutonic knights of the Livonian Order recovered from disaster at **Tannenberg** (1410) and intervened in the Lithuanian succession, supporting Swidrygiello against Zygmunt Korybut. Attacked at Wilkomierz, north of Vilna, by Zygmunt and Polish General Jakob Koblynski, the Order suffered another decisive defeat, with Grandmaster Frank von Kersdorf routed and killed (1 September 1435).

Willems I 1794 I French Revolutionary Wars (1st Coalition)

Following the surrender of **Landrécies**, in northern France, British Dragoons and Hussars under General David Dundas attacked a large infantry formation under General Jacques Bonnaud east of Lille at Willems. The heavily outnumbered cavalry managed to break the French infantry square, inflicting over 2,000 casualties as well as taking 13 guns and 450 prisoners (10 May 1794).

Williamsburg I 1862 I American Civil War (Eastern Theatre)

Early in the Peninsula campaign in Virginia, Union commander George B. McClellan pursued the Confederates west from **Yorktown** and met the rearguard under General James Longstreet at Willliamsburg. After Union General Joseph Hooker was initially repulsed, Generals Winfield S. Hancock and Philip Kearny joined the attack and Longstreet continued his withdawal (5 May 1862).

Williamson's Plantation I 1780 I War of the American Revolution

Leading Loyalist militia against rebel forces gathering under Colonel Thomas Sumter, Captain Christian Huck attacked James Williamson's Plantation in York County (modern Brattonville, South Carolina) and was surprised by partisan Colonels William Bratton and James McClure.

The Tories were routed, with Huck killed, encouraging Sumter to advance on **Rocky Mount** (12 July 1780).

Williamsport I 1863 I American Civil War (Eastern Theatre)

Confederate commander Robert E. Lee withdrew from defeat at **Gettysburg** and reached Williamsport, Maryland, on the Potomac, where he was attacked by units of George G. Meade's Union army. After a prolonged but inconclusive engagement—and action further east at **Boonsboro**— Lee withdrew into Virginia, then turned to meet a flank attack at **Manassas Gap** (6–16 July 1863).

Williams Station Massacre I 1860 I Pyramid Lake Indian War

See **Truckee**

Willmanstrand I 1741 I 1st Russo-Swedish War

Threatened by Russian claims on Finland, Sweden unwisely declared war and General Charles Erik Lewenhaupt was routed by Russian Marshal Peter Lacy and General James Keith at Willmanstrand (modern Lappeenranta) on Lake Saimaa. Lewenhaupt was later executed after surrendering 17,000 men at Helsingfors (Helsinki). The ensuing peace gave Russia part of Finland (3 September 1741).

Willow I 1848 I Cayuse Indian War

Colonel Cornelius Gilliam marched up the Columbus in pursuit of Indians who had murdered Dr **Whitman** to win at the **Deschutes**, then met the Cayuse near the Willow River on the Washington-Oregon Border. Grey Eagle and seven others were killed in a fierce action and Five Crows was mortally wounded. A month later Gilliam met another Indian force at the **Tucannon** (24 February 1848).

Willow Grange I 1899 I 2nd Anglo-Boer War

Encouraged by success south of besieged **Ladysmith** at **Chieveley**, Boer leaders David Joubert and Louis Botha advanced on Estcourt, where they were attacked at nearby Willow Grange by General Henry Hildyard. Failing to drive the Boers off Brynbella and Beacon Hill, Hildyard fell back on Estcourt with about 80 casualties. However, Joubert soon withdrew to Colenso (22–23 November 1899).

Willows I 377 I 5th Gothic War

See **Ad Salices**

Wilmington I 1865 I American Civil War (Eastern Theatre)

Advancing up the Cape Fear River from **Fort Fisher**, North Carolina, a large Union force under General John M. Schofield attacked Fort Anderson outside Confederate Wilmington. General Robert Hoke was forced to abandon the fort after heavy bombardment (19 February) and General Braxton Bragg evacuated Wilmington, the Confederacy's last Atlantic seaport (12–22 February 1865).

Wilno I 1794 I War of the 2nd Polish Partition

See **Vilna**

Wilno I 1915 I World War I (Eastern Front)

See **Vilna**

Wilno I 1919 I Lithuanian War of Independence

See **Vilna**

Wilno I 1920 I Russo-Polish War

See **Vilna**

Wilno I 1944 I World War II (Eastern Front)

See **Vilna**

Wilnsdorf I 1796 I French Revolutionary Wars (1st Coalition)

As General Jean Victor Moreau crossed the Rhine into Germany, French General Francois Lefebvre advancing on the left met Austrian General Paul Kray in a strong position at Wilnsdorf, southeast of Siegen. Lefebvre took over 600 prisoners in a hard day's fighting and Austrian commander Alexander Wartensleben ordered Kray to withdraw to the Lahn (4 July 1796).

Wilson's Creek I 1861 I American Civil War (Trans-Mississippi)

A month after tactical victory in southwest Missouri at **Carthage**, Confederate General Ben McCulloch and militia under Sterling Price met Union General Nathaniel Lyon at Wilson's Creek, south of Springfield. Lyon was killed in a bloody action with over 1,000 lost on either side. Major Samuel D. Sturgis then led a Union retreat to Springfield, buoying the secessionist cause (10 August 1861).

Wilson's Wharf I 1864 I American Civil War (Eastern Theatre)

On campaign southeast of Richmond near the James, about 3,000 Confederate cavalry under General Fitzhugh Lee attacked a Union supply depot at Wilson's Wharf, Virginia, on the north side of the river, near Fort Powhatan. Lee was defeated and driven off by black regiments under General Edward A. Wild and the Union offensive soon advanced south towards **Totopotomoy** (24 May 1864).

Wilton I 871 I Viking Wars in Britain

Following the death of Aethelred of Wessex in the Saxon defeat at **Merton** in March, his brother King Alfred continued the fight against the Viking invasion of Wessex until the Danes attacked him near Wilton, west of Salisbury, the traditional home of Saxon Kings. Lured from his position by a feigned Viking withdrawal, Alfred was defeated and paid a tribute to buy peace.

Wilton I 1143 I English Period of Anarchy

Amid anarchy following the death of Henry I, King Stephen was restored after defeating his cousin the Empress Matilda in 1141 at **Winchester** and **Oxford**. She and her half-brother Robert of Gloucester fought on and at Wilton, west of Salisbury, Stephen was routed, only just escaping capture. But when Robert died in Oc-

tober 1147, Matilda retired to Normandy (1 July 1143).

Wimbledon I 568 I Anglo-Saxon Conquest of Britain
See **Wibbandun**

Wimborne I 902 I Viking Wars in Britain

In a disputed succession following the death of King Alfred of Wessex, his son Edward the Elder found himself at war with his cousin Aethelwald, son of Aethelred of Mercia. Aethelwald fled after being besieged and defeated at Wimborne, near Poole in Dorsetshire, He returned in 905, aided by Danish Vikings, and was killed in battle on the Thames at **Holme**.

Wimpfen I 1622 I Thirty Years War (Palatinate War)

Following victory near Heidelberg at **Wiesloch**, a failed attempt by Count Ernst von Mansfeld to split his Catholic enemy left George Frederick Margrave of Baden alone to face the combined forces of Johan Tserclaes Count Tilly and General Gonzalo Fernández de Cordoba. The elderly Margrave was routed north of Heilbronn at Wimpfen and the Protestants soon lost again at **Höchst** (6 May 1622).

Winceby I 1643 I British Civil Wars

Royalist Sir John Henderson led a fresh offensive near Horncastle in Lincolnshire, attacking Parliamentary troops besieging Bolingbroke Castle. Led by Edward Montague Earl of Manchester, Oliver Cromwell and Sir Thomas Fairfax, the Ironsides cavalry routed Henderson's far superior force at nearby Winceby, capturing 800 prisoners and substantial quantities of arms (10 October 1643).

Winchelsea I 1350 I Hundred Years War

When Spanish Privateer Carlos de la Cerda entered the English Channel from Sluys, he was intercepted off Winchelsea, Sussex, by English ships under personal command of King Edward III. A large number of Spanish ships were destroyed or captured. The victory, coming after the great naval battle at **Sluys** (1340), ensured

Edward mastery of the sea route to his army at **Calais** (29 August 1350).

Winchester, England I 1141 I English Period of Anarchy

In a period of anarchy following the death of Henry I, when King Stephen was overthrown and imprisoned by his cousin Matilda at **Lincoln** in February, his wife Matilda besieged the Empress and her half-brother Earl Robert of Gloucester at Winchester. The defenders fled after six weeks, but Robert was captured at Stockbridge and was later exchanged for the King (August–September 1141).

Winchester, Virginia I 1862 I American Civil War (Eastern Theatre)

Two days after victory near **Front Royal**, Virginia, Confederate General Thomas "Stonewall" Jackson advanced along the Shenandoah against Winchester. During a decisive action at nearby Bowers Hill, Jackson and Major Richard S. Ewell routed heavily outnumbered Union General Nathaniel P. Banks, who lost over 2,000 men and retreated north across the Potomac (25 May 1862).

Winchester, Virginia I 1863 I American Civil War (Eastern Theatre)

Confederate comander Robert E. Lee prepared his new invasion of the north, sending General Richard Ewell into Virginia's Shenandoah Valley against General Robert H. Milroy at Winchester. A crushing Union defeat cost Milroy about 1,000 casualties and over 3,000 prisoners plus massive losses in supplies and guns. Two days later, Lee himself started north towards **Gettysburg** (13–15 June 1863).

Winchester, Virginia I 1864 I American Civil War (Eastern Theatre)

See **Opequon**

Windhoek I 1915 I World War I (African Colonial Theatre)

On a determined campaign into German Southwest Africa, South African commander Louis Botha advanced from Swakopmund towards Windhoek, while General Jan Smuts marched north through **Gibeon**. Windhoek and its powerful wireless station fell after the capture of nearby Karibib and two months later German Governor Theodore Seitz surrendered the whole colony (12 May 1915).

Winkovo I 1812 I Napoleonic Wars (Russian Campaign)

See **Vinkovo**

Winnington Bridge I 1659 I Royalist Rising

Despite defeat in Britain's Civil War, Royalist plotters organised a regional rising under Sir George Booth. The intended wider revolt failed and Parliamentary troops under John Lambert routed the rebels at Winnington Bridge, near Northwich, Cheshire. Booth was captured dressed as a woman and imprisoned. He was soon released upon the King's restoration in May 1660 (19 August 1659).

Winter Battle of Masuria I 1915 I World War I (Eastern Front)

See **Masurian Lakes**

Winter Line I 1943–1944 I World War II (Southern Europe)

See **Gustav Line**

Winterthur I 1292 I Habsburg-Swiss Wars

In an early confederation of Swiss cities against their Habsburg rulers, the army of Zurich marched northeast against the Austrian city of Winterthur, where they were heavily defeated. Albert of Austria then besieged and captured Zurich itself and the confederation was for the time being dissolved. The struggle resumed 60 years later at **Nafels** (12 April 1292).

Winter War I 1939–1940 I Russo-Finnish War

As World War II began, the Soviet Union attacked Finland, bombing **Helsinki** and capturing **Petsamo**, before suffering costly losses at the **Mannerheim Line** on the Karelian Isthmus, and further north at **Tolvajärvi**, **Suomussalmi** and **Raate Road**. Soviet forces regrouped for a fresh assault on the **Mannerheim Line** and Finland was forced to sue for peace (30 November 1939–13 March 1940).

Winwaed I 655 I Anglo-Saxon Territorial Wars

Amid rivalry between Northumbria and Mercia, Penda of Mercia defeated and killed successive Northumbrian Kings at **Heathfield** (633) and **Maserfield** (641). But at the River Winwaed, near modern Leeds, Penda was defeated and killed by Oswy of Northumbria, who was avenging his brother Oswald. Northumbrian pre-eminence was restored until defeat in 679 at **Trent** (15 November 655).

Wippedesfleet I 465 I Anglo-Saxon Conquest of Britain

Eight years after defeating the Britons at **Aegelsthrep** and **Creccanford**, the semi-legendary Jute warrior Hengist received reinforcements from Jutland and achieved a third victory at Wippedesfleet (probably the Wansum Channel near Thanet in Kent), said to be named for the death in battle of the Thane Wipped. The campaign gave Hengist effective control of much of southeast England.

Wisby I 1361 I Wars of the Hanseatic League

See **Visby**

Wisconsin Heights I 1832 I Black Hawk Indian War

The Sauk Chief Black Hawk campaigned in Wisconsin after defeat at **Kellogg's Grove** (25 June) and was attacked while crossing the Wisconsin River, west of Madison, by mounted volunteers led by Colonel Henry Dodge and some of General Henry Atkinson's regulars under General James Henry. Black Hawk was badly defeated but escaped to soon fight again at **Bad Axe** (21 July 1832).

Wise's Fork I 1865 I American Civil War (Western Theatre)

See **Kinston**

Wissembourg I 1793 I French Revolutionary Wars (1st Coalition)

Days after defeat near **Froeschwiller**, Austrian General Dagobert Wurmser withdrew north to Wissembourg, on the Lauter, where he was again attacked by French commander Louis Lazare Hoche. Wurmser suffered heavy casualties and, three days later, the invaders withdrew across the Rhine at Philippsburg, leaving France controlling the left bank of the Rhine (25–26 December 1793).

Wissembourg I 1870 I Franco-Prussian War

At the start of the war, Crown Prince Friedrich Wilhelm of Prussia invaded in overwhelming force east of **Saarbrucken** to attack Wissembourg and the nearby fortress of Geissberg, held by advance units of Marshal Marie MacMahon's army under General Abel Douay. The French withdrew after heavy losses—including Douay killed—and MacMahon fell back on **Wörth** (4 August 1870).

Witebsk I 1812 I Napoleonic Wars (Russian Campaign)

See **Vitebsk**

Witebsk I 1944 I World War II (Eastern Front)

See **Vitebsk**

Withlacoochee I 1835 I 2nd Seminole Indian War

Marching south from Fort Drane, Florida, 260 regulars under General Duncan Clinch and 400 militia led by General Richard Call, unaware of the **Dade Massacre** three days earlier, were attacked crossing the Withlacoochee, southwest of Ocala, near modern Dunellon, by 200 Seminole under Osceola. Clinch had 60 casualties, though the Indians suffered a major defeat (31 December 1835).

Withlacoochee I 1836 I 2nd Seminole Indian War

In a fresh offensive against the Seminole in Florida, General Edmund Gaines led 1,200 men north from Tampa and was attacked by Osceola at the Withlacoochee, near the earlier battlefield east of Dunellon. After a week's siege and 65 casualties, including Gaines severely wounded in the mouth, he was relieved by General Duncan Clinch and both sides withdrew (29 February–6 March 1836).

Wittenweier I 1638 I Thirty Years War (Franco-Habsburg War)

When Bernard of Saxe-Weimar advanced down the Rhine to besiege the city of Breisach, Emperor Ferdinand III sent a relief force under Count Johann von Gotz to support Count Friedrich von Savelli (who had escaped from capture at **Rheinfelden**). The Imperials were repulsed at nearby Wittenweier and an attempt to relieve **Breisach** in October was repulsed at **Sennheim** (30 July 1638).

Wittstock I 1636 I Thirty Years War (Franco-Habsburg War)

When Imperial forces entered Brandenberg to aid Elector John George of Saxony, they were attacked on the Dosse at Wittstock by a smaller Swedish army under Johan Banér, with Scottish Generals Alexander Leslie and James King. The Elector and General Melchior Hatzfeld suffered an awful loss, which helped avenge the Protestant defeat in 1634 at **Nördlingen** (24 September 1636).

Wodnesbeorg I 592 I Anglo-Saxon Territorial Wars

Following his defeat by the British at **Fethanleag**, King Ceawlin of the West Saxons faced a rebellion by nobles under his nephew Coel, son of Cutha, who had died at Fethanleag. Coel seized part of his uncle's land, then in battle at Wodnesbeorg (Adams's Grave, near Wanborough) in Wiltshire, Ceawlin was defeated and driven out. As a result, Coel secured the crown of Wessex.

Wodnesbeorg I 715 I Anglo-Saxon Territorial Wars

Concerned about the growing power of Wessex, Ceolred of Mercia invaded Wessex and met Ine of the West Saxons in battle at Wodnesbeorg (Adams's Grave, near modern Wanborough) in Wiltshire. After heavy losses on both sides, Ine was defeated and forced to withdraw. An attempt by King Ine to expand west into Cornwall was also defeated six years later at the **Camel**.

Woevre I 1915 I World War I (Western Front)

Attempting to take the offensive southeast of Verdun in the Woevre, French forces attacked the northern face of the German salient around St Mihiel. Although the French secured part of the heights at Les Éparges, their offensive was eventually checked with heavy losses. German attacks the following year made **Verdun** the focus of one of history's bloodiest battles of attrition (6–15 April 1915).

Wogastisburg I 631 I Frankish Imperial Wars

The Frank Samo united the Slavs against the Avars (defeated at **Constantinople** 626) to secure an area in Moravia, Slovakia, Lower Austria and Carinthia, and become King. Threatened by growing Slavic power, Dagobert I of the Franks sent a large force, supported by Austrasians. They were badly beaten at Wogastisburg (probably in Bohemia), but Samo's "empire" collapsed when he died in 658.

Wohlenschwyl I 1653 I Swiss Peasant War

Faced by a rural rising, 10,000 Swiss under Conrad Werdmüller of Zurich marched against the canton of Aargau, where they were attacked at Wohlenschwyl, near Mellingen, by a massive but poorly armed peasant force under Nicolas Leuenberger and Christian Schybi. The peasants withdrew after an inconclusive battle and within days had been beaten at **Gisikon** and **Herzogenbuchsee** (3 June 1653).

Wojnicz I 1655 I 1st Northern War

Charles X of Sweden beat John II Casimir at **Opoczno** (6 September), then besieged Cracow before moving east against Polish commanders Stanislas Lanckoronski and Aleksander Koniecpolski at Wojnicz. Although outnumbered, Charles secured a decisive victory and **Cracow** then fell. The Swedes were soon checked at **Jasna Gora** and the Poles were able to regroup (23 September 1655).

Wolchefit Pass I 1941 I World War II (Northern Africa)

Despite Italian surrender at **Amba Alagi** (19 May), remaining troops held out in central Ethiopia, where Allied forces under General Charles Fowkes converged north of Lake Tana. Some of the heaviest fighting was at Wolchefit Pass, on the road south from Adowa. An elite force of over 3,000 Italian and African troops eventually surrendered, opening the road to **Gondar** (27 September 1941).

Wolfenbüttel I 1641 I Thirty Years War (Franco-Habsburg War)

Karl Gustav Wrangel took command of the Swedish army following the death of Johann Banér and besieged Wolfenbüttel, just south of Brunswick, supported by Count Johann von Königsmarck and Jean-Baptiste Guébriant. Fierce fighting saw Wrangel drive off the approaching Imperials under Archduke Leopold William and Ottavio Piccolomini, but he was soon superseded (29 June 1641).

Wolf Mountain I 1877 I Sioux Indian Wars

In a final campaign against the Sioux following **Little Big Horn** (June 1876), General Nelson Miles took 500 men and two light guns against Crazy Horse's village on Wolf Mountain, near the Tongue River, just inside the Montana border. The Sioux were beaten and Crazy Horse surrendered just before a final action at **Muddy Creek** in May. He was shot "trying to escape" (7 January 1877).

Wolgast I 1628 I Thirty Years War (Saxon-Danish War)

Christian IV of Denmark was encouraged by Imperial failure at **Stralsund** (5 August) and took 12,000 men to Pomerania to seize the city of Wolgast in preparation for invading Mecklenberg. But Imperial commander Albrecht von Wallenstein routed the Danes near Wolgast and drove them back to their ships. Christian sued for peace and Denmark withdrew from the war (2 September 1628).

Wonju I 1950 I Korean War

As North Korean forces stormed across the border, they were delayed in the central peninsula at **Chunchon**, then fought their way south towards Wonju against determined resistance by the South Korean Sixth Division. The North Koreans finally reached Wonju and took it after heavy fighting, but General Chon U was relieved of command for falling behind the invasion schedule (2–5 July 1950).

Wood Lake I 1862 I Sioux Indian Wars

Colonel Henry Hastings Sibley relieved **Fort Ridgely**, Minnesota (22 August) and took 1,600 volunteers northwest against Santee Sioux under Little Crow. The Indians ambushed Sibley's scouts south of the Yellow Medicine, then attacked Sibley at nearby Wood Lake, where they suffered a decisive defeat and sued for peace. Thirty-nine were later hanged, but Little Crow escaped (23 September 1862).

Woodsonville I 1861 I American Civil War (Western Theatre)

See **Rowlett's Station**

Woodstock Races I 1864 I American Civil War (Eastern Theatre)

See **Tom's Brook**

Worcester I 1642 I British Civil Wars

See **Powick Bridge**

Worcester I 1651 I British Civil Wars

Pursued into England after Royalist defeats at **Dunbar** (September 1650) and **Inverkeithing**

(20 July), Charles II and General David Leslie reached the Severn, where they were invested at Worcester by Oliver Cromwell's New Model Army. Outnumbered almost two to one, the Cavaliers suffered a decisive defeat. Charles fled to France and the Civil Wars were effectively over (3 September 1651).

Worgaom I 1779 I 1st British-Maratha War
See **Wargaom**

Worringen I 1288 I German Ducal Wars
Climaxing a five-year war over the Duchy of Limburg, east of the Meuse, Duke John of Brabant decisively defeated Rainald of Guelders and his allies, the Archbishop of Cologne and Henry of Luxembourg, in battle at Worringen, a suburb of modern Cologne. Henry was killed in battle, after which Limburg was joined to Brabant, while Cologne secured self-government (5 June 1288).

Wörth I 1793 I French Revolutionary Wars (1st Coalition)
See **Froeschwiller**

Wörth I 1870 I Franco-Prussian War
Crown Prince Friedrich Wilhelm of Prussia invaded France through **Wissembourg** and over 100,000 men marched on Wörth, where Marshal Marie MacMahon held the village of Froeschwiller. Hard fighting saw the Prussians suffer greater casualties, but MacMahon lost a third of his army and fled towards **Metz**. France suffered another defeat the same day northwest at **Spicheren** (6 August 1870).

Wounded Knee Creek I 1890 I Sioux Indian Wars
Attempting to suppress the messianic Ghost Dance movement, Colonel James Forsyth attacked Indians at Wounded Knee Creek, north of Pine Ridge, South Dakota. In a one-sided disaster, about 150 Indians were killed, including Chief Big Foot and many women and children. Forsyth lost about 30 killed, many to "friendly fire," in this last action of the Indian Wars (28 December 1890).

Wrotham Heath I 1554 I Wyatt's Rebellion
With Queen Mary of England planning to marry Catholic Philip II of Spain, rebels in Kent under Sir Henry Isley set out to support insurrection by Sir Thomas Wyatt. Near Wrotham, they were met and routed by Henry Lord Abergavenny, with the survivors hunted down at nearby Hartley Wood. Isley escaped but was among about 100 rebels executed after the rebellion ended at **Temple Bar** (28 January 1554).

Wuchang I 1852–1853 I Taiping Rebellion
Taiping forces repulsed at **Changsha** soon captured Hanyang and Hankou, then besieged strategic Wuchang across the Yangzi, supported in the field by General Xiang Rong. Joined by Heavenly King Hong Xiuquan, the Taiping stormed the city, followed by a terrible massacre. But facing a costly siege, they advanced downriver towards **Anqing** (23 December 1852–12 January 1853).

Wuchang (1st) I 1854 I Taiping Rebellion
Leading a fresh Taiping offensive west from **Nanjing**, Huang Zaixing occupied Hanyang and Hanchow, then again besieged strategic Wuchang, defended by Governor Chonglun (later by Qinglin). Although Wuchang fell to Taiping General Weijun after very heavy fighting, it was soon retaken. Qinglin escaped, but he was subsequently executed for abandoning the city (16 February–26 June 1854).

Wuchang (2nd) I 1854 I Taiping Rebellion
After checking the Taiping Western Expedition in Hubeh, Zeng Guofan's Xiang Army advanced down the Yangzi to retake Wuchang, held by a reduced Taiping garrison under Shi Fengkui. In a massive assault by land and river, Zeng destroyed the Taiping fleet and took the city by storm for a great Imperial victory. The Taiping then continued east towards **Jiujiang** (12–14 October 1854).

Wuchang ∎ 1855 ∎ Taiping Rebellion

While Taiping commander Shi Dakai delayed Imperial commander Zeng Guofan at **Jiujiang**, he sent Generals Qin Rigang and Chen Yucheng up the Yangzi to attack Wuchang, where they were later joined by reinforcements under Weijun. The city was taken for the last time by a furious Taiping assault and held out against a massive siege a year later (23 February–3 April 1855).

Wuchang ∎ 1856 ∎ Taiping Rebellion

Imperial Generals Luo Zenan and Hu Linyi led a renewed offensive against the Taiping on the Yangzi, where they besieged Wuchang, held by Weijun and Shi Fengkui. Luo was killed repulsing a Taiping sortie (6 April) and a Taiping relief force under Gu Longxian was driven off. Wuchang was finally relieved when Shi Dakai arrived with 30,000 Taiping (3 January–August 1856).

Wuchang ∎ 1911 ∎ 1st Chinese Revolution

Following a premature revolutionary bomb explosion in Wuchang, an Imperial crackdown on Republicans triggered an army rising. Governor Ruizheng of Hubei and General Zhang Biao fled and many Manchu troops died before the city fell to rebels. While nearby **Hankou** and **Hanyang** were taken and then lost, Wuchang held out until the Chinese Republic was born (9–11 October 1911).

Wuchang ∎ 1926 ∎ 1st Chinese Revolutionary Civil War

When Nationalist forces converged on Wuchang through **Tingsiqiao** and **Hesheng**, the city held off three bloody assaults by General Chiang Kai-shek, then settled down to a siege. Northern General Wu Beifu withdrew when the twin cities of Hanyang and Hankou defected, but Liu Xing held out until finally forced to surrender (7 September–10 October 1926).

Wuhan ∎ 1938 ∎ Sino-Japanese War

With **Nanjing** captured in late 1937, Japanese forces advanced west against the great Yangzi conurbation of Wuhan. A sprawling five-month battle of attrition was fought as cities and fortresses to the north and east fell to the Central China Expeditionary Army. Chiang Kai-shek finally had to withdraw and early the following year the Japanese turned south against **Nanchang** (June–25 October 1938).

Wu-hsueh ∎ 1853 ∎ Taiping Rebellion
   See **Wuxue**

Wurschen ∎ 1813 ∎ Napoleonic Wars (War of Liberation)
   See **Bautzen**

Würzburg ∎ 1796 ∎ French Revolutionary Wars (1st Coalition)

Following defeat at **Amberg**, French General Jean-Baptiste Jourdan withdrew towards the Rhine. At Würzburg he was heavily defeated by the combined Austrian forces of Archduke Charles and Generals Alexander Wartensleben and Paul Kray. After a rearguard action at **Bleichfeld**, Jourdan sought an armistice and the Austrians marched northwest towards **Aschaffenburg** (3 September 1796).

Würzburg ∎ 1866 ∎ Seven Weeks War

Ending the war against Austria's southern German allies, General Erwin von Manteuffel advanced through **Tauberbischofsheim** and **Werbach** against Würzburg, held by a small garrison after Prince Karl of Bavaria was defeated at **Gerchsheim** and withdrew across the Main. Würzburg surrendered after a brief bombardment and Bavaria signed an armistice with Prussia (28 July 1866).

Wuxue ∎ 1853 ∎ Taiping Rebellion

Following the bloody capture of **Wuchang**, Taiping forces under Shi Dakai advanced down the Yangzi and near Wuxue (Wu-hsueh) surprised and destroyed an Imperial garrison of 3,000 under General Enchang, who killed himself in shame. Imperial Comissioner Lu Jianying, approaching with reinforcements, disgracefully turned and fled through **Anqing** to **Nanjing** (15 February 1853).

Wynberg I 1795 I French Revolutionary Wars (1st Coalition)
See **Cape Colony**

Wynendael I 1708 I War of the Spanish Succession
French commanders Louis Duke de Vendôme and James Duke of Berwick were unable to relieve besieged **Lille** and sent General Louis du Fosse Comte de la Motte against a massive convoy travelling south from Ostend. At Wynendael, near Torhout, Motte's superior force was routed by the escort under Generals John Webb and Cornelius Woudernberg. Lille soon fell (28 September 1708).

Wyoming Massacre I 1778 I War of the American Revolution
Major John Butler attacked rebel militia in Wyoming, marching south from Niagara to the Susquehanna with a large force of Tory militia and Iroquois Indians. Near Forty Fort, southwest of Scranton, Pennsylvania, the patriots under Colonel Zebulan Butler were destroyed, followed by slaughter of fugitives and prisoners and terrible destruction in the Wyoming Valley (3 July 1778).

X

Xaquixaguana ▌ **1548** ▌ **Spanish Civil War in Peru**

After seizing Peru at **Anaquito** (January 1546) and defeating a Royalist counter-offensive at **Huarina** (October 1547), Gonzalo Pizarro faced a fresh Royalist army under Viceroy Pedro de la Gasca. In a battle with few casualties at Xaquixaguana, near Cuzco, Pizarro was beaten. He was executed next day and Royal authority was restored, but anti-Royalists won again in 1554 at **Chuquinga** (8 April 1548).

Xeres ▌ **711** ▌ **Muslim Conquest of Spain**
See **Guadalete**

Xerigordon ▌ **1096** ▌ **1st Crusade**

Preceding the First Crusade, pilgrims of the so-called "People's Crusade" reached **Civetot** on the Asian side of the Bosphorus, where Germans under Rainald of Breis advanced and captured the castle of Xerigordon, east of Nicaea. Besieged by a large Turkish army, they were forced by terrible thirst to surrender after eight days. Most were killed or enslaved (September–October 1096).

Xiamen ▌ **1841** ▌ **1st Opium War**

New Superintendent Sir Henry Pottinger renewed war following the truce at Guangzhou by sailing northeast from Hong Kong with troops under General Sir Hugh Gough and a strong fleet under Admiral Sir William Parker. Approaching Xiamen (Amoy) off Fujian, Gough landed to take the island by storm after a naval bombard-

ment. Pottinger then sailed north against **Dinghai** (25–27 August 1841).

Xi'an ▌ **1949** ▌ **3rd Chinese Revolutionary Civil War**

During the Communist offensive into northwest China, General Peng Dehuai seized Xi'an (Sian) from General Hu Zongnan, then faced attack by Hu and Muslim commander Ma Pufang. Sent from **Taiyuan**, General Nie Rongzhen joined Peng and together they utterly defeated Ma, west of Xi'an. The Communists then pursued him further west to seize Lanzhou and Xining (20 May 1949).

Xiang ▌ **1934** ▌ **2nd Chinese Revolutionary Civil War**

Soon after Chinese Communists under Zhou Enlai and Mao Zedong began the Long March from Jiangxi, they were attacked crossing the Xiang (Hsiang) River by Nationalist commander He Jian. The most disastrous defeat of the campaign cost the Red Army perhaps 30,000 men, but the march continued west and north through victory at **Loushan** (25 November–3 December 1934).

Xiangfan ▌ **1268–1273** ▌ **Mongol Wars of Kubilai Khan**
See **Xiangyang**

Xiangji ▌ **757** ▌ **An Lushan Rebellion**

When An Lushan captured **Luoyang** and **Chang'an**, China's Imperial army regrouped for a counter-offensive under Guo Ziyi. Just south of Chang'an at Xiangji, Guo was initially repulsed before his Uighar cavalry under Pugu Huai'en helped win a decisive victory. Chang'an fell next day, followed by Luoyang (3 December). An Qingxu (son of An Lushan) withdrew to **Xiangzhou** (13 November 757).

Xiangyang ▮ 1206–1207 ▮ Jin-Song Wars

When Song forces tried to recover land in northern China, a massive Jin (Chin) army advanced to besiege Xiangyang (Hsiang-yang) on the Han in Hubei. Song commander Zhao Chun led a brilliant defence, with night raids destroying Jin boats and siege machines. After three months the Jin withdrew with heavy losses. The Jin also besieged **De'an** to the southeast (December 1206–March 1207).

Xiangyang ▮ 1268–1273 ▮ Mongol Wars of Kubilai Khan

In a massive assault on Song southern China, Mongol Kubilai Khan sent forces to besiege the powerful fortress town of Xiangyang on the Han and nearby Fancheng, held by General Lu Wenhuan. During a five-year blockade—which saw the use of trebuchets— Mongol commanders and local ally Liu Zheng repulsed relief attempts by land and river. The fall of Xiangyang was a decisive blow to the Song.

Xiangzhou ▮ 758 ▮ An Lushan Rebellion

With victory at **Xiangji** (November 757), Tang forces retook Chang'an and Luoyang, then a claimed 200,000 men under Yu Chao'en besieged An Qingxu (son of An Lushan) at Ziangzhou (modern Anyang). A relief force under Shi Siming finally arrived and inflicted a humiliating defeat on the badly led Imperial army. Shi Siming then overthrew An Qingxu and later retook **Luoyang** (7 April 758).

Xianyang ▮ 207 BC ▮ Fall of the Qin Dynasty

While rebel warlord Xiang Yu destroyed the main Qin (Ch'in) army at **Julu**, his ally Liu Bang marched on the capital at Xianyang (Hsienyang) near modern Xi'an in Shaanxi. After Qin

forces were defeated at nearby Lantian, Qin ruler Ziying surrendered himself and the city to Liu Bang. Early next year Xiang Yu looted and burned Xianyang and murdered Ziying, ending the short-lived Qin Dynasty.

Xiao ▮ 627 BC ▮ Wars of China's Spring and Autumn Era

See **Yao**

Xiaoling ▮ 1631 ▮ Manchu Conquest of China

When Manchu leader Abahai (Hong Taiji) besieged **Dalinghe**, a Ming relief army approached and part of the force under Wu Xiang and Sun Chengzong was beaten by Abahai at the Xiaoling, near Jinzhou. Heavily outnumbered, Abahai later attacked the main force of 40,000, also at the Xiaoling. Ming General Zhang Chun was beaten and captured and later changed sides (11 & 22 October 1631).

Xing-an ▮ 1900 ▮ Russo-Chinese War

In the aftermath of the Boxer Rebellion, Russian forces advanced along the Chinese Eastern Railway into Manchuria, where General Orlov captured **Ongon** then attacked a large Chinese force entrenched further east at Xing-an. Aided by Cossacks under Colonel Alexander Bulatovich, Orlov forced the Chinese to withdraw, but he was too late to support the capture of **Qiqihar** (24 August 1900).

Xinmintun ▮ 1925 ▮ Guo Songling's Revolt

Manchurian warlord Zhang Zuolin secured northern China at **Shanhaiguan** (October 1924), then faced rebellion by General Guo Songling, who invaded Manchuria and reached Xinmintun, west of Mukden (Shenyang). After initial success, cavalry threatened Guo's rear and his officers surrendered (just as allies in China won at **Tienstin**). Guo was executed and the revolt ended (23 December 1925).

Xoconochco ▮ 1498–1500 ▮ Aztec Wars of Conquest

See **Soconusco**

Xuan Loc | 1975 | Vietnam War

North Vietnamese General Van Tien Dung captured **Ban Me Thuot**, in the central highlands, then turned south towards Saigon. However, he found his way blocked by stubborn South Vietnamese resistance on the last defensive position at Xuan Loc, just 35 miles northeast of the capital. Dung lost perhaps 5,000 killed before finally breaking through to advance on **Saigon** (9–22 April 1975).

Xuge | 707 bc | Wars of China's Spring and Autumn Era

With the Eastern Zhou Dynasty threatened by feudal lords, King Huan led an army against the powerful noble Zheng Zhuang Gong, who had been ousted as Royal Chief Minister. In battle at Xuge (Hsü-ko), the King was wounded by an arrow and the Royal army was embarrassingly defeated. The Zhou became only nominal rulers of China and Zheng assumed leadership among the feudal states.

Xuyi | 451 | Wars of the Six Dynasties

Emperor Taiwu of Wei crushed a Song army at **Huatai**, near the Yellow River, then continued his southern offensive and reached the Yangzi near Jiankang, before withdrawing to besiege Xuyi (Hsu-I) on the Huai to secure food for his army. Song commander Zangzhi led a courageous defence for weeks and, on reports of a Song fleet approaching upriver, Taiwu returned north, ravaging the countryside.

Xuzhou | 1927 | 2nd Chinese Revolutionary Civil War

After securing the lower Yangzi at **Longtan**, east of Nanjing, Nationalist forces consolidated central China and General He Yingqin led a fresh offensive against Northern warlord Sun Zhuanfang at Xuzhou (Hsuchow) in northern Jiangsu. Sun launched a massive counter-offensive, though he was finally driven off and withdrew northeast into Shandong (14–16 December 1927).

Xuzhou | 1937–1938 | Sino-Japanese War

Following the Rape of **Nanjing**, Japanese forces advanced northwest against the strategic railway city of Xuzhou (Hsuchow), while other units marched south through Jinan. After months of heavy fighting north and east of the city, including the Japanese defeat at **Taierzhuang**, the Chinese had to avoid further losses and evacuated Xuzhou (23 December 1937–19 May 1938).

Xuzhou | 1948–1949 | 3rd Chinese Revolutionary Civil War

See **Huaihai**

Y

Yaguachi ▌ 1821 ▌ Ecuadorian War of Independence

After taking command of Ecuador's Patriot army at Guayaquil, General Antonio José de Sucre marched out against approaching Spanish commander Melchior Aymerich. To the northeast at Yaguachi, General José Mires destroyed a Royalist column, capturing Colonel Francisco González to avenge previous defeat at Huachi. Aymerich was defeated a month later at **Huachi** (19 August 1821).

Yahni ▌ 1877 ▌ Russo-Turkish Wars

General Mikhail Loris-Melikov supported the Russian siege of **Kars** in the Caucasus by capturing Turkish positions on nearby hills known as the Great and Little Yahni. Heavy Russian casualties made him pause and Ahmed Mukhtar Pasha led a brilliant counter-attack, driving the Russians off. However, the Turkish commander was routed ten days later at **Aladja Dagh** (2–4 October 1877).

Yai-shan ▌ 1279 ▌ Mongol Wars of Kubilai Khan
See **Yashan**

Yalu–Naval ▌ 1894 ▌ Sino-Japanese War

Marching north through Korea after driving the Chinese out of **Pyongyang**, Japanese Marshal Aritomo Yamagata soon reached the Yalu, strongly defended by General Song Qing. In a broad assault at Hushan, Jiuliancheng and Dandong, Yamagata stormed across the river, capturing massive supplies of guns and munitions, then advanced into Manchuria towards **Caohekou** (24–25 October 1894).

Yalu ▌ 1904 ▌ Russo-Japanese War

Japan's First Army (General Tamemoto Kuroki) marched north through Korea after landing at **Chemulpo** (9 February) and approached the vital Yalu crossing, weakly defended by advance Russian units under General Mikhail Ivanovich Zasulich. A mismanaged disaster near Uiju saw Zasulich sacrificed with over 2,000 casualties. The Japanese then crossed into Manchuria (25 April 1 May 1904).

Yalu (naval) ▌ 1894 ▌ Sino-Japanese War
See **Haiyang**

Yamazaki ▌ 672 ▌ Jinshin War

When Japanese Emperor Tenji died, a war of succession broke out between his son and heir Prince Otomo (later Emperor Kobun) and his brother Prince Oama, who raised forces against his nephew and advanced on the capital Otsu. South of Otsu at Yamazaki, Otomo was defeated and committed suicide. Oama took the throne as Emperor Temmu and moved his capital to Asuka.

Yamazaki ▌ 1582 ▌ Japan's Era of the Warring States

With his army besieging **Takamatsu**, Oda Nobunaga in Kyoto was attacked and then forced to kill himself by his own General, Akechi Mitsuhide. Securing Takamatsu, Loyalist commander Toyotomi Hideyoshi pursued the traitor to Yamazaki, southeast of Kyoto, where he and his allies were routed. Mitsuhide was later killed while fleeing and Hideyoshi became effective ruler (2 July 1582).

Yamen I 1279 I Mongol Wars of Kubilai Khan
    See **Yashan**

Yanacocha I 1835 I Bolivian-Peruvian War
    When Peruvian President Luis José de Obregoso was overthrown, the acquisitive President Andrés Santa Cruz of Bolivia marched into Peru, supposedly to restore Obregoso, and met former President Agustín Gamarra at Yanacocha, southeast of Cuzco near Urcos. Gamarra suffered a decisive defeat and Santa Cruz marched north for further victory near Arequipa at **Socabaya** (11 August 1835).

Yan'an I 1947 I 3rd Chinese Revolutionary Civil War
    A co-ordinated Nationalist offensive into Shaanxi saw two armies under General Hu Zongnan converge on the Communist capital at Yan'an, where outnumbered commander Peng Dehuai fought a defensive action just south of the city. Mao Zedong's Central Committee withdrew and the Nationalists took Yan'an and perhaps 10,000 prisoners. They in turn withdrew after **Yichuan** (15–19 March 1947).

Yanbu (1st) I 1916 I World War I (Middle East)
    When Sharif Hussein, Emir of Mecca, proclaimed the Arab Revolt against Turkey in the **Hejaz**, his son Abdullah took a large force against Yanbu 'al Bahr. The Red Sea port surrendered and became an important supply base for the Arab Revolt. When the revolt later began to stall, the successful defence of Yanbu helped rekindle support for the cause (27 July 1916).

Yanbu (2nd) I 1916 I World War I (Middle East)
    While Arab forces besieged **Medina**, further west Prince Feisal tried to hold the Red Sea port of Yanbu. Attacked by Turks from Medina, the Arabs were defeated and fell back into the town. British warships offshore under Captain William Boyle forced the Turks to withdraw, which enhanced the prestige of the Arab Revolt and encouraged the advance north on **Wejh** (8–16 December 1916).

Yancun I 1900 I Boxer Rebellion
    With the legations in **Beijing** besieged by antiforeign Boxers, a 20,000-strong relief force left **Tianjin** and advanced through **Beicang** to Yangcun (Yangts'un—modern Wuqing), where General Song Qing tried to defend the Bei He. In the last heavy fighting before the Allies reached Beijing, over 100 British, French, Russian and American troops were killed, many by "friendly fire" (6 August 1900).

Yangts'un I 1900 I Boxer Rebellion
    See **Yancun**

Yangzhou I 1645 I Manchu Conquest of China
    When the Manchu captured **Beijing**, Ming Prince Fu (Zhu Yousong) set up court in Nanjing with the Imperial name Hongguang. Manchu Prince Dodo, fresh from **Tongguan**, then attacked Yangzhou, north of Nanjing, where General Shi Kefa was defeated and killed. An exemplary massacre followed and Prince Fu fled. In 1659 the Ming were routed trying to retake **Nanjing** (13–20 May 1645).

Yangzi Incident I 1949 I 3rd Chinese Revolutionary Civil War
    When the British frigate *Amethyst* entered the Yangzi to evacuate embassy staff at **Nanjing**, she was shelled by Communist artillery and driven ashore with 17 killed, including Captain Bernard Skinner. After months of negotiation, and costly losses in a relief attempt, naval attaché Commander John Kerans eluded gunfire and *Amethyst* successfully escaped downstream (20 April–31 July 1949).

Yangzi Pass I 1904 I Russo-Japanese War
    After General Feodor Keller failed to halt General Tamemoto Kuroki's First Army at the

Motien Pass, near the Lan River north of **Port Arthur** (modern Lüshun) in Manchuria, he tried to defend the nearby Yangzi (Yang-Tzu) Pass, west of the Lan. When Keller was killed by shrapnel, his successor, General Kashtalinksi, abandoned Haichang and withdrew to **Liaoyang** (31 July 1904).

Yanling I 575 BC I Wars of China's Spring and Autumn Era

Following a period of truce on the Yellow River, the state of Zheng transferred its allegiance from Jin in the north to Chu in the south and Duke Li of Jin sent a large army under Luan Shu and Shi Xie (victor in 589 at **An**). At Yanling in Zheng, King Gong of Chu and Marshal Zifan suffered a decisive defeat and Zifan killed himself. Duke Li was soon overthrown in a coup which weakened Jin.

Yannina I 1912–1913 I 1st Balkan War
See **Jannina**

Yanshi I 618 I Rise of the Tang Dynasty

During power struggles within the ailing Sui Empire, Li Mi of Henan took a large force against Luoyang, held by Sui general Wang Shichong, who led a powerful sortie against Li's camp. In battle at Yanshi, Li was decisively defeated and fled west to Chang'an to submit to Li Yuan's newly proclaimed Tang Dynasty. In 621 Wang himself surrendered to a Tang army at **Luoyang** (5–6 October 618).

Yantra I 1810 I Russo-Turkish Wars
See **Batin**

Yanzi I 1813 I Napoleonic Wars (Peninsular Campaign)

During the weeklong "Battles of the Pyrenees," French General Honoré Reille's retreat towards France (after the defeat at **Sorauren**) was blocked in the valley at Yanzi by Spanish troops led by General Francisco Longa. The French eventually broke through and continued their withdrawal across the Bidassoa, though at the cost of more than 300 casualties (1 August 1813).

Yao I 627 BC I Wars of China's Spring and Autumn Era

The powerful Chinese states of Jin (Chin) and Qin (Ch'in) had been allies at **Chengpu** (632), but following the death of Duke Wen of Jin (628), Duke Mu of Qin determined to attack the disputed state of Zheng. New Duke Xiang of Jin took his army and met the invaders at the Yao (sometimes Xiao) Gorge, south of the Yellow River. The Qin suffered a disastrous defeat with three generals captured.

Yarmuk I 634 I Muslim Conquest of Syria

Muslim forces under General Khalid ibn al-Walid advanced from victory at **Ajnadin** (30 July) and drove the Byzantine army back to the Yarmuk River, in northeastern Jordan, and inflicted a defeat at Yaqusa. The Byzantines withdrew, effectively opening the door to the invasion of Syria, where Khalid won early next year at **Fihl** and **Marj as-Suffar** as he advanced on Damascus (September 634).

Yarmuk I 636 I Muslim Conquest of Syria

After Muslims captured **Damascus**, Emperor Heraclius sent a large army under Theodorus Trithurius, aided by Armenian Prince Vahan. Muslim General Khalid ibn al-Walid abandoned Damascus and withdrew down the Jordan to the Yarmuk, where Theodorus was defeated and killed. Khalid then re-occupied Damascus, ending a millennium of Greco-Roman Levant (20 August 636).

Yashan I 1279 I Mongol Wars of Kubilai Khan

After Mongol Kubilai Khan attacked southern China and captured the Song capital **Hangzhou** (1276), Imperial Regent Zhang Shijie fled and finally took refuge on Yashan Island near Guangzhou with the infant Emperor Bing. Defeated by Mongol ships near Macao, Admiral Lu Xiufu leapt into the sea to drown with the child. Kubilai had already declared himself Emperor (19 March 1279).

Yashima I 1185 I Gempei War

Defeated at **Ichinotani** (March 1184), the Taira fled to their stronghold at Yashima on Shikoku in Japan's Inland Sea, while Minamoto Yoshitsune took time to rebuild his army with troops from his brother Yoritomo in Kamakura. Yoshitsune then launched a powerful attack on the island fortress and Taira Tomomori withdrew west with the boy-Emperor Antoku to **Dannoura** (23 March 1185).

Yataití-Corá I 1866 I War of the Triple Alliance

Six weeks after victory at **Tuyutí**, the Argentine, Brazilian and Uruguayan allies under General Bartolomé Mitre came under attack by Paraguayan forces just to the northeast at Yataití-Corá, between the Paraguay and the upper Parana. After a drawn action, with costly losses on both sides, the Paraguayans withdrew under cover of darkness. They won a week later at **Boquerón** (11 July 1866).

Yatay I 1865 I War of the Triple Alliance

Early in Paraguay's offensive against its neighbours, Dictator Francisco Solano López sent his vanguard under Major Pedro Duarte to the Uruguay, where he was met on the Argentine side at Yatay by a small allied force under General Venancio Flores. Duarte was defeated and captured with 2,000 casualties and the Paraguayans withdrew across the river to **Uruguayana** (17 August 1865).

Yaunis Khan I 1516 I Ottoman-Mamluk War

With Mamluk Sultan Kansu al-Gauri killed in northern Syria at **Marj-Dabik** (24 August), his nephew Touman Beg marched to meet the invasion by Sultan Selim I. Near Gaza at Yaunis Khan (now Khan Yunis), Ottoman Vizier Hadim Sinan destroyed the Mamluks with artillery and seized Gaza, killing the garrison. Meanwhile, Touman withdrew and met the invaders at **Ridanieh** (28 October 1516).

Ybate I 1868 I War of the Triple Alliance

See **Ita Ybate**

Ybibobo I 1934 I Chaco War

As the Paraguayan army advanced north into the Chaco Boreal through victory at **Yrendagüe**, a Paraguayan detachment under Colonel Nicolás Delgado reached the Parapití and surrounded the outnumbered Bolivians at Ybibobo. Delgado won, capturing 2,000 prisoners and massive supplies, but the Paraguayan advance was checked in the following April at **Boyuibé** (27–30 December 1934).

Ye I 528 I Wei Dynastic Wars

Amid rivalry to control the Wei Court at Luoyang, Erzhu Rong appointed a puppet Emperor then turned east with his General Hou Jing against the rebel Ge Rong. Outside Ye, near modern Anyang, Ge Rong's much larger army was defeated and he was captured and executed. Within two years Erzhu Rong was killed in a palace coup and in 532 his successor Erzhu Zhao was defeated near Ye at **Hanling**.

Yecla I 1813 I Napoleonic Wars (Peninsular Campaign)

Opening a new French offensive in Valencia by Marshal Louis Suchet, General Jean-Isidore Harispe attacked an isolated Spanish force under General Francisco Elio at Yecla, inland from Alicante. Elio's Murcian army was routed and fled south towards Jumilla, while Suchet's main force continued east to another victory next day at **Biar** (11 April 1813).

Yelizavetpol I 1826 I Russo-Persian Wars

After Persian forces invaded Russia and lost at the **Shamkhor**, Prince Abbas Mirza raised his siege of **Shusha** and marched north towards Yelizavetpol (later Kirovabad and Gandzha) against Russian Generals Ivan Paskevich and Valerian Gregorevich Madatov. Russian artillery destroyed the Persian cavalry, but war continued until the fall of **Erivan** and Tehran (13 September 1826).

Yellow Bayou I 1864 I American Civil War (Trans-Mississippi)

At the end of his Red River Campaign in Louisiana, repulsed at **Mansfield** and **Pleasant**

Hill, Union commander Nathaniel P. Banks won at **Mansura**, then two days later sent General Joseph A. Mower against General Richard Taylor's Confederates further east at Yellow Bayou, near Simmesport. Both sides withdrew after indecisive action and Banks escaped over the Atchafayala (18 May 1864).

Yellow Creek I 1774 I Cresap's War

Daniel Greathouse campaigned against Indians on the Ohio, where he attacked the settlement at Yellow Creek, north of modern Weirton, and killed a number of people, including the wife of leading Shawnee warrior James Logan. The massacre triggered war against militia under Michael Cresap (which became Lord Dunmore's War) eventually decided in October at **Point Pleasant** (30 April 1774).

Yellow Ford I 1598 I Tyrone Rebellion
See **Blackwater**

Yellow River I 1227 I Conquests of Genghis Khan

The last campaign of the Mongol Genghis Khan saw him march against the Tangut of Xi Xia in northwest China, where he inflicted a decisive defeat at the frozen Yellow River (Helanshan Mountain). He later besieged the Tangut capital at Ningxia, but died before it fell. In accordance with Khan's deathbed wish, when Tangut Emperor Li Xian surrendered, he was put to death. Ningxia was destroyed.

Yellow Sea I 1592 I Japanese Invasion of Korea
See **Hansan**

Yellow Sea I 1894 I Sino-Japanese War
See **Haiyang**

Yellow Sea I 1904 I Russo-Japanese War

With besieged **Port Arthur** (modern Lüshun) exposed to Japanese artillery fire, Russian Admiral Vilgelm Vitgeft was ordered to Vladivostok and sailed into the Yellow Sea with six battleships, three cruisers and eight destroyers. In a bloody fleet action with Admiral Heihachiro

Togo, Vitgeft was killed. Most of the Russian ships fled back to Port Arthur and were later sunk (10–11 August 1904).

Yellow Tavern I 1864 I American Civil War (Eastern Theatre)

While the Union and Confederate armies fought a massive action at **Spotsylvania Court House**, Union General Philip Sheridan led cavalry deep into Confederate Virginia and was blocked by General James "Jeb" Stuart just north of Richmond at Yellow Tavern. Stuart was defeated and mortally wounded and Sheridan continued south to join the Union army on the James (11 May 1864).

Yemama I 633 I Muslim Civil Wars
See **Akraba**

Yemoji I 1892 I British Conquest of Nigeria

Governor Gilbert Carter resolved to extend British rule in Nigeria and sent Colonel Francis Scott of the Gold Coast Constabulary north from Ipe. Falling back through Pobo and Majoda, Ijebu warriors tried to defend a pass on the Yemoji River near Imagbon. Heavy fighting saw Scott's Hausas distinguish themselves and the nearby capital Ijebu Ude surrendered next day (19 May 1892).

Yenan I 1947 I 3rd Chinese Revolutionary Civil War
See **Yan'an**

Yenangyaung I 1942 I World War II (Burma-India)

Withdrawing north from the fall of **Prome** (1 April), British under General Bruce Scott tried to hold Yenangyaung and the nearby Magwe oilfields, boldly supported to the north by Chinese General Sun Liren. Fighting in extreme heat, the Allies secured some local success against General Shozo Sakurai before they finally had to withdraw with heavy losses in men and equipment (10–19 April 1942).

**Yenbo ▍ 1916 ▍ World War I
(Middle East)**
See **Yanbu**

Yenikale ▍ 1855 ▍ Crimean War
See **Kerch**

**Yenikale Strait ▍ 1790 ▍ Catherine the
Great's 2nd Turkish War**
After attacking Turkish harbours on the Black
Sea, Admiral Fedor Ushakov's 16 ships met 18
Turkish ships under Kapudan Pasha Hussein in
the Strait of Yenikale, south of Kerch, attempting to land forces in the Crimea. The resulting
two-hour action was fierce but indecisive and the
damaged Turks withdrew. The rival fleets met
again in late August west of the Crimea at
Tendra (8 July 1790).

Yenisehir ▍ 1481 ▍ Ottoman Civil Wars
Sultan Bayazid II faced rebellion by his
brother Cem, who captured Bursa in northern
Anatolia and declared himself Sultan (28 May).
However, 30 miles to the east at Yenisehir, Cem
was overwhelmed by Imperial janissaries under
Ahmad Gedik Pasha. The defeated rebel fled to
Egypt and later to the Christians in Europe, who
used him as a pawn in international politics (20
June 1481).

Yenitsá ▍ 1912 ▍ 1st Balkan War
See **Jannitsa**

**Yen-ling ▍ 575 BC ▍ Wars of China's
Spring and Autumn Era**
See **Yanling**

Yen-shih ▍ 618 ▍ Rise of the Tang Dynasty
See **Yanshi**

**Yerbas Buenas ▍ 1813 ▍ Chilean War
of Independence**
Following their repulse in central Chile at
Cancha Rayada (29 March), Patriots under
Juan de Dios Puga Córdova pursued guerrilla
leader Ildefonso Elorreaga into the hills of Yerbas Buenas, south of the Maule, where they
unexpectedly met the entire Royalist army of

Antonio Pareja. Puga Córdova suffered a terrible
defeat and his attempted withdrawal became a
disastrous pursuit (26 April 1813).

Yerua ▍ 1839 ▍ Argentine Civil Wars
In renewed resistance to Argentine Dictator
Juan Manuel de Rosas, Juan Galo Lavalle en-
tered the Uruguay River with French aid. At
Yerua, south of Concordia, he heavily defeated
Federalist General Pascual Echague, Governor
of Entre Rios. However, forces loyal to Rosas
soon won in the south at **Chascomús** and
Echague defeated Lavalle in July 1840 at **Sauce
Grande** (22 September 1839).

Yevpatoriya ▍ 1855 ▍ Crimean War
See **Eupatoria**

**Yichuan ▍ 1948 ▍ 3rd Chinese
Revolutionary Civil War**
Communist General Peng Dehuai led an offensive in Shaanxi, where he encircled Yichuan
then savaged the relief force of General Liu Kan.
Severe fighting saw Liu and perhaps 5,000 killed
and 18,000 captured, with 5,000 more killed
with the fall of Yichuan itself. As a result, on 22
April, Nationalist General Hu Zongnan had to
abandon nearby **Yan'an** (29 February–1 March
1948).

**Yiling ▍ 222 ▍ Wars of the Three
Kingdoms**
To avenge the execution of his sworn brother
Guan Yu after **Fancheng** (219), Liu Bei of Shu
led a large army against Sun Quan of Wu. An
extended campaign along the Yangzi around
Yiling (modern Yichang) saw Liu Bei and his
commander Huang Quan decisively defeated by
the brilliant young Lu Xun. Victory secured
Wu's control of Jingzhou and led to uneasy
peace between Wu and Shu.

Yingchuan ▍ 548–549 ▍ Wei Dynastic Wars
Taking advantage of rebellion by Hou Jing of
Eastern Wei, a Western Wei army under Wang
Sizheng advanced deep into enemy territory and
occupied the fortified town of Yingchuan on the
Wei, southeast of Luoyang. A large Eastern Wei

army under Gao Yue besieged the city and, after costly assaults, diverted the river to flood the area. Wang finally surrendered to Gao Cheng of Eastern Wei.

Yingkou I 1895 I Sino-Japanese War

Continuing Japan's offensive in southern Manchuria, General Motoharu Yamaji marched from **Taipingshan** against Yingkou, joined by General Taro Katsura advancing west from **Niuzhuang**. Crossing the frozen Liao towards nearby Tianzhuangtai for one of the largest battles of the campaign, Yamaji decisively defeated Chinese commander Song Qing to effectively end the war (9 March 1895).

Yongchon I 1950 I Korean War

North Korean forces launched a major assault on the north of the **Pusan Perimeter**, in southeast Korea, attempting to advance through Yongchon and threaten **Taegu**, under attack to the west. Intense fighting by South Korean troops, with American support, saw Yongchon change hands several times before the Communist offensive was finally repulsed with very heavy losses (5–13 September 1950).

York, England I 866–867 I Viking Wars in Britain

On a major offensive into Northumbria, a large Danish force from East Anglia under Ivar, Ubba and Halfdan—sons of the warrior Ragnar Lodbrok—captured the key city of York. A few months later, the local rulers, Aelle and Osbeorht, united to regain York, but both were killed in a terrible Saxon defeat. The city then became capital of Danish England (November 866–21 March 867).

York, England I 1069–1070 I Norman Conquest of Britain

Resisting the Norman conquest of northern England after **Hastings**, Northumbrian Earls Waltheof and Gospatrick and a large Danish force under Asbiorn attacked York, which fell after eight days with the 3,000-strong Norman garrison massacred. King William I later persuaded the Danes to withdraw, then retook the

undefended city and devastated the entire district.

York, England I 1644 I British Civil Wars

In the wake of Royalist defeat at **Selby** (11 April), William Cavendish Earl of Newcastle withdrew to York under siege by Ferdinando Lord Fairfax and Scottish forces under Alexander Leslie Earl of Leven. Royalist forces reached York (31 June), but after their defeat at nearby **Marston Moor**, Newcastle fled abroad and Sir Thomas Glenham surrendered the city (22 April–16 July 1644).

York, Maine I 1692 I King William's War

In a French counter-offensive against the British in Acadia (modern Nova Scotia), Governor Joseph Robineau de Villebon reoccupied Port Royal, then sent Canadians and Abnaki Indians against York, on the coast of Maine, northeast of Kittery. Attacking in heavy snow, they killed 48 colonists then withdrew with perhaps 70 prisoners. The next major offensive was against **Wells** (5 February 1692).

York, Ontario I 1813 I War of 1812

Captain Isaac Chauncey and 1,700 troops under General Zebulan Pike attacked the British naval base on Lake Ontario at York (modern Toronto) and overwhelmed General Sir Roger Sheaffe, who had to withdraw. The town was looted and destroyed, but the magazine exploded killing many Americans, including General Pike. The British soon retaliated at **Sackets Harbour** (27 April 1813).

York River, Virginia I 1644 I Powhatan Indian Wars

Hearing of civil war in England, Opechancanough of the Algonquin Confederacy renewed war against Colonial Virginia, where a coordinated attack on outlying settlements on the York River saw about 300 settlers killed. Governor Sir Wiliam Berkeley then led local militia and friendly Indians and crushed the confederacy. Opechancanough was later captured and shot in custody (18 April 1644).

Yorktown I 1781 I War of the American Revolution

Withdrawing from New York to Virginia, British commander Charles Earl Cornwallis defended Yorktown, on Chesapeake Bay, against a large American and French force under General George Washington and Jean-Baptise Comte de Rochambeau. Earl Cornwallis surrendered after costly assaults and naval defeat off **Chesapeake Capes** and Britain lost her American colony (6–19 October 1781).

Yorktown I 1862 I American Civil War (Eastern Theatre)

At the start of the Peninsula campaign in Virginia, Union commander George B. McClellan marched on Yorktown and General Fitz-John Porter besieged the city, held by Generals John B. Magruder and Joseph E. Johnston. After needless delay and about 300 casualties, the Confederates slipped away through **Williamsburg** just as McClellan was ready to attack (5 April–4 May 1862).

Youghiogany I 1754 I Seven Years War (North America)

See **Great Meadows**

Young's House I 1780 I War of the American Revolution

Colonel Joseph Thompson led about 250 Connecticut troops on a mid-winter patrol into Westchester New York and was met near Mt Pleasant by a larger force of British, Hessians and Tories under Colonel Chapple Norton. Sharp fighting around Joseph Young's House cost the Americans 14 killed, many wounded and over 100 captured, including Thompson and his officers (3 February 1780).

Ypacarai I 1868 I War of the Triple Alliance

See **Ita Ybate**

Ypres I 1794 I French Revolutionary Wars (1st Coalition)

See **Hooglede**

Ypres I 1914 I World War I (Western Front)

German General Erich von Falkenhayn launched a large-scale offensive to break the line in Flanders, sending forces against the Belgians on the **Yser**. He then attacked British Sir John French and French Ferdinand Foch around Ypres. Action at **Langemark**, **Gheluvelt** and **Nonne Boschen** cost both sides terrible losses, but the Allies held the vital Ypres salient (15 October–15 November 1914).

Ypres I 1915 I World War I (Western Front)

The first use of gas on the Western Front reputedly occurred when Duke Albrecht launched a huge advance against the Allied salient around Ypres in the Second Battle of Ypres. Severe fighting at **Hill 60**, **Gravenstafel**, **St Julien**, **Frezenberg** and **Bellewaarde** saw the salient substantially reduced at the cost of 70,000 Allied and 35,000 German casualties, but Ypres did not fall (22 April–25 May 1915).

Ypres I 1917 I World War I (Western Front)

Following success at **Messines** (14 June), commander Sir Douglas Haig ordered the bloody offensive called Third Ypres, or Passchendaele. Fighting at **Pilkem Ridge**, **Langemark**, **Menin Road**, **Polygon Wood**, **Broodseinde**, **Poelcappelle** and **Passchendaele** saw the British salient only slightly enlarged at the cost of over 300,000 Allied and 250,000 German casualties (31 July–6 November 1917).

Ypres I 1918 I World War I (Western Front)

See **Lys**

Yrendagüe I 1934 I Chaco War

Paraguayan Colonel Eugenio Garay marched north to the Chaco Boreal from victory at **Cañada el Carmen** (16 November) to attack Bolivia's Colonel David Toro at Yrendagüe, while Colonel Rafael Franco attacked to the east at Picuiba. A decisive rout saw Bolivia sacrifice up to 4,000 dead (many from thirst and heat) and

3,000 captured. They lost again at **Ybibobo** (8–11 December 1934).

Yser I 1914 I World War I (Western Front)

The Belgian army was driven out of **Antwerp**, then tried to defend the River Yser in Flanders, between Ypres and the port of Nieuwport. Attacked by German forces under Prince Albrecht, the Belgian and French Allies fought a bold defence. In the face of terrible losses, they flooded the area to halt the German advance, then moved east to join the main battles around **Ypres** (18–29 October 1914).

Ystradowen I 1032 I Anglo-Welsh Wars

In one of the decisive battles between England and Wales, Saxon forces landed at the mouth of the Dawen and advanced against Cynan Seisyllt (Cecil) at Ystradowen, west of Cardiff. Cynan and his two sons were killed in very hard fighting, but his brother Robert arrived overnight from the Wye and routed the invaders at nearby Llancwywan, driving them back to their ships.

Ytororó I 1868 I War of the Triple Alliance

Pursuing the defeated Paraguayan army south of Asunción, the Argentine, Brazilian and Uruguayan allies under Marshal Luíz Aldes, Marquis of Caxias, met General Bernadino Caballero attempting to defend the Ytororó River near Ypané. Heavy fighting saw 1,200 Paraguayans and 3,000 Brazilians killed and Caballero fell back towards **Avaí** (6 December 1868).

Yubi I 546 I Wei Dynastic Wars

After Western Wei was halted at **Mangshan** (543), fighting resumed between the great rivals in northern China when Gao Huan of Eastern Wei advanced down the Fen to besiege Yubi. (His previous attempt in 542 failed in the face of a great snowstorm.) The Western garrison under Wei Xiao Kuan held out against tunnelling and assault and after two months Gao withdrew. He died a few weeks later.

Yugoslavia I 1941 I World War II (Southern Europe)

See **Belgrade**

Yü-hsien I 1232 I Mongol Conquest of China

See **Yuxian**

Yuhuatai I 1862 I Taiping Rebellion

Imperial commander Zeng Guoquan advanced against the Taiping capital at Nanjing, seizing nearby Yuhuatai Hill (30 May), where his 20,000 men eventually faced assault by perhaps 200,000 Taiping under Generals Li Xiucheng and Li Shixian. The Taiping were defeated and withdrew after six weeks of bloody fighting and Zeng maintained his siege of **Nanjing** (13 October–26 November 1862).

Yung'an I 1851 I Taiping Rebellion

As a massive Taiping army withdrew through Guangxi, pursued by Imperial Commissioner Saishanga and Generals Xiang Rong and Wulantai, rebel General Luo Dakang surprised Yung'an (modern Mengshan) on the Meng River. The strategic town fell by storm and was held against siege until April 1852, when the Taiping withdrew through the **Dadong Mountains** (25 September 1851).

Yungay I 1839 I Chilean War of the Confederation

When President Andrés Santa Cruz of Bolivia seized Peru after victory at **Socabaya** and imposed confederation, Chile felt threatened and sent General Manuel Bulnes, who captured Lima. The following year Bulnes met the Bolivian army southeast of Concepción at Yungay. Santa Cruz was defeated and overthrown—fleeing to Ecuador—and the confederation came to an end (20 January 1839).

Yungchen I 1949 I 3rd Chinese Revolutionary Civil War

See **Chenguanzhuang**

**Yuxian I 1232 I Mongol Conquest
of China**

In renewed invasion of northern China, the
Mongols Ogedai and Tolui (sons of Genghis
Khan) and General Subetai crossed the Yellow
River. After capturing Luoyang, they met the
outnumbered Jin army near Yuxian in Henan,
where Jin General Wan Yen Yi was defeated and
executed. The Mongols then marched northeast to
besiege the Jin capital at **Kaifeng** (February 1232).

Yzer Spruit I 1902 I 2nd Anglo-Boer War

Jacobus de la Rey resumed his offensive in the
western Transvaal after **Kleinfontein**, attacking
a convoy and 700 men sent by Colonel Stanley
von Donop northeast from Wolmaranstad to
Klerksdorp. At Yzer Spruit, 13 miles from
Klerksdorp, the British lost 53 killed and the rest
wounded or captured. De la Rey seized hundreds
of horses and half a million rifle rounds (24
February 1902).

Z

Zab I 130 BC I Later Syrian-Parthian War

Marching into Mesopotamia with a huge army to recover land lost to the Parthians, Seleucus Antiochus VII of Syria defeated Phraates II of Parthia in a great battle on the upper Zab River. While the victory enabled Antiochus to recapture the key cities of Babylon and Ecbatana, his defeat and death near **Ecbatana** the following year ended Syrian ambition east of the Euphrates.

Zab I 591 I Byzantine-Persian Wars
See **Ganzak**

Zab I 627 I Byzantine-Persian Wars
See **Nineveh**

Zab I 750 I Muslim Civil Wars

In a decisive move to suppress the rival Caliph Abdu'l-Abbas (who was descended from the Prophet's uncle Abbas) the last Umayyad Caliph, Merwan II, took a large army to Mesopotamia and was defeated at **Karbala** in August 749. On the River Zab, near the ruins of ancient Nineveh, he was again defeated and fled. Abdu'l-Abbas then established the Abbasid Caliphate (25 January 750).

Zabern I 1525 I German Peasants' War

Erasmus Gerber led peasant rebels in Alsace, where they seized the city of Zabern (modern Saverne), northwest of Strasbourg, provoking intervention by Duke Antoine of Lorraine. With 60,000 French, Spanish and other troops, the Duke attacked and utterly routed about 7,000 peasants at nearby Lupstein. He then regained Zabern and subdued Alsace with terrible violence (16 May 1525).

Zabid I 525 I Aksum-Sabaean War

At the height of Aksumite power in Ethiopia, Emperor Ella Asbeha took a large force across the Red Sea against Saba (in modern Yemen) whose Jewish rulers were persecuting Christians. On the beach at Zabid, King Yusuf Dhu Nuwas was defeated and killed, ending the once-mighty Empire of Saba (biblical Sheba). In 570, Persian allies of Saba seized the country and forced Aksum to withdraw.

Zacatecas I 1914 I Mexican Revolution

With Federal forces in central Mexico retreating after **Torreón** and **Paredón**, Venustiano Carranza sent Pánfilo Natera—and later Francisco (Pancho) Villa—against stubbornly held Zacatecas. After ten days of bombardment the ruined city fell by storm, with perhaps 6,000 Federal troops killed in the costliest defeat of the war. Carranza then overthrew President Victoriano Huerta (12–23 June 1914).

Zag I 1980 I Western Sahara Wars

Polisario guerrillas from Western Sahara captured **Lebouirate** (August 1979) and besieged Zag in southeast Morocco, triggering a fresh Moroccan offensive (Operation Iman). The relief force was twice severely repulsed outside Zag, but a renewed effort broke the siege in early May. Morocco then began to build a sand wall to seal off part of Western Sahara (1–11 March 1980).

Zagonyi's Charge I 1861 I American Civil War (Trans-Mississippi)
See **Springfield, Missouri**

Zahara I 1481 I Final Christian Reconquest of Spain
Opening the last Muslim offensive against Christian Spain, Mulei Abdul-Hassan, the new King of **Granada**, refused the annual tribute to Ferdinand and Isabella and invaded Andalusia. There he surprised and destroyed the fortress of Zahara, on the Guadalete River, killing or enslaving most of the population. Muslim Spain was finally destroyed in the war that followed (26 December 1481).

Zahle I 1981 I Lebanon Civil War
On the offensive in the Bekaa Valley, Syria attacked Christian militia at Zahle, on the Beirut-Damascus highway. Militia General Bashir Gemayel sent reinforcements and the town held out for three months against severe shelling. A brief Israeli air raid persuaded Syria to talk and both sides withdrew, though failure of the Syrian army left the Lebanese Christians to claim victory (2 April–30 June 1981).

Zakataly I 1853 I Russian Conquest of the Caucasus
Imam Shamil of Dagestan took advantage of impending war between Russia and Turkey to attack Russian Prince Girgori Orbeliani at Zakataly in southwest Dagestan. Orbeliani drove the rebels off, then came under siege at nearby Meseldeger. Shamil was repulsed with costly losses and a relief army under Prince Moisei Argutinsky finally forced him to withdraw (5–19 September 1853).

Zalankamen I 1691 I Later Turkish-Habsburg Wars
See **Slankamen**

Zalgiris I 1410 I Later Wars of the Teutonic Knights
See **Tannenberg**

Zallaka I 1086 I Early Christian Reconquest of Spain
When Alfonso VI of Castile took **Toledo** (May 1085) and advanced into Andalusia, Almoravid Emir Yusuf ibn Tashufin of Morocco landed in force at Algeciras and met the huge Christian army on the Plains of Zallaka near Badajoz. His horsemen destroyed the Spanish force, with Alfonso severely wounded and forced to retreat. The victory secured Yusuf most of southern Spain (23 October 1086).

Zallaqa I 1086 I Early Christian Reconquest of Spain
See **Zallaka**

Zama I 202 BC I 2nd Punic War
Marching his veterans inland, away from Carthage in modern Tunisia, Carthaginian leader Hannibal Barca took up position at Zama against Roman General Publius Scipio the Younger and his Numidian allies. The Carthaginians were utterly destroyed in a classic set-piece battle and the war came to an end. Hannibal fled and Scipio was granted the honorific "Africanus" (19 October 202 BC).

Zamora I 873 I Christian Recapture of Zamora
King Alfonso III of Castile and Leon secured his greatest victory over the Muslims of Cordova when he destroyed a large army at Zamora, north of Salamanca. The rebel Kalib of Toledo was heavily defeated and his ally Abdul-Kassim was killed in the battle. Alfonso the Great then rebuilt Zamora as he advanced the Christian frontier to the Douro River and the Guadarramas.

Zamora I 939 I Christian-Muslim Wars in Spain
See **Simancas, Vallidolid**

Zamora I 981 I Later Christian-Muslim Wars in Spain
See **Rueda**

Zamora I 1072 I War of Castilian Succession

After defeating his brother Alfonso VI at **Golpejerra** in January, Sancho II of Castile seized Leon, then faced a local rebellion supported by his sister Urraca. Sancho besieged Zamora, north of Salamanca, but was assassinated by Vellido Adolfo, apparently at Urraca's instigation. The siege ended and Alfonso returned from exile to take the Kingdoms of Castile and Leon (October 1072).

Zamosc I 1920 I Russo-Polish War

With Russia's main army defeated near **Warsaw**, Soviet forces and Cossack Calvary under Symeon Budenny in Galicia were soon encircled by Polish General Wladyslaw Sikorski ncar Zamosc, southeast of Lublin. One of the last cavalry battles saw Polish General Juliusz Rómmel secure bloody victory at nearby Komárow, but the Russians were allowed to escape (30 August–2 September 1920).

Zamosc-Komárow I 1914 I World War I (Eastern Front)
See **Komárow**

Zand I 1900 I 2nd Anglo-Boer War

As British commander Lord Frederick Roberts advanced north along the railway from Bloemfontein towards Pretoria with 38,000 men and 100 guns, about 5,000 Boers under Christiaan de Wet and Louis Botha attempted to defend the Zand River. The Boers were driven back in heavy fighting and the British marched north to take nearby Kroonstad and east to **Lindley** (10 May 1900).

Zanzibar I 1503 I Portuguese Colonial Wars in East Africa

At the start of Portugal's campaign along the east coast of Africa, commander Rui Lorenco Ravasco took a force against the strategic island of Zanzibar (part of modern Tanzania). A sharp bombardment forced Mwinyi Mkuu, King of Zanzibar, to accept Portuguese suzerainty. Portuguese forces further north soon captured

Muscat and **Hormuz** to command the Persian Gulf.

Zanzibar I 1652 I Later Portuguese Wars in East Africa

Imam Sultan ibn Sayf of Oman took **Muscat** (1650) then despatched his son Sayf ibn Sultan with 28 ships and 10,000 troops against Portuguese settlements in Zanzibar. The Portuguese suffered heavy losses, including Viceroy Manoel de Nazareth killed. Omani forces gradually secured the island, deposing Queen Fatima and expelling the remaining Portuguese after the fall of **Mombasa** in 1698.

Zanzur (1st) I 1912 I Italo-Turkish War

Despite summer heat, Italian commander Carlo Caneva in Tripoli launched an unexpected offensive west against Turko-Arab forces entrenched in an extended line from Zanzur through Sidi Abd-al-Jalil. Over 13,000 Italians with field artillery inflicted heavy casualties and occupied Sidi Abd-al-Jalil, but they failed to secure Zanzur and had to fight again four months later (8 June 1912).

Zanzur (2nd) I 1912 I Italo-Turkish War

Four months after a bloody but unsatisfactory Italian offensive west of Tripoli towards Zanzur, Generals Ottavio Ragni and Felice de Chaurand advanced again with 12,000 men and 34 guns. Intensive fighting saw the Turks and Arabs finally driven out at bayonet-point with about 1,400 killed. Peace was signed within a month, securing Italy possession of Libya (20 September 1912).

Zapote Bridge I 1896 I Philippines War of Independence

Spanish Governor Ramon Blanco faced rebellion in Cavite and sent a small force under General Ernesto Aguirre against Emilio Aguinaldo, who attempted to defend the Zapote Bridge, near Bacoor. The insurgents suffered a costly defeat and Aguinaldo narrowly escaped capture. Aguirre soon returned to Manila for reinforcements and days later resumed his offensive at **Imus** (3 September 1896).

Zapote Bridge ▍ 1897 ▍ Philippines War of Independence

On a fresh offensive south of Manila, new Spanish Governor Camilo de Polaveija and General José Lachambre were met at Zapote Bridge, near Bacoor, by rebels Emilio Aguinaldo and Edilberto Evangelista. An heroic victory saw Evangelista killed holding the Spanish at bay, but **Silang** and **Dasmariñas** soon fell and Aguinaldo fell back through **Imus** to defeat at **Naic** (17 February 1897).

Zapote River ▍ 1899 ▍ Philippine-American War

Sent to combat fresh insurgency in southern Luzon, American General Henry W. Lawton was reinforced after humiliation at **Sucat** (10 June) and attacked General Artemio Ricarte entrenched on the Zapote, near Cavite. After a costly action—with 75 American and over 500 Philippine casualties—the insurgents withdrew. Nearby Imus fell next day without resistance (13 June 1899).

Zara ▍ 1202 ▍ 4th Crusade

Seeking transport to Palestine, leaders of the Fourth Crusade asked Venice for ships and were induced to pay the debt by helping besiege and recapture the former Venetian city of Zara in Hungarian-ruled Dalmatia. Though Europe was shocked at Crusaders attacking a Christian city, the Crusaders then also agreed to assist Venice in seizing **Constantinople** in July 1203 (10–15 November 1202).

Zara ▍ 1346 ▍ Hungarian-Venetian Wars

Soon after Venice seized Dalmatia from Hungary, the Adriatric city of Zara (Zadar in modern Croatia) rose in revolt and was besieged by Venetian commander Marino Faliero. Louis I of Hungary arrived with a large force to assist Zara but he suffered a costly defeat and was forced to withdraw. Two further campaigns (1337–1358 and 1378–1381) saw Louis gradually regain most of Dalmatia.

Zaragoza ▍ 1118 ▍ Early Christian Reconquest of Spain
See **Saragossa**

Zaragoza ▍ 1710 ▍ War of the Spanish Succession
See **Saragossa**

Zaragoza ▍ 1808 ▍ Napoleonic Wars (Peninsular Campaign)
See **Saragossa**

Zaragoza ▍ 1937 ▍ Spanish Civil War
See **Saragossa**

Zarghan ▍ 1730 ▍ Persian-Afghan Wars

Advancing into Persia against its Afghan conquerors, Persian General Nadir Kuli (later Nadir Shah) won great victories at **Mehmandost** and **Murchakhar**, driving the usurper Ashraf Khan south towards Shiraz, where he rallied his troops. However, Ashraf was utterly defeated just to the north at Zarghan. He was murdered returning to Kandahar and Nadir was created Sultan (15 January 1730).

Zarnesti ▍ 1690 ▍ Later Turkish-Habsburg Wars
See **Zernyest**

Zarnow ▍ 1655 ▍ 1st Northern War
See **Opoczno**

Zarnowiec ▍ 1462 ▍ Thirteen Years War
See **Puck**

Zatec ▍ 1421 ▍ Hussite Wars

Recovering from defeat at **Vitkov Hill** (July 1420), a fresh expedition of Imperial Princes entered Bohemia against the Hussite heretics and besieged Zatec (German Saaz), northwest of Prague. On false reports of an approaching army under the great Jan Zizka, the so-called Second Crusade withdrew with costly losses inflicted by the pursuing garrison of Zatec (19 September–2 October 1421).

Zborov I 1649 I Cossack-Polish Wars

With his army in the Ukraine beaten at **Korsun** and **Pilawce**, John II Casimir of Poland led a new force against Cossack rebel Bogdan Chmielnicki, now besieging Zbarazh, north of Ternopol. While the King was surprised and defeated just to the west at Zborov, Chmielnicki's fickle Tatar allies withdrew and he had to accept peace until decisive battle in 1651 at **Beresteczko** (15–17 August 1649).

Zeebrugge I 1918 I World War I
(War at Sea)

Determined to bottle up German destroyers and U-boats at Bruges in Belgium, Admiral Roger Keyes led an ambitious raid against the ports of Zeebrugge and **Ostend**. Troops landed at Zeebrugge failed to silence shore batteries and blockships were not correctly positioned. The raids cost over 500 Allied casualties and saw eight Victoria Crosses won, but Zeebrugge was quickly reopened (22–23 April 1918).

Zeelandia I 1661–1662 I Chinese
Conquest of Taiwan
See **Fort Zeelandia**

Zehdenick I 1806 I Napoleonic Wars
(4th Coalition)

As the Prussian army retreated north across Germany after the twin defeats at **Jena** and **Auerstadt**, French Generals Antoine Lasalle and Emmanuel de Grouchy attacked their flank at Zehdenick, north of Oranienberg. As at **Potsdam**, Prince Friedrich-Ludwig of Hohenloe's retreating force suffered a sharp loss, soon followed by defeat and surrender at **Prenzlau** (26 October 1806).

Zela I 67 BC I 3rd Mithridatic War

When Mithridates VI of Pontus tried to recover his kingdom, lost five years before at **Cyzicus** and **Cabira**, local Roman Governor Lucius Valerius Triarius, a legate in the army of Lucius Licinius Lucullus, allowed himself to be attacked near Zela (modern Zile) in northern Turkey. Triarius suffered a terrible defeat, losing

7,000 men. Mithridates was routed the following year on the **Lycus**.

Zela I 47 BC I Roman-Pontian Wars

King Pharnaces of Bosporus attacked Roman forces in Asia Minor and defeated Julius Caesar's General Domitius Calvinus at **Nicopolis** (48 BC). Caesar himself then hastened from Egypt and gathered an army in Syria. In northern Turkey at Zela (modern Zile), the Pontians were routed and Pharnaces fled. Caesar reported to the Senate: "Veni, Vidi, Vici—I came, I saw, I conquered."

Zella I 1866 I Seven Weeks War

After defeating Hanover at **Langensalza**, Prussians invaded Bavaria and Prussian General August von Goeben sent General Ferdinand von Kummer south from Dermbach against General Friedrich von Zoller at Zella, near Neidhartshausen. Fierce action forced the Bavarians to fall back on Diedorf. After victory that day at **Wiesenthal**, the Prussians regrouped to advance on **Kissingen** (4 July 1866).

Zenta I 1697 I Later Turkish-
Habsburg Wars

Sultan Mustafa II renewed the Turkish offensive in Hungary, where his army was attacked while crossing the Tisza River at Zenta (modern Senta) by an Imperial force only one-third as large under Prince Eugène of Savoy. The Turks were destroyed, with Grand Vizier Elmas Mehmed among thousands killed. The ensuing peace saw the Habsburgs secure Hungary (11 September 1697).

Zenteno I 1933 I Chaco War
See **Alihuatá**

Zernyest I 1690 I Later Turkish-
Habsburg Wars

In a renewed Turkish offensive in Europe, renegade Hungarian Count Imre Thokoly was sent to invade Transylvania. At Zernyest (modern Zarnesti) Thokoly defeated a Habsburg-Transylvanian army and the Turks made him Prince. However, he and Grand Vizier Fazil

Mustafa were defeated a year later at **Slanka-men** and Transylvania was secured by the Habsburgs (11 August 1690).

Zhapu ❙ 1842 ❙ 1st Opium War

Reinforced by Admiral Sir George Elliot, Superintendent Sir Henry Pottinger and General Sir Hugh Gough withdrew troops from Ningbo and attacked Zhapu, the port of Hangzhou, held by 10,000 Chinese regulars and Tatars. Gough took the city by storm with over 1,200 Chinese dead. Wusong and Shanghai soon fell without fighting and Gough advanced up the Yangzi to **Zhenjiang** (18 May 1842).

Zhawar ❙ 1986 ❙ Afghan Civil War

Following up a government offensive into the **Parrot's Beak** region, southeast of Kabul (September 1985), Brigadier Abdol Safar took about 12,000 men against the Mujahaden supply base of Zhawar, defended by General Jalaluddin Haqqani. A massive air and ground assault saw Zhawar fall with heavy losses, but the government forces soon withdrew and it was reoccupied (2–20 April 1986).

Zhejiang-Jiangxi ❙ 1942 ❙ World War II (China)

Supposedly in response to the **Doolittle Raid** on Tokyo in April, General Shunroku Hata led nine Japanese divisions on a massive offensive into East **Zhejiang** and **Jiangxi** Provinces, where they took Qingtian (30 July) and destroyed several Allied airfields. Chinese General Gu Zhutong eventually counter-attacked near Wenzhou and the Japanese were forced to withdraw (15 May–27 August 1942).

Zhelte Vody ❙ 1648 ❙ Cossack-Polish Wars

See **Zolte Wody**

Zhengrong ❙ 404 ❙ Wars of the Sixteen Kingdoms Era

In the bloody struggle for the middle Yangzi, Huan Xuan seized the upper reaches then advanced to seize Jiankang and depose the Jin Emperor (403). Loyalist General Liu Yu assembled a large fleet and, at Zhengrong Island

near modern Echeng, Huan was routed, then killed in the pursuit. Liu Yu restored Emperor An, but in 420 he seized the throne and began the Southern Song Dynasty (June 404).

Zhenhai ❙ 1841 ❙ 1st Opium War

Campaigning northeast from Hong Kong, General Sir Hugh Gough and Admiral Sir William Parker captured **Xiamen** and Dinghai, then attacked the fortified city of Zhenhai at the mouth of the Yong, held by almost 4,000 Chinese. Zhenhai fell by assault after a heavy bombardment and defeated Commissioner Yu Qian commited suicide. **Ningbo** quickly fell three days later (10 October 1841).

Zhenjiang ❙ 1842 ❙ 1st Opium War

After storming **Zhapu**, General Sir Hugh Gough advanced up the Yangzi, strongly supported by Admiral Sir William Parker, but was blocked at Zhenjiang (Chenkiang). In some of the war's hardest fighting—with many British killed by heatstroke—Zhenjiang fell by assault. With Nanjing threatened, China ended the war, ceding Hong Kong and opening key ports to British trade (21 July 1842).

Zhenjiang ❙ 1856 ❙ Taiping Rebellion

Determined to relieve Zhenjiang (Chenkiang), east of Nanjing (under Imperial siege since May 1853), Taiping commander Qin Rigang attacked and routed the besieging force. After capturing nearby Yangzhou, he returned and, just west of Zhenjiang, defeated and killed Imperial commanders Liu Cunhou and Ji'er Hang'a. Qin was soon recalled to defend **Nanjing** (1 April & 1 June 1856).

Zhijiang ❙ 1945 ❙ World War II (China)

While Japanese forces seized the airbase at **Laohekou**, General Ichiro Sakanishi, south of the Yangzi, led 70,000 men towards the major airfield at Zhijiang. Despite suffering terrible losses, Chinese General He Yingqin halted the advance and Japan's last offensive was repulsed. Commander Yasuji Okamura ordered continued withdrawal and the war soon came to an end (8 April–7 June 1945).

Zhitomir I 1920 I Russo-Polish War
See **Berezina**

**Zhitomir I 1943 I World War II
(Eastern Front)**

At the centre of the Soviet offensive towards the **Dnieper**, General Nikolai Vatutin took **Kiev** before his forward units raced west and seized the key rail centre of Zhitomir. It was retaken within days by General Hasso von Manteuffel's Seventh Panzer Division, then lost again to the Russians. The front stabilised and the Russians turned south against the pocket at **Korsun** (12–31 December 1943).

**Zhongdu I 1214–1215 I Conquests of
Genghis Khan**
See **Beijing**

Zhovnyne I 1638 I Cossack-Polish Wars

Despite disaster at **Kumeiky** in late 1637, Yakiv Ostrianyn continued Cossack revolt in the Ukraine. Between Kremenchuk and Poltava at Hotva he routed a Polish force under Stanislas Potocki. The Poles regrouped and a month later at Zhovnyne, northwest of Kremenchuk, Ostrianyn was defeated and fled. Rebellion died down until the great rising of 1648 at **Bazavluk** (15 May & 13 June 1638).

Zhovti Vody I 1648 I Cossack-Polish Wars
See **Zolte Wody**

**Zhumadian I 1927 I 1st Chinese
Revolutionary Civil War**

Nationalist Tang Shengzhi opened a new offensive north from **Wuchang**, crossing into Henan to attack Northern General Wu Beifu attempting to make a stand on the Beijing-Hankou railway at Zhumadian (Chumatien). Wu was decisively defeated and fled and Tang continued north against Zhang Xueliang (son of Marshal Zhang Zuolin) at **Linying** (14 May 1927).

Zhuozhou I 1920 I Anhui-Zhili War

As warlords struggled for northern China, Manchurian leader Zhang Zuolin joined Kao Kun of the Zhili against the ruling Anhui faction of Duan Qirui in Beijing. A ten-day war saw Allied General Wu Beifu defeat Duan's army southwest of the capital at Zhuozhou and then Liulihe. The Anhui government collapsed, but the allies fell out two years later at **Changxindian** (14–18 July 1920).

Zielenice I 1792 I Polish Rising

When Poland declared an independent constitution in 1791, Catherine the Great sent Field Marshal Alexander Suvorov to impose Russian authority. At Zielenice (modern Selenez), northeast of Warsaw, Josef Poniatowski (nephew of the Polish King) held off the Russians with heavy losses on both sides. Despite further Polish resistance at **Dubienka**, the rising was doomed (18 June 1792).

Zieriksee I 1304 I Franco-Flemish Wars

After Guy of Namour's Flemish victory at **Courtrai** (July 1302), he attacked southern Holland to no avail, then besieged Zieriksee on the eastern Scheldt. Count William of Hainault sought help from Philip IV of France and off Zieriksee the Flemish navy was destroyed with Guy taken prisoner. The siege was lifted and further Flemish defeat a week later at **Mons-en-Pevele** ended the war (10 August 1304).

**Zieriksee I 1575–1576 I Netherlands
War of Independence**

In a courageous assault on the Zealand island of Duiveland, Spanish General Don Osorio de Ulloa waded ashore under heavy attack (28 September) and Dutch General Charles Boisot was killed. Christoforo de Mondragón then besieged Zieriksee. After Admiral Louis de Boisot was killed attempting to break the blockade, Arend van Dorp finally capitulated (26 October 1575–2 July 1576).

**Zijpe I 1799 I French Revolutionary Wars
(2nd Coalition)**
See **Zuyper Sluys**

**Zilikats Nek (1st) I 1900 I 2nd Anglo-
Boer War**

Boer commander Jacobus de la Rey recovered from the fall of Pretoria and attacked 240 men under Colonel Henry R. Roberts attempting to secure the strategic pass to the west at Zilikats Nek, near Rustenberg. Trapped under heavy fire, with no sign of relief from Colonel Walter P. Alexander, Roberts surrendered shortly after sunset with 17 killed, 55 wounded and 189 captured (11 June 1900).

Zilikats Nek (2nd) ∎ 1900 ∎ 2nd Anglo-Boer War

Determined to recover the Zilikats Nek, a strategic pass through the Magaliesburg to western Transvaal (lost to the Boers two months earlier), General Ian Hamilton marched west from Pretoria with over 7,000 men. After a sharp attack, with light casualties on either side, the Boers under Commandant Petrus Coetzee fled and Hamilton reached Rustenberg three days later (2 August 1900).

Zitácuaro ∎ 1811 ∎ Mexican Wars of Independence

When insurgent forces seized Zitácuaro, west of Mexico City, Royalist Captain Juan Baustista de la Torre was bloodily repulsed (20 February and 22 May 1811). Ignacio López Rayón then took command of the insurgents and faced another attack by Colonel Miguel Emparan. The Royalists were defeated once again and a national revolutionary Junta was established in Zitácuaro (22 June 1811).

Zitácuaro ∎ 1812 ∎ Mexican Wars of Independence

Royalist General Félix María Calleja resolved to destroy the insurgent Junta at Zitácuaro, west of Mexico City, and took a large force against the rebel stronghold, defended by Ignacio López Rayón. After bloody fighting, Calleja took Zitácuaro by storm, then sacked the city with terrible casualties and destruction. Months later, he attacked rebel leader José María Morelos at **Cuautla** (1–2 January 1812).

Zivin ∎ 1877 ∎ Russo-Turkish Wars

When Russian commander Mikhail Loris-Melikov advanced into the Caucasus to relieve General Arzas Artemevich Tergukasov at **Tahir**, he attacked Izmail Hakka Pasha at Zivin, south-west of Karaugan, even though Tergukasov had already retreated. Izmail fled with over 1,000 casualties, but the cautious Loris-Melikov feared a counter-attack and also withdrew (25 June 1877).

Zizkov ∎ 1420 ∎ Hussite Wars

See **Vitkov Hill**

Zlatitsa ∎ 1443 ∎ Turkish-Hungarian Wars (Long Campaign)

The Christian army of King Ladislas IV of Hungary and General Janos Hunyadi advanced across the Balkans after victory in Serbia and once again met Kasim Bey, Governor of Rumelia, now escaped from capture at **Nish**. Battle at Zlatitsa (Izladi), west of Sofia, saw the Christians halted and in deepest winter they turned for home, harried at **Melshtitsa** and **Kunovica** (12 December 1443).

Zlatoust ∎ 1919 ∎ Russian Civil War

During a powerful counter-offensive in the Urals by General Mikhail Tukhachevski, the Red Army captured **Ekaterinburg**, then advanced on Whites attempting to defend Zlatoust. A massive encircling movement routed and almost captured the forces of General Vladimir Kappel, before the city was taken by storm and the Whites withdrew east towards **Chelyabinsk** (24 June–13 July 1919).

Zloczow ∎ 1675 ∎ Turkish Invasion of the Ukraine

After beating the Turks in Moldavia at **Khotin** (1673), John III Sobieski of Poland was abandoned by his former ally Michael Pac of Lithuania in the face of an invasion by 20,000 Turks and Tatars. Determined to recover the Ukraine, Sobieski met the invaders east of Lvov at Zloczow (modern Zolochev) and inflicted a heavy defeat. He then won again at **Soczawa** and **Zurawno** (24 August 1675).

Zlota Lipa ∎ 1914 ∎ World War I (Eastern Front)

As Austrians advanced into eastern Poland through **Krasnik** and **Komárow**, further south Russian commander Nikolai Ivanov sent Generals

Nikolai Ruzskii and Aleksei Brusilov on a counter-offensive across the Zlota Lipa, a tributary of the Dneister. Austrian General Rudolf von Bruderman was routed and fell back in disorder to the **Gnila Lipa**, southeast of **Lemberg** (26–28 August 1914).

Znaim ▮ 1809 ▮ Napoleonic Wars (5th Coalition)

In the aftermath of Archduke Charles of Austria's loss at **Wagram**, French General Auguste Marmont intercepted the Austrians on the far bank of the Danube at Znaim (modern Znojmo). Henry Prince of Reusse attempted a counter-attack but was repulsed with heavy losses when Marshal André Masséna arrived with the main French army. An armistice was signed next day (10–11 July 1809).

Zojila ▮ 1948 ▮ 1st Indo-Pakistan War

As Pakistan-backed forces invaded northern Kashmir, some of the fiercest action occurred at the strategic 11,500-foot Zojila Pass, east of Srinigar. The Indians had to withdraw from some key positions (7 July), but Brigadier Kanhya Lal Atal—with a record high-altitude use of tanks—stormed the pass to retake Kargill and relieve **Leh**. The war soon came to an end (23 May–1 November 1948).

Zolte Wody ▮ 1648 ▮ Cossack-Polish Wars

Bogdan Chmielnicki's Cossacks began rebellion against Poland in the Ukraine at **Bazavluk** (21 January) and John II Casimir sent Hetman Mikolaj Potocki, whose son Stefan's advance guard was surrounded by Cossacks and Crimean Tatars under Tuhai-Bei, at Zolte Wody, south of Kremenchuk. Stefan Potocki was defeated and captured and his father was soon beaten at **Korsun** (16 May 1648).

Zonchio ▮ 1499 ▮ Venetian-Turkish Wars

See **Lepanto**

Zongzhou ▮ 771 BC ▮ Wars of the Western Zhou

Having overthrown the Shang at **Muye** (1045 BC), the Western Zhou ruled at Zongzhou (near modern Xi'an) gradually losing influence to feudal lords and "western barbarians." With King You distracted by a family dispute, Quan Rong "barbarians" attacked and sacked Zongzhou. You was killed, ending the Western Zhou Dynasty. The Eastern Zhou fled east to Chengzhou (trad date 771 BC).

Zorawno ▮ 1676 ▮ Turkish Invasion of the Ukraine

See **Zurawno**

Zorndorf ▮ 1758 ▮ Seven Years War (Europe)

General Count Wilhelm Fermor led a renewed Russian invasion of East Prussia and advanced towards the Oder to besieged Kostrzyn (Custrin), where Frederick II attacked at nearby Zorndorf. While both sides suffered enormous losses in a bloody action, General Friedrich von Seydlitz's Prussian cavalry finally won the day and the Russians withdrew to Königsberg (25 August 1758).

Zornoza ▮ 1808 ▮ Napoleonic Wars (Peninsular Campaign)

After advancing into Biscay to recapture **Bilbao**, Spanish General Joachim Blake was attacked to the southeast at Zornoza by French Marshal Francois Lefebvre and General Francois Sébastiani. The outnumbered Spanish managed to disengage, but Blake had to abandon Bilbao three days later. He withdrew west through **Valmaseda** to further defeat in two weeks at **Espinosa** (29 October 1808).

Zouar ▮ 1986–1987 ▮ Libyan-Chad War

When rebel leader Goukouni Oueddei changed sides to support President Hissen Habré, his former Libyan sponsors attacked his strongholds at Bardai and Zouar. Heaviest fighting was at Zouar, where the Toubou garrison was finally overwhelmed by 8,000 Libyans. Habré sent troops north to join the rebels and Zouar was retaken with very costly Libyan losses (December 1986–2 January 1987).

Zouerate I 1977 I Western Sahara Wars

With Morocco and Mauritania attempting to seize former Spanish West Africa, Polisario guerrillas attacked Mauritania's vital iron-ore mines at Zouerate, destroying major facilities. The raid led to Morocco sending troops to assist, though attacks continued on the ore railway to the coast. A year later President Mokhtar Ould Daddah was deposed and Mauritania abandoned the war (1 May 1977).

Zsibó I 1705 I Rákóczi Rebellion

Prince Ferenc II Rákóczi of Transylvania raised rebellion against Austria and faced a major offensive by Count Ludwig von Herbeville. Rákóczi tried to block the Austrian advance in the mountains of northwest Romania, but near Zalau at Zsibó (modern Jibon), he suffered a decisive defeat, losing perhaps 5,000 killed. Herbeville quickly retook most of Transylvania (11 November 1705).

Zubiri (1st) I 1836 I 1st Carlist War

French Foreign Legion Colonel Joseph Bernelle was sent to support the Spanish government and attacked Carlists threatening the garrison at Zubiri, northeast of Pamplona near Larrasoaña. Fighting in heavy snow, the Carlists were driven off with over 100 casualties and 30 prisoners executed as a reprisal. Another Carlist attack was driven off a month later at nearby **Tirapegui** (24 March 1836).

Zubiri (2nd) I 1836 I 1st Carlist War

Following his costly success near Larrasoaña at **Tirapegui**, northeast of Pamplona in Navarre, French Foreign Legion Colonel Joseph Bernelle joined a Spanish government force in a second assault on the Carlists further east at Zubiri. A one-sided disaster saw the Carlists driven off with about 1,500 casualties, but Bernelle was soon replaced in command (1 August 1836).

Zug I 1531 I Swiss Religious Wars

Amid open warfare between Catholics and Protestants in Switzerland, a large Catholic army defeated and killed Reformation leader Ulrich Zwingli at **Kappel** (11 October) before facing a better-organised Protestant force from Berne and other cities. South of Zurich at Zug, the Catholics were again victorious and Switzerland was permanently divided along religious lines (24 October 1531).

Zuili I 496 BC I Wars of China's Spring and Autumn Era

In the struggle between Wu and Yue for the fertile Yangzi Delta, King He-lü of Wu invaded neighbouring Yue against King Goujian. In battle at Zuili, near modern Jiaxing in Zhejian, He-lü's army was badly defeated and He-lü himself died of wounds. His son and successor Fuchai had his revenge against Goujian two years later at **Fuqiao**.

Zullichau I 1759 I Seven Years War (Europe)

See **Kay**

Zulpich I 496 I Frankish-Alemannic War

When Alemanni tribesman from the Rhine attempted to expand west into the territory of King Sigebert of the Ripuarian Franks, his powerful Frankish kinsman, King Clovis, came to his aid. The Alemanni were utterly defeated at Zulpich, southwest of Cologne. The Frankish King was wounded in the leg and became known as Sigebert the Lame.

Zumelzu I 1875 I 2nd Carlist War

See **Treviño**

Zunyi I 1935 I 2nd Chinese Revolutionary Civil War

See **Loushan Pass**

Zurakow I 1676 I Turkish Invasion of the Ukraine

See **Zurawno**

Zurawno I 1676 I Turkish Invasion of the Ukraine

Recovering after defeat at **Zloczow** and **Soczawa**, a reputed 200,000 Turks and Tatars under Ibrahim Shetan besieged John III Sobieski of Poland in his fortified camp at Zurawno (modern

Zhuravno), on the Dniester east of Stryy. The Turks withdrew after costly losses, but they returned the following year to make a final attempt on the Ukraine at **Chigirin** (September–October 1676).

Zurich (1st) I 1799 I French Revolutionary Wars (2nd Coalition)

French General André Masséna fell back from a bloody encounter east of Zurich at **Wetzikon** and days later found himself facing a fresh offensive with superior numbers by Archduke Charles of Austria. In four days of inconclusive battle near Zurich, both sides suffered heavy casualties before Masséna was forced to continue withdrawing west and the Austrians occupied the city (4–7 June 1799).

Zurich (2nd) I 1799 I French Revolutionary Wars (2nd Coalition)

Two months after being driven into western Switzerland by the much larger Austrian army of Archduke Charles, French General André Masséna attempted a counter-offensive and advanced on Zurich. Costly fighting saw him again repulsed and he withdrew to prepare for a second and more successful offensive six weeks later (14 August 1799).

Zurich (3rd) I 1799 I French Revolutionary Wars (2nd Coalition)

With Archduke Charles of Austria absent in Germany, French Generals André Masséna and Charles-Nicolas Oudinot launched an offensive in Switzerland against Russian General Alexander Korsakov, who was routed in a two-day battle at Zurich. General Alexander Suvorov arrived from Italy too late to prevent the disaster and was in turn driven back to the Rhine (25–26 September 1799).

Zurmat I 1869 I Later Afghan War of Succession

Despite defeat at **Kila Alladad** in late 1867, Sher Ali and his son Yakub Khan gradually recovered Afghanistan from the usurper Azim Khan, retaking Kandahar (April 1868) and Kabul (September 1868). The decisive mid-winter campaign in Zurmat, east of Ghazni, saw Sher Ali's brother Azim and nephew Abdur Khan finally defeated. Britain then recognised Sher Ali as Amir (January 1869).

Zusmarshausen I 1648 I Thirty Years War (Franco-Habsburg War)

French Marshal Henri de Turenne and Sweden's Marshal Karl Gustav Wrangel led a renewed advance into Bavaria and pursued the Bavarian-Imperial army of Marshal Peter Melander and Count Raimondo Montecuccoli to the Danube. Melander was defeated and killed in a rearguard action at Zusmarshausen, west of Augsburg, and the allies overran Bavaria as far as the Inn (17 May 1648).

Zutphen I 1586 I Netherlands War of Independence

Prompted by the fall of **Antwerp** (August 1585), England's Queen Elizabeth sent Robert Dudley Earl of Leicester to the Netherlands, where he besieged Zutphen, near Arnhem, defended by Spanish commander Juan Bautista Tassis. Leicester was routed by a relief column under the Marques del Vasto (his nephew Sir Philip Sidney was killed) and he returned home (22 September 1586).

Zutphen I 1591 I Netherlands War of Independence

With Alexander Farnese Duke of Parma occupied in France, Prince Maurice of Orange began an offensive along the Dutch Coast. After capturing **Breda** (March 1590), he besieged Zutphen, which had held out against attack five years earlier. Supported by his cousin William Louis of Nassau, Maurice took the city after just seven days and went on to capture Deventer and Nijmegen (24–30 May 1591).

Zuyder Zee I 1573 I Netherlands War of Independence

As Spanish forces under Don Fadrique Alvarez besieged the Dutch city of **Alkmaar**, the defenders opened the dikes to flood the area to the east and Spanish ships under Maximilien de Henin Count Bossu came up to support the siege. On the nearby

Zuyder Zee, Dutch Admiral Kornelius Dirkszoon defeated and captured Bossu and the siege of Alkmaar ended (11 October 1573).

Zuyper Sluys | 1799 | French Revolutionary Wars (2nd Coalition)

General Sir Ralph Abercromby and advance units of the expedition to northern Holland landed at **Groote Keeten** and marched on Zuyper Sluys, near Alkmaar, where they were attacked by French General Guillaume Brune with Dutch support. Brune was driven off with 2,000 casualties and Frederick Augustus Duke of York arrived three days later with the main Allied force (10 September 1799).

Zwettl | 1427 | Hussite Wars

On campaign against Sigismund of Bohemia, Bohemian Hussite leader Prokob the Bald raided into Silesia, then marched into Austria against Sigismund's son-in-law Duke Albert. Northwest of Linz at Zwettl, Prokob routed an Austrian army with massive casualties—the first major Hussite victory on foreign soil—then returned home to meet a new invasion at **Tachov** (12 March 1427).

Appendix

This project was conceived as a dictionary of battles and sieges, not a dictionary of wars. However, some wars do not have specific recorded battles but remain sufficiently significant in their own right to be included in this appendix. For fuller details on these wars, and on history's many low-level conflicts and insurgencies, the reader is referred initially to the multi-volume Cambridge History series; the *Encyclopedia of Military History* (Dupuy and Dupuy) or the *Dictionary of Wars* (Kohn). This chronological appendix does not include the many low-level wars fought since 1945, which are well summarised in the existing literature, including *Wars in the Third World since 1945* (Arnold), *An Encyclopedic Dictionary of Conflict and Conflict Resolution, 1945–1996* (Jessup) and *Conflicts after World War II* (Ciment).

Nubian Conquest of Egypt | 750–730 BC

After King Kashta of Nubian Kush conquered Upper Egypt and became ruler of Thebes, his son and successor Piankhy led a massive force into Egypt itself. Following his bloody capture of Memphis, Piankhy overthrew the Lybian Dynasty and reunited Egypt. When Esarhaddon of Assyria invaded Egypt in 671 BC the last Nubian Pharaoh Taharqa withdrew to Napata and continued to rule Kush.

1st Messenian War | 736–716 BC

With Dorian forces from northern Greece gradually conquering the Peleponnese, Sparta attacked Messenia in the southwest, greedy to control the fertile Pámisos River Valley. Despite prolonged resistance by the native population around Mount Ithome, King Theopompus of Sparta finally captured the region and established the Messenians as helots, or state serfs, bound to hand over half their produce to Sparta.

Lelantine War | 725–700 BC

One of the most important military conflicts of the early period of Greek history involved the cities of Chalcis and Eretria, on the island of Euboea, in a prolonged struggle to control the fertile Lelantine Plain. As allies joined either side, the Greek world split into rival trade blocks, and fighting spread across the entire area. But there is no certain information about the war, its time frame or the exact outcome.

2nd Messenian War | 650–630 BC

A bloody rebellion against their Spartan masters (the Great Revolt) saw Messenians rise up under the semi-legendary leader Aristomenes. After initial success, the Messenians were defeated at the so-called Battle of the Great Trench and withdrew under siege to Mount Eira. When the stronghold fell, reputedly after 11 years, Aristomenes fled into exile and Messenia continued as a serf state.

Median-Persian War I 553–550 BC

Opening a brilliant career, Cyrus II of Anshan (part of Persia) started a revolt against his grandfather and overlord, Astyages (Ishtuwegu) of Media. After prolonged war, the Median army mutinied, allowing Cyrus to capture Astyages and the capital Ecbatana. Cyrus secured Media then began building the great Achaemenid Persian Empire by defeating Croesus of Lydia (Astyages' son-in-law) at **Pteria**.

Persian War of Succession I 521–519 BC

In the disputed succession following the death of Cambyses II of Persia, his cousin Darius seized the throne, then fought a complex war to defend it against usurpers and other claimants. In a far-reaching campaign, he put down repeated revolts in Babylonia, Media, Susiana, Armenia and inside Persia itself, as well as in Egypt. With internal order restored, he then set about rebuilding the glory of the Persian Empire.

Persia's Scythian Expedition I 516–509 BC

Having restored authority within Persia, Darius attacked the Scythians east of the Caspian (519 BC), then turned west against the Scythians in Thrace. In the first attack of Asia upon Europe, Darius advanced beyond the Danube while his satraps turned towards Macedonia. A Scythian scorched-earth policy eventually forced Darius back across the Bosphorus, but he soon returned to attack Greece itself.

3rd Messenian War I 464–455 BC

When a severe earthquake struck Sparta, the helots (state serfs) of Messenia once again rose in revolt and won some early victories. But King Archidamus II of Sparta soon brought heavy forces to bear, and the rebellion was crushed when the fortified position on Mount Ithome fell, and many survivors fled into exile. Messenia was eventually liberated after Spartan defeat in 371 BC at **Leuctra**.

2nd Sacred War I 449–448 BC

In an effort to exert influence with the Oracle in the Temple of Apollo at Delphi, Sparta sent an armed force to Delphi, and encouraged the citizens to renounce control by Phocis and declare independence. The intervention caused a major rift within the Sacred League and Athenian forces under Pericles marched into Delphi to reinstate the Phocians in control of the sacred city.

Wars of the Mauryan Empire I 321–232 BC

In the wake of Alexander the Great's invasion of India, Chandragupta Maurya seized the throne of Magadha and began a campaign to unite the north of the sub-continent. His son Bindusara and grandson Ashoka further extended the empire and Ashoka conquered Kalinga (Orissa) to unite nearly all of India. He then renounced war and adopted Buddhism, and the Mauryan Empire soon fell into decline.

Damascene War I 280–275 BC

Following the death of the great Seleucid King Seleucus I, Ptolemy II Philadelphus, the Macedonian King of Egypt, campaigned against Antiochus I in Asia Minor, then marched into Seleucid Syria. In a confused campaign, the capital Damascus appears to have changed hands several times before Ptolemy eventually withdrew. Soon afterwards, Antiochus invaded Egypt to trigger the 1st Syrian War.

1st Syrian War I 274–271 BC

When war resumed between Ptolemy II Philadelphus of Egypt and the Seleucid King Antiochus I, Syrian forces marched south into Phoenicia and other territory claimed by Egypt. Ptolemy defeated his half-brother Magas, Governor of Cyrenaica, who had allied himself with the Seleucids and, by the time Antiochus sued for peace, Ptolemy had secured significant parts of Syria, as well as land in Asia Minor.

2nd Syrian War I 260–255 BC

After victory in the Chremonidian War, Antigonus II of Macedonia joined the Seleucid Antiochus II against their rival Ptolemy II Philadelphus of Egypt. Antigonus won a largely naval war in Asia Minor, while Antiochus retook

Phoenicia, which had been seized from his father. Ptolemy made peace, marrying his daughter Berenice to Antiochus, but her subsequent murder (246 BC) triggered the 3rd Syrian War.

War of Demetrius ❙ 239–229 BC

With Macedonia struggling in the Peloponnese after the loss of **Corinth** (243 BC), the new King Demetrius II faced an unexpected coalition of the Aetolian and Achaean Leagues. A complex and obscure war of changing alliances ended when Demetrius was killed by invading Dardanians. Macedonian influence in Peloponnese effectively came to an end, and the Achaean League reached its greatest extent.

2nd Greek Social War ❙ 219–217 BC

Antigonus III of Macedon secured much of the Peloponnese through the Achaean League after victory at **Sellasia** (222 BC). After his death, his teenage cousin Philip V faced war when the Achaeans sought Macedonian aid against the rival Aetolian League. Philip defeated the Aetolian League and its allies and eventually secured the Peace of Naupactus (this is also known as the War of the Allies).

1st Macedonian War ❙ 215–205 BC

As Rome struggled in the early years of the 2nd Punic War, Philip V of Macedon launched a campaign against Roman Illyria along the Adriatic coast. After years of indecisive action, Philip turned south against the Greek city-states, where Rome supported an anti-Macedonian coalition led by Aetolia. With Rome now winning the war against Carthage, Philip finally sued for peace.

Lusitanian Wars ❙ 154–138 BC

Lusitanians in modern Portugal and western Spain, led by the warrior Punicus (and later Kaisaros), ravaged Roman territory and inflicted heavy losses until they finally agreed to peace (151 BC). A new leader, Viriathus, later renewed the war (147 BC) and defeated several Roman forces. Consul Servilius Caepio then bribed three of the leader's friends to murder Viriathus and the war came to an end.

Celtiberian Wars ❙ 153–133 BC

As Roman forces conquered the Iberian Peninsula, they met fierce resistance from Celtic tribes in the mountainous regions of north central Spain. After suffering some very costly losses, Rome gradually gained the upper hand. However, Rome's preoccupation with the 3rd Punic War (149–146 BC) saw renewed resistance and further heavy fighting. Celtic resistance was finally crushed at the siege of **Numantia**.

Syrian-Parthian War ❙ 141–139 BC

Parthians under Mithridates I invaded Babylonia, where they were checked by the Seleucid Demetrius II Nicator. While details of the war are uncertain, Demetrius was decisively defeated by the invaders on the Iranian Plateau. After ten years in captivity, he was released as a possible counter to his brother and successor Antiochus VII, who was routed in the Later Syrian-Parthian War at **Ecbatana**.

Chinese Conquest of Vietnam ❙ 111 BC

The Trieu Dynasty in Nam Viet (the northern part of modern Vietnam) came under increasing Chinese influence until the Han Emperor Wu Di sent a large force under General Lo Bac Duc to seize the country. The young King Trieu Vuong Duong was defeated and killed, beginning 1,000 years of almost uninterrupted Chinese domination, which was finally overthrown at **Bach Dang** in 938.

2nd Servile War ❙ 104–99 BC

Slave war broke out again in Sicily, where a leader named Salvius besieged the city of Murgantia in the east, while Athenion in the west attacked Lilybaeum. The two forces united, but were defeated near Triocala by Lucius Lucullus, who was then forced to withdraw. A fresh Roman force under Consul Marcus Aquilius eventually defeated and killed both leaders, and the survivors were hunted down.

Lepidus Revolt **|** 77 BC

Roman Consul Aemilius Lepidus attempted to rescind some reforms of the late Dictator Sulla and took an army from northern Italy against Rome. Outside Rome at Milvian Bridge, Lepidus was repulsed by Quintus Lutatius Catulus and driven back to Etruria, where he was defeated again by Pompey. Lepidus' ally Marcus Junius Brutus was besieged then murdered, in Mutina. Lepidus himself died soon after in Sardinia.

1st Satavahana-Saka War **|** 80–106

The Satavahana built the Andhra Empire, which covered most of southern India, then faced a prolonged campaign by the Saka Chiefs (Western Satraps) who seized Malwa and northern Deccan. A powerful new ruler, Gautamiputra Satakani, then inflicted a crushing defeat on the Sakas and regained lost land as well as Gujarat and Rajputana. The gains were lost soon after his death.

2nd Jewish Rising **|** 115–117

The Cyrenian Messianic leader Lukuas-Andreas began a campaign to free Palestine from Roman rule, and costly rebellion broke out in Cyprus, Cyrenia, Egypt and Mesopotamia. Emperor Trajan sent General Marcius Turbo and the Mauretanian Lusius Quietus to crush the rising, which was put down with very heavy Jewish losses. A few years later, a final rising under Bar-Cocheba was crushed at **Aelia**.

2nd Satavahana-Saka War **|** 126–131

Gautamiputra Satakani of the Satavahana defeated the Sakas (Western Satraps) of northwest India, but when he died, his son Pulumayi was attacked by the powerful Saka Chief Rudradamani, who seized Malwa, Gujarat and Rajputana. Driven back to the Deccan, Pulumayi made peace and married one of Rudradamani's daughters, but within 100 years the Andhra Empire had disappeared.

Egyptian-Nubian War **|** 641–652

When Muslims conquered Egypt, their cavalry under Nafi ibn Abd al-Kays marched into Christian Nubia (641–642) but were heavily repulsed. A second, much larger, invasion under Abd Allah ibn Sa'd (651–652) laid siege to the Dongala (Dunqulah), capital of Makurra. The ensuing peace treaty regulated Egyptian-Nubian relations for 600 years and saw the flowering of Nubian Christianity.

Shi'ite Rebellion **|** 814–819

The Shi'ite leader Abu 'l-Saraya raised rebellion against Caliph al-Ma'mun and, after defeating an Abbasid Imperial army at Kufa, marched to threaten Baghdad. Loyalist General Harthama ibn Ayan defeated Abu 'l-Saraya, who was later executed, and Mecca was recaptured. Al-Ma'mun declared a Shi'ite successor and withdrew, but in 819, he returned to rebuild the caliphate and restore Sunni authority.

Paulician War **|** 867–872

Successive Byzantine Emperors persecuted the Paulicians, a heretic sect in Armenia, who eventually established a powerful base at Tephrike (modern Divrig, Turkey). Under Karbeas, and later Chrysocheir (Chrysocheres), the Paulicians fought with the Arabs against Byzantium until Emperor Basil I launched an offensive which killed Chrysocheir, crushed the sect and dispersed the survivors.

Muslim Civil War **|** 936–944

When Caliph Ahmad ar-Radi appointed Muhammad ibn Raiq amir al-umara (Army Chief), he drove the Ikhshids of Egypt out of northern Syria and defeated the Hamdanids. He was killed by an assassin sent by al-Hasan of Syria, who took over Baghdad as Amir, with the title Nasir al-Dawla. After further fighting, Nasir was driven out by the Turk Tuzun, who made peace recognising Nasir in northern Syria.

Muslim Civil War **|** 945–948

During war over Syria between the Hamdanids of Baghdad and the Ikhshids of Egypt, Muhammad ibn Tughdj, Governor of Egypt, invaded Syria and defeated Sayf al-Dawla, forcing a partition. But when Ibn Tughdj died (947), al-Dawla twice advanced on Damascus, where he was defeated by Kafur, effective ruler of Ikhshid Egypt. The ensuing peace saw Cairo keep Damascus and Baghdad retain Aleppo.

Muslim Civil War ▮ 968–978

In the continuing struggle for Syria, Karmati leader Hasan al-A'sam of Bahrein defeated the Ikhshid army in Damascus, then faced the new Fatimid rulers of Egypt. Al-A'sam, with Hamdanid aid, twice repulsed the Fatimids and advanced to besiege Cairo. But, in September 978, new Fatimid Caliph al-Aziz personally led a massive army to defeat the Karmati at Ramleh and secure southern Syria.

Arduin's Wars ▮ 1004–1014

When Arduin, Marquis of Ivrea, proclaimed himself King in Lombardy, Emperor Henry II took a large force into Italy, where Arduin was defeated and forced to flee. Henry had himself crowned in Pavia (1004), then burned much of the city. In 1014 Arduin encouraged further rebellion and Henry returned. The Pope proclaimed Henry Emperor and his Germans again defeated Arduin, who withdrew to a monastery.

Chola-Pala War ▮ 1021–1024

Rajendra Chola continued his father's expansion of the South Indian kingdom, conquering the Andaman and Nicobar Islands, then turned north to invade the great Pala Kingdom of Bengal. In a brilliant campaign, he inflicted a decisive defeat on Mahipala I, leading to the decline of the northern dynasty. However, within fifty years, the Chola Dynasty was in turn eclipsed by the Chalukya.

Byzantine-Venetian War ▮ 1171–1177

Emperor Manuel attacked Venetians in Byzantium, and Doge Vitale Michiel II retaliated by leading a force which seized Ragusa (Dubrovnik), then attacked Chios. Driven off by plague, Vitale returned home, where he was murdered. Venice later supported the failed siege of **Ancona** (1173), and when they formed an alliance with Sicily (1175), Manuel made peace, and Venetian trading privileges were restored.

Muslim War of Succession ▮ 1196–1200

When Ayyubid Sultan Saladin died (1193), his empire was divided between his sons and brother al Malik al-'Adil (Sayf al-Din). In the ensuing dispute, al-'Adil supported Prince al-'Aziz in Egypt against his brother. But when al-'Aziz died (1198), al-'Adil pursued Prince al-Afdal from Syria to Egypt, where he defeated his forces. Al-'Adil proclaimed himself Sultan in Cairo, sharing the empire with his own sons.

Mongol Conquest of Korea ▮ 1231–1241

At the start of a new era of Mongol expansion, Ogedai (son of Genghis Khan) sent General Subetai to Korea. There he secured some of the main cities and left Mongol Governors in charge when he returned to China to defeat the Jin at **Yuxian**. In the face of local rebellion, Ogedai sent a second expedition in 1235, which gradually retook the country, and Mongol puppet Kings ruled until 1392.

Rise of Mali ▮ 1235–1332

After the fall of Sosso at **Kirina** (1235), a prolonged war of consolidation and expansion saw the rise of the massive Mandingo Empire of Mali in West Africa, reaching its maximum extent under the military leader Mansa Musa (1312–1332). However, from the mid-fourteenth century, dynastic struggles, border raids and outlying revolt saw the empire steadily decay. In 1433, Timbuktu itself fell to Tuareg invaders.

Mamluk-Nubian War ▮ 1272–1275

When Mamluks seized Egypt, Sultan Baibars began an aggressive new policy towards Christian Nubia, and sent a large army to support Shekanda, who was claiming the throne from his uncle Dawitt II. After heavy fighting, Dawitt fled from Dongala and Shekanda was installed. But years of royal intrigue followed and, in 1315, Egypt appointed a Muslim-converted Prince as a puppet in northern Nubia.

Hungarian War of Succession ▮ 1301–1308

The 400-year Arpad Dynasty of Hungary came to an end in 1301 with the death of King András III, last of the male line, plunging the country into civil war between rival claimants Wenceslaus III of Bohemia, Duke Otto III of Bavaria and Charles Robert of Anjou. After eight years of warfare and dispute, Charles Robert was elected King Charles (Károly) I and ruled Hungary until 1342.

Khalji Invasion of Pandya ▌ 1310–1311

Sultan Ala-ud-din seized Kakatiya at **Warangal** (1310), then sent Malik Kafur into southern India, where he overcame Vira Ballala III of Dhorasamudra, then invaded Pandya. Kafur defeated the brothers Vera and Sundara Pandya, and looted the kingdom and its capital Madura. He returned with the largest booty ever taken to Delhi, but soon lost favour in court intrigue (19 October 1310–24 April 1311).

1st Ethiopian-Ifat War ▌ 1320–1332

Amda Siyon (Tseyon) of Christian Ethiopia declared war on his Muslim neighbours and invaded Ifat, where he defeated and killed King Haqedin (Hakk al-Din). He then overwhelmed Haqedin's son and Ifat became a tributary state. A revolt in 1332 by Sabredin was put down and his ally the King of Adal was killed. Siyon also seized a number of other Muslim princedoms.

War of the Eight Saints ▌ 1375–1378

In revolt against the French Pope Gregory XI, Florence joined Milan and other cities. Led by a council of magistrates—the Eight Saints—Florence enjoyed initial success before the rebellious states were ravaged by a Papal army under Cardinal Robert of Geneva (later, anti-Pope Clement VII). Florence was eventually able to negotiate a peace, and Gregory returned the Papacy to Rome.

2nd Ethiopian-Ifat War ▌ 1415

When Yeshak became Emperor of Christian Ethiopia (1414), be began an aggressive new policy and took a large army against Sultan Sa'd ad-Din, who had launched a fresh rebellion in Muslim Ifat, roughly modern Somalia and Djibouti. The army of Ifat was crushed and Sa'd ad-Din escaped to an offshore island, where he was pursued and killed. Ifat was annexed and ceased to exist.

Scandinavian Revolt ▌ 1433–1439

Erik XIII of Sweden, who ruled Denmark, Norway and Sweden (the Kalmar Union), faced armed rebellion in Sweden under Engelbrekt Engelbrektsson, which soon spread. Erik was deposed and Engelbrektsson became Administrator of Sweden, but was murdered in 1436. Erik was restored but fresh revolt broke out, and rebel leader Karl Knutsson became Administrator. Erik was finally deposed in 1439.

Hungarian-Bohemian War ▌ 1469–1478

When the Hussite George of Podebrad became King of Bohemia, Pope Paul III induced Matthias I Corvinus of Hungary to invade in support of the Catholic nobility. After initial defeat, Hungarian troops seized Brno, where Matthias was declared King (3 May 1469). George and then his son Ladislaus fought on until 1478, when two Kings of Bohemia were recognised, and Matthias kept his conquests until his death.

Spanish Conquest of Haiti ▌ 1494–1509

When Christopher Columbus returned to Haiti (Española), his brother Bartholomew and Alonso de Hojeda crushed the native Taino and seized their Chief Caonabo. The Magua Chief Guarionex was also defeated, and a fresh force under Nicholas Ovando crushed the Zaraguayans and hanged their Queen Anacaona. Within a few years the original Haitians were annihilated by slavery and European diseases.

Funj-Nubian War ▌ 1504–1505

With the Christian kingdom of Alwah, south of Dongala, crumbling in the face of Arab pressure from the north, nomadic cattle herdsmen in the mountains of the Blue Nile, known as the Funj, began to assert their presence. They invaded to defeat a local force and Amara Dunqas built his capital at Sennar to establish a new "Black Sultanate" in the region of Khartoum. The Funj soon converted to Islam.

Spanish Conquest of Puerto Rico ❙ 1508–1511

Conquistador Juan Ponce de Leon arrived in Puerto Rico in 1508 and was initially welcomed by the Taino Chief (Caicique) Agueybana. But in the face of brutal suppression, Agueybana began a belated revolt which was crushed by the well-armed Spaniards. Agueybana was shot dead, and his brother Agueybana II eventually accepted a peace which saw his people decimated by slavery and smallpox.

Spanish Conquest of Cuba ❙ 1511–1513

Governor Diego Columbus of Española (Haiti) sent an expedition under Diego Velásquez de Cuélla to seize Cuba. He and his lieutenant, Pánfilo de Narváez, met determined resistance led by the Taino Chief Hatuey, who had also crossed with his supporters from Española. After a harsh guerrilla war, Hatuey was betrayed and burned at the stake (12 February 1512) and remaining resistance was soon crushed.

Maya Revolt ❙ 1546–1547

Leading a final Spanish expedition against the Northern Maya of the Yucatan (1540), Francisco de Montejo the Younger rapidly seized much of the western peninsula, where he founded the city of Merida (1542). But a few years later, the Spanish faced an upsurge of resistance in the east. In a series of harsh actions, the so-called revolt was crushed and most of the upper peninsula was secured for Spain.

Morisco Revolt ❙ 1568–1570

In the face of religious persecution, Spanish Moors who had converted to Christianity (Moriscos) led a revolt in southern Spain, which began on Christmas Day 1568 in Granada. A brutal war saw the rebels crushed by Iñigo Lopez de Mendoza, Marquis of Mondéjar, and later by Don John of Austria. The survivors were dispersed in northern Spain, but after 1609, perhaps 300,000 were expelled to North Africa.

1st Dutch-Khoikhoi War ❙ 1659–1660

Soon after Jan van Riebeeck established the first permanent settlement in South Africa for the Dutch East India Company (1652), land-hungry free settlers in Western Cape came into armed conflict with native Khoikhoi (formerly known as Hottentots), led by Doman of the Goringhaiqua. Well supplied with horses and rifles, the settlers soon crushed resistance and the Khoikhoi signed a peace treaty.

Revolt of the Three Feudatories ❙ 1671–1681

Three former Qing Generals who helped overthrow the Ming were given feudatories in southern China, but turned against the Kangxi Emperor. Wu Sangui proclaimed a new Zhou Dynasty with himself as Emperor, but he soon died. His followers were routed in bloody fighting and his allies Shang Kexi and Geng Jimao were defeated and executed as the rebellion was crushed. Some survivors fled to Taiwan.

2nd Dutch-Khoikhoi War ❙ 1673–1677

Under renewed Dutch pressure for land in the Western Cape, Khoikhoi under leadership of Cochoqua Chief Gonnema struck back against settlers and traders. A series of punitive, costly expeditions caused heavy Khoikhoi losses, but failed to capture Gonnema. However, he eventually agreed to make peace, and his people went into steep decline. In 1713 the Khoikhoi were utterly ravaged by smallpox.

Rise of Dahomey ❙ 1724–1727

The powerful warrior Agaja Trudo of Dahomey defeated and killed the King of Allada (March 1724) and later defeated King Huffon of Whydah (Ouidah) to establish the new kingdom of Dahomey. While Agaja was forced to pay tribute to Oyo from 1730, he built a major power in West Africa, which played a dominant role in the lucrative Atlantic slave trade.

Funj-Ethiopian War ❙ 1730–1755

Badi IV of Funj began a major campaign against Ethiopia, where he and his ally Shaykh Kamis of Nubia defeated an Ethiopian army near Sennar. The Funj marched into Kordofan and, after an initial loss, General Muhammad Abu Likaylik took command and secured victory.

Likaylik then deposed Badi, who was later killed. Protracted intrigue ruined the sultanate, and in 1821 it submitted meekly to Egypt.

Tupac Amaru Revolt ❙ 1780–1782

In a prelude to wars of independence throughout South America, Indians in the Peruvian Andes rose in revolt under Jose Gabriel Condorcanqui, who took the name of his ancestor Tupac Amaru. The rebels failed to take Cuzco, where Tupac Amaru was publicly tortured to death. Resistance continued elsewhere and rebels took Bogota and twice attacked La Paz before the rising was finally crushed.

Haitian Invasion of Dominica ❙ 1822

During the Napoleonic War, Spanish forces drove the French out of **Santo Domingo** (1809). But when Lieutenant Governor José Nuñez de Cáceres declared an independent state of Spanish Haiti, new President Jean-Pierre Boyer of Haiti led a swift invasion. The Spanish were expelled and Boyer briefly united the entire island of Hispaniola until the Dominican War of Independence in 1844.

Great Java War ❙ 1825–1830

When a Dutch-supported claimant succeeded to the throne of Jogjakarta, Prince Dipo Negoro opposed Dutch land reforms designed to weaken the Javanese nobility. A prolonged guerrilla struggle—cast as a Jihad (Muslim Holy War)—was eventually quelled by General Hendrik Merkus de Kock. Dipo Negoro attended peace talks under safe conduct, but was arrested. He died in exile 25 years later.

Spanish Civil War ❙ 1840–1843

In the wake of the First Carlist War, General Baldomero Espartero became Regent for Queen Isabella II and assumed dictatorial power. Popular risings in Pamplona and Barcelona were severely crushed and when Espartero dissolved the Cortes, General Ramón Narváez marched on Madrid. He seized the capital and Espartero fled.

Aged just 13, Isabella assumed government with Narváez as Chief Minister.

Dominican War of Independence ❙ 1844

With the overthrow of President Jean-Pierre Boyer of Haiti, rebellion began in Dominica, led by Juan Pablo Duarte, Francisco del Rosario Sánchez and Ramón Mélla, who forced the Haitians to flee. Caudillo Pedro Santana then had himself declared President of the Dominican Republic and imprisoned his former allies. Santana assumed dictatorial powers and repulsed Haitian invasions in 1849 and 1855.

Caste War of Yucatan ❙ 1846–1901

Not long after Mexico won independence from Spain, war broke out, pitting the Maya of the Yucatan against European-descended Yucatecans and distant central government. A prolonged and bloody struggle ensued, which spilled over into British Honduras. After more than five decades, a Mexican offensive into rebel-held eastern Yucatan virtually ended the war, though skirmishing continued for years.

Dominican War of Restoration ❙ 1863–1864

President Pedro Santana returned the Dominican Republic to Spain (1861), which soon faced guerrilla resistance and later open rebellion under José Antonio Salcedo. Santana took command of Spain's largely mercenary army but, after he died, the nationalists soon prevailed. Spain eventually annulled the annexation and withdrew from Dominica. In early 1865, Dominica's second independence was declared.

Waziristan Campaign ❙ 1936–1937

Following a legal dispute over the marriage of a Muslim schoolteacher and an under-age Hindu girl, rebellion broke out in Waziristan, fanned by a Mullah, the Faqir of Ipi. A large-scale Indian Army presence eventually secured order at high cost in men and resources. Intermittent resistance continued, with further British losses, until the creation of independent Pakistan in 1947. The Faqir died in 1950.

Bibliography

No dictionary of battles could fail to acknowledge the pioneers who led the way—starting with the Reverend Thomas Harbottle whose 1904 *Dictionary of Battles* was revised and reprinted by George Bruce from 1971 onwards, before it was retitled in 1995 because, as Bruce claimed: "the new title Dictionary of Wars reflects the changed character of war, set battles having long since become antiquated."

Similarly, every military enthusiast owes an enormous debt to Ernest and Trevor Dupuy, the father-and-son team whose monumental *Encyclopedia of Military History* has been continuously in print since 1970; and the late Brigadier Peter Young, who tragically completed only two volumes of his planned four-part master work, *A Dictionary of Battles 1816–1976* (1977) and (with Michael Calvert) *A Dictionary of Battles 1715–1815* (1979).

Other useful publications across the full scope of history include David Eggenberger's *An Encyclopedia of Battles* (1985); John Sweetman's *A Dictionary of European Land Battles to 1945* (1984); Michael Sanderson's *Sea Battles, a reference guide* (1975) and George Kohn's *Dictionary of Wars* (1988) later retitled *Encyclopedia of Wars*.

Beyond these publications, the research for this project has recorded well over one thousand separate titles, including national and campaign dictionaries of battles and military history, as well as dozens of national and subject encyclopedias, national dictionaries and databases of biography. Typical of these are the scores of individual national volumes in the monumental Historical Dictionaries series published by Scarecrow Press of Lanham, Maryland, and their outstanding companion series Historical Dictionaries of War, Revolution and Civil Unrest. In addition a priceless debt is owed to the contributors to the magisterial multi-volume series, *The Cambridge Ancient History*, *The Cambridge Medieval History*, *The Cambridge Modern History* and *The New Cambridge Modern History* as well as the multi-volume Cambridge histories of individual countries such as China, India, Iran and Japan. The research has also included a very large number of invaluable online resources and databases.

The bibliography which follows contains a large number of general books or those covering several major historical eras.

Where possible, however, the sources have been categorised into broad historic periods (adapted from Dupuy and Dupuy) namely: The Ancient World to 600 AD; Medieval Warfare 600–1500; The Early Modern Era 1500–1750; The Century of Revolution 1750–1850; The Rise of Modern Professionalism 1850–1900; World War and Revolution 1900–1939; World War II 1939–1945; War after 1945.

General Books or Sources across Several Major Eras

Adamec, Ludwig W. *Dictionary of Afghan Wars, Revolutions and Insurgencies.* Lanham, MD: Scarecrow Press, 1996.

Allen, William E. D. and Muratov, Paul. *Caucasian Battlefields: A History of Wars on the*

Turco-Caucasian Border 1828–1921. London: Cambridge University Press, 1953.

Arnold, Guy. *Historical Dictionary of Civil Wars in Africa.* Lanham, MD: Scarecrow Press, 1999.

Baker, G. P. *A Book of Battles.* London: Hurst, 1935.

Barker, Ralph. *Against the Sea: True Stories of Disaster and Survival.* London: Chatto and Windus, 1972.

Barthorp, Michael. *The Northwest Frontier: British India and Pakistan 1839–1947.* Poole: Blandford Press, 1982.

Bartlett, Thomas and Jeffery, Keith (Eds). *A Military History of Ireland.* Cambridge: Cambridge University Press, 1996.

Bennet, Matthew. *Hutchinson Dictionary of Ancient and Medieval Warfare.* Oxford: Helicon, 1998.

Bhuttacharya, Sachchidananda. *A Dictionary of Indian History.* Calcutta: University of Calcutta, 1967.

Black, Jeremy. *European Warfare 1453–1815.* London: Palgrave Macmillan, 1999.

———. *European Warfare 1494–1600.* London: Routledge, 2002.

Black, Jeremy (Ed). *The Seventy Great Battles in History.* London: Thames and Hudson, 2005.

Brice, Martin. *Forts and Fortresses.* London: Quarto Publishing, 1990.

Brooks, Richard. *Cassell's Battlefields of Britain and Ireland.* London: Weidenfeld and Nicolson, 2005.

Bruce, George. *Harbottle's Dictionary of Battles.* London: Granada, 1979.

Burne, Alfred H. *The Battlefields of England.* London: Methuen, 1950.

———. *More Battlefields of England.* London: Methuen, 1952.

Cairns, James F. *The Eagle and the Lotus: Western Intervention in Vietnam.* Melbourne: Lansdowne, 1969.

Calvert, Michael and Young, Peter. *A Dictionary of Battles 1715–1815.* New York: Mayflower Books, 1979.

Chandler, David. *The Art of Warfare on Land.* London: Hamlyn, 1974.

Chandler, David (Gen Ed). *Dictionary of Battles: Key Battles from 405 BC to Today.* London: Ebury Press, 1987.

Charney, Michael W. *Southeast Asian Warfare 1300–1900.* Leiden: Brill, 2000.

Cline, Eric H. *The Battles of Armageddon: Megiddo and the Jezreel Valley from the Bronze Age to the Nuclear Age.* Ann Arbor: University of Michigan Press, 2000.

Clodfelter, Michael. *Warfare and Armed Conflicts: A Statistical Reference.* Jefferson, NC: McFarland and Co, 1992.

Clowes, William Baird. *The Royal Navy: A History* (7 vols). 1st ed 1898. New York: Ams Press, 1966.

Coates, William P. and Zelda K. *Six Centuries of Russo-Polish Relations.* London: Lawrence and Wishart, 1948.

Connell, Charles. *The World's Greatest Sieges.* London: Odhams, 1967.

Cook, Chris and Stevenson, John. *The Atlas of Modern Warfare.* London: Weidenfeld and Nicolson, 1978.

Cook, H.C.B. *Battle Honours of the British and Indian Armies 1662–1982.* London, Leo Cooper, 1987.

Creasey, Sir Edward. *Fifteen Decisive Battles of the World: From Marathon to Waterloo.* 1st ed 1852. New York: Dorset, 1987.

Cross, Robin (Ed). *The Guinness Encyclopedia of Warfare.* London: Guinness Publishing, 1991.

Davis, Paul K. *One Hundred Decisive Battles: From Ancient Times to the Present.* Santa Barbara, CA: ABC-Clio, 1999.

Di Cosmo, Nicola (Ed). *Warfare in Inner Asian History 500–1800.* Leiden: Brill, 2002.

Dupuy, R. Ernest and Trevor N. *The Encyclopedia of Military History: 3500 BC to the Present.* London: HarperCollins, 1993.

Dupuy, Trevor, Johnson, Curt and Bongard, David L. *The Harper Encyclopedia of Military Biography.* New York: Castle Books, 1995.

Edgerton, Robert. *Warriors of the Rising Sun: A History of the Japanese Military.* New York: W. W. Norton, 1997.

Eggenberger, David. *An Encyclopedia of Battles: Accounts of over 1,560 Battles from 1479 BC to the Present.* New York: Dover, 1985.

Falls, Cyril (Ed). *Great Military Battles.* London: Spring Books, 1969.

Fass, Virginia. *The Forts of India.* London: Collins, 1986.

Fenby, Jonathan. *Generalissimo: Chiang Kai-shek and the China He Lost.* London: Free Press, 2003.

Fortescue, Hon Sir John. *A History of the British Army* (13 vols). London: Macmillan, 1889–1930.

Frankland, Dr Noble (Ed). *The Encyclopedia of Twentieth Century Warfare.* London: Mitchell Beazley, 1989.

Frere-Cook, Gervis and Macksey, Kenneth. *The Guinness History of Sea Warfare.* Enfield: Guinness Superlatives, 1975.

Fuller, John F. C. *The Decisive Battles of the Western World.* London: Eyre and Spottiswoode, 1954.

Gerolymatos, André. *The Balkan Wars: Conquest, Revolution and Retribution from the Ottoman Era to the Twentieth Century and Beyond.* New York: Basic Books, 2002.

Goldstone, Jack K. (Ed). *Encyclopedia of Political Revolutions.* Washington, DC: Congressional Quarterly Inc, 1998.

Graff, David A. and Higham, Robin (Eds). *A Military History of China.* Boulder, CO: Westview Press, 2002.

Grey, Jack. *Rebellion and Revolutions: China from the 1860's to the 1980's.* Oxford: Oxford University Press, 1999.

Haswell, Jock. *The British Army: A Concise History.* London: Thames and Hudson, 1975.

Haws, Duncan and Hurst, Alex. *The Maritime History of the World* (2 vols). Brighton: Teredo Books, 1985.

Haydn, Joseph and Vincent, Benjamin. *Haydn's Dictionary of Dates.* 1st ed 1910. New York: Dover, 1969.

Hayes-McCoy, Gerard A. *Irish Battles: A Military History of Ireland 1014–1798.* Belfast: Appletree Press, 1989.

Heathcote, Thomas A. *The Afghan Wars 1839–1919.* London: Osprey, 1980.

Hodgkin, Thomas. *Italy and Her Invaders.* Oxford: Oxford University Press, 1879–1899.

Hogg, Ian V. *The Hutchinson Dictionary of Battles.* Oxford: Helicon, 1995.

Holdinger, Erik. *Warriors of the Steppe: A Military History of Central Asia 500 BC:1700 AD.* New York: Sarpedon, 1987.

Holmes, Richard. *World Atlas of Warfare.* London: Mitchell Beazley, 1988.

Holmes, Richard (Ed). *The Oxford Companion to Military History.* Oxford: Oxford University Press, 2001.

Jansen, Marius B. (Ed). *Warrior Rule in Japan.* Cambridge: Cambridge University Press, 1995.

Kar, Hemendra C. *Military History of India.* Calcutta: Firma KLM Private, 1981.

Keegan, John and Wheatcroft, Andrew. *Who's Who in Military History (1495 to Present).* London: Hutchinson, 1987.

Kierman, Frank A. (Ed). *Chinese Ways in Warfare.* Cambridge, MA: Cambridge University Press, 1974.

Kinross, John. *The Battlefields of Britain.* Newton Abbot: David and Charles, 1979.

Kinross, John Balfour, Lord. *The Ottoman Centuries: The Rise and Fall of the Turkish Empire.* London: Jonathon Cape, 1977.

Kohn, George. *Dictionary of Wars.* New York: Anchor Doubleday, 1988.

Laffin, John. *Brassey's Battles: 3500 Years of Conflict, Campaigns and Wars from A-Z.* London: Brassey's Defence Publishers, 1986.

Lane-Poole, Stanley. *Medieval India under Mohammadan Rule 712–1764.* Delhi: Universal Publishing, 1963.

Leung, Edwin Pak-Wah. *Historical Dictionary of Revolutionary China 1839–1976.* Westport, CT: Greenwood Press, 1992.

Livesey, Anthony. *Battles of the Great Commanders.* London: Michael Joseph, 1987.

Longmate, Norman. *Defending the Island: From Caesar to the Armada.* London: Hutchinson, 1989.

Lucas, James (Ed). *Command: From Alexander to Zhukov.* London: Bloomsbury, 1988.

Macksey, Kenneth. *The Guinness History of Land Warfare.* Enfield: Guinness Superlatives, 1973.

Majumdar, Ramesh C. *Outline of Ancient Indian History and Civilization.* Calcutta: Sri Narasimha, 1927.

Malkasian, Carter. *A History of Modern Wars of Attrition.* Westport, CT: Greenwood, 2002.

Margiotta, Franklin D. (Ed). *Brassey's Encyclopedia of Military History and Biography.* Washington, DC: Brassey, 1994.

Marren, Peter. *Grampian Battlefields: Historic Battles of Northeast Scotland AD 84 to 1745.* Aberdeen: Aberdeen University Press, 1990.

Marriott, John. *Disaster at Sea.* London: Ian Allen, 1987.

Mazumdar, A. Kumar. *Early Hindu India: A Dynastic Study* (3 vols). 1st ed 1917. New Delhi: Cosmo, 1981.

McConnell, Brian. *Assassination.* London: Leslie Frewin, 1969.

McCormack, John. *One Million Mercenaries: Swiss Soldiers in Armies of the World.* London: Leo Cooper, 1993.

McHenry, Robert (Ed). *Webster's American Military Biographies.* Springfield, MA: Merriam-Webster, 1978.

McKee, Alexander. *Against the Odds: Battles at Sea 1591–1949.* London: Souvenir Press, 1991.

Melegari, Vezio. *The World's Greatest Regiments.* London: Spring Books, 1972.

Moodie, Duncan C. F. *Battles and Adventures in Southern Africa 1495–1879.* Adelaide: George Robertson, 1879.

Moon, Sir Penderel. *The British Conquest and Dominion of India.* London: Gerald Duckworth and Co, 1989.

Mordal, Jacques. *25 Centuries of Sea Warfare.* London: Souvenir Press, 1965.

Moreman, Tim R. *The Army in India and the Development of Frontier Warfare 1849–1947.* London: Macmillan, 1998.

Morgan, Owen. *The Battles of Wales.* Liverpool: D. Salesbury Hughes, 1920.

Mote, Frederick W. *Imperial China 900 1800*. Cambridge, MA: Harvard University Press, 1999.

Naravane, M. S. *Battles of Medieval India (1295–1850)*. New Delhi: APH Publishing, 1996.

Needham, Joseph, Yates, Robin D. S. et al. *Science and Civilization in China Volume V Part VI Military Science: Missiles and Siege*. Cambridge: Cambridge University Press, 1994.

Newark, Tim. *Turning the Tide of War: Fifty Battles That Changed the Course of Modern History from 1792–1995*. London: Hamlyn, 2001.

Norman, C. B. *Battle Honours of the British Army (1911)*. Newton Abbot: David and Charles, 1971.

O'Balance, Edgar. *Afghan Wars 1839–1992*. London: Brasseys, 1993.

Pakenham, Thomas. *The Scramble for Africa*. London: Weidenfeld and Nicolson, 1991.

Paterson, Thomas W. *Canadian Battles and Massacres*. Langley, BC: Stagecoach, 1977.

Pemsel, Helmut. *Atlas of Naval Warfare* (transl. Major G. D. Smith). London: Arms and Armour Press, 1977.

Perrett, Bryan. *Last Stand!: Famous Battles Against the Odds*. London: Arms and Armour Press, 1991.

———. *Battle Book: Crucial Conflicts 1469 BC to the Present*. London: Arms and Armour Press, 1992.

———. *At All Costs: Stories of Impossible Victories*. London: Arms and Armour Press, 1993.

Polmar, Norman and Merskey, Peter B. *Amphibious Warfare: An Illustrated History*. London: Blandford Press, 1988.

Purcell, Edward. *Encyclopedia of Battles in North America 1517–1916*. New York: Facts on File, 2001.

Regan, Geoffrey. *Someone Had Blundered*. London: Batsford, 1989.

———. *The Guinness Book of Military Blunders*. London: Guinness Publishing, 1991.

———. *The Guinness Book of Decisive Battles*. London: Guinness Publishing, 1992.

Revie, Alastair, Foster, Thomas and Graham, Burton. *Battle*. London: Marshall Cavendish, 1974–1984.

Roy, Kaushik. *India's Historic Battles: From Alexander the Great to Kargil*. Delhi: Permanent Black, 2004.

Sanderson, Michael. *Sea Battles, A Reference Guide*. Melbourne: Wren Publishing, 1975.

Sawyer, Ralph D. *Fire and Water: The Art of Incendiary and Aquatic Warfare in China*. Boulder, CO: Westview Press, 2004.

Seward, Desmond. *The Monks at War: The Military Religious Orders*. London: Eyre Methuen, 1972.

Seymour, William. *Decisive Factors in Twenty Great Battles of the World*. London: Sidgwick and Jackson, 1988.

———. *Great Sieges of History*. London: Brasseys, 1991.

Shepherd, William R. *Shepherd's Historical Atlas*. 1st ed 1928. New York: Barnes and Noble, 1973.

Shrader, Charles (Ed). *Reference Guide to United States Military History*. New York: Facts on File, 1993.

Simpson, Keith. *History of the German Army*. London: Bison Books, 1985.

Singh, Sarbans. *Battle Honours of the Indian Army 1757–1971*. New Delhi: Vision Books, 1993.

Smith, E. D. *Valour: A History of the Gurkhas*. New York: Overlook Press, 1997.

Smith, Vincent A. *Early History of India: From 600 BC to the Mohammedan Conquest*. Oxford: Clarendon Press, 1924.

Smurthwaite, David. *Ordnance Survey Complete Guide to the Battlefields of Britain*. Exeter: Webb and Bower, 1984.

Smyth, Sir John. *Great Stories of the Victoria Cross*. London: Arthur Barker, 1977.

Stillwell, Richard (Ed). *Princeton Encyclopedia of Classical Sites*. Princeton, NJ: Princeton University Press, 1976.

Sugar, Peter F. *Southeast Europe under Ottoman Rule 1354–1804*. Seattle: University of Washington, 1977.

Sweetman, Jack (Ed). *Great American Naval Battles*. Annapolis, MD: Naval Institute Press, 1998.

Sweetman, John. *A Dictionary of European Land Battles to 1945*. London: Robert Hale, 1984.

Thomas, Hugh. *Cuba: The Pursuit of Freedom* (2 vols). London: Eyre and Spottiswoode, 1971.

Uden, Grant and Cooper, Richard. *A Dictionary of British Ships and Seamen*. London: Allen Lane, 1980.

Vandervort, Bruce. *Wars of Imperial Conquest in Africa 1830–1914*. London: University College Press, 1998.

Verma, Amrit. *Forts of India*. Delhi: Ministry of Information, 1985.

Weir, William. *Fifty Battles That Changed the World: The Conflicts That Most Changed the Course of History*. Franklin Lakes, NJ: Career Press, 2001.

Wheatcroft, Andrew. *The World Atlas of Revolutions*. London: Book Club Associates, 1983.

Windrow, Martin and Mason, Francis K. *A Concise Dictionary of Military Biography*. Reading: Osprey, 1975.

Wolf, Eric R. *Peasant Wars of the Twentieth Century*. London: Faber and Faber, 1971.

Wolf, John B. *The Barbary Coast: Algiers under the Turks 1500–1830*. New York: W. W. Norton, 1979.

Young, Peter. *A Dictionary of Battles 1816–1976*. London: New English Library, 1977.

The Ancient World to 600 AD

Bagnall, Nigel. *The Punic Wars*. London: Hutchinson, 1990.

Bradley, Keith R. *Slavery and Rebellion in the Roman World 140–71 BC*. London: B.T. Batsford, 1989.

Brion, Marcel. *Attila, the Scourge of God* (transl. H. Ward). London: Cassel and Co, 1929.

Cartledge, Paul. *Agesilaus and the Crisis of Sparta*. London: Duckworth, 1987.

Caven, Brian. *The Punic Wars*. London: Weidenfeld and Nicolson, 1980.

Connolly, Peter. *Greece and Rome at War*. London: MacDonald, 1981.

Cottrell, Leonard. *Enemy of Rome: The Battles of Hannibal*. London: Evans Brothers, 1960.

Curchin, Leonard Andrew. *Roman Spain: Conquest and Assimilation*. London: Routledge, 1991.

De Crespigny, Rafe. *Northern Frontier: The Policies and Strategy of the Later Han Empire*. Canberra: Australian National University, 1984.

———. *Generals of the South: The Foundation and Early History of the Kingdoms State of Wu*. Canberra: Australian National University, 1990.

Dikshitar, V. R. Ramachandra. *War in Ancient India*. 1st ed 1944. Delhi: Motilal Bamarsidass, 1944.

Dodge, Theodore Ayrault. *Hannibal* (2 vols). 1st ed 1891. London: Greenhill, 1993.

Ellis, John R. *Philip II and Macedonian Imperialism*. London: Thames and Hudson, 1976.

Ellis, Peter Berresford. *Celt and Saxon: The Struggle for Britain AD 410–937*. London: Constable, 1993.

Forde-Johnston, James. *Hadrians Wall*. London: Michael Joseph, 1977.

Fox, Robin Lane. *Alexander the Great*. London: Allen Lane, 1973.

Graff, David A. *Medieval Chinese Warfare 300–900*. London: Routledge, 2002.

Hamilton, Charles D. *Agesilaus and the Failure of Spartan Hegemony*. New York: Cornell University Press, 1991.

Hammond, Nicholas G. L. *Philip of Macedon*. London: Duckworth, 1994.

Heather, Peter J. *Goths and Romans 332—489*. Oxford: Oxford University Press, 1991.

Herzog, Chaim and Gichon, Mordechai. *Battles of the Bible*. London: Weidenfeld and Nicolson, 1978.

Howarth, Patrick. *Attila, King of the Huns*. London: Constable, 1994.

Kagan, Donald. *The Peloponnesian War*. New York: Viking, 2003.

Lau, D. C. and Ames, Roger T. *Sun Pin: The Art of Warfare*. Boulder, CO: Westview Press, 1993.

Liddell Hart, Basil. *A Greater than Napoleon: Scipio Africanus*. London: Blackwoods, 1926.

Loewe, Michael. *Crisis and Conflict in Han China, 104 BC–9 AD*. London: G. Allen and Unwin, 1974.

Loewe, Michael and Shaughnessy, Edward L. (Eds). *The Cambridge History of Ancient China: From the Origins of Civilization to 221 BC*. Cambridge: Cambridge University Press, 1999.

Maspero, Henri. *China in Antiquity* (transl. Frank A. Kierman). 1st ed 1927. Armherst: University of Massachusetts Press, 1978.

McGregor, Malcolm F. *The Athenians and Their Empire*. Vancouver: University of British Columbia, 1987.

Michell, Humfrey. *Sparta*. Cambridge: Cambridge University Press, 1952.

Miller, J. Maxwell and Hayes, John. *A History of Ancient Israel and Judah*. London: SCM Press, 1986.

Pan, Ku. *A History of the Former Han Dynasty*. (3 vols transl. Homer H. Dubs). Baltimore: Waverley Press, 1938–1955.

Renault, Mary. *The Nature of Alexander*. London: Allen Lane, 1975.

Richardson, John S. *The Romans in Spain*. London: Blackwell, 1996.

Salmon, Edward Togo. *Samnium and the Samnites*. Cambridge: Cambridge University Press, 1967.

Thomas, Carol G. and Conant, Craig. *The Trojan Wars*. Westport, CT: Greenwood, 2005.

Thompson, E. A. *A History of Attila and the Huns*. Oxford: Oxford University Press, 1948.

Tritle, Lawrence A. *The Peloponnesian War*. Westport, CT: Greenwood, 2005.

Warmington, Brian H. *Carthage*. London: Robert Hale, 1960.

Watson, Burton. *The Tso Chuan: Selections from China's Oldest Narrative History*. New York: Columbia University Press, 1989.

Watson, George R. *The Roman Soldier*. London: Thames and Hudson, 1969.

Webster, Graham. *Rome Against Caratacus*. London: B.T. Batsford, 1981.

———. *The Roman Invasion of Britain*. London: B.T. Batsford, 1993.

Wells, Peter S. *The Battle That Stopped Rome: Emperor Augustus, Arminius and the Slaughter of the Legions in the Teutoborg Forest.* New York: W.W. Norton, 2003.

Wright, Arthur F. *The Sui Dynasty.* New York: Knopf, 1978.

Medieval Warfare 600–1500

Babinger, Franz. *Mehmed the Conqueror and His Time.* Princeton, NJ: Princeton University Press, 1978.

Barron, Evan Macleod. *The Scottish War of Independence.* London: James Nisbet, 1914.

Bartos, Frantisek. *Hussite Wars 1424–1437.* New York: Columbia University Press, 1986.

Beckwith, Christopher I. *The Tibetan Empire in Central Asia: A History of the Struggle for Great Power among Tibetans, Turks, Arabs and Chinese during the Early Middle Ages.* Princeton, NJ: Princeton University Press, 1987.

Bennett, Michael. *Lambert Simnel and the Battle of Stoke.* Stroud: Alan Sutton, 1987.

Bhakari, S. K. *Indian Warfare: An Appraisal of Strategy and Tactics of War in the Early Medieval Period.* New Delhi: Munshiram Manoharlal, 1981.

Billing, Malcolm. *The Cross and the Crescent: A History of the Crusades.* London: BBC Enterprises, 1987.

Boyle, John A. *The Mongol World Empire 1206–1370.* London: Varorium Reprints, 1997.

Bradford, Ernle. *The Sword and the Scimitar.* London: Victor Gollancz, 1974.

Brent, Peter. *The Mongol Empire: Genghis Khan, His Triumph and His Legacy.* London: Weidenfeld and Nicolson, 1976.

Bridge, Anthony. *The Crusades.* London: Grenada Publishing, 1980.

Brown, R. Allen. *The Normans and the Norman Conquest.* London: Constable, 1969.

Browning, Robert. *Byzantium and Bulgaria.* London: Temple Smith, 1975.

Burne, Alfred H. *The Crecy War: A Military History of the Hundred Years War to the Peace of Bretigny 1337–1360.* London: Eyre and Spottiswoode, 1955.

———. *The Agincourt War: A Military History of the Latter Part of the Hundred Years War 1369–1543.* London: Eyre and Spottiswoode, 1956.

Burns, William. *The Scottish War of Independence* (2 vols). Glasgow: James Maclehose, 1874.

Collins, Roger. *The Arab Conquest of Spain.* London: Blackwell, 1989.

Contamine, Philippe. *War in the Middle Ages.* Oxford: Basil Blackwell, 1984.

Douglas, David C. *William the Conqueror.* London: Eyre Methuen, 1964.

Downey, Glanville. *A History of Antioch in Syria: From Seleucus to the Arab Conquest.* Princeton, NJ: Princeton University Press, 1961.

Farris, William Wayne. *Heavenly Warriors: Evolution of Japan's Military 500–1300.* Cambridge, MA: Harvard University Press, 1992.

Fennell, John L. I. *Ivan the Great of Moscow.* London: Macmillan, 1961.

Fitzgerald, Charles P. *Son of Heaven: A Biography of Li Shih-Min, Founder of the T'ang Dynasty.* Taipei: Ch'eng Wen Publishing, 1970.

Gibbons, Herbert Adams. *The Foundation of the Ottoman Empire 1300–1403.* 1st ed 1916. London: Frank Cass, 1968.

Glubb, John. *The Great Arab Conquests 630–680.* Englewood Cliffs, NJ: Prentice Hall, 1967.

———. *Haroon al Rasheed and the Great Abassids.* London: Hodder and Stoughton, 1976.

Goodman, Anthony. *The Wars of the Roses.* London: Routledge and Kegan Paul, 1981.

Grey, Ian. *Ivan III and the Unification of Russia.* London: English Universities Press, 1964.

Gulzar, Ahmed. *The Battles of the Prophet of Allah.* Lahore: Islamic Publications, 1985.

Habib, Muhammad. *Sultan Mahmud of Ghazni.* New Delhi: S. Chand and Co, 1967.

Haigh, Philip. *The Military Campaigns of the Wars of the Roses.* Stroud: Alan Sutton, 1995.

Hallam, Elizabeth (Ed). *Chronicles of the Crusades: Eyewitness Accounts.* London: Weidenfeld and Nicolson, 1989.

Hartog, Leo De. *Genghis Khan: Conqueror of the World.* London: I. B. Tauris and Co, 1989.

Harvey, Leonard P. *Islamic Spain 1250–1500.* Chicago: University of Chicago, 1990.

Held, Joseph. *Hunyadi: Legend and Reality.* New York: Columbia University Press, 1985.

Heymann, Frederick Gotthold. *John Zizka and the Hussite Revolution.* New York: Princeton University Press, 1969.

Hookham, Hilda. *Tamburlaine the Conqueror.* London: Hodder and Stoughton, 1962.

Hopkins, Andrea. *Knights.* London: Collins and Brown, 1990.

Howell, Thomas Evans. *Wales and the Wars of the Roses.* Oxford: Oxford University Press, 1915.

Kaminsky, Michael. *A History of the Hussite Revolution.* Berkeley: University of California, 1967.

Kennedy, Hugh. *The Early Abbasid Caliphate.* London: Groom Helm, 1981.

Khan, Yusuf Husain. *The First Nizam: Life and Times of Nizam-ul-Mulk.* Bombay: Asia Publishing House, 1963.

Lamb, Harold. *The March of Muscovy: 1400–1648.* New York: Doubleday, 1948.

Lewis, Bernard. *The Assassins.* London: Weidenfeld and Nicolson, 1967.

MacKay, James A. *Robert Bruce: King of Scots.* London: Robert Hale, 1974.

Marshall, Christopher. *Warfare in the Latin East 1192–1291.* Cambridge: Cambridge University Press, 1992.

Marshall, Robert. *Storm from the East: From Genghis Khan to Khubilai Khan.* London: BBC Books, 1993.

Miller, William. *The Latins in the Levant: A History of Frankish Greece 1205–1566.* London: John Murphy, 1908.

Morillo, Stephen. *Warfare under the Anglo-Norman Kings 1066–1135.* Woodbridge: Boydell Press, 1994.

Morris, John E. *The Welsh Wars of Edward I.* Oxford: Oxford University Press, 1901.

Nazim, Muhammad. *The Life and Times of Sultan Mahmud of Ghazni.* New Delhi: Munshiram Manoharlal, 1971.

Neillands, Robin. *The Hundred Years War.* London: Routledge, 1990.

Newark, Tim. *The Barbarians: Warriors and Wars of the Dark Ages.* Poole: Blandford Press, 1985.

Nicolle, David. *The Mongol Warlords.* Poole: Firebird Books, 1990.

Norwich, John Julius. *The Normans in the South.* London: Longmans Green, 1967.

O'Reilly, Bernard F. *The Contest of Christian and Muslem Spain.* Cambridge, MA: Blackwell, 1992.

Ostrogorski, George. *History of the Byzantine State* (transl. Joan Hussey). Oxford: Basil Blackwell, 1968.

Payne, Robert. *The Dream and the Tomb: A History of the Crusades.* London: Robert Hale, 1984.

Phillips, Eustace D. *The Mongols.* London: Thames and Hudson, 1969.

Pollard, Anthony J. *The Wars of the Roses.* London: Macmillan, 1988.

———. *Northern England during the Wars of the Roses.* Oxford: Oxford University Press, 1990.

Prevenier, Walter and Blockmans, Wim. *The Burgundian Netherlands.* Cambridge: Cambridge University Press, 1986.

Ratchnevsky, Paul. *Genghis Khan: His Life and Legacy.* Oxford: Basil Blackwell, 1991.

Rice, Tamara Talbot. *The Seljuks in Asia Minor.* London: Thames and Hudson, 1961.

Riley-Smith, Jonathon. *The Crusades: A Short History.* London: Athlone Press, 1987.

Rizo, Takeuchi. *The Rise of the Warriors.* Cambridge: Cambridge University Press, 1998.

Rossabi, Morris. *Khublai Khan: His Life and Times.* Los Angeles: University of California Press, 1988.

Runciman, Steven. *The Sicilian Vespers.* Cambridge: Cambridge University Press, 1958.

Salik, Saiyed A. *The Early Heroes of Islam.* Calcutta: University of Calcutta, 1926.

Sastri, K. A. Nilakanta. *The Pandyan Kingdom from Earliest Times to the Sixteenth Century.* London: Luzac, 1929.

———. *The Colas.* 1st ed 1935. Madras: University of Madras, 1955.

Soulis, George C. *The Serbs and Byzantium during the Rule of Tsar Stephen Dusan 1331–1355.* Washington, DC: Dumbarton Oaks Library, 1984.

Sumption, Jonathon. *The Hundred Years War.* London: Faber and Faber, 1990.

Turnbull, Stephen R. *The Samurai: A Military History.* London: Osprey, 1977.

Vaughan, Richard. *Philip the Good: The Apogee of Burgundy.* London: Longman, 1970.

Wise, Terence. *The Wars of the Crusades 1096–1291.* London: Osprey, 1978.

Wollaston, Arthur N. *The Sword of Islam.* London: John Murray, 1905.

Wood, Michael. *In Search of the Dark Ages.* London: BBC Books, 1981.

The Early Modern Era 1500–1750

Allouche, Adel. *The Origins and Development of the Ottoman-Safavid Conflict 1500–1555.* Berlin: Klaus Schwarz Verlag, 1983.

Anderson, Mathew S. *The War of the Austrian Succession 1740–1748.* London: Longman, 1995.

Argenti, Philip R. *The Occupation of Chios by the Venetians 1694.* London: Bodley Head, 1935.

Ashley, Maurice. *The English Civil War.* London: Alan Sutton, 1990.

Barker, Thomas M. *Double Eagle and the Crescent: Vienna's 2nd Siege.* New York: University of New York, 1967.

Barnett, Correlli. *Marlborough.* London: Eyre Methuen, 1974.

Begley, Wayne and Desai, Ziyaud. *The Shah Jahan Nama of Inayat Khan.* Delhi: Oxford University Press, 1990.

Bengtsson, Frans G. *Life of Charles XII, King of Sweden 1697–1718.* London: Macmillan, 1960.

Bennett, Martyn. *Civil Wars in Britain and Ireland 1638–1651*. Oxford: Blackwell, 1997.

Berdan, Frances. *The Aztecs of Central America*. Belmont: Wadsworth, 2004.

Bobrick, Benson. *Fearless Majesty: Life and Reign of Ivan the Terrible*. New York: Putnam and Sons, 1987.

Boxer, Charles R. *Fort Jesus and the Portuguese in Mombasa 1593–1729*. London: Hollis and Carter, 1960.

Bradford, Ernle. *The Great Siege: Malta 1565*. London: Hodder and Stoughton, 1961.

———. *The Shield and the Sword: The Knights of St John*. London: Hodder and Stoughton, 1972.

Brown, M. Kathryn and Stanton, Travis W. (Eds). *Ancient Mesoamerican Warfare*. Walnut Creek, CA: AltaMira Press, 2003.

Buchan, John. *Montrose: A History*. 1st ed 1928. Boston, MA: Houghton Mifflin, 1975.

Burne, Alfred H. and Young, Peter. *The Great Civil War: A Military History of the First Civil War 1642–1646*. London: Eyre and Spottiswoode, 1959.

Cassels, Lavendar. *The Struggle for the Ottoman Empire 1717–1740*. London: John Murray, 1966.

Childs, John. *The Nine Years War and the British Army 1688–1697*. Manchester: Manchester University Press, 1991.

Church, Benjamin. *Diary of King Philip's War 1675–1676 (1716)*. Chester, CT: Pequot Press, 1975.

Corbett, Julian S. *England and the Mediterranean 1603–1713* (2 vols). London: Longmans Green, 1917.

Cust, Sir Edward. *Lives of the Warriors of the 17th Century* (3 vols). London: John Murray, 1865–1869.

Danvers, Frederick Charles. *The Portuguese in India* (2 vols). 1st ed 1894. London: Frank Cass and Co, 1966.

Data, Piara Singh. *Banda Singh Bahadur*. Delhi: National Bookshop, 1987.

Davies, Nigel. *Aztecs: A History*. London: Macmillan, 1973.

Dening, Walter. *The Life of Toyotomi Hideyoshi*. 1st ed 1904. Kobe: J. L. Thompson and Co, 1930.

Dhillon, Dalbir Singh and Bhullar, Shangana Singh. *Battles of the Guru Gobhind Singh*. New Delhi: Deep and Deep Publications, 1990.

Duffy, Christopher. *Russia's Military Way to the West 1700–1800*. London: Routledge and Kegan Paul, 1981.

———. *The Military Experience in the Age of Reason*. London: Routledge and Kegan Paul 1987.

Early, Abraham. *The Mughal Throne: The Saga of India's Great Emperors*. London: Weidenfeld and Nicolson, 2003.

Eccles, William J. *Frontenac: The Courtier Governor*. New York: McLelland Stuart, 1968.

Ellis, George William. *King Philip's War*. New York: Grafton Press, 1906.

Engels, Friedrich. *The Peasant War in Germany*. 1st ed 1850. New York: International Publishers, 1926.

Evans, Susan Toby. *Ancient Mexico and Central America*. London: Thames and Hudson, 2004.

Ferishta, Mahomed Kasim. *History of the Rise of Mohammadan Power in India (to 1612)* (4 vols transl. Jon Briggs). Calcutta: Editions India, 1966.

Finkel, Caroline. *The Administration of Warfare: The Ottoman Military Campaigns in Hungary 1593–1606*. Vienna: VWGO, 1988.

Fisher, Sir Godfrey. *Barbary Legend: War, Trade and Piracy in North Africa 1415–1830*. Oxford: Clarendon Press, 1957.

Francis, David. *The First Peninsular War 1702–1713*. London: Ernest Benn, 1975.

Fraser, Antonia. *Cromwell: Our Chief of Men*. London: Weidenfeld and Nicolson, 1973.

Gascoign, Bamber. *The Great Moghuls*. London: Jonathon Cape, 1971.

Geyl, Pieter. *The Netherlands Divided 1609–1648*. London: Williams and Norgate, 1936.

Gordon, Linda. *Cossack Rebellions: Social Turmoil in the Sixteenth-century Ukraine*. Albany: State University of New York Press, 1983.

Grey, Ian. *Ivan the Terrible*. London: Hodder and Stoughton, 1964.

———. *Boris Godunov: The Tragic Tsar*. New York: Scribner, 1973.

Harding, Richard. *Amphibious Warfare in the Eighteenth Century: The British Expedition to the West Indies 1740–1742*. Suffolk: Boydell Press, 1991.

Harrison, Peter D. *The Lords of Tikal: Rulers of an Ancient Maya City*. London: Thames and Hudson, 1999.

Hassig, Ross. *Aztec Warfare*. Norman: University of Oklahoma, 1988.

Hatton, Ragnhild M. *Charles XII of Sweden*. London: Weidenfeld and Nicolson, 1968.

Hilton, Anne. *The Kingdom of Kongo*. Oxford: Clarendon Press, 1985.

Ingrao, Charles W. *In Quest and Crisis: Emperor Joseph I and the Habsburg Empire*. West Lafayette, IN: Purdue University Press, 1979.

Irvine, William. *The Later Moghuls 1707–1739* (2 vols). Calcutta: M. C. Sarker, 1922.

Jones, Grant D. *The Conquest of the Last Maya Kingdom.* Stanford, CA: Stanford University Press, 1998.

Kamen, Henry. *The War of Succession in Spain 1700–1715.* London: Weidenfeld and Nicolson, 1969.

Kenyon, John P. *The Civil Wars of England.* New York: Alfred Knopf, 1988.

Knight, Alan. *Mexico: From the Beginning to the Spanish Conquest.* Cambridge: Cambridge University Press, 2002.

Kulkarni, Govind T. *The Moghul-Mahratta Relations 1682–1707.* Poona: Deccan College, 1983.

Kunt, Metin and Woodhead, Christine (Eds). *Suleyman the Magnificent and His Age.* London: Longman, 1995.

Lamb, Harold. *Babur the Tiger.* New York: Doubleday, 1961.

Majewski, Wieslaw. *The Polish Art of War in the 16th and 17th Centuries.* Cambridge: Cambridge University Press, 1982.

Majumdar, Ramesh C. (Ed). *The Age of Imperial Kanauj.* Bombay: Bharatiya Vidya Bhavan, 1955.

Malik, Arjan Dass. *An Indian Guerilla War: The Sikh People's War 1699–1768.* New Delhi: Wiley Eastern, 1975.

Malleson, George Bruce. *Akbar and the Rise of the Moghul Empire.* Oxford: Oxford University Press, 1899.

Martin, Simon and Grube, Nikolai. *Chronicles of the Maya Kings and Queens.* London: Thames and Hudson, 2000

Martin-Leake, Stephen. *The Life of Sir John Leake* (2 vols). London: Navy Records Society, 1920.

Massie, Robert K. *Peter the Great.* London: Victor Gollancz, 1981.

Mattingley, Garrett. *The Defeat of the Spanish Armada.* London: Jonathon Cape, 1959.

Michael, Franz. *The Origin of Manchu Rule in China.* 1st ed 1942. New York: Octagon Books, 1972.

Oman, Sir Charles. *A History of the Art of War in the 16th Century.* London: Greenhill, 1989.

Pares, Richard. *War and Trade in the West Indies 1739–1763.* Oxford: Oxford University Press, 1936.

Park, Yun-Hee. *Admiral Yi Sun-Shin and His Turtleboat Armada.* Seoul: Hanjin Publishing, 1978.

Parkman, Francis. *Count Frontenac and New France under Louis XIV.* Boston, MA: Little Brown and Co, 1907.

Parsons, James Bunyan. *The Peasant Rebellions of the Late Ming Dynasty.* Tucson: University of Arizona, 1970.

Payne, Robert and Romanoff, Nikita. *Ivan the Terrible.* New York: Thomas Y. Crowell and Co, 1975.

Perdue, Peter C. *China Marches West: The Qing Conquest of Central Eurasia.* Cambridge, MA: Harvard University Press, 2005.

Perjes, Geza. *The Fall of the Medieval Kingdom of Hungary: Mohacs 1526 to Buda 1541.* New York: Atlantic Research and Publishing, 1989.

Porter, Harry C. *The Inconstant Savage: England and the North American Indian 1500–1660.* London: Duckworth, 1979.

Prebble, John. *Glencoe.* London: Secker and Warburg, 1966.

Putnam, Ruth. *William the Silent, Prince of Orange.* New York: G.P. Putnam Sons, 1911.

Restall, Matthew. *Seven Myths of the Spanish Conquest.* Oxford: Oxford University Press, 2003.

Richmond, Sir W. H. *The Navy in the War of 1739–1748* (3 vols). Cambridge: Cambridge University Press, 1920.

Roberts, Michael. *Gustavus Adolphus: A History of Sweden 1611–1632.* London: Longmans, 1953–1958.

Rogers, Colonel Hugh C. B. *Battles and Generals of the Civil Wars 1642–1651.* London: Seeley Service, 1968.

Royle, Trevor. *Civil War: The Wars of the Three Kingdoms 1638–1660.* London: Little, Brown, 2004.

Sardesa, Govind S. *New History of the Mahrattas* (3 vols). 1st ed 1948. Bombay: Phoenix Publications, 1968.

Sarkar, Sir Jadunath. *Shivaji and His Times.* Delhi: Longmans, 1973.

Savory, Roger. *Iran under the Safavids.* Cambridge: Cambridge University Press, 1980.

Setton, Kenneth M. *Venice, Austria and the Turks in the 17th Century.* Philadelphia, PA: American Philosophical Society, 1991.

Skrine, Francis Henry. *Fontenoy and Great Britain's Part in the War of Austrian Succession 1741–48.* London: William Blackwood, 1906.

Steinberg, Sigfrid Henry. *The Thirty Years War and the Struggle for European Hegemony 1600–1660.* London: Edward Arnold, 1966.

Strandes, Justus. *The Portuguese Period in East Africa.* 1st ed 1899. Nairobi: East African Literature Bureau, 1971.

Struve, Lynn A. *The Southern Ming 1644–1662.* New Haven, CT: Yale University Press, 1984.

Subrahmanyan, Sanjay. *The Portuguese Empire in Asia 1500–1700.* New York: Longman, 1993.

Thomas, Hugh. *Conquest: Montezuma, Cortés and the Fall of Old Mexico.* New York: Simon and Schuster, 1993.

———. *The Conquest of Mexico.* London: Hutchinson, 1993.

Turnbull, Stephen R. *Battles of the Samurai.* New York: Arms and Armour Press, 1987.

———. *Samurai Invasion: Japan's Korean War 1592–1598.* London: Cassell Military, 2001.

Wakeman, Frederic. *Great Enterprise: The Manchu Reconstruction of the Imperial Order in Seventeenth-century China* (2 vols). Berkeley: University of California Press, 1985.

Webster, David. *The Fall of the Ancient Maya.* London: Thames and Hudson, 2002.

Wedgewood, Cicely V. *William the Silent.* London: Jonathon Cape, 1945.

———. *The King's War 1641–1647.* London: Collins, 1958.

———. *The Thirty Years Wars 1938.* London: Methuen, 1981.

Woolrych, Austin. *Battles of the English Civil War.* London: B.T. Batsford, 1961.

Young, Peter and Holmes, Richard. *The English Civil War.* London: Eyre Methuen, 1974.

Zolkiewski, Stanislas. *Expedition to Moscow.* London: Polonica Publications, 1959.

The Century of Revolution 1750–1850

Alden, John R. *A History of the American Revolution.* London: Macdonald, 1969.

Allen, Gardner W. *The Naval History of the American Revolution.* New York: Russell and Russell, 1962.

Baddeley, John F. *The Russian Conquest of the Caucasus.* New York: Russell and Russell, 1969.

Bauer, K. Jack. *The Mexican War 1846–1848.* New York: Macmillan, 1974.

Becker, Peter. *Path of Blood: The Rise and Conquests of Mzilikazi of the Matabele.* London: Longman Green, 1962.

Beeching, Jack. *The Chinese Opium Wars.* London: Hutchinson, 1975.

Bence-Jones, Mark. *Clive of India.* London: Constable, 1974.

Berton, Pierre. *The Invasion of Canada 1812–1813.* Toronto: McClelland and Stewart, 1980.

———. *Flames across the Border 1813–1814.* Toronto: McClelland and Stewart, 1981.

Bidwell, Shelford. *Swords for Hire: European Mercenaries in Eighteenth-century India.* London: John Murray, 1971.

Bill, Alfred H. *Rehearsal for Conflict: The War with Mexico 1846–1848.* New York: Cooper Square Publishers, 1969.

Black, Jeremy. *War for America: The Fight for Independence 1775–1783.* Stroud: Sutton Publishing, 1991.

Blanco, Jose Luis. *Maximilian: Emperor of Mexico.* New Haven, CT: Yale University Press, 1934.

Blease, Walter L. *Suvorof.* London: Constable, 1920.

Boatner, Mark M. *Encyclopedia of the American Revolution.* Mechanicsburg, PA: Stackpole Books, 1994.

Bruce, George. *The Burmese Wars 1824–1886.* London: Hart-Davis, 1973.

Bryant, Arthur. *The Years of Endurance 1793–1802.* London: William Collins and Co, 1944.

———. *Years of Victory 1802–1812.* London: William Collins and Co, 1944.

Caratini, Robert. *Dictionnaire des Personnages de la Revolution.* Paris: Le Pre aux Clercs, 1988.

Carrington, Henry B. *Battles of the American Revolution 1775–1781.* New York: Promontory Press, 1973.

Cavaliero, Roderick. *The Independence of Brazil.* London: British Academic Press, 1993.

Chandler, David. *Dictionary of the Napoleonic Wars.* London: Arms and Armour Press, 1979.

———. *The Campaigns of Napoleon.* London: Weidenfeld and Nicolson, 1993.

Chang, Hsin-Pao. *Commissioner Lin and the Opium War.* Cambridge, MA: Harvard University Press, 1964.

Clinton, Herbert R. *The War in the Peninsula.* London: Frederick Warne, 1878.

Collis, Maurice. *Foreign Mud: The Opium Imbroglio and Anglo-Chinese War.* London: Faber and Faber, 1946.

Compton, Herbert. *A Particular Account of the European Military Adventurers of Hindustan 1784–1803.* Karachi: Oxford University Press, 1976.

Cook, Hugh C. B. *The Sikh Wars: The British Army in the Punjab 1845–1849.* London: Leo Cooper, 1975.

Corbett, Julian S. *England in the Seven Years War* (2 vols). London: Longmans Green, 1907.

Coverdale, John F. *The Basque Phase of the First Carlist War.* Princeton, NJ: Princeton University Press, 1984.

Crecelius, Daniel. *The Roots of Modern Egypt: The Regimes of Ali Bey al-Kabir and Muhammad Bey Abu al-Dhahab 1760–1775.* Minneapolis, MN: Bibliotheca Islamica, 1981.

Curtiss, John Shelton. *The Russian Army under Nicolas I 1825–1855.* Durham, NC: Duke University Press, 1965.

Dakin, Douglas. *The Greek Struggle for Independence 1821–1833*. London: B. T. Batsford, 1973.

Datta, Kalikinkar. *Shah Alam II and the East India Company*. Calcutta: World Press Private, 1965.

Davie, A. Mervyn. *Clive of Plassey*. London: Nicholson and Watson, 1939.

Deardon, Seton. *A Nest of Corsairs: The Fighting Karamanlis of Tripoli*. London: John Murray, 1976.

Dillon, Richard H. *North American Indian Wars*. New York: Facts on File, 1983.

Downey, Fairfax. *Indian Wars of the United States Army 1776–1865*. New York: Doubleday and Co, 1963.

Duffy, Christopher. *The Army of Frederick the Great*. Melbourne: Wren Publishing, 1974.

———. *Frederick the Great: A Military Life*. London: Routledge and Kegan Paul, 1985.

Eisenhower, John. *So Far from God: The US War with Mexico*. New York: Random House, 1989.

Elting, John R. *Swords around the Throne: Napoleon's Grand Army*. London: Weidenfeld and Nicolson, 1989.

Esposito, Vincent J. and Elting, John R. *A Military History and Atlas of the Napoleonic Wars*. London: Faber and Faber, 1964.

Fane, John, Earl Westmoreland. *Memoir of Operations of the Allied Armies under Schwarzenberg and Blucher 1813–1814*. London: John Murray, 1822.

Fernandes, Praxy. *Storm over Seringapatam: The Incredible Story of Haidar Ali and Tippu Sultan*. Bombay: Thacker and Co, 1969.

Finlay, George. *History of the Greek Revolution 1877*. London: Zeno, 1971.

Forrest, Denys M. *Tiger of Mysore, Life and Death of Tipu Sultan*. London: Chatto and Windus, 1970.

Fowler, William M. *Jack Tars and Commodores: The American Navy 1783–1815*. Boston, MA: Houghton Mifflin, 1984.

Fregosi, Paul. *Dreams of Empire: Napoleon and the First World War*. London: Hutchinson, 1989.

Gammer, Moshe. *Muslim Resistance to the Tsar*. London: Frank Cass, 1994.

Garrett, Richard. *Robert Clive*. London: Arthur Barker, 1976.

Gates, David. *The Spanish Ulcer: A History of the Peninsular War*. London: George Allen and Unwin, 1986.

Geraghty, Tony. *March or Die: France and the Foreign Legion*. London: Grafton Books, 1986.

Gibson, Arroll Morgan. *The Kickapoos: Lords of the Middle Border*. Norman: University of Oklahoma, 1963.

Gordon, Rev J. *History of the Rebellion in Ireland 1798*. London: T. Hurst, 1803.

Gorton, Thomas. *History of the Greek Revolution* (2 vols). London: William Blackwood, 1844.

Gough, Gen. Sir Charles. *The Sikhs and the Sikh Wars*. 1st ed 1897. Delhi: National Bookshop, 1984.

Graham, Gerald S. *Empire of the North Atlantic: The Maritime Struggle for North America*. Toronto: University of Toronto, 1950.

Gupta, Pratul C. *Baji Rao II and the East India Company 1796–1818*. London: Oxford University Press, 1939.

Haber, Grace. *With Pipe and Tomahawk: Logan the Mingo Chief*. New York: Pageant Press, 1958.

Hafin, Leroy and Young, Francis. *Fort Laramie and the Pageant of the West 1834–1890*. Glendale, CA: Arthur Clark and Co, 1938.

Halbert, Henry S. and Ball, Timothy H. *The Creek War of 1813–1814*. 1st ed 1895. Tuscaloosa: University of Alabama Press, 1995.

Hamilton, Holman. *Zachary Taylor: Soldier of the Republic 1941*. Hamden, CT: Archon Books, 1966.

Hartley, M. *The Man Who Saved Austria: Baron Jellecic*. London: Mills and Boon, 1912.

Hasrat, Bikrama J. *Life and Times of Ranjit Singh*. Hathikhana: Pub by the author, 1977.

Haythornthwaite, Philip. *Sourcebook of the Napoleonic Wars*. New York: Facts on File, 1990.

Hernon, Ian. *Britain's Forgotten Wars: Colonial Campaigns of the Nineteenth Century*. Stroud: Sutton, 2003.

Hibbert, Christopher. *Redcoats and Rebels*. London: Grafton Books, 1990.

Hickey, Donald R. *The War of 1812: A Forgotten Victory*. Chicago: University of Illinois, 1989.

Hodson, Major Vernon C. P. *Officers of the Bengal Army 1758–1834* (4 vols). London: Constable, 1927–1947.

Holt, Edgar. *The Opium Wars in China*. London: Putnam, 1964.

———. *The Carlist Wars in Spain*. London: Putnam, 1967.

Hook, Jason. *American Indian Warrior Chiefs*. Poole: Firebird Books, 1989.

Hooper, John P. *Admirable Warrior: Marshal Sucre*. Detroit, MI: Baline-Etheridge, 1977.

Horward, Donald D. *Napoleon and Iberia: The Twin Sieges of Ciudad Rodrigo and Almeida 1810*. Tallahassee: Florida State University, 1984.

Howarth, David. *The Greek Adventure: Lord Byron and Other Eccentrics in the War of Independence*. New York: Atheneum, 1976.

Hozier, Henry Montague. *The Seven Weeks War* (2 vols). London: Macmillan, 1867.

Inglis, Brian. *The Opium War*. London: Hodder and Stoughton, 1976.

James, Cyril L. R. *The Black Jacobins: Toussaint L'Ouverture and the San Domingo Revolution*. London: Secker and Warburg, 1938.

Jeffrey, William H. *Mitre and Argentina*. New York: Library Publishers, 1952.

Kantak, Madhav R. *The First Anglo-Mahratta War*. Bombay: Popular Prakashan, 1993.

Keene, Rev Henry G. *Madhava Rao Sindhia (Mahadji)*. Oxford: Oxford University Press, 1891.

Kelly, John B. *Britain and the Persian Gulf 1795–1880*. Oxford: Oxford University Press, 1968.

Ketchum, Richard M. *Winter Soldiers*. Garden City, NY: Doubleday, 1973.

Kirchberger, Joe H. *The French Revolution and Napoleon*. New York: Facts on File, 1989.

Klapka, Gyorgy. *Memoirs of War of Independence in Hungary* (2 vols). London: Charles Gilpin, 1850.

Lachouque, Henri. *Anatomy of Glory* (transl. Anne Brown). Providence, RI: Brown University Press, 1962.

Lancaster, Bruce. *The American Revolution*. Boston, MA: Houghton Mifflin, 1971.

Laurie, William F. B. *Our Burmese Wars*. London: W.H. Allen, 1880.

Lawford, James P. *Clive: Proconsul of India*. London: Geo Allen and Unwin, 1976.

MacLennan, Ben. *A Proper Degree of Terror: John Graham and the Cape's Eastern Frontier*. Johannesburg: Ravan, 1986.

Macrory, Patrick. *Signal Catastrophe: The Retreat from Kabul 1842*. London: Hodder and Stoughton, 1966.

Madriaga, Salvador De. *Bolivar*. London: Hollis and Carter, 1952.

Mahan, Alfred Thayer. *Seapower in Its Relation to the War of 1812*. London: Sampson, Low, Marston, 1905.

Mahon, John K. *The Second Seminole War 1835–1842*. Gainesville: University of Florida, 1967.

Makriyannis, Yannis. *Makriyannis: Memoirs of General Makriyannis*. London: Oxford University Press, 1966.

Malleson, George Bruce. *History of the French in India 1674–1761*. London: Longmans, Green, 1868.

———. *Final French Struggles in India and on the Indian Sea*. London: Wm H. Allen, 1878.

———. *The Decisive Battles of India 1746–1849*. 1st ed 1883. New Delhi: Associated Publishing, 1973.

Masur, Gerhard. *Simon Bolivar*. Albuquerque: University of New Mexico, 1948.

Maxwell, W. H. *History of the Irish Rebellion in 1798*. London: Baily Brothers, 1854.

Miller, Charles. *Khyber: British India's North West Frontier*. New York: Macmillan, 1977.

Minney, Reuben J. *Clive of India*. London: Jarrolds, 1957.

Mitford, Nancy. *Frederick the Great*. London: Hamish Hamilton, 1970.

Morrison, Samuel Eliot. *John Paul Jones: A Sailor's Biography*. Toronto: Little, Brown and Co, 1959.

Mostert, Noel. *Frontiers: The Epic of South Africa's Creation*. London: Jonathon Cape, 1966.

Nafziger, George. *Napoleon's Invasion of Russia*. Novata, CA: Presidio, 1988.

Napier, Sir William. *History of the Peninsular War* (6 vols). London: Thomas and Wm Boone, 1886.

Nevin, David. *The Mexican War*. New York: Time Life Books, 1978.

Nijjar, Bakhshish Singh. *Anglo-Sikh Wars 1845–1849*. New Delhi: K. B. Publications, 1976.

Norris, John A. *The First Afghan War 1838–1842*. Cambridge: Cambridge University Press, 1967.

O'Leary, Daniel Florencio. *Bolivar and the War of Independence*. Austin: University of Texas, 1970.

Oman, Sir Charles. *History of the Peninsula War* (7 vols). Oxford: Oxford University Press, 1902.

Osipov, K. *Alexander Suvorov*. London: Hutchinson, 1941.

Ouchterlony, John. *The Chinese War 1839–1842*. New York: Praeger, 1970.

Pakenham, Thomas. *The Year of Liberty: The Irish Rebellion of 1798*. London: Hodder and Stoughton, 1969.

Palmer, Alan. *An Encyclopedia of Napoleon's Europe*. London: Weidenfeld and Nicolson, 1984.

Palmer, Michael. *Stoddert's War: Naval Operations during the Quasi War with France 1798–1801*. Columbia: University of South Carolina, 1987.

Parkinson, C. Northcote. *War in the Eastern Seas 1793–1815*. London: George Allen and Unwin, 1954.

Parkman, Francis. *The Conspiracy of Pontiac* (2 vols). Boston, MA: Little, Brown and Co, 1851.

———. *Montcalm and Wolfe*. 1st ed 1884. London: Eyre and Spottiswoode, 1964.

Paxton, John. *Companion to the French Revolution*. New York: Facts on File, 1988.

Pecham, Howard H. (Ed). *The Toll of Independence: Engagements and Battle Casualties of the American Revolution*. Chicago: University of Chicago, 1974.

Pemble, John. *The Invasion of Nepal: John Company at War*. Oxford: Oxford University Press, 1971.

Perry, John. *Karim Khan Zand: A History of Iran 1747–1779*. Chicago: University of Chicago, 1979.

Petre, F. Lorraine. *Napoleon's Campaign in Poland 1806–1807*. London: Sampson Lane Marston, 1901.

———. *Napoleon's Conquest of Prussia 1806*. London: John Lane, 1907.

———. *Napoleon's Last Campaign in Germany 1813*. London: Bodley Head, 1912.

———. *Napoleon at Bay 1814*. London: John Lane, 1914.

———. *Napoleon and the Archduke Charles Germany 1809*. 1st ed 1890. London: Greenhill Books, 1991.

Phillips, Christopher. *Damned Yankee: The Life of General Nathaniel Lyon*. Colombia: University of Missouri, 1990.

Phillips, W. Alison. *The War of Greek Independence*. London: Smith Elder, 1897.

Phipps, Ramsay Weston. *The Armies of the First French Republic and the Rise of the Marshals of Napoleon*. Oxford: Oxford University Press, 1926.

Pope, Dudley. *The Devil Himself: The Mutiny of 1800*. London: Secker and Warburg, 1987.

———. *The Black Ship*. London: Weidenfeld and Nicolson, 1988.

Porch, Douglas. *The French Foreign Legion: A Complete History*. New York: Harper Collins, 1991.

Powell, Geoffrey. *The Kandyan Wars: The British Army in Ceylon 1803–1818*. London: Leo Cooper, 1973.

Prebble, John. *Mutiny: Highland Regiments in Revolt 1743–1804*. London: Secker and Warburg, 1975.

Priestley, Herbert I. *France Overseas: A Study of Modern Imperialism*. London: Frank Cass and Co, 1996.

Quaife, Milo (Ed). *Life of Black Hawk by Black Hawk*. 1st ed 1916. New York: Dover, 1994.

Rait, Robert S. *Life and Campaigns of Hugh First Viscount Gough* (2 vols). London: Archibald Constable, 1903.

Richards, Donald Sydney. *The Savage Frontier: A History of the Anglo-Afghan Wars*. London: Macmillan, 1990.

Ripley, Roswell. *The War with Mexico* (2 vols). New York: Burt Franks, 1849.

Robinson, William Davis. *Memoirs of the Mexican Revolution* (2 vols). London: Lackington, Hughes, 1821.

Rojas, Ricardo. *San Martin: Knight of the Andes*. New York: Cooper Square, 1967.

Roosevelt, Theodore. *The Naval War of 1812*. New York: G.P. Putnam Sons, 1927.

Ross, Michael. *Banners of the King: The Vendee War of 1793*. London: Selley Service and Co, 1975.

Ross, Steven. *Historical Dictionary of the Wars of the French Revolution*. Lanham, MD: Scarecrow Press, 1998.

Savary, Gen. Sir Reginald. *His Britannic Majesty's Army in Germany in the Seven Years War*. Oxford: Oxford University Press, 1966.

Seton-Watson, Hugh. *The Russian Empire 1801–1917*. Oxford: Oxford University Press, 1967.

Sherrard, Owen A. *Lord Chatham: Pitt and the Seven Years War*. London: Bodley Head, 1955.

Singhnayyar, Gurbachan. *The Sikhs in Ferment: Battles of the Sikh Gurus*. New Delhi: National Book Organisation, 1992.

Skrine, Francis Henry. *The Expansion of Russia 1815–1900*. Cambridge: Cambridge University Press, 1903.

Smith, Justin. *The War with Mexico* (2 vols). New York: Macmillan, 1919.

Smithers, A. J. *The Kaffir Wars: 1779–1877*. London: Leo Cooper, 1973.

Snodgrass, John J. *Narrative of the Burmese War*. London: John Murray, 1827.

Southey, R. *History of the Peninsula War* (3 vols). London: John Murray, 1823.

Spear, Percival. *Twilight of the Moghuls*. Cambridge: Cambridge University Press, 1951.

Srinvasan, C. K. *Baji Rao, The Great Peshwar*. Bombay: Asia Publishing, 1961.

Stanley, George F. G. *The War of 1812: Land Operations*. Toronto: Macmillan, 1983.

Syrett, David. *The Royal Navy in American Waters 1775–1883*. Aldershot: Scolar Press, 1989.

Thrapp, Dan L. *Encyclopedia of Frontier Biography* (3 vols). Spokane, WA: Arthur Clark and Co, 1988.

Tilley, John A. *The British Navy in the American Revolution*. Colombia: University of South Carolina, 1987.

Urwin, Gregory J. W. *The United States Cavalry: An Illustrated History*. Poole: Blandford Press, 1983.

Van Aken, Mark J. *King of the Night: Juan Jose Flores and Ecuador*. Berkeley: University of California, 1989.

Vucinich, Wayne S. (Ed). *The First Serbian Uprising 1803–1814*. New York: Brooklyn College Press, 1982.

Ward, Christopher. *The War of the Revolution* (2 vols). New York: Macmillian, 1952.

Weems, John. *To Conquer a Peace: The War between the US and Mexico*. College Station: Texas A&M University, 1988.

Wood, William J. *Battles of the Revolutionary War 1775–1781.* Chapel Hill, NC: Algonquin Books, 1990.

Worcester, Donald. *Sea Power and Chilean Independence.* Gainesville: University of Florida, 1962.

The Rise of Modern Professionalism 1850–1900

Ambrose, Stephen E. *Crazy Horse and Custer: The Parallel Lives of Two American Warriors.* London: Macdonald and Janes, 1976.

Amery, Leopold S. (Gen Ed). *The Times History of the War in South Africa* (6 vols). London: Sampson Low, Marston, 1907.

Arnold, Guy. *Historical Dictionary of the Crimean War.* Lanham, MD: Scarecrow Press, 2002.

Asiegbu, Johnson U. *Nigeria and Its British Invaders 1851–1920.* New York: NOK Publishers, 1984.

Ball, Charles. *The History of the Indian Mutiny* (2 vols). 1st ed 1858. Delhi: Master Publishers, 1981.

Baring Pemberton, W. *Battles of the Crimean War.* London: Batsford, 1962.

Barthorp, Michael. *To Face the Daring Maoris: Soldiers Impressions of the First Maori War 1845–1847.* London: Hodder and Stoughton, 1979.

———. *The Zulu War: A Pictorial History.* Poole: Blandford Press, 1980.

———. *War on the Nile: Egypt, Britain and the Sudan 1882–98.* Poole: Blandford Press, 1984.

Beasley, William G. *The Meiji Restoration.* Stanford, CA: Stanford University Press, 1972.

Belich, James. *The New Zealand Wars and the Victorian Interpretation of Racial Conflict.* Auckland: Auckland University Press, 1986.

Blume, Wilhelm. *The Operation of the German Armies in France 1870–1871* (transl. E. M. Jones). London: Henry S. King and Co, 1872.

Boatner, Mark M. *The Civil War Dictionary.* 1st ed 1959. New York: Vintage Books, 1991.

Bond, Brian (Ed). *Victorian Military Campaigns.* London: Hutchinson, 1967.

Bonner-Smith, D. and Lumby, Esmond W. R. *The Second China War 1856–1860.* London: Naval Records Society, 1953.

Brackenbury, Henry. *The Ashanti War 1873–1874* (2 vols). London: Wm Blackwood and Sons, 1874.

Brown, Dee. *The Fetterman Massacre.* London: Barrie and Jenkins, 1972.

———. *Bury My Heart at Wounded Knee.* London: Pan Books, 1973.

Chalfont, William. *Cheyennes at Dark Water Creek.* Norman: University of Oklahoma, 1997.

Churchill, Winston S. *The River War: The Sudan, 1898.* London: Eyre and Spottiswoode, 1930.

Civil War Sites Advisory Commission. *Report on the Nation's Civil War Battlefields* (Tech vol 2). Washington, DC: National Park Service, 1993.

Compton, Piers. *The Last Days of General Gordon.* London: Robert Hale, 1974.

Cowan, James. *The New Zealand Maori Wars* (2 vols). Wellington: NZ Government Printer, 1922.

Curtiss, John Shelton. *Russia's Crimean War.* Durham, NC: Duke University Press, 1979.

Datta, Kalikinkar. *Biography of Kunwar Singh and Awar Singh.* Patna: K.P. Jayaswal Institute, 1984.

Davis, Burke. *Our Incredible Civil War.* New York: Holt, Rinehart and Winston, 1960.

Doveton, Frederick B. *Reminiscences of the Burmese War.* London: Allen and Co, 1852.

Drechsler, Horst. *Let Us Die Fighting: The Struggle of the Herero and Nama against German Imperialism 1884–1915* (transl. Bernd Zollner). London: Zed Press, 1980.

Dunlay, Thomas W. *Wolves for the Blue Soldiers: Indian Scouts and Auxiliaries with the United States Army 1860–1890.* Lincoln: University of Nebraska, 1982.

Dunn, Ross E. *Resistance in the Desert: Moroccan Responses to French Imperialism 1881–1912.* Madison: University of Wisconsin, 1977.

Dusgate, Richard H. *The Conquest of Northern Nigeria.* London: Frank Cass and Co, 1984.

Edgerton, Robert B. *Like Lions They Fought: The Zulu War.* London: Weidenfeld and Nicolson, 1988.

Edwardes, Michael. *Battles of the Indian Mutiny.* London: Batsford, 1963.

———. *Red Year: The Indian Rebellion of 1857.* London: Hamish Hamilton, 1973.

———. *A Season in Hell: Defence of the Lucknow Residency.* London: Hamish Hamilton, 1973.

Farwell, Byron. *Prisoners of the Mahdi.* London: Longman Green, 1967.

———. *Queen Victoria's Little Wars.* London: Allen Lane, 1973.

———. *For Queen and Country.* London: Allen Lane, 1981.

———. *Eminent Victorian Soldiers.* London: Viking, 1985.

Featon, John. *The Waikato War.* Auckland: Brett Publishing, 1923.

Fehrenbach, Theodore R. *Comanches: The Destruction of a People.* London: George Allen and Unwin, 1975.

Ffrench-Blake, Robert L. *The Crimean War.* London: Leo Cooper, 1971.

Flint, John E. *Sir George Goldie and the Making of Nigeria.* London: Oxford University Press, 1960.

Foner, Phillip S. *The Spanish-Cuban-American War and the Birth of American Imperialism 1895–1902* (2 vols). New York: Monthly Review Press, 1972.

———. *Antonio Maceo: The Bronze Titan.* New York: Monthly Review Press, 1977.

Foote, Shelby. *The Civil War* (3 vols). London: Bodley Head, 1991.

Forrest, George W. *A History of the Indian Mutiny* (2 vols). London: William Blackwood, 1904.

Furneaux, Rupert. *The Zulu War: Isandhlwana and Rorke's Drift.* London: Weidenfeld and Nicolson, 1963.

Gabre-Selassie, Zewde. *Yohannes IV of Ethiopia: A Political Biography.* Oxford: Oxford University Press, 1975.

Gardner, Brian. *Mafeking: A Victorian Legend.* London: Cassell, 1966.

Garrett, Richard. *General Gordon.* London: Arthur Barker, 1974.

Gates, John M. *Schoolbooks and Krags: The US Army in the Philippines 1898–1902.* Westport, CT: Greenwood Press, 1973.

Genov, Tsonko. *The Russo-Turkish War of 1877–1888.* Sofia: Sofia Press, 1977.

Gibson, Tom. *The Maori Wars: The British Army in NZ 1840–1872.* London: Leo Cooper, 1974.

Glass, Stafford. *The Matabele War.* London: Longmans Green, 1968.

Glassley, Ray H. *Pacific Northwest Indian Wars.* Portland, OR: Binfords and Mort, 1953.

Goldfrank, David M. *The Origins of the Crimean War.* London: Longman, 1994.

Graham, Martin and Skoch, George. *Great Battles of the Civil War.* Lincolnwood, IL: Publications International, 1990.

Grant, Sir Hope. *Incidents in the Sepoy War.* London: William Blackwood, 1884.

Greeley, Horace. *The American Conflict* (2 vols). Hartford, CT: O. D. Case, 1864–1867.

Grew, Edwin S. et al. *Field Marshal Lord Kitchener: His Life and Work.* London: Gresham, 1917.

Grinnell, George Bird. *The Fighting Cheyennes.* 1st ed 1915. Norman: University of Oklahoma, 1983.

Gupta, Pratul C. *Nana Sahib and the Rising at Cawnpore.* Oxford: Oxford University Press, 1963.

Haley, James L. *The Buffalo War: The Red River Uprising of 1874.* New York: Doubleday, 1976.

Hallam, W.K.R. *The Life and Times of Rabih Fadl Allah.* Ilfracombe: Arthur H. Stockwell, 1977.

Hamnet, Brian. *Juarez.* London: Longman, 1994.

Hansen, Hans Jurgen. *The Ships of the German Fleets 1848–1945.* London: Hamlyn, 1974.

Hibbert, Christopher. *The Great Mutiny: India 1857.* London: Allen Lane, 1978.

Hole, Hugh M. *The Passing of the Black Kings.* London: Philip Alan, 1932.

Holt, Edgar. *The Strangest War: The Maori Wars 1860–1872.* London: Putnam, 1962.

Holt, Peter M. *The Mahdist State of the Sudan 1881–1898.* Oxford: Oxford University Press, 1958.

Horne, Alistair. *The Fall of Paris: The Siege and Commune 1870–1871.* London: Macmillan, 1960.

Howard, Michael. *The Franco-Prussian War.* London: Macmillan, 1961.

Hozier, Henry Montague. *The Campaign of 1866 in Germany: Prussian War Ministry* (record transl. Hozier). London: Her Majesty's Stationary Office, 1872.

Humble, Richard. *The Illustrated History of the American Civil War.* London: Multimedia Books, 1991.

Hurd, Douglas. *The Arrow War: An Anglo-Chinese Confusion 1856–60.* New York: Macmillan, 1968.

Hurley, Vic. *Swish of the Kris: The Story of the Moros.* New York: E.P. Dutton, 1936.

James, Lawrence. *The Savage Wars: British Campaigns in Africa 1870–1920.* London: Robert Hale, 1985.

Jen, Yu-Wen. *The Taiping Revolutionary Movement.* New Haven, CT: Yale University Press, 1993.

Johnson, Robert U. and Buel, Clarence C. (Eds). *Battles and Leaders of the Civil War: For the Most Part Contributions by Union and Confederate Officers.* New York: The Century Co, 1884–1888.

Josephy, Alvin. *The Nez Perce Indians and the Opening of the Northwest.* New Haven, CT: Yale University, 1965.

Jourdan, E. C. *Historia das Campanhas do Uruguay 1864–70* (3 vols). Rio de Janeiro: Impensa Nacional, 1893.

Judd, Denis. *Someone Has Blundered: Calamities of the British Army in the Victorian Age.* London: Arthur Barker, 1973.

———. *The Crimean War.* London: Hart Davis, 1975.

———. *The Boer War.* London: Hart Davis, 1977.

Keene, Rev Henry G. *Fall of the Moghul Empire.* London: William H Allen, 1876.

Keown-Boyd, Henry. *A Good Dusting: The Sudan Campaigns 1883–1899.* London: Leo Cooper, 1986.

———. *The Fists of Righteous Harmony: The Boxer Uprising.* London: Leo Cooper, 1991.

Kikrick, Robert. *Lee's Generals.* Dayton, OH: Morningside Press, 1979.

Knight, Ian. *Great Zulu Battles.* London: Arms and Armour Press, 1998.

———. *The National Museum Book of the Zulu War.* London: Sidgwick and Jackson, 2003.

Kolinsky, Charles. *Independence or Death: Story of the Paraguayan War.* Gainesville: University of Florida, 1965.

Laband, John. *Rope of Sand: The Rise and Fall of the Zulu Kingdom in the Nineteenth Century.* Johannesburg: Jonathan Ball, 1995.

———. *The Rise and Fall of the Zulu Nation.* London: Arms and Armour Press, 1997.

———. *The Transvaal Revolution: The First Boer War 1880–1881.* London: Pearson Longman, 2005.

Lambert, Andrew D. *The Crimean War: British Grand Strategy 1853–1856.* Manchester: Manchester University Press, 1990.

Lee, Emanoel. *To the Bitter End: A Photographic History of the Boer War 1899–1902.* London: Viking, 1985.

Lee, Fitzhugh and Wheeler, Joseph. *Cuba's Struggle against Spain.* New York: American Historical Press, 1899.

Lindley, Augustus. *The History of the Taiping Rebellion 1866.* New York: Praeger Publishing, 1970.

Lloyd, Alan. *The Drums of Kumasi: The Story of the Ashanti Wars.* London: Longmans, 1964.

Lockwood, Frank. *The Apache Indians.* 1st ed 1938. Lincoln: University of Nebraska, 1987.

Lone, Stewart. *Japan's First Modern War: Army and Society in the Conflict with China 1894–1895.* London: Macmillan, 1994.

Longford, Elizabeth. *Jameson's Raid: The Prelude to the Boer War.* London: Weidenfeld and Nicolson, 1982.

Longstreet, Stephen. *War Cries on Horseback.* London: W.H. Allen, 1979.

Lowe, Thomas. *Central India during the Rebellion of 1857–1858.* London: Longman Green, 1860.

Macmillan, William M. *Bantu, Boer and Briton.* Oxford: Oxford University Press, 1963.

Malleson, George Bruce. *The Indian Mutiny of 1857.* London: Seeley and Co, 1906.

Malleson, George Bruce (Ed). *Kaye's and Malleson's History of the Indian Mutiny* (6 vols). 1st ed 1897–1898. Westport, CT: Greenwood Press, 1971.

Martin, Christopher. *The Boxer Rebellion.* New York: Abelard-Schuman, 1968.

Martin, Percy F. *Maximilian in Mexico: French Intervention 1861–1867.* London: Constable, 1914.

Martinez, Jose Luciano. *Batalla de Palmar: Campana 1836–1838.* Montevideo: Imprenta Militar, 1935.

Mason, Philip. *A Matter of Honour: The Indian Army, Its Officers and Men.* London: Jonathon Cape, 1974.

Maxwell, Leigh. *The Ashanti Ring: Sir Garnet Wolseley's Campaigns 1870–1882.* London: Leo Cooper, 1985.

Mcaleavy, Henry. *Black Flags in Vietnam: the Story of a Chinese Intervention 1884–1885.* London: George Allen and Unwin, 1968.

Mcloughlin, William. *After the Trail of Tears: The Cherokee's Struggle for Sovereignty 1838–1880.* Chapel Hill: University of South Carolina, 1993.

McPherson, James (Ed). *Battle Chronicles of the Civil War* (6 vols). New York: Macmillan, 1989.

———. *Atlas of the Civil War.* New York: Macmillan, 1994.

Meintjes, Johannes. *The Anglo-Boer War 1899–1902.* London: Macdonald and Janes, 1976.

Michael, Franz and Chung-Li, Chang. *The Taiping Rebellion: History and Documents* (3 vols). Seattle: University of Washington, 1966–1971.

Miller, Stuart Creighton. *Benevolent Assimilation: The American Conquest of the Philippines 1899–1903.* New Haven, CT: Yale University Press, 1982.

Misra, Anand Swarup. *Nana Saheb Peshwa and the Fight for Freedom.* Lucknow: Uttar Pradesh Government, 1961.

Morris, Donald R. *The Washing of the Spears: The Rise and Fall of the Zulu Nation.* London: Jonathon Cape, 1966.

Mukherjee, Rudrangshu. *Awahd in Revolt 1857–1858.* Delhi: Oxford University Press, 1984.

Myatt, Frederick. *The March to Magdala: The Abyssinian War of 1868.* London: Leo Cooper, 1970.

Neillands, Robin. *The Dervish Wars: Gordon and Kitchener in the Sudan 1880–1898.* London: John Murray, 1966.

Nevill, Hugh L. *Campaigns on the North-west Frontier.* London: John Murray, 1912.

Obichere, Boniface I. *West African States and European Expansion 1885–1898.* New Haven: Yale University Press, 1971.

O'Connor, Richard. *The Spirit Soldiers: A Narrative of the Boxer Rebellion.* New York: G.P. Putnam and Sons, 1973.

Paine, S.C.M. *The Sino-Japanese War of 1894–1895: Perceptions, Power and Primacy.* Cambridge: Cambridge University Press, 2003.

Pakenham, Thomas. *The Boer War.* London: Weidenfeld and Nicolson, 1979.

Palmer, Alan. *The Banner of Battle: The Story of the Crimean War.* London: Weidenfeld and Nicolson, 1987.

Pando, Magdalen M. *Cuba's Freedom Fighter: Antonio Maceo 1845–1896.* Gainesville, FL: Felicity Press, 1980.

Phelps, Gilbert. *Tragedy of Paraguay.* London: Charles Knight and Co, 1975.

Porch, Douglas. *The Conquest of the Sahara.* New York: Alfred A. Knopf, 1984.

Presland, John. *Vae Victis: The Life of Ludwig von Benedek.* London: Hodder and Stoughton, 1934.

Preston, Diana. *The Boxer Rebellion: The Dramatic Story of China's War on Foreigners That Shook the World in the Summer of 1900.* New York: Walker, 2000.

Purcell, Victor. *The Boxer Uprising: A Background Study.* Cambridge: Cambridge University Press, 1963.

Quesada, Gonzalo De. *Free Cuba: The History of the War of Independence.* New York: Publishers Union, 1898.

Rana, Pudma Jung Bahadur. *Life of Maharaja Sir Jung Bahadur of Nepal.* Kathmandu: Rastna Pustak Bhandar, 1980.

Reitz, Deneys. *Commando: A Boer Journal of the Boer War.* London: Faber and Faber, 1929.

Remini, Robert. *Andrew Jackson and the Course of American Empire.* New York: Harper and Row, 1977.

Ricarte, Artemio. *Memoirs of General Artemio Ricarte.* Manila: National Heroes Commission, 1963.

Ridley, Jasper. *Maximilian and Juarez.* London: Constable, 1993.

Roberts, David. *Once They Moved Like the Wind: Cochise, Geronimo and the Apache Wars.* New York: Simon and Schuster, 1993.

Robson, Brian. *Fuzzy-Wuzzy: The Campaigns in Eastern Sudan 1884–1885.* Tunbridge Wells: Spellmount, 1993.

Roeder, Ralph. *Juarez and His Mexico* (2 vols). New York: Viking Press, 1947.

Ryan, Tim and Parham, Bill. *The Colonial Wars in New Zealand.* Wellington: Grantham House, 1986.

Scroggs, William O. *Filibusters and Financiers: The Story of William Walker.* New York: Macmillan, 1916.

Seaton, Albert. *The Crimean War: A Russian Chronicle.* London: B.T. Batsford, 1977.

Sen, Surendra Nath. *Eighteen Fifty-Seven.* Delhi: Indian Government Publications, 1957.

Shadwell, Lucas. *Life of Colin Campbell, Lord Clyde* (2 vols). London: William Blackwood, 1881.

Spence, Jonathan D. *God's Chinese Son: The Taiping Heavenly Kingdom of Hong Xiuquan.* New York: W.W. Norton, 1996.

Stoecker, Helmut (Ed). *German Imperialism in Africa.* London: C. Hurst and Co, 1986.

Stowers, Richard. *Forest Rangers during the New Zealand Wars.* Hamilton, NZ: Print House, 1996.

Sumner, Benedict H. *Russia and the Balkans 1870–1880.* Oxford: Oxford University Press, 1937.

Sweeney, Edwin R. *Cochise: Chiricahua Apache Chief.* Norman: University of Oklahoma, 1991.

Tan, Chester C. *The Boxer Catastrophe.* New York: Octagon Books, 1975.

Tatsios, Theodore George. *The Megali Idea and the Greek-Turkish War of 1897.* New York: Columbia University, 1984.

Taylor, P.J.O. (Ed). *A Companion to the Indian Mutiny of 1857.* Delhi: Oxford University Press, 1996.

Taylor, Stephen. *Shaka's Childen: A History of the Zulu People.* London: HarperCollins, 1994.

Temperley, Harold W. V. *England and the Near East: The Crimea.* London: Frank Cass and Co, 1964.

Thayer, William R. *Life and Times of Cavour* (2 vols). New York: Howard Fertig, 1971.

Totman, Conrad. *The Collapse of the Tokugawa Bakufu 1862–1868.* Honolulu: University of Hawaii, 1980.

US Navy Department. *Official Records of the Union and Confederate Navies in the War of the Rebellion* (30 vols). Washington, DC: Government Printing Office, 1894–1922.

US War Department. *The War of the Rebellion: Official Records of the Union and Confederate Armies* (128 vols). Washington, DC: Government Printing Office, 1880–1901.

Utley, Robert M. *Frontier Regulars: The United States Army and the Indian 1866–1891.* New York: Macmillan, 1973.

———. *Frontiersmen in Blue: The United States Army and the Indian 1848–1865.* New York: Macmillan, 1976.

———. *The Indian Frontier of the American West 1846–1890.* Albuquerque: University of New Mexico, 1984.

———. *The Lance and Shield: Life and Times of Sitting Bull.* New York: Henry Holt and Co, 1993.

Viotti, Andrea. *Garibaldi: The Revolutionary and His Men.* Poole: Blandford Press, 1979.

Volpicelli, Zenone. *The Japan-China War 1894–1895.* London: Sampson, Low, Marston, 1896.

Wallace, Robert L. *Australians at the Boer War.* Canberra: Australian War Memorial, 1976.

Warner, Philip. *The Crimean War: A Reappraisal.* London: Arthur Barker, 1972.

———. *Dervish: The Rise and Fall of an African Empire.* London: Macdonald, 1973.

Wawro, Geoffrey. *The Austro-Prussian War.* Cambridge: Cambridge University Press, 1996.

Whitmore, General Sir George. *The Last Maori War in New Zealand.* London: Sampson, Low, Marston, 1902.

Wilson, Andrew. *The Ever-Victorious Army: The Chinese Campaign of Colonel Gordon and the Suppression of the Taipings 1868.* London: Greenhill Books, 1991.

Wilson, Ruby E. *Frank J. North: Pawnee Scout and Pioneer.* Athens, OH: Swallow Press, 1984.

Wood, Sir Evelyn. *The Revolt in Hindustan 1857–1859.* London: Methuen, 1908.

Woodward, Ralph Lee. *Rafael Carrera and the Emergence of the Republic of Guatemala 1821–1871.* Athens: University of Georgia, 1993.

Wooster, Robert. *Nelson Miles and the Twilight of the Frontier Army.* Lincoln: University of Nebraska, 1993.

Worcester, Donald. *The Apaches: Eagles of the Southwest.* Norman: University of Oklahoma, 1979.

Wright, Patricia. *Conflict on the Nile: The Fashoda Incident of 1898.* London: W. Heinemann, 1972.

Yates, Charles L. *Saigo Takamori: The Man behind the Myth.* London: Keagan Paul, 1995.

Zaide, Gregorio F. *The Philippine Revolution.* Manila: Modern Book Co, 1968.

Ziegler, Philip. *Omdurman.* London: Collins, 1973.

World War and Revolution 1900–1939

Aguinaldo, Emilio. *Memoirs of the Revolution.* Manila: National Heroes Commission, 1967.

Anderson, Ross. *The Forgotten Front: The East African Campaign 1914–1918.* Stroud: Tempus, 2004.

Ashmead-Bartlett, Ellis. *With the Turks in Thrace.* London: W. Heinemann, 1913.

Askew, William C. *Europe and Italy's Acquisition of Libya 1911–1912.* Durham, NC: Duke University Press, 1942.

Banks, Arthur. *A Military Atlas of the First World War.* London: W. Heinemann, 1975.

Barker, Arthur J. *The Civilising Mission: A History of the Italo-Ethiopian War 1935–1936.* New York: Dial Press, 1968.

———. *The Neglected War: Mesopotamia 1914–1918.* London: Faber, 1976.

Battersby, H. F. Prevost. *Richard Corfeld of Somaliland.* London: Edward Arnold, 1914.

Becvar, Gusta. *The Lost Legion: A Czechoslovakian Epic.* London: Stanley Paul, 1939.

Bennet, Geoffrey. *Naval Battles of the First World War.* London: B.T. Batsford, 1968.

Bigham, Clive, Viscount Mersey. *With the Turks in Thessaly.* London: Macmillan, 1897.

Bley, Helmut. *Southwest Africa under German Rule 1894–1914.* London: W. Heinemann, 1971.

Blount, James H. *American Occupation of the Philippines 1898–1912.* New York: Putnam and Sons, 1913.

Bradley, John F. *Civil War in Russia 1917–1920.* London: St. Martins Press, 1975.

Bridgman, Jon M. *The Revolt of the Hereros.* Berkeley: University of California, 1981.

Brown, Malcolm. *The Imperial War Museum Book of the Somme.* London: Sidgwick and Jackson, 1996.

———. *Verdun 1916.* Gloucestershire: Tempus, 1999.

Bruce, Anthony. *An Illustrated Companion to the First World War.* London: Michael Joseph, 1990.

———. *The Last Crusade: The Palestine Campaign in the First World War.* London: John Murray, 2002.

Bury, David F. and Purcell, L. Edward. *Almanac of World War 1.* Lexington: University of Kentucky, 1998.

Chi, Hsi-Sheng. *Warlord Politics in China 1916–1928.* Stanford, CA: Stanford University Press, 1976.

Clark, Alan. *The Eastern Front 1914–1918: Suicide of the Empires.* London: BPC, 1971.

Clendenen, Clarence C. *The United States and Pancho Villa.* New York: Cornell University Press, 1961.

Connaughton, Richard M. *The War of the Rising Sun and the Tumbling Bear.* London: Routledge and Kegan Paul, 1988.

Coogan, Tim and Morrison, George. *The Irish Civil War.* London: Weidenfeld and Nicolson, 1998.

Coox, Alvin D. *Nomohan: Japan against Russia 1938* (2 vols). Stanford, CA: Stanford University Press, 1985.

Curran, Joseph M. *The Birth of the Irish Free State 1921–1923.* Tuscaloosa: University of Alabama Press, 1980.

Davies, Norman. *White Eagle—Red Star: Polish Soviet War 1919–1920.* London: St. Martins Press, 1972.

Del Boca, Angelo. *The Ethiopian War 1935–1941.* Chicago: University of Chicago Press, 1969.

Denikin, Anton I. *The White Army.* London: Jonathon Cape, 1930.

Deutsch, Hermann B. *The Incredible Yanqui: The Career of Lee Christmas.* New York: Longman Green, 1931.

De Watteville, Herman. *Waziristan 1919–1920.* London: Constable, 1925.

Divine, David. *Mutiny at Invergordon.* London: Macdonald, 1970.

Dreyer, Edward L. *China at War 1901–1949.* London: Longmans, 1995.

Durham, M. Edith. *The Struggle for Scutari.* London: Edward Arnold, 1914.

Estigarribia, Jose Felix. *The Epic of Chaco: Marshal Estigarribia's Memoirs of the Chaco War 1932–1935* (transl. Pablo M. Ysnfa). 1st ed 1950. New York: Greenwood Press, 1969.

Estonian National Historical Committee. *Estonian War of Independence 1918–1920* 1st ed 1939. New York: Eesti Vabadusvoitlejate Liit, 1968.

Falls, Cyril (Ed). *Military Operations in Macedonia* (2 vols). London: His Majesty's Stationary Office, 1933.

Farrar-Hockley, Anthony. *The Somme.* London: Severn House, 1976.

Fleming, Peter. *Bayonets of Lhasa: The First Full Account of the British Invasion of Tibet.* London: Rupert Hart, 1961.

Footman, David. *Civil War in Russia.* Allen and Unwin, 1987.

Fung, Edmund S. K. *The Military Dimension of the Chinese Revolution 1911.* Canberra: Australian National University Press, 1981.

Gilbert, Martin. *Atlas of the First World War.* New York: Dorset Press, 1970.

Gillin, Donald G. *Warlord: Yen Hsi-Shan in Shansi Province 1911–1949.* Princeton, NJ: Princeton University Press, 1967.

Gilly, Adolfo. *The Mexican Revolution* (transl. Patrick Camiller). Norfolk: Thetford Press, 1983.

Gleichen, General Edward (Ed). *Chronology of the Great War 1918–1920.* London: Greenhill Books, 1988.

Gordon, Alban. *Russian Civil War.* London: Cassell, 1937.

Gray, Randal. *Chronicle of the First World War* (2 vols). New York: Facts on File, 1990–1991.

Haldane, Sir Aylmer. *The Insurrection in Mesopotamia 1920.* London: William Blackwood, 1922.

Hannula, Joose Olavi. *Finland's War of Independence.* London: Faber and Faber, 1939.

Herbert, Edwin. *Small Wars and Skirmishes 1902–1918: Early Twentieth-century Colonial Campaigns in Africa, Asia and the Americas.* Nottingham: Foundry Books, 2003.

Herman, Gerald. *The Pivotal Conflict: A Comprehensive Chronology of the First World War.* Westport, CT: Greenwood Press, 1992.

Herwig, Holger and Heyman, Neil. *Biographical Dictionary of World War I.* Westport, CT: Greenwood Press, 1982.

Hogg, Ian V. *Historical Dictionary of World War I.* Lanham, MD: Scarecrow Press, 1998.

Hoisington, William A. *Lyautey and the French Conquest of Morocco.* New York: St. Martins Press, 1995.

Horne, Alistair. *The Price of Glory: Verdon 1916.* London: Macmillan, 1962.

Howard, Harry N. *The Partition of Turkey 1913–1923.* New York: Howard Fertig, 1966.

Howarth, David. *Desert King: A Life of Ibn Saud.* London: Collins, 1964.

Howe, Sonia E. *Lyautey of Morocco.* London: Hodder and Stoughton, 1931.

Hseuh, Chun-Tu. *Huang Hsing and the Chinese Revolution.* Stanford, CA: Stanford University Press, 1961.

Iliffe, John. *Tanganyika under German Rule: 1905–1912.* Cambridge: Cambridge University Press, 1969.

Jackson, Robert. *At War with the Bolksheviks: The Allied Intervention in Russia 1917–1920.* London: Tom Stacey, 1972.

Jardine, Douglas. *The Mad Mullah of Somaliland.* London: Herbert Jenkins, 1923.

Johnson, John H. *Stalemate: The Great Trench Warfare Battles of 1915–1917.* New York: Arms and Armour Press, 1985.

Jordan, Donald A. *The Northern Expedition: China's Nationalist Revolution of 1926–1928.* Honolulu: University of Hawaii Press, 1976.

Kautt, William H. *The Anglo-Irish War of 1916–1921: A People's War.* Westport, CT: Praeger, 1999.

Keenan, George F. *The Other Balkan Wars.* Washington, DC: Carnegie Endowment, 1993.

Kenez, Peter. *Civil War in South Russia 1918.* Berkeley: University of California, 1971.

———. *Civil War in South Russia 1919–1920.* Berkeley: University of California, 1977.

Khoury, Philip S. *Syria and the French Mandate 1920–1945*. Princeton, NJ: Princeton University Press, 1987.

Kiraly, Bela and Djordjevic, Dimitrije (Eds). *East Central European Society and the Balkan Wars*. Boulder, CO: Social Science Monographs, 1987.

Knight, Alan. *The Mexican Revolution* (2 vols). Cambridge: Cambridge University Press, 1986.

Kostiner, Joseph. *The Making of Saudi Arabia 1916–1936*. New York: Oxford University Press, 1993.

Kuropatkin, General Aleksei N. *The Russian Army and the Japanese War* (2 vols). London: John Murray, 1906.

Lensen, George Alexander. *The Russo-Chinese War 1900*. Tallahassee, FL: Diplomatic Press, 1967.

Leroy, James. *The Americans in the Philippines* (2 vols). 1st ed 1914. New York: AMS Press, 1970.

Liddell Hart, Basil. *History of the First World War*. London: Cassell, 1970.

Lincoln, W. Bruce. *Red Victory: A History of the Russian Civil War*. New York: Simon and Schuster, 1989.

Liu, Frederick F. *Military History of Modern China 1924–1949*. Princeton, NJ: Princeton University Press, 1956.

Longrigg, Stephen H. *Syria and Lebanon under French Mandate*. London: Oxford University Press, 1958.

Luckett, Richard. *The White Generals: An Account of the White Movement and the Russian Civil War*. London: Longman, 1971.

Lyttelton, Adrian. *The Seizure of Power: Fascism in Italy 1919–1929*. London: Weidenfeld and Nicolson, 1973.

Macdonald, Lyn. *1915: The Death of Innocence*. New York: Henry Holt, 1993.

Machad, Manuel. *Centaur of the North: Pancho Villa, the Mexican Revolution and Northern Mexico*. Austin, TX: Eakin Press, 1988.

Macias, Silvio. *La Guerra del Chaco: Paraguay vs Bolivia 1932–36*. Asuncion: La Tribuna, 1936.

Mack Smith, Denis. *Mussolini's Roman Empire*. London: Longman, 1976.

Manstein, Erich Von. *Lost Victories*. London: Methuen, 1958.

Mason, David. *Verdun*. Gloucestershire: Windrush, 2000.

Maurois, Andre. *Marshal Lyautey* (transl. Hamish Miles). London: Bodley Head, 1931.

Mawdsley, Evan. *The Russian Civil War*. London: Faber and Faber, 1961.

McClure, William K. *Italy in North Africa: An Account of the Tripoli Enterprise 1913*. London: Constable, 1913.

McCullagh, Francis. *Italy's War for a Desert: Tripoli 1911*. London: Herbert and Daniel, 1912.

McLoughlin, Leslie. *Ibn Saud: Founder of a Kingdom*. New York: St. Martins Press, 1993.

Middlebrook, Martin. *The First Day on the Somme: 1 July 1916*. London: Allen Lane, 1971.

Mockler, Anthony. *Haile Selassie's War*. Oxford: Oxford University Press, 1984.

Moyse-Bartlett, Hubert. *The King's African Rifles: Military History of East and Central Africa 1890–1945*. Aldershot: Gale and Polden, 1956.

Palmer, Alan. *The Gardeners of Salonika*. London: Andre Deutsch, 1965.

Palmer, Frederick. *With Kuroki in Manchuria*. London: Methuen, 1904.

Pilsudski, Josef. *The Battle of Warsaw during the Polish Soviet War*. London: Pilsudksi Institute, 1972.

Pitt, Barry. *Zeebrugge: St. George's Day 1918*. London: Cassell, 1958.

Pope, Stephen and Wheal, Elizabeth-Anne. *Macmillan Dictionary of the First World War*. London: Macmillan, 1995.

Porch, Douglas. *The Conquest of Morocco 1900–1914*. London: Jonathon Cape, 1986.

Powell, Ralph. *The Rise of Chinese Military Power 1895–1912*. Princeton, NJ: Princeton University Press, 1955.

Preston, Diana. *The Boxer Rebellion*. New York: Walker and Co, 2000.

Pretorius, Fransjohan. *Life on Commando during the Anglo-Boer War 1899–1902*. Capetown: Human and Rousseau, 1999.

Price, G. Ward. *In Morocco with the Legion*. London: Beacon Library, 1937.

Pugsley, Christopher. *Galllipoli: The New Zealand Story*. Auckland: Reed, 1998.

Ramaciotti, Gustavo. *Tripoli: Principal Engagements of the Italo-Turkish War 1911–1912*. London: Hugh Rees, 1912.

Rankin, Sir Reginald. *In Morocco with General d'Amade*. London: Longmans Green, 1908.

———. *Inner History of the Balkan War*. London: Constable, 1914.

Rose, William Kinnaird. *With the Greeks in Thessaly*. London: Methuen, 1897.

Ross, Colonel C. *Outline of the Russo-Japanese War*. London: Macmillan, 1912.

Rutherford, Ward. *The Tsar's War 1914–1917*. Cambridge: Ian Faulkner, 1992.

Schurmann, Jacob G. *Tha Balkan Wars 1912–1913*. Princeton, NJ: Princeton University Press, 1914.

Sheik-Abdi, Abdi. *Divine Madness: Mohammed Abdulle Hassan*. London: Zed Books, 1993.

Sheridan, James E. *The Chinese Warlord: The Career of Feng Yu-Hsiang.* Stanford, CA: Stanford University Press, 1966.

Smythe, Donald. *Guerilla Warrior: The Early Life of John J. Pershing.* New York: Charles Scribners, 1973.

Somin, Ilya. *Stillborn Crusade: The Tragic Failure of Western Intervention in the Russian Civil War 1918–1920.* New Brunswick, NJ: Transaction Publishers, 1996.

Stewart, George. *The White Armies of Russia: A Chronicle of Counter-Revolution and Allied Intervention.* New York: Macmillan, 1933.

Stone, Norman. *The Eastern Front 1914–1917.* London: Hodder and Stoughton, 1975.

Storey, Moorfield and Lichuaco, Marcial P. *The Conquest of the Philippines by the United States 1898–1925.* New York: G. P. Putnam's Sons, 1926.

Strawson, General John. *Gentlemen in Khaki: British Army 1890–1990.* London: Secker and Warburg, 1989.

Tarulis, Albert N. *Soviet Policy toward the Baltic States 1918–1940.* Notre Dame, IN: University of Notre Dame, 1959.

Taylor, A.J.P. (Ed). *History of World War I.* London: Octopus, 1974.

Terraine, John. *Mons: The Retreat to Victory.* London: B.T. Batsford, 1960.

———. *To Win a War: 1918, the Year of Victory.* London: Macmillan, 1978.

Theobald, Alan B. *Ali Dinar: Last Sultan of Darfur 1898–1916.* London: Longmans Green, 1965.

Thomas, Hugh. *The Spanish Civil War.* London: Eyre and Spottiswoode, 1961.

Tong, Te-Kong and Li, Tsung-Jen. *The Memoirs of Li Tsung-jen.* Boulder, CO: Westview Press, 1979.

Turner, Ernest S. *Dear Old Blighty.* London: Michael Joseph, 1980.

Walder, David. *The Short Victorious War: The Russo-Japanese Conflict 1904–1905.* London: Hutchinson, 1973.

Warner, Denis and Peggy. *The Tide at Sunrise: A History of the Russo-Japanese War 1904–1905.* New York: Charterhouse, 1972.

Warner, Philip. *Kitchener: The Man behind the Legend.* London: Hamish Hamilton, 1985.

War Office. *The Official History of the Operations in Somaliland 1901–1904.* London: HMSO, 1907.

———. *The Abyssinian Campaigns: The Official Story of the Conquest of Italian East Africa.* London: His Majesty's Stationary Office, 1942.

Warren, Alan. *Waziristan: The Faqir of Ipi and the Indian Army: the Northwest Frontier Revolt of 1936–1937.* Oxford: Oxford University Press, 2000.

Wavell, Archibald. *The Palestine Campaigns.* London: Constable, 1928.

Westwood, John N. *Russia against Japan 1904–1905.* London: Macmillan, 1986.

Wilson, Sir Arnold T. *Loyalties: Mesopotamia 1914–1917.* London: Oxford University Press, 1930.

———. *Mesopotamia 1917–1920: A Clash of Loyalties.* London: Oxford University Press, 1931.

Wolff, Leon. *Little Brown Brother: America's Forgotten Bid for Empire Which Cost 250,000 Lives.* New York: Doubleday, 1960.

Woolman, David S. *Rebels in the Rif.* Stanford, CA: Stanford University Press, 1969.

Wright, Mary Clabaugh (Ed). *China in Revolution: The First Phase 1900–1913.* New Haven, CT: Yale University Press, 1968.

Young, Ernest P. *The Presidency of Yuan Shih-Kai.* Ann Arbor: University of Michigan Press, 1977.

Younger, Calton. *Ireland's Civil War.* London: Frederick Muller, 1968.

Zamoyski, Adam. *The Battle for the Marchlands.* New York: Columbia University Press, 1981.

Zook, David H. *The Conduct of the Chaco War.* New York: Bookman Associates, 1960.

World War II 1939–1945

Archer, Jules. *Twentieth-century Caesar: Benito Mussolini.* Folkestone: Bailey Bros, 1972.

Barnett, Correlli. *The Desert Generals.* London: William Kimber and Co, 1960.

Campbell, James. *The Bombing of Nuremberg.* London: Futura, 1974.

Carell, Paul. *Hitler's War on Russia: German Defeat in the East.* London: George Harrap, 1964.

Carew, Tim. *The Fall of Hong Kong.* London: Anthony Blond, 1960.

Chandler, David G. *Battles and Battlescenes of WW II.* London: Arms and Armour Press, 1989.

Collier, Basil. *The Battle of Britain.* London: B.T. Batsford, 1962.

Craig, William. *Enemy at the Gates: The Battle for Stalingrad.* London: Hodder and Stoughton, 1973.

Dear, I.C.B. (Gen Ed). *Oxford Companion to the Second World War.* Oxford: Oxford University Press, 1995.

D'este, Carlo. *Bitter Victory: The Battle for Sicily July–August 1943.* London: Collins, 1988.

Devereux, James P. S. *Wake Island*. Canoga Park, CA: Major Books, 1978.

Dunnigan, James F. and Nofi, Albert A. *The Pacific War Encyclopedia* (2 vols). New York: Facts on File, 1998.

Garland, Albert N. and McGaw Smyth, Howard. *Sicily and the Surrender of Italy*. Washington, DC: Department of Army, 1965.

Goralski, Robert. *World War II Almanac 1931–1945*. London: Hamish Hamilton, 1981.

Greene, Jack and Massignani, Alessandro. *The Naval War in the Mediterranean 1940–1943*. London: Chatham Publishing, 1999.

Hastings, Max. *Das Reich*. London: Michael Joseph, 1981.

Holland, Jeffrey. *Aegean Mission: Allied Operations in the Dodecanese*. Westport, CT: Greenwood Press, 1988.

Hu, Pu-Yu. *Brief History of Sino-Japanese War 1937–1945*. Taipei: Chung Wa Publishing, 1971.

Hutchison, Kevin D. *World War II in the North Pacific*. Westport, CT: Greenwood Press, 1994.

Keegan, John (Ed). *Who Was Who in WWII*. London: Bison Books, 1978.

Lucas Philips, C. E. *The Greatest Raid of All*. London: Heinemann, 1958.

Lyall Grant, Ian. *Burma 1942: The Japanese Invasion*. Chichester: Zampi Press, 1999.

Mason, David. *Who's Who in World War II*. London: Weidenfeld and Nicolson, 1978.

McCombs, Don and Worth, Fred. *World War II: Strange and Fascinating Facts*. New York: Greenwich House, 1983.

Mockler, Anthony. *Our Enemies the French: The War between the French and the British, Syria 1941*. London: Leo Cooper, 1976.

Moreman, Tim R. *The Jungle, the Japanese and the British Commonwealth Armies 1941–1945*. London: Frank Cass, 2005.

Owen, Frank. *The Fall of Singapore*. London: Michael Joseph, 1960.

Parrish, Thomas (Ed). *Simon and Schuster Encyclopedia of WWII*. New York: Simon and Schuster, 1978.

Perrett, Bryan and Hogg, Ian. *Encyclopedia of the Second World War*. London: Longman, 1989.

Polmar, Norman and Dorr, Carpenter. *Submarines of the Imperial Japanese Navy 1904–1945*. London: Conway Press, 1986.

Romanus, Charles F. and Sundeland, Riley. *Stillwell's Command Problems*. Washington, DC: US Army, 1956.

———. *Time Runs Out in China-Burma-India*. Washington, DC: US Army, 1959.

Roscoe, Theodore. *United States Submarine Operations in WW II*. Annapolis, MD: US Naval Institute, 1949.

Rotunda, Louis (Ed). *Battle for Stalingrad: 1943 Soviet General Staff Study*. London: Pergamon-Brassey, 1989.

Salisbury, Harrison E. *The Long March*. London: Macmillan, 1985.

Sandler, Stanley (Ed). *World War II in the Pacific: An Encyclopedia*. New York: Garland Publishing, 2001.

Seaton, Albert. *The Russo-German War 1941–1945*. London: Arthur Barker, 1971.

Seth, Ronald. *Stalingrad: Point of No Return*. London: Victor Gollancz, 1959.

Smith, Colin. *Singapore Burning: Heroism and Surrender in World War II*. London: Viking, 2005.

Smith, Peter C. and Walker, Edwin. *War in the Aegean*. London: William Kimber, 1974.

Snyder, Louis. *Historical Guide to World War II*. Westport, CT: Greenwood Press, 1982.

Taylor, James and Shaw, Warren. *The Third Reich Almanac*. New York: World Almanac, 1987.

Trotter, William R. *A Frozen Hell: The Russo-Finnish War of 1939–1940*. Chapel Hill, NC: Algonquin Books, 1991.

Tsuji, Masanobu. *Singapore: The Japanese Version*. Sydney: Ure Smith, 1960.

Upton, Anthony F. *Finland 1939–1940*. London: Davis-Poynter, 1974.

Warner, Geoffrey. *Iraq and Syria 1941*. London: Davis-Poynter, 1974.

Warren, Alan. *Singapore 1942: Britain's Greatest Defeat*. Singapore: Talisman, 2002.

Wells, Anne S. *Historical Dictionary of WW II: The War against Japan*. Lanham, MD: Scarecrow Press 1999.

Wheal, Elizabeth-Anne and Pope, Stephen. *Macmillan Dictionary of the Second World War*. London: Macmillan, 1995.

Zabecki, David (Ed). *World War II in Europe: An Encyclopedia*. New York: Garland Publishing, 1999.

War after 1945

Alexander, Bevin. *Korea: The Lost War*. London: Arrow, 1989.

Allen, Thomas B., Berry, F. Clifton, and Polmer, Norman. *War in the Gulf: From the Invasion of Kuwait to the Day of Victory and Beyond*. Atlanta, GA: Turner Publishing, 1991.

Arnold, Guy. *Wars in the Third World since 1945.* London: Cassell, 1991.

Barker, Arthur J. *Fortune Favours the Brave: The Battle of the Hook, Korea 1953.* London: Leo Cooper, 1974.

Bell, John P. *Crisis in Costa Rica: The 1948 Revolution.* Austin: University of Texas Press, 1971.

Bennet, Christopher. *Yugoslavia's Bloody Collapse.* London: Hurst and Co, 1995.

Bickerton, Ian and Pearson, Michael. *43 Days: The Gulf War.* Melbourne: Text Publishing, 1991.

Brigot, Andre and Roy, Olivier. *The War in Afghanistan.* London: Harvester-Wheatsheaf, 1988.

Bullock, John and Morris, Harvey. *The Gulf War: Its Origins, History and Consequences.* London: Methuen, 1989.

Burg, Steven L. and Shoup, Paul. *The War in Bosnia and Herzogovina.* Armonk, NY: M.E. Sharpe, 1999.

Burr, J. Millard and Collins, Robert O. *Africa's Thirty Year War: Libya, Chad and the Sudan 1963–1993.* Boulder, CO: Westview Press, 1997.

Carver, Michael. *War since 1945.* London: Weidenfeld and Nicolson, 1980.

Chabal, Patrick. *Amilcar Cabral: Revolutionary Leadership and People's War.* Cambridge: Cambridge University Press, 1983.

Chassin, Lionel Max. *The Communist Conquest of China 1945–1949.* London: Weidenfeld and Nicolson, 1966.

Ciment, James (Ed). *Conflicts after World War II.* Armonk, NY: Sharpe Reference, 1999.

Clayton, Anthony. *The Wars of French Decolonisation.* London: Longman, 1994.

Close, David H. (Ed). *Greek Civil War 1943–1950: Studies of Polarization.* London: Routledge, 1993.

Connell, Dan. *Against All Odds: A Chronicle of the Eritrean Revolution.* Trenton, NJ: Red Sea Press, 1993.

Cordesman, Anthony H. and Wagner, Abraham R. *The Lessons of Modern War.* Boulder, CO: Westview Press, 1990.

Davidson, Basil. *The Liberation of Guine.* London: Penguin, 1969.

De St Jorre, John. *Nigerian Civil War.* London: Hodder and Stoughton, 1972.

Dupuy, Trevor. *The Military History of the Chinese Civil War.* London: Franklins Watts, 1969.

———. *Elusive Victory: The Arab-Israeli Wars 1947–74.* London: Macdonald and Janes, 1978.

Edgerton, Robert B. *Mau Mau: An African Crucible.* New York: Macmillan, 1989.

Fall, Bernard. *Two Vietnams: A Political and Military Analysis.* Boulder, CO: Frederick A. Praegar, 1984.

Freedman, Lawrence and Karsh, Efraim. *The Gulf Conflict 1990–1991.* London: Faber and Faber, 1993.

Gerard-Libois, Jules. *Katanga Secession.* Madison: University of Wisconsin Press, 1966.

Hartman, Tom. *A World Atlas of Military History 1945–1984.* London: Secker and Warburg, 1984.

Hastings, Max and Jenkins, Simon. *The Battle for the Falklands.* London: Michael Joseph, 1983.

Herzog, Chaim. *The War of Atonement.* London: Weidenfeld and Nicolson, 1975.

———. *The Arab-Israeli Wars.* London: Arms and Armour Press, 1982.

Hiro, Dilip. *The Longest War: The Iran-Iraq Conflict.* London: Grafton Books, 1989.

———. *Desert Shield to Desert Storm: The Second Gulf War.* London: HarperCollins, 1992.

———. *Lebanon: Fire and Embers: A History of the Lebanese Civil War.* London: Weidenfeld and Nicolson, 1993.

Ho, Kan-Chih. *History of the Modern Chinese Revolution.* Peking: Foreign Language Press, 1960.

Hodges, Tony. *Western Sahara: The Roots of a Desert War.* Westport, CT: Lawrence Hill and Co, 1983.

James, Harold and Sheil-Small, Denis. *The Undeclared War: The Story of the Indonesian Confrontation 1962–1966.* London: Leo Cooper, 1971.

Jessup, John E. *An Encyclopedic Dictionary of Conflict and Conflict Resolution 1945–1996.* Westport, CT: Greenwood Press, 1998.

Judah, Tim. *Kosovo: War and Revenge.* New Haven, CT: Yale University Press, 2000.

Karnow, Stanley. *Vietnam: A History.* London: Penguin, 1984.

Lambeth, Benjamin S. *NATO's Air War for Kosovo.* Santa Monica, CA: Rand, 2001.

Liao, Kai-Lung. *From Yenan to Peking: The Chinese People's War of Liberation.* Peking: Foreign Language Press, 1954.

Maley, William. *The Afghanistan Wars.* Basingstoke: Palgrave Macmillan, 2002.

Malkasian, Carter. *The Korean War 1950–1953.* Oxford: Osprey, 2001.

Marolda, Edward J. and Schneller, Robert J. *Shield and Sword: The United States Navy and the Persian Gulf War.* Annapolis, MD: Naval Institute Press, 1992.

Newell, Clayton R. *Historical Dictionary of the Persian Gulf War 1990–1991.* Lanham, MD: Scarecrow Press, 1998.

Niven, Sir Rex. *War of Nigerian Unity 1967–1970.* Totowa, NJ: Rowan and Littlefield, 1970.

O'Ballance, Edgar. *The Sinai Campaign 1956.* London: Faber and Faber, 1959.

———. *The Indo-China War 1945–1954.* London: Faber and Faber, 1964.

———. *Greek Civil War 1944–1949.* London: Faber and Faber, 1966.

———. *Civil War in Bosnia 1992–1994.* New York: St. Martins Press, 1995.

———. *Civil War in Lebanon 1975–1992.* London: Macmillan, 1998.

Olson, James S. *Dictionary of the Vietnam War.* Westport, CT: Greenwood Press, 1988.

Oren, Michael B. *Six Days of War: June 1967.* New York: Oxford University Press, 2002.

O'Shea, Brendan. *Crisis at Bihac: Bosnia's Bloody Battlefield.* Stroud: Sutton, 1998.

Packham, Eric. *Success or Failure: The UN Intervention in the Congo.* Commack, NY: Nova Science Publishers, 1998.

Pepper, Suzanne. *Civil War in China: The Political Struggle 1945–1949.* Lanham, MD: Rowman and Littlefield, 1999.

Pimlott, John. *Vietnam: The Decisive Battles.* London: Michael Joseph, 1990.

Rézette, Robert. *Western Sahara and the Frontiers of Morocco.* Paris: Nouvelles Editions Latines, 1975.

Rogel, Carole. *The Breakup of Yugoslavia and the War in Bosnia.* Westport, CT: Greenwood Press, 1998.

Scales, Robert H. *Certain Victory: The US Army in the Gulf War.* Washington, DC: Brassey, 1994.

Schwartz, Richard A. *Encyclopedia of the Persian Gulf War.* Jefferson, NC: McFarland, 1998.

Smith, Hempstone. *Rebels, Mercenaries and Dividends: The Katanga Story.* New York: Frederick A. Praegar, 1962.

Somerville, Keith. *Foreign Military Intervention in Africa.* London: Pinter Publishers, 1990.

Tucker, Spencer (Ed). *Encyclopedia of the Vietnam War* (3 vols). Santa Barbra, CA: ABC-Clio, 1998.

———. *Encyclopedia of the Korean War* (3 vols). Santa Barbra, CA: ABC-Clio, 2000.

US News and World Report. *Triumph without Victory: The Unreported Story of the Persian Gulf War.* New York: Times Books, 1992.

Urban, Mark. *War in Afghanistan.* London: Macmillan, 1988.

Westd, Odd Arne. *Decisive Encounters: The Chinese Civil War 1946–1950.* Stanford, CA: Stanford University Press, 2003.

Woodhouse, Christopher M. *Struggle for Greece, 1941–1949.* London: Hart-Davis, MacGibbon, 1976.

Young, John. *Peasant Revolution in Ethiopia: The Tigrayan People's Liberation Front 1975–1991.* Cambridge: Cambridge University Press, 1997.

Index

Hatvan (Hungarian Revolutionary War), 438, 788, 923
Hatzfeld, Melchior (General), 486, 1083, 1109
Haughton, John (Lieutenant), 227
Hausen (Napoleonic Wars (5th Coalition)), 438
Hausen, Max von, 228
Hautai (Wars of the Six Dynasties), 1116
Hautefort, Louis de (Marquis de Surville), 1030
Hauteville, Roger d', 216, 769
Havana (Sack of Havana), 438–39
Havana (Seven Years War (Caribbean)), 439
Havana (War of the Austrian Succession), 439
Havelberg (Thirty Years War (Swedish War)), 439See Werben
Havelock, Henry (General), 22, 57, 112, 143, 214, 349, 604, 627, 773, 1054
Havelock, Henry (Major) (Son), 112
Haviland, William, 683
Havré (Netherlands War of Independence), 439
Havrincourt (World War I (Western Front)). See Épéhy
Hawaiian Wars. See Chronological Reference Guide
Hawke, Edward (Admiral), 193, 196, 467, 833
Hawkins, Edgar (Captain), 368
Hawkins, Edward (Major), 513–14
Hawkins, Richard, 32
Hawkwood, John, 209
Hawley, Henry (General), 346
Haw River (War of the American Revolution), 439
Haws Shop (American Civil War (Eastern Theatre)), 439
Hay, Arthur (Major), 893
Hay, Francis (Earl of Errol), 397
Hayakawa, Mikio, 758
Hayashi, Yoshihide (General), 470
Hayat, Mohammad (Brigadier), 383
Haydon, Charles (Brigadier), 595, 1057
Hayfield Fight (Red Clouds War), 439
Hayib, al- (Taifa of Lérida), 324
Haynau, Julius von (Baron), 163
Haynau, Julius von (General), 923, 1006
Haynes' Bluff (American Civil War (Western Theatre)). See Snyder's Bluff
Hayredin, Pasha, 917
Hays, Alexander (General), 687–88
Hays, Jack (Captain), 1091
Hays, Jack (Colonel), 799
Hazarasp (Eastern Muslim Dynastic Wars), 439–40
Hazen George B. (General), 364
Hazrat Mahal (Begum of Oudh), 698
Head, Francis, 1027
Heald, Nathan (Captain), 360

Hearsey, Hyder (Captain), 515
Heartbreak Ridge (Korean War), 146, 440
Heath, Lewis (General), 642, 951
Heathfield (Anglo-Saxon Territorial Wars), 440, 1108
Heathfield (Baron). See Elliot, George (General)
Heavenfield (Anglo-Saxon Territorial Wars), 440
Heavy Runner (Chief), 635
Hébert, Louis (General), 954
Hecatombaeum (Cleomenic War), 440, 924
Hechuan (Mongol Conquest of China). See Diao Yu
Hedgeley Moor (Wars of the Roses), 440
Hedges, Richard (Major), 205
He Dog, 815
Heemskerk, Jacob van (Admiral), 393
Heeringen, Josias von (General), 599, 695
Hefei (Taiping Rebellion). See Luzhou
Hefiz, Achmet (Pasha), 404
He Haiming (commander), 711
Heidelberg (Thirty Years War (Palatinate War)), 440
Heiden, Lodewijk (Count), 717
Heigoutai (Russo-Japanese War). See Sandepu
Heiji War. See Chronological Reference Guide
Heijo (Sino-Japanese War). See Pyongyang
Heiligerlee (Netherlands War of Independence), 440
Heilman, Julius (Major), 360
Heilsberg (Napoleonic Wars (4th Coalition)), 441
Heinrich of Schwerin, 154, 672
Heinrichs, Erik (General), 629
Heirax, Antiochus, 50
Heister, Siegbert (Field Marshal), 1033
Hejaz (Turko-Wahhabi War), 441
Hejaz (World War I (Middle East)), 441, 1118
He Jian, 1114
Heke, Hone, 1002
Hekimoghlu, Ali Pasha (Vizier), 105
Hekmatyar, Gulbuddin (warlord), 484, 500
Hel (World War II (Western Europe)), 441, 806, 1094
Helena, Arkansas (American Civil War (Western Theatre)), 441
Helena, France (Roman-Frankish Wars), 441
Helfstein, Ludwig von (Count), 1097
Helgeaa (Norwegian Wars of Succession), 441, 967
Helgeaa (Scandinavian National Wars), 721
Helgoland (2nd Schleswig-Holstein War), 441

Helgoland (World War I (War at Sea)), 918
Helgoland Bight (World War I (War at Sea)), 442
Helicopter Valley (Vietnam War). See Song Ngan
Heliopolis (French Revolutionary Wars (Middle East)), 442
Heliopolis (Muslim Conquest of Egypt), 442, 785
Helles (World War I (Gallipoli)), 290, 339, 381
Hellespont (Roman Wars of Succession), 244, 442
Helmed (1st Muscovite-Lithuanian War), 442, 928
Helmstadt (Seven Weeks' War), 390, 442, 1099
Helsingborg (2nd "Great" Northern War), 379
Helsingborg (Wars of the Hanseatic League), 260, 442–43, 1081
Helsingfors (Finnish War of Independence). See Helsinki
Helsinki (Finnish War of Independence), 443, 814, 943, 993
Helsinki (Russo-Finnish War), 443, 1107
He-lü (King), 150, 1136
Helvetia (2nd Anglo-Boer War), 443
Hely-Hutchinson, John (commander), 30
Hely-Hutchinson, John (General), 183, 211
Hemmingstedt (Wars of the Kalmar Union), 443, 865
Hemu (General), 295, 774
Henao, Braulio (General), 887
Henderson, George (Captain), 870
Henderson, John, 1106
Henderson, Melvin (General), 795
Hendley, Israel (Captain), 685
Henestrosa, Juan (Colonel), 661
Hengist, 270, 1108
Hengist's Down (Viking Raids on Britain). See Hingston Down
Hengyang (World War II (China)), 226, 419
Henin, Maximilien de (Count Bossu), 1137
Henley, Austin (Lieutenant), 910
Hennebont (Hundred Years War), 164, 443, 833
Hennersdorf (War of the Austrian Succession), 443–44, 961
Henni (Italo-Turkish War). See Sidi El Henni
Henningsen, Charles, 899
Henri (Comte de Rigny), 717
Henri, Francois (Duke of Luxembourg), 228
Henri Comte d'Harcourt, 863
Henriques, Alfonso, 63, 909–10
Henry (Count of Burgundy), 909
Henry (Duke of Bouillon), 565–66
Henry (Duke of Guise), 267, 572

About the Author

TONY JAQUES is an independent scholar. Mr. Jaques was born in New Zealand and graduated in political science, then started his professional life in journalism in New Zealand and London before moving to political speechwriting. He now works and teaches in the field of Corporate Communication and Issue Management, where he has published extensively, for a Fortune 500 company. A schoolboy enthusiasm for World War II became a lifetime passion for military history in all eras. He is currently a resident of Melbourne, Australia.